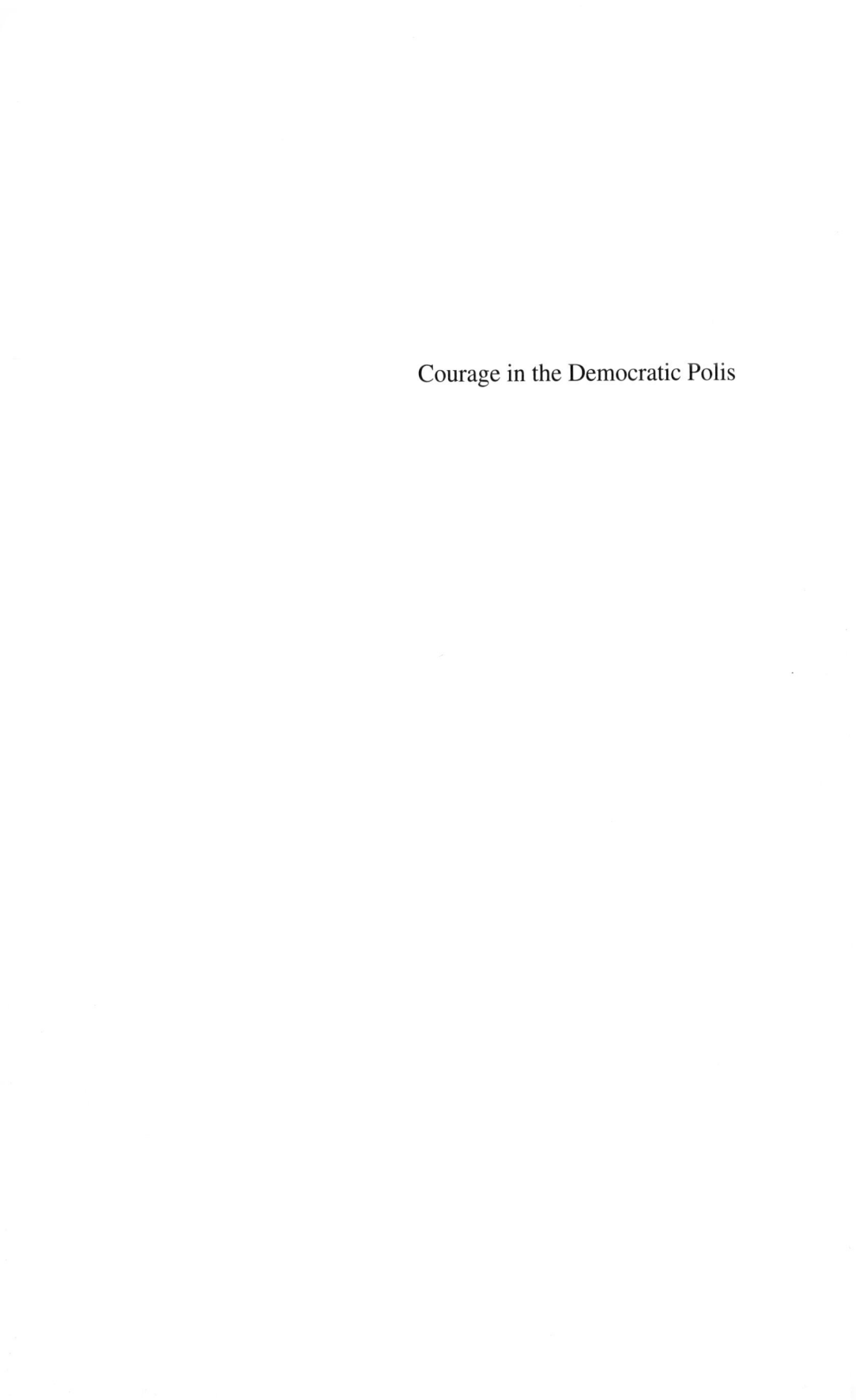

Courage in the Democratic Polis

Courage in the Democratic Polis

Ideology and Critique in Classical Athens

RYAN K. BALOT

OXFORD
UNIVERSITY PRESS

Oxford University Press is a department of the University of Oxford.
It furthers the University's objective of excellence in research, scholarship,
and education by publishing worldwide.

Oxford   New York
Auckland   Cape Town   Dar es Salaam   Hong Kong   Karachi
Kuala Lumpur   Madrid   Melbourne   Mexico City   Nairobi
New Delhi   Shanghai   Taipei   Toronto

With offices in
Argentina   Austria   Brazil   Chile   Czech Republic   France   Greece
Guatemala   Hungary   Italy   Japan   Poland   Portugal   Singapore
South Korea   Switzerland   Thailand   Turkey   Ukraine   Vietnam

Oxford is a registered trademark of Oxford University Press
in the UK and certain other countries.

Published in the United States of America by
Oxford University Press
198 Madison Avenue, New York, NY 10016

© Oxford University Press 2014

All rights reserved. No part of this publication may be reproduced, stored in a
retrieval system, or transmitted, in any form or by any means, without the prior
permission in writing of Oxford University Press, or as expressly permitted by law,
by license, or under terms agreed with the appropriate reproduction rights organization.
Inquiries concerning reproduction outside the scope of the above should be sent to the Rights
Department, Oxford University Press, at the address above.

You must not circulate this work in any other form
and you must impose this same condition on any acquirer.

Library of Congress Cataloging-in-Publication Data
Balot, Ryan K. (Ryan Krieger), 1969-
Courage in the Democratic Polis : Ideology and Critique in Classical Athens / Ryan K. Balot.
pages cm
Includes bibliographical references and index.
ISBN 978-0-19-998215-8   1. Courage.   2. Conduct of life.
3. Athens (Greece)—Politics and government—Early works to 1800.
4. Democracy—Greece—History.   I. Title.
BJ1533.C8B27 2014
320.01'9—dc23
2013020156

9 8 7 6 5 4 3 2 1
Printed in the United States of America
on acid-free paper

To Carroll

CONTENTS

Acknowledgments ix

CHAPTER 1 Introduction: A Theory of Democratic Courage 1

PART ONE | The Periclean Ideology and Its Critics

CHAPTER 2 The Periclean Model 25

CHAPTER 3 Free Speech, Democratic Deliberation, and Courage 47

CHAPTER 4 Writing Courage into Democratic History: Aeschylean and Herodotean Perspectives 74

CHAPTER 5 New Faces of Athenian Courage: The Pursuit of Imperialism 109

CHAPTER 6 Democratic Courage and the Platonic *Laches* 129

CHAPTER 7 Isocratean Reflections: Athens's Courage, Imperialism, and Eudaimonism 149

PART TWO | Equality, Emotion, and Civic Education

CHAPTER 8 Courage, Equality, and Military Recognition in Democratic Athens 179

CHAPTER 9 Revisiting the "Standard Model" of Greek Courage 198

CHAPTER 10 The Courageous Passions of Democratic Athens 218

CHAPTER 11 Shame, Honor, and the Constitution of Role Models 243

CHAPTER 12 Cocky Athenian Men? 256

CHAPTER 13 Tragic Explorations of Courage, Freedom, and
Practical Reason 278

PART THREE | Athens's Ideology of Eudaimonism

CHAPTER 14 Athenian Eudaimonism in Thought and Action 297
CHAPTER 15 Eudaimonistic "Paradoxes" and Resolutions 309
CHAPTER 16 Conclusion: Three Challenges 330

Bibliography 353
Index 385
Index Locurum 395

ACKNOWLEDGMENTS

It has taken me a long time to write this book. I would like to acknowledge the many friends, family members, colleagues, and institutions that have helped me in the process. I began work on this volume when I was in the Department of Classics at Washington University in St. Louis. While I was in St. Louis, George Pepe's friendship and guidance made a great difference to me; he has given me the benefit of his energy and rare intelligence throughout my work on this project. I was fortunate in the colleagues I had at Washington University, especially Cathy Keane, Eric Brown, Hillel Kieval, Joe Loewenstein, Bob Lamberton, and Susan Rotroff. Among many other things, they helped me think through the basic themes of the volume. Generous support from Washington University in St. Louis and from the National Endowment for the Humanities enabled me to take a sabbatical leave during 2003–2004, without which my early progress would have been limited.

In the course of my work on courage, I joined the Department of Political Science at the University of Toronto. Arlene Saxonhouse and Stephen Salkever helped me to make this transition, and they have been friendly and supportive critics throughout. My colleagues in Political Science have helped me expand and deepen my appreciation of these issues in a variety of ways. Cliff Orwin has been a demanding critic and a superb friend. I am grateful to Ed Andrew, Ronnie Beiner, Alan Brudner, David Cameron, Joe Carens, Simone Chambers, Ran Hirschl, Rebecca Kingston, Jeff Kopstein, Jennifer Nedelsky, and Melissa Williams. Among my colleagues in Classics at the University of Toronto, I am especially happy to acknowledge the support of Brad Inwood and Victoria Wohl. My research assistants, Larissa Atkison and Kiran Banerjee, made many contributions to the project, including important substantive improvements. I am also grateful to the Social Sciences and Humanities Research Council of Canada, which provided generous funding for my research on courage.

Other colleagues have always been willing to read chapters, to answer questions, and to talk with me about Greek history and the history of political thought. I would particularly like to thank Josh Ober, Robin Osborne, Matt Christ, Sara Forsdyke, Greg Anderson, David Pritchard, Peter Hunt, Charles Hedrick, Paul Cartledge, Chris Bobonich, Jill Frank, Sara Monoson, Bob Wallace, John Wallach, Kurt Raaflaub, Gerry Mara, David Rosenbloom, Ben Akrigg, Donna Orwin, and Ewen Bowie. I would also like to thank audiences in Berkeley, Minnesota, St. Louis, Toronto, Chicago, North Carolina, Sydney, Aix-en-Provence, Berlin, Washington, DC, New York, and Seattle for helping me to sharpen my ideas.

I finished a draft of this book while I was on sabbatical leave in Aix-en-Provence in 2011–2012. I am indebted to the staff of the Centre Paul-Albert Février and to the librarians at the Maison méditerranéenne des sciences de l'homme. Among many colleagues in Aix, I would particularly like to thank Christian Boudignon, Frédéric Trajber, and Emmanuèle Caire for their generosity and hospitality.

I am also grateful to my agent, Jill Marsal, for her confidence in the project and for her patience, and to my editor Stefan Vranka, whose good judgment steered me smoothly through the production process.

During my work on courage, my daughters Julia and Corinne were born. They have shown a great deal of understanding as I prepared this volume. Watching them (and hopefully helping them) grow up has given me extraordinary joy. My mother, Liz Miranne, and my aunt, Mary Joe Krieger, have helped me for a very long time, as have my earliest mentors, Grégoire C. Richard, Stephen L. Pearce, and the Rev. Claude P. Boudreaux, S.J. I dedicate this volume to my wife, Carroll, a model of courage.

Throughout the volume, I have drawn on my own previously published material, often in a revised form:

"Pericles' Anatomy of Democratic Courage," *American Journal of Philology* 122.4 (2001) 505–25; "Free Speech, Courage, and Democratic Deliberation," in *Free Speech in Classical Antiquity*, edited by I. Sluiter and R. M. Rosen (Leiden: Brill, 2004), 233–59; "The Dark Side of Democratic Courage," *Social Research* 71.1 (Spring, 2004), 73–106 (www.socres.org); "Courage in the Democratic Polis," *Classical Quarterly*; 54.2 (2004) 406–23. © 2004 The Classical Association. Reprinted with the permission of Cambridge University Press; "Democratizing Courage in Classical Athens," in *War, Culture, and Democracy in Classical Athens,* ed. D. Pritchard.

(Cambridge: Cambridge University Press, 2010), 88–108.© 2010 Cambridge University Press. Reprinted with permission.

I am grateful to the publishers of these essays for permission to reuse this material freely in the present volume.

Chapter 14 contains a brief extract from the following chapter:

"Democracy and Political Philosophy: Influences, Tensions, Rapprochement." In *The Greek Polis and the Invention of Democracy: A Politico-Cultural Transformation and Its Interpretations*, edited by Johann P. Arnason, Kurt A. Raaflaub, and Peter Wagner, 181–204. Oxford: Blackwell, 2013.

I am grateful to Wiley-Blackwell for permission to reprint this extract.

In the interests of economy and coherence, I have chosen not to reprint here my previously published work on Plato's *Gorgias*, *Apology*, and *Republic*: the relevant arguments can be found in Balot 2007, Balot 2008, and Balot forthcoming c. Translations of ancient and modern texts are generally my own, although occasionally they are taken or adapted from the following works, for which full details are given in the bibliography:

Adams 1988; Barker (rev. Stalley) 1995; Burtt 1980; Campbell 1990; Crawley (rev. Strassler) 1996; de Sélincourt (rev. Marincola) 1996; deWitt and deWitt 1949; Fagles 1990; Freese 1994; Gerber 1999; Godley 1975; Grube 1997; Grube (rev. Reeve) 1997; Hamilton 1971; Henderson 1998, 2000, 2002; Herrman 2009; Knox 1967; Kovacs 1995, 1998, 1999, 2002; Lamb 1988; Lattimore 1961; Lembke and Herington 1981; Maidment 1982; Mansfield and Winthrop 2000; Nolla/Schleifer 2010; Norlin 1991, 1992; Pangle 1980; Rackham 1952, 1994; Rhodes 1984; Ross 1908; Rowe 1995; Saunders 1970; Scott-Kilvert 1960; Sprague 1997; Todd 2000; Tredennick 1989; Vince 1986, 1989; Vince and Vince 1999; Warner 1972; Woodruff 1993; Worthington, Cooper, and Harris 2001; Zeyl 1987.

ABBREVIATIONS

Ael.	Aelianus
V.H.	*Varia Historia*
Aesch.	Aeschines
Andoc.	Andocides
Ar.	Aristophanes
Ach.	*Acharnians*
Eccl.	*Ecclesiazusae*
Lys.	*Lysistrata*
Thesm.	*Thesmophoriazusae*
Arist.	Aristotle
Ath. Pol.	*Athēnaiōn Politeia*
EE	*Eudemian Ethics*
EN	*Nicomachean Ethics*
Pol.	*Politics*
Rhet.	*Rhetoric*
DA	Alexis de Tocqueville, *Democracy in America*
Dem.	Demosthenes
Ex.	*Exordium*
Eur.	Euripides
Hipp.	*Hippolytus*
Or.	*Orestes*
Supp.	*Suppliants*
fr.	Fragment
Hdt.	Herodotus
Hom.	Homer

Il.	*Iliad*
Od.	*Odyssey*
Hyp.	Hyperides
IG	*Inscriptiones Graecae* (1873–)
Isocr.	Isocrates
Lyc.	Lycurgus
Lys.	Lysias
ML	R. Meiggs and D. Lewis, *A Selection of Greek Historical Inscriptions to the End of the Fifth Century BC*, rev. edn. (1988)
Pl.	Plato
Ap.	*Apology*
Gorg.	*Gorgias*
Lach.	*Laches*
Prot.	*Protagoras*
Symp.	*Symposium*
Tim.	*Timaeus*
Plut.	Plutarch
Mor.	*Moralia*
Them.	*Themistocles*
Polyb.	Polybius
Thuc.	Thucydides
tr.	translator
Tyrt.	Tyrtaeus
Xen.	Xenophon
Mem.	*Memorabilia*

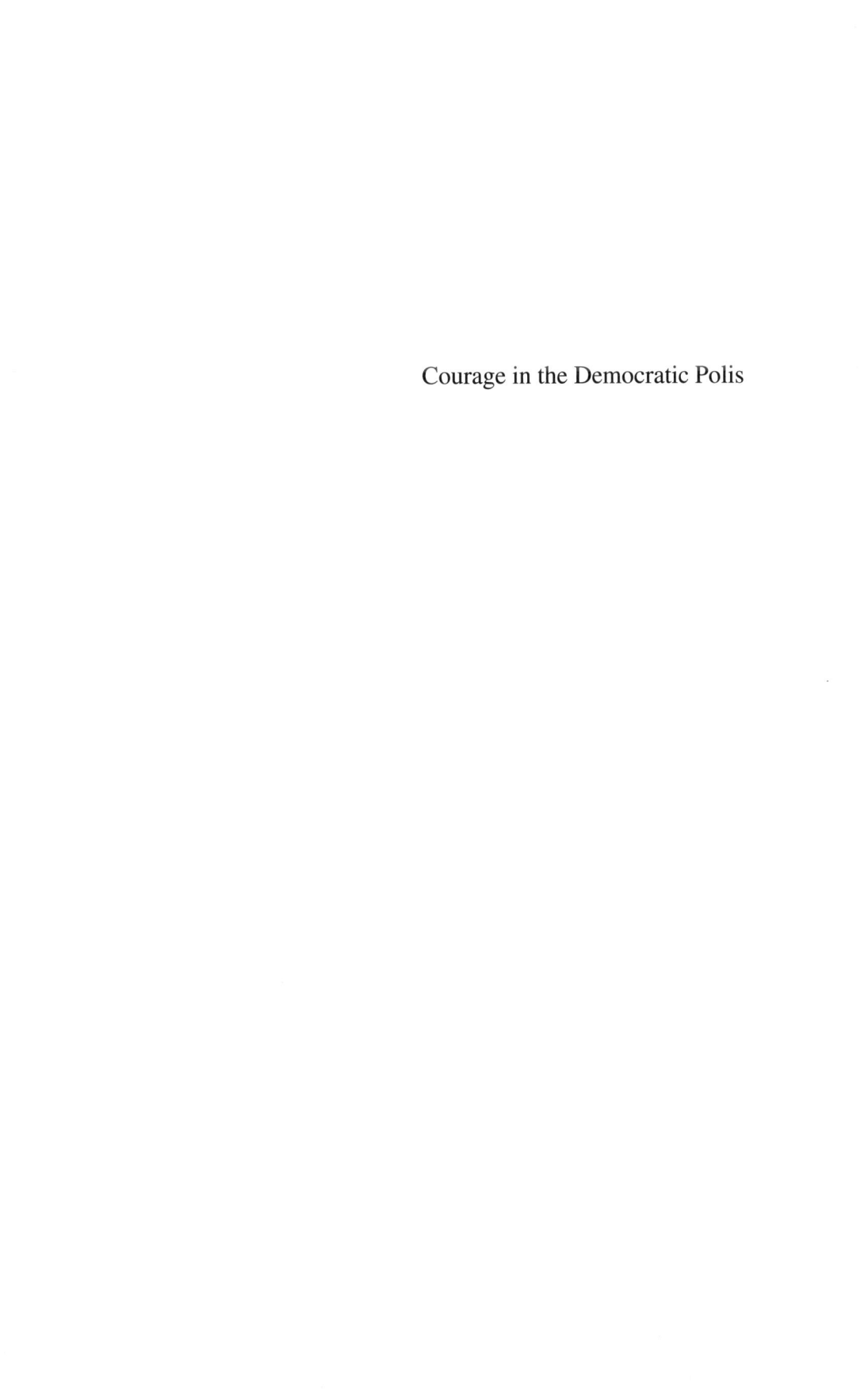

Courage in the Democratic Polis

CHAPTER 1 | Introduction
A Theory of Democratic Courage

COURAGE IS THE MOST exciting and elusive of the traditional virtues. Where moderation is boring, courage is dangerous; where justice is impartial, courage is dedicated to special causes.[1] Recent controversies show that courage is just as crucial to our self-image as ever, even if its precise character is hard to unpack. Susan Sontag's assertion that the 9/11 terrorists were courageous, for example, led to a furious but inconclusive debate over the ethical significance of courage.[2] In frustration, our leading intellectuals have called courage a "mysterious" or even an "impossible" virtue.[3] Philosophers continue to work at cross-purposes in grappling with questions such as the "courage of the villain" or the proper motivations and ends of courage.[4] Meanwhile, democratic citizens care deeply about courage. Far from being old-fashioned, it is politically expedient for our politicians to don military garb in artificial displays of courageous leadership.[5] Most importantly, we send young soldiers into the field—into

---

[1] For an illuminating discussion of the ancient Greeks' cardinal virtues, see Low 2007: 134–44; Whitehead 1993; on the tendency of courage and "manliness" to show partisanship to particular causes, see Mansfield 2006.
[2] For a detailed examination of this controversy, see Balot 2004c: 74–79.
[3] Mysterious: Miller 2000b; impossible: Kateb 2004: 39.
[4] See, for example, Walton 1986: 52–55; Bauhn 2003: 33–44; Von Wright 1963: 153, quoted in Walton 1986: 52; Foot 1978: 124–25; Miller 2000b: 8; Geach 1977: 150–70, esp. 160; Wallace 1978. For a more culturally specific attempt to explain courage philosophically, see Lear 2006, which connects courage to the theme of "radical hope" in the face of the devastation of the cultural and conceptual landscape of the Crow nation.
[5] For example, in a television drama called "DC 9/11: Time of Crisis," which was reportedly sanctioned by the White House, George Bush donned a flight suit and reminisced about his days as a pilot fighting the Vietcong (see Rich 2003 and Balot 2004c: 75–77). Equally, at the 2004 Democratic National Convention, presidential hopeful John Kerry appeared in a naval uniform and saluted his constituents. Kerry's gambit was countered by a strident oppositional group that

Iraq or Afghanistan, and elsewhere—in order to fight courageously for democratic principles of freedom and equality. We want and need an understanding of courage related to those principles. We owe at least that much to the soldiers commanded to stand and possibly die for democratic ideals.

The goal of the present volume is to begin to address such questions by returning to ancient Athens. I offer an account of courage as a central virtue of the Athenian democracy. In particular, I try to make sense of the Athenians' claim that they had developed a specifically democratic ideal of courage. By exploring the case of courage in Athens, I investigate the hypothesis that virtues vary according to regime type. Are there specifically democratic virtues—as opposed to the virtues of nondemocratic societies such as Persia, Sparta, and Macedon? Certainly, the Athenians were proud to declare that they had established a novel ideal of courage, that they had democratized this formerly heroic virtue. They proclaimed their superiority in this respect, specifically because they came to view their own courage as an outgrowth of admirable democratic ideals, such as freedom, equality, and political rationality.

Yet we will not rest content with reconstructing the Athenians' own most ambitious, and possibly self-serving, declarations about themselves. Rather, we will reconsider their ideal or ideology of courage within their complex social, political, and military worlds. Envisioning courage within that wider framework will involve examining tensions, gaps, and criticisms. To anticipate our conclusion: the case of ancient Athens brings to light not only an attractive and meritorious ideal of democratic courage, but also conceptual and ethical ambiguities that threaten that ideal. On the one hand, by connecting courage to democracy specifically, the Athenians made sense of the motivations, ends, and ethical significance of courage in ways that can illuminate our own democratic aspirations and commitments. On the other hand, the Athenians' otherwise attractive ideal covered over the desire to rule—an ambition that seemingly inexorably characterizes the powerful.[6]

---

called itself, tellingly, Swift Vets and POWs for Truth. Because the swift-boat veterans group has now disbanded, one convenient place to obtain information about the group and its attacks on presidential candidate John Kerry is http://en.wikipedia.org/wiki/Swift_Vets_and_POWs_for_Truth, retrieved February 17, 2012. For historically informed discussion of the role of the military in presidential politics, see Corbett and Davidson 2009.

[6] On the Athenians' desire for power and "rule," see especially Raaflaub 1994.

What Is "Democratic Courage"?

When Athenians emphasized the distinctiveness of democratic courage, they had several related ideas in mind. Above all, they meant that they were transforming what had traditionally been the hero's or the hoplite's cardinal virtue into a feature of the democratic character, by linking their ideal of courage with democratic freedom, innovation, equality, and rational deliberation. The Athenians acknowledged that all citizens, including the poor, could exhibit courage equally.[7] This extension of the formerly heroic virtue to all citizens, even the lowliest among them, in itself constituted a central democratic achievement—even if we find that, in practice, Athenian equality itself always remained ambiguous and contested.

The Athenians also located courage within new contexts and endowed it with a new substance. This new context was free and equal debate in Athenian public life. In democratic ideology, courage was informed by the deliberation, purposiveness, and rationality characteristic of democratic institutions and practices. Hence, democratic courage was cognitively richer, more deliberate, and more purposive than the courage of nondemocrats, such as Persians or Spartans. In substance, courage was newly recognized as the virtue that enabled Athenians to flourish as human beings, or to achieve *eudaimonia*, by living as free and equal citizens in the democratic polis. The Athenians recognized both the intrinsic goodness of courage, as a virtue, and the instrumental importance of courage as the "footstool of the virtues," which made possible secure lives of freedom, equality, and solidarity within their democracy.[8]

In this book I do not specifically engage with the numerous debates over the character of courage altogether.[9] Rather, I begin with a broad but widely shared view of courage: courage is an intrinsically worthwhile excellence of character, on the basis of which ethical agents knowingly strive to overcome difficult, dangerous, painful, or frightening obstacles or uncertainty, with a view to achieving noble ends. One of the purposes of the book is to arrive at a clearer account of the Athenians' own conception

---

[7] Among modern theorists, Walton 1986 (e.g., 14–17, 40–52) is distinctive in the attention he pays to the problem of heroic, as opposed to democratic, courage.

[8] The phrase "footstool of the virtues" is most often attributed to Robert Louis Stevenson in the essay "The Great North Road." For further treatment of this idea in the democratic Athenian context, see Balot 2007.

[9] Solid recent treatments include Walton 1986; Bauhn 2003; Foot 1978; Miller 2000b; Geach 1977: 150–70; Wallace 1978; and Casey 1990: 51–103. On courage in modern democracies, see particularly Scorza 2001.

of courage and its links to democracy. Accordingly, it is important not to prejudge the case. Yet it may be helpful to specify, at least provisionally, how the Athenians made the foregoing conception of courage more concrete. First, the Athenians envisioned courage not only as an intrinsically admirable quality of individuals, but also as the virtue whose precise function was to protect the city—thereby enabling the Athenians to live freely and equally, to participate regularly in political life, and to cultivate the virtues of character and the practical intellect. Second, unlike most traditional Greeks, the Athenians understood courage as informed by free, public deliberation on central questions of political and ethical life. Third, the Athenians recognized, as many contemporary authors do not, that courage, properly understood, must be guided by appropriate, proportionate, and well-informed emotions.

One of the Athenians' chief innovations within Hellenic culture at large was the recognition that courage is intrinsically linked to practical reasoning. Nowadays, this connection is often the centerpiece of philosophical accounts of courage; but it is important that this idea first arose within the democratic political context of ancient Athens.[10] Among the Athenians, such reasoning concerned both the goodness of particular choices and the choice of life trajectories as a whole. Courage requires deliberateness and intentionality: it is "about" certain things and "for" certain purposes. The Athenians saw that their greater self-consciousness about these features of courage made their practices of courage more adequate to the essence of this virtue than were the incomplete expressions of courage found in other polities.

Athenian practical reasoning had both immediate and long-term dimensions. In certain situations, it is correct to emphasize the strategic or technical or prudential reasoning characteristic of courage—think of a soldier who sees that he must jump from the third storey of a building and does so without hesitation. In other situations, it makes more sense to emphasize the longer arc of practical reasoning about life as a whole—that is, the reasoning about one's flourishing—in the light of which immediate risks make sense. The Athenians developed a fertile, complex discourse on both types of practical reasoning. It was a source of pride that the democratic regime enabled individuals to achieve this level of consciousness about their practices of courage.[11]

---

[10] Walton 1986, for example, focuses heavily on this component.
[11] Here I am self-consciously developing certain Hegelian ideas about the importance of self-consciously acknowledging one's own ideals, rather than being immersed within them unreflectively. I interpret Hegel's ideal modern state to be one in which the inner rational principles

Equally, unlike most contemporary authors, the Athenians linked courage to particular emotions. Intuitively, courage most often involves acting well in spite of fear. As the Athenians recognized, though, fear can be well placed or misplaced; the virtue of courage demands that agents act with the knowledge of how seriously they should attend to their fears.[12] They cannot allow themselves to be so "driven" by fear as to lose their capacity to reason well or act appropriately. The same holds true with respect to shame, emulation, anger, pride, and confidence. Although these emotions can distort our perceptions or interfere with our efforts to behave virtuously, they can also inform us and inspire us to do what is right for the right reasons. As recent theorists of the emotions have recognized, the emotions themselves are constituted, at least in part, by beliefs, ideas and ideals, and evaluative judgments (see chapters 10 and 11). The Athenians did not, like most contemporary theorists of courage, ignore these emotions and their relationship to courage. Instead, in addition to their emphasis on democratic deliberation, they also developed a discourse on the normatively desirable and cognitively informed emotional responses related to courage.[13]

Critics might charge that Athenian democracy itself (let alone democratic courage) was not distinctive. I have argued the contrary in other places.[14] I do not make the case again here, except to say that in my view

---

of social organization are well known by, explicit among, and self-consciously endorsed by the citizens as the fundamental ground on which they are able to actualize their freedom. Without this level of explicit understanding, individuals could not self-consciously endorse the state. Hence, they would experience its authority as alien, as imposed by others, rather than as self-chosen. For individuals or cultures to subordinate themselves to such external authorities is unworthy of the dignity and rational freedom of which human beings are naturally capable. Such subordination, indeed, makes their social forms and individual lives inadequate to our essential human capacities to live well. As Hegel finally relates, "It was when men had not yet plumbed the depths of self-consciousness or risen out of their undifferentiated unity of substance to their independence that they lacked strength to look within their own being for the final word" (*PR* 279R). Thus I mean to exempt the Athenians from the criticism that Hegel generally lodges against the ancient polis—that is, that its citizens were unreflectively beholden to its laws and customs and did not self-consciously acknowledge that they themselves had created law and custom and continued to endorse them as sources of authority.

[12] Aristotle says that fear makes men inclined to deliberate (*bouleutikous*) (*Rhet.* 1383a6-7). For a discussion of fear as penetrated by cognition, cf. Konstan 2006: 129–44; for fear and manliness in Athenian oratory, see Roisman 2005: 186–203.

[13] Most political theorists have ignored the political role of the emotions; for a helpful corrective, see Kingston 2011.

[14] See in particular Balot 2010a, along with the other essays in Pritchard 2010b. It is important to see the Athenians' transformations of courage against the backdrop of wider currents in Athenian war making and politics in the fifth and fourth centuries BC; for an illuminating treatment of these questions, see Pritchard 2010a.

Athens's democrats established a distinctively democratic ideology, institutional organization, and politico-military regime. By "ideology" I mean a set of relatively consistent beliefs about human nature, flourishing, psychology, and political life—beliefs that were popularly available and that mostly consisted of self-justifying interpretations of ethical and political phenomena.[15] By "democracy," I mean "people power"—which is a direct translation of the Greek word *dēmokratia*. As recent scholars have abundantly documented, people power is the central feature of the Athenians' lived experience of their own political regime. Democracy is the particular regime in which the *demos*—that is, the ordinary citizens, including the poor—made decisions in its own name, controlled the symbolic language of public debate, invented and enforced the laws, voted on war and peace, and regulated status and membership in the community.[16]

I favor the view that the Athenian democracy, in this sense, arose in 508 BC during the "Cleisthenic revolution," although scholarly differences on this point will not materially affect the arguments that follow.[17] It is more important, albeit less controversial, that, at least after 462 BC, Athens was a heavily participatory democracy, in which citizens of all classes and statuses regularly exercised their privileges of voting, regularly attended local and polis-wide assemblies, and occasionally even held office and made their opinions known in public.[18] To avoid any blurring of categories, I reserve the term "democracy," not for Greece's widespread and generally egalitarian constitutions (which have been aptly designated "isonomic"[19]), but rather for constitutions in which all citizens, including the poor, were involved in the processes of making decisions and rendering justice. "Democracy" in this sense is not a special term of art, but rather an appropriately restrictive usage corresponding to the Athenians' own inclusive self-presentation.[20] It laid unusual emphasis on freedom (especially free speech) and equality, which are the two principal ideals I will discuss in relation to courage.[21]

---

[15] Cf. Balot 2004c: 408–9; Ober 1989: 38–40; Harris 2001: 24.

[16] On these questions, see especially Ober 1989, 1996b, and 1997.

[17] On the debates over the character of the regime established by Cleisthenes' reforms, see now the articles assembled in Raaflaub, Ober, and Wallace 2007, which revise earlier discussions.

[18] On the participatory character of Athenian democracy, see Sinclair 1988; Hansen 1991.

[19] On this term, see, e.g., Raaflaub 1997a, 1997b.

[20] I assume without argument that, contra Robinson 1997, the uses of *dēmokratia* by Hellenistic Greek historians were informed by local ideology and foundation myths; for this criticism of Robinson, see Hansen 1999.

[21] On free speech and equality as the central political ideals of democratic Athens, see Ober and Hedrick 1996.

The Ambiguities of Democratic Courage

Whatever their distinctive and meritorious features, the Athenians' discourses on and practices of courage were shot through with ambiguity. We must neither whitewash the Athenians nor denigrate their achievements. Even as we appreciate the Athenians' novel connections between courage and democracy, then, it is worthwhile to keep in mind that their conception of courage itself carried with it unsettling and distinctly unappealing features. At its root, "courage" for the Athenians was "manliness" or the "manly virtue" (*andreia*). In its guise as "manliness," Athenian courage was always implicated in the subordination of women and in the desire to rule others. The Athenian citizen body was an exclusively male group whose solidarity was constituted in part by the exclusion of women, slaves, and foreigners. The Athenians frequently intended to extend imperial power over other Greeks. The Athenians' "manliness" or "courage" was often toxically invested in the projection of power over others, in the execution and enslavement of enemies, and in the maintenance of hierarchies over women.

Any "recovery" of classical Athenian courage, therefore, should avoid celebration, however fertile the resources of Athenian courage might be for our own ways of linking courage to contemporary democracy. Hence, whatever the attractions of the Athenian ideal, it is impossible to endorse that ideal fully. Yet, before we approach questions of endorsement or critique, it is necessary to clarify the ideology of democratic courage and to discuss its place in Athenian political life, as well as its ambiguities. This project of exploration and clarification is ambitious enough in its own right. This is why I have conceived of the present volume as a predominantly historical treatment of the ideology of democratic courage—a treatment that is informed by philosophical questions, no doubt, but one that stops short of taking an explicitly normative stance on the issues.

The ideology of democratic courage presents a complex picture along several dimensions. First, it wobbled between a robustly democratic conception and a more traditional conception. On the one hand, democratic courage often exemplified Athenian novelty and embodied the fruits of free and open deliberation. On the other hand, the Athenian orators sometimes envisioned courage as based on shame and the fear of punishment, rather than deliberative rationality and free, purposeful choice. Thus the Athenians did not depart from the traditional Greek ethos at all times or in a watertight fashion. There was a conflict between the ideology of democratic courage and the Athenians' reliance on traditional Greek *andreia*.

Second, the Athenians' practices of courage did not always align closely with their ideals. Admittedly, we would be hard-pressed to explore any particular psychological experience of courage on the ancient battlefield or in the Athenian Assembly, as contemporary psychologists might do in the laboratory.[22] Yet, to the extent that we can make a judgment on such questions, it is clear that the Athenians were not always as fair-minded and generous toward their imperial subjects (for example) as their ideology suggested. They acted out of fear, anger, and wounded pride—when they were not unabashedly pursuing their own imperialistic self-aggrandizement. Even during the Persian Wars, their leaders were driven by a tendency to focus on their own narrowly construed self-interests.

In these ways, "democratic courage" turns out to be, not the essential truth of the Athenian experience, but rather an interesting and fertile ideological construct—one worth exploring for its historical importance and potential philosophical value. This remains true even if the claim to distinctiveness was contradicted by other ideological principles and by other facets of the Athenians' lived political experience. This type of complexity in the relation between idea and experience is familiar from other examinations of Athenian democratic "values," such as equality and freedom. As Raaflaub has shown, for example, equality was vaunted as a central plank of the Athenian democracy, and yet, in central military and political forums, the city's public ideology tended to neglect, ignore, or despise the lower classes.[23]

Even so, studying the idea of democratic courage is still important for three reasons. First, whatever its ambiguities or contradictions, the Athenian ideology was influential in shaping later philosophical models of courage—in particular, those of Plato and Aristotle. The Athenians maintained that courage should be understood with reference both to practical rationality and to correctly educated emotions; the idea of unifying reason with passion represented a theoretical advance in the understanding of courage. Both Plato and Aristotle later developed theories of courage that included both cognitive understanding of the good life and emotional training designed to shape our desires appropriately and to combat inappropriate fears whenever necessary. Acknowledging Athenian influence on the philosophers does not, however, limit the originality of the philosophers'

---

[22] Moreover, as I argue in the conclusion, any judgment about a person's or a people's courage must engage with normative and not simply empirical questions: see chapter 16. For empirically based psychological work on courage, see, e.g., Rachman 2004.

[23] Raaflaub 1996. We consider this question in more detail in chapter 8.

own explorations of courage or cast doubt on their decisive break with the democratic political experience.

Second, the Athenian ideology, suitably reimagined and "updated," and used selectively, might still hold out a promising ideal of democratic courage for us today—one based on free speech, deliberation, equality, and rationality; one that was oriented toward human flourishing; and one that also included appropriate attention to the emotional development of citizens. This would constitute a novel challenge indeed to the liberal models of courage or, rather, to the liberal ignorance of courage that prevails in our anodyne contemporary discourses.[24]

Third, investigation of the relationship between ideas and historical realities is interesting in its own right, as a way to throw light on the democratic experience of classical Athens. We want to know, among other things, how the Athenians constructed idealizing images of themselves as citizens and democrats, why their self-image took the precise forms it did, and how well that self-image matched Athenian practice and behavior. It would be interesting to learn that the classical Athenians' practices differed markedly from their ideology, self-presentation, and self-understanding, particularly if we can explain precisely how, when, and why the fault lines arose as they did. As Peter Hunt has argued, however, it is important not simply to indulge the scholarly desire to "unmask" the Athenians' motives and self-conceptions, as though their ideology and self-presentation were simply a "cover" for their underlying desires for power, status, and wealth.[25] It is also worthwhile to lay bare the logic of the Athenians' own self-understandings, as expressed in oratory, drama, public monuments, and historical texts, because these self-understandings both helped to construct the Athenians' particular desires, and they were, conversely, informed by those very desires.

Toward a Regime-Specific Interpretation of Courage

For the sake of argument, at least, let us grant that the Athenian democracy was founded on two distinctive ideals—freedom and equality—and that its political practices, social relations, and cultural rituals were deeply informed by those ideals. Is it possible, similarly, to think of courage itself

---

[24] For criticism of the neglect of courage as a virtue within liberal political theory, see Mansfield 2006, Rabieh 2006.
[25] Hunt 2010: 2–10.

as a regime-specific attribute, rather than as a general or universal human quality? Is it not true that all peoples, always, have prized at least physical courage, if not the diverse moral, psychological, political, and even philosophical expressions of courage with which we are now familiar? In what sense were the Athenians entitled, if at all, to think of their courage as qualitatively different from that of others? Are we entitled to think of courage, in general, as qualitatively different across regimes and perhaps across times and places?

At least initially, it is helpful to approach these questions at a more general level, by considering whether emotions and virtues altogether are susceptible of historical, political, social, and cultural analysis. To be sure, we will have to investigate Athenian courage on its own terms, in order to discern whether it was, at bottom, distinctively a product of the Athenians' democratic regime. But the idea itself may gain initial plausibility if we consider that theorists and historians working on the emotions and virtues have typically come to see our ethical psychology as informed by social, political, and cultural contexts. Students of this subject increasingly accept that emotions and ethical virtues—such as justice, jealousy, self-control, and anger, not to mention courage—are expressed in distinctive ways across societies and political regimes, and diversely throughout different historical epochs.[26] As Aristotle emphasized, the citizen's virtue or excellence is relative to the regime (*Pol.* III.4.1276b16-35).

Consider several examples drawn from recent work on the Athenians' emotions, virtues, and cultural ideals. Classical Athenians democratized traditionally aristocratic *kalokagathia* (nobility) by making nobility the property of all Athenians considered as a collective group.[27] Among the democratic Athenians, moreover, *phthonos* (envy) arguably evolved in the context of class struggle to become an ethically respectable emotion directed at undeserving recipients of good fortune.[28] More generally, anger evolved from playing a notoriously destructive role in the Homeric epics to taking on a morally ambiguous role in classical Athens to being severely criticized in Hellenistic philosophy and early Christianity.[29] If we turn to work on global cultures and traditions, we find that different societies have

---

[26] In the case of the emotions in ancient Greece, see especially the landmark study of Konstan 2006, which argues for the "disparities, sometimes subtle and sometimes conspicuous, between their emotional repertoire and ours" (x). On justice, see MacIntyre 1988; on virtue in general, see MacIntyre 1984.
[27] Ober 1989: 259–66.
[28] Konstan 2004.
[29] For the long history of anger in classical antiquity, see Harris 2001; cf. Konstan 2006: 76.

adopted either "offensive" or "defensive" styles of courage; they have viewed courage as supererogatory or as a minimum standard required of all citizens or adults; and they have diversely emphasized the martial, civic, or spiritual dimensions of courage, depending on the larger ethical frameworks in which their ideals of courage were embedded.[30] The same holds true of important recent work on the emotion of shame in diverse global cultures.[31]

Recognition of the cultural contexts that inform courage and other virtues, not to mention the emotions, is not peculiar to the modern investigation of such topics. Herodotus (5.78) and the author of the Hippocratic *Airs, Waters, and Places* (16) specifically connected courage and cowardice with particular political regimes. Tyrannies were held to produce cowardly citizens because soldiers fighting under tyrants were fighting for the benefit of others, not themselves (Hdt. 5.78, 5.91; Thuc. 1.17).[32] The tyrant must work hard to eliminate brave citizens from his territories, for fear of rebellion; instead of a free and self-respecting citizenry, tyrants must cultivate docile, even servile, subjects (Xen. *Hiero* 5.1–4).

On the other side of the political spectrum, Thucydides argued that the courage of the Spartans was unrivaled (5.72). In Plato's *Republic*, Socrates described democracy as having a characteristically immoderate view of *andreia* (560c–e), while in the Platonic *Laws* the Athenian Stranger characterized the Dorian regimes as unhealthily elevating courage over all other virtues (625c–630d). In the "historical" sections of the *Laws*, moreover, the Athenian Stranger proposed that the egalitarianism that had prevailed under Cyrus made the Persians courageous (694ab); by contrast, the increasing despotism of his successors made the kingdom militarily weak (697c–e). For Polybius, who wrote centuries after the Athenian democracy, Roman *virtus* was deliberate and self-disciplined as well as ambitious; it thereby promoted the cause of Roman greatness more effectively than (for example) Macedonian courage, which, however fearsome, was not managed carefully within a framework of free republican institutions.[33]

Confirmation of these points can also be found in the writings of Alexis de Tocqueville, particularly in his most important work, *Democracy in*

---

[30] Miller 2000: 106–26, 182–84, 254–70.
[31] On shame, see Williams 1993; Taylor 1985; Schweder 2003; Konstan 2003; and Tarnopolsky 2010.
[32] Cf. Thomas 2000: 102–34 for a searching discussion of such questions, especially in Herodotus.
[33] See Eckstein 1995: 171–73, Balot 2010b.

America (two volumes, published in 1835 and 1840). Whatever institutional, ideological, or religious differences may separate Tocqueville from the democratic Athenians, Tocqueville provides strong support for the possibility of a distinctively democratic model of courage.[34] Tocqueville sees a clear relationship between the enlightenment of the citizens within democratic society and their discipline once they are recruited into the army: "Have enlightened, well-ordered, steady, and free citizens, and you will have disciplined and obedient soldiers" (*DA* II.3.22). In Tocqueville's view, the democratic statesman should strive to make "reflective, intelligent, and stable tastes" (*DA* II.3.22) out of the citizens' instinctive hatred for despotism; this would help to create an army "pervaded by the love of liberty and the respect for rights" that characterize the people in general (*DA* II.3.23).

Tocqueville argues explicitly that the democratic regime itself engages in a form of soul-craft that shapes the military experience of democratic soldiers (*DA* II.3.25). Military courage in democracies is different from military courage in aristocracies. Calling democratic courage "intelligent," Tocqueville argues that its source is "in the very will of the one who obeys; it rests not only on his instinct, but on his reason" (*DA* II.3.25). Democracies practice a more "rational," self-conscious, and individualistic form of military courage than previous centuries had known. The serf who populates aristocratic armies, on the other hand, "acts without thinking." We may question the degree to which this is possible, but, for Tocqueville, this type of traditional soldier is merely "a very ferocious animal trained for war" who displays the "blind, minute, resigned, and always constant obedience" that characterizes the lower orders of an aristocratic society (*DA* II.3.25).

Tocqueville's analysis illustrates not only that democratic courage exists, but also that democracy in America brought about transformations in the traditional ideal of courage. It was *democracy*—that is, the democratic regime, or *politeia*—that was "doing the work" of transforming courage into a rational, articulate, and more explicitly purposive virtue than had been known previously. This is an exciting parallel that, at least

---

[34] It is worth noting, however, that because of its slaveholding, Tocqueville himself viewed ancient Athens, not as a genuine democracy, but rather as a limited, aristocratic republic (*DA* II.1.15). I develop the theme of "democratic courage" with respect to Tocqueville more fully in Balot forthcoming a.

initially, vindicates our inquiry into the regime-specific virtues of the classical Athenian democracy.[35]

Source Material and Progression of the Argument

The Athenians did not, of course, leave a complete or systematic record of democratic courage. Hence, we must rely on a wide variety of sources produced in ancient Athens during its classical, democratic period. Principally, this means that we will focus on the public speeches of the corpus of Attic oratory—a body of roughly 150 speeches delivered by members of the Athenian upper classes to ordinary democratic citizens. These speeches are a fertile source for understanding the Athenians' commitment to liberty, equality, security, and social solidarity. "Free speech," or even "frank speech," expressed by the Greek terms *parrhēsia* and *isēgoria*, was the classic ideal and distinguished the Athenian democracy from its more traditional and less outspoken nondemocratic rivals.[36]

Within the oratorical corpus, the "epitaphic" speeches, or funeral orations, will occupy a central place in our investigation. I have made this choice for two reasons. First, these speeches reflect seriously on the character of Athenian life, on the essential nature and function of Athenian ideals, and on the role of democracy in defining the Athenian ethos. This is precisely the register of discussion that will help us see in a distilled form how the Athenians constructed an ideal of democratic courage. Second, these speeches focus especially on the virtue of courage, because they were delivered in order to commemorate the Athenian soldiers who had fallen in war in a particular year. Even as they emphasized the democratic regime, the funeral orators respected the commemorative occasion by highlighting the specific qualities—indeed, the characteristic merits and dignity—of Athenian courage.

---

[35] Very few classicists or political theorists have seen the importance of this connection. But George Kateb has recognized that "reading him [Tocqueville] is an ideal preparation for thinking about the revision of courage as a virtue" (Kateb 2004: 66). As Kateb 2004: 66 correctly argues, Tocqueville "familiarizes us with the idea that democracy changes all values in a democratic direction, even courage and honor." In her study of shame in the Platonic dialogues, Christina Tarnopolsky also argues that "all emotions have the possibility of becoming an integral part of our democratic virtues and vices" (2010: 6). Avramenko 2011 includes a discussion of both the Athenians and Tocqueville on courage, but his Heideggerian focus on "care" leads to a very different, and to my mind much less plausible, account of courage as a feature of democratic mentality or practice.

[36] See especially the essays in Rosen and Sluiter 2004.

The funeral oration attributed to Pericles in Thucydides' *History* is the starting point of my investigation. The status of this speech has been the subject of frequent controversy: To what extent does it reflect the speech that Pericles actually delivered? Does it capture the Athenians' own ideals or represent subtle Thucydidean criticisms of those ideals? I follow many students of this oration in holding that Thucydides himself composed the speech; consequently, what we have is not a word-for-word rendition of Pericles' actual oration. Nonetheless, in keeping with his famous methodological declaration (1.22), Thucydides presented Pericles' underlying democratic principles, arguments, and sentiments. This is why, I think, the speech makes a genuinely powerful case for the merits of Athenian democracy, articulated by its foremost leader in the late fifth century BC. Even if the speech does not correspond exactly to the one delivered by Pericles, students of the funeral oration as a genre have convincingly argued that the speech offers a clear statement of the political and ethical ideas that characterize the genre.[37] Since Pericles' oration was widely witnessed, and since Thucydides was writing contemporary history, his record of the speech could have been tested by at least some of his readers. He would have reduced his own credibility if he had fabricated its basic arguments or underlying principles.[38]

---

[37] Loraux 1986: 220, for example, writes that "this epitaphios develops more brilliantly the thought of other orations.... It is neither an isolatable document of its genre nor an isolated exception in the midst of more traditional orations. On the contrary, Pericles' epitaphios attests the unity of the funeral oration." See also Ziolkowski 1981: esp. 180–81; Mills 1997: 46–47. Even so, we should not assume that the speech provides unmediated access to the *vox populi,* without referring to a wide range of other, more directly engaged democratic texts (see Balot 2006: 50–51). This is why we will have occasion to indicate how the ideals expressed in Pericles' speech were reformulated in other democratic contexts, so as to suit the needs of particular democratic occasions, rituals, and performances in Athens, as they arose. I take a middle-of-the-road view in general on Thucydides' speeches: the speeches were not delivered in the form in which we have them, and Thucydides used them to instruct his readers (cf. Yunis 1996). But Thucydides himself, virtually alone among ancient authors (cf. Hornblower 1991: 59), raises the question of their veracity (1.22), and says explicitly that he will try to present to his readers the essential point of the speeches. For a discussion of the various possibilities, see Ziolkowski 1981: 188–95.

[38] The treatment of this speech in the text and footnotes adapts my earlier treatments in Balot 2001a: 136–37, 145; 2004b; 2004c; and 2006: 50–51. There are, in fact, two separate but linked questions about the speech: first, the relationship between Thucydides' own views and those of his character Pericles; second, the relationship between Pericles the Thucydidean character and Pericles the historical statesman. On the former, the issue is straightforward: whatever his admiration for Pericles, Thucydides also criticizes views he attributes to Pericles and in particular Pericles' misunderstanding of his own role in the democratic system: see Balot 2001a: 148–49. The latter issue will likely never be resolved conclusively. My account shares elements with those of Orwin 1994: 207–12, Loraux 1986, Yunis 1996: 61–66; Hornblower 1987: 45–72; and Swain 1993. For arguments endorsing the historicity of the speeches, see Garrity 1998, Bosworth 2000. On the near impossibility of providing a verbally accurate account, see Woodman 1988: 1–69, esp. 11–15, recently challenged by Munn 2000: 11–12, 292–94, 305–7, who argues that

This speech captures democratic ideals of courage in a particularly striking way, as Pericles not only distinguishes Athenian courage from Spartan courage, but also links democratic courage to *eudaimonia*, or flourishing, within the democratic city in ways that other speakers and writers adapted to their own contexts. Because of its importance and complexity, Pericles' funeral oration deserves its own chapter (chapter 2). Then, in a subsequent chapter (chapter 3), I argue that we can deepen our conception of the Periclean ideal by concentrating on the relationship between courage and free speech. The orators' discussions of free speech as supportive of, and dependent upon, courage further the case for the distinctiveness of democratic courage. Yet I stress that in the present volume I intend only to *explore* the extent to which Pericles' ideal surfaces in other evidence from classical Athens; I do not take this for granted. Thus, after offering an extended interpretation of Pericles' "anatomy of democratic courage" and of the relationship between courage and free speech in the Attic orators, I investigate how widespread this conception was in classical Athenian life and thought in general. To what extent was Pericles' ideology of distinctively democratic courage attractive and useful to classical Athenians altogether? To what extent did Athens differ from others in its ideals of courage?

To confirm the importance of the ideology expressed by Pericles, I proceed to show that both Aeschylus' *Persians* and Herodotus' *Histories* represented democratic courage in action during the Persian Wars (chapter 4). The ideal of democratic courage circulated well beyond Thucydides' text. Both Aeschylus and Herodotus present the Persian Wars in such a way as to vindicate, rather than to question, the Athenians' claim to a distinctive ideal (and even practice) of democratic courage. But Herodotus also raised questions about the ends to which Athenian courage and power were directed. As admirable as democratic courage may have been, its praiseworthy features stood in tension with the darker and more problematic facts of Athenian aggression and bellicosity. Even Pericles had praised Athenian expansionism in his otherwise attractive representation of democratic courage.

Thucydides worked from written notes. For treatment of what can be known about the historical Pericles, see Podlecki 1998, Stadter 1989, and Stadter 1991. Todd 2007: 151 stresses, following Loraux and Ziolkowski, that Pericles' oration is similar to the fourth-century funeral orations that we have in expressing democratic principles, but he also points out that it is different from those fourth-century orations in suppressing the mythological narratives that seem to have been typical of the genre.

In order to investigate the pugnacity and injustice of Athenian imperialism as fully as possible, I build upon my analysis of Herodotus and interpret Thucydides' *History* through the lens of democratic courage (chapter 5). Pericles' funeral oration was presented within a larger narrative designed, in truth, to cast doubt on the Periclean ideal. Thucydides balances the approbatory Periclean representation of Athens by raising questions and criticisms of his own. Thucydides' challenges will further our understanding of the dialectic between the Athenians' subscription to distinctively democratic courage and their retreat to more traditional, and possibly more harmful, models of *andreia*.

To add strength to Thucydides' challenges, I show that Plato, too, engaged with the discourse on free speech, courage, and democratic deliberation, in his dialogue *Laches* (chapter 6). The chief characters in this dialogue are Socrates and two generals, Laches and Nicias, both of whom are also characters in Thucydides' *History*. At many levels, Plato's dialogue advances the criticisms leveled against democratic courage by Thucydides. Even though Thucydides and Plato criticized the ideals of Pericles and the Athenian orators, these authors show that contemporaries were attuned to the ideology of democratic courage and thought it worth their time to engage seriously with it. In the fourth century, similarly, Isocrates showed through his recollections of Athenian imperialism that Athens had striven to embody a new ideal of courage that gave certain benefits to the wider Greek world (chapter 7). In Herodotus, Thucydides, and Isocrates, though, the very case for democratic distinctiveness and superiority gave way to anxieties about the Athenians' desire to put their daring and innovativeness in the service of their imperialism.

Throughout these discussions, I think, it becomes clear that to understand the Athenians' development of a distinctively democratic model of courage in the most complete way possible, we must explore the treatments of courage found not only in the Athenian orators, but also in the narratives of historians, and in the more overtly philosophical works of Isocrates and Plato. These sources are complex, neither fully pro-democratic nor entirely hostile to democracy. Herodotus, Thucydides, Isocrates, and Plato all leveled powerful criticisms against the Athenian demos, ones with which twenty-first century observers are likely to sympathize. And yet, perhaps with the exception of Plato's *Laches*, they also put on display certain meritorious and noble dimensions of democratic courage. In order to grasp the totality of the Athenian experience of courage, it is as important to present critical allegations as it is to offer an account of the Athenian ideology on its own terms. It is not only possible but also exciting, as we will see, to uncover the dialectic between pro-democratic arguments and critical responses to the demos's ideology and behaviors.

With this interpretation of Isocrates, we conclude our examination of the "Periclean model" in both its wide-ranging, positive expression in Athenian culture and in the responses and criticisms of historians and philosophers. Part I concludes that the Athenians' claim to novelty and superiority is overshadowed by the charge that, beneath the surface of their ideal, the Athenians were similar to others, whether Greeks or non-Greeks, in their desires to become preeminent and even to rule their Aegean neighbors.

By contrast, Part II explores the associations of courage with equality, emotion, and civic education. Having reconstructed the interdependence of courage and democratic freedom, we are well positioned to understand the complex relationship between courage and democratic equality (chapter 8). Beginning with a study of Athens's most important practices of military commemoration, we grasp the tension between the Athenians' desire for egalitarian military recognition and their dependence on a social imaginary in which the traditional Greek hoplite was central. For all their innovativeness, the Athenians did not make a clean break from hierarchical notions of honor and glory associated with the hoplite. Whatever their tendency to embody the ideal of equality in practice, they did not ever give their rowers, their chief source of military power, equal public recognition for their military successes.

In their everyday speech and practices in general, then, how well did the demos and its leaders live up to the claim that Athens practiced a distinctively democratic form of courage? In order to approach this question, we revisit, albeit more systematically, what I call the "standard model" of Greek courage—courage motivated chiefly by the fear of social shame, humiliation, and legal punishment (chapter 9). Here we recall that Pericles himself highlighted both rationality and emotion in his anatomy of democratic courage, without ever doubting that Athenian courage was different from and superior to the Spartan alternative. In order to make sense of his claims and to confront the possible instability of Pericles' vision, I turn to an exploration of courage and the emotions in the next two chapters (chapters 10 and 11).

At first glance, at least, "distinctively democratic" courage overlaps with the standard Greek sources of motivation for courage. For the classical Athenians, too, courage was sometimes driven by anger, shame, pride, and even fear. The question is whether these emotions drew the Athenians away from their deliberative ideals and their dispositions to innovate. Were

Pericles and the other orators simply distorting manifest realities, then, as they made their claim to democratic distinctiveness, or did Athens's democratic culture modify the traditional emotions so as to cast the apparent "overlap" in a different light? Is it possible that these "emotions of courage" were shaped and tutored within Athenian democratic culture by the individual's experience of the city's festivals, orations, rituals, artwork, and theatrical productions? In other words, was there also a democratic form of shame, anger, and so on, that corresponded to democratic courage?

Here the evidence is ambiguous, as befits the complex, lived experience of a large, democratic city-state that evolved continuously over some two centuries. Through examining forensic cases, deliberative oratory, and public monuments, we find that the Athenians sometimes failed to adhere to their ideals of thoughtful, purposive courage. Instead, they occasionally adopted more traditional approaches. To that extent, at least, the democratic associations of Athenian courage receded. At certain times and in certain places, the Athenians showed themselves to be more similar to other Greeks, or other Mediterranean peoples, than their ideology had suggested, because they too relied, at times, on social humiliation and the fear of punishment in order to motivate citizens to act courageously.

On the other hand, it is possible to recognize in other cases that the Athenians cultivated their normative emotional responses in a more intentional, deliberate, and thoughtful way than their nondemocratic rivals. They publicly discussed the emotional education offered by the city. And, more specifically, they debated the nature of the role models offered to their children in order to cultivate proper emotional responses, particularly those related to shame and honor.[39] Such debates were possible only because of the Athenians' institutionalized free speech and open deliberation, along with their habits of self-criticism.[40]

In addition to public discussions in the Assembly and the courts, as well as informal discussions in a variety of other venues, this emotional education took place during comic and tragic theatrical productions (chapters 12 and 13). The theater embodied democratic thoughtfulness and openness. In discussing a variety of plays, we will discover that Aristophanes and Euripides, in particular, invited their audiences to rethink their seemingly "reflexive," knee-jerk emotional responses. Perhaps they recognized that

---

[39] For a helpful discussion of role models in certain Platonic texts, see Hobbs 2000: 59–68 and passim.

[40] For a very different assessment of the motivations for Athenian courage, and of the role of "manliness" (*andreia*) in Athenian political life, see now Crowley 2012.

it was possible to experience shame, anger, fear, and other emotions in ways that were healthy or unhealthy, reasonable or hidebound, mature or "primitive." Because the demos reflected seriously upon such questions, we have reason to accept the claim to democratic distinctiveness, even or especially with regard to the city's emotional education of its citizens. The democratic culture of freedom, innovation, and self-criticism led to a heightened self-consciousness in the production of emotion—a self-consciousness that we would be hard pressed to find in other regimes, particularly Persia or Sparta.

If it seems difficult to accept that emotions, too, varied according to the regime, then we might at least note that in fashioning his "Callipolis" in the *Republic*, Plato's Socrates agreed that it was possible—indeed, necessary—to train the citizens' emotions in ways that suited the particular purposes of his unusual regime (375a–376e, 387b–d, 388d–e, 390c–391b, 395c–396e, 401e–402d). His strategy was designed to correct the supposedly misguided education offered by traditional poetry and the theater (377a–403c). Socrates emphasizes the importance of self-consciousness and even vigilance in these respects (385b–c, 401b–402a), just as the Athenian orators, similarly, called upon their fellow citizens to show just the same vigilance in educating the emotions of the Athenian young (e.g., Aesch. 3.245–47). Other, more traditional cities adopted different, less healthy and sound, modes of emotional education through music and physical training. At all events, these chapters indicate that it takes substantial interpretative work to reconstruct emotional experiences from the past. We would be less historically sensitive than necessary, if we accepted at face value the Athenians' apparent traditionalism in these respects without digging further into the particular qualities of their experience.

With these investigations we conclude Part II, having worked through the associations of courage with freedom and equality, and having discussed the two most prominent psychological dimensions of democratic courage—practical reasoning and the emotions. At this stage it becomes necessary to examine, finally, the ends served by Athenian courage. As Pericles himself emphasized, it is impossible to diagnose or appreciate democratic courage without an adequate conception of the ends served by that virtue. This is why I spend two subsequent chapters (chapters 14 and 15) describing the democratic ideology of *eudaimonia*. The Athenian orators contended that Athens's free and secure cultivation of the virtues in general led to the best life possible for Athens's democratic citizens. This ideology helped to make sense of courage as an intrinsically good and meritorious element of a well-lived life of democratic citizenship. Courage was both an intrinsically good and admirable attribute of citizens, and an instrumentally valuable means by which the city enjoyed security, freedom, and equality. Within the democratic polis, all citizens could flourish by developing their human capacities for the social and intellectual virtues.[41] Courage made this type of flourishing (*eudaimonia*) possible.[42]

The orators' arguments for democratic eudaimonism are big claims, difficult to sustain in any event, and especially in public speeches written for specific occasions and delivered before large, diverse democratic audiences. Hence, as exciting as their arguments may be, we should keep in mind that the ideology of *eudaimonia* was one among several images of Athens, one way of constructing the Athenian self-image that competed with others over two centuries of democratic self-government. (Other images, for example, were those of the demos as tyrant and the demos as hero, with which the Athenians flirted from time to time.) Yet with this qualification in mind, it is fair to say, I think, that the Athenians' eudaimonism was deep, significant, provocative, and philosophically interesting. This is why I speculate, at least, that the Athenian discourse on *eudaimonia* helped to shape the accounts of *eudaimonia* found in Plato and Aristotle.[43] The philosophers' account of human ends was influenced in both structure and content by that of the democratic city. However that may be, the Athenian self-presentation helps to explain why the Athenians were able to claim, at least, that their regime was just, healthy, and sound, despite their imperialism, despite their slaveholding, and despite their disturbing exclusion of women from political life.

---

[41] For an exciting application of social scientific theory to the study of Athenian democracy, see Ober 2008. I agree with Ober that the Athenian democracy's distinctive institutions, practices, and ethos differentiated it not only from authoritarian regimes, but also from its generically "republican" counterparts; but readers will note that my sense of "flourishing" in the following pages differs considerably from Ober's focus on "aggregate material flourishing" (Ober 2008: 39), even though the two are not incompatible or, a fortiori, mutually exclusive.

[42] In speaking of "flourishing," the development of "natural capacities," "capabilities," and so on, I am using the language of contemporary theorists who have developed ancient (largely Aristotelian and Stoic) ideas of *eudaimonia*, particularly Martha Nussbaum (see, e.g., Nussbaum 1986, 1988, 1990, 2001b, along with other works) and Richard Kraut (especially 2007 and 2011). What is different about my account, though, is that I am eliciting these ideas from the pre-philosophical context of democratic Athens and thus showing that these important philosophical ideas grew out of a rich legacy of Greek, and specifically democratic, political thinking altogether.

[43] In other, related work (Balot 2013 and Balot, forthcoming b), I demonstrate that the vision of emotional education offered by Socrates in Plato's *Republic* was heavily influenced by Athenian democratic thinking about the moral psychology of shame, honor, and fear, as well as the possibility of a civic education that focused on these emotions.

In conclusion, I put the Athenians into dialogue with their critics once again. I argue that the Athenians' claim to superiority is surprisingly successful in meeting the challenges posed by political and philosophical rivals. A chastened and more self-consistent Athenian ideal may yet prove attractive to us as we reflect again, in their company, upon our own democratic quandaries, deficits, and aspirations.

PART I | The Periclean Ideology and Its Critics

CHAPTER 2 | The Periclean Model

OUR STARTING POINT IS the Athenians' cognitively rich model of courage that derived from the deliberative rationality of Athenian institutions and political practices. The most explicit formulation of this model comes from Pericles' funeral oration, as reported by Thucydides.[1] According to Pericles, the democratic Athenians, by contrast with others, either develop the city's policy or at least make judgments about it; and their democratic processes have a significant impact on the quality of their courage:

> We do not think that words (*tous logous*) are harmful to deeds (*tois ergois*); instead, it is harmful not to be instructed in advance by argument (*logōi*) before going in deed (*ergōi*) to what is necessary. For we differ in this: that we ourselves, the same men, both dare the most and calculate about what we undertake; whereas for others ignorance brings boldness, and calculation hesitation. Those would rightly be judged most courageous who both know most clearly pains and pleasures and nevertheless (*dia tauta*) do not turn away from danger (2.40.2–3).

Kenneth Dover has argued that "an archaic mode of indicating that a man was all that a man should be confined itself to two aspects of his character, his valour on the battlefield and his wisdom in discussion (sc. of tactics, organization, and other matters relevant to victory or survival in war)."[2] These two aspects of the ideal could be connected as dual but largely unrelated attributes of an individual (as in the case of Homer's

---

[1] For my stance on the historicity of this speech, and related methodological questions, see the Introduction, pp. 14–15.
[2] Dover 1974: 161. On these varying formulations, cf. Thuc. 2.11.5 with Hdt. 3.4.1, Thuc. 1.71.1; see further Edmunds 1975: 39n.48, Rusten comm. ad 2.11.5, 2.40.1.

Odysseus) or opposed to each other in a way that emphasized thinking (as in the philosophical tradition) or action (as in the popular tradition).[3] Thucydides' Pericles developed these two facets of the ideal by explaining their precise relationship with one another. Pericles argued that, at least ideally, Athenian institutions and political life educated the Athenians to exemplify a wise sort of daring that was peculiarly democratic. By the end of the classical period, both Plato and Aristotle were firmly convinced that courage requires knowledge along with a properly habituated character.[4]

Pericles' statement has given rise to a revealing philological controversy. On this controversy hangs the question of whether courage is founded primarily on an intellectual basis or partly on an intellectual basis and partly on the basis of character. The crux of the matter is the grammatical interpretation of *dia tauta*, which is generally understood to refer to the knowledge of what is fearful and what is pleasant.[5] On a concessive reading, the sentence would be translated as follows: "Those would rightly be judged most courageous who understand both the fearful and the pleasant and do not turn away from risks on account of this (*dia tauta*)." On a causal reading, it would be translated, "Those would rightly be judged most courageous who understand both the fearful and the pleasant and on account of this (*dia tauta*) do not turn away from risks."[6]

---

[3] Parry 1988: 15–57.
[4] For Aristotle's composite conception of virtue as requiring both practical wisdom and a properly trained character, see, e.g., *EN* 1103b21–25, 1144a18–b1, 1144b30–32. On Aristotle's critique of Socratic intellectualism, see *EN* 1144b17–30, *EE* 1216b3–26, with Nehamas 1999: 27–28, 46. With Plato the situation is more ambiguous: in the *Protagoras* (360d4–5), Socrates argues that "Wisdom about what is fearful and what is not fearful is courage" (*Hē sophia ara tōn deinōn kai mē deinōn andreia estin*); the *Laches* of course ends aporetically (see 199e11); while in the *Republic*, on the other hand, Books 2–3 are devoted to describing the correct education of character, which is then later complemented by the acquisition of philosophical knowledge (at 430c2–3 Socrates qualifies his discussion of courage by suggesting that he has now defined civic courage (*politikēn andreian*), which seems to be a qualified form of courage dependent not on knowledge but on true belief; cf. Cooper 1999e: 140–41). Penner (2000: 165–71) seems to me right to contrast the Socratic intellectualism of the earlier dialogues with Plato's emphasis in the *Republic* on both character and intellect. Smoes 1995 touches on these themes in Thucydides, implicitly following Parry in seeing the growth of a more intellectualist expression of courage that is specifically Athenian; but Smoes ties this expression too closely, in my view, to the rise of technical and strategic knowledge of warfare, rather than to the knowledge of human excellence and human flourishing, which I believe the Athenians, followed by Plato and Aristotle, emphasize.
[5] See Classen-Steup 1889 comm. ad loc.; Gomme 1956 comm. ad loc.
[6] Translators and commentators are sharply divided on the issue: Woodruff 1993, 42–43; Marchant 1961 comm. ad loc.; Yunis 1996: 76; and Williams 1998: 122 favor the concessive reading; Sharples 1983 and perhaps Gomme 1956 comm. ad loc. favor the causal reading.

At first glance, the word order appears to support the causal reading, since *dia tauta* comes before the negative *mē* and arguably should not be understood within the negative clause. To this R. W. Sharples (1983: 139–40) has added considerations of context: "It is true that [Pericles] has just mentioned the Spartans (by implication) as being bold through ignorance, so there may indeed be something of a paradox in the idea that knowledge too can cause men to face dangers; but it is this, that knowledge causes men to face dangers, that must be the primary meaning of Thucydides' words, rather than that the Athenians are brave *in spite of* their knowledge" (his emphasis).

If we read *dia tauta* in a concessive sense, however, then Pericles will be identifying two equally significant and potentially antithetical facets of courage: intellectual understanding of what is fearful and pleasant and the disposition of character that drives such men to face danger in spite of their rational reflection. There are equally strong contextual reasons for interpreting the expression in this way. As Pericles has just said, "[A]nd we ourselves (*autoi*) either judge (*krinomen*) at any rate (*ge*) or formulate our policy correctly (*enthumoumetha orthōs*), not supposing that words harm deeds, but believing rather that harm comes from not being taught in advance in words before going in deed to what is necessary. For we differ in this also that we ourselves, the same men (*hoi autoi*), both dare the most and calculate about things which we undertake; whereas for others ignorance brings confidence, and calculation hesitation" (2.40.2–3).[7] The concessive *dia tauta* implicitly contrasts Athenians with Spartans on the

---

[7] Like many other sentences in the oration, this one is opaque and difficult to interpret grammatically. On the general issues involved, see most recently Hornblower 1991: 305–6, who, following Meyer, shows that *krinomen* and *enthumoumetha* refer to two distinct intellectual processes. Edmunds 1972, with Rusten 1989 comm. ad loc., shows that *ge* lays emphasis on the likelier member of the pair. On the reading *autoi* (rather than *hoi autoi*) at the beginning of the quoted passage, I follow Rusten (comm. ad loc.) and Hornblower 1991: 305. I believe that the *autoi* of 2.40.2 (not the *hoi autoi* 2.40.3) intensifies the subject "we" without emphasizing the notion of "sameness." Rather, it stresses that the Athenians deliberate and judge in person—they do it themselves. That fact of democratic participation will figure in my later discussion of the democratic context of Pericles' account of courage. This interpretation, and the translation offered in the text, requires a manuscript reading (*kai autoi...krinomen* rather than *kai hoi autoi...krinomen*) that is different from the one accepted by editors who believe that the idea of sameness is emphasized in this part of the sentence. Pericles means that even if not all Athenians formulate policy in the Assembly, they all grasp the speakers' different proposals and make informed judgments on them in person; that is why it makes sense for Pericles to attribute a superior, cognitively demanding type of courage to his audience. Their courage is not only not undermined by a grasp of what is good and bad in life, but is actually informed by their understanding of the relevant issues.

ground that Athenians are unusual in combining what are apparently two antithetical activities—judging rationally and acting daringly.

Throughout the paragraph (2.40), in fact, Pericles emphasizes that the Athenians are uniquely capable of uniting apparently antithetical qualities.[8] The Athenians enjoy fine things with restraint and they are lovers of wisdom but are not soft (2.40.1). Care for both private and political matters can be found in the very same men (*tois autois*) at Athens, while those devoted to their own business have an adequate knowledge of politics (2.40.2). Pericles uses the pronoun *tois autois* in order to emphasize that the *very same men* are able to do things that are typically believed to be antithetical. The pronoun is picked up toward the end of the sentence quoted above: Pericles says that the Athenians themselves, the very same men (*hoi autoi*), both think about their actions and act daringly. Hence, the tenor of the paragraph suggests that knowledge is a constituent of the ideal form of courage for Pericles; but it must be accompanied by, and can also be antithetical to, a willingness to run risks.

Thus the contested prepositional phrase *dia tauta* lies at the heart of a paradox in Pericles' funeral oration. The "solution" may be that Pericles' enigmatic formulation expresses an ambiguity that is not fully articulated by Thucydides.[9] If we move outward, then, from Pericles' contested statement to his vision of courage throughout his speeches as represented by Thucydides, then we find that Pericles holds a composite view of courage that requires both a knowledge of human flourishing and a daring character that has been properly trained to act in accordance with one's judgments. Pericles typically discusses these attributes in a paratactic "both/and" construction: *tolman te…kai…eklogizesthai* (2.40.3) and *gignōskontes kai…mē apotrepomenoi* (2.40.3). These expressions are paralleled by another paratactic participial formulation later in the oration, where Pericles urges his audience, "When it [Athens] seems great to you, lay it to heart that men who dared and knew their duty and had a sense of shame in their actions acquired these things" (2.43.1).[10] Pericles impresses

---

[8] On the unification of opposites, compare the illuminating discussions of Mills 1997: 70–75 and Manville 1997.
[9] Parry 1988: 166 rightly sees this passage as ambiguous and suggests, at least implicitly, that its ambiguities have a larger thematic and even philosophical significance: "the rest of the world may well admire the Athenians for achieving so much in action despite their concern with the intelligence; but we know that the one is an effect of the other." Gomme 1956: 137 also correctly remarks on 2.43.1 that "true Athenians, they did not dare only, without knowing the reason why."
[10] There is a well-known ambiguity in this sentence: the subject "it" might refer to the city of Athens, but it might also refer to the power of Athens; cf. Hornblower 1991: 311. This ambiguity

upon his listeners that the courage of the fallen soldiers is constituted by three different but related elements: their daring (*tolmōntes*), their knowing (*gignōskontes*) what it is right to do (*ta deonta*), and their having a sense of shame or honor (*aischunomenoi*).[11] It is useful to deal in turn with the components of Pericles' vision of courage—intellect (knowing) and character (daring and having a sense of shame).

Courage and Knowledge

First, then, the intellectual element, which, as we will see, has two components in its own right—a knowledge of ultimate or long-term ends, and a knowledge of what to do in particular situations in order to achieve those ends (which I call "practical" or "technical" knowledge).[12] The intellectual component of courage can be illuminated by a comparison and contrast with Aristotle's more elaborate exploration of courage. In assessing Aristotle's account of courage, David Pears has argued that in the heat of battle the individual must evaluate, among other things, both the importance of the external goal—for example, saving his city, along with the corresponding benefits that saving his city will bring to himself and his family—and also the "disvalue" of the "countergoal"—that is, death or physical trauma.[13] The individual must evaluate these respective goals and deterrents correctly in order to act consistently with his *eudaimonia*.

It is important to see, however, that this judgment does not consist in any felicific or utilitarian calculus. Why not? The reason is that the individual could not understand his own flourishing properly without recognizing the harmony that is supposed, ideally, to connect his own excellent behaviors with the good of his family, friends, and city. Hence, when Pears speaks of the "disvalue" of the courageous person's "countergoal," we must acknowledge that neither Aristotle's nor Thucydides' ethical agents are envisaged as calculating in accordance with "rational choice" theory.

---

further suggests that Pericles' vision of the Athenians' good life carried overtones of his admiration for the city's projection of imperial power.

[11] For a contrasting account of the Periclean conception of courage, see Avramenko 2011: 87–98, which argues that Pericles "is thus encouraging Athenians to a courage that aims at democratic leisure" (91). In offering this interpretation, however, Avramenko ignores Pericles' own emphasis on the deliberative rationality that distinguishes Athenian from Spartan courage, on the way to developing an anachronistically liberal presentation of ancient Athens—one in which "reason and speech are instrumental" (92) and one that finds its highest significance in a vaguely described hedonism.

[12] Santas 1969 makes a similar distinction in his discussion of Plato's *Laches*; cf. chapter 6.

[13] Pears 1980: 183.

Their judgments are both practical and ethical; the "goods" involved in their judgments are not given in advance, but rather depend upon ethical evaluations and a special concentration on the ethical features of the situation. Hence, the Athenians as envisioned by Pericles had to take into account their own potential destruction, as well as the importance of the objectives they set for themselves, in order to make a reasonable, ethical judgment about what courage and the other virtues demanded in that particular situation. They should never risk likely death in order to achieve limited or unimportant goals. This claim results not from any utilitarian calculation, but rather from a fair-minded, prudent, and virtuous assessment of the worth of their own lives, the ethical dimensions of their proposed actions, and the limits of what courage or solidarity with others could require.

Throughout the speech, Pericles suggests that the external goal of fighting is the security of the city and, by extension, the flourishing lives of its citizens. In his judgment, the polis is worth risking one's life for because of its practices (*epitēdeuseōs*), its regime (*politeias*), and its way of life or character (*tropōn*)—all of which have made the city great and its citizens' lives free and flourishing (2.36.4, 2.38). In a famous sentiment, he captures the Athenians' relationship with their polis through an erotic metaphor: "Gaze, day after day, upon the power of the city and become lovers (*erastas*) of it" (2.43.1). Given Pericles' emphasis on the democracy and its way of life, it is important to acknowledge that even if "become lovers of Athens" is the standard translation of this sentence, it is nonethless grammatically possible to take Pericles to mean "become lovers of the city's power."[14] This grammatical ambiguity prompts reflection, already, on the ends that the Athenians are called upon to pursue. On the one hand, Pericles dazzlingly evokes the flourishing lives of democratic citizens as the *telos* of Athenian courage; on the other hand, he also points his audience toward the city's expansionist power and its capacity for impressive imperial "achievements," such as its imperial "monuments" (2.41).

Even though this ambiguity remains in play throughout the speech, Pericles exhorts his audience to acknowledge the irreducible worth and dignity of the reciprocal relationship between the individual and the polis. In a detailed examination of the erotic metaphor, in fact, Monoson has argued persuasively that "[t]he metaphor urges citizens willingly and affectionately to offer their city fine and extraordinary gifts in the form of

---

[14] Cf. Hornblower 1991: 311.

public service of a variety of sorts and patiently to tend to the city's developing needs."[15] Equally, however, the *erastēs* (here, the citizen) derives at least commensurate benefits from his reciprocal relationship with the *erōmenos* (the city). He is handsomely rewarded for his labors and risks by the city's guarantee of political and personal freedoms, its stable social order, its civic education of Athenians, and the massive material benefits it offers, as head of an empire, to individual citizens and their families. *Erōs* is a metaphor that expresses, not destabilizing individual passion for a fellow human being, but rather the citizens' appreciation of the excellence of their city and a willingness to act on the basis of that appreciation, along with an awareness of the civic education and ritual and social advantages that they would receive in turn.

Aristotle maintained, by contrast, that *erōs* is an irrational emotion that makes men bold through passion, but not genuinely courageous (*EE* 1229a20–24). Pericles' use of the metaphor can withstand this criticism, however, since his "erotic" notion of citizenship captures fundamental features of the Athenians' loyalty to their city, which he explains as a thoughtful desire for their own *eudaimonia*. As he tells his fellow citizens, "You yourselves now emulate them [the war dead] and judge that well-being (*to eudaimon*) is freedom (*to eleutheron*) and freedom (*to eleutheron*) is courage (*to eupsuchon*); do not stand on the sidelines and watch the risks of war" (2.43.4).[16] Pericles of course does not mean to equate freedom with courage, but rather to propose that courage is the defender of freedom; freedom in turn is a central ingredient of Athens's democratic way of life and hence of the city's well-being.

Pericles' evocation of *eudaimonia* helps to explain the ends to which the Athenians' courage is ideally directed: the excellent development of all Athenian citizens with respect to their intellectual, practical, and social capacities. This means, in particular, that the democratic way of life is especially capable of producing citizens who are admirable, excellent human beings. This is why Pericles emphasizes that "each one of us presents a person that is independent and ready to take on the most various types of behavior, with every grace and exceptional versatility" (2.41.1). Athens is superior to other cities in cultivating its citizens' virtues: by cultivating, for example, the citizens' benevolence toward others, which is informed by courage and "trust in our freedom," not by a "calculation

---

[15] Monoson 1994: 270–71; cf. also the theoretically sophisticated treatment of Wohl 2002: 55–72.
[16] On the translation "stand on the sidelines," see Rusten 1989: 171.

of advantage" (2.40.4–5). By thus linking courage to *eudaimonia*, which is understood as the city's cultivation of freedom and human excellence, Pericles points toward the "eudaimonistic" ideology that other Athenian orators would later develop as the most appropriate context within which to understand democratic courage (see chapters 14 and 15).

Pericles' specific formulation enables him to manage a neat transition from the city's welfare, which is promoted by individual patriotism, to the individual's flourishing, which is guaranteed by the safety of the city, in the first instance, and by its civic education and political practices, altogether.[17] The city guarantees the democratic way of life, and even the glorious imperialism, which makes the individual's life worth living. Pericles' reference to *erōs* thus emphasizes reciprocity between individual citizens and the city, and he integrates the erotic metaphor into a plausible, and rationally defensible, conception of the citizens' flourishing as democratic citizens (cf. 2.60.2).[18] In Pericles' view, then, it is rational and prudent for the Athenians to become lovers of their polis, since their polis and its democratic ethos guarantee the citizens' freedom and, thus, their individual *eudaimonia*.[19] Against Aristotle's criticisms of *erōs*, Pericles' vision of courage includes a rational understanding of ultimate goods—the good of the polis in general and of the citizens' flourishing—which is carefully and self-consciously articulated in terms of *eudaimonia*.

Yet it is necessary to add two important qualifications to this account of democratic "knowledge." First, and more important, Periclean knowledge of long-term ends does not make any particular reference to justice.[20] This in itself casts Pericles' conception of *eudaimonia* in a very different light from the conceptions of human flourishing found in Plato and Aristotle. Pericles explicitly, and at length, exhorts his audience to admire their ancestors' successful projection of imperial power throughout the Aegean (2.36, 2.41); he even adopts a triumphal attitude toward the Athenians' ability to control the other Greeks and their "memorials" of "vengeance or

---

[17] On the reciprocity between city and citizen, Connor 1984: 65–69 remains a superior treatment.
[18] This idea extends the excellent treatment of Monoson 1994. For further discussion of the reciprocity that characterized relations between the city and its citizens, see Christ 2012: 68–93.
[19] Orwin 1994 is right to say that "Pericles sketches a society in which the fullest development of the citizen is compatible with the greatest devotion to the city" (16; cf. 15–29 as a whole); we will explore the theme of eudaimonism in democratic ideology more fully in chapters 14 and 15.
[20] Orwin 1994: 15–29 offers an especially helpful treatment of the tensions and ambiguities related to justice in Pericles' speeches.

aid" (*kakōn te kagathōn*, 2.41.4).[21] These soldiers longed to punish their enemies (2.42.4). Pericles' own admiration for Athenian preeminence and expansionism issues in an insistence on punishing those who resist the Athenian desire to rule. Hence, we discover that Pericles' representation of the democratic city is shot through with the following tension: Athenian self-restraint and service of the common good also serve the project of imperialism, which involves the acquisition of power meant both to punish the Athenians' enemies and to satisfy the Athenians' desire for more (*pleonexia*).[22] Their "knowledge" of their own flourishing coexists with their willingness to harm others in order to win glory and imperial profits (2.38, 2.41).

Elsewhere, in fact, Pericles does not avoid likening Athens to a "tyranny" that may have been "unjust" for them to acquire in the first place (2.63.2). The city's power, and the citizens' love of that power, helps to explain why the city needs no Homer to glorify it (2.41.4); its glory is already inscribed in the hearts of all Athenians. Pericles' newly democratic model of courage takes as its end not only the protection and development of a flourishing democratic way of life, but also the traditional desire to become preeminent among the city's rivals and even to rule them and to punish them when necessary. This complicates the otherwise admirable picture of thoughtful and cognitively demanding courage that Pericles attributes to Athens because of its democratic way of life.

Second, "knowledge of long-term ends" is merely one half of the meaning of "knowing what must be done" (*gignōskontes ta deonta*), the other half being a practical knowledge of what to do in particular situations. To be more precise, knowledge of long-term ends is a precondition of knowing what must be done in particular situations; particular actions must be undertaken in the light of overarching goals that make sense of them both practically and ethically. If the Athenians and their leaders take a long-term view of their own good, then they must also be able to understand how to act in particular situations in order to attain their overall good. In Pericles' analysis, then, the Athenians must judge correctly what particular circumstances demand of them in light of their larger vision of civic and individual flourishing. Before treating the more practical type of knowledge possessed by the Athenians, it is necessary to discuss their

---

[21] The translation in the text is that of Rusten 1989: 161; Rusten assimilates the passage to the traditional idea of "helping friends and harming enemies."
[22] On Thucydides' representation of Athenian *pleonexia*, see Balot 2001a: 136–78.

daring characters, which will lead directly back to a discussion of the Athenians' practical understanding.

The Athenians' Courageous Character

Pericles says that the Athenians are both daring and equipped with a proper sense of shame. As a first step in explaining the Athenians' daring character, Pericles distinguishes Athenian courage from Spartan courage: "We willingly run risks even though we have a relaxed lifestyle rather than one of rigorous training, and we do so with courage (*andreias*) derived not from laws more than from our habits (*tropōn*)" (2.39.4).[23] To Pericles, the Athenians' understanding of their long-term ends helps them act in appropriate ways, but their courage is also based on their character and their dispositions. Pericles does not offer a detailed explanation of the ways in which the Athenians have arrived at a national character with this specific makeup. In this respect he is similar to the Corinthians at Sparta (1.68–71), who explain the Athenian national character (*tropoi*) as full of *polupragmosunē* (restlessness, meddlesomeness) and *pleonexia* (greed), without offering any account of the ways in which the Athenians came to embody these attributes. Indeed, Pericles' emphasis is on the Athenians' relaxed lifestyle (cf. *aneimenōs diaitōmenoi*, 2.39.1), in spite of which they are still "naturally" courageous and run risks "willingly" (*ethelomen kinduneuein*, 2.39.4)—that is, in the right spirit.

My suggestion is that shame, understood in a distinctive way, is the primary rhetorical and emotional tool enabling Pericles to encourage his audience to live up to the standards set by their ancestors. Through helping the Athenians develop a proper sense of shame, Pericles encourages them to restrain their short-term desires and to internalize their ancestors' behavior as an ideal.[24] Thus, Pericles exemplifies in his rhetoric the importance of pre-rational training for producing courageous citizens. As we have seen, Pericles' interventions in the Assembly sometimes take the form of education through explicit arguments about the Athenians' long-term goals, ends, and properly construed interests. But his rhetoric also helps him to foster a proper sense of shame in his listeners and to train their desires appropriately.

---

[23] For the translation of the genitives (of cause) as "derived from" see Rusten comm. ad loc.
[24] For a useful discussion of the ancestors as a source of motivation for the Athenians, see now Hunt 2010: 123–33.

Aristotle considered shame to be a (quasi-)virtue of character rather than intellect (*EN* IV.9.1128b10–35), and he believed that "civic courage" was grounded in an attitude of appropriate shame (*EN* III.8.1116a17–29). As Cottingham has described this conception, "One ought not to be brave under compulsion, but because it is a fine thing (*kalon*), and hence civic courage (the first and most important in the list of states analogous to courage) is grounded in a proper sense of shame, and a 'desire for something noble..., and avoidance of reproach, which is a disgrace.' "[25] This captures an important feature of the Periclean conception without entirely doing justice to that conception. We will discover, in fact, that democratic courage went beyond what Aristotle and Cottingham designate as merely "civic" courage, because the Athenians' sense of shame often was, in its own right, based on carefully reasoned, articulate ideas about the appropriate ends for human beings and for the cities that nurtured them. Those ideas themselves derived from democratic practices of free speech.

The habits of courage, Pericles declares, have been displayed by each generation of Athenians; he urges members of his audience to live up to the ideals of their ancestors. As he says, "When it [Athens] seems great to you, lay it to heart that men who dared and knew their duty and had a sense of shame in their actions acquired these things. If they ever failed when they attempted something, they did not on that account think it right to deprive the city of their excellence (*aretēs*), and they put forward for Athens the best contribution they could" (2.43.1). In his view, the empire had been won through the toil of several generations, all of them striving, to whatever extent they were able, to live up to an exceptionally high standard of honor and excellence. They were ashamed to compromise that standard.

Pericles urges his audience to develop a similar set of standards: "Don't show yourselves to be inferior to your ancestors on two counts, since they took the empire through their own toil and did not receive it from others; moreover, they kept it safe and passed it on to you (it is more shameful (*aischion*) for those who already control an empire to have it taken away than to fail in attempting to acquire more)" (2.62.3). In the funeral oration, in its own right, the Athenians received an education in appropriate shame through images of the behavior of the fallen fellow citizens, who had admirably lived up to the ideals embodied by their ancestors.[26] Pericles argues

---

[25] Cottingham 1996: 59.
[26] Cf. Monoson 1994: 268, which also explores the *paideia* (education) offered to the city by those who have given their bodies in battle.

that his contemporaries must resolve to be no less daring than the dead (2.43.1), who "fled a shameful reputation, but stood up to their task at the risk of their lives" (2.42.4).[27] The rhetorical power of Pericles' evocation of shame results from his appeal to the Athenians' emotions and desires. Pericles was trying to cultivate in his listeners a respect for the dead and for the traditions of the city, both of which he presents in terms of shame.[28] Because of the Athenians' institutionalized practices of free speech and independent reflection, these emotions and desires were themselves fostered in novel ways by the Athenians, who penetrated their emotions with thoughtful reflection and thereby moved beyond the traditional Greek experience of shame and the desire for honor. To see why this is so, we will need to explore Pericles' appeal to democratic shame more carefully.

Through offering the Athenians an education in recent history and in appropriate conduct on the battlefield, Pericles undertook to train their desires and to offer them a self-image that contributed to their ability to administer and defend their empire courageously. This training contributed to the Athenians' sense of shame because, as Bernard Williams has shown, "The basic experience connected with shame is that of being seen, inappropriately, by the wrong people, in the wrong condition."[29] Through the operations of shame, the Athenians internalized an "other"—here, their ancestors or those lost in battle—whose critical gaze drove them to live up to the ideals articulated by Pericles.[30] Pericles' words helped to lay bare a set of imagistic responses that defined and consolidated the Athenian character. At the end of his final speech in the *History*, he exhorted the Athenians in language that draws together and echoes his account of courage and the necessity of avoiding shame: "You should make a judgment with a view to winning honor in the future and to avoiding shame at present…Whichever men are least distressed about calamity in their minds,

---

[27] Rusten 1989: 162 points out, correctly in my view, that in 2.43.1–2 Pericles encourages his audience to "develop the same resolution as the dead (*dianoian* 43.1 and *tês gnômês* 43.3 refer to the attitude described in 42.4)."

[28] Note too that Pericles links the Athenians' courageous response to the vicissitudes of war to the customs of their ancestors, and he urges his audience not to let those customs lapse in the present generation (2.64.2).

[29] Williams 1993: 78.

[30] As Williams 1993: 82 explains, "Even if shame and its motivations always involve in some way or other an idea of the gaze of another, it is important that for many of its operations the imagined gaze of an imagined other will do." The expression "internalized other" is from Williams 1993: e.g., 85.

and yet hold out against it most firmly in their actions, these are the most powerful cities and individuals" (2.64.6).[31]

Pericles' ideal vision requires in particular that the Athenians give up their attachment to their private wealth. Hence, for example, Pericles encourages the citizens to view themselves as islanders (1.143.5), in the hope that they will base their deliberations less on striving to maintain personal property than on courageously envisioning their own well-being in an irreducible relationship with that of the city as a whole. In a similar vein, Pericles teaches the Athenians to take a thoughtful and carefully reasoned perspective on their farmland: "although you may think it a great loss to be deprived of your land and houses, still you must see that this power is entirely different; and instead of worrying on that account, you should really regard them in the light of the gardens and other accessories that embellish a great fortune, and as, in comparison, of little moment. You should know too that liberty preserved by your efforts will easily recover for us what we have lost, whereas, if you submit, you will lose what you already have (2.62.3).[32] Thus the "countergoal" or "deterrent" in Pericles' argument is the loss of personal property in the short term, but the significance of this personal property is negligible; indeed, the loss will easily be recuperated, he says, as long as the Athenians defend their city. Pericles' creation of this highly Athens-centric self-understanding for individual Athenians is complemented by his reflection upon the dead soldiers' determination to check the enemy's aggression, even if it meant dying in the effort and never living to become rich (2.42.4).

Of course, the Spartans too utilized shame and honor in order to motivate their fighting forces. In the words of the King Archidamus, "We are both good warriors and men of sound judgment, because we are well ordered. We are good warriors because our moderation (*sōphrosunēs*) is guided by our sense of shame (*aidōs*), and our courage (*eupsuchia*) is based upon honor. We have sound judgment because of our rigorous education, which makes us too ignorant to have contempt for our laws and too moderate to disobey them" (1.84.3).[33] Archidamus emphasizes that these

---

[31] The second sentence is similar in theme and terminology to the passage from 2.40.3 with which this discussion began.
[32] This proper understanding of the relative values of wealth and the city allows the Athenians to alienate their bodies, as the Corinthians say at Sparta (1.70.6). Similarly, Saxonhouse (1996: 68) insightfully argues that Pericles urges the Athenians to disregard their physical sufferings through an act of mental transcendence: "It is only by casting off attachments to bodies that we can unite the city into one—and, as one, make the city have one mind, not many minds."
[33] In interpreting the relationship between the key abstractions in this sentence, I follow Woodruff 1993 and Nussbaum 1986: 508n.24; see also Hornblower 1991: 128–29.

ideals and virtues have been handed down from the Spartans' ancestors (1.85.1); like the Athenians, the Spartans were trying to live up to ideals of behavior laid down in advance by their own civic traditions. Their ideals were directed toward promoting the success and safety of Sparta in war and in peace (1.82.1).

How, then, knowing these things, did Pericles intend to distinguish Athens from Sparta with respect to courage, and specifically with respect to the use of shame as a motivation for courage? As de Romilly has emphasized, Pericles envisions the Spartans as unreflectively carrying out duties imposed by their laws and *paideia* (2.39).[34] The Spartans utilized shame as a strict mechanism of social control (2.37, 2.39), with the result that Spartans live and fight in fear of humiliation rather than in enjoyment of their city's festivals and freedoms (2.38), as the Athenians do. Spartan shame was unreflective (2.40), inculcated by rote education (2.39), and punitive, rather than carefully reasoned (2.40) and prospective (2.40). Adapting Christina Tarnopolsky's work on shame in the Platonic *Gorgias*, we might call Spartan shame "rigid" and "primitive" and Athenian shame "deliberate" or "sophisticated" or "carefully reasoned."[35]

Since the Spartans cultivated courage through rigorous training and through imposing harsh legal penalties on defaulters (2.39), their courage did not especially depend on the citizens' grasp of the dignity and merits of their city's attractive way of life. The Spartans were beholden to the past and were largely unreflective followers of tradition, whereas the Athenians were innovators and self-consciously reflected on the links between their practices, their virtues, their emotions, and their democratic regime. This is why, in his culminating stroke, Pericles charges that the

---

[34] De Romilly 1980: 309–10.

[35] See Tarnopolsky 2010: 6–21 for an excellent discussion of what she calls "flattering" shame, "Socratic respectful" shame, and "Platonic respectful" shame. Tarnopolsky right points out that shame, properly understood and adapted to the democratic context, can be central to the healthy functioning of specifically democratic politics: "If our own current problems arose in part from the lack of self-regulation and self-limitation within each of our polities' economic and political institutions and practices, I hope to show that such self-regulation and self-limitation are at the heart of a very important kind of democratic shame" (2010: 9). A failure to make such distinctions in the quality of social shame weakens the interpretation of Avramenko 2011: 23–98. Somehow, for Avramenko, the Spartans' "fundamental care" is "honor" (28), which is supposed to distinguish Sparta from Athens, because at Athens "the demands of honor are antithetical to democratic leisure" (96)! Few Athenians would agree, though, that their regime was devoted to "leisure" or that their regime was fundamentally opposed to the demands of honor. Millender 2002a: 50–51 offers yet another treatment of Pericles' attitudes toward shame, but this treatment does not fully take into account the interior dynamics of shame as an internalized emotion among both Spartans and Athenians.

Spartans believed that open deliberation and speeches make men cowards; whereas the Athenians held that their courage results from both the intellectual and character training produced through free conversations about the city (2.40). In an ideologically perfect moment, Pericles has shown that Athenian courage is not only distinctively democratic, but also superior to Spartan courage for precisely this reason.

We have now arrived at the point of convergence between forming well-reasoned opinions about long-term ends and training desire appropriately. On the one hand, Pericles believes that if the Athenians really understand what is good for them and for the city, then they will consider their property to be essentially worthless as compared with the freedom of their city. Given his claim that *eudaimonia* consists in liberty, and liberty in courage, Pericles appropriately invokes liberty as a human good that takes precedence over land and houses and that links courage and *eudaimonia*. On the other hand, Pericles says that the war-dead correctly restrained their desire for wealth in the interests of acting courageously for the city: "No one of these men grew soft because he preferred to continue to enjoy his wealth or deferred facing death in the hope that he might escape poverty and become rich" (2.42.4). Pericles focused his audience's attention on the dead soldiers' proper disciplining of their private desires for the sake of promoting the common good. This self-restraint in regard to wealth is an element of the excellent character that he demands of his fellow citizens.

Athenian History and Practical Knowledge

Pericles' development of his fellow Athenians' ethical character has a strongly historical dimension, not only because Pericles persistently refers the Athenians to paradigms drawn from Athens's history, but also because the Athenians themselves initiated their own tradition of daring in the Persian War period. As Pericles tells it, the Athenians' ancestors "thrust away the Persians more through intelligence (*gnōmēi*) than good fortune (*tuchēi*), and through daring (*tolmēi*) rather than power (*dunamei*)" (1.144.4). The Athenians, under Themistocles' leadership, combined intellectual insight with a daring character in order to ward off the Persians. Speaking of the Athenians' decision to abandon the city during the Persian War, Steven Forde has argued, "The astonishing deed of the Athenians, which seems to display the greatest courage, seems also to bear a certain tincture of impiety. It might go beyond what merely human courage is permitted. It is audacity; it is daring."[36] Pericles would undoubtedly reject this formulation. Elsewhere, Thucydides clearly distinguishes reckless daring from courage: it is in the perverse conditions of the Corcyraean *stasis*, not in successful Athens, that the two tend to be conflated (3.82.4).[37]

What then does Pericles' understanding of Themistocles' *gnōmē* entail? In the quoted passage, Pericles emphasizes the perception of which practical alternatives exist and which are likely to materialize.[38] This is not of course to suggest that Themistocles lacked long-term judgments about the good of Athens. After all, he developed path-breaking strategies to promote Athens's long-term welfare both before the Persian Wars, by using the silver from Laureion for ships (1.14.3), and afterward, by rebuilding Athens's walls before rebuilding individual houses (1.90.3).

In this quotation (1.144.4), however, Pericles' contrast between intelligence (*gnōmē*) and good fortune (*tuchē*) suggests that he is referring to specific, pragmatic judgments about when and how to fight the Persians in order to win. The Athenians won because they appreciated particular facts about the situation (e.g., the respective sizes of the fleets at Salamis, or which side was more likely to win in a confined space as opposed to the open sea), not because they were lucky. Similarly, as much as his funeral oration emphasizes the knowledge of long-term objectives, Pericles, like Themistocles before him, makes a rational judgment about the war on the basis of the Athenians' naval expertise and their overwhelming financial advantages. Pericles must consider factual knowledge, as well as the knowledge of long-term ends, in determining a proper course of action, and he must persuade his democratic audience that his approach does justice to both kinds of knowledge. Courage certainly involves appropriate ethical consideration of goals and deterrents, but, practically speaking, it must also engage our capacity to understand the facts and our sensitivity to the "odds"—that is, the likelihood that one or another eventuality will result.

---

[36] Forde 1986: 437.

[37] A similar distinction between courage and reckless daring can be found at *Laches* 196e–197b (cf. de Romilly 1980: 314); cf. Aristotle, *EN* 1115a18–19, 1115b24–33; *EE* 1229b22–30.

[38] In discussing Socrates' cross-examination of Laches in the *Laches*, Santas 1969: 446 invokes a distinction between practical knowledge of particulars and long-term knowledge of what is valuable: "a distinction between being wise or knowing *what* the alternatives before one are and which alternative is likely to materialize, *and* being wise or knowing the comparative *values* or worth of the alternatives before one." Pericles' conception of courage, in my reconstruction, includes both practical knowledge and the long-term knowledge of value, along with the proper habituation of civic character.

In his speech in indirect discourse, for example, Pericles convinces the Athenians that they possess the technical and financial resources to meet the Spartan threat with confidence (2.13). Presenting a conversation between Socrates and Plato's brother Glaucon, Xenophon later showed in excruciating detail that technical financial knowledge was a cardinal element of successful leadership (*Mem.* 3.6). In Thucydides' final verdict, moreover, Pericles inspired the Athenians to take heart when they were wrongly afraid, while also reducing their hubristic tendencies whenever they became overconfident (2.65.9).[39] He did this by persuading the Athenians to consider not only ultimate goals, but also facts about their situation, such as their naval training and their financial advantages, both of which figured into his attempts to strike the mean between recklessness and unreasonable fear. It is difficult to see what that mean could be unless one had a sense both of the importance of winning the war generally and of the particular strategic conditions of participants on both sides.

Pericles usefully supplements Aristotle's dismissal of technical and tactical knowledge in the *Eudemian Ethics*, where the philosopher attributes to Socrates, perhaps inaccurately, the idea that bravery is knowledge of a technical sort (1230a6–8). In order to show that technical knowledge is the basis only of a deficient form of courage, Aristotle says, "Sailors who know how to climb the sails are not brave through their knowledge of what is frightening, but because they know how to protect themselves from the dangers" (1230a8–10).[40] In other words, men should be thought *less* brave (or "defectively" brave) because their technical competence, rather than knowledge of what is truly significant in human life, makes them less fearful. By contrast, Pericles offers a more complex picture in which technical knowledge realistically figures in decisions that his fellow citizens make with an eye toward ultimate ends. It is only within the framework of those larger ends that Pericles' rational judgments could become meaningful. Courage is in Pericles' view the virtue that enables individuals to put into practice their underlying ideals and their explicit rational judgments in the appropriate way. In describing Athenian courage, Pericles strikes an appropriate balance between the knowledge of facts and the knowledge of ends.

Interestingly, it is the Spartan general Brasidas, not Pericles, who explicitly offers a more sophisticated account of technical knowledge than

---

[39] On Pericles' notion of appropriate fear, see Williams 1998: 127–28; Edmunds 1975: 52–60; for a general study of fear in Thucydides, see de Romilly 1956.
[40] Compare also Aristotle's discussion in *EN* 1115a35–b4, 1116b3–23.

Aristotle allows for in his example of the sailors. After Phormio's defeat of the Spartans off the headland of Rhium, Brasidas encourages his troops to see that courage is a necessary feature of deploying technical knowledge in frightening situations: "Their [the Athenians'] knowledge of these things, which you fear most of all, if it is combined with courage, will enable them to remember in the midst of danger how to do what they have learned, but, without courage, no skill will prevail in the face of danger" (Thuc. 2.87.4).[41] For Brasidas, courage is that feature of character that enables people to maintain their technical knowledge in circumstances in which they are apt to forget it through fear of losing their lives. It is the ability, in other words, to maintain one's knowledge in situations of pleasure and of pain.[42] This is a reasonable point, as Plato saw when he urged that the Guardians of his Callipolis be tested for their ability to maintain true belief in the face of pleasure and pain (*Republic* 429c5–430c1).

What is missing from Brasidas's conception, however, is an explanation of when, how, and why the Spartans should be fighting in the first place— that is, an explanation of the ultimate goals or ideals for which Spartans should fight at all. Whereas individual Athenians were expected to understand, in a deep and articulate way, why they were behaving as they did, ordinary Spartans tended to have a vaguer, less self-conscious understanding of their behavior and ultimate goals, at least in Pericles' representation. The characteristically Spartan emphasis on the collective good meant that there was correspondingly less interest in individual *eudaimonia* in Sparta than in Athens. There was no Spartan funeral oration because of the deep differences between Sparta and Athens in self-image and political organization.

In comparison with the Athenians, to be more specific, the Spartans lacked the ability to articulate the long-range goals that alone provide a ground for courage. They obey the laws ignorantly; they believe that the way in which general principles of their culture should be applied to particular circumstances, such as their allies' complaints, is self-evident. In his hawkish speech to the Assembly, Sthenelaidas urges the Spartans to put an end to the Athenians' injustice against Sparta's allies (1.86.1–2), presumably believing that he and the other Spartans recognize injustice when they see it, without needing to make long speeches about it. For Sthenelaidas, a lengthy speech is merely a ploy designed to delay action

---

[41] Crane 1998: 225–29 offers an interesting general discussion of this episode and its debates over courage. For an interesting alternative reading, see Millender 2002a: 52–54.
[42] Cf. Konstan 2006: 139–44.

or retribution, not a method of figuring out more precisely the fundamental grounding of one's own actions (1.86.4–5). By contrast with the Athenians' imagination and innovation, the Spartans are hidebound by their belief in the importance of tradition, which both gives them their ultimate objectives and militates against their reflecting deeply upon those ends. Yes, their tradition provided them with a self-image of self-control, shame, and courage, which guided their decisions in particular situations, with a view to making Sparta successful and keeping control over its allies. It is open to them to believe that they are going to war in order to fight injustice. However, Pericles has made a convincing case for the superiority of democratic courage based on thoughtful deliberation and a qualitatively different type of shame.

Herodotus provides at least one hint that might help to explain the Athenian democracy's unique focus on the individual's assent to and understanding of the human goods that guide particular decisions. After describing how Athens finally eliminated its tyranny, Herodotus explains that the Athenians then became all the better at fighting their neighbors because they were fighting for themselves rather than a master: "when they [the Athenians] were held down [by the tyrants], they were slack in their duties, since they were working for a master; but once they were free, then each one of them was eager to work for his own sake" (5.78). Athens's military success, in other words, was based on the recognition by ordinary Athenians that they were fighting for what was significant to themselves as individuals. The transformation charted by Herodotus implies that ordinary Athenians had also transformed their relationship to their city and their understanding of their own new commitments and ideals. It is not accidental that such a transformation also affected their ability to fight successfully. Democracy generated a specific form of courage, which was based on the Athenian individual's correct apprehension of his own *eudaimonia* as a citizen—and, implicitly, of an appropriate understanding of his relationship to the polis. The Athenians' new self-understanding, according to Herodotus, made them more courageous.

By sharply contrasting Athens with Sparta, Thucydides elaborates Herodotus' insights into courage as a specifically democratic ideal. At least implicitly, Thucydides poses the question of whether soldiers can be truly courageous if they merely know how to follow someone who knows, perhaps blindly, as in Sparta. Or must they, rather, understand for themselves why they are entering into dangerous situations and how to do so appropriately?

Pericles' speeches emphasize the latter option—that courage has a necessary epistemological component. This conception of courage is more plausible and deeper than the Spartan conception. It arguably arose in Athens because of Athens's democratic politics, where the burden of understanding how to act during crises was placed on the citizens. In a democracy, by definition, the citizens themselves must choose which policies to follow, all the more so in a direct democracy in wartime when ordinary Athenians had to vote on policies at meeting after meeting.[43] They conceived of courage in a way that derives from the participatory democracy evoked by Pericles. In order to participate effectively in democratic politics, individual Athenians had to have an intellectual understanding of the issues involved in making any decision, both in terms of the society's core ideals (the knowledge of the fearful and the pleasant) and in terms of their ability to predict outcomes accurately.[44] Pericles democratized the traditionally and exclusively heroic virtue of courage, making it available to, and even necessary for, the entire democratic citizenry.[45] The fallen soldiers knew what they had to do because their entire public life had been an education in the long-term ends that guided their actions and decisions.

Conclusion: Reason, Emotion, and Democratic Courage

Taking a long view of Greek thinking about courage, the democratic context has led to a more discursive conception of courage. The Athenians did not abandon the traditional emphasis on character. But Pericles' discourse helps to explain how a daring character is to be put into action at the right time, in the right place, and with the right intentions. This particular combination of character and intellect as key constituents of courage held sway for the rest of the classical period and was adopted in a suitably modified

---

[43] Here the translation of *krinomen* and *enthumoumetha* (2.40.2) again becomes important (cf. above, n.11): as Hornblower 1991: 305–6 points out, Thucydides' grammar lays stress on *krinomen* (we judge), which suggests that individual Athenians are masters at judging policy correctly, even if they do not formulate it personally (cf. also the defense of democratic decision making offered by Athenagoras, 6.39.1). The point is that, by contrast with the Spartans, the Athenians practice a deep, reflective form of judging that continually forces them to re-evaluate both their values and the facts of their situation in light of present circumstances.

[44] For *logismos* and *logos* as rational calculation, see the excellent chapter of Edmunds (1975: 7–88).

[45] Loraux (1986: 15–76, esp. 52–56) offers an illuminating survey of the ways in which the funeral oration as a genre appropriates formerly heroic privileges for all the citizens of the polis; Ober 1989: 259–70 shows that fourth-century oratory created a general "democratization of birth privilege" (259).

form by Plato and Aristotle, despite their criticisms of democracy. Hence we are left with the paradox that the dominant fourth-century philosophical account of courage was initially established by the discourses and political structure of the Athenian democracy, against which Plato and to a lesser extent Aristotle directed stern political criticisms. Even so, we should keep in mind that the philosophers introduced their own novel conceptions of virtue that pertained to the philosophical rather than the political life. By contrast with the Athenians, they saw the question of the good life or human flourishing as a persistent one, rather than as a matter that could be grasped with certainty through a prevailing public ideology.

Needless to say, the foregoing is an account of Pericles' idealized vision of democratic courage. The possible gap between ideal and reality leads me to offer two concluding remarks. First, whatever Pericles the orator or the Thucydidean character believed about democracy, Thucydides himself does not allow that the Athenian demos is an informed democratic citizenry capable of rational reflection about its own ideals. Rather, the demos needs Pericles' guidance to achieve success and *eudaimonia*.[46] From Thucydides' perspective, then, Pericles' ideal vision must remain contingent on the wise leadership of men like Themistocles and Pericles.[47] The irony is that Pericles, even as he evokes the democratic ideal, does not understand his own importance within the democratic system.[48] In his account of the Mytilenian and Sicilian debates, and in numerous other episodes, Thucydides shows that once Pericles' successors had taken charge, the democratic Assembly was divided by lies, greed, and a general fragmentation of interests. If Pericles occupies a position of such special prominence within the democracy (e.g., 2.65), then his democratic construction of courage, with its novel emphasis on the epistemology of each citizen, falls apart at the seams—or so Thucydides might explain. In chapter 5, we will explore additional perplexities and ambiguities in Thucydides' presentation of Athenian courage.

---

[46] Aristotle said that Pericles exhibited practical wisdom (*phronēsis*) as a statesman (*EN* 1140b7–11). For Aristotle, *phronēsis* is an intellectual excellence in virtue of which human beings correctly deliberate about what is best for themselves or their communities and find the virtuous mean in the practical world in light of their conception of *eudaimonia*. See further Macleod 1983: 127 on Pericles' connections between practical wisdom and courage.

[47] This is argued by Ober 1998, 52–121; cf. Ober 1993, Balot 2001a: 142–45. Pope 1988 rightly points out that Thucydides criticizes both oligarchs and democrats on moral and prudential grounds. Even though Thucydides offers an extensive critique of Athenian democracy, it must be emphasized that he also criticizes nondemocrats, such as the Melians, the Athenians oligarchs of 411 BC, and the Spartans, for their political rashness and irresponsibility.

[48] Balot 2001a: 148–49.

Second, the idea of uniting daring and knowledge as constituents of courage, however, was not foreign to the democratic experience. In Manville's judgment, for example, democracy's strength lies in its ability to integrate apparent contradictions—the democracy united individualism with consensus, and political equality with social inequality.[49] If Manville's argument is correct, then Pericles captures something true and important about democratic experience altogether, despite Thucydides' criticisms of the demos. In other words, Pericles' articulation of what constitutes courage derives from, and depends upon, actual democratic practice. This is a proposition that we explore in greater detail in chapter 3. We will discover that the Athenians drew links between courage and freedom in such a way as to emphasize that Athenian courage was informed by the rationality characteristic of democratic deliberation. Investigating these links will deepen and extend Pericles' arguments for the superiority of democratic courage.

As we continue to explore these exciting connections, however, we should resist the temptation to celebrate the Periclean ideal in any unqualified way. For although Pericles highlights the pleasures and flourishing characteristic of democratic Athens, he also stresses that the Athenian way of life was built upon the city's successful imperialism. He continually exhorts his fellow citizens to admire their forefathers, and he urges them to internalize sensitivities to the shame of yielding to their enemies in even the smallest of respects. He also encourages his audience to fall in love with the city itself and perhaps even with the city's power—a dramatic expression of the associations between democratic courage and the desire to rule. Even if democratic courage holds out promise for citizens of contemporary democracies, it is impossible to ignore the machismo and expansionism that were so closely associated with this ancient ideal in its Periclean expression.

---

[49] Manville (1997: 73–84) has ingeniously related this arguably unique capacity of democracy to what he calls the "both/and" (as opposed to "either/or") thinking characteristic of the most outstanding private corporations in modern America, arguing in particular that Pericles' language illustrates his rhetorical, and sometimes paradoxical, unifying of opposites. On these points, see further Ober 1989: 332–39; Mills 1997: 70–75.

CHAPTER 3 | Free Speech, Democratic Deliberation, and Courage

WITHOUT LOSING SIGHT OF Pericles' references to the Athenians' normative emotional responses, we can fairly say that Pericles' emphasis on the cognitive "work" of the democratic experience was one of the keys to transforming courage into a distinctively democratic virtue. But how widely did Pericles' account of "deliberative courage" circulate in the democracy's public forums? Would Pericles' articulation of a rationalized conception of courage have been plausible to Athenians? If so, then what functions could it have served for the democracy at war?

In answering these questions, I would go further than most commentators and contend that Pericles' account of Athenian rationality was dependent upon his conception of the democracy as a deliberative form of self-government. Pericles' ideal of courage originated in his understanding of democracy as a particular regime type—a regime that was superior to others in that its practices of free speech and open deliberation produced a deeper cognitive understanding of courage than was available in other regimes. If the Athenian democrats could forge connections between democratic freedoms and their own conceptions and practices of courage, then they could legitimately understand themselves as producing a distinctively democratic model of courage. They did, in fact, forge such links by developing a theory of democratic deliberation according to which open, no-holds-barred debate in the Athenian Assembly informed Athenian decision making with intellectual clarity and political prudence.

Free Speech, Democratic Deliberation, and "Cognitive Work"

It was a deep conviction among Athenians that their structures of democratic deliberation had a special claim to practical rationality.[1] Therefore, they were able to justify their claim to a rationally informed conception of courage through appeal to the demanding forms of political reflection undertaken by democratic citizens in the Athenian Assembly and in other public forums. Demosthenes' *Exordia* help to clarify this point. Since the *Exordia* were standardized preambles, they could serve as introductions for a variety of possible speeches.[2] In so far as they express characteristic ideological claims, they are especially useful for our purposes.

In *Exordium* 50, Demosthenes envisioned a close connection between democratic civic rationality and the Athenians' expression of courage. He started off urging his fellow citizens to reconsider the unreflective belief that, whatever the circumstances, courage required them to take the field in a show of manly bravado: as he said, "I ask only so much of you, that you not reckon those urging you to fight to be brave (*andreious*) for that reason alone, nor that you reckon those trying to argue against them to be for that reason cowardly (*kakous*)" (50.1). Although standard hoplite ethics demanded taking the field in a show of manhood, deeds of genuine courage had to be carefully planned in accordance with the wisdom that results from democratic deliberation.[3] This is why Demosthenes went on to argue that genuine courage must follow from clear-sighted deliberation about the particular demands of each situation. As he said, "For the test of speech and the test of deeds, men of Athens, are not the same; but it is necessary for us right now to show ourselves to have deliberated well (*eu bebouleumenous*) and then, if we eventually adopt this proposal, to display the deeds of courage (*ta tēs andreias*)" (50.1). Demosthenes emphasized that the Athenians should moderate their knee-jerk bellicosity in order to

---

[1] On the democratic deliberative context, see Balot 2006: 63–68; Monoson 2000: 51–63 (a slightly adapted version of Monoson 1994). On democratic rationality, see also Herman 2006: 65–66, 142.
[2] On the arguments establishing the authenticity of these preambles, see Yunis 1996: 287–89.
[3] For a related discussion of the "rhetoric of war and peace," see Roisman 2003: 132–36. For another contemporary attempt to say what courage demands of citizens, compare the passage in Plato's *Laws* (943e–945b) where the Athenian Stranger writes into Magnesia's law-code a distinction between "throwing away one's shield" through shameful cowardice and losing one's weapons for perfectly legitimate reasons, such as being caught in a storm or being thrown down from a cliff (944a–b). For further consideration of Plato's revision of the Greek tradition of courage, and particularly of Homeric models, see Hobbs 2000: 7–8, 175–78, 199–219.

deliberate well and to ensure that their military activities would benefit the city in a large sense.

That Demosthenes had to make these arguments shows that his point was not universally accepted, or tacitly understood, by the Athenians. Even so, his arguments drew on and contributed to the discourse on democratic courage that we have begun to excavate, and they had enough currency to be plausible to an Athenian audience. Like Pericles, Demosthenes proceeds by emphasizing the interdependence of speech and action. Demosthenes declares, "So, when you march out of the city, whoever is leader has authority over you, but now each one of you yourselves is a general" (50.3). The metaphor both links and separates Athenian public discourse and military action. On the one hand, Demosthenes argues that democratic equality cannot and should not pertain on the battlefield. Then as now, military leaders must act with power, authority, and vision, so as to make lightning-fast and unquestioned strategic decisions.[4] On the other hand, the metaphor also suggests that in the context of public reasoning about the dangers of warfare, each citizen is an independent political agent, individually responsible for articulating and judging proposals.[5] By metaphorically envisaging ordinary citizens as generals of the Assembly, Demosthenes advanced a logocentric understanding of courage that placed dispositions and physical actions within the larger rational frameworks generated by democratic politics and institutions.

This claim to rationally informed courage was important to the Athenians' democratic self-image. In Demosthenes' funeral oration, delivered after Athens's defeat at Chaeronea in 338 BC, the speaker argues that "of all virtue, the beginning is understanding (*sunesis*), and the end (*peras*) is courage (*andreia*); through the one we form opinions about what must be done, through the other this is carried to success" (Dem. 60.17–18). Demosthenes held that it might in principle be possible to separate *andreia* from the other elements of virtue (Dem. 60.3; cf. Isocr. 12.196–97, 12.242), but he shows that courage cannot do its proper work without being linked to wise judgment, to nobility and justice (Dem. 60.6–7), to loyalty to the other Greeks (Dem. 60.8, 10–11), and to piety (Dem. 60.8). Thus, Demosthenes not only linked courage to practical rationality, but

---

[4] Van Wees 2004: 108–13 reminds us, however, that the classical battle line was much more fluid and less disciplined than we might expect, and that ancient Greek generals could expect much less obedience from their soldiers than generals of armies in our day.
[5] On the "autonomy" expected of Athenian citizens, see Monoson 2000: 56, 61–63.

also embedded it within a wide range of coordinate virtues and excellences of the Athenian citizenry.

According to Demosthenes, the Athenian soldiers' "understanding" (*sunesis*) is not simply a matter of having technical or factual knowledge. Rather, it involves the ability to comprehend what must be done, both in light of their beliefs about how to live flourishing human lives in the democratic city and as leaders of the Greeks. In fact, Demosthenes adds, the Athenians were distinctly superior to others in these respects, precisely because they could foresee dangers and challenge other Greeks to fight for their own freedom—which was, in his view, a demonstration of "sound judgment" (*gnōmēs*) that was also "loyal" (*eu phronousēs*) to the Greek cause (Dem. 60.18). Demosthenes contrasts the Athenians' virtues with the "folly mixed with cowardice" (*agnoias memeigmenēs kakiai*, Dem. 60.18) displayed by the other Greeks. At each turn, Demosthenes contends that the Athenians' courageous behavior was informed by sound judgment and a carefully reasoned sense of why their leadership was worthwhile and meritorious.

A similar emphasis is at work in a roughly contemporary speech of Hyperides, from which only a single fragment is preserved. The Loeb translator reads the passage as follows: "Rash men do everything without reflection, whereas the brave reflect on the dangers they encounter and meet them unafraid" (Hyp., fr. A.4). To be more precise, the passage is designed to emphasize that the "brave" (*hoi tharraleoi*) remain unafraid in withstanding the dangers that befall them, precisely because they act "with reflection" or "with reckoning" (*meta logismou*). In this sentence, there is no doubt (as there may have been, at least initially, in Pericles' funeral oration; see chapter 2) that the reasoning associated with genuine bravery is one of the causes of that bravery.

This idea corresponds closely to Hyperides' account of the Athenians' courage in his own funeral oration. The orator begins by praising the city of Athens for its "thoughtful choice" (*proaireseōs, to proelesthai*) to fight for freedom in such a way as to rival the ancestors of the present generation (Hyp. 6.2).[6] The men of Athens showed *andreia* in battle (Hyp. 6.3, 6.22–24) and are praised as "prudent" (*sōphrosi*, Hyp. 6.5) and "virtuous" (*epieikesi*, Hyp. 6.5).[7] The general Leosthenes guided the city to a

---

[6] On "prohairetic choice" as a central motif of the funeral orations, cf. Allen 2010, along with the discussion of this term's Aristotelian overtones in chapter 4.

[7] See Herrman 2009: 62, who rightly connects the orator's praise of the fallen soldiers' courage to Leosthenes' "courage and cunning" (Hyp. 6.38) and to other, similar passages in the other funeral orations, including Thuc. 2.40.3 and Dem. 60.17.

thoughtful and deliberate choice (Hyp. 6.3), and he wins praise for sound deliberation at the time of the battle. He even proved superior to Miltiades and Themistocles in "courage and practical intelligence" (*andreiai kai phronēsei*) because, unlike them, he did not allow the enemy force to invade (6.38). Equally, the Athenian soldiers courageously risked their lives for Greek freedom, "thinking that the clearest proof of their desire that Greece be free was to fight and die on its behalf" (Hyp. 6.16). Hyperides maintains from the outset that prudence, deliberation, and long-term reflection lay behind the soldiers' willingness to fight Philip despite the Macedonians' numerical advantages (Hyp. 6.19). But what was the nature of the soldiers' own reflections on their purposes in fighting?

In Hyperides' representation, the soldiers had a clear vision of their goals, which were linked specifically to democratic freedom, equality, and self-government. This point emerges when Hyperides cites examples of the "arrogance" (*huperēphanian*), injustice, and disrespect for law that prevail wherever the Macedonians rule—especially the worship of the Macedonian king in place of the gods (Hyp. 6.20–22). It was to avoid vulnerability to this sort of hubris, or even servitude, that the Athenian soldiers had given their lives. The fallen soldiers died for the freedom of Greece as well as for the cause of equality, justice, and security (Hyp. 6.5). Hyperides is very specific about what this meant to them: they fought for *eudaimonia*, for "self-government" (*autonomias*), for the rule of law that enables citizens to flourish, and for freedom from groundless accusations (Hyp. 6.24–25). They sacrificed themselves so that their fellow citizens could live well (*kalōs zēn*, Hyp. 6.26). This is why it made sense for Hyperides to say that the courageous met danger confidently, because they had thought through their own fundamental purposes and ideals, which provided a rationale for their courage in action. They believed in their cause. In particular, they always kept in mind the end of securing the democratic city, so that their descendants and fellow Athenians could "live well" (6.26), that is, enjoy lives of freedom, equality, and flourishing.

Where, precisely, did this democratic reflection take place? Did the Athenians themselves understand the relationship between democratic reflection and democratic expressions of courage? Democratic ideology answered this question in the affirmative, and it could rely on democratic institutions and practices in order to support its claim. The Athenian Assembly, courts, and public festivals were the principal forums in which an unusually reflective form of courage came to sight. The public debates of political leaders and the judgments required of ordinary citizens demanded that individuals reflect independently and submit their political ideas to public scrutiny. The Athenians forged links between democratic courage and freedom by developing a fertile understanding of democratic deliberation. Wide-ranging debate in the Athenian Assembly imbued Athenian decision making with intellectual clarity and political prudence. In the course of exploring these connections, we will discover that the Athenians invented a novel discourse on "civic courage" by adapting this traditionally martial virtue to the contexts of democratic debate.[8]

Athenian practical rationality should be distinguished from the calculating, utilitarian rationality of modern social-scientific literature. The Athenians conceived of their rationality with reference to intellectual virtues, such as practical wisdom. They cherished these virtues as both intrinsically admirable and instrumentally useful. The Athenians did not presume to know, a priori, just what "goods" would constitute the city's flourishing. Instead, they devised public forums in which the citizens could explore significant questions of virtue, flourishing, and success in concert with one another, even as they responded to the practical and immediate questions of war and peace, diplomacy and expenditure. The Athenians' intellectual virtues cooperated with and even made possible their exercise of courage as a virtue. As we saw in chapter 2, however, Athenian rationality was not divorced from the emotions and passions, nor was its primary purpose seen to be that of controlling the passions. The Athenians' exercise of rationality was closely linked to and informed by the Athenians' emotions, and vice versa: Athenian emotion was recognized at the same time to be penetrated by self-conscious cognition. At least ideally, the Athenians understood themselves to be motivated to courageous behavior by the cooperative psychological activities of prudence, self-respect, a proper sense of shame, and a desire for what is good.[9]

Free Speech and Democratic Deliberation

The Athenian orators argued that specifically democratic practices of free speech led to a superior ideal of courage. Building on the arguments of

---

[8] Roisman 2003 applies the term "civic courage" to Demosthenes' prosecution of Meidias, but he does not theorize the idea at a broader level.

[9] We should also keep in mind that in the contentious struggles for power among Athens's leaders, particularly, Athenian politics did not always live up to these ideals; not only did the rationalistic associations of courage recede at times, but also politicians hurled slurs and abuse at one another in order to humiliate and shame their rivals (see, for example, Aesch. 2.148, 3.148, 3.152; with Roisman 2005: 64–83). We will approach these topics more fully in chapters 9–11.

Monoson, Saxonhouse, Roisman, and Ober,[10] I will focus on the orators' attempts to use free speech as the basis for claims of superiority over the Athenians' nondemocratic rivals.[11]

In ancient Athens the democratic citizenry wielded power through actively debating political proposals and through voting on competing proposals in an open-air Assembly, at least four times a month. Both the process of decision making through active, public deliberation and the eventual legislation produced by voting were important. If either element had been lacking, then Athens's *politeia* would not have been democratic according to the Athenians' own standards. If the Athenian citizenry had merely been able to vote on proposals made by elected officials or a hereditary elite, then their political practices would have resembled those of (nondemocratic) Sparta or Rome. Contrasting democratic and oligarchic practices, Aeschines says that "in oligarchies it is the powerful man who makes public speeches, not just anyone who wants to speak; whereas in democracies whoever wants to speak can speak whenever it seems right to him" (3.220; cf. Dem. 2.30).[12]

If, on the other hand, the Athenian citizenry had merely been able to debate the issues without the ability to transform its considered judgments into law, then the citizens themselves would not have held meaningful political power. Even debates and decrees by themselves meant little; after making prudent judgments in the Assembly, the Athenian citizens had to embody those judgments in action (Dem. 3.14–15; cf. Dem. 1.6, 2.12–13; Ober 1996a). The Athenian democracy provides us with antiquity's most exemplary expression of both elements of democratic political power, as well as a plausible, substantive account of democratic deliberation and its positive consequences. This account adds significant depth to Pericles' and other orators' connections between democratic courage and the democracy's practical rationality.

The key to this account was democratic free speech. As a political term, "free speech" was often expressed by the Greek word *isēgoria*, which emphasizes the equal opportunity of all citizens to speak freely in political forums. "Free speech" was also commonly expressed by the word *parrhēsia*, which lays stress on frank and outspoken speech.[13] In the

---

[10] Monoson 1994, 2000; Saxonhouse 1996, 2006; Ober 1989. Roisman 2003: esp. 136–41; Roisman 2005: 75–79.
[11] For further reflections on democratic deliberation in both the Assembly and the theater, see now Burian 2011 and Hesk 2011, along with chapters 12–13.
[12] See Hansen 1991: 81–85, 305–7, 311–13.
[13] On the "constant interplay" of freedom and equality in Athenian political thought and practice, see Hansen 1991: 85. On the limitations imposed on free speech in cases of slander

political world of democratic Athens, freedom of speech was a privilege that derived from a citizen's status qua citizen. Unlike slaves, foreigners, metics, and Athenian women, Athens's citizen males were both permitted and encouraged to engage in frank discussion about matters of public concern.[14] A well-known symbol of this privilege is the herald's standard question before the Assembly: "Who wishes to speak?" (Dem. 18.170, cf. Aesch. 1.24, 3.4). Beyond its status as a privilege of citizenship, however, free speech was always a central element of democratic ideology, particularly in arguments that democracy was superior to other forms of political organization. For example, Demosthenes observed with pride that in Sparta one could not praise the laws of Athens or any other state; whereas in Athens one could praise whatever laws one liked (20.106; cf. Eur. *Suppl.* 438–41; Hdt. 5.78; Hansen 1991: 77).

In the classical period it was easy to attack free speech and democratic deliberation. Attacks on democracy often focused on the ways in which free speech was practiced and the political results to which it led. The infamous Theban herald in Euripides' *Suppliant Women*, for example, criticized both the deception and the social subversion made possible by free speech: "The city I come from is ruled by one man and not by a disordered crowd (*ochlōi*). Nor is there anyone to puff up the city through speech and turn it now here and now there for the sake of private profit.... And this is a sorry condition in the view of the better citizens, when a worthless man wins a reputation by enthralling the demos with his tongue, having previously been nothing" (410–25). The herald criticizes democracy because its cherished freedom of speech, he says, leads to deception and to the political elevation of, in his view, unworthy citizens.

Other critics, such as Thucydides, represented democratic free speech and deliberation as a potentially combustible mixture of lies, deception,

---

and defamation, that is, uttering abusive words that were in Attic law considered *aporrhēta* and therefore punishable, see MacDowell 1978: 126–29.

[14] See Carter 2004 for a thoughtful reconsideration of whether the language of "rights" can be applied to Greek conceptions of freedom, and in particular Athenian conceptions of free speech (*parrhēsia* and *isēgoria*). As my use of the word "permitted" (rather than "entitled") indicates, I take a minimalist position on using the language of rights in relation to democratic free speech. As Ostwald 1996 has demonstrated, Greeks understood citizens as organically "sharing in" their communities: they had access to certain privileges (like holding office) and special duties to their communities, but did not understand this relationship in terms of claims, rights, or entitlements. For a largely similar verdict on the question, see Cooper 1999a, who argues, however, that we could usefully apply the language of rights to study of the ancient world, so long as we recognize the corollary importance of duties, and so long as we distinguish ancient "rights" from the more metaphysically grounded "rights" familiar from the modern tradition. For a different view of the case, see Monoson 2000: 51–63.

and narrowly self-interested greed.[15] During the Mytilenian debate, for example, Diodotus argues that "it is established practice now that good things spoken straight out are no less suspect than bad things, so that it is equally necessary for a speaker who wants to recommend terrible policies to attach the people to himself through deception and for a speaker with better advice to become trustworthy through lying" (Thuc. 3.43). Diodotus' point is that in practice democratic free speech and deliberation do not guarantee reasoned discussion; rather, they tend to promote irrationality and bad faith.[16] Still other critics emphasized the excessive freedom and tolerance of democracy (Plato, *Rep.* 557b–558c), or the likelihood that *parrhēsia* would be offensive (Eur. *Or.* 902–05). In pointing out the recklessness of Athens's current political advisors, Isocrates even claimed that true freedom of speech does not exist in Athens, because the people will not listen to those who rebuke them (8.14).[17] The self-conscious arguments in favor of democratic free speech and deliberation originated in a climate of contentious political discourse in Athens.[18]

Against such assaults on their cherished free speech, democrats replied by offering an alternative account of democratic deliberation—one that, in their view at least, supported the idea that free speech led to choiceworthy results for the city. In order to explain the benefits and demands of the democratic process, the orators developed an understanding of democratic deliberation that emphasized the advantages of permitting free speech and dissent, and the wisdom of the decisions that resulted from the process.

The most important element of their vision was that democratic audiences profited from hearing citizens frankly express novel or dissenting views.[19] As Demosthenes put it, "As I see it, men of Athens, no one with sense would reject the idea that it is best of all for the city to do nothing disadvantageous at the beginning; but, if that does not happen, no one would deny the value of having those who will immediately object present" (*Ex.*

---

[15] For this point in general, see Ober 1998: 94–104; Balot 2001a: 159–72.

[16] Hesk 2000 is an important contribution to our understanding of deception in democratic ideology; on the Mytilenian debate in particular, see Hesk 2000: 248–55 for a compelling analysis of the "rhetoric of anti-rhetoric."

[17] Cf. "Old Oligarch" (ps.-Xen. *Constitution of the Athenians*) 1.6–8, 1.12.

[18] The best recent discussion of the critics of Athenian democracy, with particular reference to democratic free speech as a "speech act," is Ober 1998.

[19] My view of free speech and democratic deliberation shares elements with Monoson 2000: 54–61, who emphasizes *parrhēsia* as a form of critical and educative political speech; and Ober 1989: 163–65, 295–98. Whereas Monoson emphasizes intellectual autonomy as the central virtue enabling the system to work (56), however, I would stress civic courage (see "The Athenians' Virtue of Civic Courage," below), which the orators themselves highlight in addressing the demos.

49.1). His assumption is that members of the audience would benefit from examining suitably justified challenges to their own preconceptions (cf. Dem. 3.32; 10.54; *Ex.* 44.1, 47.3; Isocr. 8.14).[20]

This emphasis on dissent qualifies another common sentiment expressed by the orators—that they should try, if possible, to give voice to the ideals and beliefs that they share with the many. As Demosthenes says in *On the Crown*, "But it is not the speech of a rhetor, Aeschines, or the power of his voice which are his worth, but it lies rather in his preference for the same things as the many and in his hating and loving the same things as his homeland. If he has such a disposition, everything a man says will be patriotic" (18.280).[21] The demos wanted to believe, though, that its speakers were not simply patriotic and loyal, but also capable of raising intelligent objections and refining or even reversing previous decisions. Hence, speakers could argue that patriotism was shown paradigmatically in the attempt to persuade the demos, against its own inclinations, to do what was best for the city, instead of gratifying fleeting desires for pleasure (cf. Aesch. 3.127; Dem. 3.3, 3.21–22, 6.3, 9.3–4, 9.63, 10.54; Ober 1989: 321–22).

A major benefit of hearing objections raised in public is that individuals might come to prefer more sensible proposals and begin to revise their own opinions; indeed, the demos as a whole might vote for revised proposals on the basis of intelligent objections to previous decisions. Thucydides' Diodotus asserted that the revisability of decisions and norms is a central source of political strength in the democracy (3.42).[22] This revisability extends beyond the Assembly's collective reconsideration of decisions already taken, such as the decision to execute the Mytilenians, to the citizens' individual revision of viewpoints they once held, if good reasons were presented to the contrary (*Ex.* 44.2). Even if the Athenians were not persuaded by what they heard, they still benefited from listening to contrary positions, since they could then feel more confidence in their previous decisions and achieve greater unanimity in supporting them (*Ex.* 47.2).[23] All things considered, these arguments suggest that it is a matter

---

[20] Cf. Monoson 1994: 181–82.

[21] The translation is adapted from Ober 1989: 167. See Ober 1989: 166–74, for an illuminating discussion of this passage. Monoson's discussion (Monoson 1994: 174–85) does not fully take into account the expectation that orators will both articulate and help to refine the views of the demos, both of which require civic courage.

[22] For the importance of the revisability of democratic decisions and norms as expressed in this speech, see Saxonhouse 1996: 72–79. For an interesting statement, however, of the potential pitfalls of revising an earlier decision made on good grounds, see Dem. 10.75.

[23] Political theorists will notice the Millian overtones of these ancient discussions of free speech.

of prudence and self-interest for the demos to permit all Athenian citizens to speak freely, especially if their views were novel or dissenting. This is why Demosthenes could argue that it was a matter of patriotic duty for Athenians, as lovers of the city, to grant "frank speech" (*parrhēsia*) to those willing to address the Assembly (*Ex.* 27.1).

In the contentious, and often antidemocratic, world of classical Greek political thinking, the Athenians found it important to buttress these interlocking claims with an explanation of the prudence of decisions reached through collective deliberation. In part, their explanation focused on the good judgment of democratic audiences. For example, Thucydides has Athenagoras, the Sicilian orator, say, "I believe that the rich are the best guardians of money, that intelligent men provide the best counsel, and that the many, having listened to arguments, judge best" (6.39). Others emphasized the demos's cleverness in comprehending speeches (Dem. 3.15), its general good judgment (Dem. 23.145–46), and its reputation for superiority in political deliberation (Dem. 23.109). Speaking of its laws rather than its decisions in the Assembly, Aeschines argues that the demos (qua jury) is "naturally more clever than others" (1.178). Naturally, these arguments are highly contextual and can be balanced against others (e.g., Thuc. 3.38, Isocr. 8.14; Dem. 10.75) in which speakers berate the demos for its irrationality, fickleness, and lack of insight.[24] But in general, speakers praised their fellow citizens for intelligence and good sense, emphasizing in other words the collective "wisdom of the masses."[25]

A linked, but not identical, idea can be found in Aristotle's well-known "summation argument" in the *Politics*: "As for the many, each of them may not be a good man; nevertheless, it is possible for them, having come together, to be better than the few best men, not individually but all together...for, when they are many, each one has his share of excellence and practical understanding" (1281a42– b5).[26] In Aristotle's view the demos is a better judge of music and poetry than are a few aristocrats because different individuals can judge different parts of artistic works, and all of them can judge the works as a whole (1281b7–10). This is often called the "summation argument" because Aristotle assumes that the virtues and intelligence of individual members of the demos work according to an additive

---

[24] See Roisman 2004, 2005: 130–62 for a highly illuminating discussion of the orators' occasional questioning of the demos's wisdom, which he interprets as part of the power struggle between the demos and its leaders.

[25] Ober 1989, 163; on the democratic claim to wisdom, see further Monoson 1994: 179–85.

[26] A strong analysis of the summation argument in its philosophical and democratic context can be found in Ober 1998: 319–24; cf. Ober 1989: 163–65.

principle—added all together, they amount to more than the virtues and intelligence of a few oligarchs or other nondemotic participants.

Athenian orators could be sympathetic to this view, insofar as it shows how the demos could function intelligently and make wise decisions. However, they typically went beyond the additive principle in arguing for democratic rationality. They explained the key role of free speech in its incarnation as confidently spoken dissent. Frank speech allowed differences of opinion to be expressed, and therefore more cogent arguments to be produced and better judgments formed, in the Athenian Assembly.[27] Implicitly contrasting Athens with Sparta, Thucydides' Pericles had said that action should be informed by prudent speech, rather than opposed to it (2.40). Rational decision making resulted not so much from an Aristotelian, quasi-mystical summation, or adding up, of individual perceptions, but rather from the free play of debate within the assembled group, and from the citizens' willingness to revise previous points of view based on these debates. As the speakers knew well, this required an audience willing to listen to the debates and to learn from them (Dem. *Ex.* 49.1). One speaker, therefore, openly criticized his fellow citizens for not waiting to hear all sides of a question explored by a range of diverse speakers, but instead asking impatiently and prematurely what to do (Dem. 10.11, 10.28–29).

The ideal suggested that democracy has a particular way of making the native perceptiveness of individuals count, that is, by encouraging freely expressed dissent, novel ideas, and challenges to convention. Individuals willing to make arguments in the Assembly had to confront the disagreements of others and to refine or revise their own views accordingly. Thus, Athenians believed deeply that the democratic Assembly could produce rationally justified decisions when individuals expressed their own views publicly, articulated their reasons before others, gave an impartial hearing to reasoned alternatives, and voted for measures after due reflection (Thuc. 2.40; 6.39; Dem. 1.1, 2.31, 8.1; Aesch. 1.178). Every citizen potentially had something to contribute (Isocr. 12.248). In the ideological constructions of the orators, therefore, the Athenians' free speech created the greatest political benefits because of the context of respectful and rational public deliberation.

Strikingly, the Athenians' system, at least in this ideological representation, overlaps to some extent with the theories of deliberative democracy offered by modern political theorists such as Seyla Benhabib. Writing about

---

[27] See Monoson 1994: 179–84, Monoson 2000: 56–63 for further exploration of this view.

the public discourse characteristic of "deliberative democracy," Benhabib argues, "Central to practical rationality is the possibility of free public deliberation about matters of mutual concern to all.... Such processes of public deliberation have a claim to rationality because they increase and make available necessary information, because they allow the expression of arguments in the light of which opinions and beliefs need to be revised, and because they lead to the formation of conclusions that can be challenged publicly for good reasons."[28] Although Benhabib is discussing modern democracies in large, bureaucratic nation-states, her argument can help us articulate the context of deliberation in which Athenians located their practices of free speech. In classical Athens, that context was underwritten by political equality and mutual respect, and, in democratic ideology, it helped to provide an explanation for the Athenians' traditional claim to be intellectually superior to others. I note that Benhabib is making the case that free public deliberation leads to greater political rationality in actual fact, not simply in ideological representation. This may make us reflect, albeit speculatively, on whether the Athenians' ideology of political wisdom was, to some extent at least, a reality.[29]

By examining the deliberative frameworks developed by the Athenian orators, we have arrived at a clearer understanding of the deliberative rationality that was critical to Pericles' arguments for the distinctiveness of democratic courage. In fact, the orators provided an even more intransigently and self-consistently demotic perspective on such questions than Pericles did. For Pericles had said, "We ourselves either make judgments on practical matters, at least, or reflect on them correctly" (2.40.2)—which perhaps indicates, as many commentators have argued, that Pericles expected the Athenians' leaders to formulate policies and the people to (at least) make intelligent judgments about them.[30] But the more demotic Athenian orators proposed that all Athenians should debate the issues for themselves, reflect on them personally, voice opposition when necessary, and vote independently according to their best understanding of what was good for the city. It was in that way that the Athenians could best internalize the articulate and self-conscious understandings of courage that distinguished Athenian courage from that of nondemocratic cities.[31]

---

[28] Benhabib 1996: 87.
[29] For modern investigations of such questions, see Estlund 2009; Marti 2006.
[30] Rusten 1989: 154–55; Hornblower 1991: 305–6.
[31] It is undoubtedly true, as Hansen 1991: 266–68 (relying on his earlier, more detailed treatments) has argued, that few Athenians proposed measures or made speeches on a regular basis. Given the state of our evidence, we have virtually no records of the dense habits of political participation at local, deme levels, no records of conversations in the Boule, and no real records of Assembly

Hazards and Obstacles: The Ideology and Practice of Free Speech

As every speaker recognized, however, contributing to public debate could be hazardous: speakers could be shouted down, informally harassed for their views, or, perhaps worst of all, haled before a court of law on the charge of making an illegal proposal. Even if free speech had substantial benefits to offer the citizenry, then, it also entailed grave risks in practice for the speaker. This is why the foregoing model of practical deliberation was by no means taken for granted, even by the orators themselves. The orators showed concern that their idealistic vision of democratic deliberation could be undercut by the realities of political competition, by the (alleged) character flaws of both other speakers and the demos, and by the audience's tendency to interrupt speakers.[32] Hence, their ideological model had to be responsive both to putative character problems, themselves a part of oratorical representation, and to the competitive realities of political speech at Athens, which were a part of Athens's institutions and ordinary political practices. They had to take into account both other representations and political realities in order to make their model of democratic deliberation plausible.

The Athenians' democracy held individual orators accountable to the demos and forced them to compete with one another for the approval and votes of the demos.[33] As David Cohen has argued, a central facet of this competition was the use of the courts to wage political warfare against one's rivals.[34] Since the legal risks associated with proposing illegal measures in the Assembly and with being an active public speaker generally, are well known, I do not discuss them here in detail,[35] except to note that

---

debates. Yet in these forums, too, individual Athenians debated the issues, spoke in public, offered critically dissenting views, and so on, in much larger numbers than we see in the fragmentary record for Assembly debates. For deme politics, see Osborne 1985a and Whitehead 1986; for the flow of knowledge in bodies such as the Boule, see Ober 2004b, 2008. For political discussion in the agora and in the people's workshops, see Hansen 1991: 311, with Aesch. 3.1, Isocr. 7.15. For the ideology that all Athenians were expected to speak from time to time, see Hansen 1991: 266–68, who cites Aesch. 3.220, Dem. 22.37, 23.4, 24.66.

[32] Therefore, as I will explain in this section, I disagree with the view of Monoson (2000: 55): "The risks were not thought by the Athenians to undermine or even conflict with the practice of frank speech"; though cf. Monoson 1994: 182–83, Monoson 2000: 60–61.

[33] On accountability in Athenian politics, see Roberts 1982 and Hansen 1991: 267; on elite competition for the demos's approval, see Ober 1989.

[34] See Cohen 1995. Johnstone 1999: 46–69 provides illuminating analysis of how litigants shaped their narratives of the immediate past to win advantages for their own cases. For further exploration of the "agonale Moment," see Piepenbrink 2001: 9–100.

[35] For a full treatment of the risks of political leadership, see Sinclair 1988: 136–61.

the orators themselves foregrounded the dangers of free speech and argued that they deserved credit for their courage in running risks for the sake of Athens's welfare (Dem. 1.16, 3.11–13, 3.32, 4.51, 8.71–72, 10.70–72, 23.5; Isocr. 8.14; cf. in general Andoc. 2.4, Lys. 7.32).[36]

There was a legitimate basis for their arguments in the penalties, both formal and informal, that might result from political participation. Participants' property, citizenship, and even lives were at stake in such legal procedures as the *graphē paranomōn*, *eisangelia*, *probolē*, *endeixis*, and *apophasis*.[37] To these can be added the less formal risks derived from shame—unpopularity, humiliation, and loss of credibility—as well as slander (Aesch. 3.227). These could, like the others, be overwhelmingly damaging to an individual's career in politics, since, as Finley once showed, every speaker's position was only as secure as his latest speech.[38] Since the Athenian system did not grant official status to public speakers and advisors, a speaker's political status depended entirely on his ability to persuade the audience on each issue as it arose. These political realities of elite competition made free speech in the deliberative context of the democracy an enormously risky venture.

The performative dimension of Athenian democratic leadership led directly to a well-developed discourse on the ethical pitfalls to which political speakers were susceptible, because the informality of their political status increased the importance of perceptions of their character.[39] In the context of such intense competition, political speakers argued that their courage enabled them to overcome the temptation to resort to illicit, or at least shameful, means of acquiring or maintaining political power. At the level of character, the deliberative model sketched earlier requires individual independence (Dem. *Ex.* 50.3) and patriotism (Dem. 23.190) from speakers, as well as impartiality (Dem. 8.1, cf. 23.19; cf. Andoc. 1.2) and a self-controlled and long-term perspective (e.g., Dem. 1.11, 1.14–15, 6.27) from listeners.

In the view of the orators, none of these attributes were secure or to be taken for granted. The primary problem is that speakers tend to "channel" the short-term desires of the demos, in order to win adulation and respect. In his *On Organization*, for example, Demosthenes told the audience, "The speakers never make you either bad or good, but you

---

[36] See Ober 1989: 109–12; Piepenbrink 2001: 146–47; Roisman 2005: 142–45.
[37] On the mechanisms of political control over the politicians, see Piepenbrink 2001: 144–48.
[38] Finley 1962.
[39] Piepenbrink 2001: 148–50.

make them whichever you wish; for you do not aim at what they wish for, but they aim at whatever they think you desire" (13.36). This tendency was heightened because the system of political rewards encouraged ambitious individuals to make their proposals compatible with the desires of the demos. Thus, in the critical remarks of democratic orators themselves, speakers could easily become the people-pleasing creatures of the demos (see "Free Speech and Democratic Deliberation," above; cf. Ar. *Knights* passim; Thuc. 2.65.10; Pl., *Gorg.*, esp. 515c–519b; Arist. *Pol.* 1305a3–7, 1320a4–6). This tendency was driven, according to the orators, by the speakers' desire to enrich themselves at the expense of the polis and by the unfair privileging of their own interests over those of the polis (Dem. 3.29; 23.208; 24.8–9; Isocr. 8.124, 12.140; Aesch. 3.173; Piepenbrink 2001: 116–119). These problems were exacerbated by the demos's alleged tendencies to play favorites (Isocr. 8.3, cf. Isocr. 15.22; Dem. 23.19–20) and to mistake short-term benefits for the city's greater welfare (Dem. 4.39). In both ideology and practice, therefore, speakers were strongly discouraged from proposing bold, independent resolutions that challenged the assumptions and preconceptions of their audiences, that is, from doing their part in the ideal deliberative workings of the democratic assembly.

Finally, in the *thorubos* (disorderly noise, "hubbub"), we find another impediment to speakers' exercising their citizen-based privilege of speaking freely, but this time the impediment comes from the audience. It turns out, in fact, that many justifications of free speech are also exhortations to the democratic audience to be quiet and let others have their say. Demosthenes argued that it was important to allow speakers to speak freely, because they might have useful advice to offer; moreover, he said, if the audience chose to shut down a particular speaker, then other speakers, too, would give up their independent ideas and merely parrot back to the assembly whatever it wanted to hear (Dem. *Ex.* 10.1, cf. Dem. 10.28). At the same time, the *thorubos* was a clear indication that the community's interests and desires took precedence over those of any individual.[40] Moreover, through the *thorubos*, the Athenians made it clear, through either interrupting or not, that the demos was all powerful, and ultimately responsible for the speakers' freedom to speak.[41] What are we to make of

---

[40] See Wallace 2004.
[41] See Roisman 2004.

the apparent tension between Demosthenes' argument and the common practice of the *thorubos*?

First, although there are cases in which a speaker stirs up the *thorubos* on purpose (cf. Dem. 18.23), there are many more cases in which the speaker was anxious not to be interrupted by the audience (e.g., Dem. 5.15, 13.3, cf. Aesch. 1.35; cf. Tacon 2001: 182–84). However much this sounds like a simple contest of wills, the deeper significance, as the passage just mentioned (Dem. *Ex.* 10.1) shows, is that speakers could make strong arguments for the ethical and practical significance of free speech and dissent. Should they refuse to listen to all sides of the question, and all relevant viewpoints, the citizens would deprive themselves of potentially useful insights into policy matters. At a more abstract level, they would deprive themselves of deeper understandings of what virtues such as justice and courage required in their particular circumstances—and even what the point of those virtues may have been, altogether. Therefore, the ideal model of democratic deliberation, as I have sketched it above, would break down to the extent that the demos interrupted speakers.

Second, such arguments directed toward practical efficacy and knowledge of the intrinsic merits of the virtues are different from any modern arguments to the effect that individual freedom of speech should be "protected" by virtue of the dignity and equality of individual citizens.[42] The Athenian democracy did not need any doctrine of "protected free speech" in order to recognize the pitfalls of the *thorubos*. Even on the Athenian democracy's own premises, there are good grounds, in the orators' arguments for allowing and encouraging dissent, for disapproving of the *thorubos*. This held true even despite the very interesting possibility that the *thorubos* could act as a kind of effective free speech for members of the demos who would not ordinarily participate actively in the Assembly debates.[43] The speakers' attractive model of democratic deliberation should limit the approval that recent reassessments have granted to the *thorubos*.[44]

---

[42] Therefore, this argument adds strength to David Carter's view that free speech is not conceived of as a "right" and also illustrates a possible avenue of disagreement with Wallace's generally favorable construction of the Athenians' utilitarian system (see Carter 1994; Wallace 2004).

[43] For this possibility, see Tacon 2001: 180; cf. Bers 1985: 12–15.

[44] I note that even though the *thorubos* was a common practice, it is hard to find a rational justification of this practice within the framework of democratic ideals and commitments—even among the highly (by modern standards) community-oriented Athenians.

The Athenians' Virtue of Civic Courage

Because free speech played a special role in democratic deliberation, and because, nevertheless, free speech was seen as entailing substantial risks, the orators' courage was a uniquely significant part of the democratic system. The orators strove to define their courage in a novel democratic idiom that corresponded to Athens's novel egalitarian political structures and ideology of free speech. Civic courage, as they conceived of it, was central to the viability of democratic deliberation because it was the precondition of exercising democratic free speech. The orators' understanding of civic courage helped to make their public, ideologically informed conversations about democracy and free speech more plausible. The Athenians' efforts to develop a novel understanding of military courage cooperated with, and even to some extent issued in, an innovative theory of civic courage.[45] The orators maintained, quite plausibly, that their courage enabled them to make a unique contribution to the quintessentially democratic ideals of deliberation to which they subscribed.

Hence, whatever the importance of the *thorubos*, speaking before one's fellow citizens required the ability to take risks, to confront social dangers such as humiliation or shame, and to maintain a level-headed composure when expressing one's own opinions before one's opinionated political equals. In short, if the key to successful deliberation was free speech, and if speakers were confronted by threats and pressures of all sorts, then speakers needed courage. In the first essay of *The Human Condition*, Hannah Arendt argued for the intrinsic dignity of courage in similar ways: "To leave the household...demanded courage because only in the household was one primarily concerned with one's own life and survival. Whoever entered the political realm had first to be ready to risk his life, and too great a love for life obstructed freedom, was a sure sign of slavishness. Courage therefore became the political virtue par excellence."[46] As important as the distinction between *oikos* and *polis* may be, however, the Athenians' legitimate fears resulted rather from political competition and legal constraint than any existential transition from the protected space of the household to the forums of political engagement.

The problem with such a competitive democratic ethic was that individuals could easily become the victims or casualties of the system. If free

---

[45] On the Athenians' "civic courage," see Roisman 2005: 142–45.
[46] Arendt 1958: 36.

speech and dissent benefited the community, then, by contrast, the hazards of dissent fell entirely on individuals (cf. Dem. 4.51). These hazards gave orators the opportunity to claim courage for themselves and to show that their courage made a unique contribution to democratic deliberation. By contrast with the honorific language of decrees, that of courage was usually self-asserted, and such self-assertion was a delicate matter: it had to be embedded in the framework of patriotically doing one's duty and counseling the city to do what was best for it.[47] In the hands of the orators, a novel conception of civic courage enabled speakers to become the "real men" of their day—but this was now redefined as a form of speaking freely and boldly, so as to promote democratic deliberation, and thus wisdom about human excellence and human flourishing.

Athenian orators argued that their willingness to run risks in order to speak freely indicated their sincerity and patriotism. In his speech *On the Chersonese*, for example, Demosthenes imagined a rival charging him with declining to make proposals or run risks, which allegedly shows that he is "a weak coward" (*atolmos ei kai malakos*). (8.68). In defending himself, Demosthenes formulated civic courage as the ability to speak freely even against the demos' inclinations: "Yet I think that I myself am braver than many of your reckless politicians. For, Athenians, if anyone, neglecting what will benefit the polis, judges, confiscates, bribes, and makes accusations, he does not do these things because of any courage. Rather, ensuring his own safety through speaking and passing measures to please you, he is 'safely bold.' But whoever often opposes your wishes for the sake of what is best, and never speaks to win favor, but always to promote your best interests, and chooses that policy in which chance rather than calculation has more power, and yet makes himself accountable to you for both—that man is truly brave, and he is the useful citizen" (8.68–70).[48] In this passage, Demosthenes voices the familiar criticism that democratic leaders tend, for selfish reasons, to parrot back to the demos exactly what it wants to hear. Everyone, he implies, would like to be called *andreios*, but other speakers pilfer a counterfeit form of that approbation by gratifying the demos's unruly desires and thereby ensuring their own safety. True courage, for Demosthenes, enables a speaker to undertake risks in the

---

[47] Thus, for reasons I offer in the following pages, I would modify Roisman's claim (2003: 129) that "courage could not be securely self-claimed."

[48] As Roisman 2003 has made clear, courage is sometimes defined as an internal stance of moderation with relation to desires to get more (especially *philotimia* and *pleonexia*). Glimmers of that conception can be found in this passage, along with Demosthenes' more characteristic idea that it takes courage to transcend the fears associated with possible political failure.

most uncertain of circumstances, and to do so for the sake of the common good. Demosthenes' courage is focused on the common good in so far as it provides for the confident expression of dissent, and therefore promotes democratic deliberation.

Cicero definitively established courage as an appropriately civic virtue in the first book of his *De Officiis*.[49] Especially in any post-Ciceronian era, this civic redefinition of courage will appear largely unproblematic. However, as Rosen and Sluiter (2003) have shown, and as we have assumed, the "prototype" of *andreia* is military courage.[50] The Athenians' development of a conception of civic courage therefore challenged the traditional military interpretation of this virtue. Contrary to that narrow interpretation, Athenian democratic ideology was invested in making courage, the formerly heroic military virtue, available to all participants in the free-speaking, egalitarian civic arena.[51]

What was needed was a translation of courage from the military to the civic realm. To make this transition plausible, orators used military metaphors to describe their courage in speaking freely.[52] Demosthenes' speech *Against Meidias* illustrates this strategy and illuminates the ways in which courage, free speech, and equality were inextricably linked in the forging of the speakers' democratic self-image.[53] Characterizing Meidias as an authoritarian, tyrannical figure, Demosthenes argues that his wealth and power posed a considerable threat to both himself and to democratic free speech and equality. Relating the story of Meidias' revenge on the arbitrator Strato, an ordinary citizen who had once entered a verdict against Meidias, Demosthenes exhibits Strato himself, now disenfranchised and

---

[49] See *de Officiis* I.61–92 on *magnitudo animi*. It is striking that Cicero explicitly draws on Athenian civic traditions to formulate a conception of courage (cf. *de Officiis* I.61, 75–76, 84); note also his use of Platonic political thought (I. 64, 85) in order to establish his novel conception of "greatness of soul."

[50] For Aristotle, at the end of the classical tradition, courage is shown in confronting the greatest of all fearful things, i.e., death, and in the noblest arena, i.e., specifically hoplitic battle (not, for example, in facing death through drowning or disease): *EN* 1115a25–32. For Aristotle on courage, see Deslauriers 2003: esp. 188–92. For courage associated with free speech, we may note that Aristotle believes that the *megalopsuchos* is a "frank talker" (*parrhēsiastēs*) because of his contempt for others (*dia to kataphronētikos einai*) (1124b29–30), whereas hiding one's feelings is considered cowardly, because it involves caring more for one's own reputation than the truth (1124b27–29). On Aristotle and free speech, see Mulhern 2004.

[51] Smoes 1995: 9–97 provides a helpful overview of what he calls "conceptions préphilosophiques du courage" [prephilosophical conceptions of courage]; see in particular his discussion of the evolution from "mythic" courage to "rational" courage in Herodotus and Thucydides (81–97).

[52] On a comparable use of military metaphors to describe the Aristophanic poet and Roman satirists, see Rosen and Sluiter 2003: 15–20.

[53] Compare Roisman 2003: 136–40; Ober 1996; Wilson 1991; Piepenbrink 2001: 116–19.

therefore unable to speak before the jury: "[N]ow he stands in silence, deprived not only of the other privileges we hold in common, but also of speaking and complaining; and he is not permitted even to tell you whether he has suffered justly or unjustly" (95).

Strato's literal excommunication from the polis makes him unable to participate in the community's collective constructions of right and wrong, and therefore, in Aristotle's terms, he is a man without a polis (*Pol.* 1253a14–18). No wonder, then, that many of Meidias' victims held their peace (*hēsuchian eschon*), as Demosthenes puts it, cowed by his self-confidence, wealth, and gang of thugs (21.20).[54] The histrionic display of Strato gives added point to Demosthenes' summation: "We must not overlook things like this, nor must we suppose that the man who, by frightening us, tries to keep any one of us from obtaining justice from him for his crimes is doing anything other than taking away our share in free speech (*isēgorias*) and freedom (*eleutherias*)" (21.124). Free speech appears here in the guise of "equality of speech," *isēgorias*, since Demosthenes is eager to emphasize the connections between the intimidation, silencing techniques, and anti-egalitarian hubris of Meidias.[55] Demosthenes is in the process of making civic courage a principal element of Athenian politics, by placing it alongside freedom and equality and demonstrating the interconnections of all three factors.

To make his conception of civic courage plausible, Demosthenes now evokes the martial connotations of this virtue, which, he tries to show, are still operative in the political context. As he argues, the only antidote to a Meidias is the courageous citizenship exemplified by Demosthenes. In his own case, Demosthenes says, Meidias trumped up accusations of desertion (*lipotaxiou*, 21.103) and murder against him in order to keep him from bringing charges. He did this, Demosthenes alleges, "as though it were right for a man to be expelled beyond our borders without a chance of being let go, if, having been insulted by this man, he thought it right to seek justice and not to remain silent; as though it were necessary also to be convicted on a charge of desertion and to face murder charges and

---

[54] In Athenian democracy, keeping quiet (*hēsuchian agein*) is usually considered a repellent condition of passivity, often brought about by the machinations and oppressiveness of rich and powerful individuals. At 8.67, for example, Demosthenes accuses other speakers of trying to silence the demos in order to continue manipulating and abusing it. The negative evaluation of political silence is the ideological converse of the positive evaluation of free speech and all its attendant political benefits.

[55] On hubris and the contest between civic and elitist codes of political discourse enacted in this speech, see Ober 1996. On Demosthenes' use of Strato, see Allen 2000: 230–32.

only just escape crucifixion" (21.105). Desertion is of course a quintessential act of cowardice; by contrast, therefore, this element of Meidias' accusation played a central role in Demosthenes' picture of himself as a courageous freedom fighter. Demosthenes turned Meidias' accusation on its head by activating the prototypically military associations of *andreia*. He argued that he was, right before the jury's eyes, courageously speaking freely in order to defend liberty: "I think the opposite: if I had let Meidias go," he says, "then I would have abandoned the post of justice" (21.120). For Demosthenes, democrats need courage in order to safeguard their democracy against threats from within—both from real tyranny and the more subtle forms of tyranny that restrict democratic freedoms, subvert equality, or diminish the force of law. Elsewhere, along the same lines, Demosthenes invoked the tyrannicides as the quintessential instance of democratic civic courage and freedom fighting (20.160–62). The courage to speak freely enables Demosthenes to defend not only himself, but also democracy.

Demosthenes used a military metaphor, that is, deserting one's post, to describe a civic function in which free speech played an integral part. By using military metaphors to describe acts of speaking freely, the orators developed a plausible and attractive conception of civic courage. Their conception both explained how their model of democratic deliberation could work, despite the hazards of free speech and dissent, and why it proved attractive as a form of approbation for speakers themselves.[56]

Several further examples will illustrate the Athenians' conception of civic courage. In *Against Theomnestus I* (10.24–25) Lysias' client figures the courtroom as a site of armed conflict even more dangerous than military campaigns. In *On the Embassy* (2.181–82) Aeschines renders a startling image of his own courageous free speech before Philip of Macedon, by contrast with Demosthenes' cowardly tendency to faint before the king. He concludes that his willingness to expose himself to the risks of slander after the embassy shows that he is superior in courage even to conspicuously brave soldiers. Elsewhere (15.32–33) Demosthenes urges that speakers should be deprived of the privilege of giving advice if they adopt oligarchical attitudes and thereby "desert the political post handed down by our ancestors" (cf. Pl. *Lach.* 190e4–6). Democratic civic courage

---

[56] My study of military metaphors used to describe civic functions is methodologically indebted to Bynum (1995), who argues that "ideas are sometimes elaborated and sometimes betrayed (in the several senses of the word *betray*) in the specific metaphors that clothe them" (xvi).

consists in the appropriate use of free speech to defend and promote the democratic institutions handed down by the Athenians' ancestors.

We normally associate this brand of civic or political courage, and even the military metaphor itself, with the speeches of Socrates in Plato's *Apology*. Socrates subtly transformed the democratic metaphor by emphasizing concern for his own soul rather than concern for the polis.[57] As Socrates argued, "I would have done a terrible thing, men of Athens, if, when the archons whom you elected to command me had assigned me to a post at Potideia, Amphipolis and Delium, I had remained where they assigned me, just like everyone else, and run the risk of dying, but then, when the god assigned me (as I believed) to live as a philosopher and to examine myself and others, then, fearing death or anything else whatever, I had left my post" (Plato, *Ap.* 28d10–29a2). Socrates' view is that it is his divinely ordained duty to speak candidly to his fellow citizens about the state of their souls, even if the democracy should somehow outlaw his practice of philosophy. Even in that case, he says, he will never stop practicing philosophy and exhorting his fellow citizens to search for the truth in his company (29d4–7).

Although Socrates evidently has the courage to speak freely, he famously disavowed active political participation in the democratic city (Plato, *Ap.* 31e–32a), even though he equally famously presided over the Assembly during the trial of the Arginusae generals (Plato, *Ap.* 32b–c). The Socratic military metaphor is an example of Socratic or Platonic uses of democratic conventions for a different purpose—that is, to explain and justify Socrates' own dedication to the pursuit of wisdom, even if that pursuit might come into conflict with prospective democratic laws. Although Plato later became a significant figure in the development of a wider, non-military conception of courage, it is plausible to argue that this Socratic

---

[57] Although Mulhern 2004 rightly points out that Greek ethical thinking took place within the framework of, and normally with a view to, politics, Socrates himself (whether he is the Platonic character or historical figure) complicates the picture. As Brown 2000 argues, Socrates practiced an extraordinary politics that aimed to improve the souls of his interlocutors without recognizing any special obligations to his fellow Athenians. Thus, although Socrates' ethical practices might still have a vaguely political orientation, Socrates' "politics," such as they were, should be sharply distinguished from the ordinary civic, and later Aristotelian, conceptions of politics. If, as Socrates claims at *Gorgias* 521d6–e2, he is Athens's only true politician, then his current *askēsis* and self-development, along with his care for individual others, must be distinguished from the cultivation of virtue one normally finds in Athens or in the ideals of its advocates, such as (the Platonic) Protagoras. It could be reasonably argued, by extension from the *Gorgias* passage, that Socrates practices ethics for the sake of the "true politics" which does not yet exist. See further Balot 2008.

conception originated in the structures, requirements, and language of democratic participation.[58]

The speakers' assertions of their own courage, and their military metaphors, occasionally enabled them to claim the demos as a courageous ally in the attempt to protect freedom of speech against the encroachments of rival members of the elite. In *Against Ctesiphon*, Aeschines used a military metaphor to inspire the demos to imagine itself as courageously defending democratic free speech by casting its vote against Ctesiphon and by extension Demosthenes. He reminded his listeners that there were three forms of government—tyranny, oligarchy, and democracy—and argued that democracy, uniquely, was administered by laws rather than the inclinations of the rulers. "Let no one of you fail to recognize this," he says, "but let each man know clearly that when he enters a court to judge a suit against an illegal proposal, on that day he will be voting about his own freedom of speech (*parrhēsias*)" (Aesch. 3.6). Freedom of speech is represented in this argument as the quintessential ideal promoted and protected by democracy. Aeschines used it metonymically to stand for the democracy itself and its laws.

Having raised the stakes to the level of the regime, Aeschines now had a firm basis upon which to warn the jury explicitly against those, such as conspiratorial generals and rhetors, who had sidestepped the laws for their entire careers and approached government with the mentality of tyrants or oligarchs. His conclusion? "But just as each one of you would be ashamed to abandon the post to which he had been assigned in war, so also now you should be ashamed (*aischunthēte*) to abandon the post to which you have been assigned by the laws, as guardians (*phulakes*) of the democracy this day" (Aesch. 3.7). Free speech and democracy were continually in need of defense by citizens willing to imagine their political participation as a form of military activity. In the midst of discussing the rationality of democratic deliberation, we should notice the appearance of shame as an emotion leading the Athenians to express courage in action. Shame, as Aeschines presents it, was shot through with the Athenians' own deliberate understandings of the goodness of being "guardians of the democracy" for reasons that they had long discussed in their public forums of communication about the city's highest ideals.

---

[58] Balot 2008; Balot 2013.

Public-Spirited Deliberation: A Democratic Safety Net

Despite the Athenians' novel discourse on civic courage, the orators also found resources within the democratic system, which, they argued, made the practice of free speech less hazardous than might be thought at first glance. These resources defused competition among speakers, thereby making responsibility for political decisions more diffuse, and extraordinary acts of individual courage less necessary. Freedom for everyone to speak, and from all sides of the issue, paradoxically offered protection to both the demos and its individual counselors. As Demosthenes says, "Those who have most persuaded you of certain proposals derive great advantages from having rivals who can speak. For if those rivals are able to teach you that the proposals of these men are not in fact best, when nothing has yet gone awry, then, in doing this, they will reduce the risks for them; but if they are not able to persuade you, then they will not be able to blame you later. For you listened to them—which it is your duty to do. Hence, if they are unsuccessful, then they will rightly accept this, and they will share in the consequences, whatever they may be, with all the others" (*Exordium* 26.2–3).

The very dangers that civic courage was meant to confront could themselves be minimized, in this account, by free speech itself. Free speech is capable not only of catalyzing competition among Athens's leaders but also of helping to defuse that competition by distributing responsibility more evenly among the various speakers and the entire assembled demos. Free speech enabled the democracy to establish a powerful cooperative framework within which the requisite rhetorical competition could be both more meaningful and less risky. This does not reduce the importance of the Athenian discourse on courage, but it tends to suggest that, upon reflection, democratic discourse is powerful and effective enough to be capable of dispensing with any extraordinary display of courage. This belief in Athens's deliberative resources stood in some degree of tension with speakers' (often self-interested) emphasis on their own courageous free speech. But it shows, on the other hand, that the Athenians' efforts to realize the common good could be furthered significantly by acts of independent thought and frank speech. What emerges from this investigation as a whole, then, is the highly productive capacity of free speech—not only to make proper deliberation possible, but also, as the orators argued, to produce courage itself, and to alleviate the dangers of being an active public speaker.[59]

---

[59] Following Hansen 1991: 143–44, 266–71, I use the term "public speaker" (and sometimes

The Athenians' understanding of democratic deliberation was not simply a self-justifying ideological fantasy; rather, it overlaps with the best modern theories of the deliberative prudence of democratic citizen bodies.[60] The Athenian discourse makes two noteworthy additions to those modern theories. First, the pursuit of enlightened deliberation, and even of practical wisdom through deliberation, requires virtues that democracy is peculiarly well suited to produce. Principal among these is the virtue of civic courage. Second, democratic deliberation itself involves risks and hazards, but it also has the resources to reduce those risks, provided that a virtuous citizen-body is oriented toward seeking the common good.

Conclusion: Disseminating Deliberative Results

The free-ranging debates of the democratic Assembly—not to mention those of the councilors in the Council of 500, or (at least speculatively) those of the assemblies of each individual deme—had a special claim to rationality and prudence.[61] But the Athenians' practices of free speech also had two additional consequences relevant to courage. First, the institutions of the Athenian democracy distributed the Athenians' self-understanding widely, so that all citizens of the democracy, encouraged as they were to participate on a regular basis, would have been exposed to this self-understanding and would have kept it in mind as they made decisions and went to war. Osborne estimates, in fact, that "perhaps 70% of Athenians over thirty served at least once" on the Boule.[62] The Athenians took special pains to understand the system and its distinctive benefits, as well as the reasoning behind each political decision.

Ober's recent work on systems of knowledge in democratic Athens adds texture to this picture.[63] As Ober has demonstrated, the Athenian

---

"orator") to refer to those who were prominent in the community's political life, as opposed to those who made proposals or spoke only occasionally.

[60] See Estlund 2009; Marti 2006.

[61] Whitehead 1986: 324 cautiously asserts that "the demes offered a fairly gentle introduction, for those who wished to avail themselves of it, to the workings of a democratic assembly and the duties of its officials," but he emphasizes that for politically ambitious young citizens there were many other (and perhaps better) routes to acquire political understanding, e.g., within the family. Osborne 1985a argues for the continuing entanglement of demes and city center during the classical period, particularly via the bouleutēs, the demarch, and propertied individuals: "The deme was the essential link, forging strong bonds of service and obligation between men of various social circles, and connecting the humble demesmen to the network of the well-to-do through which the main power flowed" (92).

[62] Osborne 1985a: 237n.56, with Osborne 1985a: 91.

[63] Ober 2008.

democratic system was distinctively capable of producing and disseminating what he calls "useful knowledge," so as to acquire military and economic advantages over its nondemocratic rivals throughout the ancient Aegean. Knowledge was dispersed throughout the demos through a variety of means, starting with Cleisthenes' institutional refinement of the Council of 500, where councilors from all over Attica met in the city and worked together intensively to grapple with the city's most pressing public issues.[64] The rules for participation in this Council implied that a large percentage of Athenians would have thought carefully about the city's ideals and practical problems, based on first-hand experience of self-government. The same holds true for local politics at the deme level, despite our comparative lack of evidence for the character of micro-political deliberation and judgment.[65] As Ober has shown, the Athenians infused their systems of politics, economics, and warfare with knowledge disseminated by public notices, free speech, laws, and other democratic institutions and practices. Although Ober has focused on "useful" knowledge, his arguments apply equally to the Athenians' knowledge of their own ideals, particularly the links between their virtues and their democratic regime.

Second, the process of publicly airing one's beliefs and hearing the beliefs of others expressed publicly led to greater confidence in the justice and correctness of the eventual conclusions. This did not create democratic dogmatism, as though Athenian citizens could never make a mistake or never wish to revise their views. Exactly the opposite is true. Yet, in taking their decisions, the Athenians could be assured that they had left no stone unturned in their quest to grasp the best and most prudent possible course of action for the city. The Athenians' practices of democratic deliberation, and their ritual dramatic performances, produced well-founded confidence in the Athenians' democratic decisions. Even if the Athenians, like every other decision-making body, still made mistakes, they were not likely to have missed important and foreseeable considerations or other relevant factors when they made their political decisions. It is now time to investigate how democratic courage was thought to work in practice.

---

[64] See especially Ober 2008: 134–51.
[65] Whitehead 1986: 97–120 and Osborne 1985a: 74–92 outline what little we can know positively about the business of deme assemblies: their most important function of citizen registration, as well as, for example, their capacity to pass honorific decrees or to arbitrate disputed land claims, and their management of cults and festivals.

CHAPTER 4 | Writing Courage into Democratic History: Aeschylean and Herodotean Perspectives

WE HAVE NOW ACQUIRED a clear understanding of the role of democratic deliberation in Pericles' ideology of democratic courage. In particular, we have seen that Pericles' ideal was refashioned in Attic, and particularly epitaphic, oratory, so as to suit the needs of later democratic projects and contexts. Do we have evidence from fifth-century Athens, however, that this ideology of democratic courage was influential? The answer is yes: in the representations of the Persian Wars found in Aeschylus and Herodotus, we find specific evidence that the main features of the Periclean expression of democratic courage were already in place in the fifth century, even before the Peloponnesian War.

Aeschylus' *Persians*

In Aristophanes' *Frogs*, Euripides and Aeschylus debate which poet can save the city. Dionysos has difficulty choosing between them; they are evenly matched. Athens needed both the democratic intelligence supposedly cultivated by Euripides (951–58, 971–79) and the boldness, anger, and warlike attitudes allegedly cultivated by Aeschylus (1021, 1025–27, 1039–43). In fact, the city needed the synthesis of these cognitive and emotional qualities, which the Athenians represented as constitutive of democratic courage. If Aristophanes presents Aeschylus as educating citizens in the angry, daring, and warlike postures characteristic of ancient Mediterranean masculinity, however, then it will be especially striking, and particularly revealing of the democratic qualities of the tragic theater, if even Aeschylus' plays turn out to present an image of democratic masculinity that depends on both daring and intelligence.

This is precisely what we find in Aeschylus' *Persians*, which offers a critique of the Persian political system juxtaposed with an admiring representation of democratic courage. This critique shows up Persian ideals as the antitheses of the Athenians' own self-conscious network of associations between courage, freedom, and practical rationality.[1] As Rosenbloom has stressed, Aeschylus' *Persians* "underscores the lack of democratic values in Persia—freedom (*eleutheria*: 241–43, 369–71, 1038–77), equality under the law (*isonomia*: 211–13), equality of self-presentation (*isegoria*: 150–58), and freedom of speech (*parrhesia*: 215–30, 591–94, 694–96, 700–702)—by depicting their absence in Persia."[2] Persian courage, in particular, is defective in a variety of ways—for example, because the Persian troops were motivated not by clear-eyed, rational dedication to the common good, but rather by fear of Xerxes' punishments (369–71).[3] Persian freedom is highly circumscribed: the chorus, for example, not only bows to Atossa rather than discussing matters frankly (152, 215–25, 548–57, cf. 170–72, 694–702); they also regret the novel possibility of free speech that arises after Xerxes' defeat, because they lack the self-knowledge to see that freedom is in their interests (584–97).[4] They are willing slaves, having died the double death of slavery and the loss of any consciousness of freedom's significance.

Perhaps most importantly, the Persians of this play lack political awareness and understanding. The apparently prudent Atossa makes elementary mistakes, such as believing that victory is dependent on wealth or

---

[1] Hall 1989: 80 emphasizes a different but not incompatible set of characteristics: "[T]he three main flaws in the barbarian psychology selected for repeated emphasis are its hierarchicalism, its immoderate luxuriousness, and its unrestrained emotionalism: all three find correlative virtues, however briefly implied, in the idealization of the egalitarian, austere, and self-disciplined Greek character." In offering a political line of interpretation that opposes Persian monarchy to Athenian democracy and its specific virtues, I develop the arguments of Euben 1986d; Goldhill 1988; Hall 1989; Hall 1996; Harrison 2000; Forsdyke 2001; Rosenbloom 2006; and Rosenbloom 2011.

[2] Rosenbloom 2011: 364; cf. Rosenbloom 1995 and 2006 and Harrison 2000 for developments of the political interpretation with which my reading shares elements. I view the play as less jingoistic than Harrison, however, who sees in it "the high-water mark of Athens' conviction in her imperial project" (Harrison 2000: 110); but I also view the play as less self-critical than Rosenbloom 1995. Garvie 2009: xvi-xxxii favors a "tragic" reading over this explicitly political interpretation. In support of not only a political but also a democratic interpretation, Rosenbloom 2011 correctly points out that it is difficult not to see the *ensemble* of the political characteristics identified in the text as referring specifically to democracy, even if other, nondemocratic poleis practiced one or another of them individually.

[3] Cf. Euben 1986c: 363–64.

[4] Cf. Harrison 2000: 83–85.

hierarchical political control (236–45; cf. 167) or numbers of ships or soldiers (235, 331–44).[5] Even after the Persians had been defeated, Atossa remained unsure where Athens was located (231–32)! Xerxes yoked the Hellespont, in an extraordinary failure of self-knowledge (65–72, 100–106). Every Persian agreed that Darius had established genuine prosperity among the Persians by making Persia fabulously wealthy through his imperialism (852–908). This play, though, invites its audience to think again about the authentic constituents of ethical and political prosperity. By pointedly contrasting his fictional Persians with the democratic Athenians, Aeschylus taught the Athenians to recognize the very great potential of their political system to produce virtues and patterns of behavior that they could legitimately endorse and take pride in.[6]

The episode involving the ghost of Darius (681–842) draws particular attention to the Persian regime's failure to produce proper forms of courage—precisely, as we will discover, because of its lack of freedom and self-knowledge.[7] Darius' ghost appears on the scene specifically because Atossa is wracked with fear over the disastrous reports arriving from Greece. Atossa assumes that the Persians' suffering has been sent by the gods and therefore proposes to make offerings to Darius (598–622). How do political communities deal with their most urgent fears? When the Athenians were terrified at the impending Persian invasion in the late 480s BC, they sought practical and prudent solutions, such as developing a navy and abandoning their city, having debated various proposals and entertained different interpretations of the famous Wooden Walls oracle (see the next section on Herodotus).[8] When the Athenians were terrified at their disastrous losses in Sicily, they reacted by collectively and purposefully controlling their expenditures and appointing a body of experienced advisors (Thuc. 8.1). By contrast, Atossa tries to address her fears through a strange religious practice, which in itself reveals the problems that plague the Persian monarchy.

---

[5] Harrison 2000: 76–77; Goldhill 1988: 190–91.
[6] Hall 1989: 93–98 provides an excellent discussion of Aeschylus' oppositions between the Persian monarchy and Athenian democracy, although she finds that "[a] crude contrast of Persian monarchy and Greek (i.e. Athenian) democracy was precluded by the poet's desire to contrast within that framework good monarchy under Darius with the irresponsible despotism of Xerxes" (97); though cf. the different view expressed in Hall 1996: 12; compare also Garvie 2009: 273–75 and then Harrison 2000: 85–87, who argues that the poet represents Xerxes as continuing the policies and practices of Darius.
[7] For a helpful reading of the scene in general, see Rosenbloom 2006: 89–121.
[8] Cf. Harrison 2000: 87.

The chief problem comes to sight at the end of Darius' analysis of the Persians' defeat. After a long diatribe against hubris, impiety, and self-deception, he says, "Seeing such punishments for these deeds, remember both Athens and Greece, in order that no one will despise present good fortune and pour away great wealth through lust for other things" (823–26). Any alert Athenian, upon hearing this, would be forgiven for recognizing the ironies of Darius' speech: Darius' own westward expansionism had led to the Persians' defeats in Scythia and, ultimately, in Greece (cf. Hdt. 3.134–35).[9] Darius' specific verbal formulation in this passage makes these ironies even more salient, since Darius himself had supposedly reacted to news of the burning of Sardis by shooting an arrow into the air, vowing to punish the Athenians, and ordering a servant to repeat, three times at dinner time, the words, "Master, remember the Athenians" (Hdt. 5.105).[10] Darius himself, while alive, did not model the behavior that he now recommends to the Persians, and especially to his son.

Yet Darius blames his son for forgetting what he had taught him (782–83). He has many salutary teachings to offer his audience under the headings of self-control, pious reverence, and the avoidance of self-deception (*atēs*, 822; cf. 808, 816–22). In fact, as a ghost, he criticizes Xerxes for invading Greece and for the imprudence, even senselessness, of yoking the Hellespont (722–25, 742–51) and desecrating temples and altars (809–12). How shocking it is, though, that Darius has become Xerxes' self-professed teacher of moderation. When Darius says that his son has finally been forced to "know himself" or to "be prudent" (*sōphronein*) (829), then, the audience will appreciate that the dead king is betraying, or unwittingly confessing, his own self-deception and self-ignorance. Darius may counsel moderation, but he shows no signs of the humility and hard-won self-understanding that are characteristic of authentically wise advisors. Darius himself is guilty of the very faults for which he blames Xerxes.[11]

To appreciate the political implications of this scene fully, however, we need to see that Darius' self-deception is not simply an individual failing.

---

[9] Garvie 2009: xvi-xxxii offers a helpful treatment of the play's political and ethical themes, although his treatment is tarnished by his anachronistic distinction between the "moral" and "amoral" "explanations of human suffering" (xxxi). Garvie correctly recognizes, though, that the figure of Darius poses many problems and ambiguities: "It seems so unfair that Darius, who criticizes his son for not being content with his present fortune and for trying to extend the bounds of the Persian empire, did exactly the same himself, and was not punished for it" (Garvie 2009: xxx); cf. Rosenbloom 2006, Harrison 2000: 80–91, Euben 1986d: 363–64.
[10] On the importance of memory in the play, see Hall 1996: 1–3.
[11] See Harrison 2000: esp. 76–91 for an important discussion of the continuities between Darius and Xerxes and of the general imprudence generated by the Persian system.

Instead, it is a marker of widespread social and political corruption. Darius is not an isolated megalomaniac with a distorted and self-serving memory of the past. The entire citizenry of Persia, including Atossa, and including the chorus, accepts Darius' bizarrely celebratory account of the Persians' military record. Darius himself recalls the glorious monarchs who had previously led Persia—Medus, Cyrus, and so forth (765–86); he laments that the wealth he had famously won would now be lost (751–52); Atossa glorifies the triumphs and prosperity that were established by the reign of her god-like husband (709–14); and, most impressively, the chorus of Persian elders barbarically celebrates the numbers of cities conquered by Darius, along with the courage of his soldiers and the casualty-free wars he once fought (853–902).[12] The reason for such distortions of the past is that free speech was not practiced in Persia; nor, accordingly, were the political authorities held accountable for their mistakes. These were problems of the regime rather than defects of individual character.

In general, in Aeschylus' presentation, the Persian regime systemically lacks dedication to the truth because of its autocratic rejection of free speech. The Persian leaders' self-deception had once led Xerxes to adopt a self-destructive ideal of manliness.[13] As Atossa says to Darius: "Reckless Xerxes learned these things through keeping company with bad men. They say that you acquired great wealth for your children by using the spear, whereas he, through lack of manliness, merely played with spears in the palace, and did nothing to increase his ancestral prosperity. Hearing such reproaches from bad men, many times over, he planned this armed expedition against Greece" (753–58). Xerxes was accused of cowardice (*anandrias*, 755) and felt ashamed that he was not a successful imperialist like his predecessors. Xerxes had not learned, apparently, that his own father had been imprudent in seeking to conquer the Scythians and the Greeks; he had heard only the celebratory stories that Darius, Atossa, and the Chorus repeated about the greatness of Darius' conquests.

These stories instilled a deep sense of unworthiness in Xerxes. Recall that Atossa's dream of the two horses showed Xerxes unable to bridle the noble and free Greek horse, which inspired Darius to pity—pity which, in turn, inspired shame in Xerxes, as Atossa explains when she describes Xerxes' shredding his regal clothing upon noticing Darius' pity (197–99). Readers have long taken note of the way in which Xerxes arrives home,

---

[12] See especially Rosenbloom 2006: 97–103.
[13] For a related discussion of Herodotus' representation of the character of Xerxes and the challenges he faced in ruling, see Immerwahr 1966: 176–83.

fresh from defeat, wearing tattered clothes and showing all the visible signs of his shameful loss. These tangible expressions of shame outwardly manifest the shame that had motivated Xerxes to undertake the expedition in the first place. The motif of tattered clothing is unmistakable.[14] Xerxes was susceptible to taunts of cowardice because he believed that he had failed to live up to the standards of Darius—standards which, as the audience will have recognized, were never fulfilled even by Darius. Xerxes' own display of aggressive masculinity—his invasion of Greece—was based on an ill-informed dedication to self-deceptive cultural ideals.[15] His sense of the significance of courage as an ideal was informed not by rational prudence but by ignorance and dishonesty. When the chorus continues to shout that this expedition was "in vain," or "all for nothing," which is expressed by the Greek word *matan* (e.g., 268, 288), they are communicating, more deeply than they themselves are aware, that Xerxes' display of manly anger was, quite literally, for the sake of culturally informed ideals of expansionist kingship that had long been self-destructive.

Persian courage is defective, first because the soldiery is motivated by fear of punishment, but second, and more importantly, because the monarchical leader himself, who should provide guidance for the army, fails to recognize the emptiness of his own ideals. His courage was motivated by shame, like that of many Greek soldiers, from Homer onward (see chapter 9), but the cognitive "inputs" into his shame are entirely empty. His sense of shame is literally based on nothing—as opposed to the sense of shame cultivated by Pericles, which was based on the real, albeit unjust and expansionist, accomplishments of the Athenians' ancestors. Even Spartan courage, which Pericles had disparaged as motivated by hierarchical authorities and enforced by punishment, was not as empty as Persian courage, because the role models that provided direction to the Spartan sense of shame had at least a certain meaning and respectability. The Spartans' shame-driven courage was at least dedicated to the common good and based on shared, and to some degree truthful, memories of military victory and defeat. The Persian regime, as represented by Aeschylus, was the diametrical opposite of the Athenian regime, with Sparta and the other Greeks in between.

Darius' judgmental attitude toward Xerxes suggests that the cycle of self-deception, expansion, and disaster will not be broken in the present

---

[14] On the motif of Xerxes' tattered clothes, see especially McClure 2006; Anderson 1972.
[15] Compare the treatment of the Herodotean Xerxes in these respects in Balot 2001a: 100–108.

generation. If Darius had honestly accepted responsibility for his failures, then the present disaster would likely never have occurred. The entire scene lends itself well to a subversive interpretation: the suffering experienced by Xerxes may well have been the same sort of suffering experienced by Darius after his own losses to the Scythians and Greeks. That the cycle will continue is strongly suggested by Atossa's acknowledgment, early in the play, that Xerxes will rule unaccountably, even if he fails in his mission (211–14). Xerxes, too, will one day cover up his losses in a dishonest and distorted celebratory history. Darius' failure to "confess" his own losses is perhaps the worst act of cowardice in the play because of the train of consequences to which it leads for his family and his people, even after his death. If Xerxes should choose to follow the same path, then the audience should not be too surprised, because such secrecy, dishonesty, ignorance, cowardice, and lack of freedom were characteristic of the Persian regime, in Aeschylus' ideologically informed representation.

My conclusions are threefold. First, already in 472 BC, the Athenians placed a premium on their democratic culture of courage and practical wisdom. They believed that they had developed a distinctively democratic understanding of these virtues. More than that, they had developed ways of recognizing the interrelations among these characteristics that they held to be distinctively democratic. These points shine through clearly in Aeschylus' representation of Persia as the polar opposite of Athenian political institutions and practices.

Second, Aeschylus' tragedy created self-knowledge among the Athenians.[16] This knowledge consisted of a clear understanding of the ways in which courage, freedom, and wisdom were related to one another within the democracy, and of why those democratically informed relations were good for the city of Athens. Persia needs the self-knowledge that Aeschylus' tragedy helped to create in Athens.

Third, and admittedly more speculatively, Aeschylus' attempt to educate the Athenians about their own democratic practices helped to make them more confident about the decisions they eventually took in their Assembly. They became more and more convinced of their own justice and rationality, because they had come to understand more clearly why democratic freedom was particularly well suited to producing justice, rationality, and courage among Athenians. The *Persians* was more

---

[16] For this interpretation of Athenian tragedy, see especially chapter 13. My approach builds on that of Zeitlin 1986/90.

celebratory than pitying, but it was primarily neither; nor was it primarily a vehicle for questioning the ideals of the city or for limiting Athenian aggression through heightening the Athenians' awareness of suffering. Instead, the play was primarily a source of the Athenians' deeper understanding of themselves as courageous democrats. In retrospect, we can see that this implies the potential for either large-scale destructiveness or political greatness, or both.

Democratic Courage in Herodotus' *Histories*

Herodotus' *Histories* furthers the case that the democratic ideal of courage circulated widely beyond Pericles' funeral oration. The text engages directly with the Athenians' strategies for interpreting what were, in the Athenians' view, the impoverished expressions of courage found among the Persians and the Spartans. Herodotus both extended the democratic ideology and offered a more complex view of Sparta than the Athenians themselves.

In two recent articles on Herodotus, Ellen Greenstein Millender has helped to advance the thesis that the Periclean ideology of courage was well known in fifth-century Greece.[17] Like Sara Forsdyke,[18] Millender shows that Herodotus was familiar with and influenced by Athenian democratic ideas and self-representations. While Millender acknowledges Herodotus' oppositions between Greeks and Persians (or other non-Greeks), she argues that Herodotus persistently undermines his own apparently positive representation of Spartan courage. By contrast with the Spartans' "unreflective" and "externally induced" courage and their "rigidity and consequent fragility," she says, the Athenians, in Herodotus' telling, made a "conscious decision" and demonstrated a flexible, natural form of courage, in their determination to resist the Persians.[19] Herodotus' presentation was,

---

[17] In this and the next two paragraphs, I summarize Millender's main points, drawing particularly on Millender 2002a: 32–47 and Millender 2002b: 375–85. On reflections of Athenian democratic ideology in Herodotus' *Histories*, see not only Millender 2002a and 2002b, but also Forsdyke 2001.

[18] See Forsdyke 2001.

[19] Millender 2002a: 40–47, at 44, 40, 44, and 46. In closely related work, Sara Forsdyke agrees: "Spartan courage depends on law/custom (*nomos*) and is socially enforced through shame. Fear of social humiliation motivates Spartan courage, as can be seen by the example of those Spartans who avoided death at Thermopylae (Hdt. 7.231–32; cf. 9.71). In Athenian ideology, by contrast, men fight courageously in order to preserve their political freedom and because they know that they are fighting for themselves rather than in the interest of a single ruler (5.78)" (Forsdyke 2001: 348). Suzanne Saïd 1980/1981: 109 argues to the contrary that Herodotus' account of courage at Marathon and Thermopylae continues the models developed in epic poetry

in this central respect, shaped by the Athenian ideology that contrasted the Spartans' shame-driven courage with the Athenians' rational daring, their willingness to take the initiative, and their desire for freedom.[20] In a very helpful way, Millender has made explicit the connection between Pericles' disparaging representation of the Spartans and Herodotus' negative recollections of Spartan behavior during the Persian Wars.

Millender's focus is on Herodotus' pejorative representation of the Spartans, and particularly on the famous exchange between Demaratus and Xerxes. Before Thermopylae, Herodotus shows Demaratus explaining to Xerxes why the Spartans were such courageous fighters. Although they were free, he says, the Spartans respected a single master (*despotēs*)—law (*nomos*). The command of law was that the Spartans should not "flee any number of men in battle," and it ordered them "to remain at their posts and defeat the enemy or die" (7.104.5).[21] As Millender and Forsdyke have argued, it is fear of *nomos*, rather than the pursuit of freedom or the sentiment of patriotism, that compelled the Spartans to stand fast in battle.

---

and thus concerns a form of courage "qui n'a rien d'intellectuel, bien au contraire [which is not at all intellectual, quite the contrary]." Saïd argues that at Plataea we see a form of "modern" warfare that is more closely linked to "intelligence," by which she means tactics and strategy, that is, "un art de la guerre" (an art of war; Saïd 1980/1981: 117); cf. Smoes 1995: 81–87, who argues, similarly, that the rise of technical thinking about the art of war encouraged the evolution toward a more intellectual conception of courage.

[20] Millender's discussions had been anticipated by several notable works in prior decades—above all, by Loraux 1986: 73–75, 89, 103–4, 150, 156–59, 161–62, 204–8, 263–64, which, building on previous scholarship, argued that, in its presentation of both Spartans and Athenians, Herodotus' *Histories* incorporates many *topoi* of the Athenian funeral orations, including an emphasis on the Spartans' tendency to delay and arrive late to battles, and the idea that the Athenians were principally responsible for the Greek victory over Persia. On similar contrasts between Athens and Sparta in Herodotus, Thucydides, and elsewhere, see Mills 1997: 66–68, 73–74; for earlier literature, see now Todd 2007: 153. Thomas 1989: 211 argues that the Athenians used epitaphic material, in Herodotus (e.g., IX 27) and elsewhere, in order to "assert their superiority" and to impress their audiences "whenever defence, praise, or emulation of the ancestors was called for." Thomas 1989 argues, in general, that the epitaphic tradition came to dominate the oral histories of Athens told by Athenians; this tradition can be recognized, she says, in a variety of extant texts, such as those of Aristophanes, Thucydides, and Herodotus (225, 235). Hartog 1988: 152–56 also makes the case for the distinctiveness of Sparta—of Sparta as "other," to use Hartog's language—within Herodotus' work; see also Benardete 1969 at (for example) 181. For further contrasts between Athens and Sparta in Herodotus, see Immerwahr 1966: 199–225; Flower and Marincola 2000: 9–31; and now Cartledge 2006: (e.g.) 137, again, on the "mainly Athenian anti-Spartan strain within Herodotus's oral sources."

[21] Stressing the curiosity of Demaratus' term *despotēs*, Millender argues as follows: "As a product of neither reasoned thought nor courage but rather of compulsion and obedience, Spartan steadfastness in battle comes to resemble the motivation driving Xerxes' subjects (7.103.3–4; cf. 7.22.1, 56.1, 223.3; 8.15.1, 69.2, 86)" (Millender 2002a: 40). But this is overstated: Demaratus uses this term *despotēs* as a direct retort to Xerxes' previous claim that fighting men need to be whipped into battle by a (real) *despotēs* (7.103).

According to Millender (2002a: 39), "As a *despotes*, *nomos* exercises a type of arbitrary authority at Sparta that parallels the relationship that exists between master and slave and between absolute rulers and their subjects." The Spartans' motivations therefore resemble those of the Persians; the Spartans are "lawful only under duress" (2002a: 40). Fear becomes the "guiding principle" of Spartan involvement in the Persian Wars and leads to "insularity and hesitancy toward involvement in the conflict" (2002a: 41).

Millender emphasizes that Spartan courage at Thermopylae was "undercut" by the Spartans' use of "fear of shame and censure" as motivational tools (as in the cases of Aristodemus and Pantites), and by the lack of a "positive desire for freedom" or "interest in the greater good of Hellas" (2002a: 42). At Plataea, too, the Spartans were guilty of "base cowardice"—for example, in Pausanias' repeated changes of the battle line (9.46–48, with Millender 2002a: 42; cf. 9.58).[22] By contrast, the Athenians exhibit a "more natural and spontaneous bravery," taking the offensive at Artemisium and Salamis, and eagerly facing the Persians alone at Plataea (2002a: 45). The Athenians were motivated by "a conscious choice...to remain firm and preserve the freedom of Hellas rather than [by] any sort of compulsion" (2002a: 46). The Athenians reasoned thoughtfully and resisted the Persians out of a conscious love of freedom, which grew out of the Athenians' "constitutional shift toward democracy" (2002a: 46). At Marathon, "open debate and courage together enabled the young democracy to defeat the Persians (6.109–10)" (2002a: 47). Herodotus argues that "the Athenians' intertwined military might, freedom, and self-determination enabled them alone to make the fateful decision to save the Greeks from barbarian tyranny and slavery" (2002b: 378).

These arguments show that the Periclean ideology was well known in Athens, and even perhaps throughout Greece, in the fifth century. As an astute contemporary observer of the period, Herodotus found this ideology to be, at least in part, a plausible organizing principle for his narrative of the Persian Wars. Building on Millender's arguments, yet also modifying them, I want to revisit certain details of Herodotus' text with a more

---

[22] On the tradition of Spartan cowardice, and on the Athenians as "helpers" to the Spartans, both at Plataea, see Immerwahr 1966: 295–96. Immerwahr 1966: 304 concludes that the "human element in the battles is primarily a delineation of the divergent traits of Greek regional character, especially the contrast between Athens and Sparta." As Flower and Marincola point out (Flower and Marincola 2002: 191), "This strange episode is most likely an Athenian invention which tried to mitigate the fact that it was the Spartans who defeated the Persians whereas the Athenians fought only against other Greeks."

systematic focus on the Periclean ideology. Specifically, I will reconsider Herodotus' view of the Spartans, his attention to the Athenians' own emotions, and his emphasis on the Athenians' ideology of "necessary identities." This reconsideration will illustrate that, for Herodotus, the Spartans' strictly land-based and defensive courage was, even if admirable, also outmoded and incapable of addressing the new type of military threat embodied by Persia. Herodotus shows Spartan courage in the process of being superseded by that of Athens. Yet, even as he praised the Athenians, Herodotus was overtly critical of the Athenians' "manly" love of their city's power. His narrative showed that the novel, admirable features of Athenian democratic courage sat jarringly alongside the Athenians' ethically questionable desire to dominate their fellow Greeks.

Reconsidering the Spartans at Thermopylae

Herodotus represents Spartan courage more admiringly than Millender's account suggests. Consider his counterfactual thought experiment: what would have happened if the Athenians had yielded to fear (*katarrōdēsantes*) and had either abandoned their country or submitted to the Persians (7.139.2)? Herodotus imagines that the Spartans would have pulled back within the Peloponnese and fortified the Isthmus of Corinth (7.139.3). Without Athenian help and leadership, the Spartans—like the other Greeks—would have stood alone (*mounōthentes*), made a last display of great deeds of courage, and died nobly (*apodexamenoi erga megala apethanon gennaiōs*, 7.139.3). According to Herodotus, moreover, the Spartans' allies would not have deserted "willingly" (*ouk hekontōn*); instead, their support would have been eroded necessarily by Persian naval power (7.139.3).

Herodotus observed just such a display of noble courage in the Spartans' last stand at Thermopylae. As we have seen, Demaratus stirringly evokes the Spartans' courage and obedience to law:

> "The Lacedaimonians, when fighting one by one, are not inferior to any men, but when they fight as a group they are the best of all men. For, although they are free, they are not free in every respect: for law is their master, and they fear it far more than your followers fear you. They do whatever that master, law, commands; and it always commands the same thing, forbidding them to flee any number of men in battle, and ordering them to remain at their posts and defeat the enemy or die" (7.104.4–5).

This has often been interpreted as a stirring expression of the Spartans' intransigent attachment to the rule of law, which was the foundation of their society.[23] It is also a verbal gibe: having just been criticized for having no "despot," Demaratus trumps Xerxes by showing that the Spartans do, paradoxically, have their own despot—that is, law—which is somehow "despotic" without being arbitrary, tyrannical, and harmful to the society. Thus, rather than creating a parallel between Sparta and Persia, Demaratus' retort maintains the distinction between an arbitrary authoritarian regime and a law-governed republican regime.

Although Xerxes laughs uncomprehendingly at Demaratus' characterization of the Spartans (7.105), he later comes to see the truth of Demaratus' words after the Battle of Thermopylae (7.234.1). The Battle of Thermopylae itself, in Herodotus' description, conforms closely to Demaratus' characterization of the Spartans. The Spartan king Leonidas had personally chosen 300 Spartans to fight in this battle, all fathers of living sons (7.205). Obviously, the Spartans took their stand at Thermopylae seriously and fought with men whose fatherhood of living sons made the battle meaningful in a larger way. Sparta had sent this army specifically, Herodotus says, to rouse the other Greeks to stand firm against the Persians (7.206). As Herodotus makes clear, Sparta intended to dedicate these troops to the cause of Greek freedom.

Herodotus emphasizes the Spartans' steadfastness and purposive attitude. When the time to fight arrived, many Greeks perceived that their inferior numbers would make resistance futile; the other Peloponnesians even proposed retreating to the Isthmus. But Leonidas, having listened to both sides of the argument, calmly decided to stay put and send requests for reinforcements (7.207). Herodotus stresses the Spartans' insouciance, even their careful coiffuring (7.208–9). In response to Xerxes' incomprehension, Demaratus confirmed that these Spartans were the bravest men alive, and that they seriously intended to fight for the pass at Thermopylae (7.209). During the initial engagements, in fact, the Spartans were successful against even the "King's Immortals," who served under the critical eye of their king (7.211–12). Their "externally induced" courage worked well against the fear-induced courage of the king's best soldiers.[24]

---

[23] Thomas 2000: 109–12 offers a subtle interpretation of this exchange with reference to *nomos* and *phusis*, arguing that Herodotus intends to represent the Spartans as distinctive among the Greeks and as having surpassed their own nature in expressing courage. For Herodotus' belief in the special power of *nomos*, and for his reinterpretation of Pindar's famous phrase "*nomos* is king," see Thomas 2000: 125–26.

[24] As Dewald 1987: 198 says, "Demaratus has described in *words* to Xerxes the nature of Spartan *arete*, and Leonidas has provided proof in *action*, but Xerxes cannot imagine a system so different from his own: he discredits the one and abuses the other."

The subsequent action confirms and extends Herodotus' analysis. Once the Persians had surrounded the Spartans through Ephialtes' treachery (7.214), Leonidas sent the other troops home, but he judged that it was inappropriate for the Spartans to leave the post they were defending (7.220.1). In Herodotus' view, Leonidas was aware at this time that he would die. He sent away the other troops because he wanted to give Sparta unrivaled fame and because he had heard the oracle foretelling that Xerxes would take Sparta itself unless a Spartan king died during the war (7.220). Leonidas and the other Spartans stood fast, according to Herodotus, for noble, albeit highly traditional, reasons: obedience, their sense of honor, and their desire for glory.[25]

This is why, in fact, Herodotus called Leonidas an *anēr aristos* in his death (7.224.1) and even learned the names of all 300 other Spartans, on the grounds that they were "worthy" (*axion*) of being remembered (7.224.1).[26] Herodotus also records that the bravest Spartan, Dieneces, had quipped insouciantly, before the battle, that he would be glad to fight in the shade if the Persian arrows numbered so many as everyone had said (7.226). It is in this context that Herodotus records the famous epitaph: "O stranger, announce to the Lacedaimonians that we lie here having obeyed their orders" (7.228). Herodotus found the Spartans' behavior admirable, courageous, and even quite remarkable, even though he recognized that their last stand at Thermopylae was ineffective.[27]

For Herodotus, then, Leonidas' last stand at Thermopylae was glorious, noble, and admirable: it represented the pinnacle of traditional Greek expressions of courage, self-sacrifice, and leadership.[28] Yet the Spartans'

---

[25] It is important to see here, contra Millender (2001: 42), that Herodotus does not criticize these motivations. These are the ideals and thoughts that had always motivated Greek warriors, from the Homeric epics onward: see Smoes 1995. Accordingly, Herodotus considers these motivations understandable and to some extent admirable, even if they were highly traditional and inefficacious in the circumstances.

[26] Cf. 7.238 on Xerxes' fierce anger toward Leonidas, and 8.26 on Tritanchaemes' admiration for men who fight for honor, such as the Spartans, rather than material rewards, such as the Persians and their allies. Munson 2001: 177 (cf. Munson 2001: 246–47) says that the battle of Thermopylae "shine[s] forth not only as the superior achievement with respect to the 'fairest victory' of Plataea (9.64.1) but also as the only perfect fulfillment the *Histories* have to offer of their author's promise in the proem to celebrate heroic glory."

[27] It is at this point, especially, that I am out of accord with the treatments of both Millender (2002a: 42; 2002: 383–84) and Forsdyke (2001: 347–52), but it is worth noting that Millender 2002b recognizes much more fully than Millender 2002a the ambiguities of Herodotus' treatment of both Athens and Sparta.

[28] Cf. Immerwahr 1966: 263 on the Homeric "touches" used to describe Leonidas and the Spartans, "an extreme example of courage such as exists only in death," with Saïd 1980/1981: 111–12.

effort to stop the Persians at Thermoplyae was generically similar to any possible efforts they might eventually have made to stop the Persians at the Isthmus of Corinth. Both were potentially occasions for admirable courage and the acquisition of glory, but both were (or would be, according to Herodotus) ultimately futile in the face of the Persians' overwhelming forces on both land and sea. This is why the Spartans' war efforts could accomplish little or nothing without the Athenians' intervention at sea (7.139)—even if Leonidas and his 300 Spartans had been successful.

What is the reason for thinking that, in Herodotus' view, the Spartans' effort at Thermopylae would ultimately prove to be ineffective?[29] When Herodotus described the initial decision to guard the pass at Thermopylae, after all, he offered no criticism of the idea.[30] He even went out of his way to mention that the Greek forces were unaware that they might be surrounded (7.175). Moreover, Herodotus later explained that Leonidas and his army were only an advance force. Their goal was to arouse support for the Greek effort among the other confederates; the plan was, all along, to send the entire Spartan force to Thermopylae after the Carneia had ended (7.206; cf. 6.106–7). This sounds like an obvious ex post facto justification of the Spartans' unwillingness to commit themselves wholeheartedly to the effort. Nonetheless, Herodotus presents this opinion as his own, without qualification.

However, prior to explaining the Greeks' decision to fight at Thermopylae, Herodotus had already offered his controversial opinion that the Athenians were, after the gods, ultimately responsible for the Greek victory, since, without their fleet, the Greeks could not have resisted Xerxes on land (7.139). He then went on to explain that the Athenians deliberately chose to develop their navy, to lead the other Greeks in the person of their commander Themistocles, to rouse the other Greeks to serve in the war, and to sacrifice their own narrowly construed interests and possibly their own glory for the sake of the wider Greek military

---

[29] As Clarke 2002 points out, "Thermopylae was strategically of little help to the defence of Greece" (2002: 68, with literature cited there). Many modern scholars (e.g., Hooker 1989, cited in Clarke 2002) have explained the Spartans' decision to fight at Thermopylae as propagandistic— that is, as illustrating the Spartans' courage and the strength of their system—even though Herodotus himself (7.175) suggests that the Greeks intended seriously to guard the pass in order to stop Xerxes from progressing into southern Greece.

[30] As Saïd 1980/1981: 104–5, following de Romilly 1967: 112, has argued, in fact, Herodotus emphasized the terminology of calculation and reflection in describing the Greeks' choice of Thermopylae as the place to make a last stand. Saïd argues that this choice did indeed have the effect of limiting the advantage that the Persians enjoyed because of their numbers. Saïd notes the contrast with the Battle of Salamis (Saïd 1980/1981: 105–6).

effort. However doggedly the other Greeks, and particularly the Spartans, had clung to their own "guarding the pass" mentality, Herodotus himself declares that this approach was futile. It was the Athenians alone who "chose" that "Greece should survive and remain free" (7.139), by adopting the untraditional "island" mentality of developing a navy, taking to their ships, and abandoning their own territory. By contrast, the only good that could possibly come of the Peloponnesians' effort at Thermopylae (much less the effort in Thessaly: cf. 7.173–74) was to delay the Persian advance for several days, and no more.[31]

What does Herodotus mean, though, by saying that the Athenians were responsible for the Greek victory "after the gods" (7.139)? Perhaps, as Michael Clarke has argued, Leonidas had decided to make his stand at Thermopylae because of the oracle's pronouncement that Sparta itself would be destroyed unless one of its kings "of the house of Heracles" died first (7.220). Herodotus himself argued that Leonidas was partially motivated by this oracle when he decided to dismiss the other troops, since he knew that the Persians would win the battle (7.220). Assuming that Leonidas believed the oracle, it is impossible to denigrate the courage of Leonidas; his courage may have been, by religious means, effective. Even so, Herodotus' use of the derogatory participles *parachreōmenoi* and *ateontes* (7.223.4) strongly suggests that Leonidas was, in the process of making his last stand, recklessly and unnecessarily sacrificing the lives of the 300 other Spartans.[32] As Clarke concludes, "Here then lies the deepest tragedy of Thermopylae as Herodotus presents it: the demands of the oracle and the demands of Spartan law combine to place these men in a position where they must throw away their lives or suffer the disgrace and humiliation that came with the label *tresantes*."[33]

Herodotus found something glorious in the Spartans' last stand at Thermopylae and in the *nomos* that enabled it, but he also included

---

[31] Notice, though, the explanation of Diodorus Siculus 11.11 and Pausanias 3.4.7–8, endorsed by Hobbs 2000: 94n.32. On the other hand, it is plausible to suppose that the Greeks genuinely meant to hold the pass: as Lazenby 1993: 136 argues, "Herodotus repeatedly says that this was the intention (7.175.2, 176.5; 8.15.2), and it is difficult to see what else it can have been—suggestions that Thermopylai was some kind of 'delaying action' or 'reconnaissance force' really do not make any sense." Cartledge 2006: 123 argues that if the "Hellenes" "were genuinely serious about putting up resistance, it was obvious where the next line [after Thessaly] should be drawn: at the axis between the pass... of Thermopylae, by land."

[32] Clarke 2002 was anticipated in this point by Saïd 1980/1981: 110, who argues that the Spartans' courage was an extension of the military "frénésie [frenzy]" characteristic of "la folie guerriere des héros épiques [the military madness of epic heroes]." Saïd interestingly relates this "frenzy" to that of Aristodemos at the Battle of Plataea (Said 1980/1981: 116–17); cf. Smoes 1995: 83–84.

[33] Clarke 2002: 71.

undercurrents of criticism of the Spartan decision to sacrifice so many lives for the sake of a strategically ineffectual effort. Herodotus admired the Spartans' "last stand" at Thermopylae, but not in an unqualified way. His praise was tempered by his recognition that the Spartans' noble expression of courage was ineffective in the circumstances. The Spartans at Thermopylae exemplified an ideal of courage that was not adequate to the rapidly changing environment of wider Aegean political and military relations. This is the other sense in which the Spartans lived up to Demaratus' characterization of them. Even if they "stood fast" unto death in obedience to the law, they also obeyed an unchanging or immutable law: Spartans hold their positions and try to keep invaders out—whether at Thermopylae or at the Isthmus of Corinth—even when their intentions to "wall off" Greece were very unlikely to succeed.[34] To address changing circumstances, perhaps the law itself must change.

We have arrived at the following conclusion: Herodotus reported admiringly on the Spartans' courage in the passages we have just discussed, but he offered two criticisms of the Spartans. First, the one analyzed in detail by Millender: Herodotus criticized the Spartans' cowardice, particularly their decision to remain within the Peloponnese and "wall off" the Isthmus, instead of defending Greece in general (8.40, 8.56, 8.71–72, 8.74; cf. 7.207, 7.235.4, 8.49.2–50.1).[35] Even after Salamis, to Herodotus' surprise[36], the Spartans continued to wall off the Isthmus and allowed their decisions to be dictated by their fear (9.6–8).[37] Herodotus reinforced this

---

[34] Immerwahr 1966: 199–206. The similarities between Herodotus' account and Athenian epitaphic oratory with regard to the Spartans' rigid version of courage also help to confirm the view that Herodotus' account is similar to and constitutes an elaboration of democratic ideology and self-presentation. We have to imagine, not that the Athenians of the fourth century derived this material directly from Herodotus (though see Loraux 1986: 143 on the epitaphic tradition as indebted to the fifth-century historians), but rather that, at least from around the 460s onward, the Athenians were making and listening to such orations as we have from the fourth century, in which the Isthmus would obviously have figured as a theme. We have only six funeral orations, on a generous count; we should probably imagine that, in toto, over 100 were actually delivered in classical Athens: see Loraux 1986: 37–39.

[35] On the isthmus motif as capturing the "divisive and selfish actions" of the Peloponnesians, see Immerwahr 1966: 205, 276; cf. the Peloponnesian fears at 8.70 and Artemisia's advice at 8.68.a–b.

[36] Herodotus' expression of surprise over the Spartans' hesitancy reveals clearly, I think, that Herodotus himself endorsed the Athenians' recollections of these events; Herodotus was not simply or unthinkingly reflecting the Athenian ideology embodied in these stories.

[37] On Herodotus' attribution of fearful insularity to the Spartans, see Millender 2002a: 41–43, with earlier literature cited. On Herodotus' negative evaluation of "walls" used in order to protect cities in the latter part of the *Histories*, see Bowie 2006, esp. 132–36: "the motif of a wall as no source of salvation" (134), at Thermopylae, Plataea, and Mycale, as well as on the Athenian Acropolis, with its "wooden walls." Compare this to Thucydides' discussion of walls as a major source of military power in the Archaeology.

point by showing that the Spartans usually reacted to crises by staying home within the Peloponnese, instead of helping their Greek allies (6.106–7, 9.6–9.8).

Second, and more important, Herodotus argued that the Peloponnesians lacked a fully rational plan to address the threat of Xerxes' combined land and sea forces. Even though the Spartans' goal of saving the Peloponnese was clear, they had little idea of how to achieve that goal in practice. They were entrenched in a mentality that focused on walling off their homeland from the invader. This was a traditional strategy, but an ineffective one in these circumstances.[38] Herodotus acknowledged that the rapidly changing ecology of the ancient Aegean had rendered traditional Greek courage outmoded and unsustainable—and, at the limit, even harmful and selfish. The Spartans' traditional model of courage was both admirable in its own limited terms and, more importantly, inappropriate to the new realities of the fifth century BC.[39]

In fact, according to Herodotus, the Greeks had long known that Xerxes hoped to conquer all of Greece (7.138.1), but that knowledge had elicited diverse reactions. Medizers were in good spirits, whereas the others "were in a state of great terror (*en deimati megalōi katestasan*) because Greece had too few ships to meet the Persians, and because most Greeks were unwilling to fight" (7.138.2). The Greeks who showed a Spartan-like tenacity—a noble and admirable willingness to resist, to try to defend their homeland against the invasion, even without any hope of success—were understandably terrified, both because they had no plan to stop the Persians at sea (which, nevertheless, and somewhat incoherently, they evidently thought was a critical part of the war effort), and because they faced a life-or-death collective action problem. If all the Greeks had immediately foregone their short-term self-gratification and resisted the Persians equally, then Greece may have had a chance. If all the Greeks had, moreover, been long preparing for the coming attack through investing their resources in building a navy, then there may have been no need for panic.

---

[38] As Immerwahr 1966: 200–206 correctly explains, the Spartans' insularity and traditionalism explain both their lack of success in projecting imperialistic power during the archaic period and their lack of imagination in confronting the Persian threat effectively. But I believe that Immerwahr 1966: 206 goes astray when he says that "insularity, and not any moral weakness, also determined the conduct of the Spartans at the very end of the war" because insularity is itself a sign of excessive traditionalism and is surely intended by Herodotus to be taken as a manifestation of the Spartans' character.

[39] In this the Spartans as a whole were like their envoys Sperchias and Bulis, who showed admirable courage and self-respect at the Persian court, but failed to accomplish their mission of compensating for the Spartans' murder of Darius' envoys (7.133–36).

Yet, lacking such sources of confidence, and in particular by remaining unwilling to transform themselves into naval powers, the nonmedizing Greeks were unable to develop an effective strategy. Like the other Greeks, the Spartans and their Peloponnesian allies lacked the rationally informed and untraditional courage of Athens. Herodotus specifies that the Spartans would have faced two problems if they had fortified the Isthmus: they lacked a navy and could not count on their Peloponnesian allies. These two factors were interrelated. Even if the Spartans had fortified the Isthmus, their allies would have deserted them, because the Persian navy would have attacked the coastal towns one by one.[40] Even the Spartans' resistance at the Isthmus was insecure if Xerxes decided to terrorize the Spartans by establishing a naval base at Cythera (7.235).

Hence, it is important to distinguish between Herodotus' criticisms of the Spartans' specific failures of nerve and hesitancy and Herodotus' judgment of the Spartan ideal of law-bound, socially enforced, and highly traditional courage as such. In the case of Thermopylae, the Spartans did live up to their own ideals of courage, as represented by Demaratus and by Herodotus himself. But their application of their ideal proved to be misguided. Even when Spartan courage "worked," and even when the Spartans won glory for their expressions of valor, as at Thermopylae, the Spartans often failed to achieve their most important objective: in this case, the repulsion of the Persians' invasion. In effect, Herodotus did not rest content with criticizing particular Spartans' failures of character or nerve; rather, he elevated this criticism to a global critique of Spartan courage altogether. As traditionalists, the Spartans were incapable of seeing that genuine courage, in this situation, required innovation: that is, the willingness or even the deliberate resolution to abandon the conventional frameworks that made traditional courage meaningful. Those traditional frameworks revolved around the idea that hoplite soldiers should fight to the death, on land, in order to "save the city." Xerxes' arrival required the Greeks to develop novel frameworks for courage—that is, to transform *nomos*.

Democratic Courage: Remembering Salamis

In Herodotus' account, all the other Greek resisters (i.e., the nonmedizing Greeks, other than the Athenians) were similar to the Spartans in their

---

[40] Cf. 8.57.2: the advice of Mnesiphilus to the same effect; 8.60.a: Themistocles' arguments against withdrawing to the Isthmus.

response to the Persian invasion, as their attitudes, thoughts, and actions revealed at the decisive moment, just when the Persians were on their doorsteps. The Athenians were different. This is why Herodotus announces his controversial conclusion, even despite its unpopularity, that Athens was responsible for the Greek victory:

> As things stand, if someone should say that the Athenians saved Greece, he would not be mistaken: for they were likely to tip the scales in favor of whichever side they joined. Having chosen that Greece should survive and remain free, they were the ones who roused the rest of the Greeks — all those who did not medize—and thrust out the king, after the gods at any rate. Even the frightening oracles that came from Delphi did not throw them into a panic or convince them to abandon Greece. Instead, they stood their ground and were tough enough to face the invader of their land. (Hdt. 7.139.5–6).

Herodotus arrived at this conclusion only after fully exploring his counterfactual thought experiment and reasoning that it would have been useless to fortify the Isthmus if the Persians had controlled the sea (7.139.4).[41] It is only after this thought experiment that Herodotus launched into his praise of the Athenians as saviors of Greece.

What was required of the Athenians was precisely that they abandon the traditional Greek *nomos* of protecting the homeland by "standing fast" in battle—not in order that they might become anomic or antinomian, but rather in order to create new and untraditional *nomoi* that more adequately answered to the facts of their situation. They decided to transform themselves into a naval power, to leave Attica behind, and to take to their ships. They thereby abandoned the traditional *nomos* of protecting their fatherland; they did not "stand fast" in that sense. However, Herodotus strikingly adds that they stood their ground and had the courage to meet the invader; they did not abandon Greece. The Athenians gave a new interpretation to the traditional idea of "standing fast" in battle—one that was superior to that of the Spartans, because the new conception enabled the Athenians to utilize their courage in order to address the magnitude and the particular composition of the Persian threat efficaciously.[42] Like good

---

[41] Cf. 8.63 for Eurybiades' agreement on this point.
[42] It is striking that the most distinguished Athenian fighter at the Battle of Plataea, according to Herodotus, was Sophanes, who wore a belt fitted out with an anchor device (9.73–75); cf. Cartledge 1998; Strauss 1996; Hanson 2000. This seems to illustrate the community of sentiment between Athenian hoplites and rowers. It is also striking that the staunch Sophanes, whose

democrats, they innovatively created a new and more appropriate *nomos* for themselves.⁴³

Herodotus needed an argument for his view for two reasons. First, his view was unpopular (7.139.1). Many Greeks, such as the Spartans, the Corinthians (8.94), and the Aeginetans (e.g., 8.92–93), wanted to claim credit for the victory. Second, Herodotus, like Pericles and the Athenian orators, was engaged in the project of justifying the Athenians' claim to a different sort of courage. But his presentation was more powerful than those of the obviously patriotic Athenian orators. Herodotus presented himself as an arbitrator or judge (*histōr*) of great deeds, an impartial spectator whose opinions carried greater weight than those of the Athenians themselves.⁴⁴ He adjudicated the dispute between Athenian and Spartan courage on the side of Athens. Without merely echoing Athenian ideology, however, Herodotus integrated the Athenians' self-conception into his account and affirmed the essential truthfulness of that self-conception.

This is, in fact, why it is especially important that Herodotus praised the Spartan effort and thus did justice to Sparta's exemplary traditional courage. Having offered a just assessment of the Spartan contribution, Herodotus still found the Periclean anatomy of democratic courage to be convincing. That is why he presented Athenian democratic courage as the ultimate explanation for the Athenians' behavior during the Persian Wars and for the Greeks' victory. His presentation illustrates not only that the Periclean ideal circulated outside the text of Thucydides and the speeches of orators, as we saw in chapters 2 and 3, but also that Herodotus found the ideal of "democratic courage" to be plausible and efficacious.

Like the Athenian epitaphic orators (e.g., Hyp. 6.2, 6.3, 6.40), Herodotus emphasized that the Athenians *chose* (*helomenoi*) to have Greece survive in freedom. Initially, at least, this is puzzling: how could the Athenians possibly *choose* to win a victory? In describing the Athenians' "choice," Herodotus uses the verb *haireo*, which was used also by the funeral orators (often in its compound form *proaireo*) to describe the Athenian

---

anchor-symbol embodies the Athenians' new interpretation of "standing fast," died not in "standing fast" to protect the city, but rather in a battle to win for Athens the far-flung gold mines at Datum (9.75).

⁴³ Thomas 2000: 114–17 ably shows that the Athenians' success in war and their creation of democratic ideals were the result of mutable cultural factors, rather than any inherent or essential characteristics—and that Herodotus himself emphasized the "constructedness" of Athenian democratic ideals. Thomas 2000: 116 also connects Athenian democratic propaganda with Herodotus' admiration for Athens's rise to power at 5.78 and with Otanes' speech in the "constitutional debate."

⁴⁴ See Nagy 1990: 250–73.

soldiers' "choice" to die for the sake of their fatherland.[45] This connection is important, because the idea of "choice" occupies an important place in the Athenian ideal of courage. We should not be misled into thinking that Athenian "choice" is equivalent to "choice" as understood by the more individualistic, "rational choice" school familiar to contemporary social science. Rather, Athenian "choice" in this context is similar to Aristotelian *prohairesis*—that is, it is similar to "deliberate desire" for things that one can control (*EN* 1113a9–12).

One might go so far as to say that Athenian "choice" is the predecessor of Aristotelian *prohairesis*, because the Athenians were themselves engaged in a project of understanding and politically exemplifying the prudential wisdom, or the "prohairetic choice," involved in expressing their ethical virtues in action. When we comprehend the multiple valences of this verb, we are in a better position to recognize that in this passage Herodotus means to say that saving Greece was part of what the Athenians had desired *deliberately,* that is, after self-conscious deliberation about the appropriate means and the appropriate ends of their desire. Both the ends (or objects) of their desire, and the means to achieve those ends, were discursively formulated within the Athenians' wide-ranging conversations in the democratic Assembly. This is why Herodotus immediately follows his provocative argument (7.139) with an excursus that explains precisely what was involved in the Athenian "choice" to save Greece. Herodotus does not explain, by contrast, the decision-making process of the other Greeks, because, in their case, there was only one decision to make: whether to medize or not. If the answer turned out to be negative, then the only question was where to start building walls in order to keep out the invader.

By contrast, at 7.140–44, Herodotus describes at length the Athenian process of decision making—one that involved rational debate over the meaning of several oracles, and one that issued in the Athenians' highly untraditional decision to transform themselves into a naval power. They began to contemplate abandoning the city—not, as their soothsayers urged (7.143), in order to find a home elsewhere, but rather in order to take to their ships and save Greece. It was in this way that the Athenians decided

---

[45] On the idea that the Athenians "chose" or "decided" to die for the city, see Loraux 1986: 101–4, who also links this to Aristotelian *prohairesis* (*EN* 1111b4–1113a14); cf. Rusten 1989: 161–63 and now Allen 2010. As Loraux points out, this idea arises in numerous funeral orations and generically related texts: she cites, for example, Hdt. 8.83; Thuc. 2.42.4, 2.43.4; Lys. 2.24–26, 62; Plato, *Men.* 246d2, Dem. 60.26, 28, 37; Hyp. 6.3, 40.

to rouse the other Greeks and, in the process, fully to exemplify the principle, later enunciated by Thucydides' Nicias (Thuc. 7.77), that the city consists not in walls and buildings, but in its citizens (cf. Hdt. 8.61). By adopting an unconventional self-understanding, the Athenians became Greece's most exemplary leaders. As Herodotus shows, the adoption of this self-image constituted an extraordinary act of courage and a novel way to "stand fast" in order to resist the Persian invader.

What was the essence of the Athenians' "deliberate desire" during this meeting of the Assembly? The Athenians had received two oracles from Delphi, the first apparently predicting the destruction of Athens, and the second, seemingly less threatening, in so far as it said that the "wooden wall" alone would not be destroyed (7.141). The Athenians openly debated the interpretation of this oracle. The Athenians did not assume that they understood the oracle's meaning, nor did they submit the interpretation of the oracle to any authorities, political or religious; instead, they debated the question in an open assembly of citizens. Older citizens—perhaps those born before the Cleisthenic democracy had been established?—interpreted the "wooden walls" to refer to the old thorn hedge that had once fenced in the Acropolis (7.142; cf. 8.51–54). This sounds Spartan-like: one fences in the precious old city in order to protect it from the invader.

Another group of citizens thought that the god had ships in mind and therefore insisted on developing the Athenians' navy (Hdt. 7.142). It is striking that an entire group of citizens, not only Themistocles, had come to the same interpretation; it was the Athenian citizens, not Themistocles alone, who conjured up this novel, metaphorical interpretation of the "wooden walls." It is also striking that, on the basis of their admittedly uncertain, albeit plausible, grasp of the oracle, this group of citizens (not "older men" but "others," perhaps even younger men who had grown up amid the novelty of the Cleisthenic democracy) was willing to abandon all other preparations and to put all the city's resources into expanding its navy.

The discussion led the Athenians to recognize which lines separated the different groups of citizens, because the discussion revealed that the oracle's final couplet was the salient interpretative crux: "Divine Salamis, you will destroy the sons of women either when the grain is being scattered or when it is being collected" (7.142). This couplet was deeply unsettling to the citizens who favored taking to the ships. But Themistocles explained that the epithet "Divine" proved that the oracle was favorable to Athens, or else it would have used another epithet, such as "Hateful" (7.143). This was enough to convince the citizens to ignore the advice of their professional interpreters (not to mention their older fellow citizens) and to begin to think of themselves as a naval power (7.143).

Herodotus concludes the scene by saying that after their debate over the meaning of the oracle, they decided to fight the Persians by sea (7.144). The process described by Herodotus was a model of democratic deliberation, even if he presents its key features schematically, and even if he also shows that democratic debate did not always issue in sound or prudent judgments (e.g., 5.97). The Athenians' willingness to air their views and to challenge one another's interpretations worked very effectively. The Athenians' deliberations issued in just the decision that helped Greece resist the Persians. It is crucial that the Athenians did not allow their fear to undermine their capacity to deliberate effectively, despite the disturbance caused by the oracle. It is difficult to imagine the same scene at Sparta; we should keep in mind the other Greeks' ineffective deliberations before Xerxes' advance (7.138).

Themistocles had earlier persuaded his fellow citizens to use the silver from the mines at Laureion in order to build a large fleet, putatively in order to prosecute their conflict with Aegina (7.144). But it is clear, as Herodotus indicates (7.138), that the Greeks had known about Xerxes' invasion for a long time, and that Themistocles' objective in proposing to build this fleet was to fortify Athens to meet the Persians at sea. Themistocles made the proposal, and the Athenian citizenry, having debated the matter for itself, made a wise choice. The Athenian democracy—and Athenian democratic courage—preceded Salamis and made the Athenians' victory on that day possible.[46] The Athenians' "choice" resulted, for example, in their capacity to contribute 127 ships to the Greek forces at Artemisium (plus twenty more manned by Chalcidian crews), compared to forty from Corinth, twenty from Megara, and even fewer from elsewhere (8.1; cf. 8.43–48 for similar figures at Salamis itself).[47]

At each turn, the Athenian citizenry courageously liberated itself from conventional ways of responding to the impending military struggle. The Athenians refused to accept both the apparent hopelessness of Delphi's

---

[46] See Ober 1997.

[47] There is controversy over precisely when the Athenians decided to remove their families from Attica and to abandon Attica to the Persians (cf. Hdt. 8.40–41 with the so-called Themistocles Decree). It seems unlikely that the Athenians would have made this decision only when Xerxes' arrival was imminent, as Herodotus' account seems to suggest. Either way, Themistocles' plan to transform Athens into a naval power was moving forward unabated; and his novel vision of Athenians as seafarers enabled the Athenians to decide on this unusual strategy in the war against Xerxes, as they did later, in a different way in their war against the Peloponnesians (cf. chapter 5).

responses and the potentially disastrous traditional interpretations of the "older men," not to mention oracles that had proposed moving to Siris in Italy (8.62). They thought seriously about what constituted an adequate response to the Persian threat. They released themselves from the conventional idea that they had to stand and fight in order to protect their homeland and its religious monuments, civic spaces, and public buildings. They recognized that the most important goal was to save the lives of Athenians and to defend Greece. They saw that it was possible to achieve this objective only through collectively choosing to build a large navy, to abandon the city of Athens itself, and to take to their ships. It is not at all surprising that, in the ensuing struggle, Themistocles was the single Greek leader able to articulate a convincing rationale for making the prudent decision to fight at Salamis in the narrow straits and to do everything possible to avoid drawing the Persian king down into the Peloponnese (8.60a–c).[48]

The Athenians were under no illusion that victory was inevitable or that they would come through the battle unscathed, even if they should win. But they inventively, wholeheartedly, and courageously gave a new interpretation to the traditional mode of courageously "standing fast"; they were able to "stand fast" on their ships at Salamis and thereby to act like men, as Themistocles said to the Spartan Eurybiades (8.62).

According to Herodotus, their democratic deliberation and their untraditional model of courage were the key components of their successful effort to save Greece. If the Athenians had lived under another sort of political regime, or if they had practiced another kind of courage altogether, then they would have either fled from their city or medized, or they would have stood fast and died. Since the other Greeks were held fast in the clutches of a particular *nomos* that was not well adapted to the changing realities of the early fifth century BC—a *nomos* that commanded them, on pain of social shame and public humiliation, to stand fast, to protect their cities from invasion by land, and to die in the effort, if necessary—they could not think through the demands of their situation clearly.

Athenian Courage *Ab Origine*

Herodotus' representation of the Athenians' thoughtful, deliberative ideal of courage in these episodes was linked closely to his representation of the origins of the Athenian democracy. According to Herodotus, the

---

[48] On Themistocles' own larger vision, see, perhaps ironically, 8.83.

democracy grew out of the Athenian demos's courageous decision to resist Cleomenes' seizure of the Athenian Acropolis in 508 BC—after which they established their democracy. As Josiah Ober has argued, following Herodotus closely, the Athenian demos acted as a self-conscious political agent in seizing democratic power for itself, without the leadership of any members of the elite: "Herodotus' language (*ta auta phronēsantes*—'all of one mind') supports the idea of a generalized and quite highly developed civic consciousness among the Athenian masses —an ability to form and act on strong and communal views on political affairs."[49]

There is, to be sure, a great deal of historical controversy over this "revolutionary" moment in Athenian history.[50] It is uncontroversial at least that Herodotus himself presents the demos as acting without the support of Cleisthenes, who had left Athens (5.72). The demos acted self-consciously in order to win political freedom for itself. This is the implication of the participle *phronēsantes* (5.72.2), which Herodotus applies to the demos. The demos "thought the same things as" the Boule and resisted Cleomenes. Members of the demos were willing to think for themselves, altogether; they came to the same conclusion as the Boule; and they were capable of acting voluntarily for the city's welfare and for their own freedom from tyranny.

In Herodotus' presentation, the Athenians' expulsion of Cleomenes and Isagoras was the "primordial" act of democratic courage. In this act, the demos behaved in thoughtful, virtuous, and energetic ways, fully displaying "democratic courage" as it was described most explicitly in Pericles' funeral oration. Just after their awe-inspiring victory on their own Acropolis, the Athenians defeated the Chalcidians and Boeotians, which Herodotus interpreted as a sign of the post-tyrannical Athenians' newly found civic and military strength (Hdt. 5.77–78). Remarkably, their victories occurred after they had daringly chosen to face down a newly mustered Spartan army at Eleusis (5.74). Endorsing the Athenians' ideology, Herodotus connected these surprising and daring victories on three fronts with the Athenians' establishment of their democracy.

Herodotus himself interpreted these events by reflecting specifically on the Athenians' *isēgoria*. "FREE and equal speech" was admirable for many reasons, and its importance was illustrated by the Athenians' notable military successes after the fall of the tyranny: "...after they had

---

[49] Ober 1996b: 44, cf. 49–50.
[50] See now the essays collected in Raaflaub, Ober, and Wallace 2007 for the latest account of the debates.

won their freedom, each citizen was eager to work for himself" (5.78; cf. 5.66.1, 5.91.1). This statement implies anything but "selfishness" on the part of Athenian citizens as individuals. Rather, its significance is that the Athenians recognized that now, at last, and after the expulsion of the Peisistratid tyranny, they could work for the city in ways that benefitted themselves. Reciprocity existed between the good of the city and the good of its individuals; like Tocqueville, we now call this reciprocity "enlightened self-interest." In fact, this reciprocity was an element of the full realization of the Athenians' eudaimonistic ideal (cf. chapters 2, 14–15).

Herodotus' specific terminology probably derives from his own late fifth-century context. Yet we can recognize that his vocabulary is closely tied to the Athenians' novel ideal of courage. *Isēgoria*—free and equal speech—was the key to the Athenians' military success for two reasons. First, *isēgoria* enabled the Athenians to think carefully about their expressions of courage, to see just what courage demanded in each situation, and to think beyond traditional norms and practices. On the basis of their *isēgoria*, the Athenians not only developed the novel "island strategy" proposed by Themistocles, but also refused to accept that the brawl on the Acropolis in 508 BC was simply a matter of elite concern or elite in-fighting. The demos was able to take political responsibility for itself because the Athenian citizens, one and all, had come to understand that their polis was theirs, and that they could and should act to transform it in accordance with their own vision of what was best.[51]

Second, *isēgoria* enabled each citizen to play an important role in deliberation, in political life, and in the future organization of the city. As a result, each citizen acquired recognition or self-respect in carrying out the deliberative and military activities characteristic of civic life. Furthermore, each citizen realized that he had a stake in the outcome of both the city's deliberations and its military activities. It is no wonder that, in these circumstances, the Athenians showed *prothumia* (5.78, cf. Hdt. 9.60).

Like Pericles (chapter 2) and the Athenian orators (chapters 10 and 11), Herodotus, too, emphasized that Athenian courage was motivated, at least in part, by normatively correct emotions, such as the Athenians'

---

[51] Notice the contrast between the Athenians and the Persians on this point: the Persian advisors are unable to speak freely, which radically harms the war effort: e.g., 8.65, 8.67–69. The only advisor to the King who understood the situation well was Artemisia—and she too understood the absence of courage and manliness in the Persian army (8.68–69). On her exploits at the Battle of Salamis and the topsy-turvy world of "barbarian" "courage," which is exhibited in an exemplary way by Artemisia, see 8.87–88, where Artemisia elicits the famous quip from Xerxes that his men had turned into women and his women into men. On the demos's responsibility, see Ober 1996b.

wholehearted eagerness (*prothumia*) to lead the other Greeks (5.78, 9.46, 9.60; cf. Thuc. 2.39), their appropriate management of fear (e.g., 6.112, 7.143), and their appropriate sense of shame and honor (e.g., 6.109, 8.144, 9.7a–b, 9.26–28). The Athenians, in fact, literally "took pleasure" in ranging themselves opposite the Persians at Plataea (*hēdomenoisi hēmin*, 9.46). Later, the Spartan general Pausanias acknowledged the Athenians' unrivaled "zeal" (*prothumotatoisi*, 9.60) in fighting for the Greeks. Their *prothumia* to behave nobly for the sake of freedom was an essential emotional constituent of their admirable display of courage during the war; their courage would have been less admirable if their minds had been divided about the importance of the cause or the necessity of their virtuous behavior. Herodotus' description perfectly fits the Aristotelian idea that virtuous agents should take pleasure in doing the right things for the right reasons (*EN* II.3.1104b3–8).

Whereas Herodotus did not attribute wholehearted eagerness to the Spartans, as we have seen, he did attribute a concern for shame and honor to them. Yet, on this front, too, Herodotus presents the Spartans and the Athenians differently. Although all Greeks looked up to past heroes for inspiration, the Spartans in particular tended to inspire courage through fear of the law (7.104) and fear of social humiliation (7.231–32). As the cases of Aristodemus and Pantites, in particular, show, the Spartans practiced a "punitive" type of shame (7.231–32; discussed also in chapters 9 and 16).[52] By contrast, the Athenians' sense of shame and honor was carefully reasoned: it involved thoughtfully respecting or living up to standards that they themselves endorsed (e.g., 6.109, 8.144, 9.7a–b). This is why, in fact, the Athenians embodied discretion of a high order in their relations with the Spartans, recognizing that Greek unity was more important than gaining recognition for their own valor (cf. 8.3).[53] It is necessary to keep an eye on both the emotions and the intellect in order to understand Athenian courage fully.

---

[52] This punitive use of shame and humiliation is the focus of Millender 2002a, although Millender does not comment on the Athenians' own sense of shame and honor in Herodotus' narrative, and she makes only passing mention of the Athenians' fighting "eagerly and successfully without having to don the yoke of necessity" (2002a: 46).

[53] On the motif of Greek disunity, and alternations between friendship and hostility, see Immerwahr 1966: 225–35; on Athens's role in helping to establish unity among the Greeks, see Osborne 2009: 321–24. Konstan 1987: 72–73 makes interesting remarks on the relationship between the Greeks' disunity, the Peloponnesians' "parochial concern" for their "own territory" (72), and the Persians' excessive unity, which is connected to their belief in the significance of quantity as opposed to quality.

The Athenians were acting "enthusiastically" or "wholeheartedly" in the pursuit of their own, and the city's, flourishing. They were not only thinking self-consciously about their future flourishing as citizens of Athens. They were, moreover, psychologically disposed in just the right way to show courage willingly and voluntarily. They had appropriate "feelings" and expressed their normatively attractive emotions in practice. They were emphatically *not* acting under pressure from a stifling set of traditional norms, or *nomoi,* or from fear of social humiliation, nor, of course, were they driven by fear of displeasing a king (8.86). Nor were they simply following rules that they failed to endorse personally or rules that were based on claims to traditional authority; they were enthusiastic precisely because they were following *nomoi* that they themselves had devised on the basis of their free and prudent political judgments.

In Herodotus' presentation, the Athenians translated their thoughtful, voluntary efforts on the city's behalf to the international realm, where they chose to put all their efforts into the Hellenic cause. In the late sixth century, for example, the Athenians sent help to Plataea after the Spartans had refused (6.108). At the Battle of Marathon, Herodotus emphasizes the Athenians' courage, construed as a thoughtful, deliberate and emotionally well-informed ideal that enabled the Athenians to stand out among the Greeks for their pursuit of freedom and their rejection of tyrannical encroachments.[54] One of the ten Athenian generals, Miltiades, persuaded the polemarch Callimachus to stay and fight the Persians, rather than to adopt the "weaker" (*cheirōn*) policy of other generals who wished to flee (6.109.2). Miltiades argued that it was up to Callimachus to make the most important decision: "It is now in your hands, Callimachus, either to enslave Athens or to make it free and leave behind for all men a memorial greater than that of Harmodius and Aristogeiton. For now the Athenians are going to meet their greatest danger ever, and if they bow down to the Persians, it is clear what they will suffer from Hippias when they are given over to him, but if this city is victorious, then it will likely become the first city of all Greece" (6.109).

In Miltiades' words we see an obvious appeal to Callimachus' desire for honor and glory, which he could acquire through living up to the exploits of the tyrannicides. In the Athenians' later recollections, the Athenian generals decided to liberate the city from the Persian threat, just as their forbears had freed the city from the Peisistratid tyranny. This desire for

---

[54] Cf. Millender 2002a: 45–47 on Marathon.

honor—a desire to live up to the city's ideals—was a reflective one, based on conversations and judgments about the importance of fighting for freedom. But this case shows clearly that the Athenians' emotions of honor, the converse of shame and humiliation, were represented as thoughtful and "prospective," rather than punitive, as were the Spartans'.[55]

In this normatively appropriate spirit, and having self-consciously chosen to pursue democratic freedoms within the city, the demos now decided to pursue and extend their city's leadership throughout Greece, so as to make Athens, in Miltiades' words, "free" (*eleutherē*) and the "first city of those in Greece" (*polis prōtē tōn en tēi Helladi*, 6.109.6). In the event, the Athenians made a signal display of courage, by running to engage the Persians (6.112). Herodotus was at pains to emphasize that the Athenians were the "first" to charge at a run and the first who were tough enough to look at Persian dress without fear (6.112.3), as well as the "first" to fight at Salamis (8.84, a point disputed by the Aeginetans). Prior to this, all Greeks had been struck by terror whenever they heard the word "Persian" (6.112). By contrast, the Athenians managed their fear correctly and dared to meet the Persians in a courageous and self-respecting way; their emotions once again proved to be adequate to the situation, unlike those of the other Greeks.[56]

Both at Marathon, at Salamis, and elsewhere in Herodotus' narrative, we can see clearly the democratic sensibilities captured in such statements as that of Demosthenes: "The beginning of all excellence (*hapasēs aretēs*) is understanding (*sunesis*), and courage is the conclusion: the one forms an opinion as to what must be done and the other preserves this opinion in action. In both these qualities these men were far superior to others" (60.17–18). Herodotus' narrative shows that correct reasoning requires not only intelligence and deliberation, but also the appropriate management of fear and the praiseworthy desire for glory, sought for the right reasons. At the same time, though, we already see hints that keeping Athens "free" implied a desire for preeminence over other Greeks and even a desire to rule (cf. 8.3). Democratic courage, informed by normatively appropriate desires for honor and by thoughtful ideals of freedom, was also closely tied to the early stirrings of imperialism at Athens.

By contrast with the Athenians, the Ionians were lazy and cowardly in their pursuit of freedom (6.11–12, 6.15). Many islanders

---

[55] On "prospective shame," see Williams 1993: e.g., 83.
[56] Cf. the Athenians' management of fear at 7.143.

and mainland Greeks submitted easily to the Persians' requests for earth and water (6.48–49). The Spartans often delayed in helping the Athenians and other Greeks. The other leading Greek states, meanwhile, had their own selfish reasons for failing to support the panhellenic cause (e.g., 7.148–52: Argos, 7.153–163: Gelon of Syracuse, 7.168: Corcyra, 7.169: Crete).

Even though Pausanias won the greatest victory known to the Greeks, that is, Plataea (9.64), and even though Herodotus believed that the Spartans were (both collectively and individually) the most brilliant fighters at Plataea (9.71), the Athenians' courage and persistence were responsible for finally breaking through the Persians' stockade at Thebes and destroying the remainder of the Persian force (9.70), thereby finishing the final land battle for good. Moreover, in the important but neglected battle of Mycale (9.102–7), Herodotus gives the most credit for the Greek victory to the Athenians, who courageously rushed the Persian line of shields (9.102) and breached the Persian barricade (9.102), which led to the Persian defeat—an act befitting what Herodotus called the "second Ionian revolt" (9.104). The Athenians rushed the Persian line with great eagerness (*prothumia*), since they wanted to win the glory for this victory themselves (9.102). The Persians had no idea that the Greeks would sail to Ionia (8.130); but the Athenians were always thinking ahead, abroad, and in large terms.

Throughout his military narratives, Herodotus illustrated the Athenians' distinctively democratic combination of deliberation, forethought, clarity about their purposes, and normatively desirable emotional responses in fighting wars that other Athenians, later in the classical period, often touted as central to the Athenians' novel democratic ideal of courage. To be sure, we frequently see individual Athenians being awarded prizes of honor, or otherwise being recognized by Herodotus, for their courage or for other remarkable contributions to the war effort (8.11, 8.17, 8.93, 8.95, 8.122–23). But the main point is that the Athenians as a democratic citizenry recognized what had to be done in the circumstances in order to achieve victory. They understood their actions in a large social, ethical, and historical context. Moreover, their emotions not only did not prevent them from acting appropriately on the basis of their good judgment; their emotions also helped to inform their judgments and to inspire admirable behavior. For all these reasons, even after receiving high honors from the Spartans (8.123–25), Themistocles himself acknowledged that his honors derived in part from his leadership of the Athenians, as opposed to (he says) the Belbinites (8.125).

Athenian Courage and Eudaimonism

Herodotus illustrated that Athenian courage could be located within the framework of the Athenians' eudaimonistic ideology. The Athenians' courage during the Persian War period consisted in much more than bravery on the battlefield or at sea, and the rationality that underlay their courage involved much more than simple means-end reasoning.[57] Instead, the Athenians' newly democratic courage consisted in an entire panoply of deliberations, judgments, self-understandings, and emotions, combined with persistent, daring, and yet steadfast actions, all of which helped to bring victory to the Greeks. In their multifaceted expressions of courage, the Athenians showed loyalty to their fellow Greeks and a proper focus on their own and the other Greeks' ultimate objective—freedom.

In Herodotus' descriptions of the Themistocles Assembly, the Battle of Marathon, and the Battle of Plataea, we have found ample evidence of the Athenians' well-informed and wide-ranging expressions of courage, along just these lines. To confirm the point, though, we might recall that although the Aeginetans were admitted to have done the greatest service to the Greek cause at Salamis (followed by Athens, 8.93, cf. 8.122), the Athenians were responsible for choosing to save Greece altogether (7.139).[58] The Athenians' courage went beyond simple martial valor, whether on land or at sea, and superseded it. Mardonius also agreed that the Athenians were an especially courageous people and that they had been primarily responsible for defeating the Persian navy (8.136)—again, despite Herodotus' praise of the Aeginetans at Salamis.[59] The Spartans gave their own prize of valor to Eurybiades but granted a similar wreath to Themistocles for "his skill and cleverness" (8.124). Finally, the Athenians could recognize clearly that their leadership of Greece, and their outstanding contribution to panhellenic freedom, required them to forsake any kind

---

[57] As we will discover, what it involved was also an adequate appreciation of their sense of themselves and the destiny of their ethos: cf. 8.144. In their own self-conception, they had to act as they acted in order to live well; they had to assume leadership; and they realized that sea fighting was necessary and that they had to unite the other Greeks. In these ways, and in others, they showed an appreciation of the ultimate ends of their own lives and of the only appropriate means to achieve them—a political, practical wisdom that no other Greeks could muster, either because of fear, because of their immersion in tradition, because of unthinking subscription to a defensive mentality, and so on.

[58] And this is true, according to Herodotus, even though Pausanias is said to have won the most brilliant victory of those "that we know" (9.64), i.e., the victory at Plataea.

[59] Herodotus' praise of the Aeginetans in this way also illustrates that he was not simply "channeling" Athenian ideology at this stage of the narrative.

of self-aggrandizement or misplaced ambitions. This is why, for example, the Athenians continually waived their claims to command in favor of Greek unity (8.3; cf. 9.27, 9.46–47).

Moreover, and more importantly, the Athenians thought of their courage as an essential or defining feature of their character—one that supported their efforts to embody the other virtues in relation to their fellow Greeks. In their final response to the Persian offer of alliance (8.144), the Athenians made their reasons for unqualified opposition to the Persians explicit. They said first that their love of freedom would lead them to defend themselves in any way they could, despite the Persians' vast numerical superiority. This initial response recalls their unhesitating willingness to "stand fast" in the defense of Greek freedom. They could not reasonably consider the possibility of running away. In view of the overwhelming difficulties they faced, including their extraordinary suffering (8.142), however, would it not have made more sense to abandon Greece altogether and move to Siris in Italy, as Themistocles had suggested? Did their courage not display a certain lack of prudence?

The answer is emphatically, though not unthinkingly, no. In the course of their few decades of living together democratically, they had constructed a particular self-image for themselves, one that consisted in courageously protecting freedom, living on terms of equality, waiving their own claims for the common good of Greece, leading the other Greeks (often in spite of themselves) to pursue their own well-understood self-interests, and paying due respect to the gods. They could not act otherwise and still remain democratic Athenians, truly so called. They later explained to the Spartans that they were inspired by an appropriate sense of shame (*aidesthentes*) before Zeus (9.7a) and by "revulsion" from the idea of betraying the other Greeks (9.7a). When they themselves were betrayed by Sparta, they felt justifiably angry with the Spartans (9.7b). They added that their response to the Persians embodied their *phronēma* (9.7b), a term that captures precisely that distinctive combination of reflective intelligence and appropriate shame, honor, and anger that were the hallmarks of democratic courage.[60]

---

[60] This interpretation points up my differences with more cynical readings, such as that of Bowie 2007: 236, who writes, "Panhellenism thus marches with touches of self-importance and self-absorption"; cf. Fornara 1971: 84–86. It is true that Herodotus produced the *Histories* during the Peloponnesian War, and against the backdrop of Athens's imperialism: hence contemporary audiences would no doubt have noticed the incongruities between this Athenian speech and the Athenians' later aggression. On the other hand, Athenians continued to give speeches like this throughout the classical period, both during and after the heyday of their imperialism; and it is equally important to grasp and grapple with the underlying intellectual framework that made their self-presentation meaningful and effective—to themselves, in the first instance, and presumably to

Hence, although they themselves had self-consciously constructed their identities, and embodied those identities knowingly and enthusiastically, those identities had become, in their view (8.144), "necessary identities."[61] Having constructed these particular ideals, the Athenians could not live in any other way and still preserve their sense of themselves, their self-respect. Herodotus' presentation recalls the paradoxical statement that Demosthenes made at the end of *On the Crown*: in confronting the Macedonian threat, the Athenians *had* to exhibit the virtues, whatever their cost, or else their lives would have been rendered worthless and meaningless (see chapters 5, 10, 11, and 16 on "necessary identities"). Even though they self-consciously chose those identities, the Athenians also now *had* to live up to them. In other words, like the Spartans, the Athenians had certain *nomoi* themselves—to exhibit the virtues, such as rational prudence, courage, and justice; to show leadership, as during the Ionian Revolt or during the preliminaries to the Battle of Salamis; and to feel justified anger (e.g., 9.7b), but in the event to overcome that anger for the good of Greece (9.7b).

These virtuous behaviors derived from firm practices and essential dispositions of character, without which the Athenians' excellent, flourishing democratic life would have been meaningless.[62] The Athenians self-consciously recognized that the "good" in their lives consisted not in gold or in vast tracts of land (8.144), but in living up to their own self-consciously constructed ideals. These were the "many" (*polla*) and "great" (*megala*) things that prevented them from accepting the Persians' offer, "even if they had wished to" (8.144.2). But they were not the sort of people who would wish to accept this offer, because of their wholehearted willingness to embrace their own self-chosen ideals. They would never "willingly" negotiate with the enemy (9.7a). Their greatest reasons were the necessity (*anankaiōs echei*) of avenging the statues and houses of their gods and the recognition that it would not be well done (*ouk an eu*

---

others, to some extent at least, in the second. I agree with Hunt 2010: 1, who offers a "charitable and empathetic" reading of the Athenians' speeches discussing war and peace, and contrasts his approach "first with scholarship that portrays Athenian thinking as simple and deplorable and second with unmasking methodologies, according to which the stated grounds for war—as found in assembly speeches—only mask the truth and thus need to be stripped away rather than examined." For further exploration of Athenian thinking about foreign policy, see chapters 14 and 15 on the Athenians' eudaimonistic framework.

[61] I derive this concept from Williams 1993: 103–29, although I apply it in a novel context.

[62] The eudaimonistic framework evoked by Herodotus explains why Immerwahr's concentration on the incompatibility of Athens's self-interest, its panhellenism, and its altruisim is anachronistic and misplaced: cf. Immerwahr 1966: 217–23.

echoi) if they should betray the "Hellenic thing," the Hellenic "nation" (*to Hellēnikon*, 8.144.2). Herodotus represents the Athenians as having a clear conception of honor, and as living up to it; but they themselves had constructed this conception and rationally endorsed it. Here we see the fusion of the cognitive and the emotional in motivating the Athenians' courage to fight for Greek freedom.

Conclusion: Tensions in Herodotus' Representations of Athens

This "necessary identity" that the Athenians had constructed stood in some degree of tension with their ideal of free speech. As we learn immediately after the Athenians reject the Persians' offer, Mardonius sent yet another offer to the Athenians at Salamis, once he had re-occupied Athens ten months after Xerxes' initial capture of the city (9.3–4). A certain Lycidas, an Athenian *bouleutēs* at Salamis, proposed that the Athenians should submit this offer to the general Athenian Assembly (9.5). The other councilors, as well as "those outside," thereupon stoned Lycidas to death in a fit of rage; and the Athenian women, having learned of Lycidas' proposal, stoned his wife and children (9.5).[63]

Enraged, all the Athenians—the councilors and "those outside," as well as the Athenian women—decisively rejected even the possibility of discussing this question. There was a tension between the Athenians' commitment to the freedom of Greece and their ideal of democratic free speech. Although he records the story of Lycidas, however, Herodotus himself appears to present it as an example of the Athenians' unwavering commitment to Hellenic liberation. He does not interpret the story as we might, that is, as an ominous indication that the Athenians' "courageous" dedication to their military goals, and their anger at those who opposed those goals, sometimes overrode their fundamental democratic commitment to free speech and even their respect for the life of a fellow citizen.

Although Herodotus does not criticize the Athenians explicitly for stoning Lycidas, however, he does raise questions about the uses to which the Athenians would eventually put their novel democratic courage. As I have argued elsewhere, Herodotus sharply criticized the Athenians' emergent imperialism. In particular, Herodotus represented Solon as an

---

[63] One of the few discussions of this episode in modern scholarship can be found in Allen 2000: 142–46; the story was also recounted by Lycurgus and Demosthenes in the fourth century.

"in-house" critic of the Athenians' "leadership" of the Greek cause after the Persian Wars.[64] We have seen that the Athenians' democratic courage enabled them to undertake novel preparations and strategies to confront the Persian invader. At the same time, we find in the *Histories* a number of clues that suggest that the Athenians' novel expressions of courage during the Persian Wars were also especially suited to being transformed into a tool of Athenian imperialism. It is to this topic that we turn in the next chapter.

---

[64] Balot 2001a: 133. Thus I agree with Moles 1996, 2002 that Herodotus was highly critical of Athenian imperialism, but I believe that he (especially in Moles 2002) overemphasizes the negative dimensions of Herodotus' representation of the Athenians. The classic works in this area remain those of Strasburger 1955, Fornara 1971, and Raaflaub 1987.

CHAPTER 5 | New Faces of Athenian Courage: The Pursuit of Imperialism

IN HERODOTUS' PRESENTATION, THE Athenians, and above all their acquisitive aristocrats, were disposed to transform their leadership of the Hellenic League against Persia into what we would now call an empire. By the end of the *Histories*, the Athenians as a whole had developed a culture of *pleonexia* that resulted not only in the addition of a number of Greek islands to their league (Hdt. 9.106, 9.114), but also in an increasingly unbridled willingness to force the other Greeks to contribute money to their cause (e.g., 6.132–33, 8.111–12).[1] According to Herodotus, the Athenians' new-model courage enabled them to project imperial power in an unprecedented fashion. By contrast with Spartan traditionalism, the Athenians' courage was purposive and far-sighted—well suited, in other words, to support imperial ambitions.

Thucydides developed these lines of inquiry in order to criticize democratic courage.[2] Early in his narrative, Thucydides illustrated the workings of democratic courage in ideology and in practice. He then went on to display the shortcomings of this ideology amid the harsh conditions of war. In Thucydides' vision, the Athenian democracy could not maintain its defining ideals—freedom and equality—when pressured by foreign threats and domestic tensions. Thucydides showed up the limitations of the belief that democratic courage served the cause of justice and freedom. He showed, in fact, that there was a more traditional and more bellicose

---
[1] Balot 2001a: 114–29. I have also explored themes related to this chapter in Balot 2004c and Balot 2009a.
[2] On the general question of Thucydides' treatment of democracy, see Pope 1988; Ober 1998: 52–121; Connor 1984: 237–42; cf. Hornblower 1987: 160–65; Woodhead 1970: 31–53.

Athenian rhetoric of *andreia* that competed with and often overshadowed the admirable Periclean vision of democratic courage. By the end of the *History*, readers should be convinced by Thucydides that the Periclean ideal, however attractive and powerful, was a fragile construct, vulnerable to the pressures of war, and often utilized for less than admirable purposes.

Thucydides' Daring Athenians: The Corinthians at Sparta

Many scholars have noted what appears to be the central attribute of Thucydides' Athenians: "daring" (*tolma*).[3] Less often explored are the character, quality, history, and consequences of this attribute. Speaking at Sparta (1.68–70), the Corinthians helped to substantiate the Herodotean characterization of the Athenians.[4] For the Corinthians, the Athenians were "innovative" (*neōteropoioi*) and "quick to think of a plan and to accomplish in practice what they have decided" (*epinoēsai oxeis kai epitelesai ergōi ha an gnōsin*, 1.70.2). The Corinthians emphasized both the Athenians' courage in action and their deliberative planning, even to the extent that they praised the Athenians for alienating their bodies to the city, while using their own, independent judgment when acting on the city's behalf (1.70.6). Thucydides shaped this particular interpretation of the Athenians, but, as we have seen in the previous chapters, Thucydides' presentation had deep roots in the Athenians' culture and in the writings of those who criticized them.

In the Corinthian view, the Athenians' daring and innovative character led to their successful pursuit of *pleonexia*, as Herodotus had suggested: the Athenians want to "acquire something" (*ti ktasthai*) by going abroad (1.70.4), they invest themselves in "continually getting more" (*to aiei ktasthai*, 1.70.8), and their city is never at rest (1.70.9). The Corinthians imply that the Athenians' character, which expressed itself in the city's successful imperialism, originated in their novel political practices, that is, in their novel democratic regime (1.71). They contrast the Spartans' "old-fashioned customs" (*ta akinēta nomima*) with the Athenians' novel technologies of warfare and, indeed, of political life (1.71.3). It would be

---

[3] See especially Forde 1986.
[4] See Connor 1984: 40–41 for a helpful analysis; as Connor (1984: 40) points out, "The Sparta presented by the Corinthians is an obsolescent power, lacking the innovative and aggressive daring of the Athenians." Among other useful accounts of the Corinthians' characterization of the Athenians, see Ober 2010: 72–75; Cogan 1981: 20–26; Edmunds 1975: 89–93.

hard to find a more powerful confirmation of the Herodotean characterization of Athens.

Yet, upon reflection, the Corinthians present a more complex picture. For they also argued that the Athenians were "bold beyond their capacity" (*para dunamin tolmētai*, 1.70.3) and that they "run risks contrary to good judgment" (*para gnōmēn kinduneutai*). This is the opposite of the Athenians' self-image, which emphasized the rationally and deliberatively informed courage of democratic soldiers. In this way, at least, the Corinthians modified the Herodotean characterization of Athens, not to mention the understanding of democratic courage envisioned in Pericles' funeral oration. This modification reveals an interesting dynamic at play in the Corinthian speech—one with wider implications for the Thucydidean interpretation of Athens, altogether.

Observe that the Corinthians were trying to incite the Spartans to war.[5] They made every effort to magnify the Athenians' power, in order to convince the Spartans of the likelihood of Athenian success. Thucydides presents the Corinthians as misguidedly believing that taking thoughtless risks would promote, rather than undermine, the Athenians' projection of imperial power. Furthermore, Thucydides presents the Corinthians as slightly mis-describing the Athenians' own self-image; instead, they present a similar, but then self-contradictory, version of that self-image. In the Corinthians' interpretation, the Athenians exemplified a thoughtful and deliberative form of courage—one that enabled them to sacrifice their bodies quite easily, even while holding fast in their minds to the governing purposes of their expressions of courage. And yet somehow the Athenians also manifested a tendency to run thoughtless risks, to overstep the boundaries of good judgment.

Perhaps the Corinthians, in Thucydides' presentation, were like many other Greeks in failing to understand the necessarily close connections between courage, rational prudence, and efficacy in action. By contrast, the Athenians themselves held that those connections were crucial to a well-founded grasp of courage altogether. On the other hand, even if the Corinthians presented a self-contradictory image of the Athenians simply for Spartan consumption, it may be that Thucydides himself endorsed that self-contradictory image as the truth of the Athenian experience. I contend that Thucydides took care to represent accurately the meritorious

---

[5] See Cogan 1981: 28–33 for the argument that, in Thucydides' presentation at least, the war was far from inevitable: "Consciously or not, the Spartans *chose* to accept the Corinthian picture of the empire" (29).

Periclean ideal of democratic courage. Yet he also found that in practice the Athenians were motivated, and even controlled, by a more traditional, and more self-destructive, type of aggressive machismo than their ideology would ostensibly allow.

Ambiguities at First Sight: The Athenians at Sparta

Responding to the Corinthians, certain unnamed Athenian envoys enunciated ideals of courage that are strikingly similar to those found in Pericles' funeral oration.[6] In Thucydides' representation, these ideals at least sometimes informed the Athenians' political life, diplomatic rhetoric, and foreign policy. At the same time, though, Thucydides himself evinced from the outset a desire to question these ideals and to criticize the Athenians for their self-serving rhetoric and behavior.

The Athenians first recalled their experiences during the Persian Wars in order, they said, to illustrate the character of the city against which Sparta might choose to fight (1.73.3). Already during the Persian Wars, the Athenians were risk-takers and freedom fighters on behalf of all the Greeks, including the Spartans (1.73.2). The Athenians defeated the Persians single-handedly at Marathon and made a decisive contribution during the Persian Wars, altogether, because of their courageous decision, as an entire people (*pandēmei*), to take to their ships and defeat the Persians at Salamis (1.73.4). The Athenians provided the "greatest number of ships, the most intelligent general (*stratēgon xunetōtaton*), and the most unhesitating willingness to fight" (*prothumian aoknotatēn;* 1.74.1). The Herodotean echoes of this passage are unmistakable.

Led by Themistocles, the Athenians provided the cleverest general, the general whose strategic aptitude enabled the Greeks to win at Salamis (1.74.1). Moreover, and more importantly, they also, as an entire democratic citizenry (*pandēmei*), came through deliberation to "deem it worthy" of themselves (*ēxiōsamen*) to abandon their city, to give up their possessions, and to take to their ships (1.74.2). "We deemed it worthy": as in Herodotus' *Histories*, the Athenians listened to the sound advice of their leaders, but then they themselves, knowingly, deliberately, and on the basis of their carefully constructed self-image, took the decision to lead the Greeks courageously. This is why, in their speech at Sparta, the Athenians

---

[6] On this speech, see Orwin 1986; Forde 1986.

emphasized both their deliberative self-understanding (cf. 1.75.1) and their vision of action that was genuinely "worthy" of themselves.[7]

This specific vocabulary of "deeming worthy" recalls that of the Athenians at Plataea and that of the Herodotean Athenians when they refused the Persian offer to medize (Hdt. 8.144). Through their public and well-reasoned formation of a collective identity, the Athenians had developed a powerful self-consciousness about who they were and what they stood for. Consequently, they had a lively sense of what was "worthy" of them as leaders of the entire Greek world (as they saw themselves). Underneath the Athenians' stirring rhetoric lies the implication that their all-important victory at Salamis was in every way the product of their democratic regime—from their use of the Laureion silver mines to produce an immense navy, to their recognition of Themistocles' brilliance, to their deliberate decision to fight as quasi-islanders. At the same time, the Athenians did not emphasize the "necessity" of their leadership, as did the Athenians of Herodotus and, later, Athens's fourth-century orators; the reason for this omission will emerge presently.

The Athenians' repeated emphasis on their "most daring zeal" (*prothumian...polu tolmērotatēn*, 1.74.2, cf. 1.74.1, 1.75.1) implied that they were wholehearted, enthusiastic, and unreserved in their pursuit of the common good of Greece. They acted "without anger" (1.74.2) at the Spartans for failing to help the Greek cause sooner. The Athenians approached the Persian Wars, not only in their own distinctive, cognitively rich fashion, but also with the appropriate emotional attitudes toward their activities. They were not struggling to do the right thing against the grain of their own desires and appetites. Rather, they had formed a citizenry whose desires corresponded to their own views of what was excellent—that is, courageous and noble, if not also more just than necessary. This proper emotional response will become crucial in Thucydides' later, more critical representations of the Athenian Assembly.

According to the Athenians, their ancestors' courage had saved not only Athens, but also the rest of Greece. If the defense of Greece had been left to the other Greeks, either through fear or through thickheaded traditionalism or both, the Persians would have emerged victorious. At this point in the speech, however, the Athenians changed tack and began to defend their projection of imperial power in a different way—notoriously, in fact, on the basis of three "compulsions" or "necessities": fear, honor, and profit

---

[7] See Forde 1986: 437, 444.

(1.75.3). The Athenians described themselves as "vanquished" by these "three greatest things" (*hupo [triōn] tōn megistōn nikēthentes*, 1.76.2). They argued that it was human nature for the stronger to rule the weaker (1.76.2). While their statement that the allies asked them to take the command against Persia (1.75.2) is a staple of the epitaphic tradition, these other self-justifications diverged sharply from the discourse of the funeral orations. In effect, Thucydides has juxtaposed the Athenians' democratic ideology of courage and his own divergent account of the Athenians' motivations. In doing so, Thucydides began to bring to light the ambiguities that informed the Athenians' "courageous" pursuit of imperialism.[8]

In particular, Thucydides pointedly raised the question of the Athenians' injustice—the very question that Pericles' funeral oration ignored. Thucydides frequently had his non-Athenian speakers emphasize that injustice (e.g., 1.86–87, 3.63, 5.104). Their central idea was that the Athenian imperialists were violating canons of distributive fairness that had long characterized relations in the wider Greek world.[9] The Athenians unjustly exacted tribute from their "allies"; they crushed dissent and intervened in the internal affairs of other Greek states; and on several occasions, they destroyed entire populations in one stroke. By vividly illustrating the Athenians' injustice, Thucydides raised the following question: How could the Athenians manage the psychological contradiction between adhering to a praiseworthy ideal of courage and using that same courage to tyrannize over the other Greeks?

In raising this question, Thucydides engaged in a subtle dialectic with the Athenian discourse on "necessary identities" (see chapter 4).[10] Herodotus' Athenians had asserted that they—even paradoxically—*chose* to embody excellence in the highest degree, while also considering their status as leaders to be a *necessary* identity for them. Thucydides' Athenians, however, refused to allude to the necessity of their identity as freedom-fighting leaders, while declaring, surprisingly, that they were motivated by "necessities" of another, less admirable, sort: fear, ambition, and greed.[11] Through transforming the Athenians' discourse on necessity, Thucydides implied that the Athenians were, in truth, less capable

---

[8] On several of these ambiguities, see Orwin 1994: 44–56.
[9] Balot 2001a.
[10] Cf. Crane 1998: 241–57, 264–73 which connects Herodotus' representation of the Athenians' rejection of Xerxes' offer of peace both to Thucydides' representation of the Melian Dialogue and to the Athenian speech at Sparta, albeit in a different way.
[11] Orwin 1994 provides a searching analysis of this tension with which my treatment shares elements.

of self-consciously creating, or forming, themselves politically than they claimed—and, more importantly, less noble than they typically imagined, with regard to the fundamental emotional and psychological wellsprings of their political agency. Like figures on the tragic stage, they understood only dimly and incoherently how their claims to nobility were embroiled in a wider web of fear, greed, and anger.

Pericles' Efficacious Ideal of Athenian Courage

Yet Thucydides also did justice to the Athenians' achievement, however limited, of leading self-chosen lives and of conforming to their own noblest conceptions of necessity. Accordingly, Thucydides not only gave voice to the Periclean ideal of courage, but also showed that this ideal was efficacious.[12] In particular, Pericles' ideal of courage enabled the Athenians to carry out his long-term strategy for the Peloponnesian War.[13] At the war's outset, Pericles persuaded the Athenians that they had to concentrate themselves, their families, and their possessions within the city; they had to maintain the city's naval strength and plan on a protracted war; and above all they had to refrain from challenging the Spartans in a pitched battle in the plains before the city walls. Pericles' grand strategy was, as he himself put it, based on an attempt to reconceive of the Athenians, metaphorically, as islanders (1.143.5). The "island strategy" was aimed at preserving Athens's naval power and empire.[14]

This unorthodox proposal ran counter to the traditional ethics of the hoplite. Earlier in the century, the Athenians' victory over the Persians at Marathon in 490 BC had established the hoplite as the central paradigm of bravery, manhood, and civic virtue for the rest of the classical period. Indeed, hoplite battle had been a normative model for warfare among Greek city-states since the early archaic period.[15] The classic hoplite battle

---

[12] This section is a revised version of Balot 2004a. Contrast the views of Foster 2010 on Thucydides' representation of Pericles: "My aim is to describe Thucydides' portrait of the exemplar of this human weakness: an intelligent, devoted, and self-controlled leader who succumbed to a belief in the historical significance of Athens' empire and the armed force that made it possible" (5).

[13] The best treatment of the "grand strategy" is Ober 1985. For particular details of the strategy, see Powell 1988: 145–54; Powell 2001: 147–56. See now also Spence 2010.

[14] A valuable recent discussion of the island mentality in the context of fifth-century democratic war making can be found in Raaflaub 2001.

[15] Vidal-Naquet has argued persuasively that, despite the normative status of hoplites in the classical period in Athens and elsewhere, Athens adhered to the ideal model for the first and last time at Marathon: see Vidal-Naquet 1986: 90.

took place between two citizen armies of heavy infantry, at an agreed-upon place in an open plain, and usually concerned a borderland dispute between two *poleis*, with special rituals and unwritten rules governing the engagement, in particular that it would be over quickly and that captives would not be killed.[16]

Judged by the standard of the prevailing hoplite ethos, Pericles' strategy of avoiding a pitched battle was cowardly, and many Athenians saw it that way. Isocrates argued that Periclean Athens had apparently lost all virtue, probably because it was corrupted by the Athenian empire: "instead of defeating those who attack us, it has so educated the citizens that they do not dare to go out against the enemy before our walls" (8.77). Aristophanes' depiction of the Acharnians' anger over this decision illustrates the seeming outrageousness of Pericles' proposal and the difficulty Athenians had in accepting it.[17] As Thucydides himself pointed out (2.65), neither the rich nor the poor enjoyed living in the city and seeing their property beyond its walls destroyed. Pericles put substantial effort into persuading the Athenians of the usefulness of his innovative policy; the difficulty was to convince them, not to mention others, that they were still courageous despite lingering behind the walls.[18] A key element of Pericles' argument was the ideal of democratic courage articulated in the funeral oration.[19]

Pericles attributed true courage only to those capable of understanding the place of courage in the architecture of a life well lived as a whole. This is why he pointedly referred to *eudaimonia* in his explication of Athenian courage: in their democratic forums, the Athenians were able to articulate explicitly for themselves why courage was meaningful within the long-term narratives of their lives, both as individuals and as a people. On the other hand, Pericles denied the title of "genuine" courage to others, such as the Spartans, who, at least allegedly, were less reflective about the place of courage within larger ethical designs.[20] He built on the prevailing ideology

---

[16] The clearest treatment of the "normative" status of the hoplite can be found in several books and essays of Victor Hanson, including Hanson 1995, especially chapters 6–8, and Hanson 1996. On the "rules of war," see Ober 1996c.

[17] See also Plutarch, *Life of Pericles* 33.6, with Konstan 2010: 191.

[18] On the potential for the charge of cowardice, see Hanson 2000: 220; Cartledge 1998; on the novelty of Pericles' proposals and the difficulty of persuading the Assembly to accept them, see also Ober 1985.

[19] For a fuller elaboration of these points, see Balot 2004c.

[20] Plato makes similar points about the Spartans' overestimation of the value of courage for well-being: at *Laws* 631c5–d1, the Athenian Stranger emphasizes that courage should properly come fourth in importance among the "divine" virtues, after good judgment, self-control, and justice.

of Athenian intelligence in order to redefine courage. And his redefinition led to the Athenians' acceptance of a highly untraditional strategy that took advantage of Athens's strengths at sea and the city's walls, while avoiding any encounters with the Spartans in their own domain, on land. This constituted for Thucydides the Athenians' principal achievement of political self-formation, conformity to their own ideals, and radical originality in a world ordinarily characterized by bitter compulsions.

Thucydides' Critique of Athenian Political Practice

The central question then became whether Pericles' strategy was the right strategy for Athenians of his time. Historians debate the question. Could Athens have won the war, if the Athenians had supported their troops in Sicily more single-mindedly (cf. 2.65)? What if Pericles had lived for another decade, instead of losing his life to the plague? Whatever the interest of these counterfactual questions, Thucydides' own outlook seems clear: hypothetically, at least, Pericles' strategy could have been successful, by virtue of Athenian strength (1.140–44, 2.13) and Periclean leadership.

Contingently, however, Thucydides showed that Pericles' vision could not control the hazards of war; nor, more importantly, could Pericles ensure that his own virtuous leadership of the city would be reproduced after his death. According to Thucydides, in short, the Athenians' democratic system could not effectively carry out the Periclean strategy, because the Athenians themselves were driven not by Pericles' noble ideals, but rather by the psychological necessities of fear, greed, and "manly" anger. The historian wondered whether a traditional ideology of machismo in fact overrode the Athenians' supposedly free deliberations, so that the Periclean ideology was hypocritical and false.

Pericles' "War Speech"

Take, for example, Pericles' first speech in Thucydides' *History*, his "war speech" (1.140–44).[21] Thucydides introduces the speech by remarking that many others had delivered speeches, some arguing that the Megarian

---

[21] Edmunds 1975: 7–36 provides an excellent commentary on this speech—one that is compatible with my own emphasis on the novelty of Athenian expressions of military courage, but one that does not focus directly on questions of *andreia*.

Decree should be rescinded for the sake of peace, and others arguing for war with Sparta (1.139). Thucydides lets his readers hear only Pericles' speech. Pericles' central idea was that the Athenians must not "yield" (*eikein*) to the Peloponnesians; rather, they should feel indignant at the Peloponnesians' "orders" concerning Potideia, Aegina, and Megara (1.140.1, 1.140.3). Pericles insists that the Megarian Decree is a test of the Athenians' firmness (*bebaiōsin*) and judgment (*gnōmēs*, 1.140.5). At the far end of international brinksmanship, Pericles lost the flexibility on which the Athenians prided themselves. His advice was always the same (1.140.1): regard any claim made by equals, however small, as "enslavement" (*doulōsin*, 1.141.1).

Pericles' rhetoric is rigid and extreme. Unlike the hortatory vision of his funeral oration, these arguments are designed to control the Athenians by stimulating their anger, aggressiveness, and indignation.[22] This point emerges clearly if we recall how often the Athenians sacrificed their claims to honor or recognition during the Persian Wars for the sake of Greek unity (see chapter 4). Any claim, however small, is equivalent to slavery? Certainly, the Athenians at Plataea would not agree. Now the Athenians could be roused to a level of anger so intense that they would tolerate Pericles' potentially destructive long-term strategy for making war against the Spartans.

Thucydides introduces significant ironies in Pericles' presentation of the city's military power. For example, Pericles criticizes the Peloponnesians for failing to work in concert for the common good; their councils, he says, are divisive arenas for the pursuit of each allied member's self-interests (1.141). Unbeknownst to Pericles, however, this is precisely the criticism that Thucydides himself later leveled against the Athenian Assembly and its chief speakers (2.65). When Pericles says that the Peloponnesians will have to resort to forced contributions of money (1.141), it is ironic that the Athenians themselves had to exact more and more money from their allies over the course of the war, starting in 428 BC at the latest.[23] Pericles' apparently rational control over the details of the situation unravels in practice, as his own half-truths and ironically inflected analyses provoke the Athenians to decide to make war on the basis of their anger rather than the good judgment on which they prided themselves.[24]

---

[22] On Pericles' possible overreaction to the Megarians' and Spartans' response to the Megarian Decree, see Aristophanes, *Acharnians* 541–56, with Konston 2010: 190.
[23] Noted by Woodruff 1993: 33n.88; cf. Hornblower 1991: 228–29.
[24] The comic poet Cratinus, in what remains of his *Dionysalexandros*, is said to have ridiculed Pericles "by way of innuendo very effectively in the play for having brought war upon the

It was in this very speech that Pericles unveiled his "island strategy" (1.143), relying on the Athenians' willingness to adapt their self-image, as in the days of Themistocles, so as to become altogether a naval power, with no concern for the physical presence of Attica. Like Themistocles, Pericles wanted the Athenians to exemplify the principle that men, not possessions, make the city (1.143). The great irony is that Pericles relied on democratic flexibility in developing this strategy, even as he imposed an inflexible and indignant rule of machismo on the citizens, in failing to negotiate with the Spartans. It is not at all clear that war was necessary at this point, except that Pericles' speech helped to convince the Athenians to make it so.

Pericles' response to the Spartans' demands is unyielding: in essence, he himself demands that the Spartans dismantle the long-term structure of their alliances with other Peloponnesian cities, if the Athenians are to give their own subject-cities autonomy. But the two cases are not parallel, because the Spartans did not exact tribute, and because the Peloponnesian League members were significantly "more equal" to their leader than the subjects of the Athenian Empire were.[25] Even so, Pericles insists that his response is "just" and "fitting" for "this city" (1.144.2), and he reminds his audience of the high likelihood that they will win honor (*timai*, 1.144.3) in the course of responding appropriately to this great danger. This is why he likens his contemporaries to the Persian War heroes of the preceding generation, who fought with good judgment (*gnōmēi*) and daring (*tolmēi*) for the sake of Greek freedom and Athenian glory (1.144.4). It is implausible to think that the Spartans threatened Greek freedom just as the Persians did. Rather, most contemporaries urged that the Athenian Empire was now the successor to the Persian threat. Hence, even as he relied on the Athenian ideology of rationally informed courage, Pericles appealed instead to very traditional constructions of anger, indignation, and shame, which, in this "primitive" guise, were the traditional motivations for Greek courage.

Thucydides on "Manliness" at Corcyra

Throughout his *History*, Thucydides continued to develop the criticism that "manly courage" compromised self-restraint and prudence. The

---

Athenians" (cited in Konstan 2010: 189). On Periclean intelligence and loss of control, Edmunds 1975 remains the fundamental treatment.

[25] See Raaflaub 2004: 122–26.

Athenians were the victims of their own unjust greed and their surprisingly hotheaded ideals of *andreia*, which denigrated inactivity and overvalued aggression. In Thucydides' vision, the Athenians' susceptibility to these factors increased significantly over the course of the war.

In his excursus on Corcyra, Thucydides reflects that war teaches men violence toward each other by attacking their shared understanding of key evaluative terms. "Irrational daring was now reckoned to be the courage of a loyal partisan; thoughtful hesitation was considered disguised cowardice; moderation (*sōphrosunē*) was a screen for the lack of manliness;...Fanatical enthusiasm was considered the part of a real man...Anyone who was violent or angry was trustworthy" (3.82). All the themes of the Athenian politics of courage are revisited here, and they are highlighted by Thucydides' obvious longing for stable political values. War the teacher of violence has found an acolyte and henchman in the cultural legacy of manly courage in ancient Greece. Courage the freedom-fighting virtue tends to damage the free speech and trust upon which the Athenian democracy was based—which in turn led to a violent Greek world and, later in the narrative, to civic breakdown at Athens in 411 BC.[26]

Cleon's Instigation of Manly Anger

The process charted by Thucydides emerged in earnest in the fourth year of the Peloponnesian War (427 BC). After the Athenians had suppressed a revolt by their subject-state Mytilene, the hawkish Cleon persuaded the Assembly to put the entire male population to death. The Athenians' judgment was heavily influenced by their anger (*hupo orgēs*, 3.36.2). The next day, the Athenians wanted to reopen the debate. The decision to think again was itself a significant sign of democratic strength and lack of traditionalism.[27] Despite the occasional rigidity of Pericles' own rhetoric, the Athenians themselves lived up to his ideals of democratic openness in this important instance.

At the same time, though, the Athenians were at least susceptible to basing their decisions on anger and a sense of indignation. In this respect, they were similar to other inhabitants of the ancient Mediterranean in valorizing

---

[26] On speech and corruption in this episode, see the excellent treatment of Euben 1990: 167–201.
[27] The best treatments of the episode, especially from the perspective of its lack of traditionalism, are Orwin 1994: 142–62 and Saxonhouse 2006: 151–64, both of which offer helpful discussions that are sensitive to the debate's emotional nuances; cf. Morrison 2006: 120–32. Wohl 2002: 73–123 addresses the question of manliness in this episode from a different angle.

"manly" notions of honor and respect.[28] This tendency does not prima facie corrupt democracy, but in practice it damaged the Athenians' commitment to free speech. The ideal of "manly" courage promoted antagonistic attitudes toward those seeking to continue debating the questions of war and peace.[29] This is what we see in the debate between Cleon and Diodotus. Cleon was the "most violent" (*biaiotatos*) of the citizens and yet also the "most trusted" (*pithanōtatos*) by them at that time (3.36.6).[30] The connection between cruelty and trustworthiness calls to mind Thucydides' description of civil war at Corcyra; the Athenians were experiencing a civil war in the soul of their polis.

Cleon berated his fellow democrats for reopening the debate and for being too enthusiastic about clever speeches. Cleon advocates fixed laws and permanent decisions—even if they are "worse" (*cheirosi*, 3.37.3)— and, like the Spartan Sthenelaidas (1.86), he denigrates reflective and self-questioning speeches as opposed to "ignorance" (*amathia*, 3.37.3) and unquestioning obedience to the law (3.37.4). He derides the Athenians for what was, in effect, the central plank of the Periclean vision of deliberatively informed courage: "You are now accustomed to be spectators of speeches, but you act as a mere audience for deeds" (3.38). He accuses the Athenians of wanting to make speeches themselves and of striving to follow complex arguments.

To this, of course, the Athenians should have responded: "Precisely: that is what discursively forming a new, self-chosen political identity, one that we can be proud of, is all about." But Cleon's surprisingly successful rejection of this ideal enabled him to accuse the Athenians of showing unmanly compassion (3.37.2) to the "rebels" and of growing soft now that the danger was over (3.40). This rhetorical diatribe against the Athenians' effeminacy was intended as a goad to immediate and unreflective action[31]—action intended, that is, to shut down the free play of deliberation.

Cleon's principal focus was on restimulating the Athenians' anger toward the Mytilenians (see also chapter 10). To be sure, anger is an

---

[28] Like other Mediterranean men, moreover, they exercised a sort of "touchy" surveillance over the manhood of their citizenry (Winkler 1990). This is why the ideology of courage tended to favor war hawks throughout ancient Greece and Rome: witness the difficulties experienced by the Roman general Fabius Maximus, opponent of Hannibal, who was nicknamed "Cunctator" (the Hesitator) (cf. Raaflaub 2001: 312–13), as well as those of other ancient generals who hesitated to fight, even if for good reasons (e.g., Thuc. 4.65, 5.7.2).
[29] For sharp observations on Athenian political rhetoric along these lines, see Hunt 2010: 117–23.
[30] On the often unnoticed connections between Cleon and pleasure, see Wohl 2002: 92–105.
[31] Wohl 2002: 174–77.

emotion cognitively informed by beliefs about justice and injustice, and it is one that often proves appropriate to a sound and well-informed model of courage: think, for example, of the Athenians' anger toward the Persians at the Battle of Salamis (cf. chapters 10 and 11). But there is a difference between the well-founded anger of the Athenians toward the Persians and what we might call the "primitive" anger recommended by Cleon. Cleon's "primitive" anger is defined by its thoughtlessness: as he argues, those who suffer injury should strike back with "hot" anger immediately, rather than waiting for their initial, leonine feelings of *thumos* to settle (3.38.1).[32]

This is precisely why Cleon urges the Athenians to react furiously, like animals in danger, rather than like their carefully reasoning "best selves":

> Do not become traitors to yourselves, but come as close as possible in your minds to your moment of suffering, and recall what great importance you placed on subduing them. Now pay them back for what they did, and do not grow soft just now, forgetting the danger that once hung over you. Punish them in a suitable way and set them up as a clear example to your other allies (3.40).

Underlying his reasoning is a framework of ideas that link courage with anger, decisive action, and aggression. As Aristotle later pointed out, anger and *andreia* appeared to be closely allied (*EN* III.8.1117a4–9).

Cleon's presentation suggests that deliberation is weak and therefore imprudent; that men full of *andreia* act boldly, decisively, and in accordance with traditional laws; and that a truly political government, as opposed to an audience in love with speeches, is focused on violent retribution for wrongs suffered. Therefore, Cleon tried to use the rhetoric of *andreia* to shut down further debate and deliberation.[33] Thucydides describes this episode in the third book of his *History*, arguably in order to illustrate certain problematic features of democratic discourse.

Others have argued well that the focus of Thucydides' criticisms is the flawed epistemology of the Assembly, the difficulties of establishing a political context where rational discussion is possible, and the antidemocratic impulses of speakers like Cleon.[34] Thucydides vividly renders a

---

[32] On anger in Thucydides, see Harris 2001: 178–82; on "hot" anger in particular, see Allen 2000: 117–18, 124–25.
[33] Cf. Yunis 1996: 87–92; *contra* Wohl 2002: 95–96.
[34] Ober 1998: 94–104; Orwin 1994: 158–59, Saxonhouse 1996: 72–79. On the tensions between democracy, deliberation, and empire, as evoked by Cleon, see especially MacLeod 1978: 68–72.

context of discussion in which speakers can manipulate the dangerous potentialities of the Athenian character in order to produce devastating practical effects. By contrast with their later behavior during the Sicilian Debate, the Athenian Assembly resisted Cleon's angry seductiveness. By showing that only "Diodotus"—the "gift of the god"—could save Athens, perhaps Thucydides meant to imply that only the gods, not the Athenian Assembly itself, could save the Athenians from the most self-destructive tendencies of their political character. And, of course, there were no gods.

But we should note that when the Athenians attacked Melos in 416 BC, there was no Diodotus to save the Athenians from themselves—much less to save the Melians. The Athenians eventually realized in practice Cleon's own ideals of aggressive manliness, his intolerance of both pity and dissent, and his punitive insistence on making an example of those who attempted to defy Athenian power. Was there a genuine strategic reason to destroy Melos and to kill or enslave its population? It seems improbable. Instead, the Athenian action against Melos was intended to display superior manliness to any Greeks who may have doubted Athenian power.

This is exactly what Thucydides' interpretation of the event leads us to see. The Athenians recognize that the Melians have done them no injustice (5.89). They have come to subscribe to a rigid dichotomy in which the Melians' potential friendship would signify Athenian weakness (*astheneias*), while the Melians' hatred of Athens (and the ensuing destruction of Melos) would demonstrate Athenian power (5.95). As Cleon had recommended in the case of the Mytilenians, the Athenians must make an example of the Melians to the other Greeks. An example of what? An example of the Athenians' power to control the other Greeks, especially islanders (5.97, 5.99). In taking this position, the Athenians exhibit a surprisingly "touchy" manliness in their concern for their reputation among the subject states: according to the Athenians, the subject states believe that some cities maintain their freedom because of their power, and that the Athenians avoid attacking them out of fear (5.97). The Athenians intended their destruction of Melos to signify to the entire Greek world their unwillingness to, and their lack of any need to, accept the claims of others to power or to justice, however great and however small (cf. 1.140–44). Perhaps Machiavelli was right that any attempts to delay conflict or to abide by defensive policies are quixotic (*The Prince* 3, 21; *Discourses on Livy* 1.6, 2.19).[35]

---

[35] For interesting reflections on neutrality in the Melian episode, see Morrison 2006: 94–99. I pursue related ideas in Balot 2009a.

Overwhelming the Athenian Ideal: The Sicilian Debate

During the Sicilian Debate of 415 BC, not even the gods could save the Athenians. It was in this Assembly that the Athenian general Nicias urged his fellow citizens not to be browbeaten into supporting an unnecessary expedition to Sicily, either through fear of being called cowards, or because of a reckless passion for endless conquest.[36] If the Athenians could maintain *sōphrosunē*, he says, then they would not be persuaded by the false promises of money and reputation offered by the rival speaker Alcibiades (Thuc. 6.11).[37]

As Thucydides' narrative shows, however, Nicias' arguments could not overcome the Athenians' dedication to these self-destructive ideals. Thucydides' presentation of Nicias' speech would have been impossible had there not existed a vibrant culture of public self-criticism within the Athenian democracy. Yet Thucydides also saw clearly that, under the stresses of the war and of their own ideals of *andreia*, it was difficult for the Athenians to maintain their fundamental democratic principles. In particular, his *History* shows that the rhetoric of *andreia* could undermine the democratic commitment to free speech.

This threat grew more intense as time went on. Later, at the end of his account of the Sicilian Debate, Thucydides mentions that those who opposed the Sicilian expedition kept silent because they feared acquiring a reputation for cowardice or lack of patriotism.[38] As Nicias discovered to his cost, appropriate *sōphrosunē* could not be maintained in such a political climate. This was not an anomaly, or a figment of Thucydides' imagination. Recall that, in the fourth century, Demosthenes addressed the same issue: "Do not consider those who urge you to take the field to be for this reason brave, nor those who undertake to oppose them to be for this reason cowards" (*Ex.* 50.1). Obviously, Demosthenes was striking out against the atmosphere of intimidation that the rhetoric of *andreia* could induce.[39]

We find a nearly exact parallel in fifth-century Sparta. Just before the Peloponnesian War, Sparta's King Archidamus had urged his fellow citizens, "Let no one suppose it to be for reasons of cowardice that we, although we are many, do not rush to attack a single city" (1.83). His rival,

---

[36] Thuc. 6.13; Wohl 2002: 171–80; Balot 2001a: 159–72.
[37] Cf. North 1966: 109–10. For useful discussions of the debate, see Connor 1984: 158–68; Ober 1998: 104–20; Saxonhouse 2006: 165–71.
[38] 6.24; cf. Raaflaub 2001: 312–14, 320, along with the helpful remarks of Yunis 1996: 103–9.
[39] Cf. Roisman 2005: 114–15.

Sthenelaidas, emphasized that there was no need to discuss matters, since the injustice done against Sparta and its allies was obvious (1.86). To settle the disagreement, Sthenelaidas instituted an irregular voting procedure in order to shame the Spartans into voting for the war. Rather than simply exclaiming their vote—the standard method—the Spartans had to stand to one side or the other to vote, thereby supposedly displaying their courage or cowardice for all to see.[40]

Thucydides remarked on the political cleverness of this tactic, which took advantage of prevailing beliefs about *andreia* (1.87). Archidamus lost the debate and acquired a reputation for weakness and traitorous sympathy with Athens (2.18.3). Throughout the debate, the primary ideal urged by Archidamus should come as no surprise: *sōphrosunē*. Indeed, the Spartan king argues at length that *sōphrosunē* is not a sign of dull caution, but rather of wisdom and good sense.[41] Comparing this with political debate at Athens, we can see that the Athenian hawks' rhetoric of courage and cowardice was forcing Athens's political climate to resemble that of Sparta—a militaristic camp posing as a polis.[42] Because of their ideals of *andreia*, and their suspicion of cautious deliberation, Sparta and Athens were more politically symmetrical than Athenian democrats might have liked to think.

Later in the Sicilian Debate, Thucydides reformulated the themes of manliness, trust, and necessity in his presentation of Alcibiades, a character often said to embody Athens's adventuresome, exciting, innovative spirit. In his biography of this complex figure, Plutarch refers to Alcibiades' debauchery, drunkenness, and insolence, as well as to his ambition, strength, courage, and beauty.[43] To reduce the destructive effects of traditional courage, democracies must work to disentangle the two sides of this equation. In the Sicilian Debate, Alcibiades does just the opposite. He argues that the Athenians must be true to their aggressive, expansionist character unless they want to lead a "quiet life" like others, which is tantamount to slavery (6.18.3).

---

[40] For a helpful analysis, which is sensitive to the role of moderation, traditionalism, and courage, see Crane 1998: 203–21.

[41] Thuc. 1.84; cf. North 1966: 102–3.

[42] See Edmunds (1975: 83–88) for astute comments on the differences between Periclean Athens and Sparta in this regard: "Thus Sparta could not assert its primacy as Athens can, in the voice of Pericles, in the Funeral Oration. The Spartan constitution has no positive meaning for its citizens, but rather creates an armed camp" (84).

[43] Cf. Plato's *Symposium* with Hobbs 2000: 254–61. For a useful discussion of Alcibiades, see Ober 1998: 109–13.

This is why, according to Alcibiades, there is a "necessity" (*ananke*, 6.18.3) for the Athenians to launch their expedition to Sicily: they could not, he said, control the size of their empire, for otherwise they would risk being ruled by others. This was manifestly contrary to the principles of Pericles' strategy. Idleness and inactivity, Alcibiades argued, would wear down the city and ultimately destroy its power to rule (6.18.6). The Athenians' ideals of choosing for themselves a necessary identity as just and generous leaders of the Greek world were undermined by a new conception of necessary identities more conducive to traditional belligerence. It should come as no surprise that Alcibiades, like Cleon and Sthenelaidas before him, criticizes Athenian speech-making in favor of pugnacious action (6.18.6). Like his predecessors Pericles and Cleon, Alcibiades called forth the striking language of freedom, slavery, and tyranny in order to stimulate the Athenians' primitive fears and anger, and in order to shut down their well-informed reasoning about the Athenians' prospects in Sicily.

To all his proposed manly aggression, Alcibiades added counter-phobia: "For one defends against stronger enemies not only when they attack; instead, one also works to prevent them from attacking in the first place" (Thuc. 6.18). Alcibiades' counter-phobia is similar to that which originally motivated the Spartans to go to war (1.23). In Thucydides' presentation, at least, Athens and Sparta overlapped in their ideals of courage: they prized decisive action, power over others, and the eradication of fear. These ideals, I think, led to the Athenians' suspicion of "too much" free speech. We now see, as a result, that their ideals of *andreia* played a central role in causing both the disastrous Peloponnesian War and the notorious Sicilian Expedition. The war need not have taken place. But the primacy of *andreia* helped to create a panhellenic culture of political mistrust and fear in which fires were seen everywhere—which, supposedly, courage alone could quench.[44]

Distrust between Athens and Sparta was mirrored by distrust within Athens. Thucydides makes clear that by the time of the Sicilian Debate, the Athenians had begun to mistrust their leaders, especially the extravagant Alcibiades.[45] Like the city itself, Alcibiades was a self-indulgent and aggressive seeker of power and honor—a leader with no respect for equality (6.16). This would not have been a shocking development to Aristotle.

---

[44] Cf. Elster 2002: 11–13.
[45] 6.15; Balot 2001a: 136–78; Orwin 1994: 180.

In his critique of imperialism, Aristotle wrote that an imperialist policy teaches individual citizens that they should form the goal of ruling their own cities as tyrants (*Pol.* 1333b31-33). Foreign policy helps to educate the desires and self-understanding of the citizenry, which in turn shape foreign policy, in a sort of "negative feedback loop"—especially in the free and open political culture of democratic Athens. By virtue of the seemingly inexorable workings of its own manly courage, the Athenian democracy was coming to be a polis at war with itself. It began to resemble, not only militaristic Sparta, but also the most famous of all civil-war-ridden cities in Thucydides' *History*—Corcyra—where the problem of trust had been especially acute.[46]

If the Athenians subscribed to a polarized vision of freedom and tyranny, and if they imprudently educated their aspiring leaders to cherish tyrannical ambitions, and if their ideals of masculinity tended to shut down free discourse, then the Periclean ideology of thoughtful, deliberative courage was undermined from within, from the very practices of imperialism itself. Imperialistic aggression had the tendency sharply to reduce the efficacy of democratic courage, even if, paradoxically, democratic courage had helped to make the Athenians' imperialistic aggression successful in the first place. None of this demonstrates, by itself, that imperialism is intrinsically wrong. But Thucydides' critical examination of democratic imperialism strongly suggests that imperialism threatens the ideals of democracy. The proper corrective would appear to be a firmer commitment to freedom and equality at home, derived from a more flexible and thoughtful, and correspondingly less polarized and less competitive, conception of freedom and masculinity.

Conclusion: Thucydides and Athenian Imperialism

Thucydides offered a profound critique of Athens's democracy and imperialism—a critique that we have appreciated through examining the city's competing ideals of *andreia*. On their own behalf, the Athenians themselves argued that they were more moderate imperialists than they had to be: they went to law (in Athens, admittedly) when disputes arose with their subjects, and they treated their subjects more equally than the facts of their power demanded (1.76–77). They said that they were worthy to rule (2.41.3). And, to some extent, they enacted their democratic ideals

---

[46] Cf. Orwin 1994: 175–82.

by adhering to Pericles' "island strategy" and by revising their initially harsh judgment of the Mytilenians (3.36). All the same, at Cleon's insistence, they eventually executed 1000 Mytilenians and distributed land on Lesbos —apart from the Methymnians'—to Athenian shareholders (Thuc. 3.50). They also imposed harsh penalties on other cities, such as Scione (5.32) and Torone (5.2). Eventually, in their Sicilian venture, they proved themselves to be, not thoughtful agents of Pericles' novel democratic courage, but rather, as the Corinthians had charged, "bold beyond their capacity" (*para dunamin tolmētai*, 1.70.3) and likely to "run risks contrary to good judgment" (*para gnōmēn kinduneutai*, 1.70.3).

Despite the Athenians' imprudence and injustice, a number of recent scholars have shown a certain sympathy with the Athenians' own self-assessment as "mild" imperialists.[47] While it may be true that the Athenians were more moderate than other ancient imperialists, such as the Hellenistic Kings or the Romans, it is also the case that the Sicilian expedition was a fiasco, that the citizens themselves turned against one another in two civil wars (411 BC and 404 BC), and that Athens lost the Peloponnesian War. Thucydides' critique of Athenian *andreia* and overreaching is to that extent well founded. This critique was elaborated by Plato's investigation of the paradoxes of *logos* and *ergon*, "word and deed," to which we now turn.

---

[47] Forsdyke 2005: 206; Strauss 2009; Low 2005; Herman 2006: 360–73.

CHAPTER 6 | Democratic Courage and the Platonic *Laches*

WITH PLATO'S SHORT TEXT *Laches*, we return to the foundations of our inquiry—the distilled version of the Athenian ideology found in Pericles' funeral oration. In this brief dialogue, Socrates explores courage in the company of two Athenian generals, Nicias and Laches. The conversation gives Plato the opportunity to investigate critically the Athenian claim to unify apparently antithetical attributes in a uniquely democratic way— "opposites" such as reason and emotion, *andreia* and *sōphrosunē* (courage and moderation), daring and intellectual understanding, care for the city and care for the household.[1] In the present case Plato directs attention to the crucial relationship between *logos* and *ergon* (speech and deed): a well-known antithesis in fifth-century Athenian culture at large, and one of great consequence for the Athenian understanding of courage in particular. Among the canonical Greek virtues, courage provides a unique invitation to meditate upon the *logos/ergon* relationship, since its sphere of application is precisely that of carrying out deeds, in frightening circumstances and thus with difficulty, in accordance with one's basic ideals and preexisting commitments. According to Thucydides, the Corinthians said at Sparta, "No one can reflect upon things and pursue them in action with the same confidence; instead, we formulate opinions in safety and then fall short in the event because of our fear" (1.120.5). By contrast, the Athenians had claimed to unify "word" and "deed," "reason" and "action," in their project of developing a distinctive ideal of democratic courage. They had thereby

---

[1] On the "reconciliation of traditional opposites" in Athenian ideology, see the interesting reflections of Mills 1997: 70–75 and Manville 1997, along with the earlier discussion in chapter 2.

transcended the standard antithesis between *logos* and *ergon*. The question was whether their ideological self-image was genuinely embodied in their practices and in the lives of their leading statesmen.

The *Laches* has been the subject of renewed critical interest in recent years, both from the quarter of analytic philosophy and from that of literary criticism and history. Philosophers have vigorously debated the so-called priority of definition, the unity of the virtues, and the place of the *Laches* in the development of Platonic thinking about courage, Socrates, and his own developing corpus.[2] Contextual critics have emphasized *parrhēsia* as one of Plato's key democratic "entanglements,"[3] and have focused on the introduction of Socrates into Athens's cultural life,[4] as well as Plato's literary techniques in subtly hinting at the true, but hidden, definition of courage.[5] In the present chapter I draw on these different methodologies in order to offer a different interpretation of Plato's presentation of the setting, characterizations, and argumentation of the dialogue. Few have recognized the close connections between Plato's dialogue and the Athenian

---

[2] See Santas 1969; Devereux 1977; Woodruff 1987; Irwin 1995: 18–19, 40–41, passim; Beversluis 2000; Hobbs 2000: esp. 68–74 is particularly useful in its attention to the gender implications of Plato's treatment of the so-called manly virtue. For an interesting, although finally unpersuasive, argument about chronology, see Vlastos 1981. Cullyer 2003 examines the Stoics' reception of the questions raised but, as she argues, not answered by the *Laches*.

[3] Monoson 2000: esp. 154–61.

[4] The dialogue's lengthy introduction shows that Socrates is being introduced into Athenian culture as a sympathetic, nonadversarial figure with ties to important families and healthy relationships with political leaders. This is the burden of Emlyn-Jones's useful article (especially Emlyn-Jones 1999: 130–38); cf. Michelini 2000: 63. Since the dramatic date of the dialogue is between 421–418 BC, this introduction contrasts sharply with Socrates' portrayal in the would-be contemporary *Clouds* of Aristophanes, which was first produced in 423. On these points, see Hoerber 1968: 95–97; Schmid 1992: 61; Emlyn-Jones 1999: 125. *Clouds* was first produced in 423 BC, but the version of it we have is partially revised and probably was never performed: see Dover 1968: lxxx–xcvii on the complications of the tradition of scholarship, going back to the ancient world, on the problem of the two versions.

[5] See especially Schmid 1992; Emlyn-Jones 1999; Michelini 2000; Blitz 1975. See also the interpretations offered by O'Brien 1963 and Hoerber 1968, both of which ultimately derive from Bonitz 1886: 210–26. See, finally, the synthetic approach of Stokes 1986. Woodruff 1987: 111–13 offers a helpful overview of previous interpretations. Avramenko 2011: 138 focuses his interpretation on the sons of Lysimachus and Melesias, arguing that "[t]heir courage, which may be the result of nothing more than being treated as equals in the discourse, will enable them to participate in the hunt for the right teacher, the right weapon, the right battle, and, importantly, the hunt for justice. It [sic] will endow them with political courage, which is an absolute and permanent good." It is unclear precisely what [their courage?] will "endow them with political courage," but, even more importantly, it is unclear how the understanding of courage as "an absolute and permanent good" can be squared with the radical historicism and thus relativism of Avramenko's account of courage in general: "If the reader finds one of the types of courage preferable to another, then as much is revealed about the reader's cares and political commitments as about courage" (Avramenko 2011: 20).

ideology that we have reconstructed.[6] Yet this dialogue opens up clear and forceful lines of attack on the epistemic sophistication and civic versatility that democracy claimed for itself, particularly in relation to courage.

Alert readers will immediately recognize Plato's interrogation of the democratic system, even on the text's surface. Most obviously, Socrates questions Lysimachus' default position that voting, rather than further argumentation and expert insight, is the way to solve controversies between speakers (184c9–d6). Socrates reiterates his familiar "*technē*-criticism" of democracy: in other important areas of life, people rely on expert opinion rather than majority vote, so why not in politics? More specifically, the author's critique of Athenian democracy was conditioned by Thucydides' own reflections on Athens.[7] Many have plausibly seen an allusion to Thucydides in the suggestion that Nicias's definition of courage appears to lead, unhappily, to the view that soothsayers are the only genuinely courageous individuals (195e1–4). Ironically foreshadowing Nicias's culpable mistakes in Sicily, Socrates admonishes him, a few years (as it were) before the fact, that the general and not the soothsayer is in charge of warfare (198e2–199a3).[8] The role of "history," or *erga*, as exemplified in the lives of these generals is critical to an appreciation of Plato's exploration of courage.

Several earlier students of the *Laches* have centered their interpretations on the *logos/ergon* relationship, arguing that Plato uses this and other dichotomies to hint at his deeper meaning—that *logos* and *ergon* must be united to produce courage, and that the appropriate unification can be found in the person of Socrates.[9] On the other hand, Socrates disclaims knowledge of what courage is and thus proves, in his own right, to be out of harmony with himself as regards *logos* and *ergon* (199e, cf. 193de). The most complete exemplar of the Athenian ideal as enunciated by Pericles—that is, apparently, albeit paradoxically, Socrates—lacks

---

[6] Reading Plato in the context of democratic Athens has a long history that has recently been invigorated by conversations between historians and political theorists. See, for example, Ober 1998: 156–247. Many political theorists have come to reject the idea that Plato was antidemocratic: Monoson 1994b; Saxonhouse 1996: 87–114; Euben 1996.

[7] Monoson 1998 has plausibly argued that the *Menexenus*, likewise, refers both to the actual democracy and to the democracy as it is represented by Thucydides.

[8] Thucydides says that when the Athenian forces had their last chance to escape from Sicily, and were on the brink of leaving, Nicias delayed the army because of religious anxieties brought on by a nocturnal eclipse; he was in the thrall of the soothsayers (7.50). See further Schmid 1992: 8–9, O'Brien 1963: 143–44.

[9] See especially Bonitz 1886; O'Brien 1963; and Hoerber 1968; for criticism of this excessively neat picture, see Emlyn-Jones 1999: 128–29; Michelini 2000: 65.

conviction about his own embodiment of that ideal. Far from confidently laying claim to his own superior brand of courage, Socrates displays a novel form of self-consciousness in relation to *logos* and *ergon*; Socratic self-consciousness consists in the perpetual self-auditing that renders *logos* and *ergon*, and therewith courage, unstable. Perhaps this dissatisfaction with oneself is the proper orientation toward the mysteries of courage as a unification of *logos* and *ergon*. This is why Socrates finishes by encouraging everyone, and agreeing himself, to continue studying courage along with the sons of the Lysimachus and Melesias (201ab). We are left with the central difficulty of courage: not only how to produce *erga* that are reliably in accord with correct *logoi*, but also, and more profoundly, whether *logoi* themselves are capable of producing such *erga*.

Educating Leaders in the Democratic Polis

In the opening scene, the old man Lysimachus says that he has invited the prominent generals Laches and Nicias to watch the display of a certain Stesilaus, who claims to be a teacher of *hoplomachia* (fighting in heavy armor). As he says frankly but with a certain embarrassment, he and his friend Melesias are uncertain about educating their sons so as to make them worthy namesakes of their grandfathers, the famous statesmen Aristides the Just and Thucydides the son of Melesias. The opening scene emphasizes the visual spectacle they have just witnessed. Lysimachus and Melesias have asked the generals Nicias and Laches to be their "fellow spectators" at Stesilaus' demonstration. "Someone" (*tis*, 179e1)—a notably anonymous "someone" for such an important subject as their sons' education—had encouraged the two doddering fathers to attend such a spectacle, and they thought it best to invite Laches and Nicias to come along as *suntheatas* and *sumboulous* (fellow spectators and advisors: 179e4–6). The old men are ready to accept the advice of anyone.

Yet, as the aged scion of a glorious family, Lysimachus has access to the Athenian leadership and is disposed to ask the generals to be his fellow counselors (*sumbouloi*) in the care (*epimeleia*) of their sons. In particular, he wants to hear their opinions on whether *hoplomachia* would make their sons worthy of their famous names. There follows a set of paired speeches by Laches and Nicias, which formally resemble sophistic *antilogiai* and the paired speeches central to Thucydides' presentation of Athenian democracy. The two old men are in the position of the Athenian audience—spectators of speeches. When the generals disagree, and when

Lysimachus asks for Socrates' vote on the question, Socrates makes his first real contribution to the argument. He proposes that they first need to win clarity on the real subject of their conversation, that is, how to make the boys virtuous. A precondition of bringing that subject into focus, in this case, Socrates argues, is being able to say what courage is.[10] The Athenian Assembly had never gotten to the core of such questions so clearly or easily.

The uneducated fathers' search for an adviser is a paradigmatic scene of how one should, or should not, choose an adviser for oneself and, by extension, an educator for one's children. Their premise is that the two generals are worthy advisers in the education of young men, by contrast with the apparently unfamiliar Socrates, whose credentials must be set out at length by Laches and Nicias (180b7–181b4). For Lysimachus, Laches and Nicias can form good judgments and then state their opinions directly (*haplōs*) (178b7–8). Since they have young sons, he explains, they probably have given some thought to their education, or at least ought to have done so (179a8–b6, cf. 187c5–d1). These statements are superficially plausible, but both turn out to be false. As we will see, the generals, however forthright, are also anything but simple and direct in saying what they think, primarily because they do not have a self-conscious and articulate grasp of precisely what they think.

More importantly, though, these generals have not given special thought to their sons' education. Upon reflection, in fact, these are odd arguments for Lysimachus to make. As he goes on to say, his own father, Aristides, and Melesias' father, Thucydides, were both too busy attending to the affairs of others to care for their sons' education. Aristides and Thucydides were evidently successful in balancing different sets of antithetical duties: they accomplished a great deal in war and a great deal in peace (179c4) and they managed the affairs of both the allies and the city (179c4–5). But they could not, it appears, unite their political successes with attention to the education of their own sons, who ran wild as youths and are now ashamed of their thin records of accomplishment. They could not unite attention to public affairs with appropriate care for their own families. Why, then, should Lysimachus think that *other* men of affairs, such as Laches and Nicias, would be capable of uniting political activity with appropriate care for *their* families?

---

[10] This search for definitions is of course a very familiar Socratic move and need not be considered destructive, or at least wholly so: see Irwin 1995: 20–29.

One reason, perhaps, is that the prevailing ideology of democratic Athens said that Athenian leaders were capable of just such a unification of their duties. In the midst of his celebration of Athens in the *epitaphios*, Pericles says that, by contrast with other states, the Athenians' leaders are uniquely capable of uniting apparently antithetical attributes in their own persons. Their singular capacity for uniting opposites redounds to the glory of both Athens and themselves. "In the same men there is care (*epimeleia*) for both household and political affairs and those engaged in private work form judgments about politics that are not inadequate" (2.40.2).[11] Judging by the dramatic "evidence" provided in the opening scene, we can immediately recognize that Pericles' ideal does not correspond closely to the lived experience of Athenian leaders. Pericles' words do not correspond to the deeds of the Athenian leaders. Nor could Aristides and Thucydides the general take care of both the city and their sons. Their successful imperialism made care for the household impossible (cf. chapter 12).

Laches himself confirms this point: "What Lysimachus said just now about his own father and Melesias' seems to me very well spoken, both with regard to them, to us, and to all who manage the affairs of the city—that, as he says, we usually give short shrift to our private affairs and neglect them, both the children and other things" (180b1–7). Even Socrates alludes to this point during the lead-in to his elenchus of Laches: if the generals are too busy with the city's affairs to educate young men, then they should tell us whom to approach as a teacher (186e6–187a6). These criticisms might come as a surprise to readers of the Platonic *Meno* (94a–e). There Socrates argues that Thucydides and Aristides *did* give their sons the best Athenian education available to the wealthy, but those sons still managed, eventually, to lack virtue—evidence, he declares, that virtue cannot be taught. But perhaps the lesson is the same after all. The sons lacked virtue because their fathers failed to express the virtues of caring for their households properly.

There is an unspoken irony in this scene. At least with regard to the education of one's sons, or of children in general, there *should* be no distinction between caring for the city and caring for one's household. The distinction is not warranted. How could someone better or more appropriately care for the city than by ensuring that young men acquire courage and the other virtues? Isn't care for the city that lacks care for education a

---

[11] On the interpretation of this passage, see Edmunds 1972; Rusten 1985; Hornblower 1991: 304–5.

manifestly inadequate form of care for the city?[12] The unifications imagined by Pericles are interdependent: being appropriately disposed toward *logos* and *ergon* depends upon the appropriate relations between public and private, reason and emotion, "word" and "deed." But the public/private distinction at Athens is in disarray. If the sons of Aristides and Thucydides, architects of mid-fifth-century Athenian growth, power, and stability, are ill-educated *apragmones*, then what can we expect of the citizenry at large? At all events, the democratic education to courage and the other excellences does not occur spontaneously or simply by growing up in the democratic polis.

A Spectacular Education?

By his own criteria, Lysimachus has already chosen bad educational advisers. Now, the generals interpret the spectacle they have just seen. Structurally, the scene reproduces, and thus invites us to evaluate, spectatorship and voting based on deliberation as the means to arrive at credible decisions. The first word of the dialogue is *tetheasthe* (you have seen). Plato emphasizes spectatorship and its role in decision making in the dialogue's early exchanges. The verb *theaomai* and its cognates and associated nouns, such as *suntheates* and *thea*, appear nine times before the elenchus begins (178a twice, 179e four times, 181a8, 183d1, 183d3) and twice thereafter (188d1, 197c2). How should we interpret the spectacle of Stesilaus' *hoplomachia* in a way that makes sense for the education of young men? In their efforts to respond to that question, Laches and Nicias tie themselves into the knots of *logos* and *ergon*. Their epistemological problems and their frequent self-contradictions are evident primarily to Plato's readers. We are aware of both other evidence and other events that postdate the dramatic date of the dialogue, while this knowledge is unavailable to those who desperately need to know, Lysimachus and Melesias.

Plato was engaged with the democratic belief that watching public spectacles, especially in the theater, was a key mode of civic education (cf. chapters 12 and 13).[13] Plato made the generals both fellow audience members (*suntheatai*) and fellow counselors (*sumbouloi*). He staged Nicias and Laches as spectators and counselors in order to reveal the underlying

---

[12] Cf. Blitz 1975: 189–91; Dobbs 1986: 830–31.
[13] The bibliography here is vast: most recently, one might look to Too 2001, especially the contributions of Griffith and Ober; the essays collected in Euben 1986c; and the essays collected in Winkler and Zeitlin 1990.

nature and quality of their characters. Keep in mind that Socratic conversation concerns the character and lives of his interlocutors, instead of or in addition to the ostensible, and typically abstract, intellectual subject of the discussion (187e6–188a3). This is a broad invitation to consider the characters of the men involved when we hear how they interpret the spectacle of *hoplomachia*.

"Staging" Nicias

After watching the display, Nicias argues that studying with the likes of Stesilaus could be beneficial to young men because the *hoplomachia* requires hard exercise and the acquisition of technical skills that are useful in combat (182ab). Students in this subject will be inspired to learn other, more architectonic skills, such as how to organize a fighting unit and how to be a general (182bc). A further advantage, he mentions off-handedly, is that this skill will make a man more daring (*tharraleōteron*) and courageous (*andreioteron*) in battle (182c6). Nicias concludes by citing a final advantage: that studying *hoplomachia* will improve a young man's appearance and thus make him more "terrible" (*deinoteros*) to the enemy (182cd). Nicias' discussion of these educational benefits includes no clear organization, no analysis, and no account of how these presumed advantages fit together, if indeed they do, into a logical whole.

Several features of Nicias' speech are striking. First, its conclusion is incompatible with his later attempt to define courage as "knowledge of what is fearful and encouraging both in war and in all other circumstances" (194e11–195a1). In offering this definition, Nicias refers to an appropriate grasp of ideals of excellence—one quite similar to Pericles' definition of courage, in fact—rather than practical and technical forms of knowledge.[14] In his interpretation of Stesilaus, by contrast, Nicias presents technical skill as being capable of making someone more courageous; but, to say the least, it is unclear how technical skill could possibly be equivalent to the knowledge of "value," or how Stesilaus could possibly impart this more essential knowledge to his students. As we saw in chapter 2, technical knowledge of the sort evoked by Nicias is incomplete without the addition of this further, typologically different, and more profound knowledge of "value."

---

[14] Sharples 1983.

Second, Nicias should have known as much. For he later distinguished carefully between the soothsayer and the truly courageous individual. He pointed out that the soothsayer may know what will come to pass, but he does not know, as (Nicias argues) the courageous individual must, whether future events, such as death or disease or victory or defeat, are good or bad for someone (195e8–196a3). Nicias' denigration of the soothsayer's knowledge depends on his awareness, however dim, that courage must be appropriately located in a eudaimonistic framework. Is courage, along with its consequences, good for the individual? This is the kind of understanding that the democratic city claimed to offer its citizens, but one could hardly learn as much from Stesilaus, or Nicias. Nicias' initial equation, or at least homogenizing, of the adjectives "daring" and "courageous" violates his later, and better informed, distinction between the two.

Third, in light of his later definitions, Nicias' interpretation must be rated a failure, and a surprisingly absurd one at that: it fails to mention any empirical facts about, or relevant to, Stesilaus or his display. As we will see, the use of empirical facts is the forte of his interlocutor Laches. Nicias apparently had not heard of what a ridiculous spectacle Stesilaus had once made of himself by trying to use an innovative "scythe-spear" in a mock naval battle (183c–184a). Nicias' *logoi* are contradictory because he lacks knowledge of *erga* and fails to appreciate their significance in thinking through practical problems. His ineffective, sophistical approach mirrors that of Stesilaus himself.[15]

To make these points differently, Nicias fails to acknowledge that the subject at hand, really, is not *hoplomachia*, but rather the training of young men's souls (185c2–4).[16] Even if he can utter the sentence that virtue is wisdom, or something of the sort, Nicias cannot translate this highly generalized abstraction into useful advice in the present situation. He lacks appreciation of the particulars of this situation. He cannot recognize clearly what the present situation demands in light of Lysimachus' and Melesias' goals. Rather than deriving his ideas from scrutiny of his own psychology and experience, Nicias unreflectively believes what he hears from others, such as Damon (197d, 200b). But hearing abstract definitions of the virtues—even if they come from Damon or the like, and even if

---

[15] For a development of this parallel, see Gonzalez 1998; cf. Hoerber 1968: 99–100, who contrasts Socrates with Stesilaus and compares Stesilaus with both Nicias and Laches on the grounds that their words do not match their deeds.

[16] Benitez 2000 makes the interesting suggestion that the "image of fighting in armor" is meant "to represent cowardice," with a view to helping "us to choose and appraise actions on the basis of what is essential rather than what is accidental" (Benitez 2000: 85).

they are somehow true—is useless unless one understands how those *logoi* about courage can be translated into *erga*. Nicias is no more an expert than Lysimachus because he is incapable of understanding the connections between his military experiences and the account (*logos*) of courage that he has heard from others.

If we apply this characterization of Nicias to our knowledge of the historical Athenian leader, then we can gain a clearer understanding of Plato's purposes. For Nicias, serving as general in Sicily, abstract *logoi* connecting courage with knowledge failed to make possible appropriate *erga*; Nicias was muddled about how to proceed after the Athenians' final defeat in the Sicilian harbor, when the necessity of a quick retreat seemed obvious.[17] Nicias's presentation in the dialogue, therefore, constitutes a substantial argument for the importance of the step-by-step process of Socratic dialectic in coming to understand the truth.[18] The idea is that we need to work through abstract definitions in order to appreciate their complexity and inner logic, as well as their connections with the empirical world. Nicias has not received this sort of education from the debates of the Athenian Assembly or from the theater. Perhaps Cleon was right to criticize the Athenian demos for being "spectators of *logoi* and merely hearers of deeds" (3.38.4), and for being more like the audience of a sophist than the political body sitting in Assembly (3.38.7).[19]

Keep in mind, too, that Nicias' speeches before the Sicilian expedition, as recounted in Thucydides (6.9–14, 6.20–23), both failed to issue in appropriate *erga*. In his first speech, he tried to persuade the Athenians not to sail at all; in his second, he deceptively tried to dissuade the Athenians from undertaking the expedition by proposing that they outfit an outlandishly huge armada for Sicily (see Thuc. 6.8–24).[20] But nothing stopped them. In the dialogue as in life, his *logoi*, self-contradictory in themselves,

---

[17] Nicias' indecisiveness and muddled strategic thinking are central themes of Thucydides Book 7; see especially 7.48. On Nicias in this dialogue and his relationship to the Thucydidean Nicias, see Schmid 1992: 6–11, 168–69.

[18] For Plato's attempt to encourage his readers to undertake the dialectic for themselves, see Benitez 2000.

[19] On Cleon and the language of spectatorship, see, among others, Goldhill 1999. In constructing his Kallipolis, Plato famously rejected mimetic poetry and felt anxiety that audiences of tragedy and comedy would be wrongly educated and sensitized by what they saw on stage. In the *Laws*, Plato extended this worry by voicing regret over democratic citizen audiences' tendency to arrogate to themselves, not only the right to judge dramatic competitions, but also to become *arbitres elegantiae*, with disastrous consequences both for aesthetic taste and for the political order. On the idea of "theatrocracy" in Plato and in general, see, for example, Wallace 1997.

[20] On Nicias' speeches before the expedition, see Balot 2001a: 164–72.

do not issue in the appropriate *erga* of courage when a close connection between the two would have been most meaningful for the city.

Uncovering the Character of General Laches

Laches offers an entertaining rebuttal of Nicias's position, based on his well-known "simplicity" (*haploun to g'emon*, 188c). In interpreting the spectacle, to begin with, Laches appeals to familiar empirical facts, noting that the Lacedaimonians, renowned land warriors, do not train by staging *hoplomachiai*. They would do so, he argues, if *hoplomachia* had any real merit as an educational tool. But the fact is that no self-proclaimed expert in *hoplomachia* has ever succeeded as an actual hoplite (182e–183c), while Stesilaus has shown himself to be a buffoon (183c–184a). Unlike Nicias, Laches stands up for the evidentiary primacy of *ergon* over *logos*. He judges that whether a man is brave or cowardly, he will end up being an object of ridicule for claiming to possess special technical knowledge of *hoplomachia* (184bc). Laches is aware, but only dimly so, that the conversation should be about courage and cowardice, not *hoplomachia*. But he needs more complex *logoi* to make sense of his knowledge of *erga*.

Laches is introduced as a general attached to *ergon*. Using the language of spectating (*etheasamēn*, 181a8), for example, Laches argued that Socrates merited a part in the discussion because he remained levelheaded at the battle of Delium and helped to maintain the reputation of his father as well as helping to "set straight" (*orthounta*) his polis (180a7–b4). Later, Laches explained his ambivalence toward philosophical discussions by saying that he was annoyed by those whose words do not match their deeds, but delighted when he listens to a speaker whose deeds justify his noble words. "For when I hear a man talking about virtue or some other kind of wisdom, someone who is truly a man and worthy of what he says, I am very delighted, seeing (*theōmenos*) that the speaker and his words are suitable to one another and harmonious" (188c6–d2). Hence, although he does not know what Socrates will say, and has no experience of Socrates' words (*tōn men logōn ouk empeiros eimi*, 188e), his experience of Socrates' courage, he says, has convinced him that Socrates is "worthy" of "fine words" (*logōn kalōn*) and "every frankness" (*pasēs parrhēsias*, 188e5–189a1).

Eventually, we learn that Laches prizes deeds over words in an extreme and confused way. Laches fails to appreciate the role of *logos*, or intellectual understanding, in constituting the virtue of courage. He appears to believe that *logos* is inessential to courage. Courage consists in deeds and is knowable by experience, whereas *logos* can only ever amount to banal, traditional praise of this virtue.

In saying that a Doric harmony of words and deeds is crucial to credibility (188d), Laches presumes that he knows already which words will be forthcoming. Socrates has earned the privilege of speaking "fine words" about courage. But are those words nothing more than traditional praise, such as "Courage is a noble possession"? Because he judges Socrates' and others' courage on the basis of their deeds, in advance, Laches is certain that courageous men will live up in deed, or have already lived up in deed, to such "fine words." But how can Laches be certain that someone who behaves courageously will speak words that are worthy of his deeds? It would seem necessary to evaluate "fine words" independently — on the basis of their own merits, that is, which can only mean on the basis of their truth, and not on the basis of the speaker's record.

What is more, if the presumptively courageous agent cannot speak words that are worthy of his deeds, then are his deeds worthy of "fine words" in the first place? The Athenians' reflective ideal of courage would lead them to say "no" in response to this question. Genuinely courageous action requires a complex grasp of why, how, and when one should act courageously—a deep grasp of what courageous action is for, and why it is a meaningful constituent of a citizen's *eudaimonia*. Only *that* sort of courageous action, the kind that is already penetrated by an adequate *logos*, is "worthy" of "fine words." Is Laches himself in a good position to judge which actions are courageous, which actions are worthy of fine words, when he himself, as we now see, can hardly speak coherently about courage?[21]

It turns out, to be sure, that Laches might "have a share of courage" (*andreias metechein*; 193e); and the world might therefore praise his deeds; but his words are certainly inadequate to his deeds (193e).[22] He cannot explain why he has been led so easily to agree that "foolish endurance" (*aphrona karterēsin*, 193d) is courage, when in fact he believes that courage is fine and noble. Laches may be entitled to speak "fine words" but he is incapable of doing so. If he is incapable of speaking fine words,

---

[21] Benitez 2000: 94–97 makes interesting and related remarks about courage from a Hegelian perspective.
[22] Blitz 1975: 195 makes this very interesting point: "One reason the dialogue is named after Laches is that Socrates' eventual opening of Laches to the genuine priority of speech is the central deed of the dialogue."

then he cannot adequately appreciate the nobility of his own courage. As Laches himself puts it, he "seems to himself" to understand courage, but he cannot articulate his understanding (194b).

Prior to this conversation, in fact, Laches had failed to appreciate the difficulty involved in speaking words adequate to his deeds. In fact, he later insists that "wisdom" (*sophia*) is "certainly distinct" (*chōris dēpou*) from courage; to speak differently, like Nicias, is to babble (195ab). Laches is hostile to the Athenians' logocentric understanding of courage. Only soothsayers know "what is to be dreaded and what is to be dared" (195e; cf. 198e–199a). Laches even insists that wild animals (*ta thēria*, 197a) are courageous (*andreia*, 197a), "as everyone agrees," even though ancient Greeks typically distinguished between humanity and animals precisely by appealing to human beings' possession of *logos*. Laches the Athenian is the ultimate *misologos*.[23]

Does Laches then have the *erga* to back up his *logoi*, or to speak fine words in praise of courage? Since Laches argues vigorously for the primacy of *erga* over *logoi*, he must assume that his *erga* (at least) are adequate, assuming that he wishes to offer advice without hypocrisy. As Socrates says of the generals, "They never would have spoken so fearlessly about the practices that are good and bad for a young man, unless they were confident that they had sufficient knowledge" (186d1–3). But there are hints that Laches' own *erga* may not have been adequate. Even as Laches praises Socrates, he does not say what he himself was doing during the retreat after Delium. According to Alcibiades in the *Symposium*, however, Socrates was much calmer than Laches, and his courage, exemplified by his unmistakable swagger, enabled him to save Laches and other fellow citizens (*Symp.* 220d–221b). Using Laches' own assumptions about the evidentiary priority of deeds, we might question Laches' title to speak on courage in the present conversation.

Of course, only a well informed reader of Plato's dialogues would make that connection—the key pieces of knowledge (the *logoi* of Laches' *erga*) are unavailable to Lysimachus and Melesias. Even so, Alcibiades offered his *logos* while drunk and while eulogizing Socrates by contrast with Laches. His *logos* was anything but innocent. And it was based only on his own interpretation of another spectacle, the retreat from Delium. Alcibiades' interpretations are subject to further re-evaluation in the light

---

[23] Hence I am less optimistic about Laches' character than is Dobbs 1986: 828–29; cf. O'Brien 1963: 138; Michelini 2000: 66.

of other evidence. Quite a lot is happening behind the scenes in the *Laches*. For a reader aware of his dramatic cues, Plato powerfully dramatizes the ignorance and vulnerability of those in Lysimachus' situation, and, more broadly, of those asked to vote democratically on the basis of *logoi* that consist of the interpretations of *erga*. Those who need advice are in a quandary because there is no one available to advise them on who should advise them.[24] When the advice concerns courage, this quandary is especially acute because of the intimate relationship between *logos* and *ergon* in the practice of courage. This intensity took on special meaning in the context of the Athenian democracy, where speech was said to be a crucial prerequisite to the implementation of decisions, or, in short, to action.[25]

Still other questions can be raised about Laches' adequacy in deed. As Schmid has argued, Laches' record at the battle of Mantineia, although obscure, may have been less than honorable.[26] Along with Argive and other allied commanders, Laches made the decision to give up a fortified position on a hill and advance into the plain of Mantineia to fight the Spartans, partly in reaction to the grumbling of the soldiers. He did this even though he emphasized, in his initial rebuttal of Nicias, that the Spartans are the best hoplites of all. Whether or not Socrates makes an allusion to Mantineia in his elenchus, Laches' behavior there, as far as we can tell, did not do credit to himself or to his city. Laches' character flaws were enduring. In the Platonic drama that unfolds before us, Laches fails to persevere in the discussion after Nicias gets the better of him, and he is inspired more by *philonikia* (194a8) than by a resolute search for the truth. He ridicules Nicias for proposing that courage is wisdom (195a). He is defensive about his own *aporia* (196b). Yet Socrates has indicated that one sign of courage is the resolve to persevere in the pursuit of understanding courage, in the face of courage's elusiveness and despite the participants' murkiness as to how to proceed (194a1–5).[27] Laches is neither steadfast

---

[24] On certain paradoxes in giving advice, as presented by this dialogue, see Blitz 1975: 185–89, along with Machiavelli's *The Prince*, chapters 22–23.

[25] On the ways in which democratic speech might be thought, in its own right, to constitute action, see Ober 1998: 27–40, 53–62.

[26] Schmid 1992: 13–15.

[27] Hobbs 2000: 76–112 (on *Laches* in particular) and 235–49 (on *Republic*, and in general) proposes, along with many others (e.g., Benitez 2000: 88–89), that Plato represents philosophical courage, as opposed to military or civic courage, as the new ideal, and that philosophical courage consists in large part in searching after the truth despite difficulties and obstacles. On courage as resisting fear of uncertainty, and thus as a kind of philosophical endurance or judicial firmness or both, as suggested by the *Laches*, see Dobbs 1986.

nor wise; he certainly lacks wisdom because he lacks steadfastness (197e); perhaps he also lacks steadfastness because he lacks *logos* (196bc, 197cd).

Combined with these hints about his inadequacy, Laches' emphasis on the significance of deeds undercuts his ability to act as an advisor. After Laches fails to give an adequate account of courage, Socrates says, "Then you and I, Laches, are not in harmony in the Dorian mode, according to your own account, since our deeds do not agree with our words. For in action, it seems, someone would say that we have a share of courage, but not in speech, as I see it, if he heard us talking just now" (193d11–e4). Socrates is subtle in his criticisms; Nicias, by contrast, openly casts doubt on Laches' courage. At 197c2, Laches says, "Look (*theasai*), Socrates, how well this one adorns himself with words, as he thinks. But he is trying to take away the honorable title of courage from all those generally agreed to be courageous." Laches is talking about wild animals like lions, whom all men call *andreia*, as well as people like himself. To which Nicias responds: "No, not you, Laches; take heart (*tharrei*); for I think that you are wise, and Lamachus, and many other Athenians, if indeed (*eiper*) you are courageous" (197c5–7).

Nicias is being coldly ironic in this exchange. Student of Damon and purveyor of strange, apparently sophistical, theories about courage, Nicias emphatically does not view many Athenians as wise or courageous. Laches is obviously not wise. The particle *eiper*, which expresses the speaker's doubt about the conditional, perfectly captures Nicias' ironic stance, as does his use of the imperative *tharrei* (197c5). This is the *mot just* in the case of Laches, since Nicias has just said that "those [such as headstrong animals] which you and the many call *andreia*, I call *thrasea*," reserving the term *andreia* for those with good sense (*ta phronima*, 197b6–c1). Laches responds defensively and then retires from posing further questions to Nicias. Significantly, Laches urges Socrates to "see" what Nicias is doing; he insists that Socrates be a witness to Nicias' perversions of all ordinary opinions about what courage is and who best exemplifies it. But by now the empirically verifiable facts have ranged themselves against Laches. Nicias makes the strong point that courage is distinguished from boldness or rashness by prudence (*promēthias*, 197b; *ta phronima*, 197c). He does so even though he had earlier lumped together *tharsos* and *andreia* indiscriminately (182c). Nicias offers a comparatively compelling account of courage even though his deeds, as we know them from Thucydides, fail to justify his title to speak of courage at all.

Laches is a paradoxical figure. Although he lacks the deeds to buttress his arguments, he nonetheless produces good arguments to refute

Nicias' interpretation of the Stesilaus spectacle. His own most vivid argument derives from Stesilaus' once having made an unwitting exhibition of himself in actual combat conditions, almost literally hoisting himself on his own new-fangled petard. Fighting with an unusual scythe-spear, Stesilaus got his weapon caught in the rigging of an enemy ship, much to the amusement of both friend and foe. Of course, it is possible that Stesilaus is simply the victim of bad luck, rather than any lack of courage, but at an early stage in the argument the question is only whether studying with Stesilaus would be worthwhile, and the answer seems to be resoundingly negative. Though Laches' methodological premise that only those with deeds are qualified to speak disqualifies him from speaking, he is nonetheless a good speaker, at least at first. But in the course of the discussion he shows himself to lack the words that would make him either a speaker of words or a doer of deeds.

Laches' position therefore raises the specter of a quandary in which all advice seekers find themselves: if you know very little, like Lysimachus, then how can you find a good advisor in the first place? Once words and deeds are irrevocably pulled apart and shown to be contradictory, as they are in the speeches and lives of Nicias and Laches, then who can advise you on who can advise you? If Laches is paradoxical, and Nicias is self-contradictory, then Lysimachus is in a quandary. The generals' disagreement prompts him to call a vote—the typically democratic, pragmatic mode of making a decision and forging consensus about action in the face of conflict. But, as Socrates points out, a vote provides no necessary access to the truth or even to the best way forward (184de). This is the quandary from which democracy cannot extricate itself. Its leaders offer self-contradicting and self-undermining advice, which is sometimes good advice, sometimes bad, but the onus of judgment, and of discriminating between good and bad advice, falls on the ignorant. Through his ironies of *logos* and *ergon*, Plato is drawing attention to the quagmire in which democratic assemblies typically find themselves. The mass production of courageous citizens in democracy seems ever more elusive and unlikely. Socrates may be the democracy's best hope, but he is aware that he lacks words adequate to courage.

Socrates the Citizen?

If we turn again to Pericles' unification of apparent opposites, then further ironies of democratic courage come to light.[28] Plato emphasizes the contrast

---

[28] On this passage, see chapter 4, with Manville 1997.

between public and private in order to suggest that real-life Athenians are not capable of unifying apparent opposites in the way Pericles says they are. This point is designed to strike a major blow at Pericles' democratic vision of courage. Both characters, Nicias and Laches alike, fail to live up to Periclean ideals of democratic courage as enshrined in the funeral oration. They fail to do so because of their unsettled relationship to *logos* and *ergon*.

Pericles had touched on this point directly. According to Pericles, the democratic Athenians, by contrast with others, "do not think that words (*tous logous*) are harmful to deeds (*tois ergois*); instead, it is harmful not to be instructed in advance by argument (*logōi*) before going in deed (*ergōi*) to what is necessary. For we differ in this: that we ourselves, the same men, both dare the most and calculate about what we undertake; whereas for others ignorance brings boldness, and calculation hesitation. Those would rightly be judged most courageous who understand both the fearful and the pleasant and nevertheless (*dia tauta*) do not turn away from risks" (2.40.2–3).[29]

A number of interpreters, beginning with Meyer (1899), have argued that this passage anticipates Nicias' definition of courage as the "knowledge of what is fearful and encouraging both in war and in all other areas" (194e11–195a1). But Pericles' formulation is a biconditional depending on two participles, *gignōskontes* and *apotrepomenoi*: men must *both* know what is valuable *and* not turn away from risks. Pericles implicitly contrasts Athenians with Spartans on the grounds that Athenians are unusual in combining what are apparently two antithetical activities—calculating rationally and acting daringly.[30] This accounts for his repeated emphasis on *autoi* (the very same men), as if it were stunning that the very same men could love what is fine without growing soft, or take care of both public and private affairs, or reflect rationally on what is ethically significant and still stake everything on a fight to the death.

Whether self-consciously or not, Pericles was in the process of transforming traditional ideas about courage, according to which courage is derived from or equivalent to a strong character. He was infusing a subtle epistemological component into the conception of courage. Now, as Manville has elegantly demonstrated, democracy has a "both/and," rather than an "either/or," perspective on the ingredients required for outstanding

---

[29] I have treated the ambiguities of the translation in detail in chapter 2.
[30] See also Manville 1997 on Pericles' "both/and" strategy.

accomplishment within organizations and societies. In Pericles' vision, "the Athenian citizen incorporates a series of contradictory traits," which are expressed stylistically in the dense structure of antithesis and paradox that characterizes the funeral oration as a whole.[31] In Plato's dialogue, Laches inherits from the dominant democratic culture the very same insistence on making words match deeds. But Laches' devaluation of *logos* would be, to someone with Pericles' views, a fundamental flaw in his view of courage.

Laches first declares that courage is remaining at one's post (190e5–6). Afterward, he offers a revised definition according to which courage is "a certain steadfastness of soul" (*karteria tis...tēs psuchēs*, 192b9). Throughout the elenchus, he remains unsure whether the steadfastness should be wise or foolish if it is to be considered courage. His lack of clarity about the relationship among courage, technical knowledge, and the knowledge of "values" stands in stark contrast to the vision of democratic courage offered by Pericles. Pericles urges his audience to "gaze upon (*theōmenous*) the actual (*ergōi*) power of the city every day and become lovers of that power, and when it seems great to you, lay to heart that men (*andres*) acquired these things, daring (*tolmōntes*) and knowing what was necessary (*gignōskontes ta deonta*) and having a sense of shame in action (*en tois ergois aischunomenoi*)" (2.43.1). Becoming spectators of the city and its power is a source of education in a citizen's proper duties. Carrying out those duties requires both the daring character for which Athenians were famous, however they are supposed to have acquired it, and an understanding of what is at stake in their military risks. For Laches, by contrast, *logos* has no business preceding *ergon* or inhabiting the minds of those carrying out *erga*. In his view *logos* should occupy a position posterior to *ergon*, whereas in Pericles' view Athenians consider it harmful not to be "taught in advance" (*prodidachthēnai*) by words before going into action (2.40.2).

For Nicias, on the other hand, courage is knowledge (*epistēmē*, 195a1); but, as the ensuing argument shows, he cannot identify any marks that are peculiar to courage. In other words, he understands little of the distinctive nature of courage, which is, as Laches' comments suggest, strange to find in a statesman, though less so in a sophist (197d6–8). Judged by the standard of Pericles' ideal vision, Nicias' understanding of courage lacks the developed characterological components stressed by Pericles—daring

---

[31] Edmunds 1975: 46–47; cf. Kakridis 1961: 31; Parry 1988: 161.

and a sense of shame. In a little noticed, but significant, aside, Socrates proposes to Laches that, even though they are inharmonious thus far, perhaps they can accept that the courageous pursuit of philosophical understanding requires steadfastness in the search (194a1–5).[32] In the absence of secure knowledge about what courage is, the most proper sphere of courage, for Socrates, is that of persisting in the face of uncertainty about what courage itself looks like, and hoping still to find it, but emphatically not arriving at definite decisions based on ill-founded premises and arrogant ideological commitments. Both Laches and Nicias fail to endure the rigors of inquiry in the appropriate way: Laches because of his self-involved *philonikia* and pride (cf. 199e–200a), Nicias because he believes that his mistakes can be simply and directly repaired by his expert teacher Damon (200bc).

By comparing the words and deeds of these generals, we discover that the Athenians are unlikely to unite the apparently antithetical attributes of *gnōmē* and *tolma*. Plato depicts the shortcomings of Laches and Nicias as measured against the ideal vision of Pericles in order to suggest that the democracy is, in practice, unable to live up to, or even to understand, the highest expression of its own ideals. Laches and Nicias are exemplary of traditional confusions over word and deed, rather than a novel synthesis of these "opposites." Democratic deliberation leads nowhere. Lysimachus and Melesias are bound to repeat their ancestors' patterns, or worse.

On the other hand, the Athenians' goal of unifying these apparently antithetical attributes—in other words, their ideal of courage itself—has not been entirely discredited by this dialogue. To the contrary, this ideal seems to be best exemplified by the person of Socrates.[33] By the end of the dialogue, Socrates stands alone. He does not have a suitable definition of courage to offer, but he recognizes the importance of *logos* in carrying out *erga* appropriately. He apparently has the *erga* to match "fine words"; he has not only acted bravely in combat, but also persists wholeheartedly in the pursuit of courage. Socrates the philosopher is the exemplary democratic citizen. But Socrates himself concludes the dialogue by maintaining that his words and deeds are still inharmonious. Such is the measure of his humility before the truth of courage. This humility is what the Athenian ideal, as an ideal, lacks. The Athenians are too readily convinced of the harmony between their words and their deeds, and of the adequacy of both.

---

[32] Cf. Dobbs 1986; Benitez 2000: 88–89.
[33] This is the burden of O'Brien 1963.

In Plato's vision, their words and their deeds come to ruin with respect both to free speech and rationality (as in the *Laches*) and to justice and equality (as in the *Gorgias*).[34] Athens needs political philosophy in order to make its realities correspond to its considerable capacities; Socrates the philosopher is Athens's only true statesman (*Gorgias* 521d).

---

[34] On this theme in the *Gorgias*, see Balot 2007.

CHAPTER 7 | Isocratean Reflections
Athens's Courage, Imperialism, and Eudaimonism

BY CONTRAST WITH THUCYDIDES, Isocrates provides another type of philosophical reflection on the Athenians' *andreia* and on their relationships with the other Greeks. While criticizing the Athenians for their pursuit of selfish and greedy imperialism, Isocrates also reformulated the Athenians' ideology in order to call forth among his contemporaries a novel appreciation of the importance of courage, leadership, and justice, not only for the flourishing of other Greeks, but also for that of Athens itself. Isocrates is particularly interesting for our purposes, because he offers a vision of civic education that promotes the inculcation and exercise of virtue without remaining entrenched in the antidemocratic politics of his philosophical contemporaries.[1] Like Thucydides, he was ambivalent toward the Athenians' democratic expressions of courage, but he tended, in the texts that I will consider, to offer more robustly positive avenues for the Athenians' development of *eudaimonia* than did Thucydides. These concerns cooperate effectively with Isocrates' accounts of *doxa*, *philosophia*, and practical wisdom, which have much to offer modern educational and rhetorical theorists engaged in the search for pragmatic alternatives to Aristotelian theory.[2]

In the midst of the recent resurgence of interest in Isocrates' rhetorical and educational theory, scholars have also begun to reconsider the orator's searching analysis of politics within the community of Greek poleis

---

[1] See particularly the essays collected in Poulakis and Depew 2004.
[2] See, for example, Too 1995; Hariman 2004; and Haskins 2004.

and, more broadly, within the entire Eastern Mediterranean. As a matter of fact, Isocrates' political ideas—including his reflections on Panhellenism, Athenian democracy, and monarchy—were once the cornerstone of studies of the orator.[3] This traditional emphasis was understandable, because, through reacting to lines of political thought established by Herodotus, Thucydides, Plato, and Demosthenes, Isocrates addressed urgent contemporary questions in such a way as to elucidate permanent features of political life. Recent scholars have refined our understanding of the historical implications of individual speeches, they have brought Isocrates into conversation with the contemporary Athenian democracy, and they have re-evaluated Isocrates' ideas on warfare, rhetoric, and relations with non-Greeks altogether.[4]

We focus now on two related features of Isocrates' political thought—his exploration of political psychology and his theory of enlightened hegemony. Isocrates investigates these topics with reference to the competition between Athens and Sparta for leadership in the Greek world. Focusing on political psychology and enlightened hegemony enables us to read Isocrates both contextually and philosophically. From a historical standpoint, we can appreciate Isocrates' particular development of the Athenian epitaphic tradition and understand his response to the practical ideas of his fellow citizens—for example, regarding the Second Athenian League. Yet we might also view Isocrates' exploration of these topics in a way that goes beyond the historical context. Isocrates contributes to ongoing discussions in international relations a distinctively ancient emphasis on psychological motivation and a distinctively ancient development of eudaimonism. He thereby provides ways in which the Athenians might have responded to the Thucydidean criticisms of democratic courage, picking up on lines of thought developed in the Athenians' broader eudaimonistic ideology.[5]

---

[3] See, for example, the philosophical and contextual discussion of Mathieu 1966 (first ed. 1925), along with the probing analysis of the *Panegyricus* found in Buchner 1958 and the interesting general treatment of Bringmann 1965.

[4] Davidson 1990; Ober 1998; Walter 2003; Masaracchia 1995.

[5] For two interesting treatments of Thucydides by international relations theorists, see Monten 2006 and Welch 2003. For recent explorations of these issues by ancient historians, see Ober 2001; Crane 1998; Eckstein 2006; and Low 2007. For other, related studies of democracy, warfare, and international relations, see the classic treatment of the "democratic peace" in Russett 1994, as well as the Forum section of the *American Political Science Review* 99.3 (2005): 453–72.

Isocrates, International Relations, and Inter-State Competition

Isocrates' presentation of international relations is best understood through the lens of culture, psychology, and the virtues.[6] It is necessary to focus in particular on *andreia*, *pleonexia*, sympathy, and impartiality. Even more than Herodotus or Thucydides, Isocrates maintained the intuitively plausible thesis that domestic politics and political psychology were highly relevant to the behavior of states as international actors.[7] Isocrates traces Athens's international success to the Athenians' willingness to extend sympathy and fair-mindedness abroad, which led them, in his analysis, to adopt an impartial stance as leader within the Hellenic community. According to Isocrates, the Athenians were able to extend sympathy and to adopt an impartial stance because they correctly located *andreia* within the framework of their larger aspirations to be moderate and just. In developing his account of Athens, Isocrates also offered one of the first explanations of the ways in which hegemony could contribute to a state's enlightened conception of its own flourishing.[8]

These themes come to light in Isocrates' examination of the rivalry between Sparta and Athens. Like his predecessors, Isocrates envisioned international relations as an anarchic domain in which states inevitably compete for power and scarce resources. Isocrates was, however, less interested in which city had "won" this competition by successfully asserting its dominance within the relevant geographical sphere. Instead, more explicitly than other ancient theorists, Isocrates assumed the mantle of an ethical and political "umpire," a reflective judge of each city's claim to have done outstanding service to the Panhellenic community (12.39–41). Insofar as he offered judgments on this question, however, Isocrates also acted as arbitrator in a deeper and even more important contest—that of the regime (*politeia*). Which city—Athens or Sparta—was better at providing

---

[6] For one historically based attempt to fuse the cultural and structural approaches within international relations theory, see Johnston 1998, which focuses on the "strategic culture" of premodern China. On the language of decrees and classical texts describing the virtues of international behavior, see Low 2007: 134–44.

[7] Ned Lebow's account of international relations places this point at the center of his inquiry, drawing on ancient Greek (indeed, Platonic) psychological theories of reason, honor, and appetite, to generate a provocative, multilayered model for understanding the international behavior of states. See Lebow 2008.

[8] There is a burgeoning literature on hegemony and enlightened self-interest, which is called "hegemonic stability theory"; for an explanation and criticism of this theory, see the classic work of Keohane 1984.

for the welfare of its citizens? How did each city's international behavior reflect back upon the material conditions of life at home? Which city was more successful in pursuing its own excellent and flourishing condition, through establishing hegemony within the Greek world? Isocrates' examination of international relations always had in view the question of whether Athens or Sparta most deserved praise for making the good life possible for its citizens (12.111–37, cf. 7.84).[9]

Since competition in this sense is the premise of the *Panegyricus* and *Panathenaicus*, these speeches are my principal focus. They present a clear and politically useful vision of both proper and improper ways of exercising international power. In these speeches, Isocrates drew upon the Athenian epitaphic tradition in order to expound a normative vision of Athenian leadership in the Greek world.[10] He wrote enthusiastically of the Athenians' beneficial exercise of hegemony in the past. He envisioned the possibility of future Athenian leadership of the Greeks against the Persians. Yet this reading of Isocrates' encomiastic speeches raises the question of consistency across the corpus. Given the favorable treatment Isocrates provides in these two speeches, what explains his critical account of Athens in the related, supposedly "deliberative," speeches, *On the Peace* and *Areopagiticus*?[11] The potential problems with consistency call into question the plausibility of Isocrates' enthusiastic endorsement of Athenian hegemony.

Criticizing Imperialism, Praising Hegemony

To grapple with the charge of inconsistency, scholars have traditionally understood Isocrates to be drawing sharp distinctions between hegemony (*hēgemonia*) and empire (*archē*).[12] One prima facie problem with this

---

[9] In presenting Isocrates qua political philosopher as a judge or "umpire," I follow the lead of Strauss 1959/1988: 80–81, who argues that the "vocation" of the ancient political philosopher, so to speak, was to adjudicate between competing claims of justice and the good life, within the realm of practical political discussion and reflection. On the question of the regime in Isocrates, see Bloom 1955/1995: 15–21, Bloom 1955: 8–59; on the comparison of Athens and Sparta, see Bloom 1955/1995: 26–28. Mathieu 1925: 69–75 treats the hegemony of Athens in the context of his discussion of Athenian "propaganda."
[10] Loraux 1986: 79–97 discusses the hegemonic impulses of the funeral oration with reference to the *Panegyricus*; see also Loraux 1986: 218–20.
[11] On the issue of consistency, see Mathieu 1966/1925: 118–25; Buchner 1958: 150, Bringmann 1965; and Too 1995: 61–73. Too 1995: 13–19 helpfully illustrates the difficulties in providing an adequate generic taxonomy of Isocrates' works.
[12] See Buchner 1958; 39–41, 117–19, and esp. 150–51, which gives his general conclusion, along with the judicious remarks of Hudson-Williams 1960 and Bringmann 1965: 28–30;

approach is that Isocrates does not, in fact, maintain a rigorous distinction between the words *archē* and *hēgemonia* and their roots and compounds. A deviation from the supposed pattern occurs, for example, at *On the Peace* 91–94, where *archē* is first contrasted with tyranny and thus occupies the position that we would expect *hēgemonia* to occupy; but by the end of the passage, *archē* is itself, as usual, condemned on ethical grounds.[13] Another deviation occurs at *Panegyricus* 119, where Isocrates seems to refer to the Athenian empire as *archē*, but then immediately suggests that after 404 BC, other Greeks, that is, the Spartans, had taken the Athenians' place as "leaders" (*heterōn hēgemonōn*, 119).[14] These are, however, anomalies within a much larger and easily recognizable pattern. As scholars have understood for a long time, Isocrates generally distinguishes *archē* from *hēgemonia* at a terminological level; and, despite the slight fluidity of Isocrates' terminology, he certainly drew a conceptual distinction between hegemony and empire. Isocrates wanted to distinguish characteristics of good or enlightened leadership from abusive or tyrannical power.[15]

It is fair to say that, as a result, Isocrates unequivocally condemned the desire to institute what I will call "empire." Imperialism consisted in the selfish, aggressive, and unjust acquisition of power over others and their possessions (8.29–32). Imperialism was an operation of enslavement and tyranny (8.41–44). Through pursuing imperialism for much of the classical period, the Athenians had incurred the hatred of other Greeks (8.82) and destroyed entire armadas, armies, and even generations of Athenian

---

and Davidson 1990. Too 1995: 62–63 seems to misunderstand the implications of the general philological and conceptual patterns laid out by Buchner. Despite his rejection of the distinction between *hēgemonia* and *archē* on philological grounds in *On the Peace* (Davidson 1990: 22n.7), Davidson 1990: 31–32 argues, correctly, that Isocrates may be seen as contrasting the Athenians' tyrannical imperialism with a more enlightened leadership of the other Greeks, which Isocrates characterizes as "kingly," on the model of the Spartan kingship within Sparta: cf. 8.142–44. Davidson (1990: 36) correctly regards this idea of "kingly imperialism" as one of Isocrates' most distinctive contributions in this work, though one would need to turn elsewhere, namely to the texts considered here, to discover the precise constituents of Isocrates' "good imperialism," or what I am calling "enlightened hegemony." For interesting remarks on Isocrates' use of the hegemony/empire distinction in the context of his efforts to model practical wisdom for his students and readers, see Poulakos 1997: 82–83. These conceptual distinctions were anticipated by Mathieu 1966/1925: 123–25.

[13] Cf. Davidson 1990: 22n.7.

[14] Cf. Hudson-Williams 1960: 32.

[15] If readers are not convinced of this point already, then hopefully this chapter will persuade them of the conceptual rigor with which Isocrates pursues this distinction. My aim is to unearth the precise "ingredients" of enlightened hegemony and to demonstrate that it is Athens's capacity for this form of leadership that reveals Athens to be superior to Sparta in the contest of which Isocrates is umpire.

citizens (8.86–89). This adequately explains why, as Isocrates told the Athenians, it was both unjust and imprudent to seek *archē* (8.65–66).[16]

By contrast, Isocrates regarded what I will call "hegemony" as an enlightened form of leadership in which the Athenians cultivated the prosperity of their allies and thereby promoted their own advantage (8.75–78). Like modern theories of hegemonic stability, Isocrates' theory required that the Athenians possess dominant power, in order to enforce their decisions and choices within the Hellenic world. Yet Isocrates also viewed the hegemonic, as opposed to imperial, Athenians as contributing to the common good of Greece as a whole. The Athenians enforced justice, relative equality, and peace, which were considerable public goods in the Panhellenic world.[17] Isocrates' rhetorical appeals rested on the idea that Athenian leadership in these respects—their "proper" exercise of international power, as he saw it—contributed mightily to the flourishing of Athens and Athenians. Thus, the conceptual distinction between empire and hegemony enabled Isocrates both to criticize his Athenian contemporaries for unhealthily coveting an empire and to praise the Athenians' ancestors for exercising international power justly, responsibly, and beneficially. Isocrates' theoretical outlook was consistent in that he praised past generations of Athenians for their hegemonic behaviors and statesmanlike ideals, on the one hand, and criticized later Athenians for their imperialism, on the other.[18]

This combination of praise and criticism corresponds to a well-known chronological distinction in Isocrates' evaluation of his native city (cf. 7.15–18).[19] Roughly speaking, Isocrates reserved his praise for the foreign policy of the "ancestral Athenians," who, in his presentation, committed themselves to an old-fashioned, Solonian and self-restrained "democracy" and fought loyally to protect the Hellenes from foreign invasion (e.g., 7.20–23 and passim in the *Areopagiticus*). These praiseworthy Athenians, in particular, defeated the Persians in the early fifth century and organized the Delian League as respectful and generous leaders (7.79–80). They

---

[16] For Isocrates' treatment of Spartan and Athenian imperialism in the *Panegyricus*, see the discussion of Buchner 1958: 108–42, which, though clear and helpful, suffers at points from overemphasis on Isocrates' connections to Lysias (cf. Bringmann 1965: 29).

[17] On related themes, see Saïd 2001: 282–86.

[18] For a general treatment of hegemony as a *topos* among classical Greek historians (with little discussion of Isocrates, however), see Wickersham 1994, who also considers the relation between hegemony and empire from a conceptual, rather than a philological, perspective.

[19] Davidson 1990: 21–24 fine-tunes the chronology envisioned in Isocrates' history of Athenian and Spartan decline, as outlined in *On the Peace*. See also Bloom 1955: 28–31.

enabled the Greek world to prosper and presided over the consummate flourishing of Athens itself (7.6).

By contrast, Isocrates censured those Athenians, from relatively early in the fifth century onward,[20] who transformed this healthy and statesman-like hegemony into an odious, aggressive, and expansionistic empire, and then, in the fourth century, into a much weaker state that other Greeks still regarded with hostility and suspicion (7.6–8). The failures of the corrupt fourth-century democracy had been virtually cemented by the citizens' adherence to the guidance of sycophantic, hedonistic, and fraudulent leaders (8.3–4, cf. 12.133). The imperialistic Athenians, nurtured by the city's "radical" naval (cf. 8.48, 8.114–15) democracy, weakened Greece vis-à-vis non-Greek outsiders and corrupted the traditional virtues of the city itself.[21]

Such distinctions are maintained throughout the Isocratean corpus, even within individual speeches. Athens, especially qua naval and imperial democracy, had made significant mistakes that Isocrates warned his contemporaries not to repeat. This point became explicit even in the highly laudatory *Panathenaicus*, where, as in the *Areopagiticus* and *Peace*, Isocrates criticized the "extreme" naval democracy of classical Athens by comparison with the ancestral constitution (12.114–18, 130–33). After defeating Xerxes, Isocrates argues, both Athens and Sparta pursued the senseless policy of seeking the Great King's favor while striving to overpower other Greeks and destroy one another (12.157–63). This is the sort of intra-Greek rivalry that Isocrates hopes to repair (12.158). Similar criticisms of classical Athens occur frequently throughout Isocrates' corpus (e.g., 4.100–102, 12.63–64 on harsh imperialism; 7.6, 7.9, 7.12, and especially 7.76–77 and 7.81–83 on the myriad failings of Athenians in the late fifth and fourth centuries; and, of course, *On the Peace*, passim).[22] Such criticisms are merely softened, not eliminated, by arguments that the

---

[20] Davidson 1990: 22–23 persuasively argues that in *On the Peace*, the origins of Athenian corruption began, paradoxically, right at the high point of the "Golden Age," i.e., the institution of the Delian League in 478 BC. This scheme is, however, more difficult to maintain in the *Panegyricus*, where Isocrates praises the Athenians' fifth-century imperialism as hegemonic leadership and touts its benefits for the other Greeks (4.103–9).

[21] On Isocrates' discussion of the healthy ancestral democracy, by contrast with the corrupt "modern" democracy, see Ober 1998: 264–68, 273–75, 278–86; Loraux 1986: 218–20; Mathieu 1966/1925: 140–52; Bloom 1955/1995: 15–21.

[22] As Buchner 1958: 150 correctly observes, Isocrates occasionally tries to defend the Athenians' imperialistic actions (e.g., 4.100-110), to the extent that he can, only in order to persuade contemporaries that Athens's claim to enlightened hegemony should not be too quickly or easily dismissed. This means that, consistently with his outlook throughout the corpus, Isocrates is far from an unrepentant apologist for Athenian imperialism.

Athenians' decision to radicalize their democracy originated in the threats posed by Sparta (12.114--15, cf. 12.166), rather than any belief that the new regime would be universally admired (12.118). The "radical" democracy was still a lamentable, even if necessary, development.

Isocrates' Criticisms of Excessive Manliness

On the Peace and *Areopagiticus* lay the foundations for Isocrates' particular construction of enlightened hegemony. Isocrates recognized that enlightened hegemony did not belong to the self-abasing or cowardly. Sometimes, indeed frequently, leaders in the ancient Mediterranean had to fight in order to protect their followers, as the Athenians and Spartans had done during the Persian invasions. Yet *thumos* and *andreia* tended to overreach. The necessary development of military force for defensive purposes too often, in Isocrates' view, led to unreflective bellicosity. The major question confronting theorists of Athens's power, accordingly, was how to educate Athenian *thumos* properly. More precisely, how could Isocrates penetrate the Athenians' instinctive self-assertiveness with a correct understanding of how to maximize their own properly understood flourishing? Isocrates took his bearings by seeking to reorient Athenian *thumos* toward justice and sympathetic leadership (cf. 8.136–37). He aspired to cultivate the virtues necessary for enlightened hegemony, without stimulating *pleonexia* or inflating the Athenians' self-assertive manliness beyond legitimate bounds.

In *Peace* and *Areopagiticus*, therefore, Isocrates issued a stern rebuke to Athenians who were committed to entrenched patterns of bellicosity and corruption. He exhorted them to practice moderation and so to profit themselves and the other Greeks (e.g., 7.82–84, 8.12, etc.).[23] Isocrates

---

[23] Such an account, I think, explains Isocrates' simultaneous praise and criticism of the Athenian past, but it does not settle all the problems of theoretical inconsistency; these other difficulties, however, do not directly affect the arguments of the present chapter. The problems that I have in mind are Isocrates' treatment of the desirability of peace as opposed to the resort to war, and his evaluation of the Peace of Antalcidas. Both problems come to sight in *On the Peace* (16). In this passage, Isocrates urges the Athenians to make peace not only with their Greek allies, but also with "all human beings (*hapantas anthrōpous*)," including the Great King. He also argues that the Athenians will not find terms of peace more just or advantageous than those of the Peace of Antalcidas. Elsewhere, of course, Isocrates finds Athenian hegemony preferable to the terms of this peace (4.115), and he promotes the cause of Athens as Panhellenic leader against Persia. I deal with Isocrates' thinking about war and peace later in the chapter, with implications for his thinking about the Peace of Antalcidas.

emphasized that Spartans and Athenians share the same defect—their quick recourse to war (8.8, 8.12–13, 8.97, 8.99–100; cf. 4.125–26). They fail to recognize the genuine benefits of peace (8.5–6, 18–21). Instead of perceiving that justice, respect for others, and material advantage are closely allied, they yield too easily to cultural forces that overvalue manliness (*andreia*) and the pursuit of unjust material gain (*pleonexia*) (8.16–17, 22–23, 26, 36–37; cf. 12.219–220, 12.241–43).[24] Such impulses are particularly destructive for fourth-century Athens, according to Isocrates, because the Athenians have lapsed into laziness, cowardice, and lack of preparation for war (7.76, 7.82). In reality, however, the enlightened pursuit of one's own well-being begins with the recognition that injustice provides only apparent advantages, whereas virtuous behavior and psychological order lead to genuine "happiness" or "flourishing" *(eudaimonia)* both for states and individuals (8.29–32). Isocrates states explicitly that this teaching is the chief aim of his speech (8.18).[25]

At the level of international theory, rather than individual psychology, Isocrates thus replays the central "problematic" confronted by Plato in his *Republic*: how to show that "justice pays." Why does traditionally ethical or virtuous behavior, rather than its opposite, contribute most to the flourishing of ethical agents? By drawing attention to precisely this question, and by arguing that justice is advantageous to the just agent, Isocrates sets himself up as an exponent of political eudaimonism, in ways that are at least prima facie compatible with those found in the classical Athenian discourse (12.136–37; chapters 14 and 15). By using the term *eudaimonia*, Isocrates referred to a naturalistic theory of human flourishing in which happiness depends on the rational cultivation of virtue (8.31–34, 8.63–64, cf. 8.82–84). Like Plato, Isocrates regarded greed (*pleonexia*) and unbridled "manliness" as the central problems confronting "eudaimonist" theory in his day.[26]

---

[24] Davidson 1990: 24–29 correctly emphasizes Athenian greed as the central feature of moral decline traced by Isocrates. In his emphasis on the importance of *pleonexia* for Isocratean political thought, he was anticipated by Bringmann 1965: 28–46.
[25] My reading shares elements with the interesting discussion of Isocrates in Low 2007: 154–60, although I believe that the language of *eudaimonia* better captures Isocrates' concerns than does that of "morality," which Low prefers. On the questions of international reciprocity and international law in fourth-century Athens, see the excellent discussion of Hunt 2010: 185–236.
[26] On Plato's understanding of materialistic desires and their consequences, see Balot 2001a: 234–48; on his treatment of *thumos* and its proper cultivation, see Hobbs 2000.

The Purpose of *Panegyricus* and *Panathenaicus*

If we understand the Isocratean theory of international relations in this light, then we might regard *On the Peace* and *Areopagiticus* as also laying the foundations for the rhetorical appeals made in *Panegyricus* and *Panathenaicus*. *On the Peace* and *Areopagiticus* illustrate Isocrates' critical response to the dangers of unbridled *pleonexia* and *thumos*; the encomiastic speeches show Isocrates striving to explain the many ways in which Athens's pre-imperial hegemony benefited, not only other Greeks, but also the Athenians themselves. Obviously, these works were separated by many years, and *On the Peace* and *Areopagiticus* were written in between the others. My point is simply that *On the Peace* and *Areopagiticus* give evidence of, and criticize, the psychological tendencies that Isocrates targeted for repair and re-education.[27] The encomiastic speeches, on the other hand, provide a normative account of enlightened Athenian hegemony, based on Isocrates' vision of properly educated desires, emotions, and ideals. (Needless to say, in Isocrates' evaluations of the rivalry between Sparta and Athens, Sparta, too, was characterized as lacking political health throughout its history, because of its unwholesome and aggressive pursuit of self-aggrandizement; but Isocrates was less optimistic about the possibility of transforming Sparta into an enlightened hegemon.)

One might conceivably criticize Isocrates' encomiastic efforts for retailing mere nostalgia for Athens's hegemonic power. But we should reject the "nostalgic" interpretation of Isocrates' political thought because his encomiastic speeches were intended to be politically useful.[28] Isocrates held that Athenian mistakes could be corrected if only the Athenians should recognize and be persuaded of the genuine long-term benefits of peace. Even in offering his criticisms, therefore, Isocrates was resolutely forward looking; he aspired not to condemn, but to provoke, to catalyze, and to transform. Practically speaking, if the Athenians should understand and act upon Isocrates' political advice, then they could transform themselves into admired, respected, and unchallenged hegemons, not imperialists, among the Greeks (8.24, 8.142). Thus, if *On the Peace* illustrates the defects of character to which Athens and Sparta were particularly

---

[27] For arguments that Isocrates deliberately used the category *logos politikos* to create a sense of coherence throughout his corpus, see Too 1995: 36–73.

[28] See Poulakos 1997: 78–92 for a compatible rejection of the "nostalgic" interpretation and for arguments that Isocrates used narratives of the past in order to cultivate good judgment in the present.

susceptible, then Isocrates specifically tried to repair these defects in the *Panegyricus* and *Panathenaicus*. He did so by constructing a vision of the Athenian past that would provide the Athenians with appropriate ideals and stimulate them to aim for the just and honorable leadership of which they were capable.

In writing the *Panegyricus* and *Panathenaicus*, therefore, Isocrates' purpose was both theoretical and hortatory. On the one hand, Isocrates used these epideictic compositions to identify the benefits, both to Athenians and to other Greeks, that were within the grasp of his Athenian contemporaries, should they play the role they traditionally assigned themselves within the epitaphic tradition—namely, that of just, generous, and far-sighted leaders of the Greek world. The genre enabled Isocrates to theorize precisely which virtues and behaviors were demanded by the Athenians' laudatory self-image. On the other hand, Isocrates also exhorted his contemporaries, whether in 380 or in the late 340s, to live up to the standards he had brought to light. To this extent, he participated in the hortatory idealizations that were characteristic of Athenian funerary oratory.[29] Like other hortatory encomiasts of Athens, such as Thucydides' Pericles (Thuc. 2.35–46) and, in my understanding, Plato's Socrates (in the *Menexenus*),[30] Isocrates' judgment clearly favored Athens over Sparta as the city most likely to flourish in its own right and to lead the other Greeks successfully.

Traditional Rivalries and the Athenians' Innovative Ideology of Courage

Striving to protect the Greeks was, for Isocrates, the proper goal of the traditional rivalry between Sparta and Athens:

> Well then, our ancestors and the Lacedaimonians were always rivals of one another, but in those times [roughly, the Persian War period] they competed for the noblest things, not considering one another to be enemies but rather rivals, nor did they flatter the barbarian with a view to enslaving the Greeks; instead, they thought alike about the common safety and competed with one another over which of them would be able to claim credit for this (4.85).

---

[29] On these characteristics of the *epitaphios* tradition, see Loraux 1986 and Ziolkowski 1981, and compare the interpretation of Plato's *Menexenus* offered by Kahn 1963.
[30] On the *Menexenus* in general, see Kahn 1963; Salkever 1993; and Monoson 1998.

Historically, at least, the Spartans and Athenians had exhibited a noble Hesiodic *eris* in which honor was collectively awarded to cities promoting the panhellenic cause. Courage, risk taking, and even naturally aggressive impulses properly served the panhellenic community—and they served it well, as the victory over Persia and the incipient acquisition of military security proved. Latent in such military virtues, however, were socially destructive tendencies that, while ineradicable, could at least be contained through proper surveillance and education.

Isocrates built his account of noble rivalry on the competing theories of the previous century, when rivalry for leadership and honor was a particularly hot topic of debate. After the victory over Persia, the Greeks accounted for their success, not with reference to luck, and only rarely with reference to divine aid. Instead, as the Persian War epigrams and the Athenian *epitaphioi* indicate, the Greeks universally emphasized their own *aretē*, or military valor. Isocrates utilized the Athenian ideology of rational, logocentric, and moderate courage in his analysis of the competition of Athens and Sparta, with a view to strengthening Athenian claims to rightful leadership of the Greeks. Paradoxically, perhaps, Isocrates argued that the Athenians achieved competitive success over Sparta by reducing their single-minded focus on their own superiority.

In the first instance, this meant limiting their identification with overly narrow and pugnacious conceptions of *andreia*. It was on this score, Isocrates maintained, that the Athenians had always come out ahead of the Spartans. For example, after detailing the courageous exploits of the Athenians in defending themselves against Eumolpus, Eurystheus, the Persians, and other "barbarians," Isocrates explains why earlier generations of Athenians were so admirable:

> They remained steadfast in the character they had because of the nobility of their regime. They took more pride in the condition of their souls and in their minds than in the battles that had taken place, and they were admired by others for their resolve and their moderation rather than because of their courage (*dia tēn andrian*) in danger. For everyone recognized that many men have a warlike spirit [*eupsuchian tēn polemikēn*], even among those who are excessively bad, whereas worthless men do not have a share in the spirit that is useful to all and able to benefit everyone [*tēs de chrēsimēs (eupsuchias) epi pasi kai pantas dunamenēs ōphelein ou koinōnountas tous ponērous*]. This kind of spirit arises only in those who have been nobly born, raised, and educated. (12.197–98).

This is a critical passage in Isocrates' use of the Athenian ideology, because in it Isocrates presents the three critical elements of his analysis of the contest between Athens and Sparta.

First, and most clearly, Isocrates follows Plato's character Protagoras in arguing that courage is psychologically and practically separable from other virtues such as justice, self-control, and wisdom (cf. *Prot.* 349d). For Isocrates, courage differs from the other canonical virtues in its susceptibility to abuse; courage is too easily directed to unjust and immoral ends. According to the standard Athenian conception, virtues, as excellences of the soul, cannot be directed toward unethical ends; and so acts of bravery that fail to respect the claims of justice are, in the usual account, considered unethical or positively vicious. Isocrates, by contrast, ranks among those who regard courage as a virtue but question the absoluteness of its claim to goodness.

Second, the Athenians, by contrast with their more belligerent counterparts, practiced a form of courage based on the quality of their minds and their education (cf. 8.32). Isocrates specifically praised Athenians as the Greeks who were most gifted in the arts, in speech, in action, in manliness (*andrian*) and in virtue (*aretēn*, 7.74–75). In the quoted passage, Isocrates is specifically contrasting a warlike type of "courage" (*eupsuchia*), which is available even to unjust aggressors, with a generally beneficent sort of courage that is found only in men of noble birth, breeding, and education. The Athenians' practice of courage is ethically well-grounded, carefully reasoned, and based on appropriate emotional responses. As expressed by Athenian behavior, courage is the virtue that enables Athenians to defend themselves and others, to enjoy prosperity without fear, and generally to confer benefits on the Greek world. The reason that Athenian courage, by contrast with other, more limited forms of courage, can have such positive effects is that Athenian courage was meaningfully directed by rational reflection on the positive ends that courage can achieve.[31] As a result, the Athenians have traditionally managed to use their courage in the right way—that is, most often, to support legitimate acts of self-defense.

Finally, and as an extension of the rationality of their courage, the Athenians have correctly recognized that courage ought to rank lower than moderation and justice in their table of the virtues. Courage is ethically

---

[31] On Isocrates' endorsement of the Athenians' faltering dedication to *logos*, see his so-called "hymn to logos" (*Antidosis* 253–57 = *Nicocles* 5–9), with Poulakos 1997: 9–22, which helpfully sets Isocrates' discussion within the context of Protagorean and Aristotelian theories of civilization and deliberation.

significant, not only in itself, but also and more importantly as the necessary means to and precondition of the development of these other, higher virtues. In dangerous circumstances such as external military attacks, courage has enabled the Athenians to win security; security, in turn, enabled them to cultivate such admirable qualities as moderation, justice, and intelligence (4.48–50). Thus Athenian courage was held to be, as Robert Louis Stevenson once said, the "footstool of the virtues"—like a footstool, not to be glorified for its own sake, but valued, rather, for the positive goals it enables us to accomplish.

This analysis of Athenian courage corresponds to Isocrates' insistence elsewhere that the virtues must be appropriately rank-ordered, on the grounds that self-control and justice are the unique possessions of noble men, whereas qualities such as courage and cleverness (*deinotēs*), despite the nearly universal esteem in which they are held, are commonly exhibited by the ignoble as well as the noble (3.43). Perhaps the reason for this is that courage, to take Isocrates' standing example, can be misdirected toward unjust ends, just as much as wealth, physical strength, and— heaven forbid—oratory (3.1–4). This line of reasoning helps to explain Isocrates' unusual way of praising Heracles in his address to Philip, not for his *andreia* or bodily strength, but rather for his wisdom, his love of honor, and his justice (5.109–10). This revision of the mythological tradition speaks to the account of the virtues that Isocrates uses in comparing Athens with Sparta and to the novel exercise of international power to which Isocrates will summon his fellow Athenians. Only those able to put courage into its proper place are trustworthy enough to exercise power over the right people, at the right time, and for the right reasons. The qualities of moderation and justice to which Isocrates grants primacy are precisely suited to limit aggressive impulses and the penchant to make war (4.183–84).

To clear the way for this argument, Isocrates had to demonstrate that traditional Greek bellicosity, enshrined in the approbatory language of *aretē* and *andreia*, was of limited worth; it was even possibly dangerous. This case was, however, prima facie unpersuasive. *Aretē*, *andreia*, and the hegemony that might result from them—these could be *bad* things? For everyone from Agamemnon to Callicles and beyond, the "manly virtues" were the highest possible forms of excellence; and the material goods and power to which they potentially led were of the highest value.[32] Isocrates

---

[32] On the relationship between the manly virtues and acquisition, see Balot 2001a: esp. 5–14, 59–68.

justifies his suspicions of traditional self-aggrandizement through a "thick" redescription of early Spartan history.

Spartan History and the Achievements of Agamemnon

At the heart of Spartan political history, for Isocrates, was the desire to assert dominance over others. In Isocrates' reconstruction, those known in the classical period as Lacedaimonians behaved aggressively toward their Peloponnesian neighbors right from the start. Almost immediately upon invading the Peloponnese, the Lacedaimonians established a hierarchy of power and prestige at home. The Spartan leaders, he says, "established among themselves the sort of equality and democracy which men must have if they intend to have lasting harmony, whereas they made the ordinary citizens 'Perioikoi,' enslaving their souls like those of household servants" (12.178–79). This subjection of their unfortunate fellow Laconians had political, social, military, and material implications, as these inferiors were forced to work poor land and to occupy the most dangerous posts in the Spartan army. The Spartans' political institutions were founded on just such an immoderate assertion of *kratos* over the inhabitants of their own and the surrounding territories—immoderate, Isocrates contends, not because the exercise of power is intrinsically wrong, but rather because it is particularly susceptible to abuse.[33]

To make this distinction more emphatic, Isocrates propounds a fascinating, and to my knowledge unprecedented, revisionist history of the virtues and accomplishments of Agamemnon (12.70–90). It is worth considering this section in some detail, because in it Isocrates establishes his fundamental lines of thought on two paramount questions: What is power *for* (cf. 8.110)? What virtues are required for the proper exercise of power? Isocrates himself highlights the importance of this passage by explicitly drawing attention to the amplitude of his treatment and to the counterintuitive quality of his proposals (12.73, 12.74–75, 12.84–88). Isocrates originally introduced these topics in order to condemn the Spartans' abuses of power, specifically in laying waste to the small Peloponnesian cities that had given rise to such heroes as Nestor, Menelaus, and Agamemnon (12.70–72); he also reminds readers of this point at the conclusion of his excursus (12.90).

---

[33] On Isocrates' treatment of early Sparta and its *pleonexia*, see Bloom 1955: 123–25.

However men popularly denigrate Agamemnon, and however much they neglect his nobility (12.75, 12.78), Isocrates stresses Agamemnon's extraordinary power and his farsighted use of this power to benefit the Greek world (12.77, 12.79–80). From the outset, Isocrates stresses that power is glorious only when it enhances the prosperity, stability, and quality of life of many others outside one's own immediate circle. Although Isocrates is less than certain as to Agamemnon's initial methods of acquiring power, his first and cardinal observation is that "after Agamemnon had taken this power, he did not harm any of the Greek cities" (12.77). On the contrary, Agamemnon established unity among the Greeks and conducted the most honorable and advantageous military expedition known to history—the "panhellenic" expedition against Troy (12.78).[34] This expedition was signally advantageous to the Greeks because it eliminated internecine warfare (12.77), reduced the domestic self-aggrandizement of other Greek kings (12.79), won retribution for Paris's hubristic seizure of Helen (12.80, 12.83), and established an effective system of self-defense against the "barbarian" for the future (12.80, 12.83).

If the ends of Agamemnon's power were admirable, however, then so too were his means of winning adherence to the cause. The tradition held that other Greek leaders had followed Agamemnon solely in order to discharge their oath to Tyndareus; Thucydides had famously preferred the unconventional explanation that the other Greeks feared Agamemnon's naval power (Thuc. 1.9–1.10). By contrast, Isocrates offers his readers a rhetorical Agamemnon, who persuaded other kings to join the cause even at great personal expense (12.79). Isocrates hints that Agamemnon exploited the circumstances of Helen's outrage for rhetorical purposes, without mentioning his own statesmanlike mission to save Greece (12.80). Through avoiding the Homeric and tragic condemnations of Agamemnon, and through concentrating on Agamemnon as a hero of Hellenic international relations, Isocrates outlines a persuasive, ethically meaningful theory of both the ends and the means of international power.

Such considerations do indeed help to explain what power is for; but, to link his programmatic discussion of Agamemnon to his general theme of the competition between Sparta and Athens, Isocrates also had to diagnose the qualities of mind and character which gave rise to Agamemnon's noble accomplishments. From the perspective of ethical psychology, the central

---

[34] On both Agamemnon and Heracles as panhellenic heroes, see Saïd 2001: 280–81. For a different treatment of Agamemnon as a savior of Greece's culture, see Bloom 1955: 111–13, 176–77.

point is that Agamemnon mobilized the Trojan expedition not for the sake of glory or in order to aggrandize himself, but rather in order to benefit other Greeks (12.77–78). Isocrates strictly envisions glory as the second effect of desires that were more proper to this king of kings, namely, to establish concord and to institute an effective security system for future Greeks. Agamemnon was in control of his desires because he was unusually just and moderate, as well as virtuous in every other way (12.72). Here, too, Isocrates revises the Homeric portrait of Agamemnon, which had led its audiences to endorse Achilles' complaint that Agamemnon was the greediest, weakest, least prudent, and least fair-minded of all commanders.[35]

For Isocrates, Agamemnon's virtuous character was matched by his possession of intellectual virtues—chiefly, the practical wisdom (*phronēsis*, 12.82) that had kept his "thumotic" and ambitious soldiers in line for ten years (12.81–82). They could see that Agamemnon had a clearer grasp of their well-being than they themselves did (12.82). One example of this, for Isocrates, is that Agamemnon uniquely saw in the outrage done to Helen an opportunity to stabilize the international system for years to come (12.80). All in all, Agamemnon's ethically informed and virtuous exercise of power provided a model for his explanation of the Athenians' own virtues in the leadership of other Greeks. Like Thucydides, Isocrates fashioned an Agamemnon to provide a paradigm for Athenian power, but his different ethical orientation in doing so, and the exhortatory power of his paradigm, are now obvious.

It is no wonder, then, that Isocrates should lambaste the Spartans for taking possession of the Peloponnesian cities that deserved the greatest honors, such as Agamemnon's hometown (12.70–71). According to Isocrates, such assertions of power were motivated by Spartan *pleonexia*: the excessive desire to get more (territory, in this case), with no regard for the claims of others or prevailing standards of justice.[36] The Spartans, not the Athenians, were the true heirs of the Homeric Agamemnon; whereas the Athenians were to inherit the legacy of the Isocratean Agamemnon. Characteristically, Isocrates says, the Spartans were not "satisfied with their possessions" (12.45), because they had a competitive urge to acquire more than others, even though they eventually obtained far more than they needed (12.45–47).

---

[35] See Balot 2001a: 59–68.
[36] Balot 2001a.

What enabled Sparta to pursue its *pleonexia* on such a large scale and with such success was Sparta's concentration on the military virtues and military discipline, to the exclusion of other useful and less militaristic pursuits, including agriculture and the other arts (12.46). The Spartan outlook is one of narrowly contracted horizons. For Isocrates, the Spartans erected a state that, from the time of its founding, granted primacy to hierarchy, competition, militaristic values, and *andreia*—in short, to the ruthless drives of *thumos*. Examples of Spartan *pleonexia*, militarism, and self-assertion could be multiplied, as Isocrates extends this analysis to Spartan dominance over the helots and to Sparta's tendency to attack its "free," but only formerly autonomous, Peloponnesian neighbors (12.45–47, 12.177–81). Sparta's contracted horizons were both the expression and the cause of a narrow, and thus ill-informed, vision of what *andreia* is really for. Sparta's domestic political culture explains Sparta's lack of success as a hegemon: as Michael Doyle has aptly said, "[I]t was because Sparta was only a war machine that it could not be a large-scale empire."[37]

Hence, when his case might have appeared most unpersuasive within the framework of traditional Greek ethics, Isocrates powerfully revised the traditional picture of Agamemnon in order to show that the "manly" virtues and accomplishments could have genuine worth and dignity only if they squared with the requirements of justice and prudence. Conversely, in his representation of Sparta, Isocrates drew attention to the latently destructive characteristics of the "manly" virtues when unhinged from a controlling ethical framework. For this purpose, he recognized that it was hardly sufficient—indeed, it was irrelevant—for him to contend that Spartan "courage" was itself a sham: during the Persian Wars, the Spartans actually had to be shamed by the Athenians into acting courageously in self-defense (4.93–97; cf. Loraux 1986).[38] Instead, Isocrates dug deeper and argued that the Spartan ethos as such was detrimental to the panhellenic cause. This point becomes evident in the conclusion of the *Panathenaicus*.[39]

---

[37] Doyle 1986: 72.

[38] Even so, Isocrates does maintain Athens's superiority to Sparta in the realm of warfare strictly construed (12.60–61, 12.155).

[39] For an interesting and thorough attempt to explain the generic affiliations of this conclusion, see Gray 1994; my account shares certain elements with Gray's, but, with Allan Bloom (Bloom 1955/1995), I hold that Isocrates' view of Sparta was complex; as Bloom's account illustrates, a careful reading of the corpus shows that, despite his criticisms of Sparta, Isocrates also found elements of the Spartan *politeia* and *paideia* to be admirable.

Making the Case for Sparta?

In this surprisingly long, complex conclusion, Isocrates' "interlocutor" identifies "athletic practices," "training in courage," and "discipline for war" as Sparta's paramount contributions to Greek culture (12.217). Isocrates offers an initial rebuttal of this "interlocutor," but he does not directly contest the value of these pursuits, properly used. Instead, he condemns the Spartans' misuse of military discipline for the sake of *pleonexia* (12.220, 12.223, 12.228, cf. 12.241). But he then expresses doubts about this condemnation. Had he been excessive (12.232)? His "interlocutor" thinks so, of course, which leads him to reread against the grain in order to find praise of Sparta hidden within the ostensibly condemnatory speech. In his persona as speaker, however, Isocrates remains silent as to the substance of this radical interpretation (12.265), even though he had previously emphasized the ethical necessity of admonishing his students when they went wrong (12.203)—all of which, taken together, communicates a tangible sense of *aporia* to Isocrates' external audience of readers.[40]

Along with Isocrates' expression of self-doubt, this *aporia* indicates, I think, Isocrates' view that it is difficult, if not impossible, to locate the ethical significance of such a complex virtue as courage in the abstract, without understanding the courageous agent's motives, effective causes, intentions, and wider goals. Isocrates both appreciates the importance of the military virtues and worries seriously about the dangerous proclivities of militaristic culture. He masterfully performs the balancing act characteristic of those who write thoughtfully about courage, manly virtue, and the exercise of international power.[41]

As Isocrates' "interlocutor" says, Sparta's high-minded devotion to manliness (12.242–43) is, at least in certain respects, admirable, in so far as it expresses self-respect—a quality that Isocrates elsewhere praises in the Athenians, who refused to abase themselves before the aggressive Spartans (12.117–18). Moreover, the Spartans exemplified at least some of the ideals Isocrates articulated in the *Areopagiticus*—that is, republicanism, moderation, discipline, order—which perhaps enabled Isocrates to say that the worst Spartan excesses were not true to Sparta's own ideals

---

[40] On the aporetic conclusions of *Panathenaicus*, see Too 1995: 68–73. For other reflections on Isocrates' incorporation of a pro-Spartan interlocutor into this discourse, see Konstan 2004: 119–21.
[41] Cf. the essays in *Social Research* 2004, an issue of the journal dedicated to courage, in particular Kateb 2004.

(4.110), ideals that had once led the Spartans to expel tyrants from Greek cities (4.125, 12.153–54, cf. 7.61).[42]

Yet Spartan *andreia* has often led to ruthless aggression and *pleonexia* (4.114, 12.46–48, 12.55, 12.103, 12.187–88). Sparta itself, in fact, underwent a transition similar to that of Athens, from old-fashioned virtue to corrupting naval imperialism (7.7, 8.101–3); yet Sparta's old-fashioned virtue was not ever as admirable as that of Athens (e.g., 4.57–65). And, to repeat, Sparta's aggressiveness toward other states was remarkable even from the beginning (12.45–47). For Isocrates one thing is certain: Sparta's contracted horizons do not provide an appropriate context in which citizens can reflect appropriately on courage, locate it properly within their social scheme of ethical ideals, and correctly limit the self-aggrandizing tendencies of courage itself. As virtuous as Sparta may be, and as positive as the manly virtues are, the Spartans have no vantage point from which to educate courage itself to become peace seeking.

Spartan Politics at Home and Abroad

Isocrates' analysis of Sparta's domestic political culture is important because, in Isocratean political thought, a particular citizenry, such as that of Sparta, tends where possible to export its domestic relations to other Greeks.[43] This is the basis of Isocrates' account of Spartan foreign policy, not only in relation to other Peloponnesian states, but also in relation to the wider Greek world. Power in the international world was, for the Spartans, a zero-sum competition in which their own prestige, unfathomable desires, and power could only be, and necessarily had to be, extended through the diminution of others.

This was the logical foreign extension, for Isocrates, of a domestic political culture in which *kratos* consisted in hierarchy, competition for dominance, and ruthless displays of masculinity (12.178–81; but cf. 7.61, 8.142–44). The Spartans refused to extend their domestic advantages to others; instead, they exported decarchies to the Greek world, a form of constitution that was unprecedented and harmful (12.54–55). After the Peloponnesian War, in particular, the Spartans reduced the other Greeks to a condition of slavery worse than that experienced by their own helots

---

[42] On the ambiguities of Isocrates' presentation of Sparta, see Bloom 1955/1995; Buchner 1958: 124–27.
[43] See the insightful treatment of this general issue provided by Bringmann 1965: 31–46; cf. also Bloom 1955: 123–29.

(12.103–4). By setting up decarchies in the Greek states, Isocrates says, they acted like the minions of a helot (4.111), and in the process they brought the cities under their control into a state of anarchy (4.113). Just as the Spartans were willing to enslave others, so too were they willing to become slaves in order to pursue power. Tellingly, just as the Spartans destroyed the autonomy of their Peloponnesian neighbors, so too did they mortgage off Ionian autonomy, previously not vendible, in order to maintain their own *kratos* within Greece (4.117). The Spartan sale of their ethnic (second?) cousins turned the Ionians into abject slaves (4.123).

Spartan power within the Greek world therefore had the interesting, and perhaps paradoxical, effect of subverting *aretē* on the Ionian coast. (Notice the contrast with Agamemnon's leadership of the Greeks: having found them "full of anger and spirit and envy and ambition" (12.82), Agamemnon channeled their natural passions to the positive ends of courageous military accomplishment.) Because of the Spartans' unwise leadership, the Ionians were forced to fight on the side of the Persians against the free Greeks, with the result that they were, in effect, struggling to further their own servitude (4.124). Servitude has an enervating effect on men's fighting spirits: the Persians, Isocrates says, constantly "show arrogance toward some men, and act like slaves towards others"—a hierarchical condition that tends to produce cowards rather than courageous fighters (4.150–51).[44] Is this not the condition that the Spartans produced, in their brief periods of unchallenged ascendance, throughout the Greek world? When the Spartans were at their height at the end of the Peloponnesian War, their behavior turned out to be not only politically and economically harmful, but also ethically disastrous for all Greece, in that it led to a debasement of the Greek character.

The Characterisics of Exemplary Leadership

Isocrates' critique of the Spartans' militaristic ethos helps us to grasp his wider philosophical concerns about leadership. Traditionally, Greek thinkers had worried that leaders tend to misuse their power and to abuse the virtues that originally justified their leadership, in order to pursue *pleonexia*. They want too much. In the course of exercising otherwise positive qualities, such as courage, they usually take more than their fair share.

---

[44] Compare similar themes in Herodotus and the Hippocratic *Airs, Waters, Places*; with Forsdyke 2001.

So Achilles and Thersites reproached the great leader Agamemnon; so the other Greeks reproached the Spartan leadership after the Persian Wars; so the Greeks reproached imperial Athens; so Socrates reproached the aspiring leader Callicles; and so on. Isocrates participates in this tradition. In his own novel presentation of Greek history, though, Isocrates additionally teaches that leadership inherently presents underlying dangers. The defective character of existing leaders is not the only problem. Rather, the impulse to become a leader is suspect in itself, as are the drives necessary to maintain a position of primacy. Since prospective leaders *must* compete with others to win and maintain primacy, they tend to overvalue the competitive impulse, to pursue victory destructively, and to see hierarchy as a telos in its own right (cf. 12.98).

Such insights evoke a telling contrast between Sparta and Athens. Even after winning a position of uncontested leadership, the Spartans continued to assert their own strength and spirit by "doing down" the other Greeks, whereas the Athenians, once on top, were better able to confine *andreia* to its proper sphere, because they could see what *andreia* is really for. How did Athens escape the vices inherent, if we are to believe Isocrates, in leadership? The initial answer is that they correctly recognized that encouraging the prosperity of the other Greeks not only gave them a good name, but also benefited them politically and materially (4.104–5, cf. 8.143–44). The Athenians understood that their farsighted leadership and self-restraint were not simply altruistic; they saw that paradoxically, indeed, virtue is chiefly of benefit to the virtuous agent; Sparta's vices, by contrast, led not only to injustice toward others, but also to the diminishment of Sparta itself (12.55). Like the Spartans, of course, the Athenians, too, exported their own political culture when they led others, but their political culture was, and had been from time immemorial, fair-minded and public spirited. And so their leadership tended to be more "successful," in a profoundly eudaimonistic sense. Though referring to both ancestral Athens and Sparta, this passage clarifies Isocrates' admiration for Athens's benefactions:

> They managed the affairs of others in the same way. They showed consideration for the Greeks and did not treat them arrogantly, thinking that it was necessary to lead them in the field but not to tyrannize over them...they brought the cities to their side by benefiting them, instead of subverting them by force, keeping their word more faithfully than men now keep their oaths, and deeming it just to abide by their agreements as though they were necessities, not priding themselves on their power so much as being ambitious to

live moderately, thinking it right to have the same attitude toward the weaker as the stronger had toward themselves (4.80–81 cf. 12.47–48; 12.54–55).

Notice that Isocrates, in the midst of apparently standard epitaphic bromides, places special emphasis on impartiality. Impartiality, especially as expressed through obedience to written law (cf. 4.39–40), had long been a feature of Athenian self-presentation (e.g., Thuc. 1.75–76); but Isocrates has refashioned this ideal as the golden rule of justified, beneficial, and moderate imperialism.[45] The Athenians' willingness to subject themselves to pacts with the weaker, even to assert ethical principles that govern relations between strong and weak, provides a contrast with, for example, the Thucydidean Athenians, for whom justice cannot pertain between those who are not equals (5.89). Athenian impartiality in the Isocratean sense also provides an explanation for the Athenians' proper admiration for self-control as opposed to the ruthless assertion of *kratos* (cf. 4.176, 12.47–48). The Athenians had the political wisdom to see that by treating others as they would have themselves be treated (12.54, 12.94, cf. 8.134), they could lead the Greeks effectively, with true courage, and in the right causes. Thus their desire for leadership was regulated by their interest in achieving larger, well-formulated goals; and they clearly and certainly distinguished their courage from any excessive and reckless forms of daring (4.77). They were principled, and they were dedicated to larger principles and visions of human goodness. As Isocrates shows in his discussion of Agamemnon (12.80–82), one of the central attributes of effective international leadership is the ability meaningfully to direct the martial passions for the sake of larger, justified, and (crucially) non–martial goals.

In making these theoretical points, Isocrates clearly strove to counter the chief fifth-century accounts of Athenian imperialism. Thucydides, for one, had crafted an image of Athenian militarism in which the Athenians effectively exported their political passions, even their vices such as *pleonexia*, so as to maintain harmony in domestic politics. The Old Oligarch, by contrast, had offered a less "nationalistic" and more class-based analysis according to which the Athenian demos, construed as the poor, exercised *kratos* over the rich and extended their power, with the help of the allied poor, over the rich throughout the Greek world. Isocrates' account of Athenian success is less adversarial than that of either predecessor: for

---

[45] On Isocrates' recommendation of a cosmopolitan and Panhellenic ethos to counter parochial self-aggrandizement, see Ober 1998: 255–56, along with Saïd 2001: 276–86, who considers the question specifically from the perspective of ethnicity.

Isocrates, the Athenians' brilliance lay in their capacity to see that their interests would best be served by promoting the welfare of other Greeks, by encouraging their fledgling democracies (4.104–6), by participating, in other words, in the "long-term transactional order" of which the Spartans seemed desperately unaware (4.53).[46]

One might now be inclined to think that Athens's comparatively mild hegemony is to a certain extent praiseworthy but that, ideally, the Athenians should have left the other Greeks autonomous and given peace the opportunity to flourish. Let us therefore recall that Isocrates elsewhere envisioned peace as the ultimate goal of political and military action. No theorist with Isocrates' worries about the destructive consequences of untrammeled *thumos,* or unhinged power and courage, could possibly idealize warfare as a desirable state of human affairs (cf. 4.167–68). In his *On the Peace*, for example, Isocrates fulminates against the warlike virtues when they are not properly understood as peace seeking.[47] Yet these are, even for Isocrates, utopian reflections. Peace did not have a fighting chance. In Isocrates' view, and possibly in reality, the geopolitical world of the Eastern Mediterranean was sufficiently chaotic to make strong military leadership and preparedness necessary features of political survival. In fact, Isocrates once says that war against Persia is, uniquely, better than peace (4.182), but his concern is that Persia has always threatened Greek prosperity and will continue to threaten it in the future (4.17, 4.67, 4.183, 12.163). Accordingly, it would have been naïve to assume that domestic prosperity, such as that of Athens, would not be openly attractive to predatory foreign states.[48]

For Isocrates, both the symbol and the embodiment of domestic prosperity is Greek culture, which reached its pinnacle in Athenian *logos* and love of wisdom (4.47–48; *Antidosis* 293–96, 8.145). As the city's, and indeed humankind's, noblest achievement, philosophy is most in need of protection from barbarism.[49] Thus, even if we cannot credit Isocrates' way of deriving Greco-Persian tensions from natural hatred (4.157–59), we can perhaps "translate" his account by saying that he wrote for an audience

---

[46] For the term, see von Reden 1995. For this analysis of Thucydides and the Old Oligarch, see Balot 2001a: 136–78, 185–93.
[47] Davidson 1990.
[48] Bloom 1955/1995; Bloom 1955: 86, 107–110, 128–129.
[49] On the need to protect philosophy from external attack, see Bloom 1955/1995: esp. 27–34; Bloom 1955: 107–110, 128–134. For a helpful account of what Isocratean *philosophia* is, how it relates to the political deliberation of the city, and how it differs from its Aristotelian counterpart, see Depew 2004: 159–66.

that was understandably anxious about protecting its own most cherished goods when persistently faced with the prospect of invasion by a culturally different, wealthier, and militarily superior Mediterranean neighbor. The military virtues had to be kept in their place, to be sure, but they did play a critical role in providing the secure environment within which moderation, justice, and philosophy could be cultivated.

Thumos, Sympathy, and Impartiality

The big question, still, is how Isocrates proposed to help the Athenians retain that impartiality toward other Greek states that had held them in such good stead in previous years. For, as Plato illustrated in the *Republic*, the special weakness of *thumos*, and of *thumos*-driven individuals and states, is partiality, or prejudice in favor of asserting one's own claims and ignoring those of others.[50] *Thumos*—the source of shame, anger, and self-respect, which are all emotions that help to make courage possible—is the self-aggrandizing psychological element *par excellence*.[51] To become what it ought to be, namely, a motivation to behave honorably and to protect what is rightfully one's own, *thumos* must be correctly governed and guided by the intellect, so as to see itself, ultimately, as peace seeking. In the Platonic *Republic*, this proper ordering of psychological elements is accomplished through the elaborate education of desire described in Books 2 and 3, through the legal system of Callipolis, and in particular through inculcation of the belief that one's happiness, as an individual, can best be realized through voluntary submission to the commands of philosophers.

Isocrates holds no brief for such quasi-utopian schemes, but he does work with a similar insight into the self-aggrandizing tendencies of *thumos*. He aspired to manage *thumos* through extending the sympathies of the Athenians, through making them see that they had reason to view the entire Greek world as their own and Persia as unconditionally different. His extension of sympathy, as well as his praise of the Athenians for abiding by their duties toward their fellow Greeks, was his particular way of tempering *thumos* and encouraging the Athenians and other prospective leaders to show care for the Hellenic world altogether (4.81–83, 4.122, 12.47–52).

---

[50] This point is made clearly and enthusiastically in Mansfield 2006.
[51] On the character of *thumos* in the Platonic texts, see Hobbs 2000; Cooper 1999d. The most penetrating philosophical discussion of these emotions remains that of Taylor 1985.

At first glance, Isocrates' arguments for ethnic kinship between Athenians and other Greeks look disturbingly "ideological" or superficially rhetorical. But their point, I think, is less to persuade his audience that any real-life genealogical relationship exists, than to heighten awareness of the similarities between the leaders and the led within the Greek world. Greece was a world of small-scale republics based on the rule of law, fragile and evolving hierarchies of power, and shared concerns to protect Hellenic culture, religion, and *bios* from larger Mediterranean neighbors. Spartan *pleonexia* prevented the Spartans from seeing this point with any clarity, so that they resolutely based their actions on a narrow, ungenerous, and ultimately self-defeating conception of their self-interests. For the Spartans' own concerns were equivalent merely to the constricted interests of the Spartan authorities, and secondarily to the full complement of Homoioi. Spartans habitually confuse what is in their own interests with what is not, because they fail to recognize and respect the obligations placed on them by ethnic relations with the other Greeks (12.94, 12.184). Their sympathies do not extend far enough (4.131–32).

For the Athenians, by contrast, the notion of self-interest extended far beyond the geographical limits of Attica, not to mention the even narrower boundaries of interest pursued by the Athenian elite. And so Isocrates' presentation of ethnic bonds as a *de facto* feature of the Greek world is, in reality, a rhetorical summons to the Athenians, and perhaps to all the Greeks, to view themselves, correctly, as united in security and cultural interests that go beyond the merely local. That the Athenians were, even sometimes, able to appreciate the force of such a vision in their imperial ventures—with mistakes and lapses, as Isocrates is willing to admit—testifies to their comparatively broad comprehension of their own flourishing.

Potential Conflicts between Impartiality and Sympathy?

Since it openly promotes *philosophia* as the highest human achievement, Isocrates' analysis invites us to reflect upon his central ideals at a higher level of abstraction. One might object, in particular, that impartiality and sympathy are strange bedfellows.[52] Impartiality, in essence, calls on human beings to adopt a "view from nowhere," to reason morally in an abstract way, unencumbered by emotions or partisan ties or particular loyalties.[53]

---

[52] Friedman 1998.
[53] Nagel 1986; Nagel 1991; Friedman 1998.

Impartial individuals must appreciate that they are single agents among many fundamentally similar or equal agents, without morally substantive distinction. In the Kantian conception, indeed, "impartiality...demands that the moral agent reason in detachment from her own loyalties, projects, and emotions"; ideally, the moral agent is motivated by a sense of duty toward rationally legislated categorical imperatives.[54] But sympathy, like love, is an emotion of caring and attachment that makes impartial acts, at least in the traditional philosophical sense, impossible. Hence, ostensibly, a major conflict exists between the two.

Isocrates' reflections on sympathy and impartiality suggest that impartiality can be, and perhaps has to be, motivated by proper emotions; and sympathy is a particularly good candidate for this job. The Athenians' sympathy led them to recognize, quite properly according to Isocrates, that fair-mindedness, justice, and impartiality were the appropriate responses to other Greeks. The Athenians' impartial leadership—their willingness to abide by compacts, to extend the benefits of democracy to the other states, and so on—was no less effective for being motivated by sympathy. Rather, their like-mindedness with other Greeks, based on a clear recognition of similarity, gave their impartial stance its point. The other Greeks were very much like themselves; indeed, they were *oikeioi*, "their own," their kin. Hence they, too, deserved and could appreciate the importance of the political and economic advantages that the Athenians enjoyed at home and extended to others abroad. What is more, in the Isocratean conception, sympathy and impartiality need not conflict with prudence: the Athenians solidified their leadership through a sympathetic, and wisely impartial, approach to leading the other Greeks.

If this Isocratean explanation helps to reduce some of the tensions between sympathy and impartiality, then one might still have the reservation that Isocrates' own sympathies were limited, in that his politics was informed by an unattractive, ethnocentric dichotomy between Hellenism and barbarism. Even worse, he presents this dichotomy as based on natural differences. Thus, the impartiality he recommended as the key to effective leadership did not extend to the Persians; Isocrates was no cosmopolitan, closeted or otherwise. Would he, though, be committed to becoming a cosmopolitan if he were to follow his intrinsically admirable principles to their logical conclusions?

---

[54] Friedman 1998: 394.

Pressing this point, I think, illustrates the limitations of motivating "hegemonic impartiality" by encouraging sympathy. For, as the Hellenistic and later cosmopolitan theorists were to show, genuine "citizens of the world" rejected local, partial attachments in order to find common ground with other human beings at the level of, most often, rationality. Their rejection of local attachments was, in effect, a rejection of the chief sources of sympathy in human experience—shared language, ritual, history, and genealogy. Cosmopolitan impartiality, as admirable as it may sometimes be, is thin, even minimalist, and so has a hard time motivating political or military action.[55] Sympathy, on the other hand, is a good source of military motivation, but it tends to work through drawing boundaries between human beings, often by encouraging patriotism or nationalism or ethnic pride among members of an "in-group," and often by cultivating unappealing sentiments toward outsiders. In short, then, Isocrates made a compromise that is worth pondering, even if we eventually reject it. Isocrates prized Hellenism for its cultural achievements. In order to defend Hellenism, he evoked an ethnically based patriotism that has often been dangerous in the extreme.[56] But his form of panhellenic patriotism was also singularly capable of motivating an adequate defense of Greece in the chaotic ancient Mediterranean world. Such are the paradoxes and the limitations of Isocrates' conception of enlightened hegemony.

---

[55] Orwin 2006.
[56] Kateb 2000.

PART II | Equality, Emotion, and Civic Education

CHAPTER 8 | Courage, Equality, and Military Recognition in Democratic Athens

SO FAR WE HAVE focused on the Periclean model of democratic courage and its applications in the texts of historians, orators, and philosophers. The resulting picture is ethically complex. In the hands of both pro-democrats and democracy's critics, we have uncovered a remarkably stable set of associations between courage and democracy at Athens. Yet in other sources we will discover both ideological and conceptual ambiguity. Neither democratic orators nor citizens maintained a strict or systematic adherence to the model of courage we have investigated. We begin with the relationship between courage and equality.

From vignettes such as Demosthenes' representation of Strato, and from Hyperides' view that the soldiers' courage aimed at freedom and equality under the law (see chapter 3), it has become clear that the Athenians strove to create a more egalitarian form of courage—one that corresponded to their well-known subscription to democratic equality. It is already clear that the propensity to adhere to a rational, deliberative vision of courage advanced what has been aptly called the Athenians' "democratization of birth privilege."[1] This self-image helped Athenians distinguish themselves, not only from the Spartans, but also from the authoritative cultural ideals represented in the Homeric epics. These poems hold it up as a well-known ideal that the heroes should be "speakers of words and doers of deeds" (*Il.* 9.443). These are the two categories in which the heroes are sharply distinguished from the mass of fighters. At the beginning of *Iliad* 2, when

---

[1] The phrase comes from Ober 1989: 259–70.

Odysseus is shown chastising Thersites, a man of the lower class, he says, "My good man, sit still and listen to what others are saying, those who are better than you. You are a coward without any strength, and you are worthless in battle and in council" (200–202).

The Athenian democracy dignified the Homeric lower classes, summoning them to speak in the Assembly, to operate the machinery of the democracy, and to gain recognition by defending the city. The Athenian democracy allowed the likes of Thersites to become speakers of words and doers of deeds. The structures of democratic cognitive work and military practice democratized the formerly heroic virtue of courage by making it available to all citizens of the democracy, as a result of their recognized cognitive capacities and their courage on the battlefield.[2] Even if Homeric debate and reasoning were not as "primitive" as Finley once thought, the democratic experience was still significantly more complex than the Homeric experience, because the democracy established institutions that actively encouraged all members of society to reflect upon their ideals, their emotions, and their behaviors. This made democracy as a political form distinctive by comparison with other Greek forms of political organization.[3]

Yet, after several decades of carefully re-examining Athens's ideology and institutional practices, scholars have begun to ask whether the Athenian democracy did not also maintain certain exclusions in relation to poor Athenian citizens—in addition, of course, to its well-known exclusion of women, slaves, and metics from political participation. By "poor" Athenian citizens, I do not mean to call to mind the distinction between *hoi plousioi* (the rich, or those who did not work for a living) and *hoi*

---

[2] On the cultural significance of Homeric models among fifth-century Greeks, especially concerning warfare, see Clarke 2002. Self-representation and practice tend to part company here: anyone who wished might speak in the assembly (e.g., Dem. 18.170; cf. Aesch. 1.24, 3.4), but few regularly proposed motions. On the distinction between active and passive participation in the Assembly, see Hansen 1991: 306; on the relative sizes of these participant groups, see Hansen 1991: 267–68. As Hansen points out, though, "The level of political activity exhibited by the citizens of Athens is unparalleled in world history, in terms of numbers, frequency and level of participation" (313). The "cognitive work" I am discussing would regularly have taken place formally in the Assembly and other public forums, and informally throughout the gathering places of the city.

[3] For a clear and concise statement of Finley's view of the Homeric assembly and Homeric "counsel," see Finley 1978: 121–25; his view of Homeric reasoning as "primitive" has been criticized by Schofield 1986. In his conclusion, though, Schofield rightly points out that "[no]o council in the *Iliad* is or could be as sophisticated as the debate on Mytilene in Thucydides 3," which, I would argue, is a symptom of the novel structures of epistemological work that took place in the Athenian Assembly. See further chapter 9.

penētes (those who had to work for a living). By "poor" I refer instead to those who could not afford the heavy armor of the Greek land soldier known as the hoplite. These men served as rowers and light-armed troops in the Athenian military and belonged to the lowest Solonian census class, that of the thetes. They were craftsman, agricultural laborers, and small farmers. If they owned agricultural land at all, then their holding did not exceed roughly 3–4 acres: probably enough to support a nuclear family, but usually not an enlarged *familia* consisting of slaves or large animals.[4]

The status of these poor citizens is of special concern for historians of ancient democracy, because democracy, or "people power," implies the extension of political privileges to all free, adult male citizens, and yet these poor citizens appear to have "enjoyed" limited privileges in several key respects. For example, historians are uncertain whether Athenian thetes were formally registered as citizens in the local political districts of Athens. Controversy reigns as to whether thetes were included in the city's honorific casualty lists. Moreover, thetes were constitutionally (i.e., *de iure*, if not *de facto*) excluded from holding office in the Athenian democracy, even if this provision was a dead letter by the late fourth century (*Ath. Pol.* 7.3–4). Finally, M.H. Hansen's studies of Athenian "politicians" have demonstrated that even if all Athenians were free to initiate motions in the Assembly, very few men, and desperately few, if any, poor men, actually did so on a regular basis. These are considerable paradoxes. Even if Athenian democracy granted power to the people to an unprecedented

---

[4] There are numerous complications in the sociological analysis of hoplites and thetes and, as a result, there is considerable controversy over whether census-class thetes could serve as hoplites and over the relative likelihood that thetes (and even poorer hoplites) were subject to conscription. These points deserve further, detailed investigation. On balance, at this stage, it seems advisable not to draw rigid correlations between census class and military service. Despite the traditional orthodoxy, the armor of hoplites was not standardized and was often of the rough-hewn or even homemade variety, with the result that many census-class thetes could also have served as hoplites. If indeed a significant number of thetes served as hoplites, then the elements of Athenian ideology focusing on hoplites would thereby have become available to all Solonian classes. Even so, historical questions about the commemoration of nonhoplitic, and especially naval, service would still remain, and these questions would then concern the poorer of the thetes, who rowed in Athens's ships and provided military power to the city. For discussion of the various controversies, see, among others, Christ 2001; Gabrielsen 2002: 92–98; Raaflaub 1999: esp. 150n.49; van Wees 2002: 61–72 and 2004: 52–57. On the identity of the rowers in Athenian ships, see Graham 1992, 1998; Hunt 1998: esp. 83–101; van Wees 2004: 202–31; and Rosivach 1985 (with caution). There is an emergent consensus that thetes, along with a substantial number of slaves, rowed Athenian ships in normal circumstances. On slaveholding among the poor, the situation again deserves further study. Preliminarily, note Thuc. 7.13.2 with Graham 1992 and 1998: even relatively poor rowers sometimes brought their own slaves aboard warships, and ordered them to row in order to earn additional money, as the craftsmen of the Erechtheum building accounts (*IG* i³ 474–79) are shown to have done.

degree, democratic institutions were also filled with unresolved ambiguities about the status of Athens's poorest citizens.[5]

This chapter examines the honor granted to the courage and military spirit of Athens's poorest citizenry, through considering the city's public recognition of their military contributions, or lack thereof.[6] When it came to the commemoration of courageous deeds, were the rowers uniformly ignored, or perhaps despised and treated as second-class citizens? Were they viewed as less courageous and manly than their better-off fellow citizens? Many scholars have said so. Raaflaub, for example, has argued that the rowers' "status, unique and under constant attack by elite circles, constantly needed to be defended and supported—and to be legitimized by continuous success."[7] Gregory Anderson has called the thetes altogether a "citizen underclass."[8] Reinhardt Stupperich has noted that "the navy, despite its importance for Athenian democracy, does not play a role in the iconography of the state burial."[9] A preponderance of evidence indicates that the hoplite, not the rower, was at the center of the Athenians' military commemorations, discourses, and even imagination.[10]

Yet how then did the Athenians square their military commemorations and "imaginary" with their egalitarian ideals? For courage, citizen equality, and military glory were particularly sensitive topics in democratic Athens, the ancient Greek polis that, as Paul Cartledge has said, "most fervently preached the gospel of equality."[11] What is at stake is the extent to which Athenian citizens as a whole viewed themselves as *andreioi*, as both manly and courageous. In the Athenian culture that emphasized the male/female polarity, effeminized military rivals such as the Persians, admired pugnacity, and viewed slaves as weak and cowardly, it was crucial for

---

[5] On many of these points, Raaflaub 1996: 154–59 provides a thorough overview. On the *lēxiarchika grammateia*, the crucial piece of evidence is *IG* i² 79 = *IG* i³ 138.1–7, on which see Whitehead 1986: 34–35. For the view that thetic casualties were honored on the city's public casualty lists, see Bradeen 1969; Loraux 1986: 30–36, 361nn.27–29; Pritchard 1999; Strauss 2000: 265; *contra*, Raubitschek 1943: 48n.102; Raaflaub 1996: 156 is agnostic. On the speakers, see Hansen 1983; Hansen 1991: 144–45, 270–72.

[6] Whereas I focus on public recognition as illustrated by speeches and monuments in democratic Athens, Christ 2006: 112–18 offers an excellent account of the ways in which victorious troops (and especially generals) were forced to work through the city's democratic institutions in order to win the recognition due to them for their victories.

[7] Raaflaub 1996: 159.

[8] Unpublished lecture: Association of Ancient Historians, Ann Arbor, Michigan, 2004.

[9] Stupperich 1994: 97.

[10] See the discussions of and the evidence cited by, e.g., Osborne 1994; Strauss 1996: 312–13; Raaflaub 1996, esp. 154–59; Loraux 1986: 33–35, with 360–61; Pritchard 1999; Pritchard 2010: 16–19; Roisman 2005: 106–10.

[11] Cartledge 1996: 178. On the term "imaginary," see Pritchard 1999 and Loraux 1986.

citizens to view themselves as real men. The collective memory of military glory was the key to confirming the status of all Athenian citizens as men.

Equality was a more ambiguous democratic ideal than freedom, because it notoriously lacked determinate content. Proclaiming as one's slogan the Greek words *to ison*, or *isonomia*, or any of the related terms, theoretically left open two questions: equality of what? Equality in relation to which citizens?[12] The Greek polis, or citizen-state, had always held up formal equality of citizens as an ideal, although this implied no specifically democratic associations. Greek oligarchs, for example, typically claimed that they shared an exclusive sort of "equality" within the closed circle of the elite. In order to achieve the status of a distinctively democratic principle, equality had to become the rule for all members of the citizen body, regardless of noble birth or wealth. As a result, Athenian democrats had to extend *andreia* to all citizens equally, if they hoped to democratize courage by transforming it into an egalitarian virtue.

This did not imply that Athenians aspired to view every citizen as possessing a perfectly equal "amount" of courage. There were always visible differences among citizens, to such an extent that Athenians, like other Greeks, gave medals to recognize honor and military achievement.[13] Instead, a notional and "rough" equality that allowed for certain (though not substantial) differences in merit and natural ability, an equality of the sort imagined in Protagoras' theory in Plato's *Protagoras* (320c–28d), would be adequate. The idea of equalizing courage, even in this rough sense, was particularly challenging because manly courage had always been a heroic, Homeric, and individualistic ideal, whereas rowing on ships was a collective endeavor that required considerable technical competence along with bravery pure and simple.[14]

---

[12] By the late fifth century, at the latest, certain "equality" terms, such as *isēgoria*, had come to be particularly associated with democracy, just as others, such as *isokratia*, had come to be associated with oligarchy. But, unlike freedom, which never became an oligarchic or aristocratic ideal (Raaflaub 2004: 23–45), equality was susceptible to reinterpretation by those on all points of the political spectrum. The basic discussion of the "two kinds of equality" is Harvey 1965/6; on equality in Athenian society in general, see Raaflaub 1996.

[13] Pritchett 1974: Vol. II: 280–90.

[14] On equality, see Raaflaub 1996; Cartledge 1996; Balot 2006: 78–85. On the suspicion of rowing *qua technē*, see most forcefully Aristotle *EE* 1230a6–10, *EN* 1116a4–24, both of which argue (rather uncharitably) against the Socratic thesis that courage is *epistēmē*; cf. the discussion of Pritchard 1999. One possible response to the idea that courage cannot be displayed in the exercise of a craft is that, in some cases, the "craftsman," i.e., the rower, must "keep his head" and apply his technical skill even in dangerous and frightening circumstances, and doing so requires courage. Thucydides puts such an argument into the mouth of Brasidas (2.87.4). Along similar lines, in Plato's *Republic* Socrates calls the guardians' (later the auxiliaries') special métier *hē polemikē technē* (374b–e), and he considers their "civic" courage (430c) to consist in the maintenance of

When Athenians themselves confronted the relation of courage to equality, their first thought was reactive. They typically aspired to curb the extravagant ambitions of individual members of the elite.[15] The thought was that all soldiers and sailors who fought for the city deserved honor. For example, Demosthenes praised the fifth-century Athenians for their self-respecting distribution of honors both to military leaders and to themselves. He points out that the demos honored Themistocles, general at the naval battle of Salamis, without robbing themselves of due recognition: "Really, men of Athens (*andres Athenaioi*), they did not deprive themselves of any part of those deeds; and there is no one who would say that the naval battle of Salamis belonged to Themistocles; instead, it was the victory of the Athenians" (23.198). Likewise, in his speech *Against Ctesiphon*, Aeschines approvingly cited the ancestors' decision to honor the Athenian victors at Eion with stone monuments praising the collective achievement of the demos and omitting the names of the generals, "in order," he said, "that the inscription might not seem to be in honor of the generals, but rather of the people" (3.183).

The artistic evidence of the Eion monuments confirms the orators' ideology. The monuments themselves were three stone Hermae, that is, generic and indistinguishable busts of the god Hermes standing firm with an erect phallus. A painted pot from the fifth century probably illustrates this memorial. The placement of the herms invites the viewer, too, to step into the place of a fourth herm, to become a manly, equal, fully democratic military victor.[16] Salamis and Eion were early fifth-century battles in which the new Athenian democracy defeated the Greeks' arch nemesis Persia, a nondemocratic, nonegalitarian power. Demosthenes and Aeschines encouraged their socially and economically diverse audiences to remember these battles as exemplifying achievements in which *all* Athenians participated.

---

correct and law-inculcated beliefs about what is truly to be feared or not, despite the effects of intense pleasure or pain (429b–d). Socrates' long discussion in the *Laches* of whether learning the art of fighting in hoplite armor (which Nicias calls an *epistēmē*) can produce *andreia* is inconclusive (see chapter 6). Be that as it may, it is not obvious that writers hostile to democracy had a consistent set of criticisms to level against rowing specifically because it was a "craft."

[15] Cf. Roisman 2005: 121–23, who helpfully discusses the honors granted to generals and the tensions and conflicts between giving honor to single individuals and honoring the demos as a whole.

[16] On the evidence for the herms, see Osborne 1985c. It makes sense that aristocratic, antinaval elements in the city would "dock" (i.e., cut off the erect penises of) the herms just before the Sicilian expedition, in order to display their contempt for (or, in reality, fear of) egalitarian models of democratic courage: see Osborne 1985c.

Their arguments were rooted in the egalitarian ideology that had characterized their democracy from the beginning. The late fifth-century comedies of Aristophanes provide important indications of this ideology. In 421 BC, during the Peloponnesian War, the chorus of Aristophanes' *Peace* joked that while ordinary citizens stood firm at their posts, the typical commander, "with his triple crest and dazzling purple cloak," is the "first to flee, shaking his plumes like a nimble horsecock," having dyed his crimson uniform a deep brown out of fright (1172–78). Scatological humor targeting commanders as cowardly reinforced the democratic sense that ordinary citizens confronted danger stoutly, equally, and by themselves, and that they were correct to repudiate traditional hierarchies of valor. Historians must always, of course, handle comedy with great care, but such jokes could function as humor only if egalitarian ideas were attractive to the audience. Similarly, when it came to characterizing the lower classes, the sympathetic Aristophanic hero Dicaeopolis called the rowers men who "save the polis (*sōsipolis*)" (Ar. *Ach*. 161–63), while other characters refer in passing to the courage and military prowess of Athens's land forces, who were famously depicted as powerful, angry wasps. These plays were paid for by the demos, judged by members of the demos, and presumably found funny by democratic audiences.[17]

The sources I have just quoted speak without strain of Athens's recognition of the courage of all citizens, as though the distinctions between heavy-armed hoplites and rowers in the fleet were *not* in the forefront of the Athenians' consciousness. This is why the Athenian epigrams on the Persian Wars (from 480 BC) speak of both types of fighters alongside one another, with no difficulty: "These men's courage, imperishable forever, may the gods grant [lacuna]...For, as footsoldiers and on swift-faring ships, they stopped all of Hellas from witnessing the day of slavery" (*IG* i³ 503; Fornara 51). For democratic ideology, such distinctions between hoplites and thetes were a "nonquestion" throughout the classical period (cf. Dem. 3.16, 1.16–18).[18]

---

[17] See Pritchard 1999 especially on the ideology of manliness as represented by Aristophanes; Roisman 2005: 84–104 draws attention to the tensions and ambiguities in the Athenians' way of relating manliness to social status.

[18] Note the statement of Hall 2006: 12 with regard to Aeschylus' *Persians*: "The real hero of Aeschylus' version is the average Athenian citizen-rower. Although the play is careful to avoid neglecting hoplites in the audience by recounting their successful engagement near Salamis (447–72), there is no implication that any particular Athenians or Greeks were superior to their fellow combatants by birth, class, or rank."

Yet a noisy chorus of ancient authors rejects this picture of equalized courage, on the grounds that the navy is the home of cowardice or, at a stretch, of technical competence (*technē*), but never of courage and true manliness (cf. n.14, above). In his final work, the *Laws*, Plato had his lead character, the Athenian Stranger, argue that developing naval power fosters bad habits in cities. Speaking of the Athenians' subservience to Minos of Crete, the Athenian says, "For they would have benefited from losing many times seven children, if they could have avoided becoming marines (*nautikoi*: i.e., hoplites transported by ship) instead of steady hoplite soldiers. Marines frequently jump off their ships, then swiftly withdraw at a run back onto their ships; they don't think that they are doing anything shameful in not daring to stand fast and die when the enemy attacks. Excuses are typically made for them, and they are always ready to throw away their weapons and flee without shame, as they say" (*Laws* 706b-c).

The Stranger argues, further, that by having triremes ready to whisk away the infantry whenever necessary, "one would accustom lions to flee deer!"; the Battle of Salamis, specifically, led to a decline in manly virtue (*Laws* 707a, 707c–d). Finally, he maintains that, in their commemorative practices, naval powers inevitably go wrong, because they are forced to congratulate an entire miscellaneous crew of worthless men, that is, the rowers, instead of being able to "distribute honors correctly to each individual" (*Laws* 707a–b). Aristotle, echoing arguments from Plato's *Laws*, found death at sea inglorious, and argued that sailors could potentially be emboldened by experience and *technē*, but could not be truly courageous; death at sea is never a glorious death, precisely because it does not originate in the individual hoplite's resolve to stand fast (*EN* 1115b1–5, *EE* 1230a6–10). The elitist sympathies of these authors were nowhere so evident than in their resolute refusal to respect and honor the courage and the military contributions of a successful navy. Inspired by these passages and others like them, Hans van Wees has concluded: "The contrast between the prestige of hoplites and the disrepute of naval personnel could not be sharper."[19]

One explanation for the allegedly low prestige of the navy or of citizen rowers might be the large presence, up to 50 percent or more at any given naval battle, of slave rowers. But, as Peter Hunt has shown, slaves, too, fought honorably, perhaps as light-armed troops, in many of the most famous Greek land battles of the fifth century, and they hardly

---

[19] van Wees 2004: 200.

compromised the honor granted to the free hoplites at (say) Thermopylae, Plataea, and Delium. The standard recording practice was steadfastly to ignore the presence of slaves on Athenian ships and in Athenian land armies.[20]

Arguably, at least, many modern scholars have been led to the question of thetes versus hoplites by the antidemocratic authors residing in Athens, and not by the concerns of democratic Athenians themselves. Scholars have also been led to this question by oligarchic propaganda produced within Athens. Athenian democracy was a remarkably stable constitution, which lasted from 508 BC to 322 BC, with only two brief interruptions.[21] Those two interruptions were the oligarchic revolutions of 411 and 404 BC. The revolutionaries of 411 BC produced propaganda meant to persuade hoplites to dissociate themselves from their lower-class fellow citizens. The oligarchic theorists of 411 BC denied the democrats' belief in (so-called arithmetic) equality when they proposed distributing power to "whichever Athenians were best able in their own persons and with their property to serve the city" (*Ath. Pol.* 29.5). The oligarchs argued that only those with certain minimum property qualifications could meaningfully contribute to Athens's war effort.

The oligarchs of 404 BC, by contrast, were imposed on Athens by the Spartans and so had little need for such efforts at persuasion and propaganda. But, we are told, they immediately imposed an antidemocratic geography on the city. They changed the orientation of the bema on the Pnyx, which had long faced the sea, and made it face the land, thereby symbolically turning Athenian politics away from the sea toward the land (Plut., *Them.* 19.4). The oligarchs were invested in keeping sea power and sea people, whom they thought of as a "naval mob," from invading Athenian politics.

The seemingly unbridgeable gulf between hoplites and rowers at Athens was an oligarchic and philosophical construct. But the oligarchs and philosophers did have the weight of tradition on their side—including the Homeric epics and the long historical experience of hoplite warfare. This tradition was lasting: after the Athenian experiment in democracy ended, the Hellenistic kings and the Romans, among other nondemocrats, granted

---

[20] On the figures and on the role of slaves in Greek warfare, see Hunt 1998: esp. 83–101, on slaves in the navy; see also van Wees 2004: 202–31.

[21] Ober 1989 helps to show that Athens's political stability over two centuries was a notable fact, both within the framework of the ancient Mediterranean and in the history of democracy generally.

prestige to land soldiers at the expense of rowers, and they did so despite their own dependence on sea power.[22]

Contempt for the courage of rowers was, by contrast, unacceptable in Athens's popular, democratic courtrooms and in the public Assembly, where all Athenian citizens had an equal vote. In his speech *Against Meidias*, for example, Demosthenes represents Meidias as one of the most hubristic members of the elite, as an "outlier" out of step with the reigning egalitarianism of Athenian democracy. In order to achieve a sharp rhetorical effect, Demosthenes imagines how Meidias might express contempt for the military contribution made by his lower-class fellow citizens: "You are just like that, O men of Athens," he imagines Meidias saying, "You do not serve abroad, nor do you think it necessary to pay taxes.... Do you think that I will pay the costs for a trireme and you will not get aboard the ship?" (Dem. 21.203).

Joseph Roisman has suggested that this passage points to "the existence of elitist complaints about the people's poor military spirit."[23] It is possible to imagine such complaints, no doubt; yet Demosthenes created this representation specifically in order to illustrate the extremity of Meidias' hubris, his outrageous efforts to display superiority over the masses of ordinary Athenians. Only an aberrant, arrogant aristocrat would entertain such contempt for the willingness of rowers to fight on behalf of the community.

Without disputing the hoplite's centrality in the Athenian imaginary, we should not be too quick to question the courage or recognition of rowers—like the ancient authors who worked within a primarily elitist framework. To be sure, we find that certain elements of the democratic self-image gave pride of place to hoplites and cavalry. In the artistic evidence from classical Athens, hoplites and cavalry are prominent. The hoplite was typically the normative masculine ideal in classical Athens, as throughout the

---

[22] See, for example, Polybius 6.52, which erects a number of oppositions between the Romans and the Carthaginians along these lines. The Romans are stronger and braver on land because they are citizen-soldiers whose institutions foster martial courage; the Carthaginians employ foreign and mercenary troops who are superior at the "craft" of seamanship. Even so, the Romans are generally successful at sea because the courage of their marines (*hē tōn epibatōn eupsuchia*) typically outweighs even the naval skill of their enemies (6.52.8–9). Polybius is highly invested in the distinction between heavy-armed infantry and rowers. He tends to explain Roman naval success in a way that denigrates rowers, presenting a typically elitist picture that contrasts vividly with the self-presentation of the democratic Athenians. In this respect, he presented the ancient Romans as following Aristotle's advice to the letter. At *Politics* 1327a40–1327b15, Aristotle shows an appreciation for the military and commercial uses of the navy, but he insists that sailors should not be citizens and that "marines" should be heavy-armed infantrymen who have effective control over the ships.

[23] Roisman 2005: 128–29.

classical Greek world. On fifth-century Athenian vases, for example, this hoplite is pictured in countless scenes as an individual hero, which suggests that the individual Athenian land warrior was heroized and ennobled by the community—so much so that the city's patron god, Athena, was depicted as a hoplite herself, not as a rower.[24] Moreover, the frieze of the Parthenon, the quintessential state monument, includes a procession of cavalry. Whatever interpretation one offers of the festival and myths represented on that building, thetes as such played no *de jure* role whatever, while prominence and prestige are accorded *de facto* to the highest economic classes of Athenians, the ones who could own horses. Meanwhile, the Panathenaic procession drew attention above all to aristocratic youths, to the Athenian cavalry, and then to the hoplites, and it is unclear whether thetes participated at all; and, even if they did, they did not do so as rowers. Finally, at a public coming-of-age ceremony, hoplite armor was given to war-orphans when they reached majority.[25]

This evidence, impressive though it may appear, must be handled with care. Many of Athens's poor may have been too poor to commission painted pots for themselves, much less to pay for grave reliefs carved on durable stone, and we are largely ignorant of what might be called "popular art" in democratic Athens—for example, the painted prows of Athens's warships.[26] Moreover, the persistence of heroizing imagery on pots and state monuments might possibly be explicable on internal artistic grounds: for example, the general difficulty of painting three-decked Athenian triremes on pots.[27] Yet, all things considered, these diverse pieces of evidence make a statement about the considerable significance of hoplites and cavalry to the Athenian self-image. This belief is confirmed by literary evidence. Aeschylus' *Persians* of 472 BC, for example, prominently contrasts Athenian hoplites (and not, as might be expected, rowers) with Persians, while the fourth-century orator Aeschines opposed the normative manly hoplite to the suspicious pariah known as the *kinaidos*, or "bugger."[28]

---

[24] See Lissarrague 1989: 42–44.

[25] This paragraph briefly summarizes a great deal of evidence on which a vast bibliography exists: see, for example, Cartledge 1998; Hölscher 1998; Maurizio 1998; Osborne 1994; Pritchard 1999; Raaflaub 1996; Stupperich 1994.

[26] For these and similar points, see Strauss 1996, 2000.

[27] See Murray 2004, 2005, although we should keep in mind, to be sure, the presence of complex ships on large Geometric kraters and, as Murray 2004 points out, on black-figure vases.

[28] Goldhill 1988; Winkler 1990. However, for useful criticisms of Winkler's study of Athenian masculinity based on the polarity of hoplite/*kinaidos*, and more generally of Foucault's reconstruction of ancient discursive selfhood, see Fox 1998.

The question is whether, or to what extent, this evidence compromises the status of thetes. It might do so entirely, if we believe that public recognition is a zero-sum game in which the gains of one class must be offset by the losses of another. But there is another possibility—that Athens was a big, diverse city, and that democratic ideology was a "big tent" that developed several models of admirable manly behavior.[29] If this is the case, then we should not be looking for a specifically "thetic ideology." Instead, we should be looking for diverse indications of respect within a generally democratic ideology.[30] What then, if anything, can we set alongside the foregoing indications of hoplite centrality in Athenian self-representation?

One answer comes from commemorative poetry celebrating Athenian military victories. Already on the early fifth-century epigrams celebrating the Persian war victories (ML 26 = *IG* i³ 503), the Athenians praised the courage (*aretē*) of their men who fought on foot and on the "swift-sailing ships." Similarly, in an early fifth-century Athenian dedication at Delphi (ML 25, *SIG* 29), the inscription says that the Athenians dedicated *hopla* and *akrōtēria* that they had captured from the enemy. In parallel, egalitarian fashion, these monuments commemorate the praiseworthy contributions of both wings of the Athenian military.

Second, the material record provides evidence that celebrated naval actions were held up to the community for admiration and emulation. Most famously, there is the so-called Lenormant relief on the Athenian Acropolis, probably dedicated around 400 BC in commemoration of the activities of the crew of the state ship *Paralus* in the democratic repudiation of the oligarchs of 411 BC. The members of this crew were democratic freedom fighters whose courage stood as a model for every democrat to emulate.[31] Moreover, probably in the mid fifth century, the Athenians erected a permanent monument in stone to the Salamis victory at Cape Tropaea, mentioned by Plato (*Men.* 245a), Xenophon (*Anab.* 3.2.13), and Lycurgus (1.73).[32] These two monuments provide an important indication of public recognition of the thetic contribution to the city's military

---

[29] On the "big tent" conception, see Ober 2005: 69–91; for a different application of the "big tent" concept, albeit in a similar context, see Hanson 1996. This idea is slightly different from, but not incompatible with, Pritchard's conception of the "fractured imaginary": Pritchard 1998, 1999.
[30] Pritchard 2010a: 36–38 provides a sensitive and balanced treatment of the Athenians' commemoration of the courage of lower-class citizens; cf. also Pritchard 1999, especially on the Athenians' ideological treatment of thetes.
[31] The fundamental treatment is that of Beschi 1969–70; cf. also Strauss 2000: 265–67.
[32] On the reconstruction of these trophies, see West 1969.

success, and they gave members of the thetic class, if not of all classes, an ideal to which they could aspire.

Military practice also indicates the Athenians' willingness to grant respect to both its land and its naval forces. We do not find democrats worrying, as Plato did, that hoplites supported by triremes would be less courageous than hoplites untarnished by naval affiliations. We find, in fact, the opposite—the Athenians' increasing coordination of hoplite and nautical service in the classical period. The Aristophanic Bdelycleon referred to his father's "hard work, rowing and soldiering and laying siege" (*Wasps* 682–85)—duties that became closely affiliated as Athens began to use hoplites extensively as marines and what Hanson has called "seaborne hybridized troops" in the late fifth century.[33]

The multipronged Athenian military did not privilege, but rather coordinated, the contributions of hoplites with maritime forces.[34] During the Archidamian War, hoplites traveled aboard triremes to the coasts of the Peloponnese as raiders, and escaped when necessary on the ships (e.g., Thuc. 2.23.2, 2.25.3, 3.94–95). This army-navy affiliation had both practical and symbolic precedents earlier in the fifth century. Sophanes the Athenian, winner of the *aristeia* at Plataea (Hdt. 9.73–75), either carried an iron anchor on his belt or had an anchor device on his shield, symbolizing either way a nautical affiliation for this most storied of Athenian hoplites.[35] This mutual reliance led, correspondingly, to greater mutual understanding and respect between land and sea forces. Men who had experienced danger together came out of the experience, if they survived, feeling a bond with their fellows that reinforced the community of identity between hoplites and rowers. It is in this sense more than any other, I think, that triremes were, as Barry Strauss has argued, the "school of democracy."[36]

Since scholars have been concerned about the thetic rowers' self-respect and their status anxiety and worried that they experienced low prestige and esteem, it is particularly useful to examine directly the emotional quality of their lives as democratic citizens. Did rowers always have to be aspiring to be something or someone else, such as a hoplite or a cavalryman, if they were to win the genuine respect of their fellow citizens and come to respect themselves? This is a difficult question, because the emotions and

---

[33] Hanson 1996: 297; Rawlings 1998.
[34] Cf. Thuc. 1.141 with Hanson 2000: 216.
[35] See Cartledge 1998, Hanson 2000.
[36] Strauss 1996.

psychology of ancient citizens are elusive at our distance, and intangible even from close up.

But we can get a handle on this question if we carefully consider the emotion of "emulation," or *zēlos*, which Aristotle defined in his catalogue of emotions in *Rhetoric* Book 2 as "a certain pain at the manifest presence of goods held in high esteem, which are possible for us to obtain, in the possession of those who are similar to us by nature— pain not because they belong to another, but because they do not also belong to us" (*Rhet.* 1388a32-35). Emulation was a particular type of dissatisfaction with oneself that is characteristic of those who, in Aristotle's terms, strive to be virtuous. Aristotle explains that men tend to be emulous of honors won by their ancestors or their polis, because "they think that these honors are really their own and that they are worthy of them" (*Rhet.* 1388b9-10). Typically, those who are emulous aspire to imitate the virtues of those they take on as role models—in the ancient polis, often one's ancestors or forefathers. We can immediately recognize the close relationship between emulation, in this sense, and the "sense of shame" invoked by Pericles and other orators. Athenians were, in their representations, emulous of their ancestors' accomplishments, and, equally, they had a "sense of shame" before their ancestors as "internalized others" whose imagined judgments provided an inner compass for their own ideals and behaviors.[37]

The critical question is whether the thetes felt that they were worthy of the honors won by Athenian ancestors. Did thetes have their own role models to follow? Could rowers themselves, conversely, act as role models for the entire Athenian community? The Lenormant relief and the Salamis monument give us reason to think so. The corpus of Attic oratory presents an even more complete picture along these lines. As orators, members of the elite vied for approval before their mass audiences and therefore developed a popular democratic ideology that was consistent with the attitudes and beliefs of their listeners (Ober 1989; see also the discussion found in chapter 3). Attic oratory shows that, as rowers, thetes could act as normative role models and thereby help to define the ideals to which all Athenians were encouraged to aspire. Here the Battle of Salamis in 480 BC played an important ideological role, because it was both a naval battle and a turning point in the glorious Greek resistance to Persia.

Consider, for example, Lycurgus' invocation of the courageous heroes of Salamis during his condemnation of Leocrates. Lycurgus expressed

---

[37] On the phrase "internalized other," see Williams 1993, e.g., 85.

anger at supporters of Leocrates who, he claimed, compared Leocrates' desertion of Athens with the Athenians' decision to abandon the city before Xerxes' arrival (1.68–70). Such a comparison would obviously be preposterous. Lycurgus' rhetorical strategy, however, was to conjure up the courageous heroes of Salamis in order to condemn Leocrates' cowardice.

The Athenian sailors, he proclaims, were heroes whose *aretē* was famous everywhere (1.69). "Who is so envious," he asked, "or altogether unambitious, that he would not wish to have taken part in the deeds of those men?" (1.69). The heroic rowers of Salamis were role models and proper objects of emulation for all Athenians. They exhibited their manliness, not only by fighting Persians, but also by being ready to vent their justified anger on those who, like Leocrates, disgraced their valor (1.71).[38] The Athenians' ancestors also won a celebrated victory at land and sea at Eurymedon (Lyc. 1.72). Lycurgus' rhetorical strategy would have been impossible unless Athenians viewed rowing as an activity worthy of real men, worthy of defining what *andreia* meant for all Athenians, including the well-off Leocrates (1.136). Because of their military success, the rowers of Salamis had real authority within the Athenians' imaginations, as ideals to aspire to and as psychological reference points or "compasses" for their current efforts. The rowers, then, played a critical role in the Athenians' emotional lives; just as free speech was specially linked to the rationalistic dimensions of courage described by Pericles and others, so too was equality especially linked to the normative emotions that Pericles and others viewed as productive of courage.

It is true that both upper and lower classes manned the ships at Salamis; the battle was an effort by the entire city, not just thetes, undertaken in emergency conditions. This adds complexity to the picture and perhaps differentiates Salamis from other naval battles. Yet rowing at Salamis was a familiar object of commemoration in later oratory, and we find suggestions there that rowers, too, could be proper role models. Aeschines, for example, encouraged his fellow citizens to "imitate" their forefathers' wisdom and courage in both the land and sea battles of the Persian Wars (2.75). Funeral orators also highlighted the battle of Salamis, glorifying the courage of oarsmen, who were worthy of emulation: "Those men proved superior by far to all others in virtue (*kata tēn aretēn*), both in their counsels and in the risks of war; having left the city and taken to their

---

[38] On anger as an expression of the Athenians' manliness and honor particularly in their capacity as jurors, see Allen 2000.

ships, they ranged their own lives, however few, against the huge armies of Asia." (Lys. 2.40). Similarly, fourth-century speakers emphasized that the city's safety depended on maintaining the fleet and that the city won respect and prestige because of its naval strength.[39] These speakers often utilized the example of past success by rowers in the fleet to inspire their contemporaries to make courageous contributions to the city's welfare.

At our distance from these events, and given the state of the evidence, it is unusually difficult to recover what rowers themselves would have been thinking or feeling as they stood on the brink of battle. Battle exhortations reported by the classical historians, though, indicate that the city recognized and appreciated their *andreia*. As Thucydides reports, the general Phormio said to the rowers under his command, "You should maintain good order and stay by the ships, and respond quickly to commands....And as far as the action goes, recognize that discipline (*kosmon*) and silence (*sigēn*) are of the greatest importance....Fight these men, then, in a way that is worthy of your past accomplishments (*axiōs tōn proeirgasmenōn*)" (Thuc. 2.89).

This is probably not a verbatim account of Phormio's speech. But even Thucydides, normally a critic of democracy, showed that rowers, like hoplites, could be encouraged to fight through appeal to their desire to live up to recognized standards defined by their previous record of achievement. In exhorting the sailors under his command, Phormio praised their courage and daring, rejected the Spartans' supposed monopoly on courage, inspired the crews to fight in a way worthy of their record, and reminded them how crucial their performance in this battle would prove to be. As real democratic men, thetes helped to democratize the formerly aristocratic virtue of courage. Through their sense of shame and honor, they were living up to victorious traditions of their own success. They were not beholden to others' ideals; rather, they believed, and showed, that the traditional vocabulary could be newly and appropriately applied to their own valuable and courageous behavior. And they could, in all likelihood, look forward to seeing a golden Nike erected to commemorate their valor. The public decree preserved on stone and now catalogued as *IG* i² 368 shows that this is precisely what happened roughly a year and a half after the events.[40]

---

[39] Cf. Ober 1978: 122.

[40] Thompson 1944. On the Thucydidean passage, see Cartledge 1998: 64.

Conversely, as Aristophanes' *Wasps* (1117–21) shows, rowers, like hoplites, were also subject to the standards of shame and righteous anger inducing them to serve honorably: the chorus proclaims, "This is painful to us, if some draft dodger gulps down our pay, although he has never picked up an oar, a spear, or a blister on behalf of this land. But it seems to me that in the future whichever citizen does not have a stinger should not make off with the three obols." Not only hoplites, but also rowers, were expected to contribute militarily; not only hoplites, but also rowers, had stingers. And both hoplites and rowers fought to preserve the city's freedom.

But it was the stingers of rowers, in particular, which explain why, in the course of the fifth century, the Athenian demos transformed the city into a resolutely naval power, through its expenditure on the fleet, through its seaward articulation of public space and fortifications, and through its willingness and ability to entrust the city's defense to the fleet. In 457 BC, under the leadership of Pericles, the Athenians built their famous Long Walls in order to protect passage from the city of Athens itself to its port Piraeus, which itself had been fortified in the early fifth century. Centuries later, Plutarch, himself no democrat, envisioned these Long Walls, along with the Athenians' dockyards, to be themselves trophies of military victories (Plut. *Mor.* 349d). Then, in 431 BC, at the beginning of the Peloponnesian War, and again at Pericles' suggestion, the Athenians decided to entrust the protection of the city to its fleet, as they had done in the late 480s under the leadership of Themistocles. No wonder that Pericles, at least as he is represented by Thucydides, could encourage the Athenians to imagine themselves as islanders and their land as entirely trivial by comparison with their control over the sea (Thuc. 1.143, 2.62; with Hunt 1998: 126). Though it took effort, as we have seen, he convinced the Athenians that true courage consisted in staying within the walls and entrusting the safety of Athens to the fleet (see chapter 5). Evidence for Pericles' "island strategy" can, of course, also be found in the pages of the so-called Old Oligarch (2.14–16), which indicates clearly enough that this was not an artificial Thucydidean construct, but rather a central principle of Athenian strategy and foreign policy at the time. If anything, political decisions of this sort might have made the hoplites anxious about their status, their recognition, and their contribution to Athens's military success. But such was not the effect on hoplites, because hoplites could still find important work guarding the walls and serving as marines on the Athenians' ships.

As to the question of why hoplites did not themselves reject any association with thetes—as to why hoplites did not themselves become elitist—the answer lies, I think, in the hoplites' recognition that their own interests would best be served by forming a political coalition with the thetes and reinventing themselves, along with the thetes, as ordinary Athenian citizens, full stop.[41] The fleets brought money and food into the city, while the hoplites' lives were protected; and even their farms underwent little permanent destruction during the Peloponnesian invasions of Attica in the late fifth century.[42] The hoplites still received their portion of glory in public commemoration, despite their unambiguous need to share glory and political authority with their poorer fellow citizens.

It is of no use to construct a ledger or balance sheet in order to stack up naval monuments against memorials honoring the upper classes. Rather, we should imagine the democracy as a broad, inclusive tent in which diverse expressions of manly valor could be held up for public esteem and emulation. It is arguable that the Athenian democracy *had* to establish this ideological "big tent," because, to be militarily successful, and to reproduce a militarized citizenry, the democracy had to develop a structure of rewards and incentives to make Athenian citizens willing to sacrifice their lives for the defense of the polis. Democrats developed a sophisticated ideology that operated as a context-specific and flexible mosaic. This ideology had what Ober has called a "thin coherence."[43] Athenian ideology was coherent enough to create solidarity without imposing a uniform model of honorable achievement upon all citizens.

The important oppositions, for democrats, were not between the classes, but between the Athenian demos as a whole and certain "outsiders." It is well known, for example, that the Athenians drew oppositions between their manly courage and the Persians' effeminacy and cowardice (see chapter 9). The Athenians also continually reinforced the opposition between themselves as men and female outsiders such as the Amazons. They often repeated mythological narratives in which they celebrated their courageous protection of their territory from the invading Amazons— women who, according to Athenian ideology, presumed to act like men but who learned a lesson from the manly and courageous Athenians.[44] In both cases, the entire community worked together to reinforce the Athenians' image of themselves as manly, courageous, and equal.

From very early on, the thetes, who constituted the bulk of Athens's democratic citizenry, perhaps upwards of 50 percent in the mid fifth century,

---

[41] Hanson 1995: 365–90, 1996, and 2001a offer an explanation roughly along these lines.
[42] See Hanson 1983.
[43] Ober 2005: 69–91.
[44] Cf. Fantham et al. 1994: 128–35; Roisman 2003: 127–28.

were steely-eyed pragmatists who played a major role in defending their city from Persian attack, constructed an empire through naval power, and cultivated and reproduced their own self-respect. The self-respect of citizen rowers was, as far as we can tell, characteristic of ancient democracy. Democratic Syracuse, for example, had its own "Salamis moment" when the Syracusan navy gloriously defeated the Athenians in the Great Harbor at Syracuse. Thucydides himself pointed out that it took a democracy to defeat democratic Athens, because of the sizeable force Syracuse could mobilize and because of the city's naval power. According to Thucydides, the Syracusans were proud to have run risks against Athens and to have led the way to victory at sea (7.55–56).

Athenian democratic ideology was powerful because the Athenians' self-representation was flexible enough to preserve the dignity and traditional honors accorded to the cavalry and the hoplites, while also paying tribute to the thetic contribution to the state's military success. If one were inclined to view the matter cynically, one could argue that the politically and militarily powerful thetes made concessions to the upper classes so as to preserve *their* self-respect and thereby to maintain political stability. But a less dramatic and more plausible interpretation is that Athenian democrats developed an inclusive vision of masculinity, civic virtue, and military honor that was appropriate to the social and economic diversity of the citizen body. Certain traditional paradigms and forms of expression persisted; novel forms were created as the lower classes made political gains and enjoyed military success; and the Athenians were left with a conglomeration of different possibilities that satisfied a large number of people over a very long period of time. The ambiguities in the Athenians' equality of commemoration thus supported the city's democratic ideology and practices. Despite the necessary gestures toward civic unity found in the funeral oration and elsewhere, Athenian ideology itself was not always and everywhere unified and self-consistent; it allowed for diversity under the umbrella of unity. Be that as it may, we should not be misled by a tiny, albeit noisy, group of elite authors such as Plato into thinking that Athenian thetes were anything but self-respecting, "manly," courageous, and powerful equals within the Athenian political community.

CHAPTER 9 | Revisiting the "Standard Model" of Greek Courage

IN OUR EXAMINATION OF equality we have rendered more complex, and even ambiguous, the democratic associations of courage. The complexities of our picture invite us to subject the Periclean ideology to further conceptual scrutiny. Of special interest are the motivations of courage and the emotions relevant to courage, two subjects that have not been of principal concern to previous scholars. In particular, as we saw in chapter 2, Pericles made a strong case for distinguishing Athenian shame from Spartan shame. Now we need to probe this argument more deeply by investigating, to whatever extent the evidence permits, the ideals of courage found in Persia, Sparta, and Macedon.

The Athenians argued that their democratic institutions, culture, and ethos gave rise to new ways of criticizing the traditional ideal of courage and of understanding the role of courage in the life of the community. This transformation was supposed to rest on distinctive responses to a particular set of questions—the questions of how courage was motivated; which ends, in particular, courage was meant to serve; how self-consciously the community had reflected on those ends; and how clearly the community could articulate and defend its prevailing methods of instilling courage in the citizenry. Examining the "standard model" of Greek courage, along with the models of Persia and Macedon, will throw light on the Athenians' proud claim to distinctiveness, and perhaps begin to render that claim ambiguous or even unstable.

Conventional Greek courage had always been the product of traditional social norms sustained by fear of the law; fear of one's social superiors; and widespread, and typically quite punitive, practices of shaming cowards. Its final end and goal—its telos—was, quite simply, "honor," the esteem of one's fellow citizens. Citizens of the traditional Greek polis found little need to reflect on their civic practices of motivating soldiers to behave courageously; nor had they any need, in their own view, to question the precise elements or the ethical significance of "honor." They did not need to ask in a more general, philosophical way what was genuinely worthy of honor, as opposed to what their own societies contingently happened to esteem: what human beings, as human beings, ought to cherish and respect as the ultimate ends or objectives of their existence. This characterization of the conventional Greek polis holds true to an even greater extent among Athens's non-Greek rivals throughout the Mediterranean, such as the Persians and the Macedonians. By contrast, the Athenians' claims to distinctiveness—and even superiority—rested primarily on the idea that they had explicitly and openly thought through their conception of human flourishing and securely located courage within the framework of that conception.

We turn now to a more precise consideration of the Athenians' claims to superior courage, by examining courage in "Homeric society," Archaic Greek poetry, Sparta, Persia, and Macedon. In order to scrutinize Athenian courage against the background of conventional Greek, Persian, and Macedonian culture, however, we will have to confront familiar difficulties in handling the source materials. We focus in the first instance on the Athenians' own representations of themselves and their various culturally defined "others." It is certainly possible, if not likely, that the historical realities diverged from the ideologically informed pictures offered by our extant Athenian sources. Hence, we will also have to examine our sources critically and try to uncover the meaning and purposes of non-Athenian ideals of courage as the Athenians' rivals themselves would have understood them. Whatever the status of this question, however, we should nevertheless maintain a lively sense that the Athenians' ideological representations could and did have an impact on the Athenians' experience of their own political realities.

"Homeric Society," The "Isonomic" Polis, and Sparta

In the Homeric epics, we can already see the outlines of what I am calling the "traditional" account of courage. It was most common for Homeric warriors to be motivated to courageous action by the fear of shame and by the desire for honour or social esteem, rather than by a conception of the good life reached through discussion, deliberation, and the consideration of a broad variety of viewpoints.[1] In the Homeric epics, courage based on shame and honor was characteristically very conservative; it was a virtue that served highly traditional ideals and was driven, in particular, by a desire to conform to the culture's leading stereotypes of manhood. The heroes' subscription to traditional ideals motivated their military bravery, whether they expressed courage through aggressive acts of daring (as they do often in the *Iliad*) or through standing fast and enduring pain and suffering (as they do often in the *Odyssey*).[2] As Hector says to Andromache:

> But I would be very ashamed before the Trojan men and the Trojan women with their trailing robes if I should stay far away from battle like a coward. Nor does my spirit urge me to do this, since I learned always to be noble and to fight among the first Trojans, winning great glory for my father and for myself (*Il.* 6.441-446).

The heroes, above all, had surprisingly "complex inner lives," as Miller has written in another context—as we see especially in the case of Hector, whose attachments to his family and his polis made his subscription to the heroic quest for glory particularly ambiguous and multifaceted.[3] Most often, however, the heroes' ways of articulating courage stress their comparatively unreflective dedication to traditional ideals handed down by their fathers over the course of many generations.

Regarding the motivations for courage, we find mostly appeals to disgrace and shame, insults, and furious anger or "spirit." Shame was a battle cry among Iliadic warriors; it was also a general exhortation, as when Nestor shouted to his comrades, "Be men; put into your hearts shame before other men" (15.661; cf. 5.529–32, 6.111–15).[4] When the troops were clamoring to return home, Odysseus reproached Agamemnon with the prospect of disgrace before all living men (2.284–88). When Agamemnon was on the verge of leaving Troy after all, Diomedes taunted him for cowardice and insisted that the other Achaeans would remain in order to plunder Troy,

---

[1] See especially Smoes 1995: 17–18 on the heroes' desire for glory and honor, which was tied to "shame" (*la honte* [*aidos*]) and "courage irrationnel et passionnel" [irrational and passionate courage] (18); on the motivations for warfare in general in Homeric society, especially those of honor and status, see van Wees 1992; on Homeric battle in general, see van Wees 2004: 153–65.
[2] On this contrast between the visions of courage available in the two epics, see in general Smoes 1995: 31–68, who rightly points out the emphasis on *alkē* and *aretē* in the *Iliad* and that on *tlēmosunē* in the *Odyssey*, citing (e.g.) *Odyssey* 5.361–67, 20.10–23.
[3] See Miller 1995a on heroes' complex inner lives in a comparative context; cf. Gill 1996.
[4] On heroic *aidōs*, see Redfield 1975: 115–19; Williams 1993: 78–86; Cairns 1993; Bassi 2003: 33; Smoes 1995: 45–46; van Wees 1992.

since they had sailed to Troy with the gods (9.32–49). The heroes (and even the gods) ranged through the battle lines insulting slackers, including other heroes, by calling them "fawns," "disgraces," cowards, and weaklings (4.242–49, 4.338–48, 4.370–75, 5.470–77, 5.633–46, 5.811–13, 7.96–102, 8.93–96, 13.95–124, and so on).

These insults were reinforced by the heroes' powerful commands to their troops to fight—commands that were backed up by the threat of dire punishments. For example, the troops often fight before the harshly critical eyes of their leaders, under the threat of death and lack of proper burial if they default (2.357–59, 2.391–93, 4.428–32, 12.248–50). Troops were forced to fight in the center of the line if they were seen to be cowards (4.299–300). At other times, the gods drove the troops onward and made them furious for battle, intoxicated with its thrill, driving "spirit" (*menos*) into their hearts (2.450–54, 5.512–13, 7.38–42, 13.47–58).[5]

What, precisely, were the models of courage on offer in the Homeric epics? How did "Homeric society" represent courage to itself? Smoes (1995) has argued that Homeric courage was based on the warlike, aristocratic, and manly heroes' carefully trained character—a set of dispositions that enabled them to be daring, like lions, when confronting the dangers of war (e.g., 5.780–83, 12.40–50, for the similes),[6] and equally steadfast in persevering through periods of suffering and distress (e.g., 13.47–58). To be more specific, the epic poet typically represented courage and cowardice as character-based, and even bodily, states. For example, early in the narrative, when Paris catches sight of Menelaus marking him as a target, the poet says that "he was shaken in his heart" (*kateplēgē philon ētor*; 3.31) and compares Paris to a mountain climber whose knees shake and whose cheeks grow pallid when he encounters a snake (3.33–35). At other times, and most often, courage was a matter of "nerve" and "fighting strength" (*thouridos alkēs*, 4.234) or "spirit" (*menos*, e.g., 6.407) or "heart" and "daring" (*thumos* and *tharsos*, 7.152–53). Speaking with Meriones, the Cretan Idomeneus sums up his view of courage as follows:

> I know what sort of man you are and your courage (*aretēn*). Why is it necessary for you to speak of this? If we all gathered ourselves into formation right now beside the ships for an ambush, there the courage of men is most

---

[5] Cf. van Wees 2004: 162–65 for a conventional account of the "psychology of combat" in the *Iliad*.
[6] As Smoes 1995: 47 points out, there are sixty-five comparisons of heroes to animals in the *Iliad*, forty of them to lions, which symbolize the hero par excellence.

clear, there the cowardly man and the brave man are apparent. For the skin of the cowardly man changes one way and another, and the heart in his chest does not restrain him so that he sits without trembling, but he keeps changing from one leg to the other, and then stands on both feet, and his heart in his chest is pounding, since he is thinking of death, and his teeth begin to chatter. With the brave man, though, his skin does not change color, nor is he too frightened, when he first takes his station in the ambush, and he prays to mix very swiftly in mournful combat; no one would find fault with your spirit and your arms there (13.275-287).

Readers of the Homeric epics will be familiar, moreover, with the class-consciousness of the warriors' ideals of courage. As Étienne Smoes has argued, "Nous verrons que le courage homérique est d'abord une valeur sociale reflétant une société où il importe de sauvegarder l'honneur attaché à son rang" (1995: 18).[7] Ordinary soldiers were not normally rewarded for their valour, nor did they make well-informed decisions about when, where, how, and why they should fight. Needless to say, the Homeric Assembly was not a forum in which all soldiers' ideas and judgments could be openly expressed and debated. Odysseus' violent clubbing of Thersites illustrates the facility with which the heroes often shut down free speech and social criticism, whenever conflicting voices arose in order to question the leaders' decisions (2.246–77; compare the way in which Odysseus treats a man of high status, however, in 2.190–97, as opposed to 2.200–206). In almost every respect, in fact, the ordinary soldiers resembled Tocqueville's "serf," who, as we saw in chapter 1, "acts without thinking" and is "a very ferocious animal trained for war" who shows "blind, minute, resigned, and always constant obedience" (*DA* II.3.25). Only the top cadre of heroes could be "true men" and live up to the long-standing cultural ideals passed down from generation to generation (cf., e.g., *Il.* 5.348, 5.529, 6.112, 7.96–98, 8.163, etc., with Smoes 1995: 33–34, 40–42).

On the other hand, Malcolm Schofield has helpfully reminded readers that the poet meant what he said when he presented the leading heroes' conception of virtuous masculinity as summed up in the advice given by older heroes to younger ones: "always to be the best" (e.g., 6.208, 11.784) and be "a speaker of words and a doer of deeds" (9.443). *Euboulia*— "sound judgment, wisdom in council"—was a key constituent of the

---

[7] "We see that Homeric courage is first of all a social value reflecting a society in which it is important to safeguard the honor attached to one's rank."

heroic ideal, along with the more obvious virtues of martial prowess.[8] This is why Agamemnon is condemned, and even condemns himself, for losing his wits (9.377, 19.88). By contrast, heroes such as Odysseus and Nestor offer articulate, carefully reasoned judgments about difficult political and military situations—such as how to manage the initial conflict between Agamemnon and Achilles with respect to justice on both sides (Nestor: 1.254–91), or how the heroes, despite being wounded, might give the Achaeans confidence to fight on (Odysseus: 14.83–102, with Diomedes: 14.128–32). The heroes also mention, albeit briefly, certain deliberative virtues known to the democratic Athenians: more eyes see better than fewer (10.224–26) and the *thorubos* inhibits public communication (19.78–82).[9]

In light of Schofield's arguments, it is misguided to maintain the "primitivist" view of the epics, that of Finley for example, which held that the heroes' conceptions were naïve or simplistic; it was certainly possible for the heroes to have, as Miller has said in another heroic context, "deep inner lives."[10] The ideal of *euboulia* that was prized so highly by the fourth-century philosophers began to be practiced in earnest among the heroes of the Homeric epics (even in limited ways in the seconds of battle: cf. 11.401–13). Individuals such as Achilles or Odysseus (not to mention the poet himself) were undoubtedly capable of profound reflection on the nature and significance of ideals such as justice (9.309–37, 12.310–28) or self-control and anger (9.252–60). In the company of bards such as Phemius and wise advisors such as Phoenix or Nestor, the heroes could begin to think through their highly traditional paradigms of courage, such as the figures of Herakles and Meleager.

---

[8] Schofield 1986. For a more searching and profound account of Homeric practical reasoning, see Gill 1996: 41–93, reacting against the older pictures of psychology offered by Snell and Adkins. Especially helpful is Gill's discussion of Hector's motivations for battle, including his sense of shame and his adherence to social roles: see Gill 1996: 81–93. Gill does not, however, engage explicitly with the politics of courage and shame, either in the Homeric poems or in Greek society, focusing strictly on questions of ethical psychology and engaging with larger discourses developed by Kant, MacIntyre, and Williams. Contrary to both Schofield 1986 and Gill 1996, Smoes 1995: 82 argues that both Homer and Herodotus often dissociated wisdom in counsel from martial prowess. My own view is that both authors—like others—offer us diverse glimpses of the relationship between wisdom and daring in exploring both the possibilities and the limitations of the ideals of courage held by their characters. On the other hand, Smoes 1995: 57 is surely right to emphasize, implicitly *contra* Schofield, that courage in the *Iliad* is far from the virtue described by Aristotle, because it is constituted by "ardeur physique," "l'aggressivité, force innée ou occasionnelle recue des dieux, souci de son rang et des privileges, etc." [physical zeal, aggressiveness, innate force or occasionally force received from the gods, concern for one's rank and privileges, etc.].

[9] See Schofield 1985: e.g., 13.

[10] See Finley 1978 and Miller 1995a.

What was different, I think, was that such self-conscious reflection was not actively encouraged by the institutions and traditional practices of "Homeric society,"[11] and it did not extend "below" the level of a tiny handful of high-ranking heroes. Even within that narrow elite, instead of deliberative rationality, we often see the heroes, such as Agamemnon, taking the advice of soothsayers and prophets, such as Calchas, or ignoring that advice when their status is threatened (cf. 12.195–250); we often see them arguing on the basis of authority and power, and they did not make free speech into an explicit ideal.[12] Agamemnon's private councils were much less complex—and diverse—than the Athenian Assembly. Even if we can see outlines of the later, more developed conceptions of good judgment, human excellence, and human flourishing in the Homeric epics, the poet did not present a society whose institutions and discourses manifested anything like the complexity and self-consciousness found in Athenian democratic institutions and discourses.[13]

Working within a traditional framework, Archaic Greek poets, warriors, and political leaders alike relied on the fear of shame and disgrace as the chief motivational sources of courage. Exhorting his comrades to fight

---

[11] On "Homeric society" as the poet's construct, one of the best recent treatments is Raaflaub 1999; cf. also van Wees 1992; for a critique of this construct on the grounds of incoherence, see Osborne 1996.

[12] Raaflaub 2004: 29–37.

[13] Schofield 1986: 18n.26 readily admits that "in a sense the whole paper is an Aristotelian reading of the *Iliad*." As my interpretation of the Athenian democracy reveals, I am supportive of such efforts to use later Greek philosophical concepts in order to help us understand the conceptual lineaments of those concepts in earlier instantiations in the wider culture. However, one of the weaknesses of Schofield's paper, despite its usefulness, is its tendency to attribute to the Homeric heroes a self-consciousness about what they are logically committed to, by virtue of their respect for *euboulia*, even when they do not themselves manifest or articulate this self-consciousness. Does Agamemnon or Hector, for example, know or care that he is logically committed to listening to reason even when it conflicts with honor? The poet may implicitly expect his audience to entertain such questions, but it is very atypical for the heroes themselves to do so. On the other hand, to his credit, Schofield concludes by saying, "There is no question that the social world represented in the *Iliad* or *Odyssey* is simpler in organization than the society of (for example) classical Athens. Nor should it be disputed that its relative simplicity of structure determines and is reflected in simpler and less analytical ways of talking and thinking about most other things, including human nature: no council in the *Iliad* is or could be as sophisticated as the debate on Mytilene in Thucydides 3" (Schofield 1986: 31). That is correct. See Smoes 1995 for further exploration of the distinctions between Homeric culture and the culture of Athenian democracy. Smoes makes clear that Greek conceptions of courage had been transformed by the fourth century, but, like many students of classical antiquity, he sees this transformation as the result of the writings of a philosophical elite that included Thucydides, Plato, and Aristotle. A notable gap in Smoes's book is the vast literature produced by the Athenian democracy in the classical period—a literature which illustrates, as we will see, that the Athenian democracy underlay the changes observed by Smoes as we move from the Homeric epics and archaic poets, on the one hand, all the way to the fourth-century philosophers, on the other.

steadily against their political rivals, for example, Alcaeus wrote, "Let us not dishonor through our cowardice (*mē kataischunōmen anandriai*) our noble fathers lying under the earth" (fr. 6.13-14). One of the few surviving fragments of Callinus reads: "When will you stop lying around? Young men, when will you have a strong heart? Are you not ashamed (*oud' aideisth'*) before those who live around us of being so slack? You think that you are sitting in a state of peace, but war grips the whole land" (fr. 1.1–4). These poetic discourses relied chiefly on the fear of disgrace to motivate young men to fight, as well as the self-control and camaraderie produced by men in the hoplite battle line.[14] There is very little sense that the soldiers deliberated carefully about their ideals, or that they self-consciously linked those ideals to any developed conception of a flourishing human life. The institutions of their society did not invite them to reflect on such topics, nor did the early polis produce much of a sense of the intrinsic merits of human excellence as the foundation of leading a good life.

Alcaeus and Callinus, to be sure, held a more egalitarian outlook than the Homeric poet or poets, but their imagined audiences were meant to subscribe just as surely and unreflectively as their Homeric counterparts to the twin stimuli of shame and honor. Young men in the clutches of this traditional ideology were unlikely to reflect on the demands of courage or to make strides toward locating courage within a well-developed framework that helped to explain why courage was intrinsically good for the individual. The individual's welfare was strictly subordinated to the security and thriving of the community as a whole.

The underlying reason for the traditionalism of Greek culture in this respect is that, prior to the advent of the Athenian democracy, the Greeks had not developed political institutions or cultural practices that invited regular questioning of their own ideals. As we saw in the case of "Homeric society," we must be careful not to overstate the contrast between the early Greeks and the democratic Athenians. The Athenians did not stop being Greeks as soon as they became democratic. The early Greeks had assemblies, they cherished a certain "rough" sense of equality, and they discussed and voted on political measures. Their views of life were not naïve and simplistic. And, admittedly, we are not terribly well informed about the inner workings of their political (much less individual) lives. As far as we can tell, however, they did not prize freedom of speech; they did not

---

[14] Cf. Smoes 1995: 69–73, 78–81. On early hoplite warfare in general, see van Wees 2004: 166–77.

develop a discourse on deliberative rationality; they did not extend their fundamental virtues to all citizens, including the poor; and they did not construct an ideal of courage linked to deliberative institutions or to freedom or to the equality of all citizens.

By contrast, the Athenians developed a more authentic, self-conscious, explicit, and self-chosen ideal of courage, which they located carefully within their incipiently eudaimonistic framework (see chapters 14–15). The Athenians' political institutions, cultural rituals, and social practices encouraged all citizens, including the poor, to reflect upon the questions of courage for themselves, and to interrogate existing paradigms. They also reflected on the worth and soundness of their emotional responses and responded thoughtfully to the challenge of the emotional education of their young (e.g., Aesch. 3.245–46; Lyc. 1.10). In their ideological understanding, if not always in their behavior itself, the Athenians proved to be remarkably successful at balancing the claims of the community or the common good with those of the individual and his good, through locating courage carefully within a virtue-oriented account of *eudaimonia* (chapters 14 and 15).

The Spartans and other "isonomic," or nondemocratic, Greeks were the chief heirs of Homer and the Archaic Greek poets in emphasizing *la belle mort* and traditional notions of manly *aretē*, which rested on the social foundation of *aidōs*, or the "sense of shame."[15] Herodotus emphasized that Spartan courage was rigorously enforced through social mechanisms of control, especially the sense of shame and fear of the law (see chapter 4). The Spartan Aristodemus, who had contracted an eye infection just before the Battle of Thermopylae, was greeted with reproach upon his return to Sparta, because, unlike another Spartan with the same affliction, he did not go out to fight anyway. Because he was a humiliated survivor, Herodotus reports, "No one of the Spartans would give him a light for his fire, or speak with him," and he had to bear the ignominy of being called a "trembler" (7.231).[16]

---

[15] On these themes, see Loraux 1977, 1986; Smoes 1995, especially 10–14, 69–73, although both Loraux and Smoes tend to assimilate Athenian funerary oratory, not to mention Athenian oratory in general, to the aristocratic or Homeric model, and thus fail to appreciate the distinctively democratic features of the Athenian discourse. Clarke 2002: 72–77 also explores the relationship between Spartan and Homeric models of courage, with special reference to Herodotus, concluding that in his depiction of Aristodemus, and of the Three Hundred Spartans at Thermopylae, Herodotus "invites us to consider both instances of battle-fury in terms of the problematic aspects of Homeric heroism" (75).

[16] On these themes, see my discussion in chapter 4, along with Millender 2002a, Millender 2002b, Forsdyke 2001.

Tremblers faced specific legal and social disabilities: according to Xenophon, they found it difficulty to marry; they could not be manifestly cheerful; and they could not assert their status in relation to younger men, an extreme form of public humiliation in a display-oriented, honor-conscious society.[17] It is no wonder, then, that Pantites, another Spartan survivor of Thermopylae, allegedly hanged himself out of shame for failing to die in the battle like his fellow citizens (Hdt. 7.232).[18] The basic picture of Spartan shame was punitive: Spartans were severely punished if they failed to conform to social expectations regarding martial valor; these social expectations were not "up for grabs" among a diverse Spartan citizenry.

As we have seen (chapter 2), Sparta's King Archidamus offers a more sympathetic, but altogether consistent, representation of Spartan shame-driven courage: "We are both good warriors and men of sound judgment, because we are well ordered. We are good warriors because our moderation (*sōphrosunēs*) is guided by our sense of shame (*aidōs*), and our courage (*eupsuchia*) is based upon honor (*aischunēs*). We have sound judgment because of our rigorous education, which makes us too ignorant to have contempt for our laws and too moderate to disobey them" (1.84). Thucydides presents Archidamus as the most intellectual, sophisticated, and forward looking of all the Spartan speakers; but even the great Spartan king emphasizes discipline, self-control, and shame as the keys to Spartan courage. These virtues had been handed down by the Spartans for generations (1.85), according to Archidamus, and had been inculcated through a severe education that harshly censured cowardice (1.84). Although Archidamus reflects meaningfully on the Spartan ideal of courage, he is certainly an unusual product of the Spartans' militaristic culture. And, in his presentation, Spartan courage is highly traditional, based on the most rigorous kind of training (1.84), and the result of traditional discipline and austerity (1.85).

---

[17] See *Lak. Pol.* 9.5 with Powell 1988: 234; Powell 2001: 238. Miller 2000: 15–24 offers a probing treatment of Aristodemus, emphasizing the "politics of courage" (23) involved in the Spartans' refusal to grant Aristodemus public honors after Plataea, where he had fought superbly in order to make amends for his earlier humiliation.

[18] As Sara Forsdyke (2001: 348) has argued, "Spartan courage depends on law/custom (*nomos*) and is socially enforced through shame. Fear of social humiliation motivates Spartan courage, as can be seen by the examples of those Spartans who avoided death at Thermopylae (Hdt. 7.231–32; cf. 9.71)." Christ 2006: 116–17, 118–24, notes that, by contrast with the Spartans, the Athenians were not keen to censure or publicly humiliate groups of routed soldiers, although individuals "could find themselves under pressure to defend their participation in a rout" (117).

In Thucydides' presentation, however, the most important point is the reception of Archidamus' speech. The Spartan king was followed immediately by the ephor Sthenelaidas, who, after denigrating further public discussion of the decision to go to war, unconventionally forced the Spartans to take a vote by moving to one side of the assembly or the other. Sthenelaidas' departure from convention served the purpose of stirring up enthusiasm for the war, Thucydides says (1.87), precisely by publicly shaming any Spartans who might have harbored reservations about the quick decision to fight.

Our sources also associate the Spartans with courage inspired by the fear of punishment or of the law. This is the point of the conversation we examined in chapter 4, in which the exiled Spartan king Demaratus explained Spartan courage to the Persia's King Xerxes as follows: "Although the Spartans are free, they are not wholly free; for law is their master and they fear it far more than your men fear you; for indeed they do whatever law orders; and it always orders the same thing; it does not permit them to flee any mass of men in battle, but commands that they remain in their battle ranks and either conquer or die" (7.104–5).[19] Although it is reasonable to doubt the historicity of this conversation, of course, we may plausibly suppose that this conversation reflects Herodotus' best understanding of the respective ideologies of Persians and Spartans at the time of the Persian Wars. Seen in that light, Demaratus' explanation draws attention to several noteworthy features of the highly traditional Spartan approach to courage.

Most importantly, the Spartans embodied the courage of the traditional hoplite soldier-citizen, who conformed out of patriotism to the laws of his city. Spartan soldiers fought to the death, not because they had a self-conscious conception of their own flourishing as human beings, but because they were commanded to do so by their laws, and they feared the harsh punishments that awaited any who ignored the laws. Moreover, because they shared laws, customs, and patriotism in common with their fellow hoplites, they also fought out of solidarity with their comrades-in-arms. Such solidarity has always been common to most soldiers, ancient or modern, and, in itself, it is hardly objectionable. Even so, it is necessary to "unpack" the origins and emotional constituents of solidarity within fighting units, ancient or modern, in order to lay bare what glues particular military units together. In this particular case, as Demaratus' account

---

[19] The translation is from Forsdyke 2001: 347–48. See my discussion in chapter 4, along with Forsdyke 2001, Millender 2002a, Millender 2002b.

reveals, fear lies at the root of the Spartans' dedication to the law: they fear law like a master, in ways, paradoxically, that resemble the Persians' fear of *their* master.[20] And to fear or respect law as a good Spartan should, the Spartans had to recognize, as Demaratus says, that the law always says the same thing, that is, either to conquer or die. This implies that the law is invariable, that it is not an object of rational scrutiny, questioning, or reflection. (Nor, notably, were the Persian troops encouraged to question Xerxes' commands to *his* troops to fight to the death for the welfare of the king.)

Such was the Spartans' highly traditional, even hypertraditional, model of courage—based on a disciplined character, harsh training, punitive applications of social shame, and fear of legal punishment and social ostracism. The Spartans hardly idealized self-reflection or self-criticism, even to the extent offered by the "rogue" king Archidamus: there was no Spartan funeral oration, because the city saw no need to reflect on its own history, ideals, or regime.

Nevertheless, one might object, the Spartans had a sparkling reputation for courage, even among the Athenians. They were genuinely steadfast on the battlefield. According to Thucydides, in fact, the capture of Spartan prisoners on Sphacteria was the most surprising event of the entire Peloponnesian War, especially to the Athenians (4.40). As a result, one can easily imagine a Spartan reply to any such effort to denigrate traditional Greek courage, as exemplified by the Spartans. In the fifth book of Thucydides (5.9), for example, Brasidas urges the Spartan allies to "[u]nderstand that in order to fight well a soldier needs desire, shame (honor), and obedience to his commanders." In the view of this most successful of Spartan commanders, the Spartans and their allies had nothing to be ashamed of in adhering to what Ellen Millender has called their "compelled bravery," especially since shame-driven discipline seemed to work so well as a motivational force in practical circumstances.[21] What, then, is the reason for criticizing the Spartans' conception and practice of traditional, normative Greek courage? In what sense were both shame and the fear of legal punishment defective as motivational sources of courage?

The principal defect of these motivations is that both were expressions of fear. As the Athenian Stranger says in the Platonic *Laws* (646e–647a), in summarizing the traditional Greek view of fear, there are two kinds of

---

[20] Cf. Millender 2002a, 2002b.
[21] Millender 2002b: 384.

fear. The first is the expectation of evil in the future—such as the "evil" of dying in battle or of being legally punished for cowardice. "And," the Athenian says, "[W]e often fear for our reputation, when we imagine we are going to get a bad name for doing or saying something disgraceful. This is the fear which we, and I fancy everyone else, call 'shame.'"[22] In the case of the Spartans in Herodotus, these two types of fear were closely linked. The Spartans' legal punishments concretely embodied and enforced the punitive standards of shame that acted upon Spartan soldiers whenever they began to entertain the possibility of defaulting on their duties. Both shame and the fear of punishment were mechanisms of emotional control through which the community rigidly enforced its demands on individual citizens. And, like Machiavelli, the Spartans knew that fear, whether of social ostracism or other forms of punishment, constituted a motivational force that could powerfully counteract the hesitations and anxieties of those confronting difficulty or danger.

But, as philosophers have frequently urged, it hardly makes sense to imagine forms of courage—the very virtue dedicated to overcoming fear—that are motivated by, of all things, fear itself. Fear-inspired courage should not count as properly courageous, because courage (of all things) should not be motivated by fear. Fear-inspired "courage" actually consists of a selfish calculation of pain avoidance, rather than a less self-absorbed willingness to take risks in order to achieve larger, well informed, and ethically justified objectives.[23] Many philosophers, beginning with Plato and Aristotle, have objected to this "countervailing strategy," in which emotions are balanced or set against one another (cf. Hirschman 1977), on the grounds that virtues should properly be motivated by a love of what is noble (*to kalon*) or good for its own sake, not by fear of disgrace or physical punishment if one defaults.

These motivations lack the self-consciousness, and thus the dignity, of other forms of courage that are motivated by higher degrees of purposive rationality or self-awareness. What makes courage an intrinsically worthwhile attribute is that courageous individuals themselves recognize the intrinsic goodness of courage and express courage in the right ways, at the

---

[22] It is possible of course to make a distinction between "shame" considered as the experience of disgrace and humiliation—noting that at the time when a person experiences the disgrace, he presumably is not fearing it any longer, though he may fear its continuation—and "shame" considered as Plato does in this quotation, namely as the sensibility that makes us fear a loss of reputation: on the difference between an occurrence of shame and the disposition to feel shame, see Cairns 1993; Elster 1999; Williams 1993.

[23] Cf. Hunt 1997: 21–51.

right times, and for the right reasons. They grasp the point of courage more adequately than do those who are trapped in the clutches of tradition, legal norms, and political or military authority. In doing so, they realize courage as an intrinsic good of their own psychology, of their own lives, without ever failing to appreciate courage as an instrumental good that protects their communities and promotes their flourishing at other levels.

Be that as it may, the standard Greek model is now clear enough. It is the model familiar from epic and lyric poetry and from the historians' presentations of the Spartans and other "isonomic" Greeks. Yet we should ever keep in mind that the Athenians strove to distinguish themselves not only from other Greeks, above all the Spartans, but also from their non-Greek rivals, such as the Persians and the Macedonians. It will be useful to explore the Athenians' strategies for establishing these other distinctions firmly, too, before moving on to consider how well these distinctions held up in practice.

Courage and the non-Greek "Other"

In examining courage among Athens's non-Greek rivals, we again rely necessarily on ideologically informed Greek (and often Athenian) sources, which offer unfavorable impressions of Persians and Macedonians. As in the previous cases, therefore, we are dealing with rhetorical and ideological constructs, rather than with a realistic picture of courage as it was actually produced, discussed, and experienced among non-Greeks. We are not well positioned to offer an even-handed evaluation of the Persians and Macedonians. Yet it was often with such ideological constructs in mind that the Athenians developed the ideology of courage that we are investigating. As a result, pictures of the "other" had a reality of their own: they constituted useful foils for the Athenians' own self-image. These ideological representations indicate to us precisely what the Athenians wanted to avoid or to exclude in constructing their own understandings and social practices of courage.

Scholars have discussed the Persian "other" in great detail, and there is no reason, for our purposes, to rehearse this familiar material in its entirety here.[24] With specific regard to courage, however, it is worth distilling the central ideas for present purposes. The Athenians' underlying idea was that the Persians were weak, effeminate, irrational, incapable of self-government, and subject to the untrammeled authority of

---

[24] The classic discussion remains that of Hall 1989; on Herodotus and the "other," specifically, see Hartog 1988.

their king. Although Xerxes himself was worthy to hold power, according to Herodotus (7.187; though cf. 8.103, 118–19 for Xerxes' fearfulness), there were few "real men" in the Persian army (7.210; though see, to the contrary, 9.62, where Herodotus says that the Persians were not inferior to the Spartans in courage or strength, but rather only in experience, armour, training, and skill). Symbolic of the Athenians' construction of the Persian "other" was the Eurymedon oenochoe, which showed an effeminate Persian being buggered by a powerful Athenian hoplite.[25] The Persians' world was a topsy-turvy one: in his description of the Battle of Salamis, for example, Herodotus praised Artemisia as King Xerxes' most courageous fighter (8.87), and he had the king himself remark that his men had turned into women, and his women into men (8.88). The absence of normative Greek masculinity among the Persians was a basic and virtually unalterable feature of the standard account.

More interesting for us are the ways in which Greek authors represented the typical motivations for courage among the Persians, along with the location of courage within the Persians' network of cultural ideals and social relationships. As Herodotus emphasizes, the Persian soldiers were fighting, not for themselves, but for the personal safety and welfare of their king. This is why stories abounded in which Persian nobles sacrificed their lives for the sake of the king (8.118, though Herodotus himself doubts the story: 8.119), and why the Persians at Susa reacted to the king's defeat at Salamis with distress over the personal safety of the King, rather than with a mournful attitude toward the loss of so many ships—according to Herodotus (8.99; cf. Aeschylus, *Persians*, with chapter 4). Persians fought under the king's watchful eye (8.69, 8.86) and were either duly enlisted as king's Benefactors for good service (8.85, 8.89, 8.90, 8.118) or severely punished if anything went wrong (8.90, 8.100, cf. 8.15).[26] (By contrast, of course, the Athenians, once liberated from the Peisistratid tyrants, became stronger and stronger because they were fighting for themselves (5.78).)[27]

Aeschylus presented the Persians as ignorant of the proper sources and ends of courage (see chapter 4). For example, all the Persians steadfastly maintained that Xerxes' fabulous wealth (rather than the excellence of

---

[25] See Balot 2004c, with Cartledge 1998: 56–57; Smith 1999: 128–41; Fisher 2001: 47–48; and now also Miller 2010, which offers an interestingly unconventional interpretation.

[26] After the Persian loss at Salamis, Mardonius tried to blame the defeat on the cowardice of the Persians' allies, rather than on the Persians themselves (8.100), thereby illustrating the importance of courage within the Persians' own conception of themselves.

[27] On these themes, which are now familiar among ancient historians and classicists, see Konstan 1987.

its citizens) made Persia as a whole prosperous and healthy (852–908). Xerxes' mother, Atossa, is represented as believing that wealth and hierarchical political control would bring victory over the Greeks, and that the size of the Persian army, in itself, virtually guaranteed victory (236–45, 331–44). In his own Persian logos, Herodotus says that, after courage in battle, the Persians consider the chief sign of "manly virtue" (*andragathia*) to be that of having many sons, because "they think that numbers are equivalent to strength" (Hdt. 1.136).[28] In sum, Persian men and Persian political culture embodied everything abhorrent to the Athenians: ignorance, effeminacy, enslavement to the king, political hierarchy, and lack of self-assertion.

Even in the fourth century, the same constructs continued to be developed. Isocrates, for example, argued that the Persians were cowardly because their education amid political hierarchy made them fit for slavery—that is, insolent toward inferiors and cowardly and abject in relation to superiors (Isocr. 4.146–52). Ordinary Persians, according to Isocrates, were brought up to be servile, while Persian leaders showed no respect for equality or the common good (4.151). Instead of proudly working for the common good, even the Persian nobles humiliated themselves by cringing at the royal palace (4.151–52). The Athenians took themselves to embody prototypically the attributes and dispositions that most completely opposed the contemptible alternative represented by Persia.

As a different candidate for the status of "other," the Macedonians have been much less carefully studied than the Persians.[29] Whatever the reasons for Philip II's political and military success, we have clear evidence that the Athenians described the Macedonian king by reworking their traditional opposition between the self-aggrandizing monarchical imperialist (such as Xerxes) and themselves as courageous freedom fighters and protectors of the Greek world. By contrast with their representations of the Persian "barbarians," though, the Athenians focused less on the Macedonian political regime than on the character of Philip himself. In fact, far from monolithically condemning Philip, our most important sources offered diverse views on the Macedonian king, ranging from Isocrates' quixotic efforts to cultivate and instruct him, to Demosthenes' systematic denigration of his

---

[28] See Konstan 1987: 62–69 for an interesting discussion of Herodotus' opposition between Xerxes' passion for seeing and counting—for quantity—as opposed to the Greeks' concern with qualities and dispositions of soul.
[29] Yet see the notable contributions of Hall 2001 and Saïd 2001.

brutality and aggressiveness. Either way, though, the differences between Macedon and Athens remained clear.

Prior to the Battle of Chaeronea, Demosthenes focused single-mindedly on the necessity of courageously blocking Philip's advances in order to preserve the freedom of the Greeks. Hence, Demosthenes argued, the Athenians should remain vigilant concerning Philip's military aggression (1.25–27, 4.42–43, 9.27–29, 9.35), his deceptive speech and practices (2.6–7, 6.29, cf. 18.144, 18.147), and his limitless capacity for bribery (6.33–36, 7.17). In making these arguments, Demosthenes attempted to contrast Philip's injustice and greed—his *pleonexia*—with the Athenians' traditional commitment to protecting themselves and the other Greeks from imperialistic encroachments. To be sure, Demosthenes professed to admire Athenian courage, particularly that of the Athenians' ancestors; but his chief goal, prior to Chaeronea, at least, was to rouse his fellow citizens to action by defiantly declaring that Philip's daring and self-assertion were making the Athenians look cowardly (4.42). The Athenians should stand and fight, as their ancestors would have done, while the opportunity was still available (1.24). In retrospect, of course, Demosthenes was eager to assert that he had often tried to rouse the Greeks to stand up to Philip and to see him for the imperialist that he was (18.62–64). It is entirely compatible with these principal themes that Demosthenes even offered grudging praise of Philip's courage when he reflected on the king's willingness to endure losing an eye, breaking his bones, and fracturing his collar bone in order to win glory (18.66–68).

When the Athenian orators discussed the Macedonian political regime, as opposed to the character of the king himself, they tended to emphasize conventional tropes such as the consequences of the king's arbitrariness, selfishness, and hubris (Hyp. 6.20), as well as his cultural barbarity (Dem. 9.31).[30] But Demosthenes also elaborated in interesting ways on the theme of despotism and its military advantages. As he was well aware, Macedon was a highly successful imperialistic monarchy. Hence, it constituted a genuine threat to the very survival of the Athenian democracy, not to mention Athens's reputation and status among the other Greeks. As Demosthenes argues, Philip had numerous advantages in fighting Athens and the other Greeks: he was more than adequately funded and his army was consistently well armed. Even more importantly, Demosthenes argues, Philip ruled as an absolute despot, accountable to no one. He was

---

[30] Hall 2001; Saïd 2001.

capable of making military and political decisions without fear of indictment at a later time (18.235–36). By contrast, Demosthenes himself could merely make speeches and try to persuade the Athenian demos—an opportunity open to every other Athenian citizen, he says, including the most worthless and traitorous (18.236, 18.244–45). In these ways Demosthenes emphasized, quite unusually, that his monarchic political regime gave Philip military and political advantages that were unavailable to Athens's democratic leaders.

Naturally, in these passages, Demosthenes was trying to reduce the burden of his failed policies and to justify his career before the Athenian demos. But it is striking that his characterization of Macedon evokes, and indeed reverses, accusations that had once been leveled by the Athenians against the Persians and their own "unaccountable" king. In the fifth century, both Herodotus and Aeschylus had recognized absolute monarchy as a politically defective system that led to effeminacy and military weakness. In the fourth century, by contrast, Demosthenes found it legitimate to offer the Macedonians' political hierarchy as an excuse for his own inability to counter Philip's aggressive movement into southern Greece. The difference, perhaps, is that no fourth-century Athenian could plausibly charge the Macedonians with being effeminate or cowardly, especially after the Battle of Chaeronea. Because they wanted to avoid the embarrassment of having lost their freedom to supposed cowards, the Athenian orators could say only that the outcome of that decisive battle was in the hands of the gods, and that both sides had fought courageously (Dem. 60.19, 21; Hyp. 6.13).

Yet the Athenians still found substantial ground on which to defend the superiority of their democratic courage. Their overarching goal was, as in the past, to show that, despite the outcome of the Battle of Chaeronea, the Athenians' ideals of courage were more worthy and admirable than those of their Macedonian adversaries. Which strategies did the Athenian orators use in addressing this difficult rhetorical and psychological quandary? The answer, in short, is that they reformulated their ideals in order to show that, despite their "bad luck" in losing the war, their democratic culture had still produced the most worthy expression of courage possible in the circumstances.

Whereas Philip had used his courage to win glory unjustly, the Athenians, like their forefathers, had always exhibited the honorable courage of striving to preserve and extend their own freedom and that of the other Greeks (e.g., Dem. 18.66, 18.95–99; Dem. 60.11; Hyp. 6.16–17). True courage, implicitly, must be grounded in and oriented toward worthwhile ideals rather than hunger for power or self-aggrandizement. It was characteristic of the Athenian democracy, specifically, to fight courageously for the integrity of the Greeks against Philip's forward advances (Dem. 18.72).[31] The Athenians were the first to recognize the threat posed by Macedon, and the first to challenge the Greeks to stand up for themselves—which exemplified their foresight, sound judgment, courage, and public spirit (Dem. 60.17–18; cf. Hyp. 6.10–11). Indeed, prior to Philip's decisive victory, the other Greeks, including even the Thebans, Demosthenes says, judged the Athenians to be more courageous and more just than Philip's soldiers, and therefore chose to make a stand with the Athenians against Philip's encroachments (18.215–16).

In the orators' recollections of the Athenians' final, decisive battle with Philip, moreover, we find interesting reformulations of the contrast between courage as produced by a democratic citizenry and courage as embodied by the soldiers of an absolute despotism. In one memorable passage, for example, Hyperides contends that the Athenian soldiers self-consciously gave up their lives for specific and admirable democratic aims. They sacrificed themselves so that the rule of law would prevail over the threats of a despot—an absolute necessity if a people wishes to flourish (to be *eudaimōn*, cf. Hyp. 6.24–25). And, in accordance with their desire for freedom, they died in order to preserve justice under the law and safety produced by civic equality rather than a politics underwritten by the arbitrary commands of a master and the self-effacing sacrifices of his minions (Hyp. 6.25).

In his own funeral oration (338 BC), similarly, Demosthenes argued that democratic free speech produced courageous citizens through the operation of social shame (Dem. 60.25–26). Oligarchs hand out rewards and punishments arbitrarily and secretly, whereas the democracy encouraged citizens to assess one another's behavior in combat freely and openly. Since they desired to avoid frank criticism in public, democratic citizens would step up to their military duties with spirit and determination. Thus,

---

[31] In addition, the presence of Philip led to intramural squabbles between the orators, in particular Aeschines and Demosthenes, over their courage or cowardice at the court of Philip. For example, Aeschines continually harps on Demosthenes' cowardice and corruption (e.g., 2.22, 2.34–35, 3.81, 3.214; cf. Dinarchus 1.79–82). Demosthenes, on the other hand, finds limitless opportunity to praise his own courage in facing down Philip in person, in his speeches at Athens, and in his political activities throughout Greece (e.g., 18.173–80). But these quarrels do not directly affect our subject, except insofar as they illustrate the importance the Athenian democrats placed on the courage of their leaders.

Demosthenes interpreted the courage of his fallen fellow citizens as a product of their status as citizens of a democracy (25):

> Democracies possess many other fine and just characteristics... In particular, it is not possible to keep frank speech (*parrhēsia*), which depends upon the truth, from making the truth clear. For it is impossible for those who do something shameful to win over everyone, with the result that a single citizen's truthful reproach is painful; for even those who would not themselves denigrate others are happy when they hear someone else utter a reproach. Fearing these things, all these men, naturally enough in view of the shame resulting from future reproaches, stoutly withstood the danger confronting them from our enemies and chose a noble death over a shameful life. (26)

Despite the obvious military successes of Philip, Alexander, and the Macedonians, the Athenians held fast to the idea that their democracy produced a form of courage that was more truly honorable and admirable than that of the Macedonians. Athenian courage was self-consciously oriented toward admirable ideals, ideals that were worthy of choice; and it was closely and intrinsically connected to democratic free speech. Perhaps such a resolute and self-affirming vision of Athenian democratic courage compensated, somehow, for the Athenians' defeat at the hands of the authoritarian Macedonian king.

It is here, though, that questions about the distinctiveness of democratic courage should arise. Demosthenes' funeral oration shows that the Athenians themselves sometimes relied on notions of honor, shame, and fear of the law in order to motivate their citizens to act courageously. In that speech, Demosthenes interestingly links shame and the fear of reproach to democratic *parrhēsia*, thereby adding yet another perspective on the Athenians' new ways of grappling with social shame. Elsewhere, however, Demosthenes encouraged his fellow citizens with apparently standard references to shame: "Don't you feel ashamed at not daring, despite your opportunities, to inflict on Philip the same sort of suffering he would inflict on you if he could?" (Dem. 1.24). This sounds very similar to the exhortations of Alcaeus and Callinus discussed earlier. Thus we might well ask the exponents of democratic courage, especially the funeral orators and Herodotus, the following questions: Did the Athenians consistently hold in their minds a self-image that linked their courage to specifically democratic ideals of freedom, equality, and deliberative rationality? Or did the contrasts upon which this self-image depended break down because of the Athenians' own implicit traditionalism? This is the issue that we pursue in the next four chapters.

CHAPTER 10 | The Courageous Passions of Democratic Athens

IN PART I WE EXPLORED the circulation of a normative ideal of democratic courage in diverse historical, philosophical, and oratorical texts. Even, or especially, when we examined critical responses to this ideal—such as those of Thucydides or Plato—we acknowledged that the critics themselves found it useful to engage with that ideal, even if only to display its limitations or incoherence. Democratic courage had a certain importance, no doubt, but perhaps it will turn out to be merely a self-serving construct—one that was useful at different moments in the city's history, but that is less applicable to everyday practices and understandings.

Before prejudging the case, we should probe the Athenians' self-conceptions and practices more widely and deeply. The epitaphic orators asserted that Athenian courage was both deliberate and rational, on the one hand, and, on the other, that it was marked by both appropriate and thoughtfully constructed emotions. Could the Athenians unify reason and emotion (the two most traditional of "opposites") in the way we have proposed? At least in the first instance, the onus is on us to make sense of the Athenians' claims, without dismissing them too quickly. Yet we should probably expect to find tensions and instabilities in the Athenian discourse, since it spanned roughly two centuries and was used in a great variety of civic contexts.

Many pieces of evidence, in fact, suggest that, in practice, the Athenians used shaming punishments and the fear of legal consequences in order to produce conformity to ideal standards of masculine behavior. As Adriaan Rademaker has shown, for example, men such as Cleonymus, Cleisthenes, and Agathon were often ridiculed in Aristophanic comedy for their cowardice or other expressions of "unmanliness" (e.g., *Knights* 1372; *Clouds*

353; *Wasps* 19–20, and many other places).[1] This corresponds closely to the Spartans' use of shaming punishments and humiliation in order to motivate potential cowards to behave courageously (see chapters 2, 4, and 9). Moreover, gossip and other mechanisms of social control—what David Cohen has called the "politics of reputation"—were extremely effective coercive forces in the domains of honor and shame.[2] Athens was home to a network of informal conversations that exerted pressure on individuals to conform to social norms. Finally, there were laws against cowardice in the fifth century.[3] In Aristophanes' *Acharnians*, for example, Lamachus predicts that Dicaeopolis is likely to be indicted for cowardice (*deilia*) because of his private peace (1128–29).[4]

It makes sense, then, that the Athenians viewed not only shame or humiliation, but also fear of the law, as productive of courage.[5] In one of his many verbal assaults on Demosthenes, Aeschines accused Demosthenes of cowardice, alleging that everyone in the audience could think of examples to prove it. That being so, he argues, he need only remind his fellow citizens of the laws: "The ancient lawgiver Solon," he says, "considered it necessary to punish all alike the citizen who avoids service, the one who deserts his rank, and the coward. You see, we allow indictments on the

---

[1] See Rademaker 2003: 122.
[2] Cohen 1991: 97. Hunter 1994: 96–119 emphasizes that gossip upholds the norms of citizenship especially in a community in which shame is particularly powerful as a tool of social control.
[3] It may be that the relationship between Pericles' ideal vision and the coercive laws is similar to that between the persuasive "preambles" and the codified laws in Plato's *Laws*: namely, that the former, in each case, encourage citizens to become their most cultivated and virtuous selves, for sound and well understood reasons, while the latter provide a "safety net" that compels citizens to adhere to a minimally tolerable standard of behavior.
[4] The first formal citation of a law on cowardice comes in Andocides' speech *On the Mysteries*, which was delivered in 399 BC. In the midst of discussing disenfranchisement, Andocides says, "All who left the line of battle, who were convicted of evading their military service, of cowardice, or of withholding a ship from action, all who threw away their shields...were deprived of the privileges of citizenship with respect to themselves, although they kept their property" (1.74). The loss of citizen rights was a severe penalty to Athenians. This was not simply a law that lay flat "on the books." An antidemocratic pamphlet, probably written in the 420s BC, by the so-called Old Oligarch, refers in passing to the Athenian citizenry sitting in court to hear cases of cowardice during the Peloponnesian War (3.5). For other references, see Lys. 14.7; Aesch. 3.175; Dem. 15.32, with MacDowell 1978: 159–61.
[5] Did such an "emotional education" have any impact on their actual behavior on the battlefield? The Athenians themselves thought so. Yet, unlike scholars able to consult national archives detailing the heroics of medal-of-honor recipients, ancient historians must rely on the small quantity of descriptions and vignettes that can be found in ancient narratives and speeches. For example, we would dearly love to have the speech given to explain Aeschines' bravery in Euboea and the public discussion preceding his receipt of the standard Athenian prize of honor, the crown and panoply (Aesch. 2.169). The fact is that we have merely a notice that Aeschines was such a recipient.

charge of cowardice. You might be amazed to learn that we hear indictments for natural faults; we do. For what reason? In order that each of us, fearing the punishments exacted by the laws more than the enemy, might prove to fight better on behalf of his fatherland" (3.175). For precisely these reasons, in a speech against the younger Alcibiades, Lysias praises the ordinary Athenian jurors, saying that by contrast with his opponent, "You did not dare to leave the ranks or to choose what you yourself found most gratifying, but you feared the city's laws much more than the risk you ran against the enemy" (14.15).

How did the soldiers' emotions operate specifically in the field? In Athens, as in other cities, men of the same district, even neighborhood, usually fought together in the same battle line.[6] In one speech, the speaker, defending his father, says, "I will prove to you that he was demotic. For, first, his demesmen could say from personal knowledge how many campaigns he went on, without any failure of duty" ([Lys.] 20.23).[7] The fourth-century philosopher Theophrastus, in a mildly satirical work devoted to character portraits, wrote of the coward: "On campaign when the infantry are marching out to the rescue, the coward is apt to call his fellow demesmen and insist that they stand near him and have a look around first—remarking how hard it is to tell which side are the enemy" (*Characters* 25.3).[8] The fear of disgracing oneself before the neighborhood was especially powerful not only because of the informal surveillance exercised by local gossip, but also because one's fellow demesmen were responsible for citizen enrollments. Disgrace among the locals went to the core of one's status as an Athenian citizen.

Hence, social pressures and the desire to conform to standard norms limited the idealized expressions of courage that we examined in Part I. This is not, however, the end of the story. In order to explore the "courageous passions" and their relationship to democratic courage more fully, we must also consider a variety of other ideas that circulated in classical Athens—some of them adhering more closely to the "idealized" vision, and others contradicting that vision.

In considering these questions, an excellent place to start is Athenian oratory. The Athenian orators provide us with a variety of narratives replete with references to the emotions most often associated with courage. Mostly delivered in the Athenian Assembly and jury courts and at rituals such as

---

[6] On the hoplite's so-called "primary group," see now Crowley 2012: 40–69.
[7] Cf. Whitehead 1986: 224–26.
[8] See Whitehead 1986: 226 for the argument and the translation.

the funeral oration, these speeches bring to light the framework of communal "truths" that defined the Athenians' experience of democratic politics.[9] Usually expressed as rhetorical *topoi*, these ideological "truths" were not dead letters. By asserting collective ideals, they mitigated the potential for hostility and conflict amongst citizens of contrasting socioeconomic statuses.[10] We focus on four different types of public speech: a scrutiny hearing, a funeral oration, a deliberative assembly, and a public prosecution. After considering each case on its own, we draw out the implications of these cases for our investigation of democratic courage.

Case Study I: Lysias' Client Scrutinized

One useful starting point is to examine particular citizens' accounts of their military and civic service, which were offered in retrospect, at public hearings to determine their fitness to hold political office. Take, for example, Lysias' aristocratic client Mantitheus, who spoke at his *dokimasia* (scrutiny) hearing in the late 390s BC; the scrutiny concerned Mantitheus' prospective membership in the Council of 500. In this case, the special concern was that Mantitheus had been accused of serving with the cavalry against the demos during the oligarchic junta of 404–403 BC (Lys.16.1–3). He wants to make clear that he has been "loyal" (*eunous*) to the existing regime and that he has "shared in the same dangers as you" (*tōn autōn kindunōn metechein humin*). From the outset his emphasis is on respect for the ordinary citizens and on his own willingness to play an equal role with his fellow citizens in responding to military threats to Athens.

In the course of clearing his name, Mantitheus plans to "give an account of his whole life" (*pantos tou biou logon didonai*, Lys. 16.9). This formulation sounds highly "Socratic," from our vantage point. In fact, it was characteristic of the democracy to encourage individuals to think of their entire lives as narrative wholes, constituted by their civic activities within Athens.[11] In the course of giving an account of himself, Mantitheus described his courageous decision to enlist in the infantry, as opposed to the cavalry, just before the Athenians' expedition to Haliartus. Having been previously enrolled in the cavalry, he says, he decided to change

---

[9] Dover 1974; Ober 1989; Hansen 1991; Morris 1996; Ober 1996.
[10] Ober 1989.
[11] Balot 2013. MacIntyre 1984: 204–25 emphasizes the importance of narrativity in making sense of one's life as a whole; for an application of narrativity in the context of Athenian oratory, see Johnstone 1999: 46–69.

tack. He saw that everyone agreed that the cavalry would be safe, whereas the infantry would be in great danger: so he approached Orthoboulos, the commander, and had himself switched, "since I thought it was disgraceful to enter the battle having taken care for my own safety, whereas the many (*to plēthos*) were ready to run risks" (Lys. 16.13).

This apparently innocent passage encapsulates a remarkably careful self-presentation. Since the upper-class cavalry were safer when retreating from battle, most people recognized that the slow, heavy-armed hoplites ran much greater risks on behalf of the city. Mantitheus aligned himself with the (normatively) ordinary citizens of Athens, all of whom were equally ready to don the hoplite's armor to fight for the city. (This is yet another example of the hoplite's centrality to the Athenian self-image; cf. chapter 8). He did so, he says, out of a sense of shame: he thought it shameful to maximize his own chances of safety while others took substantial risks. This reaction shows his sensitivity to the community's opinions or standards, and particularly to its emphasis on equality or fairness. His emotional reactions motivated him to act not only courageously but also justly.

Why did Mantitheus feel the sense of shame that he describes? How did it make sense to him? In rendering an account of his life as a whole, he presents himself as having worked to make sense of his emotions, virtues, and actions on behalf of the city: his life made sense as a narrative unity, and he was able to articulate why and how, even if he had sought help from a speechwriter.[12] His commitment to the city and its healthy functioning explains why he donated money to help his fellow demesmen serve in the army (Lys. 16.14).[13] Having established this foundation of trustworthiness with his audience, Mantitheus proceeded to give other examples of his courage: contriving to fight in the front lines in Corinth (15), a battle he says everyone knew would be dangerous; staying later in the field than Thrasybulus, who reproached everyone for cowardice (16); and insisting that his own regiment be sent in first against the Spartan king Agesilaos, despite the evident dangers (16). From his description we learn what were thought to be the exemplary emotions and behaviors of a courageous, fair-minded, and well-functioning citizen.

---

[12] Cf. Johnstone 1999: 46–69.
[13] On Mantitheus' explanation of his services to his fellow citizens, see further Roisman 2005: 23–25.

He proceeds to argue that the citizens hearing his case ought therefore, in turn, to show him respect:

> So if some of you are angry at (*orgizontai*) those who think they are worthy of handling the affairs of the polis but run away from danger, you would not be right to take this attitude toward me; for I not only did what I was commanded with enthusiasm (*prothumōs*), but I also dared to run risks (Lys. 16.17).

Mantitheus assumes, characteristically in Attic oratory, that only those willing to run risks in war can legitimately counsel the city on its political policies. Counselors who turn out to be cowards understandably incur the anger of their fellow citizens, since their advice is not appropriately informed by an unwavering, even "selfless" commitment to the city's welfare. Hence, it is especially important to this speaker to point out that his courage was willing and eager, that is, informed by appropriate emotional responses to the prospect of running risks on behalf of the city whose ideals he shared (cf. chapter 4 on the Herodotean Athenians' *prothumia*).[14] He was not forced to run risks, but rather willingly did so, because such behavior corresponded to his own and the community's ideals. He is plainly proud of what he has accomplished. His choice of risk over safety, along with his appropriate attitudes and behavior, ought to earn him the respect of the jurors.

This line of reasoning leads him to the following conclusion:

> I did this, not because I found it easy to fight with the Lacedaimonians, but in order that, if I were ever unjustly threatened at law, I would secure every sort of justice because of the good reputation I had won with you. Let the witnesses to these things come forward, if they would. [Witnesses] So, I never fell short on any other campaign or in doing garrison-duty, but on every occasion I have marched out in the first rank and withdrawn in the last. We have to recognize the honourable (*philotimōs*) and orderly (*kosmiōs*) citizens of the polis on the basis of behavior like this (Lys. 16.17–18).

---

[14] It is important to connect the speaker's emphasis on his *prothumia* (zealousness, eagerness) with the Athenians' democratic moderation regarding conscription. As Christ 2006: 63–64 has argued, "Athenians preferred to encourage patriotic behavior through persuasion rather than to force it upon free persons through the exercise of civic authority. They rejected the alternative model of Sparta, where law was *despotes* (Hdt. 7.104.4–5, with Millender 2002) and the compulsory nature of military service manifest (Lys. 1.129–30; cf. Th. 2.39.4)" (63). For other instances of the Athenians' ideal of *prothumia*, Christ 2006: 64n.51 helpfully points to Dem. 60.18, Thuc. 2.36.4 (with 1.70.6, 1.74.1–2, 1.75.1), and Lys. 2.22.

Mantitheus says that he went forward to face danger in order to protect himself, in the future, from unjust prosecutions; the more courageously he fought, the more assurances he would have of receiving justice from the demos (17). In light of the ideology of courage discussed in Part I, this statement should strike a discordant note. If what he says is true, then Mantitheus' self-proclaimed courage seems to be due more to a desire to win the demos' approval and protection than to defend the city freely and courageously. Perhaps Mantitheus is more self-absorbed, even calculating, than a courageous person ought to be. He does not say that he freely and self-consciously embraced the city's ideals as his own, whatever the consequences. The most charitable interpretation, at least, would be that he wants to convince the jurors that he has reverence for the demos's judgment. He sees that the demos judges "honorable" those who take risks and act in public-spirited ways, such as his own ancestors, and he himself respects the judgment of the demos and shares it (Lys. 16.20–21). He has a proper desire for honor (*philotimia*) from the community, as well as a desire to be judged orderly and appropriate (*kosmios*) by his fellow citizens, because he shares their opinions about these central ideals of the community.[15]

It is interesting to see that Mantitheus' speech brings out certain conflicts in the Athenian ideology of courage, freedom, and equality. On the one hand, this speech is designed to show that Mantitheus, though an aristocrat, is "democratic," in that he subscribes to the demos's judgments and egalitarian norms. On the other hand, his conformity to the demos's opinions, his willingness and even desire to yield to the demos's social pressures, flies in the face of the democratic ideals of independent thinking and free speech. In that sense, perhaps, his self-presentation is a victory for the demos, which had socialized a potentially wayward aristocrat to aspire to equality with his fellow citizens—someone who would throw off the trappings of the aristocratic cavalry and fight alongside the ordinary citizens out of respect for equality and for the demos's judgment.

Naturally, what we find in this speech is Mantitheus' self-presentation before a jury of ordinary Athenian citizens. He is making every effort to persuade them of his loyalty and justice. The genre and the context encouraged his emphasis on conformity rather than on his own careful deliberation. What is more, the speech itself was written by a logographer, a professional speechwriter. Far from thinking for himself about democratic

---

[15] On order and disorder in the representation of manly ideals, see Roisman 2005: 192–99.

ideals of courage, Mantitheus has purchased a smooth self-presentation useful only for the circumstances. Readers can be forgiven for doubting his sincerity in voicing publicly approved sentiments.

At the same time, however, Mantitheus paid "lip service" to these ideals, which were the ideals endorsed by the democratic jury. We can infer that the democratic jury found it acceptable and even desirable that Mantitheus' courage should be motivated by conformity with the demos's own judgments. Mantitheus dutifully presents himself as having internalized the community's standards of honor, order, courage, and equality. He himself could articulate those ideals and publicly espouse them in giving an account of his entire life. Mantitheus felt shame at the thought of cowardly (or even aristocratic) behavior that would maximize his own safety at the expense of the common good. He also looked back with pride on his willingness to run risks, and thereby to seek honor, in communally sanctioned ways that he also endorsed. He felt anger, like everyone else, at those who sought to participate in politics without exposing themselves to danger at the appropriate times.

In short, Mantitheus offered a complex, even if brief, account of shame, equality, and courage as three central coordinates of the exemplary democratic character that he embodied. He might strike us as seeking the demos's favor too crassly. Nor did he entirely eliminate the ambiguities and tensions of his oratorical position. Yet his speech illustrates nonetheless that citizens were meant to reflect upon and speak to the significance of their courage and then to act on their ideas in thoughtful ways and in the appropriate emotional spirit, when the city needed their help.

Case Study 2: Lysias' Funeral Oration

Because the Athenians' standards of citizenship were so closely tied to their normative understandings of *andreia*, diverse emotions (shame, emulation, eros, anger) were brought to bear, with particular force, on the social production of courage. In a scrutiny hearing, such as that of Mantitheus, we might expect the litigant to place special emphasis on his own adherence to ideals that the demos had valorized in its decrees, judgments, and laws. Beyond such venues, we can also find publicly sanctioned representations of the courageous passions in funeral orations, which commemorated the bravery of fallen warriors. Best estimates suggest that the funeral oration was instituted either just after the Persian Wars (ca. 478 BC) or in the 460s BC during a particularly bitter period of Athens's strife with

Sparta.[16] Either way, the funeral oration was a distinctively democratic and Athenian institution found nowhere else, to our knowledge, in the Greek world.[17] Its focus, therefore, was on defining the cardinal virtues of the fallen citizen-soldiers, with particular reference to the democracy's role in encouraging those virtues.

As in Mantitheus' speech, the emotions of self-assessment came to the fore throughout these orations.[18] These were the emotions—shame, pride, emulation, and anger—that required the individual to monitor himself, to be continually aware of his self-image and his (outward) performance in relation to that (inward) self-image and in relation to the accomplishments of others. To take one particularly fertile example, Lysias' funeral oration, which dates to the late 390s BC, describes the Athenians' evaluative and behavioral responses to a variety of dangerous military ventures.[19] The speaker frames the current ceremony with references to the valor of unnamed ancestors, who "accomplished many noble and extraordinary things," and with references to the trophies won by their sons "through their courage (*aretēn*)" (Lys. 2.20). By referring to the Athenian ancestors' valor and their justly won honors, the speaker offers the audience appropriate targets of emulation—dead ancestors whose ideals they were expected to live up to.[20]

During the Persian attack at Marathon in 490 BC, the Athenians' ancestors properly disregarded the dangers of war and chose a glorious death in the service of their polis. Their sense of shame inspired them to act without the other Greeks' help: "Ashamed (*aischunomenoi*) that the barbarians

---

[16] Loraux 1986: 28–31.
[17] Loraux 1986: 1–3, 42–44, citing Dem. 20.141, and distinguishing the Athenian *epitaphios* from the Roman *laudatio funebris*; for further discussion of the evidence for the funeral oration, see Ziolkowski 1981: 13–38.
[18] The term "emotions of self-assessment" comes from Taylor 1985.
[19] See especially Todd 2007: 149–64 for the status of this speech, its date, and its intertextual connections with other examples or quasi-examples of the genre, such as Plato's *Menexenus* and Isocrates' *Panegyricus*. Todd argues quite reasonably, albeit with reservations, that Lysias is the author of the speech (Todd 2007: 162); he also proposes that it was a display piece not intended for delivery, but that it constitutes, nevertheless and even paradoxically, our most "typical" example of the genre. Whether it was intended for delivery or not, I follow Todd in maintaining that the speech exhibits the central and most persistent features of the genre and is thus useful for our effort to elucidate the Athenian ideology of courage.
[20] Hunt 2010: esp. 51–71 helpfully investigates the connection among the Athenians' self-admiring historical narratives of the city, their optimism about their potential for military success, and their recourse to war. Whereas Hunt argues that the Athenians' narratives made them more optimistic about success and thus more likely to wage war, however, I would suggest that the Athenians' narratives of the ancestors propelled them to wage war through encouraging them to emulate these particularly militaristic role models. They wanted to live up to their ancestors' habits of fighting justly for the Greeks and of expanding the empire.

were in their land, they did not wait for their allies to hear the news and help them" (Lys. 2.23). Seeing the "barbarians" near their territory, these Athenians found that their self-image as defenders of their land had become vulnerable—hence the feeling of shame as an internal monitor and catalyst to action, and their immediate response to answer to the calls of that monitor, for the right reasons. Their shame was guided by an ideal of nobility that consisted in providing safety for all Greece, at the risk of their own lives. Their sense of shame led them to deliberate about the situation and to choose a position of leadership thoughtfully.

The speaker elaborates upon the ancestors' feelings when he insists that they balanced their fear of the enemy with a sense of respect for the city's laws: they were heroes who courageously gave their lives for the city, "respecting (*aischunomenoi*) the city's laws rather than fearing (*phoboumenoi*) danger when they met the enemy" (Lys. 2.25). Their "reverence" for the city's laws recalls the similar reverence evoked by Pericles in his own funeral oration, as he presumably answered critics who charged that Athenian freedom had undermined the Athenians' reverence for the law (Thuc. 2.37.3).[21] By illustrating the proper emotional responses of the Athenian ancestors, the speaker encourages his present audience to have normatively appropriate feelings in regard to the clear dangers of contemporary wars. Both the ancestors and the present audience have reverence for the laws because those laws embody carefully reasoned judgments about the proper ways to act in dangerous circumstances. Those laws were both sanctioned by the Athenians themselves and originally devised by those Athenians: the Athenians were self-governing both in respect to law and in respect to the normative emotional responses expected of citizens in relation to the law.

Later in his account, this speaker describes the civil war of 403 BC. The Athenian democrats, exiled from the city, secured their return to power by defeating the forces of a Spartan-backed junta known as the "Thirty Tyrants." He characterizes the democrats as "imitating their ancestors' ancient valor by running new risks...choosing death with freedom over life with slavery; no less ashamed of their misfortunes than angry at the enemy" (Lys. 2.62). This captures many of the emotions relevant to the Athenians' social production of courage. By illustrating the democrats' proper style of emulation, shame, and anger, the speaker educates his audience in the normative emotional responses of the Athenian citizen-soldier,

---

[21] See Ober 2005a: 149–50.

and shows how those emotional responses operated for the good of the polis in 403 BC.

Observe, in particular, that the Athenian soldiers were angry with the Thirty Tyrants for destroying the democracy and taking over the city. What is the nature of their anger, and how is it related to the Athenians' ideal of courage? Anger is the emotion that inspires a person to retaliate against threats to his self-image. According to Aristotle, anger (*orgē*) is a desire accompanied by pain to punish those who have caused a perceived offence or slight (*Rhet.* 2.2.1). Anger derives from a person's perception of injustice; feeling that one has suffered a "slight" by definition implies that the sufferer, at least, must feel that the perceived slight is undeserved or inappropriate, in that it is unworthy of the image he has of himself. Just as communities can feel anger toward individuals who fail to meet social expectations, so too can they feel anger toward outsiders, such as other states, who fail to treat them with appropriate respect. Feeling anger appropriately at assaults against one's self, along with seeking to punish aggressors, was an essential precondition of manliness throughout classical antiquity and was closely linked to courage.[22]

In the present passage, the Athenians' anger makes sense as a retaliatory gesture against those who had dishonored them—a response to the shame they experienced at the "disasters" mentioned in this passage.[23] The oligarchs' act was a practical assault on their power—an attempt to prevent them from living the flourishing democratic lives with which they had long come to identify.

Case Study 3: Cleon in the Mytilenian Debate

As Aristotle pointed out, anger was often thought to inspire courage (*EN* 1116b23-30). He observed that "sometimes we praise those who display anger as manly, on the grounds that they are able to rule" (*EN* 1126b1-2). But expressing anger appropriately required good judgment, such as the contextual judgments that the Athenians were called upon to make in their deliberations in the Athenian Assembly. According to Aristotle, too, anger (*thumos*) should not be confused with genuine courage, whatever their apparent similarities. Genuine courage must be rationally governed; it

---

[22] Scourfield 2003: 177–78; Allen 2000; Casey 1990: 56–58; Harris 2001: 96–98, 138, 194.
[23] One can fruitfully compare the principally juridical cases of anger considered by Konstan 2006: 66–71.

must be a prohairetic act undertaken for the sake of what is noble or fine (*to kalon*). At the same time, Aristotle points out that anger (presumably like the other emotions) can "work with" (*sunergei*) genuine courage and help the genuinely noble man to achieve his goals (1116b31–32)[24]—to such an extent that if acts of anger (*thumos*) are informed by practical wisdom and *prohairesis*, then they are, indeed, acts of genuine courage (1117a4–6). If this is correct, then the key issue for the Athenians' courage was the extent to which their "thumotic" courage was penetrated by the rational judgments and acts of prohairetic will that distinguish mere or primitive anger from the rationally governed *thumos* that was, in Aristotle's view, equivalent to courage.

In the Athenian Assembly, speakers often utilized the rhetoric of courage to provoke the citizenry to go to war.[25] Anger had particular motivational force in this context. In his representation of the Mytilenian Debate, Thucydides illustrates the complicated ways in which the courageous passions, particularly anger, conspired to support hawkish policies. In 428 BC the Mytilenians declared their freedom from the Athenian Empire and forcibly resisted Athenian attempts to recover their power on Lesbos. Finally, however, the Athenians regained control and had to decide how to punish (the people they viewed as) the "rebels." Cleon, a well-known war hawk and the leading politician of the day, urged the Athenians not to delay punishing the rebels: "For, when time has passed, one who has suffered injury attacks a wrongdoer with an anger that is duller, but when the sufferer seeks requital as soon as possible afterwards, he inflicts a punishment that is both greatest and most appropriate to the crime" (Thuc. 3.38).

Why are the biggest punishment and the most violent anger "most appropriate"? Cleon emphasized that the Athenians were the victims of injustice (3.39, 3.40), that the Mytilenians were insolent and traitorous (3.40), and that executing the men of military age would be both just and useful to the city. Cleon also stressed the dangers that might result from the Athenians' tendency to show compassion to others. He interprets any potential compassion as a sign of weakness and lack of manliness (*andreia*) (3.37). The Athenians' tendency to display the cowardly types of emotions, as he puts it, has made him believe that "democracy is not able to rule over others" (3.37). His comment suggests quite clearly that not only virtues, but also emotions and political capacities, are relative to particular types of regime.

---

[24] Aristotle says: "Thus the real motive of courageous men is the nobility of courage, although spirit operates in them as well" (*ho de thumos sunergei autois*, *EN* 1116b31–32).
[25] See especially Hunt 2010.

Cleon's speech takes place in the Assembly, not on the battlefield, but obviously his goal is to stimulate appropriate anger and initiative among the Athenians, in order to make them act as "real men" should. As John Casey has written, "To learn anger may be a moral achievement. One may be learning to assert oneself, to show something better than poor-spiritedness. And this may be a way of learning how to be courageous."[26] Casey's comment illustrates that anger can be experienced in many ways and with many meanings, ranging from blind or deranged rage to thoughtful and proper self-assertion. One can see how this comment might apply to the Athenians who fought against the Thirty Tyrants, in Lysias' funeral oration, or even to the demos sitting as a jury in the case of Mantitheus and elsewhere.[27] But does it apply equally well to the fulminations of Cleon?

In his final appeal to the Athenians, Cleon conjures up fear and anger in the imagination of his fellow citizens: "Do not become traitors to yourselves, but come as close as possible in your minds to your moment of suffering, and recall what great importance you placed on subduing them. Now pay them back for what they did, and do not grow soft just now, forgetting the danger that once hung over you. Punish them in a suitable way and set them up as a clear example to your other allies" (Thuc. 3.40). By admonishing the citizens to be true to themselves, Cleon evokes their collective standards of shame, honor, and pride; he explicitly refers these emotions to the Athenians' sense of themselves. He argues that considerable anger is the proper emotional response to the Mytilenians' affront to Athenian dignity. Only a nation of weak cowards, he says, would fail to respond adamantly to such an act of insult and betrayal. Or, to translate the point into Aristotelian terms, the Athenians must act vigorously and with courage in order to maintain their self-respect. For those who lack anger, Aristotle says, lack self-respect: "It seems that they do not perceive or feel aggrieved at an injury, and that someone who does not become angry will not defend himself; and it seems to be slavish for the man who has been mistreated to put up with it or to allow his friends to be mistreated" (*EN* 1126a6-8). This thought could possibly have operated in the collective consciousness of the Athenian demos to inspire hot-blooded, macho, and violent reactions to any affront to Athenian dignity.

In this case, however, the Athenians showed themselves to be free from and in control of the hot, angry passions that had often controlled

---

[26] Casey 1990: 56.

[27] On anger as a characteristic of the Athenian jury, see especially Allen 2000.

decisions concerning war and peace: think, for example, of the Spartans being whipped up into an angry frenzy by Sthenelaidas (Thuc. 1.86–1.87). The Athenians were not beholden to these angry passions; they could, instead, exercise judgment with regard to the particulars of the situation, just when good judgment was called for; and they could rethink what was required of them, as Athenians, as men, and as emotional creatures. At first, Thucydides says, the Athenians decided "under anger" to kill all Mytilenian men of adult age and to enslave their women and children (3.36.2). But then, the next day, they experienced a change of mind (*metanoia*) because of their reflection (*analogismos*) on the cruelty of their initial decision (3.36.4); hence they wanted to reconsider the situation *ab initio* (3.36.5).[28]

The eventual result was that, on the motion of Cleon, "only" the chief conspirators, some 1000 in number, were executed; the Mytilenians' fortifications and navy were destroyed; and their land was divided up into 3000 parcels to be owned by Athenian citizens (3.49). This result does not by any means show the Athenians to have been fair-minded or generous (cf. chapters 14 and 15). But the process described by Thucydides does show that while the Athenians were occasionally beholden to simplistic, unreflective, and violent outbursts of anger, they were also capable of revising their angry decisions and moving thoughtfully beyond them. They did so through understanding when and how (and how much) anger was appropriate, and in the second round, at least, they acted accordingly, without regard for any possible criticisms that they lacked manliness or were servile or incapable of running an empire.

Case Study 4: Lycurgus' *Against Leocrates*

If we have now built up a picture of the normative democratic emotions related to courage, then we might also ask: How were Athenians supposed to acquire the disposition to feel the correct emotions, at the correct time, in the correct way, and so forth? Above all, the Athenians themselves viewed democratic legal and institutional practices as having an educational effect on the citizenry. Consider the following argument-cum-exhortation, made in 330 BC by Aeschines, who argued that his inveterate opponent Demosthenes did not deserve to be publicly honored for patriotism:

---

[28] For positive assessments of the Athenians during the Mytilenian Debate, see Saxonhouse 1996: 72–79, Orwin 1994: 142–62.

> For it would be a terrible thing, men of Athens, if we cast beyond our borders sticks or stones or iron, things without a voice or a mind, whenever they fall on someone and kill him, and if someone kills himself, we bury the hand that did this apart from the body, but, men of Athens, you will honor Demosthenes, who proposed that very last expedition, and who betrayed the soldiers. In this way those who have died are insulted, while those who are alive have their spirits dampened, when they see that death is set up as the prize of excellence, and proper commemoration is lacking. And above all, the younger men ask you which standard they should live by. For know well, men of Athens, that young men are educated not only by the wrestling halls or the schools or by musical and poetic training, but much more by our public notices. The herald proclaims in the theater that someone is awarded a crown for his excellence, his nobility, and his loyalty, a man who leads a disgraceful and disgusting life. A younger man is corrupted when he sees this. Some wretched brothel-keeper like Ctesiphon is punished; the others are educated by this (Aesch. 3.244-46).

In this passage Aeschines suggests that public honoring and punishing not only instruct or corrupt the ethical character of the young, as the case may be, but also, more specifically, shape the emotional responses of all citizens. The living are "disheartened" or, in Greek, they are made *athumoteroi*, that is, they are made to have less *thumos* than they once had. As Hobbs has shown, Plato presents *thumos* as the home, within the soul, of precisely the emotions we are considering: shame, pride, emulation, and anger.[29] Aeschines is arguably evoking all of these associations when he describes the emotional consequences of honoring Demosthenes.

The larger point, made throughout Athenian oratory, is that individuals were taught to feel such emotions when they observed or participated in the community's punishment of wrongdoers and authoritative honoring of citizens who carried out their duties properly and successfully. Lycurgus argued that the city educated its young both through punishing lawbreakers and honoring the virtuous: "Looking toward each of these, they avoid the one because of their fear; but they desire the other in order to win glory" (Lyc. 1.10). This helps to explain, in the Athenians' own vocabulary, how emotional training was supposed to occur through a citizen's observation of democratic institutions and ideology at work.

---

[29] Hobbs 2000; Cooper 1999d; Taylor 1985.

It is possible, however, to offer a more subtle analysis by bringing to bear what Peter Goldie has called the "recognition-response tie": "The essential idea is that our emotions can be educated: we can be taught to recognize, and to respond emotionally, as part of the same education. For example, we can be taught to recognize things as dangerous and to respond, appropriately and proportionately, with fear."[30] As Goldie shows, this is a very ordinary part of educating the young; we teach children, for example, that tarantulas and the edges of cliffs are dangerous and therefore merit the response of fear. It is psychologically healthy that young children should learn to recognize poisonous spiders as dangerous and to fear them appropriately and proportionately. Often, as we have seen, this education takes place through observing and internalizing appropriate role models.[31] In the Athenian democracy, this sort of education went on throughout life; citizens needed an occasional "tune-up" to keep their recognition-response ties in good repair.[32] This was a realistic and useful approach to ensuring that citizens paid adequate attention, at all times, to the proper emotions.

In elaborating the relationship between recognition and response, Goldie emphasizes the "narrativity" of our understanding of emotion.[33] According to Goldie, the recognition-response tie is formed when individuals learn paradigmatic narratives embodying the relevant emotions, and specifically when they internalize images, often from those same narratives, that evoke or embody the relevant emotions.[34] Narratives have a perceptual and imagistic quality in which individuals imagine scenes and sequences of events that stimulate particular emotional responses.[35] They

---

[30] Goldie 2000: 28.
[31] Roberts 2003: 349–52; Hobbs 2000: 59–68.
[32] Cf. Nussbaum 1992: 282–83; Hobbs 2000: 64. At the end of the *Nicomachean Ethics* (1179b29–1180a14), Aristotle makes clear that normally citizens will need to be continually disciplined throughout their lives by the law, because they respond more fully to fear of punishment than to what is honorable, or to *logos*. The Athenians held, quite realistically, that their own citizens needed continual instruction by means of the law and democratic institutions in order to keep their eyes on what was genuinely honorable and carefully reasoned. They were always "learners," not phronetic sages.
[33] Goldie 2000; cf. Roberts 2003: 49–52.
[34] Goldie 2000.
[35] As Sorabji 2000: 114–16, 154–55, 222–23 has shown, ancient philosophers, particularly Posidonius, were deeply interested in the role of imagery and imagination in the education (and often in the eradication) of the emotions. The most relevant passage of Posidonius is this: "For I think you have long since observed how people are not frightened or distressed when persuaded by reason that some evil is present or approaching them, but only when they get images (*phantasiai*) of those things. For how could one excite the irrational by reason, unless you present it with a sort of picture (*anazōgraphēsis*) like a visible one?" (5.6.24–25, p.330 de Lacy, qtd. in Sorabji 2000: 114).

stimulate specific responses because individuals have learned to interpret or "decode" them in particular ways. This "decoding" process is informed by beliefs, habitual reactions, desires, and previous experiences[36]—and, in the case of the Athenians, as we have argued, through deliberate public reflection on these topics in both oratory and in the theater. In uncovering more precisely how this process worked in classical Athens, I will concentrate on the narratives, paradigms, and images that were authorized by the Athenian demos as "privileged" or as embodying its own central ideals.

A particularly intense example of emotional education can be found in Lycurgus' prosecution, in 330 BC, of Leocrates on a charge of cowardice that amounted to treason. After the Athenians' loss to Macedon at the Battle of Chaeronea (338 BC), emergency measures were taken to defend the city of Athens: women and children were to be brought within the city walls, and the generals assigned Athenians to man posts throughout the city (Lyc. 1.16). We happen to know the outcome of this prosecution because of a stray reference in Aeschines' oration of the same year: "Another private individual sailed off to Rhodes and was brought to court just recently, because he acted like a fearful coward, and the votes were equal in his case; if a single vote had been different, he would have been cast beyond our borders" (Aesch. 3.252). We do not know why Leocrates was acquitted. It is possible that his leaving the city did not fall under the scope of the emergency measures, either because of its timing or other details that are now lost.[37]

What is important is that Lycurgus' speech exemplifies one sort of education in interpretation and "decoding" that informed the response-recognition ties of Athenians. By contrast with the other speeches we have considered, however, Lycurgus' speech is one of prosecution—and, in reality, one of utter denunciation of Leocrates. It is therefore in this case that we find the most frequent appeals to the audience's fears and their desire for vengeful punishments, that is, to what is most traditional and aggressive in the Athenians' emotional repertoire. Every society, even a moderate and comparatively open democratic society, will encounter difficult cases—people who fail to respond appropriately to the rational and emotional education provided in other ways. Hence, in order to crack these "hard nuts," it was occasionally necessary to appeal to the most menacing kinds of fear.[38] This

---

[36] Nussbaum 2001a: 236–37.
[37] See Ober 2008: 183–90 for an important recent discussion of this speech.
[38] One might compare the treatment of these "hard cases" by Plato's Athenian Stranger (e.g., 853d–e), who views his introduction of the penal code in Book 9 of the *Laws* to be "shameful" in a city dedicated to the cultivation of virtue (853b).

is not what made Athens distinctive and admirable; it is what shows that Athens, too, had certain personality types, and structures, in common with other Greek cities.

Lycurgus himself highlighted the importance of presenting the demos with paradigms of behavior, as a way to implant the right images and emotions in their hearts. He praised Euripides for encouraging patriotism among the citizenry in his staging of the *Erechtheus*, a play that gave its audience examples of nobility and virtue (Lyc. 1.100). Euripides illustrated for the citizens what is noble and fine—concepts that they should come to articulate increasingly clearly, based on the city's public discussions of the importance of loving their city.

Lycurgus also commended the Athenians for reciting Homer, that famous teacher of bravery. Laws can go only so far in providing education for the citizens, but the poets, who "imitate human life" in their narratives, "pick out the finest examples of action and persuade their audiences through speech and exposition" (Lyc. 1.102). Lycurgus was sensitive to the arguments and other "cognitive work" that penetrated the Athenians' emotional responses. Lycurgus' own indictment of Leocrates can be taken, similarly, as a paradigmatic narrative intended to persuade, enlighten, and educate his fellow citizens. My focus on the narrativity of emotional stimulation and training complements other recent work on the selectivity of Athenian litigants' "hegemonic narratives," which reduce complex phenomena to a simple orientation toward Athenian law.[39]

Lycurgus frames the entire speech as a narrative, beginning with the Athenians' panicked assembly after Chaeronea (Lyc. 1.16). In order to vivify his story, Lycurgus persistently connects Leocrates' cowardice and emotional failures to the naturally inspiring monuments of the city. Leocrates was a "deserter" without pity for the harbours; he was "unashamed" before the city's walls; and he felt no proper reverence when he saw the Acropolis and the Temples of Zeus the Savior and Athena the Protector (Lyc. 1.17, cf. 1.38). These monuments symbolized the citizen's dedication to, or *eros* for, the city and its power, particularly in his capacity as a soldier and protector of Athens (cf., e.g., Thuc. 2.43, with chapter 2).

According to Lycurgus, physical artifacts also show that Leocrates abdicated his responsibility to his family: he shamefully left behind a bronze statue of his own father to be stolen or melted down (1.136). This statue enables Lycurgus to illustrate the close intertwining of public

---

[39] Johnstone 1999: 69; see in general Johnstone 1999: esp. 46–69.

responsibility and private responsibility; his failure to live up to either one or the other, not to mention both, reflects badly on Leocrates' character. Ironically, he points out, Leocrates' father had dedicated this statue in the Temple of Zeus the Savior as a sign of his own "uprightness" or "decency" (*metriotētos*, 1.136) as a democratic citizen. Lycurgus puts Leocrates' character on trial (cf. Johnstone 1999: 97) specifically by decoding public and private monuments with reference to, and in terms meant to evoke, the Athenians' normative emotional responses—in particular, anger at Leocrates' failures to live up to the ideals that they had worked out so carefully in their public explorations of and investments in courage.

In other sections of the narrative, Lycurgus charted Leocrates' self-interested movements away from, then in the vicinity of, and finally back into, the city of Athens. Leocrates first ran away, but later, after the imminent danger was gone, he lived unashamed on the borders of Athens, without paying reciprocal respect to the city that had reared him (Lyc. 1.21). Leocrates showed disrespect for the gods of the polis by exporting his family's sacred images to his new home in Megara (Lyc. 1.25–26). Eight years later, Leocrates was not ashamed to pass the graves of those who had died at Chaeronea (Lyc. 1.45). He now shamelessly exhibits himself before the eyes of mourners (Lyc. 1.142)—a clear reference to the idea that the eyes were the conventional repository of shame (cf. Arist. *Rhet.* 1384a34). The chronological framework sets up a virtually cinematographic sequence of images in the minds of the audience that explain how Leocrates' emotional defects led to cowardly behavior, and why cowardice is harmful and wrong. Specifically, Leocrates' cowardice was wrong because it forced the city to take extraordinary measures for its own safety and put unusual and unequal burdens on Lycurgus' fellow citizens. While Leocrates acted as a traitor and coward, the city placed its hopes of safety in the men over the age of fifty, who had previously been formally relieved of military duty (Lyc. 1.39–40). Those who remained felt pain and grief over being forced to free their slaves for military defense, recognizing how low Athens, once the leading state in all Greece, had now fallen (Lyc. 1.41–42). While Leocrates was moving blithely around Greece, the city of Athens struggled to keep itself intact.

All of these sentiments were, in the first instance, carefully designed to evoke indignation and anger among the jurors. But, in the process, the citizens themselves were invited to turn their attention to key features of the topography and history of the city. They were trained thereby to shape themselves so as to "feel" the proper civic emotions in relation to defending the city. Or, perhaps, they already felt the proper emotions and found themselves in the process of having their emotions clarified and reinforced in this public speech about democratic courage. Through its focus on physical monuments and topographical features, Lycurgus' narrative description provides a density of detail whose emotional content could be conveyed only through fertile images and a complex array of perceptions. Emotions contain "rich and dense perceptions of the object, which are highly concrete and replete with detail."[40] It is precisely such emotionally charged details that Lycurgus tried to capture by evoking central democratic images.

He brought those images into a wider horizon of interpretation by encouraging the audience to recall the historical events that made them meaningful. For example, he argued that those who died at Chaeronea lived on in Athenian memory as exemplars of freedom and courage (49). They were worthy models for Athenian citizens in the audience. One of their motivations, he says, was that the Athenians in particular knew how to honor courageous soldiers: "You will find that, among others, statues of athletes are erected in the agora, but your city dedicates statues of noble generals and tyrant-killers" (Lyc. 1.51). In focusing his audience's memory on the fallen soldiers, Lycurgus highlights physical objects, such as statues, because emotions, as Goldie has pointed out, have a strongly perceptual, imagistic quality.[41] Vividly imagining value-laden objects also tends to stir up strong feelings toward those objects: "When the imagining is especially vivid, the feelings will tend to be especially strong."[42]

Through conjuring up such images in an authoritative narrative, Lycurgus was helping to reinforce particular, normative emotional responses within his audience. He focused particularly on the citizens' sense of themselves and their relation to the Athenian political community. He did this, first, by eliciting in his listeners a proper sense of shame toward the city and its monuments by illustrating in painful detail the precise elements and consequences of Leocrates' shameful behavior. Athenians should shudder at seeing what shameful behavior leads to—the degradation of character such as Leocrates had suffered, and which everyone could now witness. The audience should also come to recognize the symbols that ought to evoke respect, even admiration, among properly "feeling," self-monitoring citizens. Second, Lycurgus cultivated self-respect and emulation in his audience by showing that the fallen soldiers' behavior was worthy of respect

---

[40] Nussbaum 2001a: 65; cf. Sorabji 2000: 114–16, 154–55.
[41] Goldie 2000: 72–83; Roberts 2003: 70–82, 87–89.
[42] Goldie 2000: 80.

and admiration, and by holding them up as role models for the democratic citizenry to imitate. The present democratic citizenry, too, should live up to the ideals that their fellow citizens, now fallen, adhered to at the crucial moment of life and death.

To set these points within yet broader narratives of the city, Lycurgus called to mind the heroes of the Battle of Salamis (480 BC) (68–74). Contrary to what some senseless people might think, the Athenians' ancestors were heroic in their decision to abandon the city after due deliberation about the threat posed by Xerxes. The ancestors allowed the Persians to capture the city and staked their salvation on a sea battle in the straits of nearby Salamis. This decision to change locations for the fight was far different from Leocrates' cowardly decision to abandon the city in order to win safety for himself. Lycurgus summoned up these ancestors in order to offer a decisive verdict on Leocrates:

> Do you imagine that any one of those heroes would have been ready to condone such an act? Would they not have stoned to death one who was disgracing their valor? (Lyc. 1.71).

The heroism of the ancestors not only saved Athens, but also liberated all the Greeks and set geographical boundaries, after the Battle of Eurymedon (466 BC), for the Persians. These heroes, like the heroes of Marathon, fought not to win a reputation for glory, but rather because they "valued...conduct deserving of it [glory]" (Lyc. 1.104).

Their own motivations were intrinsic and independent of external honors; they thereby avoided the sort of criticism that Aristotle later leveled against the Spartans, who, he says, had come to value the rewards of courage more than the virtue itself (*Pol.* 1271b6–10). The Athenian heroes therefore became all the purer as role models worthy of praise and emulation. But the image of such heroes stoning cowards to death also inspired a sense of shame, and perhaps even fear, in the Athenian audience. By summoning up images of heroic ancestors to serve as "internalized others" for the Athenians, Lycurgus had a powerful weapon with which to instill the appropriate feelings of shame and emulation within the present citizenry.[43]

---

[43] For the idea of "internalized others," see Williams 1993, along with my discussions beginning in chapter 2.

The converse of this emulation was the citizens' normative anger toward cowards like Leocrates: just as they praise the courageous, so also should they punish cowards—especially Leocrates, who had no respect for or shame before the demos (Lyc. 1.74). Why should an Athenian citizen show respect to the demos? As we saw in exploring Mantitheus' speech, the reason is that the demos constituted an association of fellow citizens whose communal ties, and even "civic friendship," made life meaningful. Athenian citizen-equals provided the eudaimonistic context in which individual Athenians' lives made sense (see chapters 14 and 15).

In calling these emotions to mind, Lycurgus was inculcating a proper sense of emulation toward democratic heroes and anger toward Leocrates, specifically by conjuring up these heroes as role models in the imagination of his audience (cf. chapter 8). By posing a threat to the normative status of these heroes, Leocrates made the Athenians' own self-image vulnerable and thereby incurred their anger. The audience is meant to imagine the heroes of Salamis standing in judgment of cowards and stoning them to death. The Athenians' present anger toward Leocrates thus derived directly from their emulation of the democratic heroes. The obverse of that emulation is here constituted as a sense of shame: the citizens must recognize that if they lapse into the position of someone like Leocrates, then they will find themselves the objects of anger and contempt in the eyes of heroes whom they admire, not to mention their fellow citizens, and even themselves. Their punishment would be not only death, but also disgrace and shame (91).

Moreover, if they should ever lapse into cowardice in the future, then they would have to agree that, according to the ideals to which they subscribe, they would deserve such punishment for shameful behavior. Hence, the demos also deserved respect because of its justice. This nexus of ideas was perhaps reinforced by the realization that the Athenians' ancestors themselves fought courageously in order to save the city from shame and disrepute (82). Shame and emulation were closely associated in the evaluative emotional economy of the citizenry. In other words, "it is clear that a reason for shame is, in many cases, some failure to achieve the *kalon* [the noble]; this norm is logically prior to shame and gives it its rationale."[44]

---

[44] Nussbaum 1980: 428n.2.

Reverence before the Law, Fear of Legal Punishment

Lycurgus' elaborate speech also explores the role of fear in producing, not cowardice, but courage. Lycurgus argued that the capital punishment of Leocrates could be exemplary for citizens who might otherwise waver in their resolution or dedication to the city:

> For fear that comes from one's fellow citizens is powerful; it will force men to withstand dangers when facing the enemy. For who could see a traitor punished with death and then abandon his fatherland in times of danger? (Lyc. 1.130).

Lycurgus' argument is not simply that Leocrates ought to feel shame. Instead, he deserves to die, just as those who moved to Decelea during the Peloponnesian occupation were also sentenced to death (Lyc. 1.120–21). Cowardice amounts to the capital offence of treason. The Spartans first recognized the importance of executing cowards (Lyc. 1.129). Lycurgus recommends such judicial harshness to the Athenians, on the grounds that it might help to produce courageous behavior in the other citizens. He made these arguments at the very end of the period we are examining, and he had to argue so strenuously for judicial harshness precisely because the Athenians were accustomed to producing courage through reason, persuasion, and cognitive work, rather than punitive shame and fear of the law.

As we saw at the beginning of this chapter, there are several other places where we find strong evidence of the Athenians' reverence for the law and fear of legal punishments. Like other Greek cities (and like Plato's Callipolis), classical Athens established laws against cowardice, in respect to which Pericles expected his audience to feel reverence (e.g. Ar., *Ach.* 1128–29, Aesch. 3.175, Lys. 14.15). Those who have argued that fear of the law was a distinctively Spartan variation in the Greek concept of freedom offer partial and incomplete accounts of the democratic self-presentation.[45] In these passages—and particularly in the harsher contexts of accusation—the specifically democratic and deliberative associations of courage retreated, and the Athenians fell back on emotional motivations similar to those found in other Greek cities.

Despite the ideology that had depended on sharp contrasts between Athens and Sparta, Lycurgus held up Sparta as a moral exemplar to

---

[45] See, for example, Millender 2002a, 2002b; Forsdyke 2001.

Athenians: the Spartans have laws that condemn to death those who refuse to risk their lives for their country; survival after war is subject to scrutiny that might involve disgrace and death (Lyc. 1.129–130). Lycurgus recommends that it would be expedient for the Athenians to abide by these laws as well. In the late fourth century, with Sparta out of the way militarily, it was, perhaps, a more straightforward matter to call upon the Spartan ideal in order to produce courage—even at Athens.[46]

Yet, as though to compensate for his way of breaking down the Periclean distinction between Athens and Sparta, Lycurgus made another kind of argument for the superiority of Athenian courage. Lycurgus argued that, however educational the Spartan model may be for contemporary Athenians, the Spartans got their blueprint of courage, in the deep past, from Athens itself. When the Spartans were at war with the Messenians way back in the seventh century, Lycurgus informs us, the god advised them to take a leader from Athens. The leader was no ordinary general but rather the militaristic poet Tyrtaeus who helped to make the Spartans courageous (Lyc. 1.106). The Athenian democrats continued to insist, perhaps despite themselves, that when there was thinking to be done about the virtues, whether it might be done in the Assembly, or in the militaristic poems of Tyrtaeus, the Athenians were the leaders.

We find the Athenians coming to resemble the Spartans in one of the harshest and most threatening prosecutorial speeches in the entire corpus of Attic oratory. Lycurgus (along with Aeschines before him) implied that in the hardest and most intransigent cases it was necessary to make a display of the force of Athenian law and social institutions. This was not what made Athens most distinctive and, perhaps, most noble and interesting among the ancient Greeks. All the same, it is notable that most "civilized" societies, even those of the individualistic modern nation-states, have not gotten by without threatening capital (or other very severe) punishment for those who desert the ranks.[47]

Conclusion: Democratic Courage in Practice

Our discussion illustrates clearly that Pericles' ideal of democratic courage did not pervade every corner of Athenian political practice. In fact, the

---

[46] On Athenian attitudes toward Sparta in the mid to late fourth century, see Fisher 1994.
[47] For an interesting treatment of the paradoxes involved in penalizing desertion with capital punishment, see Miller 2000: 92–97.

ideology of democratic courage whose presence we traced in Part I provided a neater and more attractive, coherent, and distinctively democratic picture than we find "on the ground" in the Athenian law courts, in the Athenians' use of legal punishments, and in Aristophanes' social humiliation of cowards. On the other hand, Lysias' funeral oration shows that the Periclean anatomy of democratic courage still resonated with Athenians of the fourth century; the speech was designed to appeal to Athenians who still endorsed an idealized image of democratic courage that prized both practical rationality and desirable emotions associated with valor. Moreover, the Athenians of Thucydides' third book showed themselves capable, in practice, of resisting the allure of the traditionally hot-headed anger to which Cleon appealed. They displayed a significant degree of harmony between their emotions and their judgments about a proportionate response to the Mytilenians—a degree of harmony and thoughtfulness that the epitaphic ideology had always tried to capture in speech.

The Athenian case appears, then, to illustrate a democracy striving to liberate itself from traditional norms, with a view to certain self-constructed ideals, and yet frequently falling short of those ideals, particularly in pressure-filled social and legal contexts. We may speculate that no society, however liberal or democratic, can genuinely free itself from the social pressures that we have identified at Athens—and even that it would not serve the interests of social cohesion or ordinary habits of lawfulness, if any society should possibly be able to do so.

However these matters may stand, there are yet other ways in which the Athenians' courageous passions corresponded much more closely to the representations we explored in Part I. Specifically, we will now consider the role of shame, honor, and role models in the Athenians' ideology and practices of courage. What we will find, I think, is that the distinctions drawn by Pericles, other Athenian speakers, and Herodotus between Athenian and Spartan shame make sense in practice, particularly when we are focused on the Athenians' democratic ways of establishing ideals, paradigms, and role models for themselves. The key was that in democracies, above all, individuals did not unreflectively inherit their sense of shame and honor from the laws or the community. Rather, citizens played a key role in fashioning, shaping, modifying, interpreting, and communicating these emotions, along with the ideals on which they were based. The result was that, in the process of socialization at Athens, the democratic citizens internalized emotions that they themselves had played a role in crafting through their participation in the city's public institutions.

CHAPTER 11 | Shame, Honor, and the Constitution of Role Models

ANCIENT CRITICS FOUND THE democratic Athenians intolerable, not because they were enmeshed in traditional structures of authority, shame, honor, reverence, and so on, but for precisely the opposite reason. The Athenians had too fully liberated themselves from the traditional Greek culture; they were too free, too lackadaisical, and too tolerant of disrespect for the law and of rampant individualism. By contrast, the criticisms of Athens posed by the modern liberal tradition are exactly the inverse: the Athenians were too immersed in traditional Mediterranean emotions and too confining with respect to the individual and his "freedom of conscience." Our picture suggests, however, that Athenian democratic culture gave rise to a third possibility, which emphasized both cognitive understanding of the good life and newly constituted emotions that were shot through with that discursive knowledge. The Athenians respected the law and their community, but they did so for sound reasons, and on the basis of clear thinking and well-informed emotions.

In this chapter we focus on shame, honor, and the related emotion of emulation.[1] We have seen that, in certain modes of exhortation, Demosthenes shamed his fellow citizens into standing up against Philip (1.24), in a very traditional deployment of shame; yet, all the same, Demosthenes' funeral oration also closely connected shaming

---

[1] For a thoughtful treatment of shame and masculinity in Athens, see Roisman 2005: 64–83, which does not, however, focus either on the question of democratic distinctiveness or on the relationship of shame to the Athenians' claim to practice a cognitively rich model of courage. For a fascinating discussion of free speech, shame, and democracy, see Saxonhouse 2006.

punishments and democratic free speech (Dem. 60.25–26). In Lysias' funeral oration, equally, the speaker emphasized that at the end of the civil war of 404–403 BC, the democrats' courageous return to Athens resulted both from imitating their ancestors and from feeling shame before them for their defeats. The ancestors thereby became both role models and internalized "others" for living Athenians (Lys. 2.62). The audience of this speech was supposed to walk away having internalized their ancestors as role models who promoted a proper sense of shame (cf. Dem. 18.95–99, 200–205).[2]

At first glance, at least, the shame evoked by these epitaphic speeches is similar to the shame utilized by many nondemocratic states in order to inspire courage (see chapter 9).[3] Yet Pericles, Herodotus, and Demosthenes all distinguished Athenian democratic shame from the shame employed by nondemocratic cities in order to motivate courage (see chapters 2, 4, and 9). Their idea was that shame might play different roles depending on the regimes in which it was cultivated—and even different roles in different contexts within the same regime. Shame might take the form of an intellectually complex emotion shot through with self-chosen commitments and aspirations; or it might be manifested as a simpler, less self-aware emotion that embodied the traditional views of one's culture and one's authority figures, taken over more or less without any criticism or self-consciousness.[4] To see how and why shame might take these different forms, we would do well to examine the Athenians' particular constructions of this emotion more carefully.

---

[2] Internalizing ideas and proper emotional responses is a common theme in the funeral orations particularly: see the emphatic statement of Hyperides: "…What speech would benefit the souls of its audience more than one that celebrates courage and brave men?" (Hyp. 6.34).

[3] In other ancient Mediterranean contexts, too, we find a similar emphasis on shame and role models: in particular, the Romans were anxious to uphold the custom of their ancestors, the *mos maiorum*; their imperialism was driven by honor and shame (see Lendon 1997); and their courage was motivated by the *exempla* (models) of previous Roman heroes, such as Horatius Cocles at the bridge (Cicero, *Laws* 2.10; Livy 2.10). Polybius argued that Roman institutions and cultural practices, such as the parade of *imagines* (masks of ancestors) at aristocratic funerals, helped to produce citizen-soldiers who were anxious to display courage (6.52–53).

[4] This idea is one of the keys to Christina Tarnopolsky's excellent work on shame in the Platonic dialogues. As Tarnopolsky argues, "Far from banishing rhetoric and emotion from his own notion of a more philosophical democratic politics, Plato's *Gorgias* shows us exactly why a rhetoric of respectful shame is integral to the kinds of reciprocal and inter-subjective relations that make self-other interactions in a democratic polity both critical and potentially transformative" (Tarnopolsky 2010: 17).

Passions, Judgments, and Civic Education: The Case of Shame

At least potentially, shame is a complex emotion that derives from an individual's self-conception, ideals, and life narrative. Certain cultures—such as, arguably, democratic Athens—think through these facets of individuality in more profound ways than others. Whether self-consciously or not, shame runs deeply into the individual's sense of himself as the product of a particular past and as the guide to a projected future. Shame—which is normally captured by the Greek terms *aidōs* and *aischunē*—was defined by Aristotle as a "certain pain or disturbance related to past, present, or future wrongdoing, concerning things that appear to lead to dishonour" (*Rhet.* 1383b12–15). The "sense of shame," by extension, connotes a character-related sensitivity to disgraceful behavior or collective prohibitions, which motivates a person to avoid acts he considers dishonorable or unworthy of him.[5] The "sense of shame" is an internal monitor that alerts us to the prospect of losing self-respect, or of doing or even of *being* something for which we have contempt. An individual's sense of shame and self-respect—his "ethical compass," so to speak—was typically governed by internalized role models.[6]

These features of shame enabled the Athenian democrats, in particular, to create a deliberate and self-conscious expression of this emotion. Because of their democratic institutions and ethos, Athens's citizens were encouraged to think carefully through their grounds for admiring particular role models. In fact, as we saw in chapter 3, the democratic city created lasting and successful institutions that invited citizens to do so on a regular basis. By contrast, there was no Spartan funeral oration, no Spartan tradition of cherishing free speech, no Spartan comic or tragic theater, no

---

[5] Like us, the ancient Greeks distinguished between "occurrent" emotions and emotional dispositions (cf. Elster 1999: 244).

[6] See the pathbreaking work of Williams 1993; Cairns 1993; Konstan 2003, 2006: 91–104; Tarnopolsky 2010; and the special issue of *Social Research* (vol.70.4) devoted to shame. Hobbs 2000: esp. 59–68 helpfully discusses shame and role models with specific reference to the Platonic corpus. Describing the Greek vocabulary of shame, Cairns writes, "[L]et *aidos* be an inhibitory emotion based on sensitivity to and protectiveness of one's self-image, and let the verb *aideomai* convey a recognition that one's self-image is vulnerable in some way, a reaction in which one focuses on the conspicuousness of the self" (Cairns 1993: 2). An individual with a sense of shame has internalized an "other"—in classical Athens, the evaluative community of democratic citizen-equals, for example, or the successful warriors at Marathon—whose judgments he himself shares. Thus, if he falls below these generally accepted standards, and disgraces himself through cowardice (for example), then he will feel shame both because others will recognize his deficiency and because he himself will endorse their judgments: he will "know" they are right.

Spartan discursive democracy, and so on. A fortiori no such institutions existed in Persia, Macedon, or the Hellenistic kingdoms. As a result, these nondemocratic cultures did not institutionalize the regular opportunity for citizens to develop richer and more cognitively demanding experiences of shame that corresponded to a qualitatively different experience of courage.

This contrast becomes all the more powerful if we agree with Plato, Aristotle, and a variety of modern theorists that emotions are penetrated by cognitive judgments of value. Traditionally, of course, the emotions have been viewed in contrast to rationality.[7] Views of emotion that stress affectivity, as opposed to cognition, have also found their champions in both antiquity and the twentieth century.[8] Following ancient thinkers, however, many contemporary theorists believe that emotions have "intelligence," or that they require cognition, or that they are compounds made up of belief and desire. For example, Martha Nussbaum has argued that emotions are "value-laden cognitive states" or "forms of evaluative judgment that ascribe to certain things and persons outside a person's own control great importance for the person's own flourishing."[9] In other words, our best theories suggest that emotions are penetrated with judgments, interpretations, beliefs, and convictions—all of which are amenable to education, persuasion, and change.

This idea was central to the Athenian democratic construction of the emotions. For it was an assumption of Athenian public oratory (for example) that the citizens' emotions could be trained through processes of reasoned discussion and interpretation. It was in this way that the Athenians developed conceptions and practices of the emotions that, through their connections with free speech and democratic deliberation, proved to be more distinctively democratic than we might have supposed initially. The shape and social functions of shame depend almost entirely upon the particular culture's strategies for cultivating sensitivities to what is honorable and dishonorable. As Tocqueville formulated this point:

> [E]very time that men gather together in a particular society, a standard of honor is immediately established among them, that is to say, an ensemble of opinions that is their own, about what one ought to praise or blame; and

---

[7] See, for example, Elster 1999: 283–87.
[8] E.g., Goldie 2000.
[9] Nussbaum 2001a: 64, 22; cf. Taylor 1985: 1–5; Cairns 1993: 5–14; Sorabji 2000: 1–7, 19–54; Konstan 2006: 21–40.

these particular rules always have their source in the special habits and special interests of the association. (*DA* II.3.18)

The Athenian democracy institutionalized reflection on the nature and ethical significance of the role models who constituted the psychological audience that gave shame its meaning, direction, and inspirational power.

In the first instance, at least, oratory and the theater were the principal loci in which Athenians were encouraged to reflect upon their ideals of shame, fear of the law, anger, emulation, and courage, as a way of taking responsibility not only for their particular actions on specific occasions, but also for the emotional and cognitive "inputs" that motivated their actions in general. In their roles as judges, deliberators, and spectators, citizens were encouraged to reflect carefully upon the *agōnes* (contests) of orators and playwrights. They were encouraged to step back and ask themselves, How important or useful are the ideals that we Greeks have always prized? I do not mean so much that ordinary citizens directly shaped the public presentations of elite speakers and playwrights—though they surely did so indirectly, through their voting and through their praise and blame—as that the democracy maintained institutions and rituals in which ordinary citizens were encouraged to interrogate their presumptive role models and to hash things out for themselves.

Athenian democrats understandably believed that citizens were educated in democratic ideals and normative emotions through listening to speeches, participating in public festivals, fulfilling civic duties, and observing Assembly decisions and judicial verdicts (e.g., Aesch. 3.245–46; cf. Plato, *Rep.* 492b–93a; Plato, *Gorg.* 513a–c). Based on this civic education, citizens were expected to have appropriate emotional responses. This is why Demosthenes could lambaste Aeschines for grieving at Athenian success and feeling joy and confidence at the moment of Athens's disastrous defeats (Dem. 18.217, 244, 287–88, 291). Whatever the empirical facts of Aeschines' emotions, Demosthenes could usefully point to Aeschines' emotions as symptoms of his deliberate intentions and attitudes. These were matters of public concern—and they were susceptible to interpretation, persuasion, and civic formation. Athenian orators assumed that emotional responses would follow upon the images, thoughts, attitudes, and beliefs of their audiences. As a result, the Athenians believed that they could train civic emotions through processes of reasoned discussion and interpretation—processes whose purpose was precisely to change the attitudes and beliefs, and thus the emotions, of their audiences.

Even more importantly, perhaps, the poets, not public speakers, were traditionally considered the educators of the Greeks. This role was manifest in the Athenian theater. In his *Frogs* (405 BC), Aristophanes staged a contest between Euripides and Aeschylus over which tragedian could render the best advice to the city (1420–21). To stake his own claim, Aeschylus asserts that his plays promoted courage among the citizens:

> But he [Homer] did teach many other brave men, such as the hero Lamachus; from which my mind, imitating his example, fashioned many outstanding men, such as Patroclus and lion-hearted Teucer, in order that I might urge on the men who are citizens to become rivalrous toward those men, whenever they hear the war-trumpet. (*Frogs* 1039–42; cf. 1053–56).

Aeschylus' point is that citizens in the audience would look up to the heroic characters he created and, at critical moments when courage was needed, aspire to live up to the standards established by those role models. The Athenians developed distinctively democratic forms of experience, discussion, reflection, and endorsement—all of which were based on democratic institutions such as the Assembly, the law courts, the dramatic festivals, and other modes of popular civic activity.[10]

What supports Pericles' claim to democratic distinctiveness was not the presence or absence of shame as a motivational resource for Athenian courage, but rather the democracy's distinctive invitation to its citizens to take part in elaborating, and taking responsibility for, the ideals, role models, and ethical paradigms that they took as the guides to their behavior. The distinction is based on clarity about one's own goals and a more profoundly voluntary adherence to certain standards of nobility or honor.[11] The key point is whether the soldier had discussed, considered, and endorsed the ideals for which he was fighting and which governed his sense of shame and honor. To be sure, the Athenian democrats were not

---

[10] My view of the Athenian theater's relationship to democracy thus shares elements with that of Burian 2011 and Hesk 2011, both of whom discuss specifically the tragic theater. See further chapters 12 and 13. In relation to the comic theater, see the persuasive remarks of Henderson 1996, who notes that the comic theater had an institutional structure that was similar to the "deliberative occasions with which the Old Oligarch aligns them," and that "the city and its citizens were the festival's theme and focus" (78–79; cf. 94–95). Henderson's piece also provides a helpful discussion of the laws against slander, which could occasionally (and within quite strict boundaries) limit comic freedom of speech.

[11] This is why Christ 2006: 92n.12 is right to say that "[w]hereas many elements of the hoplite experience are common to all Hellenes participating in hoplite warfare, Athens' institutions shaped precisely how its hoplites competed for honor on campaign and at home."

Aristotelian *phronimoi*. Yet their democracy encouraged them to reflect on the significance of courage and to achieve the sort of clarity about this virtue that others, such as the Spartans, Persians, and Macedonians, could not achieve through (merely) following the law or the king's will and acting on the basis of a more primitive and punitive type of shame.

Shame and the Tragic Experience

The tragic theater constitutes one important forum in which reflection on shame and honor could take place. Although we investigate tragedy more fully in chapter 13, considering one example now will help us to consolidate the foregoing ideas about shame. Take, as a test case, Theseus' reflections on courage in Euripides' *Suppliants*. The idea is that in his words and actions Theseus stimulated the audience to think carefully about what courage meant to them. He represented a certain kind of hero to whom the Athenians might look up and before whom they might feel a sense of shame. How did Theseus manage the quandaries of international justice and the seemingly ineradicable human propensity to make war?

When the play begins, we see Theseus' mother Aethra praying to Demeter and pitying the mothers of the Seven against Thebes.[12] Theseus enters and learns that Adrastus has come to Athens to ask for help in recovering the bodies of the fallen soldiers. It emerges that Adrastus went to war without having received good omens, and against the will of Amphiaraus (155–59). In the course of reproaching Adrastus for his reckless militarism, Theseus began to forge associations between courage, moderation, and rational understanding. First of all, Theseus upbraids Adrastus for being carried away by aggressive young men into pursuing courage at the expense of wise deliberation (160–61). Theseus himself, by contrast, praises the gods above all for granting understanding (*sunesis*) to mortal men, along with the power to communicate (201–4). Adrastus is made to see that locating courage at the top of one's table of virtues, above prudence (*euboulias*, 161), is a destructive way to rank-order the virtues

---

[12] For helpful general interpretations, see Vellacott 1975: 157–60, which is particularly concerned with war and with Athena's rebuke of Theseus; Conacher 1967: 93–108, which discusses both the victory of Theseus and the ironic overtones of the play's finale; and Michelini 1994, which discusses the play's political vocabulary and contemporary resonances for an audience of Athenians, finding in Theseus' defence of democracy a "vulnerability in democratic ideology that extends beyond this play" (236). Mills 1997: 87–128 provides a thoughtful general treatment linking the play and its treatment of Theseus to various important dimensions of Athenian democratic ideology.

(163, 219–49). Theseus wants to avoid encumbering Athens with the misfortunes brought about by Adrastus's lack of deliberation and planning (247–49). The effect of his remonstrance is to suggest that in order to be a virtue, properly understood, courage must be balanced by moderation, subordinated to justice, and meaningfully directed by practical reason.[13]

These reflections have obvious associations with the Periclean model of democratic courage. But Theseus' mother Aethra insists that her son's application of this model is incorrect in the particular circumstances. His concerns about encumbering Athens show that he has failed to orient Athenian courage toward the noble ends of generosity, piety, and justice (304–13).[14] This is why Aethra wants to say something "that brings honor" to Theseus and the city (293), even if it contradicts Theseus' initial line of reasoning. By stopping at mere criticism of Adrastus, she argues, Theseus would fail to integrate the Athenians' supposedly "deliberative courage" into the wide web of socially beneficial virtues which courage is meant to serve. By contrast, it would bring Theseus "honor" and the city "a crown of glory" to see to it that Greece's sacred laws of burial are observed (306–15). Athens flourishes, Aethra says, because of its dedication to glorious toil (323).

Theseus sees the point of his mother's challenge: while he insists that his earlier condemnation of Adrastus' bad judgment was correct, he also acknowledges the wisdom of Aethra's advice, which goes to the heart of his own self-image (334–45). As Aethra urges, helping these non-Athenians is what will give Theseus honor, properly understood (297–331). Theseus' character, his sense of self, is such that to live with self-respect, to avoid shame, and to remain true to his own self-chosen character, he must undertake difficult, dangerous tasks in order to punish wrongdoers, win glory, and satisfy the gods (339–48).[15] This is structurally and substantively close to the argument that Demosthenes made, at least in retrospect, to justify his

---

[13] Cf. Balot 2007, 2010a. For a related, and in certain respects complementary, treatment of tragedy in its social context, see Mills 1997: 104–28; Mills 2010. Burian 1985 emphasizes Theseus' reasoned rebuttal of Adrastus, but he works with what is, I think, an overly sharp dichotomy between intellect and emotion (cf. esp. 131–33).

[14] On pity and generosity in Athens's self-representation in tragedy and funerary oratory, see Tzanetou 2005, 2012; Mills 1997: 105–106.

[15] Burian 1985: 135–37 offers a helpful discussion of honor, heroism, and the *ponos* of both Theseus and Athens—"toil," a concept central to the play and to the Athenian self-image altogether. Michelini 1994: 231, on the other hand, argues that Aethra is praising a "rash Athens" and thus that her advice conflicts with the "intellectualism of her son." Mills 1997: 87–91 seems to me correct that the play carries forward the virtues of an "idealized Athens" (87) such as we see in the funeral orations.

recommendation that the Athenians confront Philip at Chaeronea despite their numerous military disadvantages (Dem. 18.199–208). Like the Athenians of Herodotus, Theseus, too, has constructed a "necessary identity" that he himself endorses, takes pride in, and feels he must live up to.

It might come as a surprise to the Athenian audience (but perhaps not as much to modern scholars[16]) that, at least in Euripides' rendition, Theseus himself, that epitome of the classical Athenian virtues, required the ethical guidance provided by conversation with his mother in order to express his own ethical virtues in their fullest and most complete form.[17] To highlight this idea, in fact, Theseus and Aethra make a specific point of discussing the possibility of a woman's giving good advice in the city (293–300). Furthermore, and in keeping with Theseus' own democratic ideals, even though he could carry the decision on his own authority, Theseus adds that if he makes a public, transparent, and rationally convincing case for recovering the Argives, then he will make the Athenian demos more zealous in pursuing this virtuous project (349–51). In the play's dramatic world, the Athenians were emboldened by understanding for themselves the importance of the proposed military action; they became more courageous as they made their projects more their own. The dramatic action and the deliberative conversations of this play invited the audience to think their way through to a more profound understanding of courage and its demands in particular situations. Athenian citizens had to reflect upon such questions on their own, after watching the play, since their democratic cultivation of thoughtful independence could never have been conducted through the rote transmission of inherited beliefs—even if those beliefs were true.

The ensuing action placed new demands on Theseus' understanding of his courage and its appropriate application in particular circumstances. As he had once criticized Adrastus' rashness, so too, we now learn, is he indifferent to the Theban herald's advice that wisdom consists in idleness and bravery in cautious forethought (509–10). Adrastus and the Theban herald represent two roads not taken in the proper evaluation of courage. In nobly undertaking to recover the Argive warriors, Theseus threads the

---

[16] Mills 1997: 107 rightly observes that "Theseus must learn, by means of his mother's persuasion, to feel fellowship with the suffering women...and thus to combine emotion and intellect in order to possess all the virtues as befits an (ideal) Athenian."

[17] On Euripides' presentation of deliberation in this scene, and its effects on the democratic audience, see Hesk 2011: 127–36. For commentary on Aethra's entry into the public sphere of masculine speech, and the surprising fact that Theseus takes advice from his mother, see Mendelsohn 2002: 164–68; Mendelsohn, however, reads Aethra's appropriation of masculine attributes such as "boldness" as a transgression, which Theseus must work to contain.

needle between Adrastus' rashness and the Theban's excessive caution, so as to act in accordance with justice and generosity, through courageous efforts, and with a detailed understanding of his own reasons for so acting.[18] He remains undeterred both in action and in conversation because he has worked his way through, with considerable effort, as we see, to a sound and balanced position.

Theseus' cognitive work paid off during his actual confrontation with the enemy. As the messenger indicates, Theseus announced before the battle that he wanted to avoid bloodshed if possible (669–72), to which the less noble Creon responds with mere silence (673–74). Once the battle was won, Theseus refused to let his anger or his greed dictate his treatment of the unprotected city.[19] The herald reports that Theseus stopped before the city walls and proclaimed that he wanted to recover the dead warriors, not to destroy the city (724–25). Theseus has deliberated about the ends of courage; he has achieved an unwavering clarity about his goals; and his careful reasoning sets limits to the violent passions to which pugnacious men are often led in the heat of the moment.[20] What would Thucydides' Cleon have done in this situation?

Such is my own way of elaborating the meaning of this text. In classical Athens there will have been many such ways, particularly, perhaps, with regard to the quasi-funeral oration given later in the play by Adrastus (857–917).[21] The play provoked its audience to think about whether courage

---

[18] Mendelsohn 2002: 176–79 interestingly argues that after his conversation with Aethra Theseus integrates feminine traits, but in his view these are primarily negative: boundary violation and incontinence. I would say, by contrast, that Theseus' integration of the feminine appears to be positive in the play's representation, in that by virtue of his conversation with his mother Theseus begins to act justly and courageously, neither indulging in excessive recklessness and anger nor yielding excessively to caution or timidity: on the themes of integrating the feminine and the masculine, see further chapter 12 and Mendelsohn's concluding remarks on this subject at 2002: 195, which suggest that the play criticizes hyper-aggressive, heroic forms of *andreia* and lauds *hēsuchia*. Michelini 1994: 232 argues that Theseus is a contradictory figure who undertakes aggressive imperialism contrary to his earlier condemnation of Adrastus.

[19] For further reflections on Theseus' moderation and its relationship with his bravery, see Burian 1985: 143–44; Mills 1997: 122–24.

[20] *Contra* Mendelsohn 2002: 182–84, who sees Theseus as "a grim reaper of young men" and as uncomfortably close to Kreon the tyrant.

[21] Burian interprets Adrastus' "epitaphios" as being full of irony and ambiguity, and even of "illustrating a disheartening failure of reason" (Burian 1985: 150): "What the Epigonoi 'learn' from their fathers' lives (and deaths) shows with disheartening clarity the failure of reasoned discourse, the foundation of Theseus' optimistic *kosmos*, to change the pattern" (Burian 1985: 149). Cf. Mendelsohn 2002: 187–96, who comments on Euripides' way of "ironizing masculine heroism" in Adrastus' *epitaphios*, by showing that Adrastus is held fast in the grip of wild and uncivilized forms of "manliness" from which Athenian democrats worked hard to dissociate themselves. *Contra* Collard 1972/2007, who finds that Adrastus "prescribes from the example of the dead a way to civic virtue and valour in its defence" (2007: 129).

could be taught, as Adrastus asserted (913–17), and whether the heroes lauded by Adrastus embodied forms of courage that they themselves could endorse. Was the courage of Adrastus' seven heroes different from that displayed by Theseus and his Athenians, and, if so, then how, and what difference did it make?

The Athenians themselves were invited to deliberate about the topics raised by Euripides' play: their role models, their native heroes' ethical outlook, the proper demands of courage, and the grounds for setting limits to the historically ingrained pugnacity of *andreia*. They would have to answer for themselves precisely what it meant to have Theseus as their role model, precisely what it meant to live up to Theseus' example. If their sense of shame was governed by having an image of Theseus in their heads, perhaps as opposed to the "Seven," then they had to take responsibility for explaining and interpreting precisely what Theseus stood for. If Theseus' conversation with Aethra had been edifying, if a hero could learn lessons of courage from his own mother, a woman, then the Athenians, too, would need to reflect on the importance of engaging in wide-ranging ethical conversations, both publicly and privately, and of revising their own ideas in order to meet the needs of present circumstances.

Through conversations with one another and through reinterpretations of their own heroes, the Athenians took responsibility for their experience of shame, along with courage, as a collective body. This is one way in which the Athenians made democratic shame a more deliberate emotion than it was elsewhere in the Mediterranean. The Athenians' culture of free speech and self-reflection helped to mitigate the ostensible conflict between the democrats' model of courage and their use of apparently pan-Mediterranean emotions to help citizens act courageously in the midst of danger or uncertainty.

If the foregoing arguments about democratic deliberation are correct, then democratic citizens are more likely than others to play an active and self-conscious role in aligning their cultural models with their own self-consciously articulated visions of the good life. The Athenians' thoughtfulness and deliberateness made their social uses of shame distinctively democratic, because they were cultural expressions of the Athenians' distinctive practices of democratic free speech. Perhaps the Athenians' courageous passions were not as traditional as they might at first appear. The cognitive and affective inputs that governed emotional responses were up for grabs among a diverse democratic citizenry that self-consciously reflected upon the city's prevailing role models. The cognitive inputs required for emotional education came from the Athenians themselves, not from an external authority, such as tradition or Plato's philosopher-rulers; Athenian citizens played for themselves the role that Plato's philosopher-rulers played for the warriors and younger trainees in the *Republic*. The democratic citizenry did not by any means have a full metaphysical and epistemology theory to explain these things; perhaps they did not need one.

Conclusion: Self-Chosen Role Models

In addition to the tragic theater, classical Athens had its own "topography of courage." The city's public monuments encouraged citizens to recall famous figures from the past as role models by whose standards their present behavior would be judged.[22] Citizens were expected, as much as possible, to live up to the ideals they embodied. Examples of this are the statues of the tyrant slayers, Harmodius and Aristogeiton, which stood in the agora, and the herm monuments commemorating the Athenians' victory over the Persians at Eion on the Strymon in 475 BC.[23] The herm statues forced viewers to meet their gaze and therefore to be judged by their example.[24] The tyrannicides were larger-than-life statues meant to be inspirational for Athenians as they aspired to practice and defend freedom—something that they were constantly urged to do throughout the classical democracy, even in the absence of apparent threats to the democratic way of life (cf. Dem. 20.160–62). The tyrannicides exemplified, in the Athenian popular consciousness, the courageous assertion of freedom both within the city and outside its borders. As references in both comedy and oratory show, they represented an ideal of masculine courage that each individual citizen was expected, in the eyes of the community, to live up to (Ar., *Wasps* 1224–27, *Lys.* 631–35; Aesch. 1.140; Lyc. 1.50–51; Dem. 20.69–70; Hyp. 6.39–40).[25]

---

[22] Raaflaub 2001 offers a helpful account of the ways in which Athens's topography, culture, public discourses, and public monuments created a militaristic landscape that constantly reminded Athenians of war, power, and empire. Specifically with reference to Athens's public monuments, see also Hölscher 1998.

[23] For the epigrams associated with this herm-monument, see Plutarch, *Cimon* 7.4–5: see especially the line "Someone in the future, seeing these things, will be all the more willing to enter combat for the sake of the common good"; cf. Aeschines 3.181–86, with Raaflaub 2001: 323–25. On the tyrannicide statues and their role in the classical Athenian "imaginary," see Taylor 1991; on the paradigmatic role of the herm monuments, see Osborne 1985a; Raaflaub 2001: 323–25.

[24] As Osborne 1985 has argued, the Herms were symbolic of democratic equality, as each Athenian met their gaze, whether on statuary or painted pottery, on equal terms with them. This constitutes one of the chief reasons why the attack on the Herms prior to the Sicilian Expedition was readily interpreted as a threat to democracy itself.

[25] For these and additional references, see Taylor 1991: 104.

With Osborne and others, I would suggest that the Athenians viewed these monuments in the light of their public discussions about equality, liberty, and resistance to tyranny.[26] As Demosthenes once argued, for example, the citizens should admire the general Conon, who, "in destroying the empire of the Lacedaemonians," had eliminated a "great tyranny," and thus was the first Athenian to be granted a bronze statue since the tyrannicides (Dem. 20.70). Lycurgus praises the Athenians for honoring generals and tyrannicides, rather than celebrated athletes, with statues; their honorable practices of commemoration further inspired soldiers dedicated to fighting for freedom (Lyc.1.47, 50–51). By contrast with other Greeks, Lycurgus argues, the Athenians took the welfare of their city and the freedom of Greece seriously; this is what explained their resoluteness in action.

When the Athenians saw the tyrannicide statues, they recollected the political significance of their fight for democracy—as well as their ancestors' repulsion of the Persian threat (cf. our discussion of Herodotus on the tyrannicides in chapter 4), and their contemporaries' courageous struggle against Philip of Macedon. The tyrannicides were role models who constituted "internal others": the Athenians had democratically thought through their ethical significance and linked these role models to their democratic way of life. When they experienced a sense of shame and emulation before them, they understood that what gave their emotions particular point was the necessity to fight for the city's freedom so as to make possible the free and flourishing lives that they enjoyed as democratic citizens (understood in their particularly eudaimonistic ways, cf. chapters 14 and 15).

In chapter 12, we will grapple with Aristophanes' own way of stimulating his fellow citizens to reflect on the ethical and emotional significance of "acting like a tyrannicide." The Athenians endorsed the tyrannicides as appropriate sources of emulation and the sense of shame, in ways that cooperated closely with their discursively constituted conception of the good life. Their social uses of the tyrannicide statues supported the general belief that cowards should feel ashamed to pass before the monuments of the war-dead (Lyc. 1.45), because cowards lacked any appropriate understanding of the significance of the city's ideals of freedom and its well-founded practices of courage. Our question now is how well Aristophanes' men understood the tyrannicides as the embodiments of appropriate masculine ideals.

---

[26] Cf. Osborne 1985.

CHAPTER 12 | Cocky Athenian Men?

WHEN SCHOLARS TELL THE story of Athenian *andreia*, they frequently emphasize masculinity, or even machismo, or male "cockiness." The story is often told with reference to the web of densely symbolic cultural images that captured and expressed abstractions such as *andreia*. A late source (Ael. *VH* 2.28), for example, records that Miltiades, the general at the Battle of Marathon, staged a cockfight during the Persian Wars in order to inspire the *andreia* of the Athenians.[1] In classical Athens, cocks symbolized the masculine ideal in sex and combat. The cock was thought to fight to the death, come what may; to achieve erections in its crest and feathers during combat; to seek to bugger a fallen opponent; and to become a sort of erect, winged phallus during combat.[2] The loser in a cockfight was called a "slave" (*doulos*). The cock perfectly captures the aggression aspired to and often achieved by Athenian men. How unusual it was for Socrates to raise the possibility that steadfast suffering, rather than gutsy fighting to the death, could count as courage (Pl., *Lach.* 191d–e).

A consequence of this "cocky" ideology was a deeply entrenched form of misogyny, which remains built into the contemporary language of courage.[3] There is an extensive (and often vulgar) vocabulary through which courage and cowardice are unmistakably gendered through reference to the sex organs.[4] This vocabulary was prominent in ancient Athens, too, but the misogyny that saturated the Athenian conception of *andreia* often ran deeper than today. In many oratorical and theatrical representations,

---

[1] Csapo 1993: 10–11.
[2] Aristotle *HA* 631b28; Csapo 1993: 13–17.
[3] Cf. Miller 2000: 232–40.
[4] Miller 2000: 232–33.

women and children were literally destroyed by men exhibiting or pursuing *andreia*.[5] Agamemnon killed Iphigeneia in Aeschylus' *Agamemnon*; Heracles killed Megara and his children in Euripides' *Heracles*; the Greeks killed Astyanax in Euripides' *Trojan Women*; and so on.

In his funeral oration, Lysias evoked a civic myth in which the very founding of Athens depended on the "courageous" repulse of the Amazons, who attacked Athens early in its history. In Lysias' account, the Amazons were "reckoned to be men on account of their courage, rather than women on account of their nature"; but, rashly invading Athens, and confronting its valiant (male) citizens, the Amazons paid the penalty of death for their recklessness and greed (Lys. 2.4–6). If the deeds of the dead provided an education for the living (Lys. 2.3), then this education startlingly rendered an equation between exhibiting courage, being a proper manly citizen, protecting democracy, and subordinating, taming, or even destroying women.[6]

Yet other texts suggest a different construction of Athenian masculinity and femininity. Even if the Athenians often subscribed to traditional ideals of machismo, their novel vision of democratic *andreia* also helped them to take other, perhaps surprising, perspectives. Consider Medea's claim that women were as courageous as men (Eur. *Medea* 248–51), or Plato's elevation of women to philosopher-king-warrior status (*Republic* 454c–457c): these ideas were not developed in a vacuum. Rather, they were artifacts of the Athenian democratic experience. It should not be shocking to find that, in his funeral oration of 338 BC, Demosthenes offered female exemplars of courage to an audience in which veterans of foreign wars were prominent.[7] I want to consider these points particularly in relation to the men of Aristophanes' *Lysistrata*.

The Men of Aristophanes' *Lysistrata*: Honor, Shame, and Self-Image

Our starting point is the familiar register of cultural abstractions such as *andreia* and *sōphrosunē*.[8] Thucydides' excursus on Corcyra illustrates that, in the volatile political cultures of late fifth-century Greece, *andreia* and

---

[5] Seidensticker 1995; Rosenbloom 1995; Mendelsohn 2002: 197–215.
[6] Fantham et al. 1994: 128–35; Roisman 2003: 127–28.
[7] I have discussed Demosthenes' funeral oration along these lines in Balot forthcoming—a.
[8] On the associations between *andreia* and *sōphrosunē* in both Athenian oratory and the Platonic corpus, see Balot 2004c; Cullyer 2003: 222; and Roisman 2003.

sōphrosunē had become "gendered" and therefore positioned in a hierarchical relationship (3.82.4). As *andreia* came to be more starkly opposed to *sōphrosunē* in political discourse, *sōphrosunē* could be considered weak and even slavish. Although it had once been a virtue of law-abiding citizens in the early democracy, it was, at least by the late fifth century, viewed as the virtue opposed to the quintessential manly excellence, *andreia*. As North has argued, *sōphrosunē* is the characteristic virtue of women and "is the most common of all tributes inscribed on memorial reliefs and tombstones" of women.[9] Thus, in a political world dominated by *andreia*, *sōphrosunē* could be suitable only for a "domesticated" woman who knew her place. At the end of the *Statesman*, Plato opposed *andreia* to *sōphrosunē* and associated the latter with everything quiet, slow, soft, lethargic, and cowardly (306b—307c).

This network of associations differentiating the masculine from the feminine plays an important role in Aristophanes' *Lysistrata*. This play has long been appreciated specifically with reference to gender typologies and constructions. Popularly, Lysistrata exemplifies the intelligent, courageous, "activist" woman who speaks out against war and organizes other women to oppose men's wars.[10] As Barbara Ehrenreich has written, "Someone, some real-life Lysistrata or analog of the much maligned Clytemnestra, might notice the circular logic linking masculinity and war—that men make war in part because war makes them men—and conclude that men *could* stop."[11] Building on these foundations, classical scholars such as Vaio, Foley, Henderson, and Konstan, have argued that, in this play, Aristophanes scrutinizes the relationships between *oikos* and polis, in order to show that the traditionally feminine virtues of the *oikos* might serve the polis better than the manly, bellicose virtues.[12]

---

[9] North 1966: 21.

[10] Taeffe 1993: 73 reads the comedy, rather, as a "play inspired by the absence of men that highlights the inauthenticity of women and reasserts the power of masculinity"; this follows Dover 1972: 159. *Contra*: MacDowell 1995: 246–50. On the significance of Lysistrata's name ("dissolving armies"), see MacDowell 1995: 240–43, who follows earlier scholarship in connecting the name to the traditional religious authority associated with Athena. Sommerstein 2009b interestingly suggests " 'she who *scatters* armies,' i.e., puts enemies to flight—with a recollection of one of Athena's own epithets, *Phobesistrate* 'she who *routs* (or panics) armies.' " (235); this translation is in service of suggesting that Lysistrata is a "warrior" and is not in principle opposed to war, but rather only to war with Sparta and to the acquisition of the most favorable terms possible for Athens, including the freedom to expand its empire when possible. This is not incompatible with my view: Lysistrata was not a peacenik, but the play did try to temper the (male) Athenians' hyperaggressive and self-defeatingly "macho" attitudes toward war and peace.

[11] Ehrenreich 1997: 131.

[12] See Vaio 1973; Foley 1982; and the early, but still magisterial, essay of Henderson 1980, esp. 185–86; though we should note that Henderson later shifted from his early endorsement of

It would be straightforward, I imagine, to propose that Aristophanes' play "questions" the male ideology of "cockiness," or that Aristophanes ridiculed the Athenians' culture of pugnacity. Perhaps he even did so, as many scholars have argued, in order to persuade his contemporaries to reconsider the possibilities of peace with Sparta.[13] Yet it is difficult to find evidence for any direct relationship between the dramas staged in Athens and the voting patterns of the Athenian Assembly. The central question, in fact, is not the "function" of the Athenian theater, as though tragedies and comedies can be explained only with reference to their social utility. The more important question, I think, is how the Athenians could pursue their wars and their imperialism, seemingly unrelentingly, and still enjoy watching plays that either brought to life the harshness of military experience or, as in the case of Aristophanes' *Lysistrata*, directly criticized their political decisions, behavior in civic life, and dedication to ideals of honor and aggression (see also chapter 13).

My own view is that the Athenian theater was a forum for the Athenians' production of self-knowledge. Roughly speaking, this is how the plays "intervened" in the democratic life of the city.[14] By watching these plays, the Athenians entertained self-conceptions, ideas about others, and debates about their governing cultural ideals, in a "safe" or "non-toxic" theatrical space that permitted their imaginations and intellects freely to pursue the

---

de Ste. Croix's position on Aristophanes' "politics." See also Burian 2011: 109–10, along with Raaflaub 2001: 329–34 specifically on the oppositions of war versus peace, individuals versus community, men versus women, and public versus private. Konstan 1993 argues that Aristophanes presents a complex, if not contradictory, vision of women in the play: they are at once "guardians of the home, prepared to fight for its values and exclusivity against danger from without," and yet, in their eroticism, they are "imagined as creatures of lawless desire, prone to violate the social order which is predicated on the integrity of the individual household" (437).

[13] Konstan 2010: 184–85 argues that Aristophanes sincerely opposed the war and developed in his plays "a subtle strategy designed to undermine popular support for the war." See also MacDowell 1995: 248–49. Sommerstein 2009: 209–10 rightly points out that Aristophanes is not a pacifist in any general sense, but directs certain of his comedies to the need to make peace specifically with Sparta, during the Peloponnesian War.

[14] My approach to Athenian tragedy and comedy builds on that of Zeitlin 1986/90; see further chapter 13. Sommerstein 2009 argues that Aristophanes was concerned with democratic themes and offered in *Knights* what Sommerstein calls "an alternative democracy," which, however, strictly limits the Athenian democracy's more "demotic" features, such as public pay for civic functions and the explicit rejection of leaders of low social status (or, as Sommerstein says, this is "the skeleton of an *anti-democratic* programme" (211)). This contains a kernel of truth, but it is possible to see in Aristophanes' plays more powerful democratic possibilities: see Balot 2001a: 197–200 on Aristophanes' *Knights*. On the other hand, Sommerstein goes astray, I think, in seeing *Lysistrata* as an alternative to democracy, i.e., monarchy (2009: 212–15). It is possible, as I suggest in the text, to read the *Lysistrata* as reinforcing certain key elements of the democratic ideology of courage.

project of understanding for its own sake.[15] As we will discover, perhaps the most that can be said about the effects of Aristophanes' *Lysistrata* on the Athenians was that they might, through watching the play, come to grasp their own *eudaimonia* more adequately. They might come to see that their *eudaimonia* depended on a more harmonious integration of *sōphrosunē* with *andreia*, however the rapport between these leading abstractions might be concretely interpreted in particular circumstances. At least it is fair to say that this play would encourage Athenian audiences to transcend "primitive" experiences of shame. They would accordingly think through, for themselves and more fully, the controlling ideals and ethical norms to which their enriched sense of shame proved responsive.[16]

Building on the important studies of feminist scholars and those influenced by them, I contend that the men and women in this play must be understood, if they are to be understood at all, as moving parts of a unified system of ideology.[17] If the women of *Lysistrata* are presumptively "intruders" into the public sphere of politics,[18] then it is worth asking what sort of world, precisely, they are intruding into, and how that world is constructed, interrogated, and even possibly transformed by their intrusion. What is the precise character, within the world of Aristophanes' play,

---

[15] For a provocative and fresh analysis of Aristophanes' political significance, see Olson 2010, which helpfully engages with both older and recent scholarship on the question. Olson emphasizes that the plays offered no political program and that they communicated to the demos that political problems were not their responsibility. My account shares elements with Olson's (as with those of Heath 1987 and Henderson 1990, 2003): that Aristophanes' political comedies are "self-consciously and outspokenly 'democratic'" (63) and that they criticize the demos for its unwise choices with respect to leadership, for example, but I disagree with Olson 2010: 66 that the comedies imply that "'democracy' has the potential to work only when it is run in a less than democratic manner." I also find that even though Aristophanes did not offer a political program, he did engage seriously and constructively with the ideological and emotional discourse of his fellow Athenians: in that sense my account shares elements with that of Ober 1998: 122–55, although I regard the play as more continuous with democratic ideology than does Ober. De Ste Croix 1972 presents an older view according to which Aristophanes was a political "conservative" of the "'Cimonian variety'" (63), who attacked the Peloponnesian War and the more demotic features of Athenian politics.

[16] Thus my approach is more ideological and cultural than that of scholars such as MacDowell 1995: 248–50, who argues that "Aristophanes is trying to prod them [the Athenians] into opening negotiations" for peace with Sparta (249). Cf. de Ste. Croix 1996: 62, who argues that "there can be no doubt at all that the *Lysistrata* is a plea for peace."

[17] Taaffe 1993 appreciates this point, but believes, by contrast, that in the play "the integrity of male identity is kept whole, while the absurdity of women in public life is played up. The play confirms and celebrates an ordered sense of gender identity in which male is stable and female is unstable, in need of control through marriage" (51). Readers will discover that, in my view, Aristophanes aspires to make "male identity" less stable rather than to strengthen or confirm any preexisting stability.

[18] Shaw 1975, with the critique and refinements of Foley 1982.

of masculine public life? How is that public life informed by the beliefs, attitudes, and emotions of the men who presumably wield authority over it? By contrast with *Wasps*, *Thesmophoriazusae,* and *Clouds*, for example, the poet does not target specific individuals as the objects of his satire (1043–46, though cf. 1092, 1105), but rather an entire array of ideals, norms, beliefs, and practices, which are constitutive of the men's world.

To be more precise, it is not Athenian men altogether that Aristophanes holds up to playful scrutiny, but rather their distinctive conception of "the political"—not in any institutional sense, but rather from the perspective of its governing ideals, its ideology. In this play, the core ideal of political life is *andreia*, the quintessentially manly virtue.[19] The *andreia* of citizens was traditionally rooted in public norms of honor and shame. This is, roughly at least, Aristophanes' starting point, too. The norms of honor and shame embraced by Aristophanes' men helped to create a distinctive self-image which they were expected to subscribe to, on pain of censure and disgrace.[20] The women of this play take as their goal a redefinition of *andreia*, and thus a reconstruction and enlargement of the men's self-image, which includes tying this "manly virtue" more closely to practical intelligence and *sōphrosunē*. This interpretation of the play helps to confirm the view that the Athenian theater was a theater of self-knowledge.[21]

Fiery Men, Watery Women

The play's founding assumption is that the men of Athens—indeed, of Greece in general—are destroying Greece, that "saving Greece" depends on the women (29–30, 32–33, 35), and that the women are capable of such

---

[19] It was common for Aristophanes to represent Athenian men as courageous: on the Athenian heroes at Marathon, see *Acharnians* 696–97, *Knights* 781, 1334; *Clouds* 985–86; *Wasps* 711; with Konstan 2010: 191–93; and on manliness and lack of manliness in Aristophanes, see Rademaker 2003.

[20] Lendon 2010 argues persuasively that the Peloponnesian War was a battle for status, for comparative rank: "The Athenian challenge to Spartan rank, rather than Spartan fear of Athenian power, was the truest cause of the war" (104). I try to show in this chapter that the Athenians, because of their democratic institutions and practices, had a way of thinking about honor and shame that was qualitatively different from the Spartan way.

[21] In light of this orientation, it is clear that I do not find it helpful to refer to Aristophanes as being on either the "right" or the "left" of the political spectrum. But I do think it impossible for an Athenian audience not to be alert to Aristophanes' engagement with their ideology of democratic courage, in the ways I will explain in the chapter. This does not necessarily imply that Aristophanes had "radical democratic credentials" (Sidwell 2009: 25), but it does imply that his *Lysistrata* (at least) helped the Athenians come to understand more fully their own commitments to a distinctively democratic conception of courage.

acts of heroism (39–41). One immediately hears an echo of the Athenian funerary ideology, where saving Greece at the time of the Persian Wars depended solely on the Athenians (i.e., the men). The women devise a two-pronged plan: the older women will occupy the Athenian Acropolis, pretending to make a sacrifice, while the younger women stage their sex strike (175–79). From the outset, the women demonstrated the possibility of reinventing the polis's key political practices, such as oath taking and decision making, by excluding the symbols of war and installing in their place the symbols of peace. For example, in swearing their oaths over the proposed strategy, they refused to slaughter animals over their shields and incorporated more peaceful, even ludic, symbols ("sacrificing" unmixed wine, 189–205).[22] The women want peace precisely because they long for their husbands and prize a stable life with them, their children, and their fellow citizens (99–106).

In introducing the men, by contrast, the poet's emphasis falls clearly on their hostility toward women. Recalling the traditional formulae of archaic Greek misogyny, the men's chorus says that their wives are a "blatant evil" that the men have "reared" in their homes (260).[23] This opening gambit is one that the women will reverse by the play's conclusion. The men's avowed hatred of women is closely linked to their self-image as warriors and protectors of the city's public space. When we first meet the men, they are marching, as a choral unit, under arms to the Acropolis—or, rather, toward "my" Acropolis (*akropolin eman*, 262)—in order to besiege the female occupiers. Insisting that they will never be ridiculed by the women "while they are alive" (*emou zōntos*, 271), they evoke memories of their successful siege of Cleomenes, the Spartan King: "Cleomenes, who first occupied this place, did not leave unharmed, but, despite breathing the Laconian spirit, he handed over his arms to me when he left" (273–77). Although Lysistrata has already drawn the audience's attention to the women's normal practice of sacrificing on the Acropolis, the Athenian men claim the Acropolis as their exclusive preserve.[24] They are swept up in the ideology of having manfully besieged the Acropolis and recovered it from Cleomenes, on the way to instituting "their" democracy.[25] Only later

---

[22] On the imagery of oath, sacrifice, and wine in this passage, see also Bowie 1993: 182–83.
[23] See Henderson 1987: 261, citing Hesiod, *Works and Days*, 55–58, Semonides 7; many other passages could, of course, be adduced.
[24] Cf. the helpful treatment of Foley 1982: 7–10.
[25] For remarks on the political and religious functions of the Acropolis, see MacDowell 1995: 232–35.

does the men's chorus actually decide to investigate what the women were doing on the acropolis (477–83).

It is on the successful military defense of the city that the men—these old men in particular—stake their reputation and their sense of self. Their honor, in their view, derives from their military exploits in the past—defeating the Spartans on land and forcing them into the humiliating surrender of arms (*thōpla*, 277). This is why they deserve the Marathonian trophy in the Tetrapolis (285). At least initially, their self-image is built up primarily in relation to, and often by contrast with, other men—above all, the defeated Spartans and Persians. For them, glory is won by inflicting humiliating defeat and punishment on other men, for the sake of preserving what is, they say, their own—the city. The men's sense of *timē* makes them construe the women's occupation of the Acropolis as an hubristic, even tyrannical assault on their honor: the women's occupation constitutes a *tolmēma* (284), an act of incredible audacity (*thrasous*, 318; cf. *hubris*, 659).

The aggressive, martial overtones of *andreia* always cast a shadow over the democratic Athenian revisions of this virtue. Such overtones are visible, for example, in our earliest extant dramas. In *Seven Against Thebes* (467 BC), Aeschylus has his messenger report to Eteocles that the seven Argives, described as "furious leaders," have sacrificed a bull outside the city gates. They swore by Ares, Enyo, and "blood-loving Fear" to destroy Thebes or to drench the land with their own blood (42–48). These violent men do not lament the fate that awaits them, because "their iron-hearted spirit breathed within them, burning with manly courage" (*andreiai*, 52–53). Though inspired by the *Iliad*, Aeschylus' imagery is not merely an example of poetic "borrowing"; rather, it maintains and even furthers the aggressive, belligerent qualities that had been embedded within Greek conceptions of masculinity for centuries. In Aristophanes' *Frogs* (produced in 405 BC), Aeschylus is depicted as asserting that his *Seven Against Thebes*, which is "full of Ares" (1021), made the Athenians more courageous and more warlike citizens (1013–42). The men of Aristophanes' *Lysistrata* were like the men of other Greek cities, archaic or classical, oligarchic or democratic, in prizing a bold and aggressive conception of masculinity.

The idea that Aeschylus' Seven were "burning with manly courage" helps to explain one of the central systems of imagery in Aristophanes' play. The old men on the march are carrying firewood; they intend to build a pyre and burn the women (269–70). The men's chorus struggles to keep its fire alight (286–95), while the men's leader proudly exclaims that his "fire is awake and lives, thanks to the gods" (306). There is no doubt that the metaphors of fire and water have strong sexual overtones in this play, too, which contributes to its humor; but the men's fire is also overlaid with fiercer and more aggressive dimensions. The men plan to charge the gates "like rams" and then, if necessary, "to set the gates on fire and press them [the women] hard with the smoke" (307–11), even at the risk of burning down their most sacred shrines (344–49). Beyond its "local" dramatic function, the men's fire symbolizes their hot-blooded anger, which, as Aristotle pointed out (*EN* 1116b24–17a9), was closely linked to (a defective form of) manliness, in the popular imagination.[26] But fiery anger is more characteristic of young men than old men. These old men have rejuvenated themselves in an unhealthy way (cf. 664–70); they need to find another, less destructive path to rejuvenation. These men see the potential for fire everywhere.[27] Their interpretation of *andreia* is highly traditional: they must ever be stripping for battle and rushing to confront emergencies (614–15).

The women's chorus enters carrying water pitchers (321–35).[28] The women are daring when necessary, but they do not present themselves as particularly bellicose. In the immediate dramatic context, they intend to use these water pitchers in order to quench the flames of the old men. The women want to quench the men's hot-blooded interpretation of manliness. The women want to save Greece from the men's fiery madness (342–43) by saving the men from their own worst tendencies. They invoke Athena as "Tritogeneia" ("thrice-born") (347), because the goddess' epithet alludes to the idea of her own birth near a body of water.[29] To the men's insults and threats of violence, the women respond by picking up their water pitchers (370) and suggesting that they will give the men a bath fit for a bridegroom (377–78). What is the precise significance of this chain of imagery, linking

---

[26] Anger was a central and defining attribute of Athenian masculinity (Allen 2000), but it was an emotion, as we saw in examining Cleon's speech in Thucydides (chapter 10), that had to be adapted correctly to the circumstances, through a well-informed training of character and practical intellect. The women eventually get angry in just this way when the men cannot be convinced to listen to them or to put down their arms (694–95): the idea is that anger on behalf of the polis is justified, whereas anger in support of machismo is self-destructive.

[27] Cf. Elster 2002: 11; Rorty 1988; on the idea of "hot-blooded" anger, see Allen 2000.

[28] On these image-systems, see especially Faraone 1997, who argues that the play depicts the women "as the bringers of salvation and civic order" (39). Faraone is chiefly concerned to elucidate the ritual, tragic, and pictorial sources of the imagery of fire and water in the play, but his analysis cooperates very closely with my own.

[29] Farnell 1906: 265–69, with Faraone 1997: 43.

the women with water, baths, marriage, Athena's own birth, and Athena's status as the goddess of new birth?

The women begin to explain the significance of this imagery, I think, when they say, "I'm watering you, so that you will grow" (384). Their goal is to help the men, however old they may be, to "grow up" into mature, independent adults. This will require the men to be free of the adolescent ideology of destructive manly honor. For this ideology threatens, in the play, to destroy the Athenian women and their Acropolis, and it threatens, in reality, to destroy Greece itself. The women stand for the transformation of the Athenian men's traditional, adolescent interpretation of *andreia* into a mature form of *andreia* that contributes to their "flourishing," i.e. their "blooming."[30] The flourishing of the city and of the men themselves (not to mention the women and children) depends on marriage, on cleanliness, and on the steadfast care shown by the women, whatever the self-absorbed manliness of the men may appear to dictate.[31] The women want to save Greece by rejuvenating the men, by making them more suitable bridegrooms, and by helping them to appreciate a more mature notion of masculinity.

As matters stand, however, the men deserve to appear before the magistrate looking as though they had just urinated on themselves like children (401–2; cf. 469–70). While the women's plans "flower" (406), the Athenian Magistrate is left making oaths by "Poseidon the salty" (*nē ton Poseidō ton halukon*, 403). Poseidon the salty may be the appropriate medium for the Athenians' ships. But Poseidon's salt water will never enable the city's plants to bloom. And Athena, after all, not Poseidon, is the city's patron deity—thank goodness.

Later in the play, the men's chorus itself reinforces this presentation of the men's immaturity. It is not uncommon for apparently insignificant or superficial jokes to have a wider thematic significance in Aristophanes' plays. Inspired by Richard Martin's work on the Lemnian women,[32] we can reconsider the passage in which the chorus idealizes the mythical figure Melanion (782–96):

---

[30] According to Faraone 1997: 53, the vocabulary of "blooming" in this passages "reflects the salvific themes inherent in the eschatological myths" that he has discussed.
[31] Notice the detail that the women "worship Adonis on the rooftops" (389) by planting quick-growing gardens.
[32] Martin 1987; cf. Bowie 1993.

> I want to tell a story to you that I once heard when I was still a child. Once upon a time there was a young man Melanion, who avoided marriage and went to the wilderness; he lived in the mountains. He had a dog and wove traps and hunted hares, and he never went back home because of his hatred. He hated women that much, and we do, too, no less than Melanion, since we have good sense.

According to Vidal-Naquet, "Melanion appears here as an ephebe, but a sort of ephebe manqué... The Athenian ephebe is in a sense the true heir of the Black Hunter... many Attic vases depict a young ephebe setting off with his hound: perhaps they do indeed, in their own way, represent the young man on the threshold of adult life."[33] For Bowie, similarly, this ephebic figure renders the men's stance "questionable in the way it prolongs a situation that is anomalous in terms of normal human life."[34]

By assimilating themselves to Melanion, the ephebic Black Hunter of Vidal-Naquet, the men are unwittingly articulating a conception of themselves as stuck in immaturity. This self-conception is not particularly attractive, since, by contrast with Aristophanic heroes who find rejuvenation in the plays, these men are declaring themselves, paradoxically, to be not fully men at all. By holding up Melanion as an exemplar, the men suggest that normative Athenian ideals of manhood, embodied in the culture's paramount virtue *andreia*, are adolescent, pre-adult, immature, and unstable. The men of Greece are living their lives in a state of arrested development. Even late in the play, when the women offer friendship (1016-17), the men say that they will never stop hating women (1018). The men are playing boys' war-games while real interests, including their own, are at stake.

The men's attitudes toward women and war are signs that they perceive a need to prove their manhood continually. This is characteristic of adolescent masculinity and plays a central role in many rites of passage and initiation. Young men like the Black Hunter must prove their manhood by leaving home, surviving in a liminal condition, hunting, killing, and then eventually returning as fully adult members of the community. Athenian men, as they are represented in this play, are arrested in precisely that stage of their normal development. Aristophanes' critique of Athenian *andreia* is of a piece with the wide-ranging evidence, collected by Winkler, which shows that Athenian men were touchy about their masculinity and

---

[33] Vidal-Naquet 1986: 119–20.
[34] Bowie 1993: 190.

exercised an oppressive surveillance over the masculinity of their fellow citizens.[35]

Manly Tyrannicides

Let us examine the particular ways in which the men of *Lysistrata* were attached to the traditional Greek culture of honor and shame. From the play's beginning, their easily nettled sense of shame drove them to attack their own women. They could not live with themselves otherwise, quite literally, since if they failed to assert themselves in this instance, they would have failed to live up to their own deeply entrenched, and self-destructive, self-image. As they point out, any real man would react violently to this act of outrageous hubris by the women (659–61). Having come to the Acropolis to get the funds for oars (420–23; cf. 488–92), the magistrate even—if quite incoherently—appears to blame the women for the disastrous motions of the democratic leader Demostratus, who had urged the Athenians to send a fleet to Sicily (390–98). The Athenian men hint at envisioning their own women as Lemnian women (299–300)—a stark contrast with the international corps of peacekeeping women, who can hardly wait to get back to their husbands' penises (715–28). In the city of cocky men, war and sex have come to sight as polarized attributes of men and women, respectively.

What drives the men to erect this harsh and self-destructive opposition? The men are motivated by a powerful and unreflective sense of shame or honor. Throughout the play, the men hark back to their past glories in driving tyranny from Athens. Occupying the Acropolis—the second prong of the women's strategy—is, after all, the standard move of aspiring tyrants. As we saw, however, the women could easily have been "occupying" the Acropolis simply in order to perform ritual sacrifices; it is the men who see in their potentially peaceful behaviors a reason to sound the military alarm. In responding to this perceived threat, Aristophanes' men evoke the memory of their culture heroes, the tyrannicides. They exclaim, "Men, they wove this scheme against us with a view to tyranny. But they will never tyrannize over me, since I will guard myself and in the future carry my sword in a myrtle branch, and I will go to the agora under arms alongside Aristogeiton, and I will stand beside him in this way" (630–34). This very sensibility is reinforced in the men's comparison of the women

---

[35] Winkler 1990.

to the Amazons depicted on the Stoa Poikile (678–79). The ideology of the funeral oration stated explicitly that Athenian political institutions and practices were founded on the exclusion, if not the destruction, of these Amazons, who were women presuming to defeat Athenian men in combat (Lys. 2.4–6).[36]

A century after this play was staged, Aristotle pointed out that people feel ashamed only before others that they respect (*Rhet.* 1384a24–25). The men of *Lysistrata* esteem their ancestors, the tyrannicides, and other fighting men, including the Spartans and their fellow citizens. Hence, if the men of Aristophanes' *Lysistrata* should remain inactive when their Acropolis is seized, then they would be in the position of Sophocles' Ajax, who, as Bernard Williams has shown, "has no way of living that anyone he respects would respect—which means that he cannot live with any self-respect. That is what he meant when he said *poreuton*, that he had to go."[37] The men of this play obviously respect the opinions, primarily, of other men; they do not reflect seriously on the meaning and larger significance of their own actions, or on the coherence of the ideals expressed by their behaviors. As Burnyeat has written, "Shame is the semivirtue of the learner."[38] The play represents the men as being badly in need of education, if they are to achieve *eudaimonia* for themselves and the city.

At present, however, Aristophanes' men are striving to imitate their culture heroes, the tyrannicides, and their glorious Athenian forbears, who had defeated the Amazons. But, as Ober has argued, there is only one form of therapeutic stasis—rising up against and defeating a tyrant.[39] Defeating the women and setting up a trophy over them within the city (318) should give the men pause. A trophy in the city is a nearly unmistakable sign that something has gone wrong in Athenian political life; it is the sign, rather, of civil war. It is doubtful that the problem is the women's "daring" (*thrasous*, 318). Lysistrata is the one, after all, who recommends not "crowbars," but "brains" and "sense" (*nou kai phrenōn*, 432). In the ideology of Pericles' funeral oration, the Athenians were said to have developed a complex conception of their *andreia* and its demands. Yet, in order to

---

[36] See Hunt 2010: 117–23 for a helpful discussion of the evidence in Athenian culture that the "exhortation to prove one's manliness by going to war" often operated as a "goading metaphor." On Lysias' representation of the Amazons, see Fantham et al. 1994: 128–35; Roisman 2003: 127–28.
[37] Williams 1993: 85.
[38] Burnyeat 1980: 78.
[39] Ober 2003.

become men, in a nonimpoverished way, these men have to enlarge their sensibilities.

Seen in this light, we might fairly say that the play's central question is, What does it mean to "love" the city and its power, as Pericles had urged in the funeral oration in Thucydides? Can traditional masculine modes of loving the polis answer to all the important elements of the polis, including the *oikos*? Perhaps the Athenians' erstwhile freedom fighting had subtly modulated, over the course of the fifth century, into an unreflective bellicosity. The Athenians' intransigence may have gained a certain psychological power from the contingent associations between courage and the Athenians' victories over Persia. The men of *Lysistrata*, as we gradually come to see, fail to recognize when, where, and why to exercise their *andreia*.

Above all, the men's bellicosity prevented them from recognizing women's contributions to the polis—ritual, sexual, ethical, and intellectual—and from recognizing the wisdom of viewing their families' welfare as a crucial component of their own flourishing as human beings.[40] They illustrate why, according to Aristotle (*EN* 1116a17–16b3) "citizen courage," based as it is on traditional canons of honor and shame, is second-best compared to the courage of the those who exercise "phronetic" courage—the kind of courage that was produced, in the minds of Pericles' Athenians, through the deliberative and psychological work of the Athenian Assembly. A culture that overestimates the importance of traditional ideals of honor and shame will inevitably tip the balance in favor of militaristic aggression over peaceful politics. The norms themselves have this force, because they tend to discourage untraditional thinking and the questioning of cultural authority, especially the authority of received tradition. Although the men's pugnacious attitudes had formerly liberated the city from the Peisistratids, they later resulted in a bellicose foreign policy: the magistrate recalls, with sorrow, the disastrous decision to sail against Sicily (391–98). Decisions like this explain why, as the women say, war is all too often a form of madness (342–43).

The image of masculine madness resurfaces in the later argument between the women and the magistrate. Although the Magistrate has difficulty in understanding the women's purposes (554), Lysistrata proposes that their first move toward peace will be to "make people stop going to the agora under arms and crazy (*mainomenous*)" (555–56). The men shop for

---

[40] Foley 1982; Saxonhouse 1980: 68–72.

groceries under arms like Corybants (557–58). The women point out that "[i]t's laughable when someone shops for sardines there with his shield and Gorgon" (559–61). There is no need—indeed, it is unhealthy—to be constantly ready to fight. To this point, the magistrate responds, "By god, men must do this" (*nē Dia: chrē gar tous andreious*)" (559). To live up to their own ideals, narrowly construed, or misinterpreted, the men have to be insane, from the standpoint of civilized, peaceful democratic culture. They even believe that they must "smell" like men (662–63). (This gives additional point to the women's project of bathing them.) However that may be, the men have brought their militaristic culture home to what should be the peaceful agora. They are looking for fires to put out without realizing that their own aggressive ideals are responsible for most fires in the first place.[41]

Free Speech, Saving the City, Human Flourishing[42]

Naturally enough, the men think of themselves as haters of war, as protectors of the polis, and as involuntarily embroiled in a welter of international chaos that has taken on a life of its own (497). In truth, the men have no idea how to stop the madness. The magistrate incredulously wonders how the women could presume to put a stop to the disorder (565–66). He recognizes, at least in retrospect, that the decision to sail against Sicily was a bad one (391–92). Despite all this, he finds it necessary to continue the war for the sake of protecting Athens (497). But there are three ways in which his ideology of courageously protecting the city is faulty. They are related to free speech, the ideology of protection, and the men's conception of "self-interest." The men's understanding of what their masculinity is, and what it demands of them, is at odds with their democratic commitment to free speech, with their belief that they are protectors of the community, and with their real flourishing as human beings, properly understood. Aristophanes' critique had staying power because it appealed to ideals to which the men were already, if unwittingly, committed.

The narrowness of the men's outlook is illustrated by their refusal to listen to the women's ideas, however imaginative or prudent. The men's pugnacity makes them ignorant of the women's stake in the polis: "What

---

[41] Cf. Elster 2002: esp. 11.
[42] On the importance of "saving the city" in this play, see Faraone 1997: 54–58, who, however, tends to view Aristophanes as focusing on saving the men themselves, rather than reforming the men's conception of what is involved in saving the city.

concern is it of yours to think about war and peace?" the magistrate indignantly asks the women (502; cf. 648–57). The magistrate is so angry that he can hardly wait for the response to this question (504). Largely because of the men's tendency to become angry in aggressive, Cleon-style ways, the women have always maintained decorum by keeping silence during political conversations about the war (506–14). The threat of force was always present. The magistrate says, "You would have cried out in pain if you hadn't kept silent" (515). To any criticism of their bellicose foreign policy, the men used to respond, "Shut up—war is the men's concern!" (520–35). The Magistrate considers it a terrible indignity that he should have to be quiet and listen to the women (530–31). The men of Aristophanes' *Lysistrata* have no interest in listening to anyone who counsels peace or self-restraint—ideas which they code as "feminine" and thereby exclude from both their own self-consciousness as men and from the public life of the city.

Legally, of course, the women had no privilege of speaking in public, institutional forums on matters of political concern. Yet what happens in this scene is all too familiar from the Athenian Assembly. In the Sicilian Debate, for example, despite Nicias' insistence on moderation, the demos sided with Alcibiades' adventuresome policy, and anyone who was opposed "held his peace for fear that he would seem disloyal to the city if he raised his hand in opposition" (Thuc. 6.24). In Athens as in Sparta, it was easy to denigrate advocates of peace as simply cowardly or effeminate. Archidamus, the Spartan King, was criticized as weak and traitorous because he had advocated *sōphrosunē* in Sparta's dealings with Athens (Thuc. 2.18.3). Because of its potential conflicts with *andreia*, *sōphrosunē* was occasionally considered the feminine virtue par excellence (cf. the discussion of Plato's *Statesman* in chapter 16).

Aristophanes brings out this feminization of peace quite literally in the play. It is one crucial element of the men's unreflective commitment to *andreia* that they typically shut down any alternatives to the hypermasculine projects of war. At its best, democratic free speech is a tool that enables the demos to search out all possible alternatives, to listen to opposing viewpoints, and thereby to come to final decisions carefully and reflectively. The women certainly have strong points to make; they certainly have a stake in the city. Contrary to what the men say, the women bear their fair share of the war's burdens, giving birth to sons and sending them on campaign (587–90, 615–30, 678); they sleep alone when their husbands are abroad (99–106, 591–92); they perform ritual transactions with the gods of the polis (638–46, 665–70), including burial of the war-dead

(599–613); and they have good advice to offer (675).[43] This play shows the men shutting down debate in the "household" and the city, which is symptomatic of their tendency to shut down debate generally.

Athenian men, both inside and outside the play, saw themselves as protectors of their *oikoi* and polis. Providing protection was one of the central aims of Greek masculinity since the Homeric epics. The problem with the men of *Lysistrata* is that their commitment to waging war was destroying the households and the city they ought to be protecting.[44] Their ideals of courage had increasingly come to be unhinged from the central, purposeful context in which those ideals made sense. Aristophanes' way of raising the problem of "courage for its own sake" leads directly to the third and most complicated issue, that of "self-interest," or, as it should really be understood, that of *eudaimonia*.

In *Lysistrata*, the men's way of life is based on a narrow and naive conception of their own well-being. Lysisistrata hints at this in arguing for the effectiveness of the sex strike. Even if the men force their wives to have sex, she advises the women to make the men suffer both in the act of sex and otherwise (162–66). The immediate point is that the women have a degree of power over men, in virtue of their intimate relationships with their husbands. More generally, the men would do well to recognize that their own well-being depends, in part, on the welfare of their wives and their households. To be sure, the women's skills and intelligence were an untapped resource for the polis. Even more important, though, in marriage the men had entrusted women with part of their own welfare. Aristophanes is signaling the costs of forgetting this crucial point.

It is not just that the men make their wives unhappy and sexually frustrated by their long campaigns (99–106). They also neglect the welfare of their children. This is made clear in the later episode in which Kinesias tries to persuade Myrrhine to resume conjugal relations. Kinesias tries to exploit Myrrhine's sympathies for their child, who has been living shabbily, without a mother. Myrrhine throws this charge back onto her husband by saying that it is his father, in fact, who doesn't care for the child (882–83). The limiting horizon of *andreia* tends to blind men to the wisdom of viewing the welfare of their families as a critical feature of their own flourishing.[45] They cannot understand their own flourishing in isolation

---

[43] See, e.g., Vaio 1973: 373–75.
[44] For a development of this point, see Shaw 1975: 264–66, Foley 1982: 6–7.
[45] By way of contrast, one may examine Aristotle's idealization of the family in the *Politics*, in which family members take the well-being of other family members to be essential to their own well-being; cf. Cooper 1999b: esp. 370–77.

from that of their families. In his attempt to broaden the Athenian men's conception of "self-interest," Aristophanes is much like the Pericles of the funeral oration. Pericles proposed that the Athenian men should come to view the good of the city as their own good. At the same time, however, Aristophanes' play suggests that Pericles has been too successful in forging a new self-image for the citizens. Overidentifying with the city as opposed to the *oikos*, these men have neglected other fundamental dimensions of themselves and their interests.

Cosmopolitanism and Androgyny

This interpretation helps to explain precisely why the women of this play are associated with both peace and cosmopolitanism.[46] The men's narrow-mindedness is exemplified in their petty, local political squabbles—such as the war between Athens and Sparta. Targeting international politics, therefore, the women persuade the men that Athens and Sparta have more in common than either side had imagined. Both cities celebrate religious festivals together, like kinsmen; they both want sex and a restored *oikos*; and they both enjoy peaceful conviviality (1128–35, 1175–80, 1280–92). Herodotus' Athenians, of course, knew as much (Hdt. 8.144). What is more, as Lysistrata argues, the Athenians and Spartans have a history of helping one another when in need (1137–61)—though she omits certain countervailing details. The women themselves, drawn from all over Greece, exemplify the model cosmopolitanism they recommend (78–92, 1050–55).[47] Aristophanes' women are well positioned to make these points vividly, because they were specifically excluded from, and subordinated to, the macho ideals of *andreia* that drove the "republican" polis.[48] It was only in that sense that they had no stake in the polis as currently constituted.

For all that, this play is not engaged in the project of providing practical solutions to real quandaries. On the other hand, the action of the play suggests, at least hypothetically, that the men's education to appropriate manhood should take the form of androgyny. Once again, the women provide an exemplary case study for the men. Throughout the play, they exhibit the

---

[46] Vaio 1973 is one of the few critics even to mention the women's cosmopolitanism, in the guise of "Panhellenism" (e.g., 370); cf. also Konstan 1993: 433–34, 441–44.
[47] Cf. Deneen 2000 for an interesting discussion of, among other things, cosmopolitanism in early and classical Greece and beyond.
[48] Cf. Konstan 1993: 433–35, 440–44.

characteristically feminine virtues: by contrast to the puerile men, the women try to restore care for others, fertility, and the institution of marriage (375–85, 395–400, 1106-87).

In practice, though, this requires the women to exhibit the manly virtue of courage: they fight down the men's assaults and claim, using another well-known Aristophanic image of manhood, to be "wasps" on the inside (450–70; cf. 439–40, 443–48, 452–54).[49] Lysistrata says that Lampito, the Spartan woman, is the only "real woman" at the assembly, because she alone agrees to give up sex in order to save Greece (142–45). As the audience of Demosthenes' funeral oration had learned, Athenian women, too, have their own traditions of courage. These traditions were not only exemplified by the courageous Lysistrata herself (1108), but also called to mind by the old woman's invocation of "Pandrosos," the daughter of Cecrops, who was traditionally recognized as an Athenian heroine (439–40; cf. 443–48, 452–54, 682). Only through becoming manly could the women exert their "feminine" virtues in the public sphere. Having learned how to manage households, like good women, the women plan to use their skills to manage the public finances better than the men (480–95). This will enable them to save the men, whether they like it or not (506)—to save the men from themselves, obviously.[50] Even the men eventually see that the women make worthy rivals (1014–15).

The women's display of courage is elaborated in an interesting and distinctive way. After Lysistrata claims war as the rightful province of the women (557), the chorus of women say: "I am willing to face any task with women as courageous as these: they have an exceptional nature, grace, daring, wisdom, and virtue that is both loyal to the city and intelligent" (541–547). As Henderson comments on this passage, "The list combines conventionally male and female attributes."[51] More than this: the passage also unifies the very same conventionally antithetical attributes that Pericles himself had attributed to the implied Athenian audience of his funeral oration (cf. Thuc. 2.40, with chapter 2).[52] The women, in other

---

[49] Taaffe registers the women's manly behaviours (1993: 59–64), but addresses these points primarily with reference to the poet's (negative) attitudes toward women and female gender roles.
[50] Cf. Faraone 1997: 54–58.
[51] Henderson 1996: 214. Foley 1982: 10 notes that "the association with Athena and with feminine religious authority neutralizes the dangerous implications usually associated with such androgynous behavior."
[52] Raaflaub 2001: 332–33 observes that "Lysistrata and her fellow women here assume roles and embody values that are explicitly praised as those of Athenian men in the prime document of Athenian civic ideology, Pericles' funeral oration in Thucydides (Thuc. 2.35–46)," without, however, noting the poet's emphasis on the unification of apparently antithetical attributes at play in this passage.

words, embodied the cognitively informed Athenian ideal of courage in a complete way, whereas the men of the play embodied the more traditional, more pugnacious, and more unreflective conception of *andreia* that Pericles and others had associated with the Spartans. The women imply that even if the men are patriotic in a narrow and limited way, they are not intelligent in their applications of their virtues: they do not possess *philopolis aretē phronimos* (546–47, cf. 708–9). In her unification of apparently opposed, albeit admired, attributes, Lysistrata is the pinnacle of such virtues and "finds her closest analogue in Athena herself."[53]

Part of the intelligent application of the virtues is the practical wisdom to understand when to display boldness and aggression, on the one hand, and when to nurture one's allies and friends, on the other. Toward the end of the play, the women help the men to "look like" real men again (1024), by putting their shirts back on them and pulling bugs out of their eyes (1019–32).[54] The leader of the women's chorus kisses the leader of the men's chorus; perhaps he has almost learned enough to become worthy of a kiss, but he childishly refuses it (1035–42). In the end, Lysistrata provides a sexually gratifying settlement for the Spartan and Athenian ambassadors, after being hailed by the chorus leader as "the manliest of all women" (*ō pasōn andreiotatē*, 1108) and after being told to be, as she surely will, both "forcible and flexible" (1109). Through the efforts of the daring and yet nurturing women, the "manly" Athenians and Spartans have a party on the Athenian Acropolis. Their drinking songs now restore their collective memories of the Persian Wars to a "proper" use, not as an incitement to violence within the city or between Greek cities, but rather as an invitation to join with other Greeks in turning their aggressions outward against the Persians (1247–72).

Conclusion

The play evokes androgyny as a compensating ideal that will counteract the narrow-minded virility of Athenian men. This resonates with contemporary feminist efforts to connect androgyny with peace: "Although some radical feminists do endorse a kind of pacifist essentialism, many of the most sophisticated theorists within this tradition argue instead that androgyny is a crucial component of peace."[55] In embodying an androgynous

---

[53] Henderson 1987: xxxvii–xxxviii.
[54] Cf. Foley 1982: 7–8 on the process of "redomesticating" the men.
[55] Tobias 1996: 232.

ideal, the women are, all over again, unifying the antithetical attributes of men and women. Hence, in addition to modeling peaceful cosmopolitanism, the women also model androgyny in relation to the virtues.

It is questionable whether the men are capable of living up to this ideal. According to their own self-conception and their understanding of the virtues, they may have too much to lose. Aristophanes leaves his audience asking whether Athenian men are capable of such a fusion of these virtues, because of their psychic investment in the gender hierarchies of the polis. When the women suggest that the men start wearing veils and sewing, and that war should be women's work, the men react indignantly, as though they are being robbed of their most important prerogatives (529–38). Beyond this literal transferral of roles, however, the women were, in effect, urging the men to integrate the "feminine" virtue of *sōphrosunē* into their *andreia*-centered paradigms of virtue. Aristophanes made this point in a sexual, rather than a political or military, register.

Much of the humor of this play derives from the Athenian men's inability to control their overabundant *andreia*, whether that "manliness" is conceived as the drive to war or sex. The men found the sex strike so punishing precisely because they proved incapable of restraining their sexual desires. In the titillating final scene, in which they are nearly overcome by sexual excitement, the men finally agree to reconcile with one another. Spartan and Athenian ambassadors offer mutual exchanges of good will and promise never to fall into the same hostility again. Through being forced to restrain their sexual desires, the men learn *sōphrosunē*—albeit in a sexual register—at last. Perhaps we should view the men's sexual self-restraint, which the women have enforced, as an analogue of the restraint they have now learned, one might hope, to exhibit in the political realm of competitive *andreia*. In Aristophanes' Athens, of course, we do not find many men voicing androgynous ideals. Aristophanes' play was a vehicle for self-exploration and self-knowledge, not a catalyst for institutional change.

It was left to later Athenians, indeed, those who excluded themselves from practical politics, to theorize more explicitly the precise character of such a fusion of apparently antithetical virtues. In the conclusion to the present volume, we will examine the reflections on this point found in Plato's *Statesman*. For now, though, let us notice that Plato's Eleatic Stranger, in that dialogue, proposes that a weaver of cloth is an appropriate model for the statesman (279a7–b6). The rationale for this model is that the statesman's expertise somehow consists in "weaving together" disparate parts of the city in a politically knowledgeable way. The image is reminiscent of the *Lysistrata* (567–86), when Lysistrata proposes that the men reconstitute the city through weaving together groups that differed in status and political role (for example, the full citizens, the resident aliens, and the colonists).[56] In Aristophanes' comedy, weaving together disparate groups in the city runs in parallel to the creation of the androgynous virtues exhibited by the women. Indeed, weaving itself is a traditionally feminine activity that Lysistrata metaphorically puts to masculine, that is, political, uses. In the *Statesman*, too, the model of weaving is intended to have both a political and a psychological significance: uniting apparently disparate groups in the city anticipates the dialogue's conclusion that the true statesman will weave together disparate virtues—*andreia* and *sōphrosunē*—in the soul. Arising from within the context of democratic debates over courage, Aristophanes' investigation of precisely these problems had a lasting impact on the philosophical discussions of courage in later centuries.

---

[56] See MacDowell 1995: 239 for a helpful political analysis of the weaving imagery.

CHAPTER 13 | Tragic Explorations of Courage, Freedom, and Practical Reason

FIFTEEN YEARS AGO, IN the wake of scholarship by Goldhill, Winkler, Zeitlin, and others, to assert that Athenian tragedy was a salient feature of democratic culture would have been obvious and banal. Now, however, in the face of attacks by Jasper Griffin, P. J. Rhodes, David Carter, and others, the political implications, if any, of Athenian tragedy are once again controversial, as is the relationship between certain apparently pacifistic plays and the Athenians' bellicose foreign policy.[1] I want to reopen these issues by asking whether tragic episodes or plays contributed

---

[1] For interpretations that link Greek tragedy to Athenian democracy, see Euben 1986a; Goldhill 1988, 1990; Winkler and Zeitlin 1990 and Ober and Strauss 1990; for interpretations that question this association, see Griffin 1999; Rhodes 2003b; Carter 2007; Carter 2011. In thinking through these debates, one might usefully note the highly flexible and capacious remarks of Griffith 2011: 1–7, which illustrate that the extant corpus of Athenian tragedy should not be reduced to any simple typology. My claim is more modest than that of some scholars: that the Athenian audiences of Greek tragedy (or at least certain Greek tragedies) would have been aware of, and alert to, certain tragedies' methods of engaging with their discourse on democratic courage. Hence, as I argue, the tragedies constituted a theater of self-knowledge for the Athenians, who were, in watching these plays, reflecting on their own governing ideals, symbols, role models, and virtues. In the case of the democratic ideal of courage that we have been reconstructing, this reflection was necessarily an engagement with democratic ideals—and, as such, it constituted a specifically democratic practice in classical Athens. My view builds on and elaborates the views of Zeitlin 1986/1990 along these lines, although Zeitlin concentrated on theatrical representations of Thebes as the antitype through which Athenians came to question their ideals and thus to know themselves; cf. also the helpful introduction provided by Euben 1986a, and the strongly political reading offered by Ober and Strauss 1990. My view also shares elements with that of Burian 2011: 95–96, who wants to show "how Attic tragedy participates palpably and at times assertively in democratic discourse through a use of dialogue and debate that has a demonstrably democratic character.... Thus, the theatre can be seen not only as a locus of debate about the merits of existing democratic ideology and practice, but as a place to imagine what, for better or worse, democracy might yet become."

to the democratic cultivation of courage that we have examined in previous chapters.

My contention is that the tragic theater encouraged the Athenians to know themselves. The tragic theater operated like the epitaphic tradition; it was, as Froma Zeitlin has said, a "theater of self and society," in which Athenian "selves" were reflected back to themselves, often in specifically democratic ways, and often in ways oriented toward self-examination.[2] To be more specific, watching these plays encouraged the Athenians to explore whether their democratic *politeia* enabled them to live distinctively good lives of freedom and equality. Their plays also taught that the Persians and Spartans, in particular, met with disaster, or lived significantly impoverished lives, because of the defects of their nondemocratic regimes. Thus, without directly affecting their political decisions, the theater deepened the citizens' appreciation of their own ideals, as well as their own limitations in living up to those ideals. The theater could play this role precisely because it was an expression of the wider democratic culture of free speech.[3] Hence, in my reading, the tragic theater, like the funeral orations, put Athenian "selves," practices, and ideals on stage for the purposes of reflection, in the specifically democratic ways I have outlined.[4] The Athenians reaped benefits from living in a democratic culture that was free to explore questions about its own behaviors and self-image, particularly when it came to the issues of manliness and courage.

Negative Paradigms

Tragedians often brought forward non-Athenians as negative paradigms of masculinity. These figures were pointedly designed to illustrate that traditional, nondemocratic manliness was corrupt or misguided in precisely the ways that the democratic construction of courage was meant to remedy. Like Pericles in the funeral oration, Euripides also specifically

---

[2] See Zeitlin 1986/1990, along with the commentary of Croally 1994: 38–43. See also Euben 1986a: 22–31; Ober and Strauss 1990; Goldhill 1990.
[3] Cf. Burian 2011: 99–107; Ober and Strauss 1990 helpfully emphasize the importance of rhetoric within tragedy and its connections to political rhetoric within democratic Athens. On the didactic role of Euripides (at least), see Gregory 1991: 1–17, who locates Euripides' "teachings" in relation to Athens's arguable need for guidance on the ambiguities associated with traditional aristocratic ideals and the new institutional structures of democratic Athens.
[4] Cf. Hesk 2011: 143n.41, which begins to move in this direction: "Citizens are made more deliberatively careful, alert, and intellectually virtuous through tragedy's staging of the problems that attend the definition and exercise of good deliberation."

set such ideals of courage apart from the ineffective and self-defeating Spartan ideals of courage. In his *Andromache*, for example, he brought forward for consideration the ugly and self-ignorant Menelaus, king of Sparta. Clearly, Euripides' representation of Menelaus contributes to the Athenians' anti-Spartan ideology. What is more important for our purposes is Euripides' revealing, and quite pointed, exploration of the precise defects of Spartan masculinity.[5]

In a dramatic replay of the opening scene of the *Iliad*, Menelaus has arrived to further the cause of his daughter, Hermione, at Neoptolemus' court, by removing Neoptolemus' war-won bride, Andromache, and her son, in chains. Away at Delphi, Neoptolemus cannot respond personally, but his grandfather Peleus takes up the Achillean mantle against this poor-man's caricature of Agamemnon.[6] When Peleus grasps the Spartan's intentions, he launches into a critical diatribe against Menelaus for his cowardice.[7] He begins by asking, incredulously, "Are you one of the men (*met' andrōn*), you terrible coward (*ō kakiste kak kakōn*)?" (590). Peleus often uses the terms *kakos* and *agathos* to elaborate his emphasis on masculinity throughout the speech. Because of this opening insult—are you "among" the *men*?—it makes sense to interpret these adjectives as evaluative terms expressing deficiency or excellence in masculinity as Peleus will describe it.

Peleus declares Menelaus a coward for a number of reasons: first, because he failed to guard his house from the depredations of Paris; second, because he "ordered" (*keleusas*, 625) his brother to kill Iphigeneia out of fear that he might lose Helen; third, because he failed to resist Aphrodite's power once he had recovered Helen; and, fourth, because he attempted to dishonor Neoptolemus' house by attacking Andromache and her son in Neoptolemus' absence (590–641). He concludes by shouting, "You are nothing!" (641). Menelaus is nothing because, despite his

---

[5] On these themes in general, see the interesting discussion of Vellacott 1975: 32–36, who connects the play's anti-Spartan ideology and "patriotism" to contemporary events in the 420s BC; see also Conacher 1967: 168–71.

[6] Sorum 1995 is a valuable discussion of Euripides' use of previous mythical models; on the relationship between Agamemnon and Menelaus, see Sorum 1995: 383–84: "Menelaus loses to Peleus as Agamemnon lost to Achilles."

[7] On Euripides' transformation of the Homeric Menelaus into a wholly unattractive coward, see Allan 2000: 20–22, 244; and on the potentially humorous or ridiculous elements of that cowardice, see Allan 2000: 67, 71. Allan 2000: 161 is right, I think, to see that Euripides' exploration of tragic women in *Andromache* is also, and necessarily, an exploration of "tragic men and issues of masculinity," though as he rightly notes (165), this is only a single feature of tragedy's wider exploration of a variety of ethical and social issues. For further thoughts on Peleus' ways of insulting Menelaus, see Conacher 1967: 178–79.

generalship, he lacks the attributes of mature masculinity outlined over the course of the speech—namely, to take them in order, protection of the household, protection of children, a dignified rejection of behaviors motivated by fear, self-control, and respect for others' property. Peleus charges that Menelaus' efforts to recover Helen also embodied both selfishness and imprudence: instead of leaving Helen in Troy, Menelaus destroyed many brave lives (611) and left many mothers and fathers bereft of their noble sons (612–13).[8]

In general, Peleus' charges might seem to evoke models of masculinity with currency throughout the Greek world. But Peleus' speech already has overtones that are characteristic of democratic courage. For example, Peleus emphasizes that self-control is one of the salient attributes of courage. As Roisman has argued, this specific way of widening the traditional concept of courage was frequently used by the Attic orators to promote a new and more flexible model of masculinity.[9] The Athenian democracy was particularly inclined to "balance" the seemingly antithetical attributes of courage and self-control.[10] Moreover, by criticizing Menelaus' supposedly courageous leadership for its lack of prudence, Peleus sounds the standard Athenian note that courage must be wise, or else it does not qualify as virtuous at all. The Athenians laid special emphasis on this point because they held that democratic structures of deliberation enabled them to express their courage in action in ways that were thoughtful and prudent. Menelaus had failed to estimate correctly the costs of bringing Helen home.

Although Greeks in general could and should have openly discussed their concerns about the destructive consequences of hotheaded masculine ventures, the fact is that the Athenians, through their open debates and self-critical comic and tragic theater, were preeminently self-critical and self-knowing in just this respect. The democrats' self-questioning culture encouraged all Athenians to reflect carefully upon their own ideals of masculinity. The Athenians questioned the potential self-contradictions involved in maintaining an ideal of courage that was supposed to "save the city," but that in the practices of bellicosity, often destroyed everything that was meaningful or deserved protection in the first place. It is indeed hard

---

[8] On the play's negative characterization of Menelaus, Hermione, and Sparta in general, see Foley 2001: 97–103. On the aspersions cast against Menelaus' manhood in particular, and on the play's associated anti-Spartan themes, see Burnett 1971: 139–41.
[9] See Roisman 2003, 2004, and 2005.
[10] See Balot 2004c, with chapter 16.

to imagine the Spartans of Sthenelaidas' Assembly holding such an open debate (cf. chapter 5).

As Peleus' speech implies, healthy masculinity is related to a man's attitudes toward women. According to Peleus, the Spartans have an improper relationship to women. He charges Spartan culture with failing to recognize the differences between masculinity and femininity, in particular with overequalization of the sexes, which leads to a general lack of *sōphrosunē* among Spartan women—and hence, more specifically, to Menelaus' problems with Helen (592–604).[11]

Peleus' most profound criticism, though, is that Menelaus' expressions of manliness are defective because they fail to make sense, because they lack wisdom. This theme begins to emerge in Menelaus' self-defense. Menelaus repeatedly asserts that he is the one, not Peleus, who manifests good judgment, because he foresees the threat posed by Andromache and her children to proper dominion over Phthia (646, 660, 666–67). But his assertion of his own good judgment is undermined by his belief that Helen's seduction and the Trojan War were god-sent gifts to the Greeks. "For the Greeks," Menelaus says, "who knew nothing about arms and battle, proceeded to manliness (*tandreion*)" through fighting against the Trojans (680–84). Shockingly, perhaps, the Trojan War was a positive development, in Menelaus' opinion, because it constituted an education to manliness.[12] Menelaus implies that the destruction of his own household was worthwhile provided that the cause of Greek manliness could thereby be advanced.

Menelaus' manliness is self-destructive because it has been unhinged from a context of noble ends. Despite his self-proclaimed wisdom, Menelaus fails to recognize that courage makes sense, as a virtue, only if it is directed toward the ends of nobility, such as justice, or toward providing the necessary preconditions of human flourishing, such as material prosperity or security. When considered to be good solely for its own sake, courage is destructive. Could the development of manliness possibly justify a protracted war filled with the deaths of "many brave men"? What is manliness for, if not the protection, rather than the destruction, of the household? Menelaus holds an immature man's perspective, reminiscent of the young men during Thucydides' Sicilian Debate, who were intoxicated

---

[11] Allan 2000: 186 (cf. 269) argues that "[t]he irascible old man adopts the rhetoric of Athenian disapproval of Spartan women's freedoms (597-601)," and considers that "many prejudices about Spartan education prevailed in popular Athenian thought."

[12] For a similar reaction, see Allan 2000: 143, who does not, however, connect Menelaus' disturbingly offensive statement with the contemporary Athenian ideology of *andreia*.

by war and manliness because they had never experienced the suffering of war (Thuc. 6.24). It is indicative of ethical shallowness that Menelaus, a Trojan War veteran, could still adopt such a perspective. Menelaus is self-ignorant because he fails to understand the genuine constituents of his people's flourishing, not to mention his own.

In order to emphasize the fragility of Menelaus' courage, in fact, Euripides has Peleus suggest that Menelaus' aggression toward Andromache results from his fear that she might attack him with a sword (721–22). If Menelaus' manliness finds expression in manhandling women, rather than in protecting them, then his manliness is not only unwise, but also incoherent and self-contradictory, in that he led the Trojan expedition allegedly in order to recover Helen.

This episode concludes with Peleus' stinging retort that the Spartans may be superior warriors, but they are not superior to others in any other respect (724–26). Their courage is not properly informed by practical wisdom or the enlightened pursuit of *eudaimonia*. We might contrast this critical view of the Spartans with Isocrates' statement that the Athenians correctly subordinated courage to wisdom and justice; Isocrates admired the Athenians for seeing that courage, in order to be properly expressed, cannot sit atop the table of culturally admired virtues (12.197–98, with chapter 7).

Aeschylus' *Agamemnon*

In the first stasimon of Aeschylus' *Agamemnon*, Agamemnon explains his decision to sacrifice Iphigeneia for the sake of appeasing Artemis and moving on with the expedition to Troy:

> The elder lord spoke as follows: "Not to obey is a heavy fate, but it is also heavy if I slaughter my child, the beauty of my home, staining a father's hands with streams of maiden bloodshed near the altar; what of these things stands apart from evil? How can I become a ship-deserter (*liponaus*) and fail the alliance (*xummachias hamartōn*)? For a sacrifice to stop the winds, and a maid's blood—it is right for them to desire these things with a passion that goes beyond anger. May it be well."

The chorus then explains:

> When he put on the yoke of necessity, breathing an unholy, unclean, impious turning of the mind, from that moment he changed to resolve an all-daring

deed; for wretched frenzy, which devises shameful things, the first cause of suffering, emboldens mortals; and he dared to become the sacrificer of his daughter, in aid of wars to avenge a woman and as first offerings for the ships. (205–27)

Scholars have often debated whether Agamemnon acted freely or under the constraints of necessity or fate.[13] If we understand the scene naturalistically, then what we see, above all, is Agamemnon's failure of leadership, combined with his willingness to destroy the "glory" (*agalma*) of his household, because he had lost control of himself during a moment of crisis. He was governed by fear for his reputation, instead of the prudent pursuit of the army's best interests and the welfare of his household and city.[14] Agamemnon was governed heteronomously, by the opinions of others, and by the militant pressures of his troops—or rather by his anxieties about the troops' presumed opinions, rather than by his own independent and well-informed judgments about the most courageous, just, and statesmanlike path to follow. Agamemnon convinced himself that the troops' bloodthirsty anger was right and appropriate. He misguidedly rationalized his choice to sacrifice his daughter as a grim necessity mandated by the gods and by his troops. In reality, though, his deed was motivated by his desire to avoid the shame of becoming a "ship-deserter" and a leader who failed his alliance.

Agamemnon's mistaken judgment was not simply a cognitive error, like the cognitive error of a hypothetical person who mistakes me for a medical doctor, just because students occasionally call me "Dr. Balot." Agamemnon's failure to appreciate the genuine demands of the situation derives rather from his character—from the excessive importance he places on avoiding humiliation and embarrassment, from his overestimation of the importance of appearing to be a real man. He rationalizes his mistaken judgment by thinking of his murder of his daughter as a way of keeping to his commitments—that is, his commitments to his troops.[15]

---

[13] For two useful treatments, see Nussbaum 1986: 32–38 and Williams 1993: 132–35, along with the classic discussion of Lloyd-Jones 1962; Lesky 1966 is an illuminating discussion, but Lesky's excessive concern with "reading too much of modern psychology into Aeschylus" (82) makes him understate the psychological realism of Aeschylus' portrayal of Agamemnon.

[14] Neither the Athenian audience nor the fictional Greeks accompanying Agamemnon really knew the will of the gods, as the chorus is at pains to communicate; this is a political and psychological drama, over which the gods exert a frightening but inscrutable control; all that the characters had, and all that we have, to go on is our own naturalistic appreciation of the physical, political, and emotional circumstances in which we find ourselves.

[15] For a different view of Agamemnon's decision, see Nussbaum 1986: 32–38.

Yet Agamemnon's interpretation is, upon closer scrutiny, precisely the wrong way to understand this murder, because Agamemnon should have been committed, above all, to saving his own and his troops' households, women, and children. Restoring the household of Menelaus was, after all, the explicit goal of the Trojan War. Hence, this was a mission to retrieve Helen, not a mission to show off Agamemnon's manliness as leader of the Greeks. In this moment, at least, Agamemnon neglected to appreciate what his courage was for.[16] Instead of being informed by prudence, Agamemnon's manliness was egoistic; these events and decisions were about Agamemnon, rather than about the noble ends that courage is meant to serve. Agamemnon's paralyzing and undeveloped sense of shame overrode any prudent or thoughtful response, and it led to a self-destructive expression of distorted manliness. The Athenians specifically devoted themselves to liberating themselves from traditional shame, so as to achieve more enlightened expressions of courage.

To make this point differently, Agamemnon's manliness was unhinged from its proper context, in which manly courage saves the household and the city. This is why, in the second stanza quoted, the chorus emphasizes that Agamemnon's mind had lost control. His daring and his anger had become ends in themselves, rather than qualities of evolved masculinity that were given meaningful direction by enlightened prudence and well-informed desires to promote the flourishing of his own family, household, and city. Agamemnon's defective sense of shame, which overrode his rationality, led to a disastrous pursuit of social honor and to a self-destructive expression of distorted manliness.

To be sure, Agamemnon was a general who made decisions that affected vast hordes of Greek soldiers; he was no ordinary Greek. Yet, in watching him, the ordinary Athenian audience was forced to reflect on the motivations of their own courage, the emotions that drive courage, and the necessity of keeping the anger and violence associated with courage in their proper places. After all, as Demosthenes said to his fellow citizens, "So, when you take the field, whoever is leader has authority over you, but now each one of you yourselves is a general" (50.3). By expressing his sense of shame, Agamemnon displayed an understandable sensitivity to the opinions of his troops and his own reputation, which the Athenian democrats also cultivated; but, by contrast with Agamemnon, the Athenians' goal was to ensure that this sensitivity was informed and directed by wisdom as

---

[16] For a helpful related discussion, see Euben 1990: 68–72.

to the proper ends, and the noblest expressions, of "manly courage." Just as Euripides' Theseus had offered a positive exemplar of Athenian courage (see chapter 11), Aeschylus' Agamemnon provided a powerful negative paradigm that furthered the Athenians' efforts to develop a more thoughtful and evolved understanding of courage.

Self-Understanding in Athens's Tragic Theater

The tragic theater did not directly affect the Athenians' political decisions. Instead, the plays we have considered deepened the Athenians' appreciation for, valuing of, and recognition of things they were already doing. The goodness of the democratic experience depended on the Athenians' own recognition that their political practices of self-formation, and the outcomes of those practices, were, in fact, key elements of their own flourishing. The tragedies we have considered contributed not so much to teaching the Athenians how to conduct their lives with courage, freedom, and wisdom, but rather to show the Athenians that they were already doing so, and that members of other political regimes were not doing so; and that the Athenians reaped extraordinary benefits from doing so, whereas members of other political regimes, particularly the Persians and Spartans, met with disaster because they did not do so.[17] In the hands of Aeschylus and Euripides, these dichotomies were given structure by the underlying principle of the regime (*politeia*), which encompassed the cultural and political worlds of the respective cities and kingdoms.

This interpretation of Athenian tragedy differs considerably from others. Many scholars have proposed, for example, that tragedy encouraged Athenian citizens to question the dominant values and norms by which they lived under the democracy. This might be called the "interrogative" interpretation of Athenian tragedy and political life.[18] My argument has shown that

---

[17] For a different, but not incompatible, interpretation of tragedy and politics in Athens, particularly in relation to the Athenian empire, see Tzanetou 2012: 10–30.

[18] See, for example, Goldhill 1990 and Raaflaub 2001, although these two treatments diverge on the question of whether tragedy "inverts" the ideology of democratic Athens: Goldhill finds that the tragedians render this ideology problematic ("Tragedy again and again takes key terms of the normative and evaluative vocabulary of civic discourse, and depicts conflicts and ambiguities in their meanings and use": Goldhill 1990: 126), whereas Raaflaub 2001: 336 speaks of the "poet's efforts to reverse official ideology." Euben 1986a: 29, though, argues that tragedy's functions of affirming, rendering problematic, and questioning existing ideology and institutions are not necessarily incompatible with one another: "As we have seen, the tragedians were popular and left none of the city's ideals, aspirations, achievements, or resolutions outside the problematizing of paradox and contradiction. They validated the city's institutions and called them into question; reaffirmed its structure of order and pushed the mind beyond that order to face the chaos those

several tragedies, at least, including Euripides' *Suppliants* (chapter 11), made a contribution to democratic culture, not by encouraging citizens to question their own ideals, but rather by encouraging citizens to understand both the importance and the reality of their own ideals. Athenian tragedy could deepen the citizens' appreciation for their own democratic ideal of courage and their democratic ideology of eudaimonism (chapters 14 and 15).

Still other scholars, by contrast, have offered a panhellenic or, we might say, humanistic, interpretation of Greek tragedy, according to which it is less closely tied to the context of Athenian democracy.[19] They have argued that tragedy has important political overtones, not so much in relation to Athenian democracy, but rather in relation to life in the Greek polis altogether. Athenian tragedy explored issues of grave concern to all polis dwellers, not just democrats—issues such as the rule of law and the relationship between *oikos* and polis, as in Sophocles' *Antigone*. In the case of many tragedies, such as *Antigone*, this might well be the case; each tragedy must be studied on its own terms, with due consideration for both the multivalence of tragedy as a dramatic form and the diversity of the audience as an interpretative community. Either way, though, the tragedies I have considered are closely connected to the Athenian democratic ideology of courage, honor, freedom, and practical rationality. The Athenians themselves saw these virtues and ideals, quite legitimately, as an outgrowth of their democratic system, which distinguished Athens from cities governed by other types of political regime. What is plausible about the panhellenic interpretation is that not all themes in tragedy are distinctively democratic in just this way. But certainly the tragedies I have considered would have resonated with Athenian audiences who were particularly sensitive to the regime-based qualities of their own ideals, such as freedom and courage.

More plausible is Martha Nussbaum's view of Athenian tragedy as a cultural mode of emotional education.[20] For Nussbaum, Greek tragedy tempered or moderated the Athenians' bellicosity. Nussbaum thus sees a direct relationship between (for example) watching the sufferings of war on stage and the Athenian decision to spare all but 1000 of the Mytilenian rebels in 427 BC. Yet the Athenians were much less compassionate than

---

structures had exorcised" (Euben 1986a: 29). For a similarly complex view, but from a more sociological perspective, see Hall 1997.

[19] Rhodes 2003b; Carter 2007; Griffin 1999.

[20] These themes emerge from the fine readings of several tragedies offered in Nussbaum 1986, and from Nussbaum 2001a: 350–53, but they come through most clearly, and with specific reference to Mytilene, in Nussbaum 1992: 280–83.

her account might suggest. In the heyday of Euripidean tragedy and Aristophanic comedy, and despite these authors' apparent orientations toward peace, the Athenians continued to commit atrocities at Scione, Melos, and elsewhere. To be sure, the Athenians acted no more atrociously on these occasions than any of their Mediterranean neighbors. Ostensibly, though, they were not schooled in special modes of sympathy or compassion by the Athenian theater.

To address precisely this problem, Kurt Raaflaub has proposed that the Athenian tragic theater helped to allay the Athenians' guilt.[21] For Raaflaub, the tragic theater enabled the Athenians to continue to prosecute their imperialism efficiently, much as a modern Christian church helps to allay the guilt of capitalist barons who focus their lives on money, except on Sundays, when they "right" themselves morally and psychologically prepare themselves for more corporate raiding. Raaflaub's view has the virtue of acknowledging that there is no direct and perceptible correlation between the performance of an apparently peace-oriented tragedy such as *Trojan Women* and the Athenians' political decisions in the Assembly. On the other hand, this view fails to offer a credible, naturalistic explanation for the psychological mechanisms through which a tragedy like *Trojan Women*, which revels in the details of suffering brought on by war, could possibly silence the Athenians' doubts and feelings of guilt over their imperialism. As Nussbaum's interpretation suggests, plays in this mold would seem likely to have had precisely the opposite effect on Athenians.

I conclude by offering brief and selective interpretations of Euripides' *Heracles* and *Trojan Women*, in order to show that the Athenians brought themselves to understand the costs, implications, and disturbingly frequent excesses of war, so as to avoid such excesses, without turning themselves into defenseless peaceniks or proposing that they needed to "give peace a chance" or in any way limiting their capacity to project military force when they determined that it was appropriate and justified, and that it could serve their own conceptions of flourishing. They wanted to resist both excess and deficiency in their displays of manliness. Not surprisingly, this meant something different for them and for us.

---

[21] Raaflaub 2001: 339–41.

Euripides' *Heracles*

Euripides had his *Heracles* produced in 416 BC. Just afterward, the Athenians voted to send their extraordinary armada to Sicily. Although divine intervention plays a prominent role in the play, it is difficult to imagine that an audience of Athenian veterans would not gravitate toward a more naturalistic interpretation of the action, according to which Heracles' madness and his murder of his family were the products of (what we now call) post-traumatic stress disorder brought on by his 12 Labors.[22] That Euripides specifically designed the tragedy to bring out this causal connection between the Labors and Heracles' destruction of his family is the best explanation for Euripides' particular way of handling the Heracles myth.[23] In the typical sequence, the Labors functioned to expiate Heracles' crime of killing his family, which was driven by madness sent by Hera. For us, the main question is what Euripides' specific exploration of "post-traumatic grief," as we would call it, might contribute to the Athenians' understanding of democratic courage.[24]

When Heracles returns to Thebes and finds that his father, wife, and children have been threatened with death by the usurper Lycus, his reaction is a mixture of disproportionate, Rambo-like aggression and a very reasonable and honorable desire to give priority to the defense of his household, over all other glorious deeds:

> Throw these garments of death from your hair, and look up at the light, gazing upon a sweet exchange for the darkness below. But, since there is work for my hands, I will first go and raze the house of the new tyrants. I will cut off his unholy head and throw it to the dogs to tear up. However many of the Cadmeans I find to be bad, despite my kindness toward them, I will overpower with this weapon, which is noble in victory. Others I will tear to

---

[22] For a challenging reading of the play that connects it to fifth-century medicine, see Holmes 2008. For an illuminating discussion of the psychological dimensions of the play's main character, see Kamerbeek 1966.

[23] On Euripides' novel presentation of the myth, see Conacher 1967: 82–90; Kovacs 1998.

[24] For an interpretation that links the play to PTSD, and contrasts it helpfully with Seneca's tragic version of the myth, see Bowman 2003, n.d. (a) and n.d. (b), who explores the play in close connection with the theories of Shay 1994 and Shay n.d. Note that before Shay 1994 had opened up his compelling psychiatric interpretation of the Homeric epics, Barlow 1982: 124 had interestingly observed that "The supposed glory and heroism of the labors is converted to hideous new circumstances where the same characteristics of the hero exist but are used in a tragically inappropriate way." See also the interesting reflections of Konstan 1999: 83–87 on Heracles' violence in war and at home.

pieces with feathered arrows. I will fill the entire Ismenus with the blood of their corpses, and the bright spring of Dirce will be bloodied. Is it necessary for me to protect someone else more than my wife, my children, and my old father? Good-bye to my labors. For in vain did I accomplish them rather than these things. It is necessary for me to die protecting them, if they were being killed on account of their father. Why will we call it noble to fight against a hydra or a lion when Eurystheus sends me on a mission, but I will not work to prevent my children's death? If that happens, then I will not be called Heracles noble in victory as I was before. (562–582).

Heracles understood that his first priority was to defend his family. As Heracles himself acknowledges, his supposedly glorious labors were actually "in vain" or "to no purpose" (*matēn*, 576), unless he could provide safety for his *philoi*. Euripides' Heracles is thus more evolved, we might say, than Sophocles' Ajax, who had to be counseled on precisely this point by his concubine Tecmessa (*Ajax* 485–524). Heracles criticizes the possession of a reputation for glory, if acquiring that reputation should mean, even unbeknownst to him, the destruction of his household. Contrast this with Agamemnon's reaction amid the crisis of military and familial roles at Aulis. To this extent, at least, Heracles has an appropriate understanding of his ethical priorities.[25] Where he misses the mark emotionally, however, is in the fanatical and self-defeating rage he feels toward Lycus and toward whichever Thebans conspired with him through acts of commission or omission. Heracles' dream is to commit the barbaric act of beheading Lycus and throwing his head to the dogs (567–68). Moreover, he is disturbingly aggressive toward the other Thebans, with whose blood he hopes to stain surrounding rivers and springs (571–73).

What we see in this play, then, is Euripides' staging of a larger-than-life character who cannot digest his pugnacious anger upon returning to his household. As the Messenger's speech indicates, Heracles believes that he is still in the killing fields, marching tactically, performing labors, and shooting down his enemies, even when his children cry out to him within his home (931–1000). I do not propose that any Greek, whether democratic or not, could find Heracles' passionate anger or his destruction of his *oikos* admirable. My point is that this play's teachings, so to speak,

---

[25] Cf. Gregory 1991: 133–35, who equally compares Heracles to both Homer's Odysseus and Sophocles' Ajax, and who also finds Heracles' care for his family attractive, but interprets this "tenderness" as one dimension of Heracles' conformity to the "epic pattern of the complete hero" (134).

both required and encouraged self-awareness about the ambiguities of the warlike emotions—a self-awareness that was a common theme in the Athenian Assembly (see chapter 3).

The honor of the warrior could yield excellent results, such as Heracles' disposition to give priority to his family's welfare over achieving glory through his military exploits. At the same time, however, the anger of the warrior, which was intensified by his combat experience, could easily become self-destructive, if that anger was not subordinated to and directed by the practical wisdom created in democratic Athens through free and open speech. Euripides' *Heracles* explored one of the primary costs of asking citizens to undertake military labors as soldiers. In this way Euripides helped the Athenians to reckon up those costs fairly and adequately when they began to deliberate about war and peace in the Assembly. Seen in this light, Euripides' character Heracles represented the ordinary ambitions and anger of the common Athenian soldier, writ large. This soldier came to know himself through confronting his fanatical *Doppelgänger*, Heracles.[26]

The importance of acquiring this self-knowledge is that the Athenian citizen, whether young or old, rich or poor, would thereby have liberated himself from the rigid canons of social shame and anger that drove Agamemnon to make the wrong decision at a moment of crisis, and from the sensitivity of Euripides' Adrastus to the shouts of the young men who spurred him on to undertake an unnecessary war against Thebes (see chapter 11). The Athenians could not have agreed with Euripides' Menelaus that warfare is good because it develops manliness. This hardly means that the Athenians would avoid war when necessary. Instead, they would make war when it served their interests, but they would do so with a clearer understanding of their own *andreia* and its role in the lives of democratic citizens.

Euripides' *Trojan Women*, staged in 415 BC, would have produced effects of similar complexity, but these effects, too, can be understood as leading the Athenians to a deeper appreciation of the suffering caused by their wars, both to themselves and others; and of the perspectives on courage and self-defense that might be taken by military losers as well as victors. Instead of questioning their decisions to go to war altogether, the playwright was teaching the Athenians the consequences and implications of decisions that they had taken and necessarily would go on taking, so

---

[26] Gregory 1991: 121–154 argues, by contrast, that Euripides transformed Heracles from an exemplar of aristocratic ideals to a hero whose "values" are "consonant with the ideology of the democratic polis." (123).

long as they were engaged in ancient politics.[27] Hence the playwright may be said to have contributed to Athenian self-knowledge.

The Trojan women with speaking parts—particularly Andromache and Cassandra—speak wisely and insightfully about the role of courage in the lives of their male relations. First of all, and most pointedly, in order to maximize the emotional intensity surrounding Andromache's memories of Hector, Euripides has Andromache explain that in Hector, she "had a man who was enough for me, great in intelligence (*xenesei*), in birth, in wealth, and in courage (*kandreiai*)" (673–74). At least in Andromache's view, Hector combines courage with intelligence as his two chief virtues; notice that the other characteristics mentioned by Andromache are socially constructed attributes of status and class, rather than character traits. In other words, apart from status and class, Hector was similar to Athenian citizens as they imagined themselves: as individuals capable of uniting courage and intelligence.

Second, and even more deeply, the crazy prophetess Cassandra offers a critique of the Greeks' actions and a defense of the Trojan men for displaying the only sort of courage that makes sense. She ridicules Agamemnon, the *sophos* as she calls him, for destroying "what was most dear to him for the sake of what was most hateful" (370–71), that is, destroying his own children for the sake of the hated Helen. Cassandra brought to the attention of the audience not questions about the necessity of going to war, but a compelling interpretation of the consequences and ethical significance of Agamemnon's defective reasons for making war. She summoned the Athenians to think carefully about their purposes in conducting expeditions abroad, and to think strategically about how to reduce the impact of war's horrors on their own city and their own families.

Cassandra next remarks on the fate of the Greek soldiers slain abroad: "When they arrived at the banks of the Scamander, they began dying, although they had not been deprived of land or of their fatherland with its high towers. The ones whom Ares took did not see their children and were not wrapped up in burial coverings by the hands of their wives but lie buried in a foreign land. Things at home were similar: wives were losing their strong husbands and dying as widows, while others died childless in their houses, having reared children in vain" (374–81). Cassandra

---

[27] For a general treatment with which my account overlaps, see Croally 1994. For a helpful study relevant to courage and warmaking, see Havelock 1968; cf. also Vellacott 1975: 164–66, Conacher 1967: 127–45: Raaflaub 2001: 334–39.

draws out the implications of making war abroad for soldiers whose first duty in fighting is to save the city and to save their households.

What are the consequences of making the decision to send a vast armada to Sicily? How was this decision connected to the cardinal purpose of saving the city? The Trojans, by contrast with the Greeks, fought in order to save the city (386–87). They understood that wise men will always avoid war, but they recognized that, amidst compulsion, a second-best alternative is to carry out the deeds of nobility even as one dies (400–402). Through exploring the implications of the decision to fight, which is often a necessary decision, Cassandra reminded Athenians of the depth and ethical significance of their choices in the Assembly, so that they could enter into those decisions with the clearest possible understanding of where their voluntary political choices would lead them. How, if at all, could the Athenians use the ideology of saving the city to accommodate or explain foreign imperial ventures? How could they avoid becoming the barbaric Greeks of *Trojan Women*, or the barbaric Persians of Aeschylus' *Persians*?

Similar points could be made about the relentless horrors put on stage in this play. There is no way, I think, that the audience could fail to feel pity and fear when hearing the chorus' description of the cries and suffering of young children throughout the city (555–67, 1091–99), or Hecuba's reaction to the news of Astyanax's death (1156–1206). Watching these scenes in the company of fellow veterans, Athenian citizen men could fully and safely experience their grief and, through doing so, return to the Athenian Assembly with a clearer sense of purpose and a strong sense of rationality, unclouded by the distortions of unaddressed suffering.[28] This interpretation offers a realistic alternative to the view that the poet—specifically Euripides in writing *Trojan Women*—made "efforts to reverse official ideology" or carried out an "inversion of official ideology."[29]

Yet Raaflaub is surely correct, as I have indicated, to say that the playwright encouraged his audience to understand causation and responsibility naturalistically, rather than religiously: as Raaflaub himself puts the point, "[I]n a remarkable prayer to Zeus (884–88) Hecuba expresses her belief that what humans attribute to Zeus, that is, to divine interference, is caused either by nature's necessity (*anankē phuseos*) or by the mortal's

---

[28] Here I evoke the notion of collective "griefwork" that Jonathan Shay has so successfully applied to the Homeric epics and, in brief compass, to Athenian tragedy: see Shay 1994 and Shay n.d.; cf. also Nussbaum 1992, 2001a.

[29] Raaflaub 2001: 336–337. On the other hand, I agree with Raaflaub (2001: 335) that the poet "induces the audience to think about important aspects of public issues that tend to be overlooked or suppressed in the heat of political debate."

mind (*nous brotōn*: 886)."[30] What the poet offers in *Trojan Women* is a naturalistic representation of suffering, courage, and warfare that made the Athenians understand their own decisions, so that they could deliberate freely and prudently on the questions of war and peace that mattered most.[31]

It goes without saying, though, that Athens was not a Kantian republic seeking cosmopolitanism and perpetual peace. It was a warlike ancient Mediterranean city that saw its best interests as served, sometimes, by pursuing imperialism to the hilt. Perhaps regrettably, therefore, the Athenians' acquisition of self-knowledge, their deepening of their own appreciation for what they were doing as democrats, and for its importance, meant emboldening the Athenians to pursue their warfare with abandon, without anxieties or qualms, whether those qualms might be ethical, religious, or practical. They understood the significance and the implications of their actions better than others, because their *politeia* encouraged them to do so; they had left no questions unasked in their explorations of warfare and suffering. Hence, perhaps, they felt emboldened to act, because they thought of themselves as the most genuinely courageous citizens that could be found in the Mediterranean, in their time, or in any previous time.[32] Those would rightly be judged most courageous who understand both the fearful and the pleasant and do not turn away from risks on account of this (*dia tauta*; compare the treatment of this ambiguous phrase in chapter 2). Is democratic courage attractive or repulsive? The Athenians themselves cannot tell us what to think.

---

[30] Raaflaub 2001: 336.
[31] Cf. Nussbaum 1992: 282–83 for a similar, but more optimistic, reading.
[32] Konstan 2010: 185 makes a similar suggestion with regard to Aristophanic comedy.

PART III | Athens's Ideology of Eudaimonism

CHAPTER 14 | Athenian Eudaimonism in Thought and Action

HOW DID THE ATHENIANS themselves understand democratic courage in relation to their imperialism, to their actual practices of political deliberation, and to their conceptions of justice both within the city and abroad? Above all, how did they understand the ends toward which their courage was directed? In order to answer these questions, we must explore the specifically ancient framework in which democratic courage was located—in particular, that of *eudaimonia*, or human flourishing. The Athenians' discourse on *eudaimonia* first came to sight as a way to address the fundamentally problematic relationship of the individual to the community.

This strategy did not, of course, embody the entirety of the Athenian self-understanding. As Kenneth Dover has illustrated, Athenian norms and ideals were complex, context dependent, and often flatly contradictory.[1] The Athenians were undoubtedly attracted to the traditional notion that Athens was a powerful, even heroic imperial city—or, at times, a hedonistic *polis tyrannos*.[2] Many were attached to the idea of Athens as the freest and greatest of Greek cities and cared little for its expressions of virtue, except to the extent that virtue was a means to expansion.[3] Thus the eudaimonistic discourse held a particular place in a contentious array of self-images. It emerged most powerfully in the Athenians' boldest and most expansive constructions of the democratic city, that is, in the funeral

---

[1] Dover 1974.
[2] On the motif of polis tyrannos, see especially Connor 1977. For examination of other metaphorical descriptions of Athens, see Morrison 2006: 133–56.
[3] See Raaflaub 2004: 166–93.

orations. The eudaimonism advanced in the funeral orations sought to make sense of the Athenians' often ambiguous values, and in particular to provide a coherent vision of why military service was good, decent, rational, and consistent with a happy life even when it led to death. The orators had to argue this case because the case itself was not obvious; rather, they strove to make sense of the diversity of possible views held by members of their audiences, so as to persuade their fellow citizens to see the attractions and coherence of the eudaimonistic picture.

The central question was how to construe courage in such a way as to answer to the claims of both the community (which sought protection and patriotic contributions to the common good) and the individual (who sought to live well as a human being). Every society, even that of the Homeric epics, requires some "sacrifice" of individual interests for the sake of the community. Courage sets this problem in particularly high relief, though, because it calls upon individuals to sacrifice their lives, at the limit, in order to protect the city. In this way courage is unlike justice (shown, for example, in paying whatever taxes one owes) or public munificence (the virtue of making generous donations to the city) or civic solidarity (illustrated in appropriate ritual behaviors or service on a jury). The Spartans and many other Greeks adopted a conventionally respectable solution: they emphasized traditional authority and entirely subordinated the individual to the community. To take an extreme example, this subordination was embodied in the Spartans' extraordinary system of education (*agōgē*).

Yet the Spartan approach is intrinsically one-sided. Envisioning the individual and the community as necessarily in conflict, this solution neglects the individual's welfare and grants respect solely to the community. By contrast, the Athenians were proud of their personal freedoms and private life; it was almost proverbial, indeed a joke, that few Athenians could be counted on to contribute their fair share to the common good (cf. Aristophanes, *Eccl.* 746–876).[4] This is the point, in fact, of studying the "bad citizen" in democratic Athens: even if other cities had bad citizens, to be sure, Athens's emphasis on individual freedom was likely to exacerbate the problem and to bring out special tensions and ambiguities between individual and community, between *idios* and *koinos*.[5] Hence, while appreciating the importance of dedication to the community as a whole, the Athenians could also

---

[4] For an illuminating discussion of the ambiguities involved in the characterization of this "bad" Athenian, see Christ 2008: 178–82.

[5] See Christ 2006. My conversations with Matt Christ and with Christian Boudignon helped bring home this point to me.

recognize—as we ourselves easily recognize, following in the footsteps of early modern political philosophers such as Machiavelli, Hobbes, and Locke—that individuals themselves have their own legitimate desires, aspirations, and commitments. These interests must be granted proper or proportionate attention if the individual's life is to be worth living.

Hence, the dilemma faced by Athens was defined by these polarities. Political regimes seemingly must follow either the rigidly collectivist Spartan model or the profoundly individualistic model familiar from our own liberal-democratic nation-states. But is it possible to uncover ways in which individual interests, properly understood, can be seen to cooperate at a deeper level with the real interests of a healthy and well-constructed city? This was the project that, in one form or another, many philosophers—such as Plato, Aristotle, Hegel, and Tocqueville—confronted in their most ambitious works of political theory. It is also a project relevant to us, right now, because contemporary accounts of courage are plagued by a markedly, but unnecessarily, one-sided approach (see chapter 1). We ask individuals to sacrifice themselves and their own good, narrowly understood, for the political community or for their fellow citizens, without providing a clear explanation of the individual's essential relationship to the political community, to his fellow citizens, and to the good of both.

Prior to the more familiar investigations of this question in Platonic and Aristotelian political philosophy, the Athenians themselves tried to sort out this apparently paradoxical knot of competing claims within their democratic political life. They tried to show that the individual's development of courage and other cardinal virtues not only instrumentally supported the community, but also intrinsically constituted a significant dimension of the individual's own flourishing as a human being. It was in this way that the Athenians attempted to bridge the gap between the community's good and the individual's good—even if they recognized, quite realistically, that it was impossible and undesirable to eliminate tensions between the two entirely. They did so by rejecting both traditional Greek efforts to subordinate individuals to the community and the modern individualism which typically sets the individual's good, understood in a narrow and circumscribed way, against that of the community. The Athenians carried out their ambitious ethical and political project in democratic and eudaimonistic ways that were unavailable to traditional Greeks and to modern political thinkers, too.[6]

---

[6] Farenga 2006 is perhaps the only existing work that explores the issue of the democratic Athenians' conceptions of the "self" in any detail. Although Farenga's ambitious book works with idioms (liberal, communitarian, deliberative democracy) that differ from my own, I believe

Athenian Commemoration as Eudaimonistic Practice

The epitaphic tradition presents us with the most fertile resources of reflection upon the flourishing of Athenians as democratic citizens. These speeches of commemoration can be interpreted as a form of "eudaimonistic practice," in that they raise to consciousness, for democratic citizens ancient and modern, the potential links between contributing excellently to the common good as democratic citizens, on the one hand, and living full and complete lives characterized by human flourishing, on the other. In order to illustrate how these orations constitute a serious public reflection on courage and eudaimonism, I focus on the detailed reading of a single *epitaphios*, whose themes I supplement with references to other, related passages in Athenian oratory, tragedy, and historiography. We will discover that the epitaphic speaker, in this case, gently but insistently leads us to the central paradox of the Athenians' eudaimonistic conception of courage—that is, how dying courageously in battle for the city can be construed as the summit and fitting conclusion of the individual's own flourishing existence.

Lysias' funeral oration (which dates to the late 390s BC) furthered Pericles' model of democratic self-understanding by arguing that democratic political life helped to perfect the Athenians' worthwhile and essential ethical capacities.[7] This cultivation of excellence among the citizenry, all by itself, illustrated the city's goodness and provided a conception of the individual's own flourishing as intrinsically dignified and choice-worthy. For the sake of civic education among the living, Lysias' speech exalted the fallen citizen-soldiers as admirable exemplars of nobility. Lysias recalled events and aspirations from the Athenian past not simply for ideological or chauvinistic reasons, but rather in order to formulate the elements of a distinctively democratic account of nobility. As Lysias himself says, the fallen soldiers were men worthy of emulation (*zēlōtoi*, Lys. 2.69: they are "to be emulated," not "envied," as in the Loeb; cf. Lys. 2.26) because "they were educated in the noble ways of their ancestors, and

---

that his careful studies of various Athenian constructions of individuality and selfhood are largely compatible with my own attempt to reconstruct the Athenians' way of relating the individual to the community, ideally. Gill 1996 also provides an excellent guide to Greek understandings of the "self," through the lens of the concept of "personality." Gill's work is less directly related to my own, however, because of its lack of engagement with democratic ideology.

[7] This discussion of Lysias' funeral oration is a revised and abbreviated version of one section of Balot 2013.

then, having become men, they preserved the reputation of their ancestors and displayed their own excellence (or courage: *aretē*)" (69; cf. 2.50–53).

Lysias' speech exemplifies the Athenians' practices of eudaimonism because, as he indicates, he is striving to make explicit three essential elements of Athenian *aretē* and *eudaimonia*. First, the orator stresses the intrinsic worth of *aretē*, which explains his emphasis on the fallen soldiers' worthiness of admiration and emulation. Second, he proposes that the activities and products of *aretē* constitute the Athenians' *eudaimonia* altogether. Third, he contends that the democratic regime (*politeia*)—that is, its way of life, its distribution of power, and its ethical ideals—educated the Athenians to develop and perfect their inborn capacities for excellence. In the course of making these arguments, Lysias shows that the Athenian soldiers were contributing to the city's common good, and even the common good of Greece, and that this contribution was a product of their own excellences of character, such as justice, courage, generosity, and fellow-feeling.

Consider, for example, Lysias' discussion of the friendship, generosity, and justice shown by the Athenians toward the sons of Heracles (11–16). Having fled the tyrannical Eurystheus, Heracles' sons found the other Greeks too afraid to help them; though ashamed of themselves, the other Greeks failed to respect their own standards of nobility, justice, and hospitality. They doomed themselves to a life that lacked self-respect. The Athenians, by contrast, carried into effect the democratic generosity exalted by Pericles (Thuc. 2.40), in ways that illustrated courage's role as the "footstool of the virtues." Out of respect for Heracles, they protected his sons at significant risk to themselves.[8] They "deemed it worthy (*ēxioun*; not "preferred," as the Loeb translates) to fight with justice on behalf of the weaker" (12; cf. 2.67–68). This statement carries forward Lysias' theme from the previous section, where he had indicated that the Athenians fought to recover the bodies of Adrastus and Polyneices at Thebes "with justice as their ally" (*to de dikaion echontes summachon*; Lys. 2.10). Courage was not truly courage unless it was allied with justice (cf. 2.14, 2.17), and unless that alliance was cemented in the Athenians' minds through an act of carefully reasoned judgment.

According to Lysias, the Athenians courageously pursued just outcomes throughout Greece only after careful deliberation on the behaviours

---

[8] On the theme of foreign "intervention," and the norm of helping others in the international arena, see Low 2007: 178–80, who also points to Lysias' funeral oration as an illuminating example of a larger pattern.

that would best embody their concern for justice, generosity, and the other virtues.[9] In this respect, the correct understanding of Lysias' verb "they deemed it worthy" (*ēxioun*) is important, because this word is meant to convey the idea that the Athenians had, on the basis of public discussion, made a shared, collective judgment that living up to their own ideals was better not only for Heracles' sons, but also for themselves. This was no simple preference, as translators suggest, but rather a well-informed judgment based on democratic deliberation. We should notice the affinities between Lysias' expression and the standard expression used to inscribe decrees of the democratic Assembly: *edoxe tōi dēmōi* (it seemed best to the demos). Uniting courage with generosity and prudence, the Athenians overcame their fears of imminent danger and steadfastly held to their purpose (Lys. 2.13). As Pericles had emphasized, Athenian courage was the embodiment of the Athenians' practical rationality and judgment about what is right or good (Thuc. 2.40).

Put differently, the Athenians strove to live with self-respect—or, as they often formulated the point, they strove to live in ways that they found "worthy" of themselves, or they strove to win a "good reputation" (2.14). Their democratic deliberation was no felicific calculus, but rather a determined and ethically informed judgment of the elements and practices conducive to, if not constitutive of, *eudaimonia*. They aspired to further the cause of freedom and justice, straight up to the limiting case of their own deaths, if necessary, because they had come to recognize that these were the only ideals worthy of them as human beings (2.13–14).

Hence, without any hopes for reciprocity from Heracles or his sons (2.13), the Athenians freely and courageously risked their lives in order to behave commensurately with their own demanding ideals of nobility. Seen in this light, their desire for a good reputation was equivalent to their desire to be recognized and praised for the right things—that is, their courageous pursuit of justice, freedom, and, as we shall see, equality. (Having constituted themselves as they did, they could hardly desire a good reputation for qualities or actions that they themselves did not reflectively endorse.) The good life—presented here as a life of self-respect won through imitating and elaborating the virtues of Greece's foremost civilizing hero, Heracles—was possible for them because they possessed and exercised the wisdom and courage to act in ways that were worthy of themselves and fully adequate to our human capacities in these respects.

---

[9] On pity and generosity in general in the Athenians' self-representation, see Tzanetou 2012.

After making these essential points about the character of Athenian courage, justice, deliberation, and generosity, Lysias stressed that the Athenians developed their noble attributes because of their city's regime of civic education. To be sure, Lysias emphasized the Athenians' inborn natural excellences (2.61), which he represented, in accordance with the Athenians' national narratives, as a feature of Athenian autochthony. Yet, having done justice to this national myth, he developed a substantial account of the regime's capacity to develop the natural capabilities of all Athenian citizens: "For they supposed that it was the task of wild beasts to be ruled over by one another by force, but that it belonged to human beings to define justice by law, to persuade by reasoned speech, and to serve these purposes in action, governed by the law and instructed by reasoned speech" (2.19). In order to cultivate their distinctively human capacities properly, the Athenians deliberately established a regime of laws, incentives, persuasive speech, and (at the limit) just punishments. Even apart from the consequences of these institutional features, the Athenians' political practices, in themselves, enabled them to perfect their abilities to dispense justice, to deliberate prudently, and to behave in thoughtful, mutually intelligible, and ethically coherent ways. Such were the goods, both individual and collective, that were internal to the Athenians' political practices.[10]

The Athenians had founded these practices in just this way, because they were aboriginally committed to the ideals of freedom and equality. Calling upon the Athenians' myth of autochthony to find an expressive language for these ideas, Lysias argued that the "beginning of the Athenians' life was just" and that their ancestors had established a "single deliberative purpose (*miai gnōmēi chrōmenois*) to fight on behalf of justice" (2.17). The Athenians were deliberate and purposeful in casting out the "ruling classes" (*dunasteias*) of the region and in founding a "democracy" (*dēmokratian*): "they thought that the liberty of all was the greatest source of common agreement (*homonoian*), and, by sharing in common with one another the hopes born of their risks, they conducted their political life with souls that were free" (2.18–19).

In this extremely dense passage, Lysias argued that democracy was founded on the basis of the Athenians' shared, deliberative courage and

---

[10] For the notion of "goods internal to practices," see MacIntyre 1984: 181–203. On the "natural capabilities" and "distinctively human capacities" of Athenians, I am developing the language and concepts of the "capabilities" approach, which Nussbaum elaborated first from a neo-Aristotelian perspective: see Nussbaum 1988, 1990; cf. also Ober 2007.

hopefulness, and that its central ideals, from the beginning, were freedom and justice. Democracy was a dangerous but exciting experiment that required courage and a collective aspiration to realize freedom and justice. In this case, and as often, however, justice is equality: the Athenians "cast out" (*ekbalontes*) the hierarchies of previous "dynasties" and shared their dangers and risks, both military and political, in common. (Note that when the Athenians were leaders of the Greeks in the fifth century BC, according to Lysias, they used their power in order to enforce the norm of political equality among their allies, too, since they could not tolerate hierarchies in which the few "enslaved" the many: Lys. 2.56). Through his complex reformulation of the Athenians' autochthony myth, Lysias emphasized dramatically that the Athenians achieved their own good as individuals through their participation in the common goods of political life—freedom, equality, justice, courage, and civic friendship. For it was through "sharing in the *politeia*" (*metechein tēs politeias*) that the Athenians realized the distinctively human excellences of justice, law, and reasoned public speech that constitute, in Lysias' presentation, the summit of human flourishing (2.18–19).

As in the Periclean funeral oration, courage was the cornerstone of the Athenians' civic and individual expression of that ensemble of excellences recognized as the constituent elements of human flourishing. At the beginning of the Persian War period, the Athenians were the Persians' chief target, because the king was aware that Athens would come to the aid of any other city attacked by the Persians (2.22). In describing the Athenians' response to the invasion, Lysias emphasized their purposefulness and their deliberate judgments (*tauta miai gnōmēi pantes gnontes*, 2.24), as well as their self-confidence (*tēi hautōn aretēi...episteusan*, 2.23). They understood clearly the importance of fighting for the liberty of Greece and were undeterred in their pursuit of this ideal. This fundamental knowledge of the value of their courage enabled them to avoid any prudential calculation of their own narrowly construed advantage (2.23). Moreover, and more importantly, it enabled them to make the best strategic choices in circumstances of extreme duress: they deserted their own city, since that was the best alternative after the battles of Thermopylae and Artemisium (2.32–33). And they managed to coordinate the naval efforts of their frequently untrustworthy Greek allies, so as to challenge the King in the most sensible and effective way (2.33–38).

Throughout these passages, Lysias emphasizes both the shared feelings and attitudes of the Athenians as a collectivity (2.35–37, 2.39–40) and the good judgment that was characteristic of the Athenians as a people and individually (2.40–42). Both the soldiers on Athenian ships, and their families at Salamis, reciprocated deep concern, fear, and anxieties on behalf of one another (2.35–36), so much so that the rowers "considered it to be the least of their present difficulties to know their own death in advance, but they considered the greatest misfortune to be whatever those whom they had removed from the city would suffer at the hands of the barbarians, if they proved victorious" (2.36). Having explained the elements of the Athenians' flourishing political life, and having evoked the terror occasioned by the Persian king's arrival, Lysias made strikingly clear how much was at stake in the Athenians' "daring" and their "counsels": "Those men proved superior by far to all others in virtue (*kata tēn aretēn*), both in their counsels and in the risks of war" (2.40). In describing the Athenian character at this pivotal moment, Lysias stressed the Athenians' cognitive appreciation for the ideals for which they were fighting (2.36–37, 2.41, 2.42), their careful and accurate deliberations as to how most effectively to meet this cataclysmic threat (2.40, 2.41–42, 2.45–46), and their capacity to behave in an excellent way amid danger, because of their shared purposes and ideals (2.40, 2.41–42, 2.44, 2.47; cf. 2.64–65, 2.67–68).

Why were the Athenian democrats distinctively capable of thinking through their own ideals, of acting honorably amid dangers, and of realizing their own individual good in the process of contributing to the common good? To respond to this type of question, the funeral orations persistently returned to the theme of perfecting nature by means of the Athenians' democratic educational regime. Lysias argued that the fallen soldiers "were first trained in the noble deeds of their ancestors (*en tois tōn progonōn agathois*), and then, having become men, they preserved their fame and displayed their own excellence (*aretēn*)" (Lys. 2.69). In his funeral oration of 338 BC, to take another example, Demosthenes contends that the fallen heroes displayed their innate nobility on the battlefield only after receiving a noble education within the city (Dem. 60.16–17). Likewise, Hyperides reminded his audience that their fellow citizens, now fallen soldiers, were trained in moderation as children; "I think we all know," he argued, "that we raise children precisely for the purpose of making them brave; and, as for those who distinguish themselves in courage during battle, it is clear that they were raised well as children" (Hyp. 6.8).

In each case, the heroic Athenian dead had achieved a standard of excellence, having been trained within the city's educational regime to realize their natural promise. The speakers intended their audiences to emulate the dead soldiers in life and in death—that is, to internalize their example of human excellence, by comprehending it within a concrete, emotionally replete narrative. The funeral oration constituted a eudaimonistic practice because the audience was exhorted not only to emulate the fallen heroes, but also to understand in a fully articulate way precisely why their lives and deaths had been admirable. In short, Lysias' projected audience learned through his narratives and analysis that the active exercise of noble and admirable qualities was its own reward, that such activity was intrinsically meritorious and worthwhile. They came to see that attaining human excellence within their lives as a whole, as a unity, constituted their full growth and flourishing. These admirable accomplishments were made possible, as Lysias' oration demonstrated, only if citizens participated wholeheartedly in the Athenians' democratic institutions, practices, and modes of civic education.

To read the oration in this way is not to make the unrealistic claim that Athenians ignored the external products of their military and political success. To the contrary, Lysias argued that such extrinsic benefits were made truly advantageous because they were conferred in the right spirit and for the right reasons (2.70). Even so, in Lysias' representation, the Athenian heroes "thought that everything was of less account than nobility and excellence" (2.71); accordingly, they willingly (even if paradoxically) abandoned their own lives, because their circumstances and their own deliberately wrought self-understanding demanded as much, even up to the limit of depriving themselves of everything else that they recognized as good, such as their own families. Their heroic final act implied, as only such an awesome act of devotion can imply, the deep paradox that their own good somehow consisted in giving up everything they cherished—and in the related paradox that the external products for the sake of which they had acted, that is, the well-being of the city and their families, were somehow less important to them than the realization, in action, of their dedication to human excellence.

As we will discover in the next chapter, the Athenians resolved or at least mitigated these paradoxes by recognizing that their own good, understood most profoundly and fundamentally, consisted in their realization and expression of human excellence, even if their expression of courage or other virtues contingently involved their own deaths. The "goods" of family and democratic political life were not worth having, were not even good at all, somehow, unless they were founded on and sustained by the Athenians' excellences of character. Athenian democratic virtue was good in itself, independent of the existence of these other goods; but these other goods were dependent on virtue in that possessing them through improper or dishonorable means (such as selling the city to the Persian King, or entering a war out of fear or distorted judgments) would tarnish these goods to such an extent that they would no longer be worth having.[11] This way of thinking establishes an extraordinarily demanding standard for the achievement of admirable human conduct. Yet Lysias pursues this already ambitious standard to its utmost limit. He insists that the Athenian soldiers would never have acted shamefully, and thus risked losing their self-respect, even if the city's safety had depended on it. They would intentionally have risked the city if somehow the demands of nobility should have required it. The good life made possible by the democratic polis is simply not worth having, not even possible, unless it is also the life of nobility or excellence.

This is not an idea confined to the funeral orations of Pericles and Lysias. In fact, in the most famous passage from his most famous speech, *On the Crown*, Demosthenes elaborated upon the paradoxes of courage and self-sacrifice in precisely this way: "I wish to say something contrary to your expectations (*paradoxon*). And, by Zeus and the gods, please do not wonder at the extravagance of what I say, but consider it in a spirit of goodwill..." (18.199). Demosthenes asked his audience to imagine that they had known in advance that Athens would lose the battle of Chaeronea and would thus, once and for all, come under the power of Philip of Macedon (18.199). Demosthenes says that, despite the protests Aeschines would have made, even then the city could not have avoided going to war, out of a sense of honor, patriotic dedication, and concern for the future standing of the city (18.199–200).

In the course of making these seemingly counterintuitive arguments, Demosthenes invites the audience to consider how Athens could have looked visitors to the city in the eye if Philip had won and Athens had not fought for Greek freedom (18.201). Athens could only have survived with shame if the citizens had stood on the sidelines and accepted Philip as their unchallenged master. In the past, Athenians had never accepted material rewards and ignobly self-regarding safety from imperial powers such as Persia; they had always considered such choices to be intolerable and inconsistent with both their nature and their national character (18.203). The Athenians' ancestors had always striven for honor, primacy, and glory.

---

[11] Here one might compare what Bobonich 2002: e.g., 131–53 has called Plato's "dependency thesis," particularly with respect to Books 1 and 2 of the Platonic *Laws*.

They rejected "servile security" and "deemed worthy" only the prospect of living freely or dying (18.204–5).[12]

Democratic formulations of *eudaimonia* established a rigorous, though not impossible, standard of human attainment. Demosthenes' account of Athens's decision to fight Philip illustrates that the Athenians were, in their own self-understanding, and as the product of a long and thoughtful discursive history, ready to sacrifice the material well-being of the city for the sake of nobility. This "self-sacrifice" was not seen to be detrimental, however, to the properly understood interests of Athenian "selves." On the contrary, acting nobly was recognized to be the only way for the "self" to live well, that is, to live with well-founded self-respect or pride. As Lysias says, in conclusion, "So it it is right to judge those most flourishing (*eudaimonestatous*) who died having run the greatest and noblest risks; not entrusting themselves to chance, nor waiting for death to come on its own, but picking out the noblest death" (2.79). The Athenians maintained demanding ideals of excellence and flourishing, based on the city's long-term narratives with which they self-consciously and deliberately identified themselves. The Athenians had reflected upon what was best in their traditions and come to identify with distinctively democratic standards of excellence for sound reasons and in well-informed ways. It is the task of the next chapter to pursue these paradoxes in connection with certain criticisms of the ancient eudaimonistic outlook altogether.

---

[12] We should keep in mind that Demosthenes' account of the decision to fight does not correspond closely to his more pragmatic speeches before Chaeronea in favor of fighting Philip; whereas he had once been steely-eyed and focused on the city's narrowly construed military and economic interests, he presented Athens in retrospect as the embodiment of nobility and self-respecting leadership. In Demosthenes' speech *On the Crown*, therefore, we have a good example of the Athenians' ideological self-presentation, which corresponded only distantly to the Athenians' actual processes of decision-making. On this tension, see especially Yunis 2001: 16–17.

CHAPTER 15 | Eudaimonistic "Paradoxes" and Resolutions

THE DEMOCRATIC ATHENIANS, AND especially their leading orators, used the central concepts of eudaimonism—natural capacity, education, perfection, and virtue—to argue that Athenian democracy was superior to all other forms of regime (*politeia*). Democracy provided the material and political conditions, and the civic education, that best enabled citizens to flourish. Hyperides argued, for example, that *eudaimonia* derives from self-governance and is impossible in tyrannies (Hyp. 6.8, 15–17, 24–25, 28–29). This idea is critical here, because the Athenians held, in general, that the active, participatory, political life was the chief arena in which virtues could be cultivated and expressed. Citizens of other forms of political organization had limited opportunities to cultivate their natural capacities in this reflective and essentially political way. This difference is especially relevant to courage, because courage had always been one of the most unreflective and conservative virtues known in Greek culture at large (chapter 9). For this reason, courage was the virtue least likely to be questioned within ordinary political life.

Democratic education, as envisioned by the orators, enabled citizens not only to do intrinsically worthwhile things, and to lead intrinsically worthwhile lives, but also to see the point of such lives, and to understand what made those lives good. Athenian virtue depended on a rational understanding of the worth and importance of virtue, of what makes it good, of its "good-making" properties.[1] We have seen that only democracy, of all regimes, makes such an understanding possible, for two reasons. First,

---

[1] My understanding of these questions has been improved by the successful application of similar ideas to the Platonic *Laws*, in Bobonich 2002.

democracy's characteristic modes of "saying everything" (*pan-rhēsia*), of free deliberation, enriched the community's understanding of the intrinsic merits of virtue as a constituent of human flourishing. Second, these same deliberative modes dispersed such understanding widely throughout the community, so that individual citizens throughout Attica were capable of seeing the point of their exercise of virtue in their lives as a whole.[2]

Courage fit within the eudaimonistic framework both as an instrumental good and as an intrinsic good. The function of courage in its instrumental guise is perhaps more obvious. Through providing security for the city, and through encouraging citizens to speak out and to innovate, courage enabled the Athenians to live excellent or worthwhile lives within the democratic city: to enjoy the city's festivals, to participate politically, and to cultivate their worthwhile capacities of character and intellect. Hence, Pericles praised the city and its way of life by arguing that Athenians were "different from most people with respect to virtue" (2.40), by which he meant specifically generosity, friendship, and courage. Courage enabled the Athenians to become excellent, fully developed individuals: According to Pericles, "Each one of us presents a person that is independent and ready to take on the most various types of behavior, with every grace and exceptional versatility" (2.41). This sounds similar to the Platonic and Aristotelian accounts of human flourishing, except that Pericles, Lysias, and other Athenians drew these conclusions from a distinctively democratic context where free speech, free choice, and personal freedoms were of cardinal importance. Democratic flourishing combined human excellence with both public and private freedom.[3] Therein, to a large extent, lies the eudaimonistic account of the ends to which Athenian courage was directed, at least in its instrumental guise.

I say "to a large extent," however, because courage was virtuous not only in its instrumental capacity, but also as an intrinsically worthwhile feature of the developed human personality. No Athenian could be considered a respectable or meritorious individual without courage: a life without courage would be incomplete and inadequate in critical respects. We want now to explain this principle more completely, because, as we saw in the previous chapter, courage raises certain paradoxical questions. Why is courage intrinsically good and worthwhile, as the Athenians asserted, for courageous agents themselves? Is courage not strictly, and obviously, "another's

---

[2] On the diffusion of knowledge that took place through Athens's democratic institutions, see Ober 2008, with my discussion in chapter 3.
[3] I have discussed this distinctive combination more fully in Balot 2009b.

good," to adapt Thrasymachus' language from Plato's *Republic*? Isn't courage good for others and good for the city, while remaining extremely harmful to oneself, as the virtue most likely to get you killed? Examining the Athenian response to this ostensible paradox will enable us to deepen our understanding of the Athenians' eudaimonistic conception of courage, and to understand more clearly why their account has advantages over other frameworks.[4]

The democratic Athenians offered a variety of explanations for the goodness of courage. Courage is useful, even essential, you might think, for getting us all the things we desire in life—pleasure, wealth, power, reputation, and so on. This is the understanding of courage (or "manliness") offered by Callicles in Plato's *Gorgias* and by the Athenians in Thucydides' *History*.[5] But if we twist the knife, then we see quickly that this response is inadequate. If we could possess those external goods (pleasure, wealth, etc.) without being courageous, would we then consider it acceptable if our children, our friends, and so on, were not courageous? Obviously not. Everyone views courage as an admirable quality. We praise and reward the courageous, even if we sometimes dispute who is courageous and why. We want those we care about—our friends, our spouses, our children, ourselves—to be courageous, because we think it is good for them, not only for others.

Why is that? In what, precisely, does the goodness of courage consist for the courageous agent himself? The Athenians offered a distinctive response to this question. In the previous chapter, we examined the origins of the eudaimonistic ancient tradition within Athenian democratic culture. Now we will find that, in order to refine their particular interpretation of *eudaimonia*, the Athenians proposed that a good life must be constructed as a coherent narrative within a *politeia* that one could be proud of.[6] This implied the belief that a good life was a life well lived as a whole, within a

---

[4] Notice that the philosophical critique offered by Isocrates and Plato (chapters 6–7) is made on ground that they shared with the Athenians, i.e., eudaimonism. For a general discussion of "virtue ethics" and eudaimonism, see the outstanding treatment of Hursthouse 2012, which connects modern virtue theory to ancient virtue theory (particularly that of Aristotle and the Stoics), and lays out the chief objections and responses to those objections. Swanton 2003 provides an excellent account from the perspective of pluralism. My purpose in the present chapter is to connect the Athenian democratic ideology to these larger ethical discourses.

[5] For my own interpretation of Callicles along these lines, see Balot 2007. It is true that, under pressure from Socrates, Callicles eventually admits that he prizes courage or "manliness" for its own sake: see, for example, *Gorgias* 498a–499c, with Barney 2004 and Cooper 1999c.

[6] As we saw in chapter 10, the Athenians thought of their lives in narrative forms, as unities. In pointing this out, I am applying to the Athenian case an analysis that MacIntyre 1984: 204–25 has developed in other contexts.

community whose ideals one could endorse and respect—indeed, a community whose ideals one had helped to formulate and institutionalize. Embedded in such a political community, a naturally sociable being will be motivated to care for others.[7] If the individual is educated correctly by the regime, then this motivation to care for others will come to light not only as one dimension of an excellent character, but also as an inner necessity—as a drive that the citizen, being who he is, simply must carry out in order to avoid irreparable damage to his integrity, or to the coherence and meaningfulness of his life as a whole.

Contemporary Objections

Two objections might plague courage when viewed as an essential constituent of human flourishing. I will call the objections the "egoistic" objection and the "altruistic" objection. Both these terms, and the objections they embody, are anachronistic: they derive from specifically modern, "moral" traditions in which self-interest and morality are sharply opposed. By contrast, the ancient Greek and Roman traditions were "ethical" as opposed to "moral." The ancients focused on questions of character, education, social development, and practical reason, rather than the production of moral rules or lists of objective goods. As a result, they did not so firmly separate individual flourishing (or "happiness," so to speak) from questions of ethically appropriate behavior. I will risk using the moderns' language for the moment, because it will help to clarify the distinctiveness, and ultimately the superiority, I believe, of the ancient Athenian outlook.

Consider this question: why should I, Theodorus the Athenian, risk my life in defending the city? On the one hand, the democratic ideology says that courage is a component of my own flourishing. I might want to save the city because it is good for me to do so, either intrinsically or instrumentally. It is said that the goodness of going out to fight the invader consists in its being a constituent of my own flourishing as a human being (not to mention all the material and other benefits I will gain by saving the city). Therefore, I will try to save the city because acting courageously is good for me; it enables me to flourish or to acquire certain goods, pleasures, powers, and status. But surely, the critics will say, this is incorrect: I should

---

[7] The Athenian realities of care for others were complicated, however, and there is evidence that Athenians often idealized respect for limits between citizens rather than civic friendship; see Christ 2012: 50–68. For a different discussion of "altruism" in Athens, see Herman 2006: 348–59.

be trying to save the city because I care for the city, not because I care for myself in such a self-absorbed way. This is what I call the egoistic objection.[8]

This is related to an objection based on the idea of moral self-importance or self-indulgence. The critics' idea is that virtue—if it has intrinsic rather than merely instrumental worth—is less important than the goods it tries to realize out in the world. To imagine that virtue is more important than those goods—such as the safety of the city, or knowledge, or other forms of achievement—is to put things the wrong way round.[9] And the reason for this mistake, presumably, is that the individual cares more for his own development of virtue than for the goods that give virtue its rationale or point. Or, to take the point even farther, I might care more for displaying my own virtues than for saving the city. At the limit, I might even have such a distorted consciousness as to view the city's danger as positively good, in that it provides me with an opportunity to display my own virtue. As Bernard Williams has argued, though, if you think to yourself how pleased you are at your own display of virtue, and especially if you act virtuously precisely in order to display your own virtues, then you have had "one thought too many."[10] You are ethically self-absorbed.

On the other hand, the more typical case is that in which courage is called upon to place others first, even when doing so involves self-sacrifice. Courageous soldiers are supposed to try to save the city, even at the risk of their lives. It is true, as Tyrtaios once suggested, that, once on the battlefield, the courageous are more likely to survive than the cowardly (fr. 11.11–13 = Stob. 4.9.16). Nonetheless, it is dubious to infer that courageous fighters have a greater chance of survival than those, like the "bad Athenians," who simply deserted or who failed to answer the call to arms at all.[11] Courage sometimes requires the "supreme self-sacrifice," as the critics might say, that is, the sacrifice of one's own life. How then (the critics will ask) can anyone say that courage is good for me, especially in the case where I die through acting courageously? Can it be good for me to be extinguished, assuming that I am in good health and have reasonable life prospects at the moment of my death? In other words, is courage too altruistic

---

[8] For one statement of these objections, see (for example) Hurka 2001: 220–24, 232–33, with Hursthouse 2012.
[9] On virtue as a "lesser good," see Hurka 2001: 129–52.
[10] For the phrase, which was initially used in arguments against utilitarianism, see Williams 1981: 18.
[11] For an excellent discussion of Athenian deserters and other "reluctant conscripts," see Christ 2006: 45–87.

to fit within the eudaimonistic framework? Surely courage is sometimes very bad for me. This is what I will call the altruism objection.

Even so, according to the critics, this line of questioning does not imply that I should avoid courage altogether. No: the critics also admire courage. Rather, this line of questioning implies that although courageous action does not necessarily, or even often, contribute to the overall good of the courageous agent himself, it does nonetheless contribute to the good of others, or even to the sum total of "goodness" in the world altogether, as certain philosophers assert.[12] Its contribution to the good lives of others, or to "goodness" altogether, gives courage its point—despite the possible destruction of the courageous agent.

These objections agree in emphasizing the self-sacrificial character of most virtues, including courage.[13] The egoistic objection holds that eudaimonistic conceptions of courage are not adequately self-sacrificial; the altruistic objection holds that, while eudaimonism appropriately regards courage as self-sacrificial, eudaimonism cannot for that very reason explain the goodness of courage for the agent himself. Within the Athenians' eudaimonistic theory, virtuous, and in particular courageous, people are often "selfless" (as opposed to "selfish") in that they frequently dedicate themselves to the good of others, in acts of generosity, justice, and friendship; but they are "selfless" in a virtuous, not a self-effacing or self-destructive, manner.[14] Their selfless activities, undertaken in a wholehearted, sincere, and enthusiastic way, constitute at least in part their goodness as human beings, their flourishing as members of this particular species. What makes their actions good for them is that these actions embody, along certain dimensions or within certain domains, their excellence as human beings. What makes their actions good for others (such as their families and fellow citizens) is, obviously, that their courageous behavior contributes to the security, prosperity, and opportunities of others. One need not, and in fact should not, ask what makes their actions good *tout court*.[15]

---

[12] See, e.g., Hurka 2001; Hooker 1996. Compare, from another angle, the criticisms of Samons 2004: 197, which also reflect precisely the noneudaimonistic dichotomies that the Athenians were trying to transcend: "Pericles described a system geared to produce a citizen who placed the advantage of the state over the virtue of the individual—or rather, a state in which acting for the (perceived) good of the state was the highest virtue.... Pericles emphasizes this utilitarian role of citizens when he encourages parents of the deceased to have more children" (197).

[13] Cf. Annas 2008: 205–6.

[14] On worries about virtue theory as "self-effacing," see Hurka 2001: 246–47; Keller 2007. For a helpful response to these worries, see Pettigrove 2011, with Annas 2008, which concentrates on the charge of egoism.

[15] On the controversies over "good" versus "good for," see the excellent discussion of Kraut 2011. Other investigations of the question include Hurka 1987, Foot 1985, and Williams 1995.

What makes this response possible is that the ancient democrats' notion of the "self" was different from the one used by modern critics. The ancient Athenians sought to reduce any unnecessarily sharp distinctions between the individual and the community. They envisioned the individual as a more "relational" being, whose "self" was constituted not atomistically, but socially and politically.[16] In fact, as the funeral orations and other political traditions make clear, Athenian individuals constituted themselves as members of the city, who "shared in" the regime (*metechein tēs politeias*), identified with its traditions and practices, and made sense of their lives as participatory Athenian democrats, as members of particular demes and localities, and as standard bearers of particular roles within their families, neighborhoods, and religious associations.[17]

Whether or not our exploration of this theoretical conflict yields a decisive outcome, though, the foregoing objections are important ones. As we saw in chapter 1, a central problem with courage, as it is understood in our own day, is that it seems to require individuals to sacrifice themselves for vague abstractions (such as democracy or freedom) that often have little concrete meaning in the lives of soldiers or of the people for whom they fight. Or, alternatively, it seems to require individuals to fight for their fellow citizens—"others" who, in the modern democratic landscape, share only the barest minimum of understanding and ethos with one another, and whose "goods" have been relativized to such an extent as to render the soldier's self-sacrifice meaningless or worse. The "egoistic" and especially the "altruistic" objections make explicit at an ethical level the problems we have canvassed at a political level. This should come as no surprise, because, even if contemporary democratic citizens do not acknowledge the close connections between ethical thought and political life, these connections run very deep.

My hypothesis is that, if we continue to think of the soldier's "self-sacrifice" merely as altruism or merely as patriotic "duty" or merely as part of a felicific calculus or a social contract, then we will never make

---

[16] The best contemporary discussion of relationality comes, perhaps not surprisingly, from feminism: see Nedelsky 2011.

[17] On "sharing in" the regime, see Ostwald 1996. This is not to say that the ancient Athenians failed to recognize a distinction between individual self-interest and the interests of others: as Christ 2006: 15–44 amply shows, the "bad citizen" was for ancient Athenians paradigmatically the "selfish" citizen, i.e., the citizen who privileged his own "private interests" (*ta idia*) over the common interests of his polis (*ta koina*). It was precisely this distinction which the Athenians tried to transcend in constructing their eudaimonistic framework—to explain, before the fourth-century philosophers, that being just, generous, and courageous is good not only for my community, but also for me, because of my natural sociality. Herman 2006: 392–95 applies rational choice theory to these questions.

sense of courage as a virtue that individuals feel called to exhibit, for themselves, both as a constituent of their own good, and as a contribution to the common good of the community in which they have a share. However, the Athenians' eudaimonistic framework will help us to make progress on this question.

Why Be Courageous? The View from Democratic Athens

We might well be tempted to charge the Athenians with holding not so much an egoistic or an overly altruistic conception of courage, but rather a destructively "ideological" view of courage. Everyone can agree that it is good for the city that its citizens should be willing to give up their lives for its sake. This should make us suspicious of the idea that courage is good for me, even when it requires me to die. Isn't this idea a repugnantly ideological one? Think of Robert Graves's line, quoting Horace, about the old lie: *dulce et decorum est pro patria mori*. Perhaps the "goodness" of dying for one's fatherland is a deception that destroys many lives in order to promote the interests of the few. From this perspective, there is no reason to believe that it is good for me to die in order to secure a good life for a politician sitting at a comfortable desk in Washington, DC. Courage therefore deserves an ideological critique, since the rhetoric of courage is nothing more than a sinister mechanism of social control.

Should I therefore undertake a complex project of "unmasking" courage? Should I teach my children to dodge the draft rather than to fight for the city? Is the eudaimonistic framework as a whole simply an ideological tool of the city informed by the agenda of a ruling elite?[18] In asking such questions, we would seem to offer not only good reasons to think that courage is bad for me (it might get me killed), but also a theory of error that explains why, despite the risks involved, people persist in holding that courage is good for me (that it suits the elite to persuade ordinary citizens to think so, and thus ordinary people are socialized to have false beliefs in this regard). What does the Athenians' eudaimonistic ideology have to say in response to these objections?

---

[18] In its rejection of the characterization of human beings as naturally sociable beings whose good lies in the exercise of social (and other) virtues, this line of thinking bears certain resemblances to Leo Strauss's interpretation of Plato's *Republic* (see Strauss 1964); and it illustrates the unnoticed alliance of Strauss and those such as Hurka 2001 and Hooker 1996, who all subscribe to the arguably misguided modern opposition between "self-interest" and "morality."

Consider Herodotus' story of Tellus the Athenian. Herodotus is describing Solon's visit to the court of Croesus. Croesus fancies that because of his wealth he is enjoying the greatest *eudaimonia* known to humankind. Solon disagrees: in his view, Tellus the Athenian is the most *olbios* man. (Later, in discussing Cleobis and Biton, the Argives who are second "happiest," Solon uses the terminology of *eudaimonia* interchangeably with that of being *olbios*; so I will assume that when Solon refers to an *olbios* man, such as Tellus, he also thinks of Tellus as a *eudaimōn* man). Here is the passage from Herodotus:

> Croesus wondered at what he had said and gave a vehement reply: "In what way do you judge that Tellus is the most prosperous?" Solon said that Tellus came from a flourishing city and had noble and courageous children. He saw that they all had children themselves, and all of these survived. He was well off in life, as we reckon these things, and the end of his life was very illustrious: for when the Athenians came to fight against their neighbors in Eleusis, he brought them aid, routed the enemy, and died in a very splendid way. The Athenians buried him at public expense right where he fell and honored him greatly (Hdt. 1.30).

This brief passage does not call forth all the elements of democratic courage or eudaimonism discussed by the ancient orators, historians, and dramatists. But Solon emphasized the Athenians' collective burial of their fallen soldiers at public expense, along with their public honoring of Tellus; and in these ways he (anachronistically) evoked the classical Athenians' public funeral ritual. In fact, Solon is evoking, in a necessarily foreshortened way, features of the Athenians' "equality of commemoration"—an important respect in which the Athenians tied their conception of courageous behavior to democratic equality (see chapter 8). In what follows, I elaborate upon Solon's narrative of Tellus by filling in the details of his motivations and purposes, where necessary, through calling to mind the Athenian ideology of courage as we know it primarily from the Attic orators.

Solon represents the best human life as a life thickly embedded in familial and social relations and as intelligible as a complete whole, in a narrative that made sense over the course of the entire life cycle. The goodness of Tellus' life consists, in part at least, of his membership in and his identification with a successful family and a prosperous city. He had developed the virtues associated with fatherhood, having raised good and noble children, and those of citizenship, maintaining close relationships with his fellow citizens and helping the city to prosper.[19] Given his natural human capacities and his life prospects, this constituted a life that he could be proud of, a good human life; and Solon agreed.

These observations help us to respond to the criticisms sketched above. Imagine that Tellus had had to die in order to save his family—if, for example, a thief had broken into his house in the middle of the night. Upon hearing a thief attack his children, Tellus' first thought would surely have been: get up and save the children! His reason for acting this way would have been his desire to save the children—because he cared for them, not because he cared for his own virtue. A similar point applies to Tellus' membership in the ethical life of the city. When his fellow citizens were fighting at Eleusis, his first and only thought was (should have been) that they needed help and he was in a position to assist; and he acted wholeheartedly on their behalf, without hesitation. Admittedly, Herodotus' presentation of Tellus is brief; but, in considering the philosophical plausibility of the Athenian ideology, it is at least reasonable to apply to a good citizen the motives normally attributed to Athenian soldiers by that ideology. Specifically, in constructing their ideology, the orators always emphasized the citizens' willingness or readiness or zeal to fight and their lack of hesitation and lack of concern to calculate the hazards of war (see especially chapters 2 and 4).

Thus, by extension at least, we can say that Tellus' courageous behavior on the battlefield was far from morally self-indulgent. He did not stop short to think about how he would look to others or to himself or about developing his own virtue. Instead, he thought only about the safety of his fellow citizens—and that, and only that, according to the Athenian tradition, was the right thought to have at the time. Tellus was motivated by his care for the city and implicitly for his fellow citizens. Tellus' story, understood in this fashion, provides the democratic eudaimonist with a helpful response to the charge of egoism.

The Athenian orators used similar concepts in their explanations of the "good-making" features of Athenian courage. For example, Lycurgus drew a contrast between the cowardice of Leocrates and the courage of those Athenians who defended the city after Chaeronea:

> But in those times no man of any age failed to offer himself for the city's safety, when the countryside was giving up its trees, the dead their graves

---

[19] Christ 2010 has argued convincingly that in reality altruistic behavior was mostly lacking among Athenian citizens; but we can find evidence for generosity toward others as an ideal in a number of texts: Thuc. 2.40, Eur. *Suppl.* 304–313, Lys. 2.11–16 and passim, Isocr. 12.69, Isocr. 4.53, Isocr. 4.61–62, and 4.80; cf. Mills 1997: 63–65.

and the temples their arms. For some took care of the construction of walls, others dug ditches, and still others worked on palisades. Everyone in the city was active (Lyc. 1.44).

Or, more grandiosely, recall what Lysias said:

> So it it is right to judge those most flourishing (*eudaimonestatous*) who died having run the greatest and noblest risks; not entrusting themselves to chance, nor waiting for death to come on its own, but picking out the noblest death (2.79).

The Athenian ideology held that the democratic Athenians, as warriors, did not stop to calculate the material risks of war, but rather went forward in order to preserve the freedom of the city without a thought for themselves. This illustrates the "selflessness" of Athenian courage. As they understood themselves, such Athenians were far from self-indulgent; they did not have "one thought too many" about their own virtue. If there is an Athenian theory of eudaimonistic virtue, then it is implausible to consider that theory vulnerable to the charge of egoism.

The Athenians were aware of what we might call "egoism," to be sure: Lycurgus' Leocrates exemplifies the selfish or "bad" Athenian who placed his own private good or affairs (*ta idia*) over those of the common good (*ta koina*). But Tellus and the other Athenians were giving up their lives to save their fellow citizens, because it was the good or noble thing to do. Furthermore, they sincerely wanted those they cared about, such as their own children, to exhibit the same virtues, because they believed that the good life for their children was impossible apart from their children's properly socialized care for the city. Given their social formation within the city, such Athenians could not live with self-respect otherwise. In moments of reflection, they could be led to see their own fulfillment or perfection as lying in such noble behaviors. Yet they saw no need, and in fact there is no need, to accept the modern opposition between egoism and altruism, in interpreting the relationship between the individual and his community. The Athenians offer us a picture of lives lived well, both inside and out, in the absence of that distinction.[20]

---

[20] In one of the most widely cited critiques of eudaimonism, Hurka 2001 argues that the eudaimonistic agent is either egoistic (in ways we have already discussed) or self-effacing (in that he can resist the charge of egoism only by avoiding any reference to his own fundamental basis for action, i.e., his own good, in answering the question of his basic motivations for action). For

What about the altruistic objection? How can Tellus' sacrifice of his own life be considered good for him, in either the hypothetical case of the "home invader" or in the Herodotean case of the battle of Eleusis? The Athenian eudaimonist holds that it is good for Tellus—and even good for him overall or "all things considered"—to protect his family or city courageously, even if he dies in the process, even if he knows in advance that he will die in the process.[21] Others take a different view. Kantians would say that individuals are required, by the moral law that they legislate to themselves, to save the city while sacrificing themselves, even if this obviously undermines their happiness. Others maintain that moral virtue is beneficial to the moral agent as a subcategory of achievement, implying that there is nothing special about moral virtue as compared to other things that make us "happy."[22] Perhaps the greatest net benefit to the agent lies precisely in not being moral, because moral behavior, such as courageously giving up one's life, often involves self-sacrifice.[23]

---

effective answers to different facets of this charge, see Swanton 2003; Kraut 2007; Annas 2008; Kraut 2011; Hursthouse 2012. I would add that in his own "recursive" account, Hurka has an impossibly difficult time explaining why anything is good *for me;* he is caught on the horns of the very dilemma that supposedly undermines eudaimonism; on the question of "good" and "good for," see Williams 1995 and Foot 1985, *contra* Hurka 1987. For, according to Hurka's logic, if the agent himself refers to the recursive account in explaining why he behaves morally, then he too must be egoistic. But if Hurka's agent doesn't refer to the recursive account in order to explain his motivations for acting, then he too will be "self-effacing" in that he can't or won't refer, as a reason for his action, to the account of why moral behavior is good for him. If the response is that it is simply "good" *tout court* for the agent to behave morally, without reference to the agent's own good, then Hurka's agent is both self-effacing (in that he fails to motivate his own actions with reference to his own understanding of what is good) and confused (in that "good" as opposed to "good for" is an empty set). Moreover, Hurka's view seems to be susceptible to the ideological critique mentioned above in connection with Robert Graves's poetry: Hurka argues that it is intrinsically good for me to love "the good," in general, but he fails entirely to explain why is it good *for me* to love "the good." (Imagine this alarming statement: it is intrinsically good for me to love "the state," in general. Whoever hears such a statement in the contemporary world will want to know, then, why it is *good for me* to love the state.) On these and other criticisms of Hurka, see Annas 2008; Hursthouse 2012; on the question of whether the very idea of "the good" *tout court* is intelligible, see Kraut 2011. Along with Kraut, I doubt it.

[21] Compared to their modern counterparts, the Athenian eudaimonists were in this sense intransigent. The firmness of the ancient Athenian position becomes especially clear when we consider that even Richard Kraut, perhaps the foremost contemporary advocate of a "neo-ancient" form of eudaimonism, softens their claim by arguing that courage or honesty is one good among many for the agent, although it may cause great harm to the agent, too: see Kraut 2007: 191–96.

[22] Hooker 1996.

[23] Cf. Hurka 2001. As Hurka says, "On this more plausible view, the extra virtue involved in pursuing others' greater pleasure can be outweighed in one's own life by the loss of pleasure for oneself" (55).

What is hidden in these objections is a narrow and inflexible understanding of self-interest. By contrast with their modern counterparts, the Athenians worked with an enlarged notion of the self or of "self-interest," which takes us outside ourselves and identifies us and our good with others and their good. We can clarify the situation by breaking it down concretely into its elements. Think of the case of the home invader. The unfortunate fact is that Tellus and his family are the victims of bad luck. It would be better for him and his family if his home had not been invaded at all. It would be better for Tellus if the Athenians had not had to fight the Eleusinians at all. Courage exists precisely in order to address difficult and dangerous circumstances, often circumstances of bad luck; and, as the case of warfare shows, "bad luck" characterizes the world in which we live.

In these circumstances of bad luck, consequentialists, such as Hurka, Hooker, and others, would theorize the agent's situation with reference to costs and benefits. They would hold that by acting courageously Tellus suffers great harm, that is, death. On the other hand, he might be doing even greater good for others. Overall, therefore, it is good for him to act courageously. He maximizes the "amount" of "goodness" that is present in the world. But this type of calculation is unsatisfactory and even dangerous, when it is not downright unintelligible. To begin with, it is susceptible to the "one thought too many" objection, in that the most appropriate response for Tellus is simply to react to the Eleusinians' attack or to the home invader without calculating the costs, in the clear understanding that he is carrying out what virtue or excellence requires. More importantly, certain agents will calculate that, based on the consequences, it is better to live than die—for example, if the agent seems to himself "likely" to go on to do great good in the world, after a certain terrible episode has passed. But that is an ugly calculation—one that no decent person could tolerate.[24] As Kant (usually no friend of eudaimonism[25]) saw clearly, such calculations utterly degrade the agent's moral worth.

By contrast, no eudaimonist could possibly say that Tellus would be better off hiding under his bed while his wife and children were being murdered, nor could any eudaimonist possibly say that Tellus would be better off deserting Athens, like Leocrates and other "bad" Athenians. No eudaimonist could agree that Tellus has any motivation whatsoever to hide under his bed: the very idea should not be tempting, nor should it figure

---

[24] Cf. Williams' discussion of a similar case in his famous study of (his character) "Gauguin" (Williams 1976: 118–120).
[25] See Wood 2001.

into a calculus. The virtuous Tellus will not do any calculations in this situation. He will immediately move to save his children and fellow citizens.

On the other hand, we are the ones trying to understand whether this act is good for Tellus, in retrospect. As external observers, after the fact, we must acknowledge that at that moment Tellus' life prospects had become severely limited by chance. As the Athenians recognized, even virtuous agents are subject to bad luck; and their lives can go less well, or even badly, if they are subjected to severely bad luck. The Athenians did not believe that the wise man can be happy on the rack or that virtue is the only good or a good that is sufficient, all by itself, to produce the good life. Tellus' choices are to hide under his bed and save himself or to die trying to save his family or city, and either choice involves loss.

It seems obvious that no decent person should weigh the hazards of the situation. Given his understandable preexisting commitments, that is, given his dignified life narrative as parent, spouse, and citizen, Tellus should try to save his family or his city without hesitation—"zealously," as Lysias' Mantitheus said (chapter 10). And this is good for him (not to mention good for his family and the city), in these extremely trying circumstances, because it is the only way that his life will make sense. Since he is a social being whose "self" is defined by his relations with family and citizens, and since those relations make sense only if the individuals concerned care deeply about one another, Tellus' life would make no sense if he acted in a cowardly way. He is better off dead, as the Athenians thought, than surviving and living an incoherent life. That incoherent life would be filled with the shame of knowing that he had abandoned everything that made his life meaningful. His life would be "broken" in that case, whatever else happened, and whatever else he might go on to do. His life would be bad for him. On the other hand, his life would make sense as a whole if he acted courageously, whether he lived or died; and the final, heroic act would confirm the goodness of his character. To borrow Hegelian terminology, it would give that meaningful life "reality."

We gain confirmation of these points if we imagine the self-image of any decent person who, in a moment of cowardice, had run away or hidden under his bed. He would regret his action and wish for the opportunity to redeem himself, even if that were to mean certain death. This is the point, in fact, of Herodotus' story of Aristodemus the Spartan, who was absent from the Battle of Thermopylae in suspicious circumstances (7.229–231), and who craved death with distinction at the Battle of Plataea in order to gain release from his shame (9.71). Aristodemus' single-minded desire for redemption indicates that those who save themselves in dishonorable ways suffer from intolerable shame after the fact. They have acted in such a way as to render meaningless all the commitments that had constituted the meaningfulness of their life thus far.

In a famous passage from Demosthenes' *On the Crown*, the orator points out the seemingly paradoxical nature of courageous behavior resulting in death. He resolves the apparent paradox by pointing to the coherence of the Athenians' lives as a whole. As we saw in chapter 14, Demosthenes argued that the Athenians had never accepted material rewards or safety from the Persians; such choices were intolerable, because they were inconsistent with both their nature and their national character (18.203). The Athenians' ancestors had always striven for honor, rejected "servile security," and "deemed worthy" only the prospect of living freely or dying (18.204–5).[26]

In these ways Demosthenes brought out clearly the importance of self-respect in explaining the Athenians' willingness to live up to the demands of virtue. The Athenians maintained a conception of themselves based on the long-term narratives of the city, with which they self-consciously and deliberately identified themselves. In their public deliberations, they had reflected upon what was best in the Athenians' civic traditions and come to identify with it. Demosthenes' argument is that, in such circumstances, the Athenians would not have, indeed could not have, purchased the well-being of the city or its inhabitants through doing something shameful. The reason is that otherwise the Athenians' lives would not have made sense; they would have been psychically incoherent. The city has no well being apart from nobility. This explains why the Athenians' so-called self-sacrifice was not, despite appearances, detrimental to the properly understood interests of Athenian "selves." On the contrary, acting nobly was recognized to be the only way for the "self" to live well, that is, to live with well-founded self-respect and thus with psychic coherence.

The ancient philosophers' responses to similar questions tend to fall back on the ideas I have just considered—ideas that we can now see as originating in democratic ideology: that a coward's life is not worth living and, more importantly, that properly motivated virtuous behavior is good for the agent himself, given our nature as sociable beings. Our

---

[26] Cf. Hdt. 8.144. For a reading of this material that emphasizes the gap between Athenian self-representation and strategic decision making, see Christ 2012: 171–76. Hunt 2010: 182–84, on the other hand, stresses the harmony between the Athenians' national narratives and the city's overriding self-interests, particularly with reference to *On the Crown*.

good consists in the appropriate care that we actively show to others—for example, through protecting our families and the city—because such is the activity of our perfected, worthwhile natural capacities.

But the democratic Athenians added something philosophically interesting to this picture, especially for us as time-traveling moderns. The Athenians envisioned the final act of courage as part of a long-term narrative that not only covered a single lifetime, but also manifested continuity over the lifetime of the city. The entirety of a citizen's life was flourishing so long as he actively exercised the social virtues. This is why Pericles said of the fallen soldiers in 430 BC, "Their life has been measured out equally to be happy in (*eneudaimonēsai*) and to die in (*enteleutēsai*)" (Thuc. 2.44.1). Despite the Athenian soldiers' unfortunate circumstances, they had steadfastly held on to the eudaimonistic narrative that made sense of their lives, without interruption. If, on the other hand, these soldiers had given up on the city's narratives, which they had internalized and actively endorsed as individuals, then their lives would no longer have made sense. Their lives would have been measured out unequally.

These ideas are closely connected to the Athenians' deliberative practices. The democratic Athenians had constructed particular traditions, had discussed their political lives with reference to the demands of virtue, and had reflected on their own decisions in all the democracy's public forums, including the Assembly, the law courts, and the theater. As Aeschines (3.245) stated most clearly, these practices of public reflection and decision making constituted an education of character for Athenians, particularly as they were growing up and learning to be citizens, but also throughout their lives, even during adulthood. This process of character formation went all the way down. The Athenians internalized particular ideals and distinctive notions of virtue and the ends of the regime; they shared a character and an ethos. As a result, having been habituated as they were, and having reasoned about their public education self-consciously, they were subject to the necessities of the character they had chosen. As men with a certain character and particular ideals instilled by the city, they could do nothing other than fight to the death, provided that they wanted to bring their lives to a satisfactory conclusion.

Given the history of psychological formation envisioned in the epitaphic speeches and in Athenian ideology generally, their characters embodied an inner necessity to act in particular ways guided by the city's table of virtues and its canons of shame, honor, and self-respect. Acting in a cowardly way or choosing material prosperity at this culminating moment would not have been a simple choice; the soldier's "choice" was not the autonomous rational "preference" of modern utilitarianism.[27] Rather, it was akin to (indeed perhaps originative of) the Aristotelian notion of *prohairesis* as a well-informed desire for that which is within reach (see especially chapter 4). The soldiers' desire to behave courageously was deliberate in the sense that they had thought through the demands of courage in the city's "public conversations," and they had self-consciously formed themselves psychologically so as to be ready to confront death when the need to do so arose. What had originally begun as a choice of the citizenry, and a social formation of its young, emerging citizens, resulted in a necessity to act in accordance with the ethical character that had been so constructed.

These considerations show, I think, that the Athenians had a plausible explanation of the goodness of courage, even when courage required death. The Athenians were motivated to act courageously because they pursued great and noble ends that existed outside themselves, such as the free, flourishing lives of their democratic fellow citizens and the freedom of all Greece. As they themselves saw, they were far from self-absorbed or egoistic. And yet they were immune to the altruistic objection, too, because they expressed in action a fitting culmination of their entire ethical education and way of life. Without doing so, their lives would have failed to make sense, and they would have experienced the deep regret of Aristodemus and the hypothetically cowardly Tellus—or even, as Bernard Williams has shown, of the Sophoclean Ajax.[28] Instead, the Athenians could die with well-founded pride, which is a great good in itself, because it represents an appropriate attitude toward a life well lived.

This account will be unattractive only if we take an implausibly narrow view of what counts as Tellus' own good or interests, or if we are obsessively focused on the continuation of life as a biological function. If we must use the vocabulary of self-interest, then we could say that by acting courageously Tellus furthers his own interests by furthering the interests of his family and his city; "self-interest," one might say, is an elastic concept. But this vocabulary obfuscates the main point, which is that Tellus' saving of his family and his city was not motivated by a calculation of "interests," much less of "self-interest." The entire picture, and with it our ethical vocabulary, must change, because we need to describe individuals whose "selves" are thickly embedded in, and differently constituted by, their social worlds. Tellus' view of the "self" goes beyond his merely individual

---

[27] Cf. Rusten 1989: 160–62.
[28] Williams 1993: 73–74, 85–86.

self, in a way that Hegel captured when he said, "Hence, in a family, one's frame of mind is to have self-consciousness of one's individuality within this unity as the absolute essence of oneself, with the result that one is in it not as an independent person but as a member" (*Philosophy of Right* 158).

The same point applies to Tellus' relationship to the city. The welfare of those fellow citizens was constitutive of his own good or interests, in that his understanding of his "self" was inextricably tied to, even constituted by, his relations to those others. From an ethical standpoint, he was, and correctly understood himself to be, a being with, for, and in relation to other beings, none of whose "good" or "flourishing" could exist independent of that of the others. Demosthenes made this point in *On the Crown*, when he evoked the praiseworthiness of the Athenians' ancestors who fought during the Persian Wars:

> Each one of them thought that he had been born not only to his father and to his mother, but also to his fatherland. But what is the difference? That the one who believes that he was born only to his parents awaits death at the appointed time, as it comes by itself; but the one who considers himself born also to his fatherland will be willing to die in order not to see it enslaved, and he will suppose that those outrages and signs of dishonor, which it is necessary to bear in an enslaved polis, are more awful than death (18.205).

We must be careful that the charge of egoism does not somehow creep back in. A critic might say: this explanation shows why, all over again, virtues as the eudaimonist describes them are in fact egoistic, in that the virtuous agent aims at the good of others which is (after all) constitutive of his own good.

Yet the objection no longer applies in the damaging way in which it is intended. Part of the goodness of Tellus' character consists in his understanding himself properly as a relational or social being. To call him "selfish" or "egoistic" now carries no sting, because he has socialized the self and its goods in such a way as to embody a just and proportionate assessment of his sociality and the importance of others in his life. In Richard Kraut's terminology, that is a positive, mature development of certain worthwhile natural human capacities.[29] Equally, this explanation insulates the Athenians from the altruistic objection: in avoiding the unnecessary contrast between self-interest and morality, the Athenians explain why

---

[29] Kraut 2007; cf. Ober 2007.

acting courageously for the city, even to the point of death, is good for anyone who does so, but not in either an altruistic or an egoistic sense.

I want to conclude with a final point about Tellus the Athenian and his Athenian descendants. Solon emphasizes the life narrative of Tellus, including even the life cycle of his family over the two generations that succeeded him. Solon provides a sparing narrative of a good life that must end at some time. The story implies that we should not be invested in the length of our lives or in the pleasurable (much less painful) continuation of our bodily or psychological experiences. In the light of Tellus' story, it is easier to imagine why a shorter, better life is better for me than a longer, worse life. In the circumstances, Tellus' life was necessarily shorter, because only by dying courageously could he complete his life in a way that made sense of all his earlier devotion to and care for his family and fellow citizens. As Socrates said to Callicles, "But, blessed man, look at whether the noble and good is not something other than to preserve life and to be preserved. For a true man, at any rate, must let go of the question of how long he will live, and he must not be too attached to his life. He should entrust these matters to the god..." (Pl., *Gorg.* 512d-e).

We are led thereby to another theory of error, this time one that supports the eudaimonistic outlook and poses a challenge to its rivals. Anyone who cannot grasp the intrinsic goodness (both for the agent and for others) of the short life expressive of human excellence, in highly special and often adverse circumstances, would seem to be overly, even viciously, dedicated to the continuation of mere life as opposed to being virtuously dedicated to the ideals that individuals such as Tellus stood for. They are like Croesus, who equated the good with material goods, such as his extraordinary wealth, which was only instrumentally good for satisfying desires of the body. At the same time, we should be clear that, to make the best sense of this framework, the fallen soldiers had to be fighting not simply for the mere lives and material prosperity of their fellow citizens or families, but rather, and more importantly, in order to give their fellow citizens the opportunity to flourish by developing *their* natural capacities. This would be the best way to show appropriate care for them.[30]

---

[30] Note that in the *City of God* (X.7) there is an Augustinian parallel to this type of care: the angels care for human beings properly by encouraging them to love God.

The funerary orators envisioned the fallen heroes' lives as part of a general life cycle within the democratic city, which provides an education and nurture from birth onward and culminates in the fully developed virtues of manhood. The outcome of this process was the development, or even perfection, of the citizens' natural capacities for virtue. On the life cycle lived within the city, consider Demosthenes' statement:

> I will try, though, to order my speech in a way that corresponds to the life of these men. From the beginning these men were outstanding in all their studies, practicing what was suitable to each stage of their lives, in a way that pleased all those it was necessary to please—their parents, their friends, their relatives. Therefore, as though they recognized footprints, the memory of their friends and relatives now carries to these men every hour in fond recollection, finding many reminders of times when they knew clearly that these were the best young men. When they arrived at manhood, they made their nature well known not only to their fellow citizens, but also to all men (Dem. 60.15-17).

In Demosthenes' evaluative language, the city renders the citizens' lives orderly, nurturing them from birth onward to the fullest expression of nobility in manhood.

The order (*taxis*) cultivated by the city was internalized by the soldiers and maintained psychologically up to the point of their death. They could not abandon their defining commitments without diminishing the psychological order of their lives. The only remaining question is whether the Athenian commitment to courage implies a commitment to bellicosity and, if so, whether it does so intrinsically or contingently. It would be most self-consistent, I think, if the Athenians should argue that the living may and should wish for more peaceful times. In that case, the courageous choice of death would be only hypothetically or conditionally or contingently the culmination of good Athenian lives, the condition being the omnipresent threat of war. Should peace become a genuine human possibility, then it would be most powerful for the democratic eudaimonists to abandon the warlike virtues altogether, or at least strive to put them to more peaceful uses (e.g., maintaining safe parks and schools for our children, or courageously saving the victims of natural disaster; cf. chapter 16 for further reflections on this transformation of courage). But one might well suspect that the Athenians themselves, as we know them, would not have taken their commitment to *eudaimonia* or self-consistency quite this far.

Conclusion: The Hard Edges of *Aretē* and *Eudaimonia*

Athenian citizens internalized, both cognitively and emotionally, distinctively democratic models of excellence through participating in the political activities of the city. By fostering these democratic excellences as intrinsically worthwhile ends of human action, the democratic city enabled its citizens to flourish as human beings—and to do so more fully, they plausibly claimed, than other cities. To adapt Aristotle's language to our purposes, the Athenians had less interest in "mere life" than in meeting the demanding standards of *eudaimonia* and *aretē* as they understood them—and, barring that, they committed themselves to abandoning their political community altogether.

"Virtue" and "happiness," our contemporary translations of *aretē* and *eudaimonia*, often fail to do justice to the severity and rigor of Athenian notions of excellence and flourishing. They are not easily relocated within the ancient framework that I have tried to lay bare. Be that as it may, democratic Athens exemplifies the possibility that democratic freedom and equality can be rendered compatible with thick and demanding standards of excellence and flourishing espoused at the center of the public square. In light of our own prevailing assumptions about state neutrality, civility, and toleration, it is especially helpful to entertain such examples.

Yet democratic Athens offers us no blueprints for political action. We cannot re-live the ancient Athenian experience, nor should we want to. Nostalgia for the ancient past is as harmful as Arendtian "polis envy" (to borrow Michael Walzer's phrase). Instead, our time travel to democratic Athens represents a thought experiment. By reconsidering the ancient Athenian example, we grasp more adequately the limitations of our own prevailing horizons. We come to see, I think, that our own categories and preconceptions constitute decisive, if narrow or one-sided, answers to fundamental and perennial questions. Through their own uncompromising pursuit of *eudaimonia* and *aretē* as political goals, the democratic Athenians force us to interrogate our own assumptions. Not all the interesting political questions have been adequately or definitively answered.

CHAPTER 16 | Conclusion
Three Challenges

I CONCLUDE BY EXAMINING three major challenges to the Athenian democratic model of courage. The Spartans posed the most important practical challenge, in that Sparta was, among all Greek cities, most renowned for its courage. How, then, should we compare Spartan and Athenian courage? Second, Plato posed the most important philosophical challenge to the Athenian model; it is worth exploring whether it is Plato (and his character Socrates) or the Athenians who have a more adequate conception of courage. Finally, certain modern theorists, including Alexis de Tocqueville, have charged democracy either with promoting a leveling or reduction of courage or with promoting an excessively bellicose and macho form of courage; and I want to investigate whether and to what extent this charge is true and damaging when leveled against democratic Athens. This investigation will lead us to our final reflections on the challenges of democratic courage.

Spartan and Athenian Courage Compared

If the Athenian democracy helped to transform the traditional belligerency of "manly courage," then were the Athenians more courageous than others in battle? It is hard to avoid wondering about this. Yet the question is far from straightforward, in part because any answer will involve an implicitly normative assessment of what constitutes admirable behavior, and in part because of the difficulties involved in obtaining the right sort of empirical evidence. Asking this question is not like asking—to take a hypothetical example—whether the Athenians were faster rowers than the Corinthians. No particular evaluative appraisal will guide inquiry into that question or determine its outcome. By contrast, our question requires the same normative analysis demanded of tribunals judging candidates for the Victoria Cross or other awards for inspirational valor.

Naturally, the ancients themselves offered opinions on such questions, often with little express awareness of the conceptual contestability of courage. Most ancients tended to admire the Spartans and the Romans (and certainly not the Athenians) as the most courageous warriors. But Athenian democrats maintained that only the Athenians were truly courageous because their courage was well informed by appropriate thoughts and emotions, and because their courage was carefully located within their lives as a whole. By contrast, they charged, the Spartans' courage was derived from excessive discipline, fear of shame and punishment, and lifelong training. Spartan courage was thus inappropriately motivated and insufficiently self-conscious. Plato and Aristotle also criticized Spartan courage (e.g., *Laws* 625c–631d; *Pol.* 1271a41–1271b10, 1333b5–26), without, to be sure, endorsing Athenian claims to superiority. We cannot appeal to any uncontroversial ancient standard in order to find stable grounds for arbitration.

It is no help, either, to suggest that what really matters about courage is achievement on the battlefield, as though we could differentiate between the courageous and the cowardly simply by adding up victories and losses. This would be misguided. Judgments of valor would not make sense unless they took into account the psychological dispositions of soldiers. Such judgments are forms of ethical approbation. If psychology and ethics were forgotten, then drunk or drugged or lucky soldiers, or even "berserkers" who happened to fight successfully, would be designated most courageous. This lacks plausibility. Even if they disputed details, the ancients themselves correctly recognized that courage has a specific ethical and psychological structure. Even the Athenians did not dispute that the Spartans were highly successful, and very scary, warriors (cf. Lys. 16.5); but, as we have seen, they did dispute the Spartans' claim to genuine *courage*.

In order to explore the importance of psychological structure, consider again the case of Aristodemus, the Spartan soldier who was dismissed from the fighting at Thermopylae because of an eye inflammation (Hdt. 7.229–31).[1] Aristodemus was disgraced because he eventually held back from the fighting, even though Eurytus, who had been excused for the same reason, rushed into battle when the Persians rounded the mountain

---

[1] Cf. Miller 2000: 15–28, who emphasizes rather the "politics" of courage in this episode.

pass. At the ensuing battle of Plataea, though, Aristodemus, Herodotus says, "was by far the most courageous (*aristos*)" (Hdt. 9.71). Despite Aristodemus' evident bravado on the field, however, the Spartans awarded the prize of valor to a certain Posidonius on the grounds that Aristodemus was not properly motivated. The Spartans "judged that Aristodemus, in fighting so ferociously and in leaving his post, had accomplished great deeds, but they thought that he clearly wanted to die because of his present guilt. They argued that Posidonius, on the other hand, had fought courageously without wanting to die; and he was a better man to that extent. But they might have said these things out of envy" (9.71).

To call someone courageous is to praise him ethically for confronting danger in the right spirit and for the right reasons. Courage is not simply a matter of defying danger, but also of how and why the soldier does so. The Spartans not only did not award Aristodemus any prizes, but also refused to grant him any public honor whatever, because he had rushed into battle like a berserker, in a spirit of reckless disregard for his own life—or indeed more than this, they thought, since he fought out of a desire to die (9.71).[2] The Spartans recognized the contribution of Aristodemus' deeds, and he was on the "short list" for military honors because he had done something notable; ultimately, though, what the Spartans had doubts about was his *courage*. Soldiers who fight well because of the "rum ration" or because they have given up hope or because they fear punishment, cannot properly be designated as courageous, whatever their exploits. When Herodotus himself praised Aristodemus for his courage, he was disagreeing with the Spartans' official interpretation, which he attributed to the Spartans' envy (9.71). In order to make his disagreement plausible, then, Herodotus had to discount the Spartans' judgment in some such way, because he implicitly agreed with the Spartans that improperly motivated courage was not courage at all. Forming such judgments demands a psychological and ethical interpretation of the facts on the ground.

On this basis I am inclined to view the Athenians as more courageous than the Spartans. The Athenians understood the point of courage, they went to battle with clarity about their own immediate and long-term goals, and they had a proportionate and just assessment of the importance of courage as compared to other virtues, such as justice. It is reasonable to

---

[2] As Loraux 1995: 65 has argued, the "austere military ethic" cultivated by Sparta prohibited any soldier from frenziedly pursuing death, even though Spartans were socialized to disregard death and accept it cheerfully when it came; cf. Tyrt. 8.5–6. To Spartans, the glorious death, compared with the good life, is nothing but a "last resort": Loraux 1995: 67.

accept the Athenians' and the philosophers' view that Spartan courage was "defective," in that it did not express a self-aware, rational, and articulate effort to achieve what is noble despite dangerous or frightening circumstances. By contrast, most Athenians, most of the time, including the poor, were more self-conscious, articulate, and independent both in their deliberations about what courage required and in their practices of courage on the battlefield. Even in the foxhole, so to speak, Athenians understood more clearly than others *why* they were doing what they were doing. As the Athenians and the ancient philosophers saw, courage involves having a clear understanding of the reasons for one's behavior. In this book we have explored precisely what such an understanding looked like within Athenian political discourse, with specific reference to the Athenians' reflections on *eudaimonia*, the democratic *politeia*, and the common good.

Plato and Democratic Athens on *Andreia* and *Sōphrosunē*

> "Of course what is best is to live boldly yet without imprudence or intemperance, but the fact is that rather few can manage that" (Foot 1978: 18).

An important dimension of our investigation has been the democratic Athenians' effort to unify apparently antithetical or traditionally opposed attributes, capacities, and qualities, such as "reason and emotion" or "*andreia* and *sōphrosunē*." We have examined *andreia* and *sōphrosunē* already in several different contexts—in the epitaphic tradition and in Aristophanes' *Lysistrata*, as well as in several episodes in Herodotus and Thucydides. As I suggested in the conclusion of chapter 12, Plato, too, returned to this opposition in his own exploration of courage at the end of the *Statesman*. Our question now is what we can learn from his treatment first in the *Statesman*, and then in his presentation of Socrates; and whether Athenian approaches to courage compare favorably to the Platonic approaches.

Altogether, Plato's *Statesman* is devoted to identifying the "statesman" (*politikos*) and his special expertise.[3] Much of the dialogue consists of the interlocutors' attempt to distinguish the statesman from other claimants to the title of "caretaker" of the "human herd," as they put it. To do so, the

---

[3] On Plato's critique of civic *andreia*, I have benefited from Salkever 1991; on the *Statesman*, I have learned from Rowe's commentary, from Cooper 1999e and 1999f, and from Hobbs 2000: 261–67, but I know of no detailed treatment of the relationship between this dialogue and the democratic discourse on *andreia* and *sōphrosunē*.

primary speaker, the "Eleatic Stranger," proposes that a weaver of cloth is an appropriate model for the statesman (279a7–b6). The rationale for this is that the statesman's expertise somehow consists in "weaving together" disparate parts of the city in a politically knowledgeable way. The image is reminiscent of the *Lysistrata* (567–86), where Lysistrata proposes that the men reconstitute the city through weaving together groups that differed in status and political role (e.g., the full citizens, the resident aliens, and the colonists; on this image, see chapter 12). In Aristophanes' comedy, weaving together disparate groups in the city runs in parallel to the creation of the androgynous virtues exhibited by the women. Indeed, weaving itself is a traditionally feminine activity that Lysistrata metaphorically puts to masculine, that is, political, uses. In the *Statesman*, too, I would argue, the model of weaving is intended to have both a political and a psychological significance: uniting apparently disparate groups in the city anticipates the dialogue's conclusion that the true statesman will weave together disparate virtues—*andreia* and *sōphrosunē*—in the soul.

Leading up to this conclusion is the Stranger's insistence that certain allied political arts, including those of the orator, the general, and the judge, important as they may be, are subordinate to the expertise of the statesman (304e5–305a10). In the case of generalship, the particular military practices that exemplify manly pugnacity are associated with a general's applied expertise, but a prior and superior expert—the statesman—must help the general to determine when, where, how, and why to apply his art at all. Thus the Stranger interprets statesmanship provisionally as the art of setting this ancillary art, along with others, within a wider framework of ethical meaning. He has created a political hierarchy that establishes a brake upon the politics of *andreia*. The nature of this "brake" is made explicit in his final description of the statesman's weaving art, which will attempt to intertwine *andreia* and *sōphrosunē*—two virtues, which, he worries, are inherently conflicting.

To be sure, he shows serious hesitation in entertaining the possibility that two virtues might come into conflict (306b6–10), since Plato's "Socrates" had typically maintained either the unity or at least the co-presence of the virtues (306b12–c1).[4] In the ensuing discussion, though, he makes clear why this conflict is possible. By conjuring up common expressions in which each virtue term is used, he can pick out the features of each virtue that we praise and regard as honorable. We praise things for *andreia*,

---

[4] Cf. North 1966: 183–85; Cooper 1999f: 182–86.

sometimes, as "quick and courageous" or as "vigorous and courageous," and we praise the *sōphrosunē* of other things, using expressions such as "quiet and self-restrained," and so on (306e2–307b2). "Brainstorming" about the common types of approbation involving the term "courage" helps us to discern the particular characteristics we cherish in this virtue, and similarly with *sōphrosunē*. Conversely, people or things can go to excess in either direction. In that case they are "aggressive and mad" or "cowardly and lethargic" and the like (307b8–c2). Our positive verbal evaluations are reserved for things done at the right time and in the right way, but the virtues can easily miss the mark and become vicious self-caricatures. For Plato this is a substantial political problem because individuals erect cultures around themselves that reflect their own dispositions (cf. *Republic* 435e1–436a3).

To counteract the tendency of either virtue to go to excess, the Stranger envisions a program of education focused on two goals: first, to teach individuals the truth about "noble, just, and good things, and their opposites" (309c5–6) and, second, to shape the citizens' characters through the intermingling of *andreia* and *sōphrosunē*. In the final words of the dialogue, the Eleatic Stranger concludes that the expertise of the statesman consists in weaving together "the disposition of the brave and the moderate, when the kingly art brings together their life in common, through harmony and friendship, fully completing the most distinguished and best of all fabrics…" (311b7–c2). If all goes as planned, then this interweaving will "tame" the disposition that tends toward *andreia* and embolden the one inclined toward moderation. This is supposed to happen through the conflicting types' willingness to share opinions and to respect the same standards of honor and dishonor (310e9–11).

Stated so baldly, however, this proposal is too vague, or even circular, to be helpful. As A. O. Rorty has pointed out, with this "checks-and-balances solution" we seem to be relying on the governance of wisdom to specify the appropriate times, places, and circumstances for virtuous action.[5] Indeed, the first prong of the Stranger's educational system is precisely to educate the citizens in wisdom. Specifying "wisdom" as the source of balance does not take us very far, because if we had wisdom, and wisdom was in charge of the soul, then any talk of "balancing" opposed virtues would be unnecessary. What is needed is an explanation of how the virtues can

---

[5] Rorty 1988: 310–11 makes the important point that the rule of wisdom in the soul would render the balancing solution superfluous. On "balancing" in a more general way, see Thompson 2001.

come to balance one another or engage in dialogue with one another, and come to a mutually satisfying agreement, that already includes the operations of practical rationality.

Another, and even more important, objection to the "balancing solution" is that it leaves untouched (and therefore treats as essential) the hotheaded conception of *andreia* that it would be desirable to defuse. Is it correct, after all, to view courage as hotheaded and bloodthirsty, when those characterizations obviously bring courage into conflict with justice, practical wisdom, and dedication to the common good? Perhaps Plato was not content with the conclusions offered in the *Statesman*. In his final work, the *Laws*, he returned to the question of unifying *andreia* with *sōphrosunē*, in considering ways (in the first instance) to criticize Spartan education and, ultimately, to devise a new system of the education to virtue in his utopian Magnesia.

On the other hand, Plato's characterization of Socrates had already suggested a completely different solution to the problem of courage—namely, that courage consists in "standing fast," in persevering with calm resolve, according to practical reason, in the face of adversity. Plato's literary representation of Socrates contributes to his expression of this ideal. Throughout the dialogues, Plato never presents Socrates as undertaking the bold, aggressive action prized (for example) by Achilles, by Callicles, or by Thucydides' Athenians. Socrates has no violent streak. Yet Socrates was a courageous warrior, indeed a hoplite, the type of soldier whose traditional goal was always to stand fast. As Alcibiades reports in the *Symposium*, Socrates saved Alcibiades during the Athenian retreat from Delium in 424 BC. The details are important. According to Alcibiades, Socrates was calmer in retreat than the elected general Laches; Alcibiades says that he continued to show good sense (*tōi emphrōn einai*, 221b1) despite the danger. It was possible to show mindful and self-aware courage in retreat. Socrates' courage enabled him to maintain his considered views on life, death, and friendship, despite the imminent threat of death. As Alcibiades reports, Socrates had enough calm resolve to stay with his wounded friend and to rescue him. Courageous Socrates did not live in fear. Courage enabled Socrates to express the ethical ideal of friendship.

To be what it was, though, Socratic courage could not be confined to the battlefield. Socrates' firm resolve extended to all areas of his life. Socratic courage consists in steadfastness and, when necessary, in the patient endurance of suffering. To explain his admiration for Socrates, Alcibiades introduces another anecdote with a line from the *Odyssey*, praising Socrates as a steadfast (*karteros*) man who dared to do something exceptional (220c2).

If we now expect Socrates to storm into battle like the Homeric Achilles, then we judge incorrectly. Alcibiades' story is that Socrates stood transfixed for twenty-four hours working on a philosophical problem in the Athenian encampment at Potidaea. This is a powerful image of courage as "standing fast." Socrates reinvents the patient endurance of Odysseus, not the hotheaded boldness of Achilles.[6] Socratic endurance is presented as an admirable form of physical courage. Alcibiades goes on to praise Socrates' endurance of hunger, thirst, and cold, and he concludes by praising Socrates' steadfast resistance to his sexual advances, saying that he "feels reverence for" (*agamenon*) Socrates' self-control (*sōphrosunē*) and courage (*andreia*) (219d4–5). This is not a balance between self-control and courage. It is a transformation of courage itself. Socrates shows why and how even physical courage can consist in self-control rather than aggressive action.

Socrates made a similar equation in the *Gorgias*. He said that the self-controlled man "would also necessarily be courageous, for it is not characteristic of the self-controlled man either to pursue or to avoid what is not fitting, but to avoid and to pursue what he must—both practical affairs and men, along with pleasures and pains, and to stand fast and endure them when he must" (507b). This is a helpful antidote to the militaristic and aggressive conception of courage whose paradigm was Achilles—especially in the context of Socrates' conversation with the young and aggressive Callicles. The problem that demanded a solution was this: how to redescribe courage so as to make it invulnerable to the charge of either weakness or overaggression, without losing anything admirable in the process. Socrates had a good answer. His model was Odysseus, the long-suffering hero who accepts fortune's blows as they come and firmly stands by his resolution to return to Ithaca. But neither Socrates nor Odysseus *identifies* with "long-sufferingness." They identify with other goals. Courage was properly the footstool of their virtues. This is why, in the Platonic *Laws*, the Athenian Stranger rated courage fourth among the "divine goods" (631b–d).

One serious problem, however, remains. In the *Laches*, Socrates explained that steadfastness or patient endurance (*karterēsis*) often turns out to be courage, provided that such steadfastness is wise (194a). Courage must, in Plato's conception, always be directed toward appropriate ends.

---

[6] Cf. Hobbs 2000: esp. 199–219, 250–61.

Even if he was outstandingly steadfast, did Socrates always know what was appropriate?

Our reflex, of course, is to say "no," and this reflex is encouraged by the typically aporetic conclusions of Socrates' dialogues; but we should acknowledge that no existing theory of courage answers this question very well, either. Determining appropriate ends in specific circumstances always calls on a high degree of appreciation of the particulars of each situation. In other dialogues, such as the *Republic*, Plato erected a vast metaphysics and epistemology in order to explore the shape and significance of such questions more fully. As modern citizens of democratic nation-states, however, we would find it difficult to follow Plato in this direction. By contrast with other Platonic solutions to this problem, the Socrates of Plato's *Apology* specifically disclaims wisdom about human ends, about the nature of virtue, about what he calls "the most important things." He is consistently presented in Plato's dialogues as someone looking for and hoping to find wisdom. Socrates' courage of standing fast was particularly well adapted to this self-image.[7] "Standing fast" could be a philosophical virtue in this context. In the *Laches*, for example, Socrates points out that persevering in argument amidst uncertainty is a difficult and onerous, if not dangerous, task (194a). Thus, even if Socrates does not always know what is appropriate, his courage can be helpfully employed in the search for what is appropriate. He knows, at least, that employing courage in this way is appropriate.

This is a very attractive conception of courage. Translating this conception slightly, we might envision courage as providing a space for rational reflection by resisting the pressures to make quick and easy decisions based on the authority of cultural paradigms. Cultural icons, like the furious Achilles, often lead us in the wrong direction. Socrates' embodiment of courage gives us the correct orientation toward this elusive virtue, assuming that we will never adequately grasp eternal Forms or laws of nature, which might guide us to correct judgments regarding every particular feature of our situation. Despite the mysteries of our human situation, Socrates illustrates how an *individual* might connect the idea of courage as steadfastness to rational reflection and to a persistent search for the truth.

How did Socrates himself, however, translate his steadfast form of courage to politics, if at all? For Socrates, standing fast in politics consists

---

[7] O'Brien 1963: 140–41 takes "steadfastness" to be the underlying theme of the Platonic *Laches*, whatever the variations in each participant's conception of what this means and what sort of knowledge it must be allied with.

in resisting harm, often simply in saying no.[8] As he argued in the *Apology*, Socrates refused to be pressured into voting to put on trial the unfortunate Arginusae generals as a group, on the grounds that an omnibus trial was illegal. Socrates also refused the command by the revolutionaries of 404 BC to fetch Leon of Salamis for execution.[9] And, as we can gather from a variety of dialogues, he refused to take part in democratic politics, which he viewed as stimulating unhealthy desires. His stance raises a welter of difficult questions.[10] His is not precisely a politics of nonviolence. He does not promote civil disobedience. We should admire his way of standing fast in relation to his reflective ethical commitments. But can we admire without ambivalence his unwillingness to work for political reform? Can we admire his participation in battles such as those of Potidaea, Amphipolis, and Delium, which were fought to further the aims of Athenian imperialism? Finally, can we imagine a city of courageous Socratic citizens? For my account suggests that even if "Socratic citizens" might possibly be, as Dana Villa has argued, "dissident, philosophical" citizens, it is unclear whether they themselves could form a political community at all.[11]

The reason for this is that Socrates' courage appears to be problematically inactive or withdrawn. Socrates wants to remain on the settled moral ground of avoiding harm. This is judicious but incomplete; perhaps it is even symptomatic of a lack of courage. For politics is always happening around us. Politics often demands decisive action in the midst of uncertainty, on pain at least of omitting to act when necessary in order to counteract evil. Politics often demands decisive action even when standing fast in practical deliberation has not yet yielded perfectly clear results.[12]

Strikingly, the democratic Athenians might help us to reduce (which is not to say resolve) this problematic feature of Socratic courage. They provide a different sort of response to the troubling features of courage. Half a century after the fall of Athens's empire, and around the time of Plato's death, the Athenian orator Demosthenes showed awareness that people who identify with courage tend to be eager to find opportunities to fight, or eager to interpret situations so as to make fighting necessary.[13]

---

[8] See Kateb 1998.
[9] We might still wonder why Socrates apparently failed to warn Leon of Salamis of his impending execution; we know little about the circumstances, of course, but perhaps Socrates' principle of saying no fails to go far enough in exhibiting the care for his fellow citizens that he claimed for himself (cf. Balot 2008).
[10] For an exploration of at least some of these questions, see Woodruff 2007, with Balot 2008.
[11] Villa 1999: 1.
[12] I thank my colleague Jennifer Nedelsky for helping me to see the importance of this point.
[13] On these worries about courage, see Rorty 1988, with Elster 2002.

Demosthenes made this point as follows: "I ask only so much of you, that you not reckon those urging you to fight to be brave (*andreious*) for that reason alone, nor that you reckon those trying to argue against them to be for that reason cowardly (*kakous*)" (*Exordium* 50.1). As we saw in chapter 3, Demosthenes was making a plea for his fellow citizens to step back, to consider alternatives rationally and calmly, and to be appropriately suspicious of the seductive rhetoric of manliness. Demosthenes' conception of courage, which involved self-restraint and further consideration of when and how to act, is admirable and shares elements with that of Socrates.

Demosthenes himself subscribed to his own conception of courage, and he exhibited this form of courage in action. In 348 BC, a rich Athenian citizen known as Meidias punched Demosthenes in the face at a major religious festival. Meidias was, in Demosthenes' description, a real-life Callicles: "In my view, he thought that whatever one man might gain at another's expense, was neither brilliant nor high-spirited enough, nor worthy of death. Unless he could humiliate a whole tribe or the council or an entire body of citizens and persecute many of you all together at the same time, he thought that life was not livable for him" (21.131).[14] For Meidias, at least, life had no meaning apart from competition, aggression, and violence. Meidias' punch was a public blow to Demosthenes' manhood. How *should* a courageous democratic citizen respond?

As Joseph Roisman has argued, Demosthenes' challenge was to demonstrate that his self-restraint had not been unmanly or cowardly.[15] His strategy was to propose that his self-restraint had been, to the contrary, an act of courage. He assumed correctly that, if confronted by the same situation, most people would—or would like to—retaliate forcibly and immediately. Demosthenes, however, referred the insult to an Athenian jury. He represented this move as positively self-restrained, as "happily inspired," as courageous. One could argue that Demosthenes was simply a coward and that he was afraid to strike back. We do not know enough details to make a judgment about this; we do not know, furthermore, the outcome of this case. But we might not "know enough," so to speak, even if all the facts were available. If Demosthenes was driven by blind fear, then he was a coward. That is clear. But if he accepted the blow without retaliating, and in order to express other ideals, then the Athenians, and we, would *still*

---

[14] On the comparison with Callicles, see Ober 2005a: 151–52.
[15] Roisman 2003, 2005: 75–79.

have a judgment to make. Could his act be called courageous? Everything depends on identifying the most powerful description and interpretation of the particulars of this case.

On a charitable reading, Demosthenes' self-restraint showed proper respect for Athens's rule of law, its impartial judicial decisions. This is one of the keys to his argument. By refusing to retaliate violently, Demosthenes stood fast in his dedication to democratic modes of justice.[16] Hence, we can agree with Gabriel Herman that the Athenians forged new ideals and new modes of behavior that went beyond the aggressive legacy of the preceding Hellenic tradition; but these new modes are better described with reference to the vocabulary of virtue and vice, and specifically with an eye to the Athenians' transformation of traditional ideals of manliness and courage, than, as Herman suggests, with an eye to "non-retaliation."[17] By referring the insult to a court, Demosthenes permitted a space for reflection and careful deliberation on the facts. This is not precisely nonviolence. Demosthenes calls upon the jurors to get angry.[18] He calls upon them to punish Meidias harshly. But his goal, he says, is to enforce democratic law, justice, and equality. If he had retaliated violently, then he would not have shown due respect for democratic law. Taking Meidias to court, on the other hand, involved risks of its own—such as the retaliation for which Meidias was well known. Demosthenes presents himself, seemingly with justification, as threading the needle between excessive aggression and excessive laxness.

Demosthenes' arguments are, of course, part of his rhetorical strategy. But we should not dismiss them for that reason, because they enlarge our conception of what courageous endurance might look like in concrete political—and indeed democratic—circumstances. We can regard it as humanly possible, and as admirable and courageous, that a high-ranking orator might risk a reputation for cowardice, and risk harmful legal and even physical consequences, in order to promote the ideals of judicial impartiality and democratic equality. As Demosthenes' extended arguments show, this was not a self-evident interpretation of courage to democratic Athenians.[19] But this interpretation was possible only because of the new modes of thinking about virtue that were characteristic of democratic

---

[16] Cf. Roisman 2005: 77, who argues that Demosthenes "presented himself as a brave defender of democratic Athens who was fulfilling his civic responsibilities."
[17] Herman 2006.
[18] Cf. Allen 2000 in general and, especially, 230–32.
[19] Cf. Roisman 2005: 76. For a different interpretation, see Herman 2006: 167–75.

Athens. We do not know the outcome of this trial, but we do know that Meidias was not dealt too extreme a punishment, since he continued to be politically active in the years after the trial. Whichever way the case was settled, though, Demosthenes offers *us* an ancient model of political (as opposed to Socratic) courage that consisted in steadfast resolve and political action in support of democratic laws and ideals. His "standing fast" was thoughtful. His courage enabled him to promote forensic deliberation and democratic justice dealt by a "third party," that is, by the Athenian jury. He thought himself out of Achillean aggressiveness and into a reflective, though hardly inactive, Odyssean style of courage. His fellow citizens were willing to entertain this new conception, because they had long been working to liberate themselves from traditional, unreflective ideals of machismo. And perhaps this is what a modified, civic, democratic form of Socratic courage would look like.

Even if he did not command universal assent among his fellow citizens, Demosthenes the democrat was able to practice a form of courage that was more admirable—both more "Socratic" and more political—than Plato might have been willing to acknowledge as characteristic of Athenian democrats and their leaders (cf. *Republic* 560c–d). Both Socrates and Demosthenes show that standing firm is an important model of political courage because it permits a space for reflection and thus for more thoughtful political decisions. It really is courage and yet it is not an excessively combative form of courage.[20] Cultures that identify strongly with Achilles' style of courage benefit significantly from the availability of different, and less aggressive, paradigms of courage. In order to defend themselves, states will occasionally need the courage of bold action, but it is only the courage of steadfastness that permits adequate reflection on the question of when, where, how, why, and within what limits bold action should be undertaken.

Perhaps the real hero of this comparison and contrast between Demosthenes and Socrates, however, is not Demosthenes, but rather the Athenian demos. The Athenian demos was willing to consider competing claims to democratic virtue, to reflect on the ethical significance of courage and self-control, and (in their assemblies, councils, festivals, ritual practices, and mythic narratives) to discuss these virtues as elements of the good life that they worked to create as individuals and as fellow citizens.

---

[20] See Roisman 2005: 76: "His justification hinged on the claim, made implicitly and woven into the legal arguments, that seeking legal redress was no less manly than violent retaliation."

The Athenians' creation of institutions that encouraged such reflection was admirable, as was their willingness to think themselves out of traditional, authoritative paradigms of the virtues when those paradigms no longer seemed necessary or useful to their common projects. In evaluating their political life, we should emphasize, not so much the "elasticity" and rhetorical usefulness of concepts of courage, with Roisman, or the shift to game-theoretical models of "non-retaliation," with Herman, but rather the Athenians' self-liberation from ancient (including religious) authorities.[21] They confidently asserted their own judgments about what was just, admirable, and best for the city. They lived flourishing lives on the basis of precisely those judgments.

The Diversity of Courageous Democracies

Yet it is possible to argue, with Plato and other critics of democracy, that democracies carry with them two significant disadvantages with respect to courage. The first is that while democracies liberate extraordinary human power and energy, they have never been successful in disentangling their conceptions of courage from destructive and ethically objectionable associations with manliness, violence, and the thrills of warfare. Therefore, whatever their capacities for brilliant and noble action, the democracies' expansion of human power does unusually enormous damage to the cause of human dignity, flourishing, and welfare. The second is that democracies degrade, rather than expand, our scope for realizing human greatness. They do this especially at the individual level, by making individuals weak. But democracies enervate human beings at a wider, cultural level, too, in that they typically produce conformity and satisfaction with (mere) material well-being. They do not encourage the courageous pursuit of excellence, whether in physical, creative, or philosophical domains.

To some extent, of course, these criticisms are at odds with one another. On the one hand, democracy seems to be unusually dangerous because it is so powerful; on the other hand, democracy is an insidious threat because it makes individuals simple, mild, self-satisfied, bourgeois, and even stupid. This paradox often surfaces in the texts of ancient critics of democracy—for example, in the works of Plato, or even, occasionally, Aristophanes. In Plato's *Gorgias*, the Athenian democracy projected extraordinary power over others, so as to indulge its passions for ships, dockyards, and

---

[21] Roisman 2003; 2005: 116; Herman 2006.

other materialistic delights—the "bread and circuses" so beloved by the Romans. Yet Socrates' very point, above all in the *Gorgias*, was to argue that democracy ultimately revealed itself to be a weak and disordered form of political organization, because its citizens typically failed to understand the purposes for which their democratic power ought, for the sake of their own good, to be discharged.[22] Similarly, Aristophanes' *Knights* and *Wasps* show Demos to be extremely powerful both domestically and internationally. Yet, at the same time, Demos was stupid and vulnerable to manipulation by its own counselors—and this is not even to mention the crudity and vulgarity of Aristophanes' Demos, even at the best of times. Democracy is both excessively powerful and excessively weak: and these defects reveal themselves glaringly in relation to manliness, courage, and power.

Is it possible, then, for democracy to avoid both of these criticisms? For Demos to hold power and to cultivate its natural capacities for excellence, while still avoiding the extremes of crude injustice and (simultaneously) weakness and disorder, with which it was often, at least in the ancient world, charged? Herodotus gave us a glimmer of hope when he showed the Athenians risking their lives in a noble cause, and in novel and remarkably adventuresome ways, during the Persian Wars. Herodotus' Athenians are hardly weak and incapable of asserting their wills. But Herodotus turned out to level the first and most important critique of the Athenian democracy as an unjust imperial power. This critique becomes especially clear if we read Herodotus alongside Thucydides. Democracy may have made Athens strong because it encouraged each man to fight courageously for himself (Hdt. 5.78), yes, but this transformation did not link the novel Athenian expressions of courage to justice: quite the opposite. The Athenians took their first opportunity to use their novel power for the sake of controlling the other Greeks (cf. Hdt. 8.3). It may be that Athenian tragedy, above all, expressed, in a series of unforgettable, phantasmagoric images, the Athenians' own profound ambivalence about the human costs levied by their pursuit of what they imagined to be imperial "greatness."

The first line of critique is also endorsed, for democracy in general, by contemporary theorists such as George Kateb. As Kateb has written, "The unfortunate general judgment is that democracy has not yet adequately revised physical courage and the honor that is accorded to it. Democracy still regularly implicates courage in terrible wrongdoing by its appeals to

---

[22] Annas 1981: 341–43 makes a similar observation about Plato's critique of art in the *Republic*; on democracy, cf. Annas 1981: 299–302.

both gullible patriotism and gullible masculinity."[23] This criticism applies to the ancient Athenians, too. The Athenians' actions did not always live up to their virtue-oriented, eudaimonistic ideology.[24] Despite their "gestures" toward more open conceptions of courage, the Athenians were often locked within the ancient world of machismo and warlike heroism.

More than this: the Athenians were able to project power to such an unprecedented extent among the Greeks not only because of the size of their citizen-body or other "natural" advantages. As we have argued, they were also capable of doing so because of their untraditional model of courage. They were willing to think and to act in novel ways for the sake of their own advantage. These factors were distinctive products of their democracy, just as much as their diverse technical and strategic innovations in prosecuting war.[25] In addition, the Athenian democracy was a "democracy of knowledge": it fully "leveraged" its capacities and forces for the sake of political, military, and economic success.[26] Hence, as much as the Athenians did to replace traditional "manliness" with a more adequate and less destructive conception of courage, as I have argued, they also retained certain attachments to damaging ideals of aggressive military behavior, which their novel expressions of courage, paradoxically, did much to promote. Athens would have been less likely to become imperialistic, and successfully so, if it had never become a democracy, or developed a correspondingly democratic ideal of courage, in the first place.

Does this imply, after all, that the Athenians' novel ideal of courage is of no importance to us today? Could the brilliance of the Athenians' democratic eudaimonism ever be disentangled from its intimate connections with destructive ideals of heroism? To be sure, democracy did not claim to create individual heroes. Rather, its claim was that the demos as a collective body proved superior in heroic terms to the greatest heroes of the Greek tradition. "Heroic democracy"—as Pericles said, one that left memorials of "both good and evil"—may be inspiring at a certain level. Yet it also carries with it precisely the intransigent disregard for justice, and for other human beings, that characterizes the "greatness" of traditional heroes. We are left with a mixed picture. In part through its novel understanding of courage and other virtues, the Athenian democracy expanded the scope of

---

[23] Kateb 2004: 68.
[24] This is not, of course, meant to imply that other societies throughout history have fared better on this front: *contra* Samons 2004.
[25] See Hanson 2001; Ober 2008; and the essays in Pritchard 2010 for further investigation of these factors.
[26] Ober 2008.

the human will and of our human capacities in general. At the same time, its incapacity to liberate itself from heroic rivalries and aspirations, such as those memorably expressed by Pericles, will always make us suspicious of even its greatest accomplishments. Athens's greatness was the enemy of its goodness.

On the other hand, we might eventually judge that Athens's courageous, democratic self-liberation may simply have been incomplete rather than misguided or hopeless. Perhaps a better version of Athens—a utopian Athens, if you wish, that lived up to its own aspirations more fully—can still prove to be not only illuminating, but also fresh and inspiring, for our own political thought and our own ways of life. In order to occupy this role, the utopian Athens of our imagination would have to be more rigorous and self-consistent than the historical Athens in pursuing its own eudaimonistic ideals to their logical conclusions. This would require, to be sure, even further revolutions in the democratic ideal of courage—not departures from democracy, necessarily, but a more complete adherence to the ideals embodied in the democratic framework of human excellence and human flourishing that we have explored. But is democracy capable of producing an antiheroic, or rather a nonheroic but still "inspired," version of itself that would promote its eudaimonistic aspirations in a more peaceful and reliable way?

Perhaps it is possible to be more hopeful than we initially thought. The Athenians' democracy opened the way to a reconsideration of courage that would, at its best, render this traditionally suspect virtue compatible with the claims of justice, equality, practical wisdom, and human flourishing altogether. As Kateb puts it, democracy has "not yet" revised its norms of courage adequately. Our argument might lead us to interpret this statement more optimistically than it seems to have been intended. Among all regime types, democracy is the most likely to disentangle courage from bellicosity, to imagine more appropriate and self-consistent ways for courage to express itself, and to transform standards of behavior so as to bring them into line with those novel expressions of courage. Because one of its key elements is continual "motion" or revision or even revolution, democracy can at least continue to strive to disentangle courage, and itself, from harmful traditional ideals or entanglements. Our reason to hope is this: Athenian courage not only promoted successful imperialism, but also, to the contrary, helped to curb the Athenians' aggressiveness and to balance it with self-control, with a concern for justice, and with wisdom. Reinterpreted in this light, Athens's "greatness" lay precisely in its (admittedly unfulfilled) aspiration to goodness.

What of the second objection to democratic courage—namely, that democracy degrades courage? To be more precise, the second objection is that democracies diminish the individual's capacity to rise above necessity or to liberate himself from bourgeois conformity. Democracies make individuals weak; and, by making states or groups stronger, they make individuals even weaker. In a more postmodern guise, one might even say that democracies give every individual the fantasy of being powerful, creative, and original, precisely in order to induce an even more profound, slumbering conformism.

Among the modern theorists, our best guide to these questions is Tocqueville. Tocqueville argued that democratic states constitute vast complexes of power and ambition, which render individuals weak, mild, orderly, acquisitive, selfish, and small: "Each individual is isolated and weak; society is agile, far-seeing, and strong; individuals do small things and the state does big ones" (*DA* II.4.8). Tocqueville finds that sovereigns in democratic centuries seek to use individuals in order to "make great things," while he himself would "want them to pay more attention to making great men" (*DA* II.4.7). Precisely because of their equality with one another, Tocqueville argues, each democratic individual comes to doubt his strength because of the power of the wider society: "The majority has no need to constrain him; it convinces him" (*DA* II.3.21; cf. II.4.6). Democracy is "prosaic" rather than heroic; the most ambitious men aim low, while men usually live their lives in the pursuit of easily obtained, albeit unimportant, things (*DA* I.2.9, II.3.19). Democracies practice despotism over the soul (*DA* I.2.7), which leaves individuals unable to think freely.

For Tocqueville, then, the principal democratic transformation of courage has led to a reduction in the traditional brilliance of that virtue:

> American honor accords with the old honor of Europe on one point: it puts courage at the head of the virtues and makes it the greatest of moral necessities for man; but it does not view courage in the same way. In the United States, warlike valor is little prized; the courage that is known best and most esteemed is that which makes one face the furies of the ocean to arrive sooner in port, to bear without complaining the miseries of the wilderness, and the solitude, more cruel than all the miseries; the courage that makes a person almost insensitive to the sudden reversal of a painfully acquired fortune and immediately suggests new efforts to construct a new one. Courage of this type is principally necessary to the maintenance and prosperity of the

American association, and it is particularly honored and glorified by it. One cannot show oneself to be lacking it without dishonor (*DA* II.3.18).

According to Tocqueville, courage has been transformed by democracy's mildness and bourgeois gratifications into a paradoxically heroic avarice. This new form of heroism, or rather anti-heroism, corresponds closely to the materialistic "ends" of the democratic regime. Whereas democratic Athens never sought or found a "moral equivalent of war,"[27] the modern American democracy, according to Tocqueville, had discovered another focal point for the expression of courage—that is, commerce.

In the light of Tocqueville's analysis, we will be inclined to suppose that democracy is in fact antithetical to courage. For courage had always consisted in brilliant exploits, in the vast expansion of desire and ambition, and in the individual pursuit of lasting, monumental greatness. By contrast, the Americans' bourgeois and democratic transformation of courage promotes idleness and weakness (*DA* II.3.18). For Tocqueville, American ambitions are many but not lofty; American passions are multiple but debased; Americans have petty virtues but lack pride (*DA* II.3.20). Perhaps it is a general truth that democratic equality sits uneasily alongside the individual pursuit of excellence. American courage appears to find its most elevated meaning in pursuing the ordinary, the everyday, the bodily—in short, what had always been derogatorily called "necessity." But isn't courage meaningful precisely because it opens us to a realm of liberation from necessity? We might well suppose, with Tocqueville, that courage must have pride or it is nothing.

Tocqueville forces us to acknowledge that modern America had established a nonheroic version of democracy, one that avoided the potentially bellicose, heroic overtones of the classical Athenian democracy. For democratic peoples, as Tocqueville argues, are brought to war only with difficulty, so thoroughly entrenched are they in their workaday economic concerns (*DA* II.3.24). But, Tocqueville wonders, is this newer version of courage good or admirable? Ever the aristocrat, Tocqueville was tempted to favor aristocratic greatness over democratic mildness, largely for aesthetic reasons. As Tocqueville himself puts it, the beautiful and dashing old society "delighted my sight," whereas "the spectacle of this universal uniformity saddens and chills me" (*DA* II.4.8). To his credit, Tocqueville does not yield to the temptations of the aesthetic. He even goes on to say that

---

[27] The phrase comes from William James's 1910 essay "The Moral Equivalent of War."

his superficial proclivity toward the aesthetic is in fact a sign of his own weakness, because "equality is perhaps less elevated; but it is more just, and its justice makes its grandeur and its beauty" (*DA* II.4.8). Democracy is humbler than aristocracy, but its greatness consists in its decency, its ordinary respect for the common, its "recognition" of all citizens.

My sense is that this comparatively feeble praise of equality does not do justice to the extraordinary possibilities of democratic courage. The Athenian example illustrates that the reduction of virtue, nobility, and brilliance is not a necessary consequence of the democratic reinterpretation of courage. Courage can be linked to democratic freedom and equality without suffering a loss of pride, dignity, or beauty. On the other hand, Tocqueville's analysis reveals that democracy has the capacity to bring about a conversion of traditional courage to nonheroic ends, and even to follow through with intense dedication in its pursuit of those ends. As Tocqueville himself observed them, those ends—all of them harnessed to the limitless pursuit of materialistic gain—were not particularly admirable. Yet what is good and admirable about American forms of honor and courage, for Tocqueville and for us, is, as Tocqueville says, that they embody admiration for "all the virtues of peace" that tend to order the society well (*DA* II.3.18).[28]

The Challenge of Democratic Courage

Our examination of these two objections has left us with a thought-provoking dialectic between ancient and modern, Athens and America, heroic democracy and egalitarian or just democracy. It is important not to rest content with the idle notion that we can or should somehow "fuse" these two visions of democracy. Rather, our consideration of these democracies alongside one another reveals both the dangers and the possibilities of the democratic reinterpretation of courage. Among the dangers, consider the following. Democracy might harm courage, either in trivializing it or in magnifying its claims and forcing it to serve hubristic aims. Conversely, courage might harm democracy, either by unfairly compromising free speech or free expression, or by fighting pugnaciously for special honors that erode equality.

---

[28] In considering these questions, of course, we should keep in mind that Tocqueville's America was not the plutocratic form of American republicanism that we now see before us. This form of American republicanism may indeed constitute the ultimate realization of James Madison's ideal, but it was hardly Tocqueville's ideal; and it can hardly be considered admirable.

At its best, however, courage can be linked closely to democratic freedom and equality. In order to do so effectively, it will have to be embedded within a eudaimonistic framework that promotes the human excellence and human flourishing of all citizens. This eudaimonistic framework will help democratic citizens understand that courage is an intrinsically good and meritorious quality of the soul, rather than a merely instrumentally useful characteristic to be called upon in order to serve other, arbitrarily chosen ends. Through locating courage within the framework of democratic eudaimonism, we will discover that courage is not the most important democratic virtue—much less, as John F. Kennedy thought, "the most admirable of human virtues."[29] It will be part of democracy's special task, in fact, to recognize that courage ranks below justice in the table of its virtues. Above all, democracy will have to recognize that its special virtue, cultivated through free speech, is wisdom—practical wisdom, to be sure, but a sort of practical wisdom that adequately respects wisdom as such, along with the courage required to pursue it. This is the most profound way in which democracy will ennoble all of its citizens, including the poor or humble.

Democracy might thus establish a sound interpretation and an admirable practice of courage that takes its pride not from rivalry with the bloody exploits of Homeric heroes, but rather from its capacity to promote ideals such as freedom or justice. Its "heroism," appropriately redefined, will be found neither on the killing fields nor in greedy boardrooms. Perhaps its courage will be expressed in the promotion of new political institutions and practices that help us more completely to realize our worthwhile natural capacities.[30] Or, it will be expressed in the physical activities of sports, such as mountain climbing or rowing alone across the ocean that put our lives at risk simply in order to enlarge our human sensitivities to the limits and the potential of human striving.[31] Or in artistic, creative, or philosophical pursuits that question received opinions and daringly explore new ideas, even ones that initially frighten or overwhelm us. Democratic courage might thereby help us to feel more at home in the world, even as it continually inspires us to reject complacency. Democracy is the best

---

[29] This phrase comes from the first sentence of John F. Kennedy's book *Profiles in Courage:* see Kennedy 1955/2006.
[30] Here I draw on the well-developed neo-Aristotelian language of Martha Nussbaum's "capabilities approach": see Nussbaum 1988, 1990, 2001b; cf. Kraut 2007.
[31] Walton 1986: 207–13 interprets mountain climbing as an act of courage in a roughly similar way, with special attention to self-knowledge.

positioned of all regimes to enable us to respect and admire nonmilitary expressions of courage.

However democratic courage might newly be expressed, it will remain true that courage is necessary for living freely in a dangerous and hostile world that is not of our own making. We can hope and strive for peace, and we can reinterpret courage in ways that are more and more fully compatible with peace; and our democratic institutions, practices, norms, and rituals will help us to do this. In the world we now know, however, we cannot completely disentangle courage from its expression on the battlefield. Nor should we fail to admire those who risk or give their lives in order to defend ideals of freedom and equality. This is precisely why it is most necessary to cultivate a democratic interpretation of courage. Of all regimes we know, democracy is the most inclined to question military courage, to explore and explain it, and to strive for clarity about its appropriate expressions and aims. By cultivating wisdom, democracy can best help us to avoid the dangers of military courage, even as it helps to inform our soldiers as to the most appropriate expressions of their characteristic virtue. How much more can we ask of a political regime that is not, as Plato's Socrates said, a *logos* in the sky?

BIBLIOGRAPHY

Adams, C. D., trans. 1988. *The Speeches of Aeschines.* Loeb Classical Library 106. Cambridge, MA: Harvard University Press.
Adkins, A. W. H. 1960. *Merit and Responsibility.* Oxford: Clarendon Press.
Allan, William. 2000. *The "Andromache" and Euripidean Tragedy.* Oxford: Oxford University Press.
Allen, Danielle S. 2000. *The World of Prometheus: The Politics of Punishing in Democratic Athens.* Princeton, NJ: Princeton University Press.
Allen, Danielle S. 2010. *Why Plato Wrote.* Blackwell-Bristol Lectures on Greece, Rome, and the Classical Tradition. Oxford: Wiley-Blackwell.
Anderson, Benedict. 1992. *Imagined Communities: Reflections on the Origins and Spread of Nationalism.* 2nd ed. London: Verso.
Anderson, G. 2003. *The Athenian Experiment: Building an Imagined Political Community in Ancient Attica, 508-490 BC.* Ann Arbor: University of Michigan Press.
Anderson, M. 1972. "The Imagery of '*The Persians.*'" *Greece and Rome* 19: 166–74.
Anderson, M. 2005. "Socrates as Hoplite." *Ancient Philosophy* 25: 273–88.
Annas, Julia. 1981. *An Introduction to Plato's Republic.* Oxford: Oxford University Press.
Annas, Julia. 1993. *The Morality of Happiness.* New York: Oxford University Press.
Annas, Julia. 1998. "Virtue and Eudaimonism." *Social Philosophy and Policy* 15.1: 37–55.
Annas, Julia. 2008. "Virtue Ethics and the Charge of Egoism." In *Morality and Self-Interest*, edited by Paul Bloomfield, 205–23. Oxford: Oxford University Press.
Aquinas, St. Thomas. 1922. *Summa Theologica.* Translated by the Fathers of the English Dominican Province. London: Burns Oates and Washbourne.
Arendt, Hannah. 1958. *The Human Condition.* Chicago: University of Chicago Press.
Avramenko, Richard. 2011. *Courage: The Politics of Life and Limb.* Notre Dame, IN: University of Notre Dame Press.
Badiou, Alain. 2010. *The Communist Hypothesis.* London: Verso.
Balot, Ryan K. 2001a. *Greed and Injustice in Classical Athens.* Princeton, NJ: Princeton University Press.
Balot, Ryan K. 2001b. "Pericles' Anatomy of Democratic Courage." *American Journal of Philology* 122: 505–25.

Balot, R. 2004a. "Free Speech, Courage, and Democratic Deliberation." In Sluiter and Rosen, *Free Speech in Classical Antiquity*, 233–59.

Balot, R. 2004b. "Courage in the Democratic Polis." *Classical Quarterly* 54.2: 406–23.

Balot, R. 2004c. "The Dark Side of Democratic Courage." *Social Research* 71.1: 73–106.

Balot, R. 2006. *Greek Political Thought*. Oxford: Blackwell.

Balot, R. 2007. "Subordinating Courage to Justice: Statecraft and Soulcraft in Fourth-Century Athens." *Rhetorica* 25.1: 35–52.

Balot, R. 2008. "Socratic Courage and Athenian Democracy." *Ancient Philosophy* 28: 49–69.

Balot, R. 2009a. "The Freedom to Rule: Athenian Imperialism and Democratic Masculinity." In *Enduring Empire: Ancient Lessons for Global Politics*, edited by David Edward Tabachnick and Toivo Koivukoski, 54–68. Toronto: University of Toronto Press.

Balot, R. 2009b. "The Virtue Politics of Democratic Athens." In *The Cambridge Companion to Ancient Greek Political Thought*, edited by Stephen G. Salkever, 271–300. Cambridge: Cambridge University Press.

Balot, R. 2010a. "Democratizing Courage in Classical Athens." In Pritchard, *War, Culture, and Democracy in Classical Athens*, 88–108.

Balot, R. 2010b. "Polybius' Challenge to Republican Triumphalism." *Political Theory* 38.4: 483–509.

Balot, R. 2013. "Democracy and Political Philosophy: Influences, Tensions, Rapprochement." In *The Greek Polis and the Invention of Democracy: A Politico-Cultural Transformation and Its Interpretations*, edited by Johann P. Arnason, Kurt A. Raaflaub, and Peter Wagner, 181-204. Oxford: Blackwell.

Balot, R. forthcoming (a). "Transformations of 'Manliness' in the Democratic Republic." In *Ancient and Modern Republicanism*, edited by Geoffrey Kellow. Toronto: University of Toronto Press.

Balot, R. forthcoming (b). "Virtue and Emotional Education in Ancient Greece: Plato and the Democrats." In *Emotions in Context*, edited by Rebecca Kingston et al. Toronto: University of Toronto Press.

Barber, Benjamin R. *Strong Democracy: Participatory Politics for a New Age*. Berkeley and Los Angeles: University of California Press, 1984.

Barber, Benjamin R. 1998. *A Passion for Democracy: American Essays*. Princeton, NJ: Princeton University Press.

Barker, Elton T. E. 2011. " 'Possessing an Unbridled Tongue': Frank Speech and Speaking Back in Euripides' *Orestes*." In Carter, *Why Athens? A Reappraisal of Tragic Politics*, 145–62.

Barker, E., trans. 1995. *Aristotle. Politics*. Revised edition by R. F. Stalley. Oxford: Oxford University Press.

Barney, D. 2011. "Eat Your Vegetables: Courage and the Possibility of Politics." *Theory & Event* 14.2: 1–25.

Barney, Rachel, "Callicles and Thrasymachus," *The Stanford Encyclopedia of Philosophy (Fall 2004 Edition)*, edited by Edward N. Zalta. Available at http://plato.stanford.edu/archives/fall2004/entries/callicles-thrasymachus/.

Bassi, K. 2003. "The Semantics of Manliness in Ancient Greece." In Rosen and Sluiter, *Andreia: Studies in Manliness and Courage in Classical Antiquity*, 25–58.

Bauhn, Per. 2003. *The Value of Courage*. Lund: Nordic Academic Press.
Beiner, Ronald S. 1992. *What's the Matter with Liberalism?* Berkeley: University of California Press.
Benardete, S. 1969. *Herodotean Inquiries*. The Hague: Martinus Nijhoff.
Benhabib, Seyla. 1996. "Toward a Deliberative Model of Democratic Legitimacy." In *Democracy and Difference: Contesting the Boundaries of the Political*, edited by Seyla Benhabib, 67–94. Princeton, NJ: Princeton University Press.
Benitez, Eugenio. 2000. "Cowardice, Moral Philosophy, and Saying What You Think." In *Who Speaks for Plato? Studies in Platonic Anonymity*, edited by G. Press, 83–98. Lanham, MD: Rowman and Littlefield.
Bentham, Jeremy. 1834. *Deontology*. London: Longman, Rees, Orme, Browne, Green, and Longman.
Bernstein, R. 1998. "The Retrieval of the Democratic Ethos." In *Habermas on Law and Democracy: Critical Exchanges*, edited by Michel Rosenfeld and Andrew Arato, 287–305. Berkeley: University of California Press.
Bers, Victor. 1985. "Dikastic *Thorubos*." In *CRUX: Essays Presented to G.E.M. de Ste. Croix on His Seventy-Fifth Birthday*, edited by P. A. Cartledge and F. D. Harvey, 1–15. London: Duckworth.
Beschi, L. 1969/1970. "Relievi votici attici ricompositi: il relievo della trireme Paralos." *Annuario Scuola Archeologica di Atene* XLVII–XLVIII: 85–132.
Beversluis, J. 2000. *Cross-Examining Socrates: A Defense of the Interlocutors in Plato's Early Dialogues*. Cambridge: Cambridge University Press.
Bhabha, H., ed. 1990. *Nation and Narration*. London: Routledge.
Blitz, Mark. 1975. "An Introduction to the Reading of Plato's *Laches*." *Interpretation* 5: 185–225.
Bloom, Allan. 1955. *The Political Philosophy of Isocrates*. Dissertation, University of Chicago.
Bloom, Allan. 1955/1995. *The Political Philosophy of Isocrates*. Dissertation, University of Chicago. Edited and excerpted by Thomas L. Pangle in *Political Philosophy and the Human Soul: Essays in Memory of Allan Bloom*, edited by Michael Palmer and Thomas L. Pangle, 15–34. Lanham, MD: Rowman and Littlefield.
Bloom, Allan. 1968. *The Republic of Plato*. New York: Basic Books.
Bobonich, C. 2002. *Plato's Utopia Recast: His Later Ethics and Politics*. Oxford: Oxford University Press.
Boedeker, D. 1987. "The Two Faces of Demaratus." *Arethusa* 1987: 185–201.
Boedeker, D. and K. Raaflaub, eds. 1998. *Democracy, Empire, and the Arts in Fifth-Century Athens*. Cambridge, MA: Harvard University Press.
Boegehold, Alan L. and Adele C. Scafuro, eds. 1994. *Athenian Identity and Civic Ideology*. Baltimore, MD: Johns Hopkins University Press.
Bonitz, Hermann. 1886. *Platonische Studien*. Berlin: Hildesheim.
Bosworth, A. B. 2000. "The Historical Context of Thucydides' Funeral Oration." *Journal of Hellenic Studies* 120: 1–16.
Bowie, A. M. 1993. *Aristophanes: Myth, Ritual, and Comedy*. Cambridge: Cambridge University Press.
Bowie, A. M. 2006. "Herodotus on Survival: City or Countryside?" In *City, Countryside, and the Spatial Organization of Value in Classical Antiquity*, edited by Ralph M. Rosen and Ineke Sluiter, 119-37. Leiden: Brill.

Bowie, A. M., ed. 2007. *Herodotus: Histories Book VIII*. Cambridge: Cambridge University Press.

Bowman, L. "The Audience of Euripides' *Herakles*." Abstract of a presentation at the 2003 American Philogical Association Meeting. New Orleans, LA. http://www.apaclassics.org/AnnualMeeting/03mtg/abstracts/bowman.html.

Bowman, L. n.d. (a). "The Audience of Euripides' *Herakles*." Unpublished paper on file with author.

Bowman, L. n.d. (b). "The Wobbly Moral Core of Euripides' *Herakles*." Unpublished paper on file with author.

Bradeen, D. W. 1960. "The Popularity of the Athenian Empire." *Historia* 9: 257–69.

Bradeen, D. W. 1969. "The Athenian Casualty Lists." *Classical Quarterly* 19: 145–59.

Bringmann, Klaus. 1965. *Studien zu den politischen Ideen des Isokrates*. Göttingen: Vandenhoeck and Ruprecht.

Brock, Roger. 2009. "Did the Athenian Empire Promote Democracy?" In *Interpreting the Athenian Empire*, edited by John Ma, Nikolaos Papazarkadas, and Robert Parker, 149–66. London: Duckworth.

Brown, Eric. 2000. "Socrates the Cosmopolitan." *Stanford Agora: An Online Journal of Legal Perspectives* 1: 74–87.

Brown, Eric. 2009. "False Idles: The Politics of the 'Quiet Life' in Greek and Roman Antiquity." In *A Companion to Greek and Roman Political Thought*, edited by R. Balot, 485–500. Oxford: Blackwell.

Brown, Michael E., Sean M. Lynn-Jones, and Steven E. Miller. 1996. *Debating the Democratic Peace*. Cambridge, MA: MIT Press.

Brown, Wendy. 1988. *Manhood and Politics: A Feminist Reading in Political Theory*. Lanham, MD: Rowman and Littlefield.

Buchner, E. 1960. *Der Panegyrikos des Isokrates*. Wiesbaden: Steiner.

Burian, Peter. 1985. "*Logos* and *Pathos*: The Politics of the *Suppliant Women*." In *Directions in Euripidean Criticism: A Collection of Essays*, edited by Peter Burian, 129–55. Durham, NC: Duke University Press.

Burian, Peter. 2011. "Athenian Tragedy as Democratic Discourse." In Carter, *Why Athens? A Reappraisal of Tragic Politics*, 95–117.

Burkert, W. 1979. *Structure and History in Greek Mythology and Ritual*. Berkeley: University of California Press.

Burnett, A. P. 1971. *Catastrophe Survived: Euripides' Plays of Mixed Reversal*. Oxford: Clarendon Press.

Burnyeat, M. F. 1980. "Aristotle on Learning to Be Good." In Rorty, *Essays on Aristotle's Ethics*, 69–92.

Burtt, J. O., trans. 1980. *Minor Attic Orators II*. Loeb Classical Library 395. Cambridge, MA: Harvard University Press.

Bynum, Caroline Walker. 1995. *The Resurrection of the Body in Western Christianity*. New York: Columbia University Press.

Cairns, Douglas. 1993. Aidōs*: The Psychology and Ethics of Honour and Shame in Ancient Greek Literature*. Oxford: Clarendon Press.

Campbell, D. A., trans. 1990. *Greek Lyric I: Sappho and Alcaeus*. Loeb Classical Library 142. Cambridge, MA: Harvard University Press.

Carter, David. 2004. "Citizen Attribute, Negative Right: A Conceptual Difference between Ancient and Modern Ideas of Freedom of Speech." In Sluiter and Rosen, *Free Speech in Classical Antiquity*, 197–220.

Carter, David. 2007. *The Politics of Greek Tragedy: Greece and Rome Live*. Exeter: Bristol Phoenix Press.

Carter, David, ed. 2011. *Why Athens? A Reappraisal of Tragic Politics*. Oxford: Oxford University Press.

Cartledge, Paul. 1996. "Comparatively Equal." In Ober and Hedrick, *Dēmokratia: A Conversation on Democracies, Ancient and Modern*, 175–85.

Cartledge, P. 1998. "The Machismo of the Athenian Empire—or the Reign of the Phaulos?" In *When Men Were Men: Masculinity, Power and Identity in Classical Antiquity*, edited by Lin Foxhall and J. T. Salmon, 54–67. London and New York: Routledge.

Cartledge, Paul. 2006. *Thermopylae: The Battle That Changed the World*. London: Macmillan.

Casey, John. 1990. *Pagan Virtue: An Essay in Ethics*. Oxford: Clarendon Press.

Castriota, David. 1992. *Myth, Ethos, and Actuality*. Madison: University of Wisconsin Press.

Chaplin, Jane D. 2000. *Livy's Exemplary History*. Oxford: Oxford University Press, 2000.

Christ, Matthew R. 2001. "Conscription of Hoplites in Classical Athens." *Classical Quarterly* 51.2: 398–422.

Christ, Matthew R. 2006. *The Bad Citizen in Classical Athens*. Cambridge: Cambridge University Press.

Christ, Matthew R. 2008. "Imagining Bad Citizenship in Classical Athens: Aristophanes' *Ecclesiazusae* 730–876." In *KAKOS: Badness and Anti-Value in Classical Antiquity*, edited by I. Sluiter and R. Rosen, 169–83. Leiden: Brill.

Christ, Matthew R. 2010. "Helping Behavior in Classical Athens." *Phoenix* 64: 254–90.

Christ, Matthew R. 2012. *The Limits of Altruism in Democratic Athens*. Cambridge: Cambridge University Press.

Clarke, M. 2002. "Spartan *Atē* at Thermopylae? Semantics and Ideology at Herodotus, *Histories* 7.223.4." In Powell and Hodkinson, *Sparta: Beyond the Mirage*, 63–84.

Classen, J. and J. Steup. 1889. *Thukydides*. Berlin: Weidmannsche Buchhandlung.

Clatterbaugh, Kenneth. 1997. *Contemporary Perspectives on Masculinity: Men, Women, and Politics in Modern Society*, 2nd. ed. Boulder, CO: Westview Press.

Cohen, David. 1991. *Law, Sexuality, and Society: The Enforcement of Morals in Classical Athens*. Cambridge: Cambridge University Press.

Cohen, D. 1995. *Law, Violence and Community in Classical Athens*. Cambridge: Cambridge University Press.

Collard, Christopher. 2007. "The Funeral Oration in Euripides' *Supplices*." In *Tragedy, Euripides and Euripideans,* 115–37. Exeter: Bristol Phoenix Press [= *Bulletin of the Institute of Classical Studies* 19 (1972) 39–53].

Conacher, D. J. 1967. *Euripidean Drama: Myth, Theme and Structure*. Toronto: University of Toronto Press.

Connor, W. R. 1977. "Tyrannis [sic] Polis." In *Ancient and Modern: Essays in Honor of Gerald F. Else*, edited by J. H. D'Arms and J. W. Eadie, 95–109. Ann Arbor: University of Michigan Press.

Connor, W. R. 1984. *Thucydides*. Princeton, NJ: Princeton University Press.

Connor, W. R. 1988. "Early Greek Land Warfare as Symbolic Expression." *Past and Present* 119: 3–29.

Connor, W. R. 1994. "The Problem of Athenian Civic Identity." In Boegehold and Scafuro, *Athenian Identity and Civic Ideology*, 34–44.

Cooper, John M. 1997. *Plato: Complete Works*. Indianapolis, IN: Hackett.

Cooper, John M. 1999a. "Justice and Rights in Aristotle's *Politics*." In *Reason and Emotion: Essays on Ancient Moral Psychology and Ethical Theory*, 378–89. Princeton, NJ: Princeton University Press.

Cooper, John M. 1999b. "Political Animals and Civic Friendship." In *Reason and Emotion*, 356–77. Princeton, NJ: Princeton University Press.

Cooper, John M. 1999c. "Socrates and Plato in Plato's *Gorgias*." In *Reason and Emotion*, 29–75. Princeton, NJ: Princeton University Press.

Cooper, John M. 1999d. "The Psychology of Justice in Plato." In *Reason and Emotion*, 138–49. Princeton, NJ: Princeton University Press.

Cooper, John M. 1999e. "Plato's *Statesman* and Politics." In *Reason and Emotion*, 165–91. Princeton, NJ: Princeton University Press.

Cooper, John M. 1999f. "Plato's *Statesman* and Politics." In *Reason and Emotion*, 165–91. Princeton, NJ: Princeton University Press.

Corbett, S. and Michael J. Davidson. 2009. "The Role of the Military in Presidential Politics." *Parameters* Winter 2009/10: 20–31. Available at http://www.carlisle.army.mil/usawc/parameters/Articles/09winter/corbett%20and%20davidson.pdf. Accessed February 17, 2012.

Cottingham, John. 1996. "Partiality and the Virtues." In Crisp, *How Should One Live? Essays on the Virtues*, 57–76.

Craig, Leon H. 1994. *The War Lover: A Study of Plato's Republic*. Toronto: University of Toronto Press.

Crane, G. 1998. *Thucydides and the Ancient Simplicity: The Limits of Political Realism*. Berkeley: University of California Press.

Crisp, Roger. 1996a. "Modern Moral Philosophy and the Virtues." In Crisp, *How Should One Live? Essays on the Virtues*, 1–18.

Crisp, Roger, ed. 1996b. *How Should One Live? Essays on the Virtues*. Oxford: Clarendon.

Crisp, Roger and Michael Slote. 1997. "Introduction." In Crisp and Slote, *Virtue Ethics*, 1–25.

Crisp, Roger and M. Slote, eds. 1997. *Virtue Ethics*. Oxford: Oxford University Press.

Croally, N. T. 1994. *Euripidean Polemic: The Trojan Women and the Function of Tragedy*. Cambridge: Cambridge University Press.

Crowley, J. 2012. *The Psychology of the Athenian Hoplite. The Culture of Combat in Classical Athens*. Cambridge: Cambridge University Press.

Csapo, Eric. 1993. "Deep Ambivalence: Notes on a Greek Cockfight." *Phoenix* 47: 1–28, 115–24.

Cullyer, Helen. 2003. "Paradoxical *Andreia*: Socratic Echoes in Stoic 'Manly Courage.'" In Rosen and Sluiter, *Andreia: Studies in Manliness and Courage in Classical Antiquity*, 213–33.

Daly, Mary. (1973) 1985. *Beyond God the Father: Toward a Philosophy of Women's Liberation*. Boston: Beacon Press.

Davidson, J. 1990. "Isocrates against Imperialism: An Analysis of the *De Pace*." *Historia* 39: 20–36.

Deneen, P. 2000. *The Odyssey of Political Theory: The Politics of Departure and Return*. Lanham, MD: Rowman and Littlefield.

Depew, David. 2004. "The Inscription of Isocrates into Aristotle's Practical Philosophy." In Poulakos and Depew, *Isocrates and Civic Education*, 157–85.

de Romilly, Jacqueline. 1956. "La Crainte dans l'oeuvre de Thucydide." *Classica et Mediaevalia* 17: 119–27.

de Romilly, Jacqueline. 1980. "Réflexions sur le courage chez Thucydide et chez Platon." *REG* 93: 3–23.

De Ste. Croix, G. E. M. 1954. "The Character of the Athenian Empire." *Historia* 3: 1–41.

De Ste. Croix, G. E. M. 1972. *The Origins of the Peloponnesian War*. Ithaca, NY: Cornell University Press.

De Ste. Croix, G. E. M. 1996. "The Political Outlook of Aristophanes." In *Oxford Readings in Aristophanes*, edited by E. Segal, 42–64. Oxford: Oxford University Press.

de Sélincourt, Aubrey, trans. 1996. *Herodotus*. Revised by John Marincola. Harmondsworth; Middlesex; Baltimore: Penguin Books.

Deslauriers, M. 2003. "*Aristotle on Andreia*, Divine and Sub-Human Virtues." In Rosen and Sluiter, *Andreia: Studies in Manliness and Courage in Classical Antiquity*, 187–211.

Devereux, Daniel T. 1977. "Courage and Wisdom in Plato's *Laches*." *Journal of the History of Philosophy* 15: 129–41.

de Witt, N. W. and N. J. de Witt, trans. 1949. *Demosthenes*. Vol. 7. Loeb Classical Library. Cambridge, MA: Harvard University Press.

Dobbs, Darrell. 1986. "For Lack of Wisdom: Courage and Inquiry in Plato's *Laches*." *Journal of Politics* 48: 825–49.

Dodds, E. R. 1963. *The Greeks and the Irrational*. Berkeley and Los Angeles: University of California Press.

Dover, K. J. 1968. *Aristophanes. Clouds*. Oxford: Oxford University Press.

Dover, K. J. 1972. *Aristophanic Comedy*. Berkeley: University of California Press.

Dover, K. J. 1974. *Greek Popular Morality in the Time of Plato and Aristotle*. Oxford: Blackwell.

Doyle, Michael W. 1986. *Empires*. Ithaca, NY: Cornell University Press.

Doyle, Michael W. 1997. *Ways of War and Peace: Realism, Liberalism, and Socialism*. New York: W. W. Norton.

Duan, D. 2010. "Reconsidering Tocqueville's Imperialism." *Ethical Perspectives* 17.3: 415–47.

Duff, A. 1987. "Aristotelian Courage." *Ratio* 29: 2–15.

Dworkin, Andrea. 1974. *Woman Hating: A Radical Look at Sexuality*. New York: Dutton.

Eckstein, A. M. 1995. *Moral Vision in "The Histories" of Polybius*. Berkeley: University of California Press.

Eckstein, A. M. 2005. "Rome and the Hellenistic World: Masculinity and Militarism, Monarchy and Republic." Paper delivered at Empire and Liberty conference, John M. Olin Center for Inquiry into the Theory and Practice of Democracy, University of Chicago.

Eckstein, A. M. 2006. *Mediterranean Anarchy, Interstate War, and the Rise of Rome*. Berkeley: University of California Press.

Edmunds, Lowell. 1972. "Thucydides ii.40.2." *Classical Review* 22: 171–72.

Edmunds, Lowell. 1975. *Chance and Intelligence in Thucydides*. Cambridge, MA: Harvard University Press.

Ehrenreich, Barbara. 1997. *Blood Rites: Origins and History of the Passions of War*. New York: Metropolitan Books.

Elshtain, Jean Bethke. 1995. *Women and War*. 2nd ed. Chicago: University of Chicago Press.

Elster, Jon. 1999. *Alchemies of the Mind: Rationality and the Emotions.* Cambridge: Cambridge University Press.

Elster, Jon. 2002. "Norms, Emotions and Social Control." In *Demokratie, Recht und soziale Kontrolle im klassischen Athen*, edited by David Cohen, 1–13. Munich: Oldenbourg.

Emlyn-Jones, C. 1999. "Dramatic Structure and Cultural Context in Plato's *Laches*." *Classical Quarterly* 49.1: 123–38.

Epstein, David F. 1984. *The Political Theory of "The Federalist."* Chicago: University of Chicago Press.

Estlund, D. 1993. "Making Truth Safe For Democracy." In *The Idea of Democracy*, edited by D. Copp, J. Hampton, and J. Roemer, 71–100. Cambridge: Cambridge University Press.

Estlund, D. 2009. *Democratic Authority: A Philosophical Framework.* Princeton, NJ: Princeton University Press.

Euben, J. Peter. 1986a. "Introduction." In Euben, *Greek Tragedy and Political Theory*, 1–42.

Euben, J. Peter. 1986b. "Political Corruption in Euripides' *Orestes*." In Euben, *Greek Tragedy and Political Theory*, 222–51.

Euben, J. Peter, ed. 1986c. *Greek Tragedy and Political Theory.* Berkeley: University of California Press.

Euben, J. Peter. 1986d. "The Battle of Salamis and the Origins of Political Theory." *Political Theory* 14.3: 359–90.

Euben, J. Peter. 1990. *The Tragedy of Political Theory: The Road Not Taken.* Princeton, NJ: Princeton University Press.

Euben, J. Peter. 1996. "Reading Democracy: 'Socratic' Dialogues and the Political Education of Democratic Citizens." In Ober and Hedrick, *Dēmokratia: A Conversation on Democracies, Ancient and Modern*, 327–59.

Euben, J. Peter. 2000. "Arendt's Hellenism." In *The Cambridge Companion to Hannah Arendt*, edited by Dana Villa, 151–64. Cambridge: Cambridge University Press.

Euben, J. Peter, John R. Wallach, and Josiah Ober, eds. 1994. *Athenian Political Thought and the Reconstruction of American Democracy.* Ithaca, NY: Cornell University Press.

Evans, J. A. S. 1991. *Herodotus, Explorer of the Past: Three Essays.* Princeton, NJ: Princeton University Press.

Fagles, Robert, trans. 1990. *Homer: The Iliad.* New York: Penguin.

Farenga, Vincent. 2006. *Citizen and Self in Ancient Greece: Individuals Performing Justice and the Law.* Cambridge: Cambridge University Press.

Faraone, Christopher A. 1997. "Salvation and Female Heroics in the Parodos of Aristophanes' *Lysistrata*." *Journal of Hellenic Studies* 117: 38–59.

Fantham, Elaine, et al. 1994. *Women in the Classical World: Image and Text.* New York: Oxford University Press.

Farnell, L. R. 1906. *The Cults of the Greek City-States.* Vol. 1. Oxford: Clarendon Press.

Faulkner, Robert. 2007. *The Case for Greatness: Honorable Ambition and Its Critics.* New Haven, CT: Yale University Press.

Finley, M. I. 1962. "Athenian Demagogues." *Past and Present* 21: 3–24.

Finley, M. I. 1978a. "The Fifth-Century Athenian Empire: A Balance-Sheet." In *Imperialism in the Ancient World: Cambridge University Research Seminar in Ancient History*, edited by P. D. A. Garnsey and C. R. Whittaker, 103–26. Cambridge; New York: Cambridge University Press.

Finley, M. I. 1978b. *The World of Odysseus*. 2nd ed. New York: Viking Press.
Finley, M. I. 1983. *Politics in the Ancient World*. Cambridge: Cambridge University Press.
Fisher, N. R. E. 1992. *Hybris: A Study of the Values of Honor and Shame in Ancient Greece*. Warminster: Aris and Phillips.
Fisher, N. R. E. 1994. "Sparta Re(de)valued: Some Athenian Public Attitudes toward Sparta between Leuctra and the Lamian War." In Powell and Hodkinson, *The Shadow of Sparta*, 347–99.
Fisher, N. R. E. 2001. *Aeschines. Against Timarchos*. Oxford: Oxford University Press.
Flower, Michael A. and John Marincola, eds. 2002. *Herodotus: Histories Book IX*. Cambridge: Cambridge University Press.
Foley, Helene P. 1982. "The 'Female Intruder' Reconsidered: Women in Aristophanes' *Lysistrata* and *Ecclesiazusae*." *Classical Philology* 77.1: 1–21.
Foley, Helene P. 2001. *Female Acts in Greek Tragedy*. Princeton, NJ: Princeton University Press.
Foot, Philippa. 1978. *Virtues and Vices*. Oxford: Blackwell.
Foot, Philippa. 1985. "Utilitarianism and the Virtues." *Mind* 94: 196–209.
Forde, Steven. 1986. "Thucydides on the Causes of Athenian Imperialism." *American Political Science Review* 80: 433–48.
Fornara, Charles W. 1971. *Herodotus: An Interpretive Essay*. Oxford: Clarendon Press.
Fornara, Charles W., ed. and trans. 1983. *Archaic Times to the End of the Peloponnesian War*, 2nd ed. Translated Documents of Greece and Rome, I. Cambridge: Cambridge University Press.
Forsdyke, S. 2001. "Athenian Democratic Ideology and Herodotus' *Histories*." *American Journal of Philology* 122: 329–58.
Forsdyke, S. 2005. *Exile, Ostracism, and Democracy: The Politics of Expulsion in Ancient Greece*. Princeton, NJ: Princeton University Press.
Foster, Edith. 2010. *Thucydides, Pericles, and Periclean Imperialism*. Cambridge: Cambridge University Press.
Foucault, Michel. 1985. *The Use of Pleasure*. New York: Vintage Books.
Foucault, Michel. 1986. *The Care of the Self*. New York: Vintage Books.
Franco, Paul. 2002. *Hegel's Philosophy of Freedom*. New Haven, CT: Yale University Press.
Frank, J. 2005. *A Democracy of Distinction: Aristotle and the Work of Politics*. Chicago: University of Chicago Press.
Freese, J. H., trans. 1994. *Aristotle. Art of Rhetoric*. Loeb Classical Library 193. Cambridge, MA: Harvard University Press.
Friedman, M. 1998. "Impartiality." In *The Companion to Feminist Philosophy*, edited by Alison Jaggar and Iris Marion Young, 393–401. Oxford: Blackwell.
Gabrielsen, V. 1997. *The Naval Aristocracy of Hellenistic Rhodes*. Aarhus: Aarhus University Press.
Gabrielsen, V. 2002. "The Impact of Armed Forces on Government and Politics in Archaic and Classical Greek Poleis: A Response to Hans van Wees." In *Army and Power in the Ancient World*, edited by Angelos Chaniotis and Pierre Ducrey, 83–98. Stuttgart: Franz Steiner Verlag.
Galston, William A. 1991. *Liberal Purposes: Goods, Virtues, and Diversity in the Liberal State*. Cambridge: Cambridge University Press.

Garrity, T. F. 1998. "Thucydides 1.22.1: Content and Form in the Speeches." *American Journal of Philology* 119: 361–84.

Garvie, A. F., ed. 2009. *Aeschylus: Persae*. Oxford: Oxford University Press.

Geach, P. 1977. *The Virtues*. Cambridge: Cambridge University Press.

Gehrke, Robert. 2003. "Staff Shakeup at Air Force Academy." CBS News online. Available at http://www.cbsnews.com/stories/2003/03/28/politics/main546607.shtml.

Gentili, Alberico. 1933. *De Iure Belli Libri Tres*. Vol. 2. Translated by John C. Rolfe. Oxford: Clarendon Press.

Gerber, Douglas E., trans. 1999. *Greek Elegiac Poetry from the Seventh to the Fifth Centuries B.C.* Loeb Classical Library 258. Cambridge, MA: Harvard University Press.

Geuss, Raymond. 2005. "Outside Ethics." In *Outside Ethics,* 40–66. Princeton, NJ: Princeton University Press.

Gill, Christopher. 1996. *Personality in Greek Epic, Tragedy, and Philosophy: The Self in Dialogue*. Oxford: Clarendon Press.

Godley, A. D., trans. 1975. *Herodotus*. Loeb Classical Library, 4 vols. Cambridge, MA: Harvard University Press.

Goldhill, S. 1988. "Battle Narrative and Politics in Aeschylus' *Persians*." *Journal of Hellenic Studies* 108: 189–93.

Goldhill, S. 1990. "The Great Dionysia and Civic Ideology." In Winkler and Zeitlin, *Nothing to Do with Dionysos?*, 97-129.

Goldhill, S. 1999. "Programme Notes." In *Performance Culture and Athenian Democracy*, edited by S. Goldhill and R. Osborne, 1–32. Cambridge: Cambridge University Press.

Goldie, Peter. 2000. *The Emotions: A Philosophical Exploration*. Oxford: Oxford University Press.

Gomme, A. W., A. Andrewes, and K. J. Dover, eds. 1945–81. *A Historical Commentary on Thucydides*. 5 vols. Oxford: Clarendon Press.

Gonzalez, F. 1998. *Dialectic and Dialogue: Plato's Practice of Philosophical Inquiry* Evanston, IL: Northwestern University Press.

Goodin, R. E. 2003. *Reflective Democracy*. Oxford: Oxford University Press.

Graham, A. J. 1992. "Thucydides 7.13.2 and the Crews of Athenian Triremes." *Transactions of the American Philological Association* 122: 257–70.

Graham, A. J. 1998. "Thucydides 7.13.2 and the Crews of Athenian Triremes: An Addendum." *Transactions of the American Philological Association* 128: 89–114.

Gray, J. Glenn. 1959. *The Warriors: Reflections on Men in Battle*. New York: Harcourt, Brace.

Gray, Vivienne. 1994. "Images of Sparta: Writer and Audience in Isocrates' *Panathenaicus*." In Powell and Hodkinson, *The Shadow of Sparta*, 223–71.

Griffin, Jasper. 1999. "Sophocles and the Democratic City." In *Sophocles Revisited: Essays Presented to Sir Hugh Lloyd-Jones*, 73–94. Oxford: Oxford University Press.

Grossman, Dave. 1995. *On Killing: The Psychological Cost of Learning to Kill in War and Society*. Boston: Little, Brown, and Company.

Grube, G. M. A., trans. 1997. "Apology." In Cooper, *Plato: Complete Works*, 17–36.

Grube, G. M. A., trans. 1997. "Republic." In Cooper, *Plato: Complete Works*, 971–1223. Revised by C. D. C. Reeve.

Guthrie, W. K. C., trans. 1994. "Protagoras." In *The Collected Dialogues of Plato*, edited by Edith Hamilton and Huntington Cairns, 308–52. Princeton, NJ: Princeton University Press.

Gutmann, A. and D. Thompson. 1996. *Democracy and Disagreement*. Cambridge: Harvard University Press.

Habermas, J. 1993. *Justification and Application: Remarks on Discourse Ethics*. Cambridge, MA: MIT Press.

Hall, Edith. 1989. *Inventing the Barbarian: Greek Self-Definition through Tragedy*. Oxford: Oxford University Press.

Hall, Edith. 1996. *Aeschylus: Persians*. Warminster: Aris & Phillips.

Hall, Edith. 1997. "The Sociology of Athenian Tragedy." In *The Cambridge Companion to Greek Tragedy*, edited by P. E. Easterling, 92–126. Cambridge: Cambridge University Press.

Hall, J. 2001. "Contested Ethnicities: Perceptions of Macedonia within Evolving Definitions of Greek Identity." In *Ancient Perceptions of Greek Ethnicity*, edited by I. Malkin, 159–86. Washington, DC: Center for Hellenic Studies.

Halliwell, Stephen. 2004. "Aischrology, Shame, and Comedy." In Sluiter and Rosen, *Free Speech in Classical Antiquity*, 115–44.

Halperin, David M., John J. Winkler, and Froma I. Zeitlin. 1990. *Before Sexuality: The Construction of Erotic Experience in the Ancient Greek World*. Princeton, NJ: Princeton University Press.

Hamilton, Walter, trans. 1971. *Plato. Gorgias*. Harmondsworth: Penguin.

Hammond, S. J. 2005. "Spiritedness Incarnate and the Unity of the Soul in Plato's *Republic*." *Polis* 22.1: 60–84.

Hansen, M. H. 1974. *The Sovereignty of the People's Court in Athens in the Fourth Century B.C. and the Public Action against Unconstitutional Proposals*. Odense: Odense University Press.

Hansen, M. H. 1983. "The Athenian 'Politicians' 403–322 BC." *Greek, Roman, and Byzantine Studies* 24: 33–55.

Hansen, M. H. 1991. *The Athenian Democracy in the Age of Demosthenes: Structure, Principles, and Ideology*. Oxford: Blackwell.

Hansen, M. H. 1995. *The Trial of Sokrates: From the Athenian Point of View*. Copenhagen: Kongelige Danske Videnskabernes Selskab: Commissioner Munksgaard.

Hansen, M. H. 1999. Review of Eric W. Robinson, *The First Democracies*. Bryn Mawr Classical Review. Available at http://ccat.sas.upenn.edu/bmcr/1999/1999-09-17.html.

Hanson, V. D. 1983. *Warfare and Agriculture in Classical Greece*. Biblioteca de Studi Antichi 40. Pisa: Giardini Editori.

Hanson, V. D. 1989. *The Western Way of War: Infantry Battle in Classical Greece*. New York: Oxford University Press.

Hanson, V. D. 1995. *The Other Greeks: The Family Farm and the Agrarian Roots of Western Civilization*. New York: Free Press.

Hanson, V. D. 1996. "Hoplites into Democrats: The Changing Ideology of Athenian Infantry." In Ober and Hedrick, *Dēmokratia: A Conversation on Democracies, Ancient and Modern*, 289–312.

Hanson, V. D. 2000. "Hoplite Battle as Ancient Greek Warfare: When, Where, and Why." In van Wees, *War and Violence in Ancient Greece*, 201–32.

Hanson, V. D. 2001a. "Democratic Warfare, Ancient and Modern." In McCann and Strauss, *War and Democracy*, 3–33.

Hanson, V. 2001b. *Carnage and Culture: Landmark Battles in the Rise of Western Power.* New York: Doubleday.

Hariman, Robert. 2004. "Civic Education, Classical Imitation, and Democratic Polity." In Poulakos and Depew, *Isocrates and Civic Education*, 217–34.

Harris, W. V. 2001. *Restraining Rage: The Ideology of Anger Control in Classical Antiquity.* Cambridge, MA: Harvard University Press.

Harrison, E. B. 1972. "The South Frieze of the Nike Temple and the Marathon Painting in the Painted Stoa." *American Journal of Archaeology* 76: 353–78.

Harrison, Thomas. 2000. *The Emptiness of Asia: Aeschylus' Persians and the History of the Fifth Century.* London: Duckworth.

Hartog, F. 1988. *The Mirror of Herodotus: The Representation of the Other in the Writing of History.* Translated by J. Lloyd. Berkeley: University of California Press.

Harvey, F. D. 1965, 1966. "Two Kinds of Equality." *Classica et Mediaevalia* 26: 101–46; 27: 96–100 (corrigenda).

Haskins, Ekaterina. 2004. *Logos and Power in Isocrates and Aristotle.* Columbia, SC: University of South Carolina Press.

Havelock, Eric A. 1968. "Watching the *Trojan Women*." In *Euripides: A Collection of Critical Essays*, edited by Erich Segal, 115–27. Englewood Cliffs, NJ: Prentice-Hall.

Heath, Malcolm. 1987. *Political Comedy in Aristophanes.* Gottingen: Vandenhoeck and Ruprecht.

Hedges, Chris. 2003. *War Is a Force That Gives Us Meaning.* New York: Random House.

Hedrick, Charles W., Jr. 1994. "The Zero Degree of Society: Aristotle and the Athenian Citizen." In Euben, Wallach, and Ober, *Athenian Political Thought and the Reconstruction of American Democracy*, 289–318.

Henderson, Jeffrey. 1980. "*Lysistrate*: The Play and Its Themes." In *Aristophanes: Essays in Interpretation*, edited by J. Henderson, 153–218. Yale Classical Studies. Vol. XXVI. Cambridge: Cambridge University Press.

Henderson, Jeffrey, ed. 1987. *Aristophanes. Lysistrata.* Edited with an Introduction and Commentary. Oxford: Clarendon Press.

Henderson, Jeffrey. 1990. "The Demos and the Comic Competition." In Winkler and Zeitlin, *Nothing to Do with Dionysos?*, 271–313.

Henderson, Jeffrey. 1993. "Comic Hero versus Political Elite." In Henderson, Halliwell, Sommerstein, and Zimmermann, *Tragedy, Comedy, and the Polis*, 307–319.

Henderson, Jeffrey, trans. 1996. *Three Plays by Aristophanes: Staging Women.* New York: Routledge.

Henderson, Jeffrey. 1996. "The Demos and the Comic Competition." In *Oxford Readings in Aristophanes*, edited by E. Segal, 65–97. Oxford: Oxford University Press.

Henderson, Jeffrey, trans. 1998. *Aristophanes: Clouds, Wasps, Peace.* Loeb Classical Library 488. Cambridge, MA: Harvard University Press.

Henderson, Jeffrey, trans. 2000. *Aristophanes: Birds, Lysistrata, Women at the Thesmophoria.* Loeb Classical Library 179. Cambridge, MA: Harvard University Press.

Henderson, Jeffrey, trans. 2002. *Aristophanes: Frogs, Assemblywomen, Wealth.* Loeb Classical Library 180. Cambridge, MA: Harvard University Press.

Henderson, J., S. Halliwell, A. H. Sommerstein, and B. Zimmermann, eds. 1993. *Tragedy Comedy and the Polis.* Bari: Levante Editori.

Herman, G. 2006. *Morality and Behaviour in Democratic Athens: A Social History.* Cambridge: Cambridge University Press.

Herrman, J. 2009. *Hyperides: Funeral Oration.* Edited, with an introduction, translation, and commentary by J. Hermann. Oxford: Oxford University Press.

Hesk, Jon. 2011. "Euripidean *euboulia* and the Problem of 'Tragic Politics.'" In Carter, *Why Athens? A Reappraisal of Tragic Politics*, 119–43.

Hirschman, A. O. 1977. *The Passions and the Interests: Political Arguments for Capitalism before Its Triumph.* Princeton, NJ: Princeton University Press.

Hobbs, Angela. 2000. *Plato and the Hero: Courage, Manliness, and the Impersonal Good.* Cambridge: Cambridge University Press.

Hoerber, Robert G. 1968. "Plato's *Laches.*" *Classical Philology* 63.2: 95–105.

Holmes, Brooke. 2008. "Euripides' Heracles in the Flesh." *Classical Antiquity* 27.2: 231–81.

Hölscher, T. 1998. "Images and Political Identity: The Case of Athens." In Boedeker and Raaflaub, *Democracy, Empire, and the Arts in Fifth-Century Athens*, 153–83.

Hooker, Brad. 1996. "Does Being Virtuous Constitute a Benefit to the Agent?" In Crisp, *How Should One Live?*, 141–55.

Hornblower, Simon. 1987. *Thucydides.* Baltimore, MD: Johns Hopkins University Press.

Hornblower, Simon. 1991–2008. *A Commentary on Thucydides.* 3 vols. Oxford: Clarendon Press.

Huart, Pierre. 1968. *Le Vocabulaire de l'analyse psychologique dans l'oeuvre de Thucydide.* Études et Commentaires, 69. Paris: C. Klincksieck.

Hudson-Williams, H. Ll. 1960. Review of E. Buchner, *Der Panegyrikos des Isokrates. Classical Review* 10.1: 31–33.

Hunt, Lester. 1997. *Character and Culture.* New York: Rowman and Littlefield.

Hunt, P. 1998. *Slaves, Warfare, and Ideology in the Greek Historians.* Cambridge: Cambridge University Press.

Hunt, P., 2010. *War, Peace, and Alliance in Demosthenes' Athens.* Cambridge: Cambridge University Press.

Hunter, V. J. 1994. *Policing Athens: Social Control in the Attic Lawsuits, 420-320 BC.* Princeton, NJ: Princeton University Press.

Hurka, Thomas. 1987. "'Good' and 'Good For.'" *Mind* 96: 71–73.

Hurka, Thomas. 2001. *Virtue, Vice, and Value.* Oxford: Oxford University Press.

Hursthouse, Rosalind. 1999. *On Virtue Ethics.* Oxford: Oxford University Press.

Hursthouse, Rosalind. 2012. "Virtue Ethics." *The Stanford Encyclopedia of Philosophy.* (Summer 2012 Edition), edited by Edward N. Zalta, Available at http://plato.stanford.edu/archives/sum2012/entries/ethics-virtue/.

Irwin, Terence H. 1995. *Plato's Ethics.* New York; Oxford: Oxford University Press.

James, William. 1910. "The Moral Equivalent of War." *McClure's Magazine*, August, 1910.

Jameson, Fredric. 1981. *The Political Unconscious: Narrative as a Socially Symbolic Act.* Ithaca, NY: Cornell University Press.

Jeffords, Susan. *Hard Bodies: Hollywood Masculinity in the Reagan Era.* New Brunswick, NJ: Rutgers University Press, 1994.

Johnston, A. I. 1998. *Cultural Realism: Strategic Culture and Grand Strategy in Chinese History.* Princeton, NJ: Princeton University Press.

Johnstone, Steven. 1999. *Disputes and Democracy: The Consequences of Litigation in Ancient Athens.* Austin, TX: University of Texas Press.

Kahn, Charles. 1963. "Plato's Funeral Oration: The Motive of the *Menexenus*." *Classical Philology* 58.4: 220–34.

Kahn, Charles. 1983. "Drama and Dialectic in Plato's *Gorgias*." *Oxford Studies in Ancient Philosophy* 1: 75–121.

Kakridis, J. 1961. *Der thukydideische Epitaphios: ein stilistischer Kommentar*. Munich: C.H. Beck.

Kallet, Lisa. 2003. "*Dēmos Tyrannos*: Wealth, Power, and Economic Patronage." In Morgan, *Popular Tyranny*, 117–53.

Kamerbeek, J. C. 1966. "Unity and Meaning of Euripides' 'Heracles.'" *Mnemosyne* 19.1: 1–16.

Kamtekar, R. 2005. "The Profession of Friendship: Callicles, Democratic Politics, and Rhetorical Education in Plato's *Gorgias*." *Ancient Philosophy* 25: 319–39.

Kateb, George. 1989. "Hobbes and the Irrationality of Politics." *Political Theory* 17: 355–91.

Kateb, George. 1992. *The Inner Ocean: Individualism and Democratic Culture*. Ithaca, NY: Cornell University Press.

Kateb, George. 1998. "Socratic Integrity." In *Integrity and Conscience. Nomos XL,* edited by Ian Shapiro and Robert Adams, 77–112. New York: New York University Press.

Kateb, George. 2000. "Is Patriotism a Mistake?" *Social Research* 67: 901–24.

Kateb, George. 2004. "Courage as a Virtue." *Social Research* 71.1: 39–72.

Keller, Simon. 2007. "Virtue Ethics is Self-Effacing." *Australasian Journal of Philosophy* 85.2: 221–32.

Kennedy, J. F. (1955) 2006. *Profiles in Courage*. New York: Harper Collins.

Keohane, R. 1984. *After Hegemony: Cooperation and Discord in the World Political Economy*. Princeton, NJ: Princeton University Press.

Keuls, Eva. 1985. *The Reign of the Phallus*. New York: Harper and Row.

Kingston, Rebecca. 2011. *Public Passion: Rethinking the Grounds for Political Justice*. Montreal and Kingston: McGill-Queen's University Press.

Knox, T. M., trans. 1967. *Hegel's Philosophy of Right*. New York: Oxford University Press.

Kochin, Michael S. 2002. *Gender and Rhetoric in Plato's Political Philosophy*. Cambridge: Cambridge University Press.

Konstan, D. 1987. "Persians, Greeks and Empire." *Arethusa* 20: 59–73.

Konstan, D. 1993. "Aristophanes' *Lysistrata*: Women and the Body Politic." In Sommerstein, Halliwell, Henderson, and Zimmermann, *Tragedy, Comedy, and the Polis: Papers from the Greek Drama Conference (Nottingham, 18-20 July 1990)*, 431–44.

Konstan, D. 1999. "What We Must Believe in Greek Tragedy." *Ramus* 28.2: 75–88.

Konstan, D. 2003a. "Shame in Ancient Greece." *Social Research* 70.4: 601–30.

Konstan, D. 2003b. "Before Jealousy." In Konstan and Rutter, *Envy, Spite and Jealousy*, 7–28.

Konstan, D. 2004a. "Isocrates' 'Republic.'" In Poulakos and Depew, *Isocrates and Civic Education*, 107–24.

Konstan, D. 2004b. "Nemesis and Phthonos." In *Gestures: Studies in Greek Literature, History, and Philosophy in Honor of Alan Boegehold*, edited by G. Bakewell and J. Sickinger, 74–87. Oakville, CT: David Brown.

Konstan, D. 2006. *The Emotions of the Ancient Greeks: Studies in Aristotle and Classical Literature*. Toronto: University of Toronto Press.

Konstan, D. 2010. "Ridiculing a Popular War: Old Comedy and Militarism in Classical Athens." In Pritchard, *War, Culture, and Democracy in Classical Athens*, 184–199.

Konstan, D. and N. Keith Rutter, eds. 2003. *Envy, Spite and Jealousy: The Rivalrous Emotions in Ancient Greece*. Edinburgh: Edinburgh University Press.

Kovacs, D., trans. 1995. *Euripides: Children of Heracles; Hippolytus; Andromache; Hecuba*. Loeb Classical Library 484. Cambridge, MA: Harvard University Press.

Kovacs, D. trans. 1998. *Euripides: Suppliant Women; Electra; Heracles*. Loeb Classical Library 9. Cambridge, MA: Harvard University Press.

Kovacs, D. trans. 1999. *Euripides: Trojan Women; Iphigeneia among the Taurians; Ion*. Loeb Classical Library 10. Cambridge, MA: Harvard University Press.

Kovacs, D., trans. 2002. *Euripides: Helen; Phoenician Women; Orestes*. Loeb Classical Library 11. Cambridge, MA: Harvard University Press.

Koziak, B. 2000. *Retrieving Political Emotion: Thumos, Aristotle, and Gender*. University Park, PA: Pennsylvania State University Press.

Krause, Sharon. 2002. *Liberalism with Honor*. Cambridge, MA: Harvard University Press.

Kraut, Richard. 2007. *What Is Good and Why: The Ethics of Well-Being*. Cambridge, MA: Harvard University Press.

Kraut, Richard. 2011. *Against Absolute Goodness*. Oxford: Oxford University Press.

LaCapra, Dominick. 1983. *Re-thinking Intellectual History: Texts, Contexts, Language*. Ithaca, NY: Cornell University Press.

Lamb, W. R. M., trans. 1988. *Lysias*. Loeb Classical Library 244. Cambridge, MA: Harvard University Press.

Lattimore, R. 1961. *The Iliad of Homer*. Chicago: University of Chicago Press.

Lazenby, J. F. 1993. *The Defence of Greece: 490-479 BC*. Warminster: Aris and Phillips.

Lear, Jonathan. 2006. *Radical Hope: Ethics in the Face of Cultural Devastation*. Cambridge, MA: Harvard University Press.

Lebow, Richard N. 2008. *A Cultural Theory of International Relations*. Cambridge: Cambridge University Press.

Lembke, J. and C. J. Herington, trans. 1981. *Aeschylus: Persians*. New York: Oxford University Press.

Lendon, J. E. 1997. *Empire of Honor: The Art of Government in the Roman World*. Oxford: Clarendon Press.

Lendon, J. E. 2010. *Song of Wrath: The Peloponnesian War Begins*. New York: Basic Books.

Lesky, A. 1966. "Decision and Responsibility in the Tragedy of Aeschylus." *Journal of Hellenic Studies* 86: 78–85.

Lessner, Richard. 1998. "Male Identity Crisis." http://fathersforlife.org/mens_issues/manliness.htm. Accessed February 17, 2012. Originally published as an editorial in the Manchester, New Hampshire *Union Leader,* August 12, 1998.

Liddel, Peter. 2007. *Civic Obligation and Individual Liberty in Ancient Athens*. Oxford Classical Monographs. Oxford: Oxford University Press.

Lissarrague, F. 1989. "The World of the Warrior." In *A City of Images: Iconography and Society in Ancient Greece*, edited by Claude Bérard and Christiane Bron, 39–51. Translated by Deborah Lyons. Princeton, NJ: Princeton University Press.

Lively, Jack. 1962. *The Social and Political Thought of Alexis de Tocqueville*. Oxford: Clarendon Press.

Lloyd, Michael. 1992. *The Agon in Euripides*. Oxford: Clarendon Press.

Lloyd-Jones, H. 1962. "The Guilt of Agamemnon." *Classical Quarterly* 12: 187–99.

Loraux, Nicole. 1977. "La belle mort spartiate." *Ktema* 2: 105–120.

Loraux, Nicole. 1986. *The Invention of Athens: The Funeral Oration in the Classical City*. Translated by Alan Sheridan. Cambridge, MA: Harvard University Press.

Loraux, Nicole. 1995. *The Experiences of Tiresias: The Feminine and the Greek Man*. Princeton, NJ: Princeton University Press.

Low, Polly. 2003. "Remembering War in Fifth-Century Greece: Ideologies, Societies, and Commemoration beyond Democratic Athens." *World Archaeology* 35.1: 98–111.

Low, Polly. 2005. "Looking for the Language of Athenian Imperialism." *Journal of Hellenic Studies* 125: 93–111.

Low, Polly. 2007. *Interstate Relations in Classical Greece: Morality and Power*. Cambridge: Cambridge University Press.

Low, Polly, ed. 2008. *The Athenian Empire*. Edinburgh: Edinburgh University Press.

Ma, John. 2009. "Afterword: Whither the Athenian Empire?" In *Interpreting the Athenian Empire*, edited by John Ma, Nikolaos Papazarkadas, and Robert Parker, 223–31. London: Duckworth.

MacDowell, D. M. 1978. *The Law in Classical Athens*. Ithaca, NY: Cornell University Press.

MacDowell, D. M. 1995. *Aristophanes and Athens: An Introduction to the Plays*. Oxford: Oxford University Press.

Macedo, Stephen. 1990. *Liberal Virtues: Citizenship, Virtue, and Community in Liberal Constitutionalism*. Oxford: Clarendon Press.

MacIntyre, Alasdair. 1984. *After Virtue: A Study in Moral Theory*. Notre Dame: University of Notre Dame Press.

MacIntyre, Alasdair. 1988. *Whose Justice? Which Rationality?* Notre Dame: University of Notre Dame Press.

MacLeod, Colin. 1978. "Reason and Necessity: Thucydides III 9-14, 37-48." *Journal of Hellenic Studies* 98: 64–78.

MacLeod, Colin. 1983. *Collected Essays*. Oxford: Clarendon Press.

MacMullen, R. 2003. *Feelings in History*. Claremont, CA: Regina Books.

Maidment, K., trans. 1982. *Minor Attic Orators*. Vol. 1. Loeb Classical Library 308. Cambridge, MA: Harvard University Press.

Manent, Pierre. 1996. *Tocqueville and the Nature of Democracy*. Translated by John Waggoner. Lanham, MD: Rowman and Littlefield.

Manent, Pierre. 2007. *Enquête sur la démocratie: Études de philosophie politique*. Paris: Gallimard.

Mansfield, Harvey C., Jr. 1971. "Hobbes and the Science of Indirect Government," *American Political Science Review* 65: 97–110.

Mansfield, Harvey C., Jr. (1979) 2001. *Machiavelli's New Modes and Orders: A Study of the Discourses on Livy*. Chicago: University of Chicago Press.

Mansfield, Harvey C., Jr. 1996. *Machiavelli's Virtue*. Chicago: University of Chicago Press.

Mansfield, Harvey C., Jr. 2006. *Manliness*. New Haven, CT: Yale University Press.

Mansfield, Harvey C., Jr., and Delba Winthrop, trans. 2000. *Alexis de Tocqueville: Democracy in America*. Chicago: University of Chicago Press.

Mansfield, Edward D. and Jack Snyder. 2005. *Electing to Fight: Why Emerging Democracies Go to War*. Cambridge, MA: MIT Press.

Manville, P. B. 1997. "Pericles and the 'both/and' Vision for Democratic Athens." In *Polis and Polemos*, edited by Charles D. Hamilton and Peter Krentz, 73–84. Claremont, CA: Regina Books.

Mara, Gerald M. 2008. *The Civic Conversations of Thucydides and Plato: Classical Political Philosophy and the Limits of Democracy*. Albany: State University of New York Press.

Marchant, E. C. 1961. *Thucydides: Book II*. London: Macmillan; and New York: St. Martin's.

Marincola, John. 1987. "Herodotean Narrative and the Narrator's Presence." In *Arethusa* 20.1–2: 121–37.

Marti, J. L. 2006. "The Epistemic Conception of Deliberative Democracy Defended: Reasons, Rightness, and Equal Political Autonomy." In *Deliberative Democracy and Its Discontents*, edited by S. Besson, J. L. Marti, and V. Seiler. Burlington, VT: Ashgate Publishing. Available at http://www.trinitinture.com/documents/martimarmol.pdf.

Martin, Richard. 1987. "Fire on the Mountain: *Lysistrata* and the Lemnian Women." *Classical Antiquity* 6: 77–105.

Martin, Richard. 1992. "Hesiod's Metanastic Poetics." *Ramus* 21: 11–33.

Mathieu, Georges (1925) 1966. *Les Idées Politiques d'Isocrate*. Paris: Budé.

Maurizio, L. 1998. "The Panathenaic Procession: Athens' Participatory Democracy on Display?" In Boedeker and Raaflaub, *Democracy, Empire, and the Arts in Fifth-Century Athens*, 297–317.

May, Larry. 1998. *Masculinity and Morality*. Ithaca, NY: Cornell University Press.

McCain, J., with Mark Salter. 2005. *Character Is Destiny: Inspiring Stories Every Young Person Should Know and Every Adult Should Remember*. New York: Random House.

McCann, David and Barry S. Strauss. 2001. *War and Democracy: A Comparative Study of the Korean War and the Peloponnesian War*. London: M. E. Sharpe.

McClure, Laura. 2006. "Maternal Authority and Heroic Disgrace in Aeschylus' *Persae*." *Transactions of the American Philological Association* 136.1: 71–97.

McNiven, Timothy J. 2000. "Behaving like an Other: Telltale Gestures in Athenian Vase Painting." In *Not the Classical Ideal: Athens and the Construction of the Other in Greek Art*, edited by Beth Cohen, 71–97. Leiden: Brill.

Meiggs, R. and D. M. Lewis. 1969. *A Selection of Greek Historical Inscriptions to the End of the Fifth Century BC*. Oxford: Clarendon Press.

Menn, Stephen. 1995. *Plato on God as Nous*. Carbondale: Southern Illinois University Press.

Mendelsohn, Daniel. 2002. *Gender and the City in Euripides' Political Plays*. Oxford: Oxford University Press.

Meyer, Ed. 1899. *Forschungen zur alten Geschichte*. Vol. 2. Halle: Niemeyer.

Michelini, A. 1994. "Political Themes in Euripides' *Suppliants*." *American Journal of Philology* 115.2: 219–252.

Michelini, A. 2000. "Plato's *Laches*: An Introduction to Socrates," *Rheinisches Museum für Philologie* 143.1: 60–75.

Milillo, D. M. 2006. "Rape as a Tactic of War: Social and Psychological Perspectives." *Affilia: Special Issue on Women, War, and Peace Building* 21.2: 196–205.

Millender, E. G. 2002a. "*Nomos Despotēs*: Spartan Obedience and Athenian Lawfulness in Fifth-Century Thought." In *Oikistes: Studies in Constitutions, Colonies, and*

Military Power in the Ancient World Offered in Honor of A.J. Graham, edited by V. Gorman and E. Robinson, 33–59. Leiden: Brill.

Millender, E. G. 2002b. "Herodotus and Spartan Despotism." In Powell and Hodkinson, *Sparta: Beyond the Mirage*, 1–61.

Miller, Margaret. 2010. "I am Eurymedon: Tensions and Ambiguities in Athenian War Imagery." In Pritchard, *War, Culture, and Democracy in Classical Athens*, 304–38.

Miller, William Ian. 1995a. "Deep Inner Lives, Individualism, and People of Honour." *History of Political Thought* 16: 190–207.

Miller, William Ian. 1995b. "Upward Contempt." *Political Theory* 23: 476–99.

Miller, William Ian. 2000a. "Weak Legs: Misbehavior Before the Enemy." *Representations* 70: 27–48.

Miller, William Ian. 2000b. *The Mystery of Courage*. Cambridge, MA: Harvard University Press.

Mills, Sophie. 1997. *Theseus, Tragedy and the Athenian Empire*. Oxford: Oxford University Press.

Mills, Sophie. 2010. "Affirming Athenian Action: Euripides' Portrayal of Military Activity and the Limits of Tragic Instruction." In Pritchard, *War, Culture, and Democracy in Classical Athens*, 163–83.

Moles, John. 2002. "Herodotus and Athens." In *Brill's Companion to Herodotus*, edited by Egbert J. Bakker, Irene J. F. de Jong, and Hans van Wees, 33–52. Leiden: Brill.

Monoson, S. Sara. 1994a. "Citizen as Erastes: Erotic Imagery and the Idea of Reciprocity in the Periclean Funeral Oration." *Political Theory* 22.2: 253–76.

Monoson, S. Sara. 1994b. "Frank Speech, Democracy, and Philosophy: Plato's Debt to a Democratic Strategy of Civic Discourse." In Euben, Wallach, and Ober, *Athenian Political Thought and the Reconstruction of American Democracy*, 172–197.

Monoson, S. Sara. 1998. "Remembering Pericles: The Political and Theoretical Import of Plato's *Menexenus*." *Political Theory* 26.4: 489–513.

Monoson, S. Sara. *Plato's Democratic Entanglements: Athenian Politics and the Practice of Philosophy*. Princeton, NJ: Princeton University Press, 2000.

Monten, Jonathan. 2006. "Thucydides and Modern Realism." *International Studies Quarterly* 50: 3–25.

Morgan, Kathryn A. 2003. *Popular Tyranny: Sovereignty and Its Discontents in Ancient Greece*. Austin, TX: University of Texas Press.

Morris, Ian. 1996. "The Strong Principle of Equality and the Archaic Origins of Greek Democracy." In Ober and Hedrick, *Dēmokratia: A Conversation on Democracies, Ancient and Modern*, 19–48.

Morris, I. 2005. "The Athenian Empire (478-404 BC)." Princeton/Stanford Working Papers in Classics. Available at http://www.princeton.edu/~pswpc/pdfs/morris/120508.pdf.

Morris, Ian and Kurt Raaflaub. 1997. *Democracy 2500? Questions and Challenges*. Archaeological Institute of America, Colloquia and Conference Papers, no. 2. Dubuque, Iowa: Kendall/Hunt.

Morrison, James V. 2006. *Reading Thucydides*. Columbus: Ohio State University Press.

Mulhern, J. J. 2004. "*Parrhesia* in Aristotle." In Sluiter and Rosen, *Free Speech in Classical Antiquity*, 313–39.

Munn, Mark. 2000. *The School of History: Athens in the Age of Socrates*. Berkeley: University of California Press.

Munn, Mark. 2002. "Speeches in Thucydides." Paper delivered at the Annual Meeting of the American Philological Association. Philadelphia, PA.

Munson, Rosaria Vignolo. 2001. *Telling Wonders: Ethnographic and Political Discourse in the Work of Herodotus*. Ann Arbor: University of Michigan Press.

Murray, Sarah. 2004. "Man Overboard: A Re-Evaluation of the Underrepresentation of Sailors and Naval Warfare in Classical Athenian Art." Dartmouth College Thesis, on file with author.

Murray, Sarah. 2005. "Man Overboard: A Re-Evaluation of the Underrepresentation of the Navy in Classical Athenian Art." Presentation at the APA/AIA. Boston, MA. Abstract available at http://www.apaclassics.org/AnnualMeeting/05mtg/abstracts/Murrays.html.

Nagel, T. 1986. *The View from Nowhere*. Oxford: Oxford University Press.

Nagel, T. 1991. *Equality and Partiality*. Oxford: Oxford University Press.

Nagy, Gregory. 1990. *Pindar's Homer: The Lyric Possession of an Epic Past*. Baltimore, MD: Johns Hopkins University Press.

Nardin, Terry. 1996. *The Ethics of War and Peace*. Princeton, NJ: Princeton University Press.

Nedelsky, Jennifer. 2011. *Law's Relations: A Relational Theory of Self, Autonomy, and Law*. Oxford: Oxford University Press.

Nehamas, A. 1999. *Virtues of Authenticity: Essays on Plato and Socrates*. Princeton, NJ: Princeton University Press.

Newell, W. R. 2000a. *What Is a Man? 3,000 Years of Wisdom on the Art of Manly Virtue*. New York: Harper Collins.

Newell, W. R. 2000b. *Ruling Passion: The Erotics of Statecraft in Platonic Political Philosophy*. Lanham, MD: Rowman and Littlefield.

Newell, W. R. 2004. *The Code of Man: Love, Courage, Pride, Family, Country*. New York: Harper.

Nino, C. 1996. *The Constitution of Deliberative Democracy*. New Haven, CT: Yale University Press.

Nolla, Eduardo, ed. 2010. *Alexis de Tocqueville: Democracy in America*. 4 vols. Translated by James T. Schleifer. Indianapolis, IN: Liberty Fund.

Norlin, G., trans. 1991. *Isocrates*. Vol 1. Loeb Classical Library 209. Cambridge, MA: Harvard University Press.

Norlin, G., trans. 1992. *Isocrates*. Vol II. Loeb Classical Library 229. Cambridge, MA: Harvard University Press.

North, Helen. 1966. *Sophrosyne: Self-Knowledge and Self-Restraint in Greek Literature*. Ithaca, NY: Cornell University Press.

Nussbaum, Martha C. 1980. "Shame, Separateness, and Political Unity: Aristotle's Criticism of Plato." In A. O. Rorty, *Essays on Aristotle's Ethics*, 395–435.

Nussbaum, Martha C. 1986. *The Fragility of Goodness: Luck and Ethics in Greek Tragedy and Philosophy*. Cambridge: Cambridge University Press.

Nussbaum, Martha C. 1988. "Non-Relative Virtues: An Aristotelian Approach." *Midwest Studies in Philosophy* 13 (*Ethical Theory: Character and Virtue*), edited by P. A. French, T. E. Uehling Jr., and H. K. Wettstein, Notre Dame: University of Notre Dame Press: 32–53.

Nussbaum, Martha C. 1990. "Aristotelian Social Democracy." In *Liberalism and the Good*, edited by Bruce Douglass, Gerald Mara, and Henry Richardson, 203–52.

London: Routledge. (Reprinted in Tessitore, 2002, *Aristotle and Modern Politics: The Persistence of Political Philosophy*, 47–104.)

Nussbaum, Martha C. 1992. "Tragedy and Self-Sufficiency: Plato and Aristotle on Fear and Pity." In *Essays on Aristotle's Poetics*, edited by A. O. Rorty, 261–90. Princeton, NJ: Princeton University Press.

Nussbaum, Martha C. 2001a. *Upheavals of Thought: The Intelligence of Emotions*. Cambridge: Cambridge University Press.

Nussbaum, Martha C. 2001b. *Women and Human Development: The Capabilities Approach*. Cambridge: Cambridge University Press.

Nussbaum, Martha C., ed. 2002. *For Love of Country?* Boston: Beacon Press.

Nussbaum, Martha C. 2006. "Man Overboard." *New Republic*, June.

Obama, Barack. 2006. *The Audacity of Hope: Thoughts on Reclaiming the American Dream*. New York: Random House/Crown.

Ober, Josiah. 1978. "Views of Sea Power in the Fourth-Century Attic Orators." *Ancient World* 1: 119–30.

Ober, Josiah. 1985. "Thucydides, Pericles, and the Strategy of Defense." In *The Craft of the Ancient Historian*, edited by J. W. Eadie and J. Ober, 171–88. Lanham, MD: University Press of America.

Ober, Josiah. 1989. *Mass and Elite in Democratic Athens: Rhetoric, Ideology, and the Power of the People*. Princeton, NJ: Princeton University Press.

Ober, Josiah. 1993. "Thucydides' Criticism of Democratic Knowledge." In *Nomodeiktes: Greek Studies in Honor of Martin Ostwald*, edited by R. Rosen and J. Farrell, 81–98. Ann Arbor: University of Michigan Press.

Ober, Josiah. 1996a. "Power and Oratory in Democratic Athens: Demosthenes 21, *Against Meidias*." In *The Athenian Revolution: Essays on Greek Democracy and Political Theory*, 86–106. Princeton, NJ: Princeton University Press.

Ober, Josiah. 1996b. "The Athenian Revolution of 508/7 BC: Violence, Authority, and the Origins of Democracy." In *The Athenian Revolution*, 32–52. Princeton, NJ: Princeton University Press.

Ober, Josiah. 1996c. "The Rules of War in Classical Greece." In *The Athenian Revolution*, 53–71. Princeton, NJ: Princeton University Press.

Ober, Josiah. 1997. "Revolution Matters: Democracy as Demotic Action (A Response to Kurt Raaflaub)." In Morris and Raaflaub, *Democracy 2500? Questions and Challenges*, 67–85.

Ober, Josiah. 1998. *Political Dissent in Democratic Athens: Intellectual Critics of Popular Rule*. Princeton, NJ: Princeton University Press.

Ober, Josiah. 2001. "Thucydides Theoretikos/Thucydides Histor: Realist Theory and the Challenge of History." In McCann and Strauss, *Democracy and War*, 273–306.

Ober, Josiah. 2003. "Tyrant Killing as Therapeutic *Stasis*: A Political Debate in Images and Texts." In Morgan, *Popular Tyranny*, 215–50.

Ober, Josiah. 2004a. "I, Socrates...The Performative Audacity of Isocrates' *Antidosis*." In Poulakis and Depew, *Isocrates and Civic Education*, 21–43.

Ober, Josiah. 2004b. "Classical Athenian Democracy and Democracy Today: Culture, Knowledge, Power." In J. Morrill, ed., *The Promotion of Knowledge: Essays to Mark the Centenary of the British Academy, 1902-2002 = Proceedings of the British Academy* 122: 145–61.

Ober, Josiah. 2005a. "The Athenian Debate over Civic Education." In Ober, *Athenian Legacies*, 28–56.

Ober, Josiah. 2005b. *Athenian Legacies: Essays on the Politics of Going on Together*. Princeton, NJ: Princeton University Press.

Ober, Josiah. 2007. "Natural Capacities and Democracy as a Good-in-Itself." *Philosophical Studies* 132: 59–73.

Ober, Josiah. 2008. *Democracy and Knowledge: Learning and Innovation in Classical Athens*. Princeton, NJ: Princeton University Press.

Ober, Josiah. 2010. "Thucydides on Athens' Democratic Advantage in the Archidamian War." In Pritchard, *War, Culture, and Democracy in Classical Athens*, 65–87.

Ober, Josiah and Charles Hedrick, eds. 1996. *Dēmokratia: A Conversation on Democracies, Ancient and Modern*. Princeton, NJ: Princeton University Press.

Ober, Josiah and Barry Strauss. 1990. "Drama, Political Rhetoric, and the Discourse of Athenian Democracy." In Winkler and Zeitlin, *Nothing to Do with Dionysos?*, 237–70.

O'Brien, Michael J. 1963. "The Unity of the Laches." *Yale Classical Studies* 18: 133–47.

Olson, S. D. 2010. "Comedy, Politics, and Society." In *Brill's Companion to the Study of Greek Comedy*, edited by Gregory W. Dobrov, 35–69. Leiden: Brill.

Orwin, Clifford. 1978. "Machiavelli's Unchristian Charity." *American Political Science Review* 72: 1217–28.

Orwin, Clifford. 1986. "Justifying Empire: The Speech of the Athenians at Sparta and the Problem of Justice in Thucydides." *Journal of Politics* 48.1: 72–85.

Orwin, Clifford. 1994. *The Humanity of Thucydides*. Princeton, NJ: Princeton University Press.

Orwin, Clifford. 2006. "Humanitarian Military Intervention: Wars for the End of History?" *Social Philosophy and Policy* 23.1: 196–217.

Osborne, R. 1985a. *Demos: The Discovery of Classical Attika*. Cambridge: Cambridge University Press.

Osborne, R. 1985b. "Law in Action in Classical Athens." *Journal of Hellenic Studies* 105: 40–58.

Osborne, R. 1985c. "The Erection and Mutilation of the Hermai." *Proceedings of the Cambridge Philological Society* 25: 45–73.

Osborne, R. 1994. "Democracy and Imperialism in the Panathenaic Procession: The Parthenon Frieze in Its Context." In *The Archaeology of Athens and Attica under the Democracy*, edited by W. D. E. Coulson et al., 143–50. Oxford: Oxbow.

Osborne, Robin. 1996. *Greece in the Making: 1200-479 BC*. London and New York: Routledge.

Osborne, Robin. 1999 [2008]. "Archaeology and the Athenian Empire." Originally in *Transactions of the American Philological Association* 129: 319–32 [= Low, *The Athenian Empire*, 211–24].

Ostwald, Martin. 1996. "Shares and Rights: 'Citizenship' Greek Style and American Style." In Ober and Hedrick, *Dēmokratia: A Conversation on Democracies, Ancient and Modern*, 49–61.

Pangle, Thomas L., trans. 1980. *The Laws of Plato*. Chicago: University of Chicago Press.

Pangle, Thomas L. 1988. *The Spirit of Modern Republicanism: The Moral Vision of the American Founders and the Philosophy of Locke*. Chicago: University of Chicago Press.

Pangle, Thomas L. and Peter Ahrensdorf. 1999. *Justice among Nations: On the Moral Basis of Power and Peace*. Lawrence: University Press of Kansas.

Parker, R. 1996. *Athenian Religion: A History.* Oxford: Clarendon Press.

Parry, Adam. 1988. *Logos and Ergon in Thucydides.* Salem, NH: Ayer.

Pears, David. 1980. "Courage as a Mean." In A. O. Rorty, *Essays on Aristotle's Ethics*, 171–88.

Pears, D. 2004. "The Anatomy of Courage." *Social Research* 71.1: 1–12.

Penner, T. 2000. "Socrates." In *The Cambridge History of Greek and Roman Political Thought*, edited by Christopher Rowe and Malcolm Schofield, 164–89. Cambridge: Cambridge University Press.

Pettigrove, Glen. 2011. "Is Virtue Ethics Self-Effacing?" *Journal of Ethics* 15: 191–207.

Piepenbrink, Karen. 2001. *Politische Ordnungskonzeptionen in der attischen Demokratie des vierten Jahrhunderts v. Chr.* Historia Einzelschriften 154. Stuttgart: Franz Steiner.

Pitts, Jennifer, ed. and trans. 2001. *Alexis de Tocqueville: Writings on Empire and Slavery.* Baltimore, MD: Johns Hopkins University Press.

Podlecki, A. J. 1998. *Perikles and His Circle.* London: Routledge.

Pope, M. 1988. "Thucydides and Democracy." *Historia* 37: 276–96.

Poulakos, Takis. 1997. *Speaking for the Polis: Isocrates' Rhetorical Education.* Columbia: University of South Carolina Press.

Poulakos, Takis and David Depew, eds. 2004. *Isocrates and Civic Education.* Austin: University of Texas Press.

Powell, Anton. 1988. *Athens and Sparta: Constructing Greek Political and Social History from 478 BC.* Portland: Areopagitica Press. (2nd edition with different pagination, 2001.)

Powell, Anton and S. Hodkinson, eds. 1994. *The Shadow of Sparta.* London: Routledge.

Powell, Anton and S. Hodkinson, eds. 2002. *Sparta: Beyond the Mirage.* London: Classical Press of Wales.

Pritchard, D. 1998. "'The Fractured Imaginary': Popular Thinking on Military Matters in Fifth-Century Athens." *Ancient History* 28.1: 38–61.

Pritchard, D. 1999. *The Fractured Imaginary: Popular Thinking on Citizen Soldiers and Warfare in Fifth Century Athens.* Dissertation. Macquarie University.

Pritchard, D. 2010a. "The Symbiosis between Democracy and War: the Case of Ancient Athens." In Pritchard, *War, Culture, and Democracy in Classical Athens*, 1–62.

Pritchard, D. ed. 2010b. *War, Culture, and Democracy in Classical Athens.* Cambridge: Cambridge University Press.

Pritchett, W. K. 1971–1991. *The Greek State at War.* 5 vols. Berkeley: University of California Press.

Raaflaub, K. 1987. "Herodotus, Political Thought, and the Meaning of History," *Arethusa* 20.1–2: 221–48.

Raaflaub, K. 1989. "Contemporary Perceptions of Democracy in Fifth-Century Athens." *Classica et Mediaevalia* 40: 33–70.

Raaflaub, K. 1994. "Democracy, Power, and Imperialism in Fifth-Century Athens." In Euben, Wallach, and Ober, *Athenian Political Thought and the Reconstruction of American Democracy*, 103–46.

Raaflaub, K. 1996. "Equalities and Inequalities in Athenian Democracy." In Ober and Hedrick, *Dēmokratia: A Conversation on Democracies, Ancient and Modern* 140–74.

Raaflaub, K. 1997a. "Power in the Hands of the People: Foundations of Athenian Democracy." In Morris and Raaflaub, *Democracy 2500? Questions and Challenges*, 31–66.

Raaflaub, K. 1997b. "The Thetes and Democracy (A Response to Josiah Ober)." In Morris and Raaflaub, *Democracy 2500? Questions and Challenges*, 87–104.

Raaflaub, K. 1998. "The Transformation of Athens in the Fifth Century." In Boedeker and Raaflaub, *Democracy, Empire, and the Arts in Fifth-Century Athens*, 15–41. Cambridge: Cambridge University Press.

Raaflaub, K. 1999. "Archaic and Classical Greece." In *War and Society in the Ancient and Medieval Worlds: Asia, the Mediterranean, Europe, and Mesoamerica*, edited by Kurt A. Raaflaub and Nathan A. Rosenstein, 129–61. Cambridge, MA: Harvard University Press.

Raaflaub, K. 2001. "Father of All, Destroyer of All: War in the Late Fifth-Century Athenian Discourse and Ideology." In McCann and Strauss, *War and Democracy*, 307–56.

Raaflaub, K. 2002. "Philosophy, Science, Politics: Herodotus and the Intellectual Trends of His Time." In *Brill's Companion to Herodotus*, edited by Egbert J. Bakker, Irene J. F. de Jong, and Hans van Wees, 149–86. Leiden: Brill.

Raaflaub, K. 2003. "Stick and Glue: The Function of Tyranny in Fifth-Century Athenian Democracy." In Morgan, *Popular Tyranny*, 59–93.

Raaflaub, K. 2004. *The Discovery of Freedom in Ancient Greece*. Rev. ed. Chicago: University of Chicago Press.

Raaflaub, K. 2009. "Learning from the Enemy: Athenian and Persian 'Instruments of Empire.'" In *Interpreting the Athenian Empire*, edited by John Ma, Nikolaos Papazarkadas, and Robert Parker, 89–124. London: Duckworth.

Raaflaub, K., J. Ober, and R. Wallace. 2007. *Origins of Democracy in Ancient Greece*. Berkeley: University of California Press.

Rabieh, Linda. 2006. *Plato and the Virtue of Courage*. Baltimore. MD: Johns Hopkins University Press.

Rachman, Stanley J. 2004. "Fear and Courage: A Psychological Perspective." *Social Research* 71.1: 149–76.

Rackham, H., trans. 1952. *Aristotle: The Athenian Constitution; The Eudemian Ethics; On Virtues and Vices*. Loeb Classical Library 285. Cambridge, MA: Harvard University Press.

Rackham, H., trans. 1994. *Aristotle: The Nicomachean Ethics*. Loeb Classical Library 73. Cambridge, MA: Harvard University Press.

Rademaker, A. 2003. "Most Citizens are *Euruprōktoi* Now: (Un)manliness in Aristophanes." In Rosen and Sluiter, *Andreia: Studies in Manliness and Courage in Classical Antiquity*, 115–25.

Rahe, Paul A. 1984. "The Primacy of Politics in Classical Greece." *American Historical Review* 89.2: 265–93.

Raubitschek, A. E. 1943. "Greek Inscriptions." *Hesperia* 12: 12–87.

Rawlings, L. 2000. "Alternative Agonies? Hoplite Martial and Combat Experience beyond the Phalanx." In van Wees, *War and Violence in Ancient Greece*, 233–59.

Rawls, J. 1971. *A Theory of Justice*. Cambridge, MA: Belknap Press of Harvard University.

Rawls, J. 1999. "The Idea of Public Reason Revisited." In Rawls, *The Law of Peoples*, 131–80. Cambridge, MA: Harvard University Press.

Raz, Joseph. 1986. *The Morality of Freedom.* Oxford: Clarendon Press.

Redfield, J. 1975. *Nature and Culture in the "Iliad."* Chicago: University of Chicago Press.

Rhodes, P. J. 1981. *A Commentary on the Aristotelian Athōnaiēn Politeia.* Oxford: Clarendon Press.

Rhodes, P. J., trans. 1984. *Aristotle: The Athenian Constitution.* New York: Penguin.

Rhodes, P. J. 2003a. *Ancient Democracy and Modern Ideology.* London: Duckworth.

Rhodes, P. J. 2003b. "Nothing to Do with Democracy: Athenian Drama and the *Polis.*" *Journal of Hellenic Studies* 123: 104–19.

Rich, Frank. "Top Gun vs. Total Recall." *New York Times,* Sunday edition, Sept. 14, 2003, section 2.

Rickman, G. 2003. "The Creation of *Mare Nostrum.*" In *The Mediterranean in History*, edited by David Abulafia, 127–53. London: Thames & Hudson.

Roberts, J. T. 1982. *Accountability in Athenian Government.* Madison: University of Wisconsin Press.

Roberts, Robert C. 2003. *Emotions: An Essay in Aid of Moral Psychology.* Cambridge: Cambridge University Press.

Robinson, E. 1997. *The First Democracies: Early Popular Government outside Athens.* Historia Einzelschriften 107. Stuttgart: Steiner.

Robinson, E. 2001. "Reading and Misreading the Ancient Evidence for Democratic Peace." *Journal of Peace Research* 38.5: 593–608.

Roisman, J. 2003. "The Rhetoric of Courage in the Athenian Orators." In Rosen and Sluiter, *Andreia: Studies in Manliness and Courage in Classical Antiquity*, 127–43.

Roisman, J. 2004. "Speaker-Audience Interaction in Athens: A Power Struggle." In Sluiter and Rosen, *Free Speech in Classical Antiquity,* 261–78.

Roisman, J. 2005. *The Rhetoric of Manhood: Masculinity in the Attic Orators.* Berkeley: University of California Press.

Rorty, A. O., ed. 1980. *Essays on Aristotle's Ethics.* Berkeley: University of California Press.

Rorty, A. O. 1988. "The Two Faces of Courage." In *Mind in Action: Essays in the Philosophy of Mind*, edited by A. O. Rorty, 299–313. Boston: Beacon Press.

Rorty, R. 1990. "The Priority of Democracy to Philosophy." In *Objectivity, Relativism, and Truth: Philosophical Papers*. Vol. I. Cambridge: Cambridge University Press.

Rosen, Ralph M. and Ineke Sluiter. 2003. *Andreia: Studies in Manliness and Courage in Classical Antiquity*. Mnemosyne Supplement 238. Leiden: Brill.

Rosenbloom, David. 1995. "Myth, History, and Hegemony in Aeschylus." In *History, Tragedy, Theory: Dialogues on Athenian Drama*, edited by Barbara Goff, 91–130. Austin: University of Texas Press.

Rosenbloom, David. 2006. *Aeschylus: Persians.* London: Duckworth.

Rosenbloom, David. 2011. "The panhellenism of Athenian tragedy." In Carter, *Why Athens? A Reappraisal of Tragic Politics*, 353–81.

Rosivach, V. 1985. "Manning the Athenian Fleet, 433–26 BC." *American Journal of Ancient History* 10: 41–66.

Rosler, A. 2005. *Political Authority and Obligation in Aristotle.* Oxford: Oxford University Press.

Ross, W. D., trans. 1908. *Aristotle: Nicomachean Ethics*. Oxford: Clarendon Press.
Rowe, C. J., trans. 1995. *Plato. Statesman*. Warminster: Aris and Phillips.
Russett, Bruce and William Antholis. 1992. "Do Democracies Fight Each Other? Evidence from the Peloponnesian War." *Journal of Peace Research* 29.4: 415–34.
Russett, Bruce. 1994. *Grasping the Democratic Peace*. Princeton, NJ: Princeton University Press.
Rusten, Jeffrey. 1985. "Two Lives or Three? Pericles on the Athenian Character (Thucydides 2.40.1–2)" *Classical Quarterly* 35.1:14–19.
Rusten, Jeffrey. 1989. *Thucydides. The Peloponnesian War. Book II*. Cambridge: Cambridge University Press.
Saïd, Suzanne. 1980–1981. "Guerre, intelligence et courage dans les *Histoires* d'Hérodote." *Ancient Society* 11–12: 83–117.
Saïd, Suzanne. 2001. "The Discourse of Identity in Greek Rhetoric from Isocrates to Aristides." In *Ancient Perceptions of Greek Ethnicity*, edited by I. Malkin, 275–99. Washington, DC: Center for Hellenic Studies.
Salkever, Stephen G. 1990a. *Finding the Mean: Theory and Practice in Aristotelian Political Philosophy*. Princeton, NJ: Princeton University Press.
Salkever, Stephen G. 1990b. "Lopp'd and Bound: How Liberal Theory Obscures the Goods of Liberal Practices." In *Liberalism and the Good*, edited by R. Bruce Douglass, Gerald M. Mara, and Henry Richardson, 167–202. New York: Routledge.
Salkever, Stephen G. 1991. "Women, Soldiers, Citizens: Plato and Aristotle on the Politics of Virility." In *Essays on the Foundations of Aristotelian Political Science*, edited by Carnes Lord and David K. O'Connor, 165–90. Berkeley: University of California Press.
Salkever, Stephen G. 1993. "Socrates' Aspasian Oration: The Play of Philosophy and Politics in Plato's *Menexenus*." *American Political Science Review* 87.1: 133–43.
Salkever, Stephen G. 2002. "The Deliberative Model of Democracy and Aristotle's Ethics of Natural Questions." In Tessitore, *Aristotle and Modern Politics: The Persistence of Political Philosophy*, 342–74.
Samons, L. J. 2002. "Democracy, Empire, and the Search for the Athenian Character." *Arion* 8.3: 128–57.
Samons, L. J. 2004. *What's Wrong with Democracy? From Athenian Practice to American Worship*. Berkeley: University of California Press.
Sandel, Michael J. 1996. *Democracy's Discontent: America in Search of a Public Philosophy*. Cambridge, MA: Harvard University Press.
Santas, Gerasimos. 1969. "Socrates at Work on Virtue and Knowledge in Plato's *Laches*." *Review of Metaphysics* 22: 433–60.
Saunders, T., trans. 1970. *Plato: The Laws*. New York: Penguin.
Saxonhouse, Arlene W. 1980. "Men, Women, War, and Politics: Family and Polis in Aristophanes and Euripides." *Political Theory* 8.1: 65–81.
Saxonhouse, Arlene W. 1983. "An Unspoken Theme in Plato's *Gorgias*: War." *Interpretation* 11: 139–69.
Saxonhouse, Arlene W. 1985. *Women in the History of Political Thought: Ancient Greece to Machiavelli*. New York: Praeger.
Saxonhouse, Arlene W. 1992. *Fear of Diversity: The Birth of Political Science in Ancient Greek Thought*. Chicago: University of Chicago Press.

Saxonhouse, Arlene W. 1996. *Athenian Democracy: Modern Mythmakers and Ancient Theorists*. Notre Dame and London: University of Notre Dame Press.

Saxonhouse, Arlene W. 2006. *Free Speech and Democracy in Ancient Athens*. Cambridge: Cambridge University Press.

Schmid, Walter T. 1992. *On Manly Courage: A Study of Plato's Laches*. Carbondale and Edwardsville: Southern Illinois University Press.

Schofield, Malcolm. 1986. "*Euboulia* in the *Iliad*." *Classical Quarterly* 36.1: 6–31 [= *Saving the City: Philosopher-Kings and Other Classical Paradigms*, 3–30. London: Routledge, 1999.]

Schofield, Malcolm. 2006. "Aristotle's Political Ethics." In *The Blackwell Guide to Aristotle's Nicomachean Ethics*, edited by Richard Kraut, 305–22. Oxford: Wiley-Blackwell.

Schweder, Richard A. 2003. "Toward a Deep Cultural Psychology of Shame." *Social Research* 70.4: 1401–22.

Scorza, J. A. 2001. "The Ambivalence of Political Courage." *Review of Politics* 63.4: 637–661.

Scott-Kilvert, Ian., trans. 1960. *Plutarch. The Rise and Fall of Athens: Nine Greek Lives*. New York: Penguin.

Scourfield, J. H. D. 2003. "Anger and Gender in Chariton's *Chaereas and Callirhoe*." In *Ancient Anger: Perspectives from Homer to Galen*, edited by S. Braund and G. W. Most. Yale Classical Studies 32. 163–84. Cambridge: Cambridge University Press.

Seaford, Richard. 2000. "The Social Function of Attic Tragedy: A Response to Jasper Griffin." *Classical Quarterly* 50.1: 30–44.

Seidensticker, Bernd. 1995. "Women on the Tragic Stage." In *History, Tragedy, Theory: Dialogues on Athenian Drama*, edited by Barbara Goff, 151–73. Austin: University of Texas Press.

Sharples, R. W. 1983. "Knowledge and Courage in Thucydides and Plato." *Liverpool Classical Monthly* 8.9: 139–40.

Shaw, M. B. 1975. "The Female Intruder: Women in Fifth-Century Drama." *Classical Philology* 70.4: 255–66.

Shay, Jonathan. 1994. *Achilles in Vietnam: Combat Trauma and the Undoing of Character*. New York. Atheneum.

Shay, Jonathan. "The Birth of Tragedy—Out of the Needs of Democracy." *Didaskalia* 2.2. http://www.didaskalia.net/issues/vol2no2/shay.html.

Sherman, Nancy. 2010. *The Untold War: Inside the Hearts, Minds, and Souls of Our Soldiers*. New York: Norton.

Shklar, Judith N. 1989. "The Liberalism of Fear." In *Liberalism and the Moral Life*, edited by Nancy Rosenblum, 21–38. Cambridge, MA: Harvard University Press.

Shklar, Judith N. 1990. *The Faces of Injustice*. New Haven, CT: Yale University Press.

Sidwell, Keith. 2009. *Aristophanes the Democrat: The Politics of Satirical Comedy during the Peloponnesian War*. Cambridge: Cambridge University Press.

Siewert, P. 1977. "The Ephebic Oath in Fifth-Century Athens." *Journal of Hellenic Studies* 97: 102–11.

Sinclair, R. K. 1988. *Democracy and Participation in Athens*. Cambridge: Cambridge University Press.

Skinner, Quentin. 1988. "Some Problems in the Analysis of Political Thought and Action." In *Meaning and Context: Quentin Skinner and His Critics*, edited by James Tully, 97–118. Cambridge: Polity Press.

Skinner, Quentin. 1988. "Language and Social Change." In *Meaning and Context: Quentin Skinner and His Critics*, edited by James Tully, 119–32. Cambridge: Polity Press.

Sluiter, I. and R.M. Rosen, eds. 2004. *Free Speech in Classical Antiquity*. Leiden: Brill.

Smith, A. C. 1999. "Eurymedon and the Evolution of Political Personifications in the Early Classical Period." *Journal of Hellenic Studies* 119: 128–41.

Smoes, É. 1995. *Le Courage chez les Grecs, d'Homère à Aristote*. Cahiers de philosophie ancienne 12. Bruxelles: Ousia.

Sommerstein, A. 2004. "Harassing the Satirist: The Alleged Attempts to Prosecute Aristophanes." In Sluiter and Rosen, *Free Speech in Classical Antiquity*, 145–74.

Sommerstein, A. 2009. "An Alternative Democracy and an Alternative to Democracy in Aristophanic Comedy." In *Talking about Laughter and Other Studies in Greek Comedy*, 204–22. Oxford: Oxford University Press.

Sontag, Susan. "Untitled." "Talk of the Town." *New Yorker*, September 24, 2001. Available at http://www.newyorker.com/talk/content/?010924ta_talk_wtc.

Sorabji, Richard. 2000. *Emotion and Peace of Mind*. Oxford: Oxford University Press.

Sorum, Christina Elliott. 1995. "Euripides' Judgment: Literary Creation in *Andromache*." *American Journal of Philology* 116.3: 371–88.

Spence, Iain. 2010. "Cavalry, Democracy, and Military Thinking in Classical Athens." In Pritchard, *War, Culture, and Democracy in Classical Athens*, 111–38.

Sprague, Rosamund Kent. 1997. "Laches." In Cooper, *Plato: Complete Works*, 664–686.

Stadter, Philip A. 989. *A Commentary on Plutarch's* Pericles. Chapel Hill, NC: University of North Carolina Press.

Stadter, Philip A. 1991. "Pericles among the Intellectuals." *Illinois Classical Studies* 16.1: 111–24.

Stokes, M. C. 1986. *Plato's Socratic Conversations: Drama and Dialectic in Three Dialogues*. Baltimore, MD: Johns Hopkins University Press.

Strasburger, H. 1955. "Herodot und das Perikleische Athen." *Historia* 4: 1–25.

Strassler, Robert B. 1996. *The Landmark Thucydides: A Comprehensive Guide to the Peloponnesian War*. New York: Free Press.

Strauss, B. S. 1996. "The Athenian Trireme, School of Democracy." In Ober and Hedrick, *Dēmokratia*, 313–25.

Strauss, B. S. 2000. "Perspectives on the Death of Fifth-Century Seamen." In van Wees, *War and Violence in Ancient Greece*, 261–83.

Strauss, B. S. 2009. "Athens as Hamlet: The Irresolute Empire." In *Enduring Empire: Ancient Lessons for Global Politics*, edited by David Edward Tabachnick and Toivo Koivukoski, 215–26. Toronto: University of Toronto Press.

Strauss, Leo. 1958. *Thoughts on Machiavelli*. Glencoe, IL: Free Press.

Strauss, Leo. 1959/1988. "On Classical Political Philosophy." In *What Is Political Philosophy?* Chicago: University of Chicago Press.

Strauss, Leo. 1964. *The City and Man*. Chicago: University of Chicago Press.

Stupperich, R. 1994. "The Iconography of Athenian State Burials in the Classical Period." In *The Archaeology of Athens and Attica under the Democracy*, edited by W. D. E. Coulson et al., 93–103. Oxford: Oxbow.

Swain, Simon. 1993. "Thucydides 1.22.1 and 3.82.4." *Mnemosyne* 46: 33–45.

Swanton, Christine. 2003. *Virtue Ethics: A Pluralistic View*. Oxford: Oxford University Press.

Taaffe, Lauren K. 1993. *Aristophanes and Women*. London and New York: Routledge.

Tacon, Judith. 2001. "Ecclesiastic *Thorubos*: Interventions, Interruptions, and Popular Involvement in the Athenian Assembly." *Greece and Rome* 48.2: 173–92.

Talbot, David. 2001. "The 'Traitor' Fires Back." Salon.com. October 16. http://archive.salon.com/news/feature/2001/10/16/susans/.

Tarnopolsky, C. 2010. *Prudes, Perverts, and Tyrants: Plato's Gorgias and the Politics of Shame*. Princeton, NJ: Princeton University Press.

Taylor, G. 1985. *Pride, Shame, and Guilt: Emotions of Self-Assessment*. Oxford: Clarendon Press.

Taylor, Michael. 1991. *The Tyrant Slayers: The Heroic Image in Fifth Century B.C. Athenian Art and Politics*. 2nd ed. Salem, NH: Ayer.

Tessitore, A., ed. 2002. *Aristotle and Modern Politics: The Persistence of Political Philosophy*. Notre Dame, IN: University of Notre Dame Press.

Thomas, R. 1989. *Oral Tradition and Written Record*. Cambridge: Cambridge University Press.

Thomas, R. 2000. *Herodotus in Context: Ethnography, Science, and the Art of Persuasion*. Cambridge: Cambridge University Press.

Thompson, D. 1944. "The Golden Nikai Reconsidered." *Hesperia* 13.3: 173–209.

Thompson, Norma. 2001. *The Ship of State: Statecraft and Politics from Ancient Greece to Democratic America*. New Haven, CT: Yale University Press.

Tobias, Sarah. 1996. "Toward a Feminist Ethic of War and Peace." In *The Ethics of War and Peace*, edited by Terry Nardin, 228–41. Princeton, NJ: Princeton University Press.

Todd, Stephen. 1993. *The Shape of Athenian Law*. Oxford: Clarendon Press.

Todd, Stephen, trans. 2000. *Lysias*. Austin: University of Texas Press.

Todd, Stephen. 2007. *A Commentary on Lysias, Speeches 1-11*. New York: Oxford University Press.

Too, Yun Lee. 1995. *The Rhetoric of Identity in Isocrates: Text, Power, Pedagogy*. Cambridge: Cambridge University Press.

Too, Yun Lee, ed. 2001. *Education in Greek and Roman Antiquity*. Leiden: Brill.

Tredennick, H., trans. 1989. "Socrates' Defense (Apology)." In *The Collected Dialogues of Plato*, edited by Edith Hamilton and Huntington Cairns, 3–26. Princeton, NJ: Princeton University Press.

Tzanetou, Angeliki. 2005. "A Generous City: Pity in Athenian Oratory and Tragedy." In *Pity and Power in Ancient Athens*, edited by Rachel Hall Sternberg, 98–122. Cambridge: Cambridge University Press.

Tzanetou, Angeliki. 2012. *City of Suppliants: Tragedy and the Athenian Empire*. Austin: University of Texas Press.

Tully, James. 2009. *Public Philosophy in a New Key*. 2 vols. Cambridge: Cambridge University Press.

Vagts, Alfred. 1937. *A History of Militarism: Romance and Realities of a Profession*. New York: Norton.

Vaio, J. 1973. "The Manipulation of Theme and Action in Aristophanes' *Lysistrata*." *Greek, Roman, and Byzantine Studies* 14: 369–380.

van Wees, Hans. 1992. *Status Warriors: War, Violence and Society in Homer and History*. Amsterdam: J.C. Gieben.

van Wees, Hans, ed. 2000. *War and Violence in Ancient Greece*. London: Duckworth and the Classical Press of Wales.

van Wees, Hans. 2002. "Tyrants, Oligarchs, and Citizen Militias." In *Army and Power in the Ancient World*, edited by Angelos Chaniotis and Pierre Ducrey, 61–82. Stuttgart: Franz Steiner Verlag.

van Wees, Hans. 2004. *Greek Warfare: Myths and Realities*. London: Duckworth.

Vellacott, Philip. 1975. *Ironic Drama: A Study of Euripides' Method and Meaning*. Cambridge: Cambridge University Press.

Vidal-Naquet, Pierre. 1986. *The Black Hunter: Forms of Thought and Forms of Society in the Ancient World*. Translated by Andrew Szegedy-Maszak. Baltimore, MD: Johns Hopkins University Press.

Villa, Dana. 1999. *Politics, Philosophy, Terror: Essays on the Thought of Hannah Arendt*. Princeton, NJ: Princeton University Press.

Vince, J. H., trans. 1986. *Demosthenes: Orations XXI-XXVI*. Loeb Classical Library 299. Cambridge, MA: Harvard University Press.

Vince, J. H., trans. 1989. *Demosthenes: Orations I-XVII, XX*. Loeb Classical Library 238. Cambridge, MA: Harvard University Press.

Vince, C. A. and J. H. Vince, trans. 1999. *Demosthenes: De Corona; De Falsa Legatione*. Loeb Classical Library 155. Cambridge, MA: Harvard University Press.

Vlastos, G. 1981. "The *Protagoras* and the *Laches*." In *Platonic Studies*, 2nd ed. Princeton, NJ: Princeton University Press.

Vlastos, Gregory. 1994. "Socrates and Vietnam." In *Socratic Studies*, edited by M. Burnyeat, 127–33. Cambridge: Cambridge University Press.

Von Reden, S. 1995. *Exchange in Ancient Greece*. London: Duckworth.

Von Wright, G. H. 1963. *The Varieties of Goodness*. London: Routledge and Kegan Paul.

Wallace, James D. 1978. *Virtues and Vices*. Ithaca, NY: Cornell University Press.

Wallace, R. W. 1994. "Private Lives and Public Enemies: Freedom of Thought in Classical Athens." In Boegehold and Scafuro, *Athenian Identity and Civic Ideology*, 205–38.

Wallace, R. W. 1997. "Poet, Public, and 'Theatrocracy': Audience Performance in Classical Athens." In *Poet, Public, and Performance in Ancient Greece*, edited by L. Edmunds and R. W. Wallace, 97–111. Baltimore, MD: Johns Hopkins University Press.

Wallace, R. W. 2004. "The Power to Speak—and Not to Listen—in Ancient Athens." In Sluiter and Rosen, *Free Speech in Ancient Athens*, 221–32.

Wallach, John. 1992. "Contemporary Aristotelianism." *Political Theory* 20.4: 613–41.

Wallach, John. 1994. "Two Democracies and Virtue." In Euben, Wallach, and Ober, *Athenian Political Thought and the Reconstruction of American Democracy*, 319–40.

Walton, Douglas N. 1986. *Courage: A Philosophical Investigation*. Berkeley and Los Angeles: University of California Press.

Wardman, A. E. 1959. "Thucydides 2.40.1." *Classical Quarterly* 9: 38–42.

Warner, Rex, trans. 1972. *Thucydides. History of the Peloponnesian War*. New York: Viking Press.

Weart, S. R. 1998. *Never at War: Why Democracies Will Not Fight One Another*. New Haven, CT: Yale University Press.

Weart, S. R. 2001. "Remarks on the Ancient Evidence for Democratic Peace." *Journal of Peace Research* 38.5: 609–13.

Weinstock, D. M. 1999. "Democracy, Value, and Truth: Saving Deliberation from Justification." Available at http://www.philo.umontreal.ca/documents/cahiers/Weinstock_Deliberation.pdf.

Welch, David. 2003. "Why International Relations Theorists Should Stop Reading Thucydides." *Review of International Studies* 29: 301–20.

West, W. C. 1969. "The Trophies of the Persian Wars." *Classical Philology* 64.1: 7–19.

Whitehead, D. 1986. *The Demes of Attica 508/7-c.250 BC*. Princeton, NJ: Princeton University Press.

Whitehead, D. 1993. "Cardinal Virtues: The Language of Public Approbation in Democratic Athens." *Classica et Mediaevalia* 44: 37–75.

Wickersham, John. 1994. *Hegemony and Greek Historians*. Lanham, MD: Rowman and Littlefield.

Williams, Bernard. 1976. "Moral Luck." *Proceedings of the Aristotelian Society*. Supplementary Volume 59: 115–35.

Williams, Bernard. 1981. "Persons, Character, and Morality." In *Moral Luck*, 1–19. Cambridge: Cambridge University Press.

Williams, Bernard. 1985. *Ethics and the Limits of Philosophy*. London: Harmondsworth.

Williams, Bernard. 1993. *Shame and Necessity*. Berkeley, Los Angeles and London: University of California Press.

Williams, Bernard. 1995. "The Point of View of the Universe: Sidgwick and the Ambitions of Ethics." In *Making Sense of Humanity and Other Philosophical Papers 1982-1993*, 153-171. Cambridge: Cambridge University Press.

Williams, Bernard. 2005. *In the Beginning Was the Deed*. Princeton, NJ: Princeton University Press.

Williams, M. F. 1998. *Ethics in Thucydides: The Ancient Simplicity*. Lanham, MD: University Press of America.

Willink, C. W. 1986. *Euripides: Orestes*. Oxford: Clarendon Press.

Wilson, P. 1991. "Demosthenes 21 (*Against Meidias*): Democratic Abuse." *Proceedings of the Cambridge Philological Society* 37: 164–95.

Winkler, J. 1990. "Laying Down the Law: The Oversight of Men's Sexual Behavior in Classical Athens." In *Before Sexuality: The Construction of the Erotic Experience in the Ancient Greek World*, edited by D. Halperin, J. Winkler, and F. Zeitlin, 171–209. Princeton, NJ: Princeton University Press.

Winkler, J. J. and F. Zeitlin, eds. 1990. *Nothing to Do with Dionysos? Athenian Drama in Its Social Context*. Princeton, NJ: Princeton University Press.

Wohl, Victoria. 2002. *Love among the Ruins: The Erotics of Democracy in Classical Athens*. Princeton, NJ: Princeton University Press.

Wolff, Christian. 1968. "Orestes." In *Euripides: A Collection of Critical Essays*, edited by Erich Segal, 132–49. Englewood Cliffs, NJ: Prentice-Hall.

Wolin, Sheldon S. 2001. *Tocqueville between Two Worlds: The Making of a Political and Theoretical Life*. Princeton, NJ: Princeton University Press.

Wood, Allen. 2001. "Kant vs. Eudaimonism." In *Kant's Legacy: Essays Dedicated to Lewis White Beck*, edited by Predrag Cicovacki, 261–282.

Wood, E. M. 1988. *Peasant-Citizen and Slave: The Foundations of Athenian Democracy*. London: Verso.
Woodhead, A. G. 1970. *Thucydides on the Nature of Power*. Cambridge, MA: Harvard University Press.
Woodman, A. J. 1988. *Rhetoric in Classical Historiography*. Portland, OR: Areopagitica Press.
Woodruff, Paul. 1987. "Expert Knowledge in the *Apology* and *Laches*: What a General Needs to Know." *Proceedings of the Boston Area Colloquium in Ancient Philosophy*. Vol. 3. 79–115. Lanham, MD: Rowman and Littlefield.
Woodruff, Paul, trans. 1993. *Thucydides on Justice, Power, and Human Nature*. Indianapolis: Hackett.
Woodruff, Paul. 2007. "Socrates and Political Courage." *Ancient Philosophy* 27: 1–14.
Worthington, I., C. R. Cooper, and E. M. Harris, trans. 2001. *Dinarchus, Hyperides, and Lycurgus*. Austin: University of Texas Press.
Yunis, Harvey. 1996. *Taming Democracy: Models of Political Rhetoric in Classical Athens*. Ithaca, NY: Cornell University Press.
Yunis, Harvey, ed. 2001. *Demosthenes: On the Crown*. Cambridge: Cambridge University Press.
Zeitlin, F. I. 1986/1990. "Thebes: Theater of Self and Society in Athenian Drama." In Winkler and Zeitlin, *Nothing to Do with Dionysos?* 130–67. (Earlier version in Euben, *Greek Tragedy and Political Theory*, 101–41.)
Zeyl, Donald, trans. 1987. *Plato: Gorgias*. Indianapolis, IN: Hackett.
Ziolkowski, John. 1981. *Thucydides and the Tradition of Funeral Speeches at Athens*. Salem, NH: Ayer.

INDEX

Acharnians (Aristophanes), 116, 219
Achilles, 165, 337, 342
Acropolis, 98, 99, 190, 262, 263, 267, 268
action, 49
Adrastus, 249–53, 291
advisers, 133, 135, 144
Aeschines, 53, 56, 68, 70, 184, 193, 216n.31, 219, 231–32, 234, 247, 324
Aeschylus, 74, 215, 286
   Agamemnon, 257, 283–86, 212
   Persians, 15, 75–81
   promotion of courage, 248
   Seven Against Thebes, 263
Against Ctesiphon (Aeschines), 70, 184
Against Leocrates (Lycurgus), 234–39
Against Meidias (Demosthenes), 188
Against Theomnestus I (Lysias), 68
Agamemnon, 163–66, 169, 171, 200, 203, 204, 257, 291, 292
Agamemnon (Aeschylus), 257, 283–86
Agathon, 218
Ajax, 290, 325
Alcaeus, 205, 217
Alcibiades, 124, 125–26, 141, 220, 336–37
altruism, 319
Amazons, 257, 268
ambition, 114
ancestors, 226–27, 238, 244, 300–301, 323, 326

Andocides, 219n.4
andreia, 7, 16, 120, 124–28, 194, 257–58
   Athenian, 160, 170, 183, 256–57
   Cleon's use of, 122
   Isocrates on, 149, 151, 156, 160, 166, 168, 170
   in *Laws,* 336
   in *Lysistrata,* 261, 265, 266, 273, 275–77
   military courage as prototype of, 66, 68
   politics of, 334
   Socrates on, 11
   and *sōphrosunē,* 258, 260, 333–36
   Spartan, 166, 168
   in *Statesman,* 334–36
   as traditional courage, 110
androgyny, 273, 275–76
Andromache (Euripides), 280–83, 292
anger, 115, 117–23, 126, 228–30, 239, 242, 264, 291
Antigone (Sophocles), 287
Apology (Plato), 338, 339
Archidamian War, 191
Archidamus, King, 37, 124–25, 207–9, 271
Arendt, Hannah, 64
Areopagiticus (Isocrates), 156, 158, 167
aretē, 329
Aristides the Just, 132–34

385

Aristodemus the Spartan, 206, 322, 325, 331–32
Aristogeiton, 254, 267
Aristophanes, 116, 218, 242, 255, 288
  Acharnians, 219
  Frogs, 74, 248, 263
  Knights, 344
  Lysistrata, 257–77, 334
  Peace, 185
  Wasps, 195, 344
Aristotle
  on anger, 228–30, 264
  on citizen's virtue relative to regime, 10
  on courage, 8, 26, 29, 31, 45, 66n.50, 269
  on death at sea, 186
  definition of emulation, 192
  eudaimonia in, 20, 329
  on fear, 5n.12
  on imperialism, 126–27
  on law, 233n.32
  on navy, 188n.22
  on shame, 35, 245, 268
  on Spartan courage, 331
  "summation argument," 57
  on technical knowledge, 41
armor, 181, 189
Artemisia, 99n.51, 212
Athena, 264–65, 275
Athenian choice, 93–94, 96
Atossa, 75–76, 78, 213

bad luck, 321, 322
Battle of Chaeronea, 215, 236, 237, 251
Battle of Eleusis, 318, 320
Battle of Mantineia, 142
Battle of Marathon, 101, 102, 104, 112, 115, 226
Battle of Mycale, 103
Battle of Plataea, 101, 103, 104, 118
Battle of Salamis, 97, 102, 104, 112, 113, 122, 184, 186, 190, 192, 193, 212, 238, 239
Battle of Thermopylae, 83, 84–91, 206, 207
Benhabib, Seyla, 58–59
berserkers, 331, 332

Brasidas, 41–42, 209
bravery, 41, 50, 83, 225, 226, 235

Callimachus, 101
Callinus, 205, 217
Callipolis, 173
capital punishment, 240–41
Casey, John, 230
Cassandra, 292, 293
cavalry, 188–89, 197, 221–22
character, 34–39, 44, 145, 324, 335
children, 257, 272
choice, 93–94, 96
Cicero, 66
citizen courage, 269
civic courage, 26n.4, 52, 64–72
Clarke, Michael, 88
Cleisthenes, 73, 98, 218
Cleomenes, 98, 262
Cleon, 120–23, 128, 138, 229–31, 242, 264n.26
Cleonymus, 218
cocks, 256
Cohen, David, 60, 219
comedy, 185, 260n.15
commemorative speeches, 300–308
  See also funeral orations
community, 298–99, 315, 319
compassion, 229, 288
Conon, 255
consequentialists, 321
Corcyra, 119–20, 127, 257
Corinthians, 110–12, 129
corruption, 155n.20
cosmopolitan impartiality, 176
cosmopolitanism, 273
Cottingham, John, 35
Council of 500, 73, 221
courage
  Aristotle on, 8, 26, 29, 31, 45, 66n.50, 269
  Athenian, 2, 34–39, 93, 159–63, 241, 254, 324–27
  civic, 26n.4, 52, 64–72
  definition of, 3, 130, 145, 146
  Demosthenes on, 48–49, 65–66, 102, 307, 339–40, 342

enthusiastic, 100–101, 113
and equality, 179–97, 304
ethical significance of, 1
    and *eudaimonism* and, 310–11, 350
and fear, 5, 210, 240
in Homeric society, 199–206
as intrinsically good, 211, 310, 325
Isocrates on Athenian, 16, 159–63, 283
and justice, 301
and knowledge, 29–34, 136, 138, 146
in *Lysistrata,* 274, 275
military, 1–2, 12, 66, 117n.21, 351
motivation for, 198, 200, 212–13
and non-Greek "other," 211–17
Periclean model, 25–47, 81,
    83–84, 115–17
Persian lack of, 75, 79
Plato on, 8, 26, 45, 161, 337
rationally informed, 49
    reckless vs. daring, 39–40
regime-specific interpretation, 9–13
and self-control, 281
and shame, 200, 207, 244
Socratic, 26n.4, 129, 131–33, 141–43,
    146, 336–39, 342
Spartan, 11, 34, 79, 81–86, 89–91, 93,
    100, 166, 198, 206–9, 241, 283
"standard model" of, 198–217
in *Suppliants,* 249–53
vs. *thumos,* 228–29
See also andreia; democratic courage
courageous passions, 218–42
cowardice, 11, 83, 89, 120, 213, 219–20,
    223, 234, 236, 240, 242, 256, 280,
    322, 323
Croesus, 317, 327

Damon, 137, 147
daring, 34, 39–40, 82, 110–12, 120, 145,
    146, 171, 203n.8
Darius, 76–80
debates, 53, 58
decision-making, 94, 135, 324
decoding, 234
deeds, 140–41, 143, 145, 179–80
Delian League, 154, 155n.20
deliberateness, 4, 94

deliberation. *See* democratic deliberation
Delphic oracles, 95, 97
Demaratus, King, 84, 85, 89, 91, 208, 209
democracy, 216–17
    Aeschines on, 70
    American, 12, 348–49
    Athenian, 5–6, 14, 53, 132, 180–85,
        187, 196, 197, 259n.14, 286, 287,
        303–4, 309, 343–46, 348–49
    criticisms of, 343–45
    definition of, 6 heroic, 345–46
    Manville on, 46, 145
    naval, 155
    Socrates on, 11, 131, 344
    Theseus' defense of, 249n.12
    Tocqueville on, 347–49
    and tragic theater, 286, 287
    and tyrannicide statues, 255
    and virtue, 309–10, 342
Democracy in America
    (Tocqueville), 11–12
democratic courage
    ambiguities of, 7–9, 18, 112–15
    American, 348
    Athenian, 80, 97–128, 215, 217, 297,
        302, 316–28, 330–31, 345
    challenge of, 349–51
    definition of, 3–6
    Demosthenes on, 68, 217
    distinctiveness of, 59
    diversity of, 343–49
    and *eudaimonism,* 104–7
    and freedom, 52
    Herodotus on, 81–84, 93
    ideal of, 2, 278n.1, 346
    ideology of, 7, 316, 317, 319
    and imperialism, 127
    ironies of, 144
    objections to, 346–49
    Periclean, 59, 93, 98, 110–12, 116, 145,
        146, 241–42, 250, 302, 310
    in *Persians,* 75
    in practice, 241–42
    reasons for, 316–28
    and self-control, 281
    theory of, 1–21
    Thucydides on, 109, 114, 149

INDEX | 387

Tocqueville on, 347–48
democratic courage (*Cont.*)
   and tragic theater, 287
   from watching *Lysistrata,* 261n.21
democratic deliberation, 50–52
   Athenian, 96, 302
   Cleon on, 122
   Demosthenes on, 48–50, 55
   and free speech, 52–59
   hazards and obstacles, 60, 65–66
   Herodotus on, 94–97, 103
   public-spirited, 71–72
democratic shame, 244, 253
democratization of birth privilege, 179
Demosthenes, 56, 61, 63, 124, 179, 285
   Aeschines on, 219, 231–32
   on Aeschines, 247
   on Athenian distribution of honors, 184
   on Athenian virtues, 48–50, 54, 106
   on civic courage, 65, 68
   on courage, 48–49, 65–66, 102, 217, 307, 339–40, 342
   on democratic deliberation, 48–50, 55
   female exemplars of courage, 257
   on free speech, 57, 62, 67, 68, 71, 216, 244
   funeral oration, 243, 305
   on life cycle in city, 328
   on Meidias, 188
   On the Crown, 56, 106, 307, 323, 326
   on Philip of Macedon, 213–16, 243, 250–51, 307, 308
   political thought, 150
   on self-respect, 323
   self-restraint, 340–41
   on shame, 217, 243–44
   on Sparta, 54
   on statue of Conon, 255
Demostratus, 267
de Officiis (Cicero), 66
desertion, 68
despotism, 216
Dieneces, 86
Diodotus, 55, 56, 121, 123
dissent, 55–56, 58, 63, 65, 66
Dover, Kenneth, 25, 297

education, 132–36, 303, 305, 335
egoism, 319, 326
Ehrenreich, Barbara, 258
Eion monuments, 184, 254
Eleusinians, 321
emotions, 4, 8, 10, 13n.35, 19, 99, 220, 222, 227–28, 231–37, 246, 247
empire, 152–55
emulation, 192, 243, 300, 305–6
enlightened hegemony, 153n.12, 154, 155n.22
enlightened self-interest, 99
enthusiasm, 100–101, 113, 120
equality, 8, 9, 51, 75, 109, 179–97, 213, 303–4, 329
Erechtheus (Euripides), 235
ergon, 129–32, 135, 139, 142, 145, 146
eudaimonia/eudaimonism
   Athenian, 43, 104–7, 116, 149, 297–308, 329
   and commemorative speeches, 300–308
   and courage, 140, 310–11, 350
   definition of, 3
   Isocrates on, 157
   paradoxes and resolutions, 309–29
   Pears on, 29
   Periclean, 15, 31–32, 39, 45, 116
   in Plato, 20
   in thought and action, 297–308
   and tragic theater, 287
   from watching *Lysistrata,* 260
Eudemian Ethics (Aristotle), 41
Euripides, 54, 74, 286, 288
   Andromache, 280–83, 292
   Erechtheus, 235
   Heracles, 288, 289–91
   Suppliants, 249–53, 287
   Trojan Women, 288, 291–94
Eurybiades, 104
Eurytus, 331
Exordia (Demosthenes), 48

Fabius Maximus, 121n.28
fear
   Athenian, 5, 100, 113, 114–15, 117, 126

and courage, 5, 210, 240
of law, 206, 208–10, 217–19, 240
Spartan, 83, 206, 208–10
types of, 209–10
"fine words," 140–41, 145, 147, 179–80
fire, 264
flourishing. *See eudaimonia/eudaimonism*
Foot, Philippa, 333
Forde, Steven, 39
Forsdyke, Sara, 81, 82, 207n.18
freedom, 6, 9, 31, 50–52, 83, 93, 104, 105, 109, 119, 179, 227, 254, 255, 303–4, 319, 350
free speech, 13, 15, 35
  Aeschines on, 70
  and *andreia*, 124
  to defuse competition, 71
  and democratic deliberation, 52–59
  Demosthenes on, 57, 62, 67, 68, 71, 216
  ideology and practice of, 60–63
  Isocrates on, 55
  Socrates on, 69
  in theater, 279
  "too much," 126
Frogs (Aristophanes), 74, 248, 263
funeral orations, 13, 225, 297–98, 305, 306, 328
  See also specific orators

gender, 258, 260n.17
generalship, 334
Glaucon, 41
glory, 165
Goldie, Peter, 233, 237
goodness, 314, 316, 320n.20, 321, 346
Gorgias (Plato), 311, 337, 343, 344
Graves, Robert, 316
greed, 114, 115, 117, 120, 157
  See also pleonexia
griefwork, 293n.28

happiness, 157, 320, 329
Harmodius, 254
Hector, 292
Hegel, G. W. F., 4–5n.11, 326

hegemonic impartiality, 176
hegemonic narratives, 235
hegemony, 151, 152–56, 166, 172
Helen of Troy, 164, 165, 281, 282, 283, 285, 292
Hellenic culture, 174, 176
Hellenic League, 109
Heracles, 162, 301, 302
Heracles (Euripides), 288, 289–91
Herman, Gabriel, 341
herm monuments, 254
Herodotus, 11, 215
  on Aristodemus, 322, 332
  on Athenian courage, 97–107
  on Athenian democracy, 344
  on Athenian self-understanding, 43
  on Athenian victories, 92–93
  concerns over imperialism, 16
  on democratic courage, 81–84, 93, 98, 102, 104–7
  on democratic deliberation, 94–97, 103
  Histories, 15, 81–84, 108, 112
  on Persians, 212, 213
  political thought, 150
  representations of Athens, 107–11
  on shame, 244
  on Spartan courage, 81–91, 206, 208
  on Tellus the Athenian, 317, 318
Hippias, 101
Histories (Herodotus), 15, 81–84, 108, 109, 112
History (Thucydides), 14, 16, 117, 122, 124, 127, 311
Homeric epics, 179–80, 189, 199–206, 235
honor, 205, 323
  Athenian, 38n.35, 100, 102, 113, 121, 160, 217
  as goal of Greek courage, 198–99
  in Homeric epics, 200
  in *Lysistrata,* 261, 267
  Spartan, 37, 160
  Tocqueville on, 246
  in tragic theater, 249, 250
hoplite battle, 115–16, 205

INDEX | 389

hoplites, 181–82, 185–91, 194–97, 208, 222, 248n.11
hoplomachia, 132, 135, 136, 139
Horace, 316
Human Condition, The (Arendt), 64
human flourishing. *See eudaimonia/ eudaimonism*
humiliation. *See* shame
humility, 147
Hunt, Peter, 9, 186
Hurka, Thomas, 320n.20, 321
Hyperides, 50, 51, 179, 216, 305, 309

ideology, 6
ignorance, 121
Iliad (Homer), 200, 204n.13, 280
impartiality, 151, 173–76
imperialism
  Athenian, 16, 46, 102, 105n.60, 107–28, 259, 288, 294
  Isocrates on, 149, 152–56, 171
  kingly, 153n.12
  pursuit of, 109–28, 259, 294
  and tragic theater, 288
indignation, 119, 120
individual, 298–99, 315, 319
infantry, 221–22
injustice, 114, 228
intentionality, 4
international relations, 151–52
Ionians, 102–3, 169, 173
Iphigenia, 283
Isagoras, 98
isēgoria, 98–99
island strategy, 115–17, 119, 12, 195
Isocrates, 17, 149–76
  on admirable qualities of Athenians, 160
  on Agamemnon, 163–66
  on Athenian courage, 16, 159–63, 283
  on Athens vs. Sparta, 151–52, 158–63, 170, 174
  criticism of excessive manliness, 156–57
  on free speech in Athens, 55
  on imperialism, 149, 152–56, 171

on leadership, 169–73
on loss of virtue in Periclean Athens, 116
Panathenaicus, 152, 158–59, 166
Panegyricus, 152, 155n.20, 158–59
on Persians, 213 praise of hegemony, 152–56
on Spartan contributions, 167–68
on Spartan history, 163–66
on sympathy and impartiality, 151, 173–76

justice, 51, 109, 157, 161, 162, 171, 249, 250, 301–2, 304, 341, 350

Kateb, George, 13n.35, 344, 346
Kerry, John, 1–2n.5
kingly imperialism, 153n.12
Knights (Aristophanes), 344
knowledge, 29–34, 39–44, 73, 136, 138, 146
kratos, 168–69, 171
Kraut, Richard, 320n.21, 326

Lacedaimonians, 139, 159, 163, 223, 255
Laches, 129, 132–35, 137, 139–47, 336
Laches (Plato), 16, 129–48, 337, 338
Laconians, 163
law, 85, 91, 121, 127, 206, 208–10, 219–20, 227, 233n.32, 235, 240–41, 287
Laws (Plato), 11, 186, 209, 219n.3, 336, 337
leadership, 169–73, 175
Lenormant relief, 190, 192
Leocrates, 192–93, 234–39, 240, 318, 319, 321
Leonidas, King, 85–88
Leon of Salamis, 339
Lesbos, 128, 229
logos, 129–32, 135, 139–42, 145–47, 172, 233n.32, 351
longevity, 327
Lycidas, 107
Lycurgus, 192–93, 234–41, 255, 318, 319
Lysias, 68, 220

on Amazons, 257
on courage, 319
funeral oration, 225–28, 230, 242, 244, 257, 300–308
scrutiny hearing, 221
Lysimachus, 131, 132–35, 137, 142, 144, 147
Lysistrata (Aristophanes), 257–77, 334

Macedonia, 51, 106, 198, 213–16
manliness, 117, 167
  of Adrastus, 252n.20
  in *Agamemnon,* 285
  Athenian, 256–77
  Cleon's instigation of anger, 120–23
  at Corcyra, 119–20
  as courage for Athenians, 7
  Isocrates' criticism of excessive, 156–57
  in *Lysistrata,* 257–77
  negative paradigms of, 279–83
  Spartan, 167, 280
Mantitheus, 221–25, 239, 322
Manville, P.B., 46, 145
Mardonius, 104, 107
Martin, Richard, 265
Megarian Decree, 117–18
Meidias, 66, 67–68, 340, 341, 342
Melanion, 265–66
Melesias, 132, 134, 135, 137, 147
Melos, 123
Menelaus, 280–83, 285, 291
military courage, 1–2, 12, 66, 117n.21, 351
military recognition, 179–97
military service, 298
military ventures, 226
Millender, Ellen, 81–83, 84, 89, 100n.52, 209
Miltiades, 51, 101, 102, 256
misogyny, 256, 262
moderation, 161, 162, 250, 305
monuments, 184, 254
morality, 1, 312
Mytilene, 120, 121, 123, 128, 229–31, 287

narratives, 233, 235
naval power, 94–97, 115, 119, 186
necessary identities, 106, 114, 126, 251
Nicias, 124, 129, 131–33, 135–39, 142–47, 271
Nussbaum, Martha, 246, 287

Odysseus, 337
Odyssey (Homer), 200, 204n.13
oligarchy, 70
On Organization (Demosthenes), 61
On the Crown (Demosthenes), 56, 106, 307, 323, 326
On the Embassy (Aeschines), 68
On the Peace (Isocrates), 153, 155n.20, 156, 158, 172
opposites, 129, 144–45, 147
oratory, 53, 55, 56, 60–61, 192, 220, 246, 247, 309
  See also funeral orations; *specific orators*

Panathenaicus (Isocrates), 152, 158–59, 166
Panegyricus (Isocrates), 152, 155n.20, 158–59
Pantites, 207
Paralus, 190
patriotism, 56, 223n.14, 235
Pausanias, 103
peace, 156n.23, 172, 260n.16, 271, 273, 275, 288, 328
Peace (Aristophanes), 185
Peace of Antalcidas, 156n.23
Pears, David, 29
Peleus, 280–83
Peloponnesian War, 115, 118–20, 126, 128, 163, 209, 261n.20
Pericles
  on action and prudent speech, 58
  on Athens, 30–34, 310
  on democratic courage, 59, 93, 98, 110–12, 116, 145, 146, 241–42, 250, 302, 310, 345–46
  eudaimonia, 15, 31–32, 39, 45, 116
  on fallen soldiers, 324

Pericles (*Cont.*)
 funeral oration, 14–15, 16, 25, 111, 112, 116, 145, 146, 227, 268–69, 274
 on good of the state, 314n.12
 identification with city, 273
 ideology of courage, 31–32, 35, 44–47, 81, 83–84, 115–17
 island strategy, 115–17, 119, 128, 195
 and laws against cowardice, 240
 on Persian Wars, 39, 40
 on shame, 34–36, 38, 119, 147, 192, 244
 on Sparta, 38–39, 41, 119
 use of practical knowledge, 40–41
 war speech, 117–19
 on wealth, 37, 39
Persia, 75, 79, 102, 172, 173, 192, 198, 211–13, 279
Persians (Aeschylus), 15, 75–81, 212
Persian Wars, 15, 39, 82–93, 101–5, 112, 113, 118, 119, 160, 166, 185, 193, 256, 304, 326, 344
personal property, 37
Philip of Macedon, 68, 213–16, 243, 251, 255, 307, 308
philosophy, 172, 174
Plato
 on *andreia* vs. *sophrosune*, 258
 Apology, 338, 339
 on courage, 8, 26, 45, 161, 337
 eudaimonia in, 20
 Gorgias, 311, 337, 343, 344
 Laches, 16, 129–48, 337, 338
 Laws, 11, 186, 209, 219n.3, 336, 337
 on naval power, 186
 political thought, 150
 Republic, 11, 19, 157, 173, 254, 311, 316n.18, 338
 on Spartan courage, 331
 Statesman, 276, 277, 333–36
 on *thumos*, 232
 on women, 257
pleonexia, 109, 110, 151, 157, 158, 165–69, 174, 214
Plutarch, 125, 195
poets, 248

political power, 53
politics, 61, 117, 149–51, 338–39
Polybius, 11, 188n.22
poor citizens, 180–82, 189
Posidonius, 233n.35, 332
power, 163–65, 169
practical knowledge, 39–44
practical reasoning, 4, 48, 52
primitive anger, 122, 126
primitive shame, 260
profit, 114
prohairetic choice, 93–94, 325
Protagoras (Plato), 183
public-spirited deliberation, 71–72

Raaflaub, Kurt, 288, 293
Rademaker, Adriaan, 218
rational choice theory, 29
reason and rationality, 4, 48–49, 246, 250
reciprocity, 99
recognition-response tie, 233, 234
Republic (Plato), 11, 19, 157, 173, 254, 311, 316n.18, 338
reputation, 302
respect, 121, 268
Roisman, Joseph, 340
role models, 244, 245, 247, 253–55
Rorty, A.O., 335
rowers, 182, 186, 187–88, 191–94, 197

Schofield, Malcolm, 202, 203, 204n.13
scrutiny hearing, 221–25
security, 51
self, 315, 322, 323, 325–26
self-consciousness, 19, 113, 132, 204n.13
self-control, 162, 170, 171, 281, 337
self-image, 226, 227, 228, 239, 245n.6, 322
self-importance, 313
self-interest, 99, 272–73, 312, 315n.17, 321, 325
self-knowledge, 278n.1, 279, 286–88, 291, 292, 294
selflessness, 314, 319
self-respect, 302, 323
self-restraint, 340–41

self-sacrifice, 307, 308, 313, 314, 315, 320, 323
Seven Against Thebes (Aeschylus), 263
sex, 272, 276
sex organs, 256
shame, 205, 210, 216, 245–49
   in *Agamemnon,* 285
   of Aristodemus, 206, 322
   Aristotle on, 35, 245, 268
   Athenian, 218, 239
   Athenian vs. Spartan, 38, 100, 198
   courage based on, 200, 207, 244
   definition of, 245
   democratic, 244, 253
   Demosthenes on, 217, 243–44
   and emulation, 239
   of Greek ancestors, 226–27
   Herodotus on, 244
   in *Lysistrata,* 261, 267
   of Mantitheus, 222
   Periclean, 35–36, 38, 119, 147, 192, 244
   and political participation, 61, 70
   Spartan, 37, 82, 83, 206–9, 219
   and tragic experience, 249–54
   of Xerxes, 79
Shay, Jonathan, 293n.28
Sicilian Debate, 123, 124–27, 271, 282
Sicilian Expedition, 124, 126, 128, 138
Sicily, 117, 131, 289
slander, 61
slavery, 168–69, 186–87, 213
Smoes, Étienne, 201, 202, 204n.13
Socrates, 351
   in Athens' cultural life, 130
   courage of, 26n.4, 129, 131–33, 141–43, 147, 336–39, 342
   on democracy, 11, 131, 344
   as exemplary democratic citizen, 147–48
   on free speech, 69
   humility, 147
   on longevity, 327
   on self-consciousness, 19
   on virtue, 134
   on voting, 131, 144, 339

soldiers, 291, 300, 301, 305, 313, 315, 324–25, 327–28, 331
Solon, 107, 219, 317, 318, 327
Sontag, Susan, 1
soothsayers, 131, 137, 141
Sophanes, 92–93n.42, 191
Sophocles, 287, 290
sōphrosunē, 124–25, 257–58, 260, 271, 276, 277, 333–37
Sparta
   vs. Athens, 105, 112–15, 151–52, 158–63, 170, 174
   contributions of, 167–68
   Corinthians at, 110–12, 129
   courage of, 11, 38, 79, 81–86, 89–91, 93, 100, 166, 198, 206–9, 241, 283, 331
   history, 163–66
   Pericles on, 38–39, 41, 119
   shame, 37–38, 82, 83, 206–9, 219
   in theater, 279, 280
   at Thermopylae, 84–91
   tradition, 43
   voting, 125, 208
   walling off of homeland, 90
   women in, 282
spectatorship, 135, 146
speech, 49
standing fast, 89, 92, 95, 97, 336, 337, 338–39, 342
statesman, 333–35
Statesman (Plato), 276, 277, 333–36
Stesilaus, 132, 135, 136, 137, 144
Stevenson, Robert Louis, 162
Sthenelaidas, 42, 121, 125, 208, 231
Strato, 66–67, 179
Strauss, Leo, 316n.18
Suppliants (Euripides), 54, 249–53, 287
sympathy, 151, 173–76, 288
Syracuse, 197

Tarnopolsky, Christina, 13n.35, 38
technical knowledge, 41–42, 139
technical skill, 136
Tellus the Athenian, 317–22, 325–27
theater, 247, 248–53, 259, 278–94

Themistocles, 39, 40, 45, 51, 87, 95–97, 99, 103–5, 112, 113, 184
Theophrastus, 220
Theseus, 249–53
thetes, 181–82, 185, 187, 189, 190, 192, 195–97
Thirty Tyrants, 227, 228, 230
thorubos, 62–63, 203
Thucydides, 27, 28, 57, 58, 171
   on Archidamus, 207–8
   on Corinthians at Sparta, 129
   on courage, 43, 45
   on daring Athenians, 110–12
   on democratic courage, 109, 114, 149
   on democratic free speech, 54
   on democratic imperialism, 127–28
   distinction between daring and courage, 40
   on manliness at Corcyra, 119–20, 257
   on Melos, 123
   on Mytilene, 229, 231
   on Periclean ideal, 45, 110, 115–17
   on Periclean war speech, 117–19
   Pericles' funeral oration, 14, 16, 25
   political thought, 117, 150
   presentation of Athenian democracy, 132
   presentation of Nicias' speech, 124
   on Sicilian Debate, 124
   on Spartan courage, 11, 126, 209
   on Spartan voting, 125
   See also History
thumos, 156, 158, 166, 172–73, 228–29, 232
Tocqueville, Alexis de, 11–12, 13n.35, 246, 347–49
tragic theater, 248–53, 278–94, 344
treason, 234, 240
trembler, 206–7
Trojan War, 164, 165, 282, 285
Trojan Women (Euripides), 288, 291–94

Twelve Labors, 289
tyrannicides, 101, 254, 255, 267–70
tyranny, 11, 70, 101, 153, 255, 309
Tyrtaeus, 241, 313

Villa, Dana, 339
virtue(s)
   Athenian thinking on, 241, 297, 322, 329
   democratic, 309–10, 342
   as intrinsically valuable, 170, 323
   Isocrates on, 157
   of manhood, 328
   material value, 313
   moral, 320
   Pericles on, 314n.12
   Socrates on, 134
   of Theseus, 251

war, 156n.23, 227, 229, 249, 258, 259, 269, 271–72, 276, 288, 292–93
Wasps (Aristophanes), 195, 344
water, 264–65
weaving, 334
Williams, Bernard, 36, 268, 325
wisdom, 172, 203n.8, 251, 335, 350, 351
women
   in *Lysistrata,* 258, 259n.12, 261–62, 264, 267–76
   misogyny, 256–57
   Spartan, 282
   subordination of, 7
wooden walls oracle, 76, 95
worthiness, 112–13, 302

Xenophon, 41, 207
Xerxes, King, 75–80, 82, 85, 86, 90, 91, 96, 107, 155, 208, 209, 212, 238

Zeitlin, Froma, 278n.1, 279

INDEX LOCORUM

Aelian
Varia Historia
  2.28   256

Aeschylus
Agamemnon
  205–227   283–84
Persians
  65–72   76
  100–106   76
  152   75
  167   76
  170–72   75
  197–99   78
  211–13   75
  211–14   80
  215–25   75
  215–30   75
  231–32   76
  235   76
  236–45   76
  241–43   75
  268   79
  288   79
  331–44   76
  369–71   75
  447–72   185n.18
  548–57   75
  584–97   75
  591–94   75
  598–622   76
  681–842   76
  694–96   75
  694–702   75
  700–702   75
  709–14   78
  722–25   77
  742–51   77
  751–52   78
  753–58   78
  755   78
  765–86   78
  782–83   77
  808   77
  809–12   77
  816–22   77
  822   77
  823–26   77
  829   77
  852–908   76
  853–902   78
  1038–77   75
Seven against Thebes
  42–48   263
  52–53   263

Aeschines
  1.24   54, 180n.2
  1.35   63
  1.140   254
  1.178   57, 58
  2.75   193

Aeschines (*Cont.*)

2.148	52n.9		
2.169	219n.5		
2.181–82	68		
2.22	216n.31		
2.34–35	216n.31		
3.1	59n.31		
3.4	54, 180n.2		
3.6	70		
3.7	70		
3.81	216n.31		
3.127	56		
3.148	52n.9		
3.152	52n.9		
3.173	62		
3.175	219n.4, 219–20, 340		
3.181–86	254n.23		
3.183	184		
3.214	216n.31		
3.220	53, 59n.31		
3.227	61		
3.244–46	232		
3.245	324		
3.245–46	206, 247		
3.245–47	19		
3.252	234		

Andocides

1.2	61
1.74	219n.4
2.4	61

Alcaeus

fr. 6.13–14	205

Aristophanes
Acharnians

161–63	185
541–56	118n.22
696–97	261n.19
1128–29	219, 240

Clouds

985–86	261n.19

Ecclesiazusae

746–876	298

Frogs

951–58	74
971–79	74
1013–42	263
1021	74, 263
1025–27	74
1039–42	249
1039–43	74
1053–56	249
1420–21	249

Knights

781	261n.19
1334	261n.19

Lysistrata

29–30	261
32–33	261
35	261
39–41	262
78–92	273
99–106	262, 271, 272
142–45	274
162–66	272
175–79	262
189–205	262
260	262
262	262
269–70	263
271	262
273–77	262
277	263
284	263
285	263
286–95	263
306	264
307–11	264
318	263, 268
321–35	264
342–43	264, 269
344–49	264
347	264
370	264
375–85	274
377–78	264
384	265
389	265n.31

390–98	267	659	263
391–92	270	659–61	267
391–98	269	662–63	270
395–400	274	664–70	264
401–2	265	665–70	271
403	265	675	272
406	265	678	271
420–23	267	678–79	268
432	268	682	274
439–40	274	694–95	264n.26
443–48	274	708–9	275
450–70	274	715–28	267
452–54	274	782–96	265–66
469–70	265	882–83	272
477–83	263	1014–15	274
480–95	274	1019–32	275
488–92	267	1024	275
497	270	1043–46	261
502	270–71	1092	261
504	271	1016–17	266
506	274	1018	266
506–14	271	1035–42	275
515	271	1050–55	273
520–35	271	1105	261
529–38	276	1106–87	274
530–31	271	1108	274, 275
541–547	274	1109	275
546–47	275	1128–35	273
554	269	1137–61	273
555–56	269	1175–80	273
557	274	1247–72	275
557–58	270	1280–92	273
559	270	*Peace*	
559–61	270	1172–78	185
565–66	270	*Wasps*	
567–86	276–77	711	261n.19
587–90	271	1117–21	195
591–92	271	1224–27	254
599–613	271–72		
614–15	264	Aristotle	
615–30	271	*Athēnaiōn Politeia*	
630–34	267	29.5	187
631–35	254	*Eudemian Ethics*	
638–46	271	1216b3–26	26n.4
648–57	270–71	1229a20–24	31

INDEX LOCORUM | 397

Eudemian Ethics (Cont.)		1333b31–33	127
1229b22–30	40n.37	*Rhetoric*	
1230a6–8	41	1378a31–33	227
1230a6–10	183n.14, 186	1383a6–7	5n.12
1230a8–10	41	1383b12–15	245
History of Animals		1384a24–25	268
631b28	256n.2	1388a32–35	192
Nicomachean Ethics		1388b9–10	192
1103b21–25	26n.4		
1104b3–8	100	Augustine	
1111b4–1113a14	94n.45	*City of God*	
1113a9–12	94	X.7	327n.30
1115a18–19	40n.37		
1115a25–32	66n.50	Callinus	
1115a35–b4	41n.40	fr. 1.1–4	205
1115b1–5	186		
1115b24–33	40n.37	Cicero	
1116a4–24	183n.14	*de Officiis*	
1116a17–29	35	1.61–92	66n.49
1116a17–1116b3	269	*de Legibus*	
1116b3–23	41n.40	2.10	244n.3
1116b23–30	228		
1116b24–1117a9	264	Demosthenes	
1116b31–32	229, 229n.24	1.1	58
1117a4–6	229	1.6	53
1117a4–9	122	1.11	61
1124b29–30	66n.50	1.14–15	61
1124b27–29	66n.50	1.16	61
1126a6–8	230	1.16–18	185
1126b1–2	228	1.24	217, 243
1128b10–35	35	2.12–13	53
1140b7–11	45n.46	2.30	53
1144a18–b1	26n.4	2.31	58
1144b17–30	26n.4	3.3	56
1144b30–32	26n.4	3.11–13	61
1179b29–1180a14	233n.32	3.14–15	53
Politics		3.15	57
1253a14–18	67	3.16	185
1271a41–1271b10	331	3.21–22	56
1271b6–10	238	3.29	62
1276b16–35	11	3.32	56, 61
1281a42–b5	57	3.183	188
1281b7–10	57	4.39	62
1305a3–7	62	4.51	61, 65
1320a4–6	62	5.15	63
1327a40–1327b15	188n.22	6.3	56
1333b5–26	331	6.27	61

8.1	58, 61	21.120	68
8.67	67n.54	21.124	67
8.68	65	21.160–62	68
8.68–70	65	21.203	188
8.71–72	61	22.37	60n.31
9.3–4	56	23.4	60n.31
9.31	214	23.5	61
9.63	56	23.19	61
10.7	56n.22	23.19–20	62
10.11	58	23.109	57
10.28	62	23.145–46	57
10.28–29	58	23.190	61
10.54	56	23.198	184
10.70–72	61	23.208	62
10.75	57	24.8–9	62
13.3	63	24.66	60n.31
13.36	62	50.3	285
15.32	219n.4	60.17	50n.7
15.32–33	68	60.17–18	49
18.23	63	60.18	50, 223n.14
18.66	215	60.3	49
18.72	216	60.6–7	49
18.95–99	215, 244	60.8	49
18.170	54, 180n.2	60.10–11	49
18.173–80	216n.31	60.11	215
18.199–203	307	60.15–17	328
18.199–208	250–51	60.16–17	305
18.200–05	244	60.17–18	102, 216
18.203	323	60.19, 21	215
18.204–05	308, 323	60.25–26	216, 217, 244
18.205	326	60.26, 28, 37	94n.45
18.215–16	216	*Exordia*	
18.217	247	10.1	62, 63
18.235–36	214–215	26.2–3	71
18.236	215	27.1	57
18.244	247	44.2	56
18.244–45	215	47.2	56
18.287–88, 91	244	49.1	58
20.69–70	254	50.1	48, 124
20.70	255	50.3	49, 61
20.106	54		
20.141	226n.17	Diodorus Siculus	
20.160–62	68, 254	11.11	88n.31
21.20	67		
21.95	67	Euripides	
21.103	67	*Andromache*	
21.105	68	590	280

Andromache (Cont.)

590–641	280
592–604	282
611–13	281
646	282
660	282
666–67	282
680–84	282
721–22	283
724–26	283

Heracles

562–582	289–90
931–1000	290

Medea

248–51	257

Orestes

902–05	55

Suppliants

155–59	249
160–61	249
163	250
201–04	249
219–49	250
293	250
293–300	251
297–331	250
304–13	250, 318n.19
306–15	250
323	250
334–45	250
339–48	250
349–51	251
410–25	54
438–41	54
509–10	251
669–74	252
724–25	252
857–917	252
913–17	253

Trojan Women

370–71	292
374–81	292
386–87	293
400–402	293
555–67	293
673–74	292
884–88	293
886	293–94
1091–99	293
1156–1206	293

Herodotus

1.130	317
1.136	213
3.4	25n.2
3.134–35	77
5.66	99
5.71	43
5.72	98
5.74	98
5.77–78	98
5.78	11, 55, 81n.19, 93n.43, 98–99, 100, 212, 344
5.91	11, 99
5.97	96
5.105	77
6.11–12	102
6.15	102
6.48–49	102–03
6.106–7	87, 90
6.108–09	101
6.109	100, 102
6.109–10	83
6.112	100, 102
6.132–33	109
7.22	82n.21
7.56	82n.21
7.103	82n.21
7.104	82, 84, 100, 223n.14
7.104–05	208
7.105	85
7.133–36	90n.39
7.138	90, 96
7.139	84, 87, 88, 92, 93, 94, 104
7.140–44	94
7.141–43	95
7.143	100, 102n.56
7.143–44	96
7.148–63	103
7.168–69	103
7.173–74	88

7.175	87, 87n.29, 88n.31	8.85	212
7.176	88n.31	8.86	82n.21, 101, 212
7.187	212	8.87–88	212
7.205–209	85	8.87–89	99n 51
7.206	87	8.89–90	212
7.207	89	8.92–94	93
7.210	212	8.93	103, 104
7.211–12	85	8.95	103
7.214	86	8.99–100	212
7.220	86, 88	8.100	212n.26
7.223	82n.21, 88	8.103	212
7.224	86	8.111–112	109
7.226	86	8.118	212
7.228	86	8.118–19	212
7.229–231	322, 331	8.122	104
7.231	206	8.122–25	103
7.231–32	81n.19, 100, 207n.18	8.124	104
7.232	207	8.130	103
7.234	85	8.136	104
7.235	89, 91	8.142	105
7.238	86n.26	8.144	100, 104n.57, 105, 106, 107, 113, 273, 323n.26
8.1	96		
8.3	100, 102, 105, 344	9.3–5	107
8.11	103	9.6–8	89, 90
8.15	82n.21, 88n.31, 212	9.7	100, 105, 106
8.17	103	9.26–28	100
8.26	86n.26	9.27	105
8.40	89	9.46	100
8.40–41	96n.47	9.46–47	105
8.43–48	96	9.46–48	83
8.49–50	89	9.58	83
8.51–54	95	9.60	99, 100
8.56	89	9.62	212
8.57	91n.40	9.64	86n.26, 103, 104n.58
8.60	91n.40, 97	9.70–71	103
8.61	95	9.71	81n.19, 207n.18, 322, 332
8.62	96–97		
8.63	92n.41	9.73–75	92n.42, 191
8.65	99n.51	9.75	92–93n.42
8.67–69	99n.51	9.102–07	103
8.68	89n.35	9.106	109
8.69	82n.21, 212	9.114	109
8.70	89n.35		
8.71–72	89	Hesiod	
8.74	89	*Works and Days*	
8.83	94n.45, 97n.48	55–58	262n.23

Homer
Iliad

1.254–91	203
2.190–97	203
2.200–202	180
2.284–88	200
2.357–59	201
2.391–93	201
2.246–77	202
2.450–54	201
3.31	201
3.33–35	201
4.242–49	201
4.299–300	201
4.234	201
4.338–48	201
4.370–75	201
4.428–32	201
5.348	202
5.470–77	201
5.512–13	201
5.529	202
5.529–32	200
5.633–46	201
5.780–83	201
5.811–13	201
6.111–15	200
6.112	202
6.208	202
6.407	201
6.441–446	200
7.38–42	201
7.96–98	202
7.96–102	201
7.152–53	201
8.93–96	201
8.163	202
9.32–49	201
9.252–60	203
9.309–37	203
9.377	203
9.443	179, 202
10.224–26	203
11.401–13	203
11.784	202
12.40–50	201
12.195–250	204
12.248–50	201
12.310–28	203
13.47–58	201
13.95–124	201
13.275–287	201–02
14.83–102	203
14.128–32	203
15.661	200
19.78–82	203
19.88	203

Odyssey

5.361–67	200n.2
20.10–23	200n.2

Hyperides

fr. A.4	50
6.2	50, 93
6.3	50, 51, 93, 94n.45
6.5	50, 51
6.8	305, 309
6.10–11	216
6.13	215
6.15–17	309
6.16	51
6.16–17	215
6.19	51
6.20	214
6.20–22	51
6.22–24	50
6.24–25	51, 216, 309
6.25	216
6.26	51
6.28–29	309
6.34	244n.2
6.38	50n.7, 51
6.39–40	254
6.40	93, 94n.45

Inscriptiones Graecae (1873–)

i² 79	182n.5
i² 368	194
i³ 138.1–7	182n.5
i³ 474–79	118n.4
i³ 503	185, 190

Isocrates
2.5–9	161n.31
3.1–4	162
3.43	162
4.17	172
4.39–40	171
4.47–48	172
4.48–50	162
4.53	172, 318n.19
4.57–65	168
4.61–62	318n.19
4.67	172
4.77	171
4.80–81	170–71
4.81–83	173
4.85	159
4.93–97	166
4.100–102	155
4.103–9	155n.20
4.104–5	170
4.104–6	172
4.110	167–68
4.111	169
4.113	169
4.114	168
4.115	156n.23
4.117	169
4.122	173
4.123–24	169
4.125	168
4.125–26	157
4.131–32	174
4.146–52	213
4.150–51	169
4.151–52	213
4.157–59	172
4.167–68	172
4.176	171
4.182	172
4.183	172
4.183–84	162
5.89	171
5.109–10	162
7.6	154–55
7.6–8	155
7.7	168
7.9	155
7.12	155
7.15	60n.31
7.15–18	154
7.20–23	154
7.61	168
7.74–75	161
7.76	157
7.76–77	155
7.79–80	154
7.81–83	155
7.82	157
7.82–84	156
7.84	152
8.3	62
8.3–4	155
8.8	157
8.12	156
8.12–13	157
8.14	55, 56, 57, 61
8.16	156n.23
8.16–17	157
8.18	157
8.19	153
8.22–23	157
8.24	158
8.26	157
8.29–32	153, 157
8.32	157, 161
8.36–37	157
8.41–44	153
8.48	155
8.65–66	154
8.75–78	154
8.77	116
8.82	153
8.86–89	153–54
8.97	157
8.99–100	157
8.101–3	168
8.110	164
8.114–15	155
8.124	62
8.134	171
8.136–37	156
8.142	158

Isocrates (*Cont.*)
8.142–44	153n.12, 168	12.157–63	155
8.143–44	170	12.163	172
8.145	172	12.166	156
12.39–41	151	12.177–81	166
12.45–47	165, 166, 168	12.178–79	163
12.46	166	12.178–81	168
12.46–48	168	12.184	174
12.47–48	171	12.187–88	168
12.47–52	173	12.196–97	49
12.54	171	12.197–98	160, 283
12.54–55	168	12.203	167
12.55	168, 170	12.217	167
12.60–61	166n.38	12.219–220	157
12.63–64	155	12.220	167
12.69	318n.19	12.223	167
12.70–71	165	12.228	167
12.70–72	163	12.232	167
12.70–90	163	12.241	167
12.72	165	12.241–43	157
12.73	163	12.242–43	167
12.74–75	163	12.248	58
12.75	164	12.265	167
12.77	164	15.22	62
12.77–78	165	15.253–57	161n.31
12.78	164	15.293–96	172
12.79–80	164		
12.80–82	171	Livy	
12.81–82	165	2.10	244n.3
12.83	164		
12.84–88	163	Lycurgus	
12.90	163	1.10	206, 232
12.94	171, 174	1.16	234, 235
12.98	170	1.17	235
12.103	168	1.21	236
12.103–4	168–69	1.25–26	236
12.111–37	152	1.38	235
12.114–15	156	1.39–40	236
12.114–18	155	1.41–42	236
12.117–18	167	1.44	318–19
12.118	156	1.45	236, 255
12.130–33	155	1.47	255
12.133	155	1.49	237
12.140	62	1.50–51	254, 255
12.153–54	168	1.51	237
12.155	166n.38	1.68–72	193
		1.68–74	238

1.71	238	2.69	300, 301, 305
1.72	193	2.70–71	306
1.73	190	2.79	308, 319
1.74	239	7.32	61
1.82	239	10.24–25	68
1.91	239	14.7	219n.4
1.100	235	14.15	220, 240
1.102	235	16.1–3	221
1.104	238	16.5	331
1.106	241	16.9	221
1.120–21	240	16.13–16	222
1.129	240	16.17	224
1.129–30	241	16.17–18	223
1.130	240	16.20–21	224
1.136	193, 235, 236	20.23	220
1.142	236		

Meiggs, R. and D. Lewis
25	190
26	190

Lysias
1.129–30	223n.14
2.3	257
2.4–6	257, 268
2.10	301
2.11–16	301, 318n.19
2.13–14	302
2.14	301
2.17	301, 303
2.18–19	303, 304
2.20	226
2.22	223n.14, 304
2.23	226–27, 304
2.24	304
2.24–26	94n.45
2.25	227
2.26	300
2.32–40	304
2.35–37	305
2.37	227
2.40	194
2.40–42	305
2.44–47	305
2.50–53	301
2.56	304
2.61	303
2.62	94n.45, 227, 244
2.64–65	305
2.67–68	301, 305

Pausanias
3.4	88n.31

Plato
Apology
28d–29a	69
29d	69
31e–32a	69
32b–c	69

Gorgias
498a–499c	311n.5
507b	337
513a–c	247
521d	148
521d–e	69n.57

Laches
178a	135
178b	133
179a	133
179c	133
179e	132, 135
180a	139
180b	134
180b–181b	133
181a	135, 139
182a–d	136

Laches (Cont.)		706b–c	186
182c	143	707a–d	186
182e–184c	139	853b	234n.38
183c–184a	137	853d–e	234n.38
183d	135	943e–945b	48n.3
184c–d	131	944a–b	48n.3
184d–e	144	*Menexenus*	
185c	137	245a	190
186d	141	246d	94n.45
186e–187a	134	*Meno*	
187e–188a	136	94a–e	134
187c–d	133	*Protagoras*	
188c	139	320c–328d	183
188d	135, 140	349d	161
188e–189a	139	360d	26n.4
190e	146	*Republic*	
191d–e	256	374b–e	183n.14
192b	146	375a–376e	19
193d–e	131, 140, 143	377a–403c	19
194a	142, 147, 337, 338	385b–c	19
194b	141	387b–d	19
194e–195a	136, 145	388d–e	19
195a	142, 146	390c–391b	19
195a–b	141	395c–396e	19
195e	131, 141	401b–402a	19
195e–196a	137	401e–402d	19
196b	142, 143	429b–d	184n.14
196b–c	143	429c–430c	42
197a	141	430c	26n.4, 183n.14
197c	135, 143	435e–436a	335
197c–d	143	454c–457c	257
197d	137, 146	492b–93a	247
197e	143	557b–558c	55
198e–199a	131, 141	560c–d	342
199e	26n.4, 131	560c–e	11
199e–200a	147	*Statesman*	
200b	137	279a–b	276, 334
200b–c	147	304e–305a	334
201a–b	132	306b	334
Laws		306b–307c	258
625c–630d	11	306e–307b	335
625c–631d	331	309c	335
631b–d	337	310e	335
631c–d	116n.20	311b	335
646e–647a	209	*Symposium*	
694a–b	11	219d	337
697c–e	11	220c	336

220d–221b	141	1.85	38, 207
221b	336	1.86	42, 42–43
		1.86–87	114, 125, 231
Plutarch		1.87	208
Cimon		1.90	40
7.4–5	254n.23	1.120	129
Pericles		1.139–41	118
33.6	116n.17	1.140–44	117, 123
Themistocles		1.143	37, 115, 195
19.4	19.4	1.143–44	119
Moralia		1.144	39, 40
349d	195	2.11	25n.2
		2.13	41, 117
Polybius		2.35–46	159, 274n.52
6.52	188n.22	2.36	30, 32
6.52–53	244n.3	2.37	38
		2.38	30, 33, 38
pseudo–Xenophon		2.39	34, 38
1.6–8	55n.17	2.40	25, 25n.2, 27, 27n.7, 28, 31–32, 37n.31, 38, 39, 44n.43, 58, 134
1.12	55n.17		
2.14–16	195		
3.5	219n.4	2.41	30, 31, 32, 33, 127
		2.42	33, 36, 37
Semonides		2.43	28, 28n.9, 30, 31, 35, 36, 36n.27, 39
7	262n.23		
		2.44	324
Sophocles		2.60	32
Ajax		2.62	35, 37, 195
485–524	290	2.63	33
		2.64	36n.28, 36–37
Thucydides		2.65	41, 45, 116, 117, 118
1.9–10	164	2.87	42, 183n.14
1.14	40	2.89	194
1.22	14, 14n.37	2.90–91	29n.11
1.23	26	3.36	120, 128, 231
1.68–71	34, 110	3.36–38	121
1.70	37n.32, 111, 128	3.37	229
1.71	25n.2	3.38	122, 138, 229
1.73–74	112	3.39–40	229
1.74–75	113	3.40	121, 122, 230
1.75	112–13, 113–14	3.42	56
1.76	114	3.43	55
1.76–77	127	3.49	231
1.82	38	3.50	128
1.83	124	3.63	114
1.84	37, 207	3.82	40, 120, 257–58

Thucydides (*Cont.*)
4.40	209
4.65	121n.28
5.2	128
5.7	121n.28
5.9	209
5.32	128
5.72	11
5.78	43
5.89	123
5.97	123
5.99	123
5.104	114
6.8–24	138
6.9–14	138
6.11	124
6.16	126
6.18	125, 126
6.20–23	138
6.24	282–83
6.39	44n.43, 57, 58
7.48	138n.17
7.50	131n.8
7.55–56	197
7.77	95
8.77	116

Tyrtaeus
fr. 8.5–6	332n.2
fr. 11.11-13	313

Xenophon
Anabasis
3.2	190

Constitution of the Lacedaemonians
9.5	207n.17

Hiero
5.1–4	11

Memorabilia
3.6	41